THE FOUR GOSPELS

AN INTRODUCTION

Other Books by Bruce Vawter

THE CONSCIENCE OF ISRAEL

THE BIBLE IN THE CHURCH

A PATH THROUGH GENESIS

THE FOUR GOSPELS

AN INTRODUCTION

Bruce Vawter, C.M.

1967
DOUBLEDAY & COMPANY, INC., GARDEN CITY, NEW YORK

Imprimatur: ✠ Joseph Cardinal Ritter
Archdiocese of St. Louis
September 20, 1966

*To the Fathers and Brothers of
the Congregation of the Mission
in Their 150th Year in America
1816–1966*

FOREWORD

Some years ago I wrote a book entitled A *Popular Explanation of the Four Gospels*. It achieved a measure of success, was reprinted, and went into a second and revised edition. It is now out of print and properly so, since it no longer represents what a popularization is supposed to be, namely, an impression for the general reader of what is present-day informed and professional thinking on its subject. This present book does, I hope, offer something of the kind. It is entirely new both in content and in format, though I have kept some of the chapter headings that I used before and, here and there, a sentence or two.

This is less a commentary on the Gospels than it is an explanation of what they are about. My intention throughout has been to let the Gospels tell their own story to the extent possible, and what comments I have added have been designed to assist the reader in hearing their story more clearly and with fewer distractions. Exegesis in the technical sense of the word is rare in this book, and still less often have I taken up the challenge of the many theological issues to which the Gospels give rise especially in our times. For these, the reader will have to be referred to the commentaries and special studies of every kind which are now available to him in abundance. If this book succeeds in its purpose he will want to move on to this other literature in any case.

This is an introduction to the Gospels through a reading of the Gospels. For reasons that I trust are justified in my first chapter, I intend that the Gospels be read concurrently. For this purpose, although it is not absolutely necessary, a "harmony" of the four Gospels should prove to be most useful. My arrangement of the text has mainly followed—though not rigidly—Kurt Aland's *Synopsis Quattuor Evangeliorum* of the Greek New Testament (second edition, 1964). There are many English harmonies on the market, practically any of which should be equally adaptable to the design of this book. I have deliberately avoided using any single one of the standard English translations of the Gospels for my citations of the text. The reader may choose the one he likes best. It is obviously indispensable, however, that he have some sort of biblical text before him as he reads.

For reasons that I judge adequate I have abandoned an earlier intention of including reading lists to assist in a continuing study of the Gospels. Continuing study will imply various things to various people. It might be thought useful, however, to mention here a few of the kind of books presupposed by an introductory volume like this, which deal not abstrusely but in detail with topics that evidently deserve more than the few lines that we have often been able to give them.

The whole gamut of contemporary Gospel study—the Synoptic and Johannine questions, form criticism, the processes and the theologies of the several evangelists, and the rest—is run in works like *New Testament Introduction* by Alfred Wikenhauser (Herder and Herder, 1958) or Robert-Feuillet's *Introduction to the New Testament* (Desclée, 1965). The sometimes fascinating story of the making of the Gospels and the New Testament, the historical tensions of which they are the product and the textual traditions which are their witnesses, can be read in Bruce Metzger's *The Text of the New Testament* (Oxford University Press, 1964) and *The Birth of the New Testament* by C. F. D. Moule (Harper and Row, 1962). The specifics of the Gospel tradition that are the raw material of form criticism are ably presented by Vincent Taylor in his *The Formation of the Gospel Tradition* (Macmillan, 1933); and in this connection Catholic readers will be well advised to consult the 1964 Instruction of the Pontifical Biblical Commission, presented with a commentary by Joseph A. Fitzmyer, S.J., in *The Historical Truth of the Gospels* (Paulist Press, 1965). The intricacies of New Testament christology may be explored from many angles. This writer has been especially indebted to Vincent Taylor, *The Names of Jesus* (Macmillan, 1962); Oscar Cullmann, *The Christology of the New Testament* (SCM Press, 1959); E. M. Sidebottom, *The Christ of the Fourth Gospel* (SPCK Press, 1961); and Asher Finkel, *The Pharisees and the Teacher of Nazareth* (Leiden: Brill, 1964).

At the end of this book the reader will find indexes of the Gospel passages and of subjects treated. The two maps should be adequate for his present purposes, though he would find it useful to have at hand a standard Bible atlas such as the *Westminster Historical Atlas to the Bible* or Grollenberg's *Atlas of the Bible*. To most of the questions which already exist in his mind or to which this reading may give rise, at least a preliminary answer can be found in a reference like *The Interpreter's Dictionary of the Bible*, *The Encyclopedic Dictionary of the Bible*, or the *Dictionary of the Bible* by John L. McKenzie, S.J., one of which should be in the library of everyone who is seriously concerned with the Gospels.

19 July 1966
Feast of St. Vincent de Paul

CONTENTS

Foreword 7
Abbreviations of Biblical References 11
Map of Palestine in New Testament Times 12
Map of Jerusalem in the Time of Christ 13

1. Some Preliminaries 15
2. The Word Made Flesh 37
3. The Term of Prophecy 46
4. Joy to the World 61
5. A Light Begins to Shine 73
6. Living Water 88
7. Acclaim in Galilee 100
8. The Keys of the Kingdom 118
9. Treasure in Heaven 133
10. Parables of the Kingdom 145
11. Rejection in Galilee 163
12. The Bread of Life 176
13. Upon This Rock 190
14. Yet a Little While 204
15. That They Who Do Not See May See 221
16. Fire on the Earth 236
17. Waiting in Perea 253
18. The Last Journey 268
19. Bethany and Jericho 285
20. Palm Sunday 299
21. Beginning of the End 314
22. A Last Supper 333
23. The True Vine and Its Branches 346
24. Agony 359
25. "What Is Truth?" 373
26. God and Lord of All 394

Index of Gospel Passages 413
General Index 417

ABBREVIATIONS OF BIBLICAL REFERENCES

Gen	Genesis	Wis	Wisdom of Solomon
Ex	Exodus	Sir	Sirach (Ecclesiasticus)
Lev	Leviticus	Is	Isaiah
Num	Numbers	Jer	Jeremiah
Deut	Deuteronomy	Lam	Lamentations
Jos	Joshua	Bar	Baruch
Jgs	Judges	Ezek	Ezekiel
1–2 Sam	1–2 Samuel	Dan	Daniel
1–2 Kgs	1–2 Kings	Hos	Hosea
1–2 Chron	1–2 Chronicles	Joel	Joel
Ezra	Ezra	Amos	Amos
Neh	Nehemiah	Mi	Micah
Tob	Tobit	Hab	Habakkuk
Job	Job	Zeph	Zephaniah
Ps(s)	Psalm(s)	Zech	Zechariah
Prov	Proverbs	Mal	Malachi
Eccl	Ecclesiastes	1–2 Macc	1–2 Maccabees
Cant	Song of Songs		

4 Ezra	The apocryphal book of 4 Ezra, also called 2 Esdras
1 QS	The *Serek* ("Manual of Discipline") of the Qumran sectaries

Mt	Matthew	Col	Colossians
Mk	Mark	1–2 Thes	1–2 Thessalonians
Lk	Luke	1–2 Tim	1–2 Timothy
Jn	John	Tit	Titus
Acts	Acts of the Apostles	Phlm	Philemon
Rom	Romans	Heb	Hebrews
1–2 Cor	1–2 Corinthians	Jas	James
Gal	Galatians	1–2 Pt	1–2 Peter
Eph	Ephesians	1–2 Jn	1–2 John
Phil	Philippians	Apo	The Apocalypse or Revelation

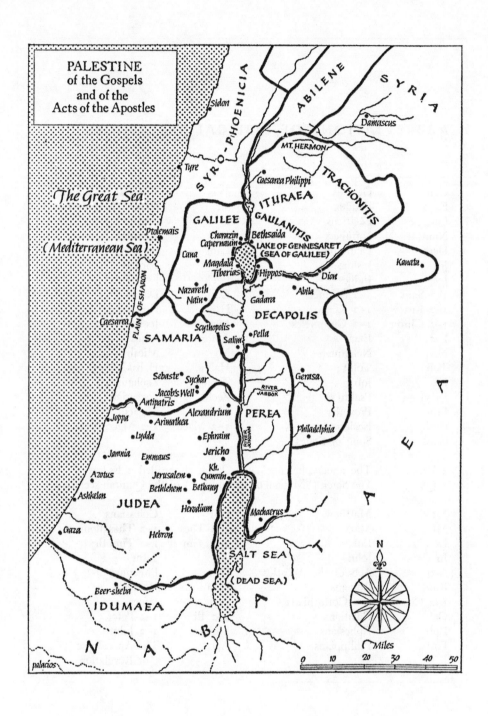

PALESTINE
of the Gospels
and of the
Acts of the Apostles

The Great Sea

(Mediterranean Sea)

SYRO-PHOENICIA

ABILENE

SYRIA

Sidon

Damascus

Tyre

MT. HERMON

Caesarea Philippi

ITURAEA

TRACHONITIS

GALILEE

GAULANITIS

Ptolemais

Chorazin

Bethsaida

Capernaum

LAKE OF GENNESARET
(SEA OF GALILEE)

Cana

Magdala

Tiberias

Hippos

Dion

Kanata

Nazareth

Nain

Gadara

Abila

DECAPOLIS

PLAIN OF SHARON

Caesarea

Scythopolis

Salim

Pella

SAMARIA

Sebaste

Sychar

Gerasa

Jacob's Well

Antipatris

RIVER
JABBOK

Joppa

Arimathea

Alexandrium

PEREA

Lydda

Ephraim

Philadelphia

Jamnia

Emmaus

Jericho

RIVER
JORDAN

Azotus

Jerusalem

Kh.
Qumrân

Bethlehem

Bethany

Ashkelon

JUDEA

Herodium

Machaerus

Gaza

Hebron

SALT SEA

(DEAD SEA)

N

Beer-sheba

IDUMAEA

N A B A T A E A

N

Miles

0   10   20   30   40   50

palacios

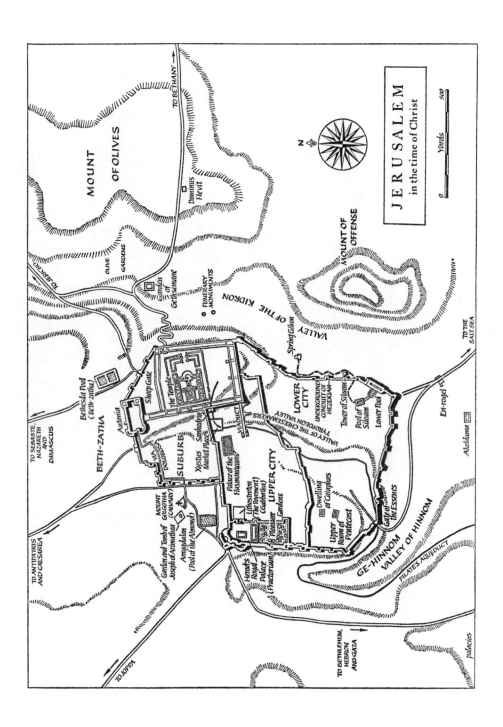

JERUSALEM
in the time of Christ

Yards 0 500

MOUNT OF OLIVES

TO BETHANY

Dominus Flevit

MOUNT OF OFFENSE

OLIVE GARDENS

Garden of Gethsemane

FUNERARY MONUMENTS

VALLEY OF THE KIDRON

Spring Gihon

TO JERICHO

Bethesda Pool (Beth-zatha)

Sheep Gate

Antonia

The Temple

VIADUCT

LOWER CITY

UNDERGROUND CONDUIT OF HEZEKIAH

Tower of Siloam

Pool of Siloam

Lower Pool

TO SEBASTE, NAZARETH AND DAMASCUS

BETH-ZATHA

SUBURB

DOLOROSA

Sanhedrin

Xystus

Market Place

Palace of the Hasmonaeans

VALLEY OF THE CHEESEMAKERS or TYROPOEON VALLEY

En-rogel

TO THE SALT SEA

TO ANTIPATRIS AND CAESAREA

MOUNT GOLGOTHA (CALVARY)

Garden and Tomb of Joseph of Arimathea

Amygdalon (Pool of the Almond)

Lithostraton (The Pavement) (Gabbatha)

UPPER CITY

Pleasure Gardens

Dwelling of Caiaphas

Upper Room of Pentecost

Gate of the Essenes

Aceldama

Herod's Royal Palace (Praetorium)

GE-HINNOM VALLEY OF HINNOM

PILATES AQUEDUCT

TO BETHLEHEM, HEBRON AND GAZA

TO JOPPA

Palacios

N

1. SOME PRELIMINARIES

When Tatian produced his *Diatessaron* sometime in the latter part of the second Christian century, he probably continued rather than began a tradition of reading the four Gospels in harmony, the tradition that justifies the arrangement of this present book. Whether or not Tatian's work was the first of its kind, it was certainly one of the most successful. For several centuries it was only in this form that the Gospels were known to a sizable part of Oriental Christianity.

There was and is both good and bad in the *Diatessaron* and the innumerable "harmonies" that have followed in its wake. On the debit side, such works have encouraged a simplistic view of the Gospels that has given a bad name to the term harmonization. This was especially true of the *Diatessaron* and its imitators, which coalesced the four Gospels into a single narrative, forming an eclectic text for which none of the evangelists was really responsible and suppressing in the process those very signs of individual genius which are the stamp of the inspired authors chosen by the Spirit of God. However ancient this kind of harmony may be, even at its best it settles for a very superficial reading of the Gospels in which matter is preferred to form, flesh to spirit. At its worst it masks a fundamental misconception of what the Gospels are all about.

To read the Gospels in concert, on the other hand, is simply to respond to the invitation the Gospels themselves offer—the first three of them, at any rate. The kind of harmony which arranges the Gospels in parallel columns to show both their similarities and differences affords us an added dimension for the understanding of each individual Gospel. The Gospels were not written in isolation from one another, at least not from the common tradition to which they all witness, and therefore they should not be read in isolation. True, they must also be read as the distinct creations of distinct authors; however, a harmony of the Gospels, if it is rightly used, can only constantly remind us of what is unique about each of the parallels.

Four Gospels or a Life of Christ? A remaining objection that may be lodged against the simultaneous treatment of the Gospels, especially when this includes the Gospel of John, is that it may

seek to pursue the outmoded approach to the Gospels that is summed up
in the title "the Life of Christ." The countless volumes that bear this title
or its equivalent (those who regarded themselves as disinterested historical
critics preferred to write a *Life of Jesus*), mainly from the latter part of
the past century and the first quarter of the present, are a monument to
an age of Gospel study that was not without value but was certainly mis-
directed. The Gospels are not a Life of Christ, for two very good reasons.
Firstly, they do not provide even the minimal amount of material that is
required to write the Life of anyone. Oddly enough, most of those who
set about writing the Lives admitted this from the outset. Secondly, and
more importantly, the Gospels were not composed, nor were their sources
formed, from any such biographical intention.

Whether by believer or unbeliever, the classic *Life of Jesus* was the
product of what has been variously termed rationalism, historical positiv-
ism, or historicism. Born of the Enlightenment and of modern critical
historical method, "the quest of the historical Jesus," as the process has
been called, was the attempt to reconstruct from the Gospels what could
be certainly known of Jesus by means of the scientific methods of the
historian. The unbeliever, who began the process, not surprisingly
found the Gospels to have been written in total disregard of modern
historical canons. As a result, he concluded that little if anything could be
said about Jesus scientifically. This in itself would not have been so bad,
of course. What proved to be bad was his reluctance to leave the matter
there. Instead, he tended to supply for a Gospel picture which by his
lights could not be historical with a highly unscientific series of recon-
structions which owed more to his sense of the fitness of things than to
historical evidence. "The so-called historical Jesus of the nineteenth-
century biographies," Albert Schweitzer wrote in 1906, "is really a modern-
ization, in which Jesus is painted in the colours of modern bourgeois
respectability and neo-Kantian moralism."

The believing Christian who wrote his *Life of Christ* in opposition to
all this usually tried to show that the Gospels were, after all, the kind
of history that the unbeliever said they were not. Very often he could not
do this in any very convincing way, but he felt it to be necessary if he
was to use the Gospels to set forth the historical person and message of
Jesus Christ. Both believer and unbeliever found it quite natural, in other
words, to measure the Gospels against a concept and standards of history
writing that are really not more than a couple of centuries old. Both were
wrong.

That the Gospels are historical documents of a high order, the writer
firmly believes. They are the work of men who were rooted in history,
who were themselves products of the history they wrote, a history that was
the very breath of their being. But the Gospels are not the self-authen-
ticating history desiderated by the modern historian. They do not appeal

to disinterested witnesses to establish as factual anything they record. They were not written to prove that certain events had really taken place; they were written to explain what those events meant and what they continue to mean. They begin by taking for granted what the modern historian considers it to be the function of his craft to demonstrate, and they immediately intrude into areas from which he feels himself debarred. In his sense of the word, they are not at all objective. They mingle narration of fact with interpretation of fact, eyewitness record with hearsay report, statistical data with theological speculation.

The Gospels acknowledge few of the conventions that the modern historian regards as essential. The exact determination of dates, places, persons, circumstances, the proper sequence of events—all this is the life-blood of history as we have been taught to know it, and yet the Gospels can be utterly casual about any or all of it. Of such stuff as are the Gospels, biographies are not made.

Synoptic   Historical records though they be, the Gospels were never
Gospels   intended to form the source material for a Life of Jesus. This
            is not to say that they were not interested in his life, which
of course they were. They were interested in it, however, not as a past event but as an enduring reality—this, as a matter of fact, is what the authors of the Gospels would have understood as the meaning of history. The Gospels contain, therefore, little if anything that is of purely bio-graphical interest. It is true, they present Jesus of Nazareth as he was known to the original eyewitnesses of the Gospel (Lk 1:2); but this Jesus is at one and the same time the Christ encountered by faith living and acting in his Church, and it is this Christ who is the Jesus of the Gospels.

For a long time it has been customary to refer to the first three Gospels as Synoptic because of the common view (*synopsis*) they assume in narrating the Gospel story. They follow basically the same order, con-tain roughly the same material, and obviously have some kind of literary affinity one with another. In all these respects they differ quite sharply from the Gospel of John, which goes its own distinctive way in order, content, vocabulary, and viewpoints.

The tradition to which the Synoptic Gospels have given literary fixation rose from the apostolic *kerygma* of the primitive Church, the "message of good news" by which the divine work of salvation achieved in Jesus Christ was proclaimed to the world by the first Christian witnesses. It is this character, in fact, which has given us our word Gospel (Anglo-Saxon *god spel*, good tidings), a literal translation of the Greek *euangelion*, Latinized as *evangelium*, from which we derive our "evangelist." The concept of salvation as the proclamation of good news which was likewise a summons to faith was already ancient in biblical tradition (see especially

Is 40:1–11; 52:7–10; 61:1–3, passages which have considerably influenced the New Testament and its authors). A good summary of the apostolic *kerygma* can be found in Acts 10:37–43, the sermon of St. Peter to the Gentiles. The attentive reader will note how this sermon is arranged according to the basic outline followed by the Synoptics: baptism by John the Baptist, the Galilean ministry, a journey to Jerusalem, and the narrative of Christ's suffering, crucifixion, and resurrection. In essence, too, the content of the Synoptic tradition is described in the few lines of this sermon.

The Synoptic Gospels are not, however, the *kerygma* itself but a development of it. The *kerygma* was and is the proclamation of revelation for acceptance in faith, the word of Christ which awakens faith (Rom 10:17). It addresses itself to those who do not yet believe. The Gospels, on the contrary, were written for believers, for Christians, both to deepen a faith that already existed and, even more importantly, to draw out for the reader all the implications of the words and deeds of Christ which formed the object of his faith (Lk 1:4; Jn 20:31). We might describe the difference by calling the *kerygma* preaching and the Gospels teaching, though of course the two are not always perfectly distinguished.

Why were the Gospels written? The answer to this question is not quite as obvious as it might seem. The Church, after all, got along without a written Gospel during the entirety of its first long generation, a generation that was also doubtless its most important from the standpoint of formation and development. The letters of St. Paul, without which a theology of the New Testament would hardly be thinkable, were all written before the emergence of the Gospels. Paul, too, and with him most of the other New Testament writers who were his contemporaries, shows what initially seems to be a surprising lack of interest in many of the things with which the Gospels are most concerned. He refers in passing to Jesus' birth and also to his death, burial, and resurrection and his institution of the Eucharist; but otherwise he hardly ever adverts to Jesus' earthly life. Never does he mention the Galilean ministry, which occupies a place of major stress in the Synoptic Gospels. It is at least conceivable, therefore, that subsequent generations of Christians could have continued like the first, without a written record of the Gospel stories that now mean so much to us.

As it happens, however, we possess the Gospels as a heritage from apostolic Christianity, a real testament and legacy of the first generation of the Church. The first Christians lived within an apostolic tradition that was not only preservative but also constitutive and creative (Acts 2:42; 1 Cor 11:23; Eph 3:3; 2 Thes 2:15; Jn 14:26; etc.). With the passing away of the apostolic age, however, it was recognized then as it is now that an era never to be recovered now belonged to history; the Church, so to speak, was now "on its own." Falling back upon the strong historical

tradition to which they belonged, the evangelists therefore produced the
Gospels as a permanent record for all time of the good news of the
Christ-event as the apostolic Church had come to know it in its witness
and experience, in its preaching and teaching, and in its meditation and
contemplation of it in the light of the Holy Spirit. It was probably inevitable that the first Gospels should have followed the outline of the
apostolic *kerygma*, the summary form in which the message of the good
news had been preached during this long generation. Neither was it
accidental that they should lay such stress on the earthly career of Jesus,
on the events that had given rise to the faith and liturgy, the life and
hope of the Church. The first heresies were already appearing, of a
Gnostic and Docetist stamp, which would reduce Christianity to a mere
philosophy by denying or declaring irrelevant its roots in history (see
1 Jn 4:1-3; 5:6; 2 Jn 7, etc.).

Form   Before we discuss briefly the separate characters of the
Criticism   several Gospels that were produced toward the end of the
               apostolic age, we must pause to consider the role played by
the apostolic Church in forming the materials that have gone into these
written Gospels. This is the dimension of New Testament study that
nowadays goes by the general name of "form criticism."

Anyone who has read the Synoptic Gospels even casually, or who is
familiar with them from their use as liturgical readings, cannot fail to have
observed how easily they may be divided into short, self-contained units
of narrative or discourse, each of which can make its own point or
points often quite independently of its immediate context. The fact becomes even more obvious when the Gospels are read in parallel, and it
can be seen that the same episode has often been assigned to different
contexts, sometimes thereby taking on a different specific application.
This phenomenon demands an explanation, which it is not hard to give.
The Synoptic tradition on which our Gospels have drawn and which
used the apostolic *kerygma* for its model was itself composed of many
prior traditions: its components were originally independent elements
of the tradition—written or oral—which had handed on the memory of
the words and deeds of the Master.

These components are the "forms" with which form criticism deals.
They are called this because they tend to fall into a certain limited
number of categories which can be distinguished one from another. One
common form, for example, is the "conflict story." In the conflict story
Jesus is pictured in controversy with one or another of the groups which
the Gospels represent as his habitual opponents, usually designated as the
scribes and/or Pharisees or the chief priests of Jerusalem. The point at
issue is some action or word of Jesus or of those identified with him—
his claim to forgive sins, his attitude toward the Sabbath or the Law of

Moses, his disciples' violation of Pharisaical ideas of propriety, and the like. Encapsulated in each conflict story is a pronouncement of the Lord which appears as its climax and gives the "moral" of the story. The stories are brief and to the point; details that could detract from the main issue have been pared away. This pattern is repeated time and time again throughout the Gospels. A series of five such conflict stories can be found gathered together in Mk 2:1–3:6, paralleled by Lk 5:18–6:11 and by Mt 9:1–17, 12:1–14, where they have been separated into two groups of three and two respectively.

The isolation and determination of the forms immediately leads to other questions. Why the preference for certain forms rather than for others? What do the forms themselves tell us with regard to the Church that transmitted the Gospel tradition? And, if we can answer these questions satisfactorily, what do we thereby conclude in respect to the historical origin of the recorded event and its significance for the evangelist and the tradition on which he drew? To consider these questions is the real task of form criticism, whose scope is better expressed by a more literal translation of the German term (*Formgeschichte*) of which it is the equivalent: "the history of the forms."

The prevalence of the conflict story involving the Jewish leadership of Jesus' day, to continue with the example taken above, can hardly be dissociated from the history of the apostolic Church as we know it from Acts and especially the Pauline epistles. This was, by and large, a history of conflict with Jews, both with Jews who refused to accept Christ and with those Jewish Christians who would have so identified the Church with its Jewish origins that the death and resurrection of Christ would have been made void. To all extents and purposes, the only opposition experienced by the Church during its formative years was Jewish. Only toward the very end of this period did the great secular power of the age, the Roman empire, begin to move against a Christianity in which it now dimly recognized a threat to its omnipotent sway over men's minds. (Characteristically, the later Apocalypse of John identifies the Antichrist with the Roman emperor, whereas the Johannine epistles consider every apostate and schismatic to be an Antichrist, and an anti-Roman bias is utterly lacking in the Gospels.) It was only to be expected that this history of Jewish controversy should have affected the transmission of the Gospel materials. Throughout this entire period the Church searched its memory for precedents, for instances in the life of its Master which paralleled its own concerns, when answers had been given in principle to what had become the burning issues of Christian survival. How better to refute the Jewish adversaries of Christianity than by appealing to what Jesus himself had done and said in analogous circumstances?

The other forms of the Gospel materials have a similar explanation. The pastoral, catechetical, apologetical, and liturgical uses of the Church have all had a considerable influence on the development of these forms. The very passages which we find it convenient to cite in making a point or teaching a lesson were, in other words, first employed by the apostolic Church for these same purposes, and it is this early Christian use that has imprinted itself on the tradition. Form critical study is, therefore, a modern approach to the ancient principle that it was the Church that produced the New Testament and that the Gospels ought not to be interpreted apart from the Church's life and belief. It will be our duty to refer to this principle often in the course of this book.

Some of the form critics, to be sure, have drawn unwarranted conclusions from their studies. Simply because it can be seen that a given passage had a role to play in the life of the Church, what the form critics call its *Sitz im Leben*, its "setting in life," is no reason to call its historical reality into question. Those critics who maintain that the Church simply invented such a passage to justify its belief or practice do so from no evidence supplied by form criticism but on the grounds of skeptical principles they have inherited from other sources. That the Gospel has an authentic *Sitz im Leben* of the primitive Church does not mean that it does not have an equally authentic *Sitz im Leben* of Jesus himself. It must be studied in both dimensions, and also, of course, in the dimension of the individual evangelist who is involved as author. While warning against exaggerations, therefore, in an historic instruction dated April 21, 1964, the Pontifical Biblical Commission wisely commended the use of form criticism to Catholic interpreters of the Gospels, and even insisted on it as necessary for a full understanding of their meaning. The substance of this instruction has been incorporated by the Fathers of the Second Vatican Council into their dogmatic constitution on Divine Revelation.

The Gospel of Mark   We should now turn to a consideration, however brief, of the specific characteristics of the four Gospels with which we shall be dealing in this book. We have already seen that the Synoptic Gospels grew out of the apostolic *kerygma*. Perhaps we can now be more precise. As far as we know, of the four Gospels that we possess, the one we know as the Gospel of Mark was the first to be written, sometime between the years 60 to 70 of the Christian era. "As far as we know," and "of the four Gospels that we possess": as we shall see, there is a possibility that there was an even earlier Gospel of Matthew, which, however, is not the work that has been preserved as our first Gospel.

The determination of the priority of Mark is very much bound up with the solution of the "Synoptic question," that is, the explanation of what seems to be an undeniable literary connection between the three Synoptic Gospels. That this connection was indeed literary and not merely the result of dependence on a common tradition is obvious to most scholars. It is not only that the three Gospels follow broadly the same

outline and contain essentially the same traditional materials; they also
sometimes agree word for word sentence after sentence, and in the process
they manage at times to use the same unusual Greek words (in some
instances, words that are found nowhere else in all Greek literature).
Particularly striking is their manner of citing the Old Testament. More
than once they agree verbally on a quotation that represents a version all
their own, corresponding precisely neither to the Hebrew text nor to the
standard Greek translation of the Old Testament (the Septuagint). The
conclusion seems to be inescapable either that they have all drawn on the
same literary source or that they have a literary dependence one on
another.

The explanation that appears to accord best both with the phenome-
nology of the Synoptic situation and with ancient Christian tradition concerning the Gospels is that Mark has been used as a literary source by
both Matthew and Luke. When the three Gospels are read in parallel
attentively, it will be seen that while Mark has practically nothing that is
not also in Matthew or Luke or both, almost invariably it is his version
of the events that is the lengthiest, the most circumstanced and detailed,
the closest to the eyewitness record from which it ultimately derives. Not
everyone will agree that this is so—there have been literally hundreds of
theories proposed to solve the Synoptic problem. But nowadays probably
most scholars would agree that one of the sources used by the Gospels of
Matthew and Luke was the Gospel of Mark. Or, if not the canonical
Gospel in the form we have it, at least a document that was almost
precisely identical with it. The attempt to explain Mark as dependent on
either Matthew or Luke, on the other hand, has been singularly un-
convincing.

There is no serious reason to doubt the consistent Christian tradition
which has identified as the author of this Gospel the New Testament
personage known to Peter and Paul as Mark (Col 4:10; Phlm 24; 2 Tim
4:11; 1 Pt 5:13) and called John Mark in the Acts of the Apostles
(12:12, 25, 13:13, 15:37). For one thing, his relative obscurity in the early
Church is warrant enough for the reliability of the tradition. Mark was not
one of the apostles or leaders in the Church. He was a cousin of Paul's
associate Barnabas; at various times he was the companion of both Peter
and Paul, with whom he had at least a temporary falling out. He was
doubtless a Jew from Jerusalem, where his mother maintained what
was evidently a substantial household.

Neither is there any reason to question the tradition, first related by
Papias, the Bishop of Hierapolis (about A.D. 130), that the basis of
Mark's Gospel was the *kerygma* as preached by Peter in Rome. Another
tradition, preserved by Irenaeus of Lyons (about A.D. 190), which places
the composition of the Gospel in Rome after Peter's death, is doubtless
also correct. There can be no doubt that Mark's Gospel is heavily in debt

to an eyewitness account which from internal considerations can hardly be other than Peter's. Furthermore, though Mark's Greek is greatly influenced by Semitisms—turns of phrase that show him to have been more at home with Palestinian Aramaic than with the Greek of the Gentile world—it also contains a surprising number of Latinisms—Latin words used in preference to Greek—which suggests that the Gospel was written in an environment where Latin was spoken.

We are not to suppose that Mark's dependence on Peter was such that he merely wrote down a Gospel of which Peter was the real author. As we have already seen, the written Gospels are an outgrowth of the *kerygma,* not the *kerygma* itself. Mark had at his disposal the materials of which we have spoken above in discussing form criticism, the written and oral forms in which the traditions about Jesus had been handed down in the apostolic Church, some still preserving their Palestinian primitiveness, others marked by the now generally Gentile character of Christianity. These he combined with Peter's testimony and worked into an art form distinctively his own, for Mark was a true author.

Mark's Gospel has suffered in comparison with those of Matthew and Luke. It has even been called simply "a passion story with an introduction." This is to do less than justice to Mark's artistry. It is true that his style tends to be laconic and unpolished, that he has expressed his own personality relatively little, that he has "done" less with the Gospel form than either Matthew or Luke. However, there is far more subtlety to Mark than appears on the surface, and there is a great deal of theology in this Gospel, as we shall have occasion to see. One of Mark's unique contributions to the Gospel record is the so-called "messianic secret," of which we shall speak later.

The Gospel of Luke   Scholars may disagree as to whether Luke's or Matthew's Gospel is the older, but probably the majority would give the priority to Luke. As indicated above, one of its main sources has been the Gospel of Mark; this source accounts for about one third of Luke's Gospel. Another major source unknown to Mark has been used by both Matthew and Luke: it is this that accounts for the special correspondence of these two Gospels within the Synoptic tradition. For many reasons that will be made plain in the commentary, however, it appears that the two Gospels were composed quite independently of each other. That is to say, while they both depend on Mark and the other common source, there is no mutual dependence.

Like Mark, Luke was a relatively obscure figure in the early Church, and we have therefore all the more reason to accept the second-century tradition which names him the author of the Third Gospel. He is the one New Testament writer whom we can identify with almost utter certainty as a non-Jew; this is the obvious sense of Col 4:14, in which Paul distinguishes Luke from Jews like Mark and Jesus Justus. In this same verse Luke is called by Paul an *iatros*. The word means "physician," but whether it was intended as a literal or a figurative designation may be debated. On the supposition that it does refer to Luke's profession, many authors have felt that a medical background may be discerned in his work (see, for example, the commentary on Lk 8:43). However this may be, it is certain that Luke was a man of some education and cultivation. He seems to have joined St. Paul during his "second missionary journey" (is Luke the Macedonian of Acts 16:9 f. who appeared to call Paul from Asia into Europe?); thereafter he became his inseparable companion.

The provenance of Luke's Gospel is something of an enigma. He was with St. Paul in Rome during the apostle's imprisonment there (about A.D. 61–63), where he could have become acquainted with Mark's Gospel or its prototype. He was also with him in Caesarea of Palestine (A.D. 59–60) where he would have had a unique opportunity to follow up the traditions handed down by the original eyewitnesses and servants of the Gospel (Lk 1:2). Again, he spent several years with Paul in Ephesus (A.D. 54–57), the home of the Johannine school of the New Testament: of all the Synoptic Gospels, Luke's has the greatest affinity for the Gospel of John. Yet nowhere within or without the Gospel are we given a hint of its place of origin. Perhaps this is part of its genius. Of all the Gospels, Luke's may be considered the most "catholic," the least identified with anything regional or partisan in Christianity. It is the Gospel of a Church that had become Catholic in fact as well as in principle.

Part of Luke's Catholicity is evidenced in his unique conception of the Gospel as the first half of a two-part work which is concluded in the Acts of the Apostles. The Acts, which has aptly been called "the Gospel of the Holy Spirit," underlines Luke's leitmotiv, which is the universality of salvation. In Acts the witness to the good news first proclaimed in the villages of Galilee is dramatically portrayed as extending to all the known world (the theme of Acts 1:8), while meantime every class of person is seen to have been embraced by Christianity: Jews both Hebrew and Hellenist, Samaritans, proselytes, Gentiles. Because the period covered by Acts ends with Paul's Roman imprisonment unresolved, it was once thought that Acts, and therefore the Gospel which preceded it, could be dated no later than A.D. 63, since otherwise Luke would have been able to describe Paul's subsequent fate. It is now recognized that this was to underrate Luke's imagination. Acts ends precisely where he intended it to end, with the Church planted at the center of the Roman world, looking forward to the limitless future that is the final stage in the history of salvation. Because Lk 19:43 f. and 21:20, 24 make it appear that the author had actually seen the destruction of Jerusalem (in A.D. 70) foretold by Jesus, most critics nowadays would date the Gospel of Luke around A.D. 80 or so.

1

Luke's Gospel is a production of high literary quality which tells us a great deal about the author. It has been cast in one of the literary forms then current, something like a travelogue: he represents Jesus' ministry as a long journey from Galilee, where all things begin, to Jerusalem, where they are consummated. (The same travelogue device is employed in Acts.) After the fashion of contemporary Gentile writing he has prefaced to his work a dedication and declaration of intention. He has imitated the existing "lives" of great men by including stories of Jesus' birth and pre-ministerial career and by collating the Gospel events to some extent with the chronology of profane history. In developing the theme of John the Baptist as forerunner of Jesus, he was not content simply to state the fact, but he has carefully paralleled the annunciation, birth, and early history of the Baptist ("the last prophet of the Old Testament") with those of Jesus ("the prophet of the New Testament") in a masterful development wherein the Baptist gradually recedes from the forefront, leaving the stage to Jesus.

In his use of the Marcan material, Luke has omitted narrations or details which would be misunderstood or unappreciated by Gentiles; he has either omitted or translated Semitic words or concepts into their Greek equivalents. His tendency throughout has been to smooth away difficulties—sometimes, it must be admitted, by the adoption of somewhat simplistic interpretations of words or events. In the passion narrative, on the other hand, he follows a version of the events which sometimes differs from that of Mark (who is followed by Matthew) and often offers a more realistic picture, as we shall see.

Together with Matthew and John, though not always in the same way or in the same passages, Luke has "actualized" the Gospel narrative far more than Mark has done. That is to say, he has related the words or deeds of Jesus in a way calculated to apply to the later times of the Church in which he lived.

The Gospel of Matthew   When we turn to the Gospel of Matthew we are immediately presented with a whole series of problems. First of all, who is the author of this Gospel? Constant tradition, beginning with the Papias whom we mentioned in connection with Mark, has identified him with Matthew the apostle, also known as Levi, one of the Twelve who lived intimately with Jesus and who were the eyewitnesses to whom Luke appeals in his prologue. However, it is evident to almost everyone that the Gospel of Matthew has used Mark as one of its main sources. Why should one who had been an eyewitness to the Gospel events employ the work of another who had not been, whose acquaintance with them had been only indirect, through another apostle? Furthermore, both Papias and Irenaeus relate that Matthew wrote his Gospel in "Hebrew," by which they doubtless meant the Aramaic lan-

guage spoken by the Jews of Palestine ("Hebrew" is used in this sense in
Acts 21:40). Our canonical Gospel of Matthew, however, as those who
have studied its Greek will testify to a man, is not the translation of anything, Aramaic or otherwise. It is a work that was composed originally in
Greek, often enough employing plays on words that make sense only in
that language. It contains rather fewer Semitisms than Mark.

On the other hand, there are numerous traits to Matthew's Gospel
which characterize it as Jewish. For one thing, it cites the Old Testament
almost as many times as all the other Gospels combined, and in its
independent use of these texts it appears to have made its own translation
of the Hebrew original. It has preserved peculiarly Jewish manners of
expression which the other Gospels have not (e.g., "kingdom of heaven"
in place of "kingdom of God"), along with peculiarly Semitic literary
or rhetorical forms like "inclusion." ("Inclusion" is the device whereby
the same catch phrase is used to introduce and to conclude a theme.
Note the repeated "by their fruits you will know them" in Mt 7:16–20,
and contrast the parallel in Lk 6:43–45.) Frequently enough a passage
paralleled in Mark or Luke will have signs of an added Jewish influence
in the Matthaean version. (See, for example, the commentary on Mt
19:3–9.)

The Jewishness of Matthew's Gospel not surprisingly has given rise to a
popular idea that it was written for Jewish Christians in contrast to
Luke's, which is obviously Gentile in its orientation. This idea, however,
can hardly be correct. When Matthew is read in the whole, it is clear
enough that for its author the period of Jewish Christianity now belongs
to the past. Not only is the Church destined to embrace all mankind
(Mt 28:19), this Gospel goes out of its way to insist that the Church is
now properly Gentile rather than Jewish (cf. 8:11 f., 21:43 f., etc.). It is
no accident that Matthew, of all the Gospels, gives the greatest space to
the relations between Jesus and scribal Judaism: the author stands in the
greatest possible opposition to the Judaizing tendencies of Jewish Christianity. There are even some passages in the Gospel which in the view of
some prove that the author could not possibly have been a Jew (see the
commentary on Mt 12:11, 21:5).

To explain all these paradoxes is not easy. Nevertheless, there are certain facts which can be reasonably connected in order to give at least a
partial solution. The common source besides Mark that has been used by
the Gospels of Matthew and Luke (called Q by the critics, from the
German *Quelle*, source), may very well have been the original Aramaic
Gospel written by the apostle Matthew and later translated into Greek.
It is interesting to note that Papias referred to this Aramaic work as the
"sayings" (*logia*) of Jesus, and that the Q material of Matthew and Luke
does largely consist of discourses, whereas Mark is almost exclusively narrative, recording the Lord's words only where they occur as pronounce-

ments in forms like the conflict stories. This Aramaic work, which would
have been treasured as an early apostolic witness, may have been circulated
in various forms throughout the Church. If we may imagine the use made
of it by the First Gospel as much more extensive and more literal than
that of Luke, we may have the explanation both of Matthew's Jewish
coloration and the persistent ascription of this Gospel to the apostle
Matthew.

However, the inspired author of our Gospel of Matthew—for it is the
Greek Gospel as we possess it that has been declared canonical by the
Church—is a later writer who, like Luke, has made use of Mark, of Q, and
other sources proper to himself, to produce this testament of apostolic
Christianity. Who he was, we do not know. The internal evidence would
indicate that the Gospel was written no earlier than that of Luke; but
whether by a Jewish Christian or a Gentile, may be debated. Its early
use by St. Ignatius of Antioch has suggested to many that its place of
composition was Syria, and doubtless it did emanate from such an ancient,
non-Jewish center of Christianity as this.

The signs of Matthew's mixed origins are plentiful. We have already
noted some indications of its Jewish background, and we shall have
occasion to note various others. The fact that Jesus' teaching appears in
the Gospel divided into five long discourses is probably one of these: it is
the new Torah. Corresponding to this is Matthew's portrayal of Jesus on
the Mountain as a new Moses once more revealing the Law to Israel.
The Gospel displays a predilection for the number seven and other
combinations reminiscent of the Old Testament. However, far more important in determining the distinctive qualities of this Gospel have been
the developments within the Church that produced it and the consequent
concerns of those for whom it was written.

Matthew's is, in point of fact, the Gospel of the Church par excellence.
It is the only Gospel in which the word "Church" is actually used. None
of the other Gospels has treated of the Church so systematically—of its
Old Testament roots, of the spirit of its law, of its structure, its sacraments,
its hierarchy, and its eschatology. It is this and other associated qualities
that give it a perennial relevance that may be seen reflected in its
customary use as the "standard" Gospel.

The Gospel   No one can think of the relevance of the Gospel message,
of John   however, or of the discourses of Jesus, without immediately
              taking cognizance of the Gospel of John. We can go
further than this. Despite all their several virtues and their indispensable
contributions, the Synoptic Gospels alone could never have transmitted
the fullness of the heritage of apostolic Christianity. For this, in God's
providence, we have been given the Fourth Gospel.

Since the second century, Christian tradition has placed the origin of this Gospel in Ephesus, the work of John the apostle, the son of Zebedee (mentioned as such by all the Synoptic Gospels, but never by John!). The Gospel itself claims to rest on the authority of an eyewitness who was an immediate disciple of Jesus, and by a process of elimination this unnamed disciple may be reasonably identified with John the apostle. It displays a familiarity with the Palestinian scene that often surpasses that of the Synoptic Gospels, and in much of its language it betrays the influence of Aramaic, the speech of a Palestinian Jew.

If there is good reason to ascribe the Gospel to the apostolic authority of John, however, there is equally good reason to suppose that he is not the literary author of the Gospel as we have it. The literary author would be, rather, a disciple of the apostle or, perhaps more precisely, a school of disciples (see especially Jn 21:24). There are various reasons for this judgment. One is the fact, recognized also from quite early Christian times, that the same person could not have been the literary author of works as diverse in style and content as the Gospel, the three Johannine epistles, and the Apocalypse—all of which, however, have been confidently ascribed to the same apostle. Even more important is the evidence which the Gospel itself gives of having been composed in stages, often with the use of variant versions of the same material. The most natural accounting for this phenomenon is the supposition that the Gospel was dictated in snatches over a considerable period of time, sometimes repetitiously, and that only after the removal of its author, presumably by death, was it put together by those who were no longer sure of the intended order or sequence. As we shall see, this supposition goes far toward explaining away what would otherwise be some insurmountable difficulties encountered in this Gospel. What is most certain, however, needs no explaining away—and that is, that this Gospel is throughout the product of a single mind that has authored its distinctive concepts and contributed to it all that makes it uniquely the Gospel of John.

It has always been generally taken for granted that John's is a "late" Gospel. Early Christian tradition regarded it as a work of the apostle's old age, a final testament intended to supplement and complete the work of the Synoptics. Led by considerations of style and of the presumed development of doctrine within Christianity itself, critics of the past century very commonly tended to make it quite late indeed, from sometime well into the second Christian century. Most of the reasons on which such judgments were grounded are no longer accorded much weight by present-day students of the Gospel and its background. Strictly speaking, there is no reason why John could not be as old as the Synoptic Gospels. Its admittedly distinctive language that sets it apart from the Synoptics is, nevertheless, just as authentically Palestinian: the so-called Dead Sea Scrolls first discovered in 1947 have helped to make this clear. The fact that we now possess a manuscript fragment of the Gospel of John (the Rylands Papyrus) that cannot be more recent than about A.D. 130–50 confirms the tradition sufficiently that would set its origins in the last decades of the first century.

The many contrasts between John and the Synoptic Gospels go to make up what has been posed as "the Johannine question." Only rarely does John coincide with the Synoptics in relating the same event or saying of Jesus, and even in these rare instances of agreement the order, lesson, or application may still be diverse. Much less obvious instances of correspondence occur in which there may be a genuine parallel between the two traditions as respects one or several events, which, however, are likely to appear as a unit in the Synoptic Gospels and as dispersed episodes in John, or vice versa. The chronology and the geographical emphases of John are quite out of harmony with those of the Synoptic Gospels. Most importantly however, the picture of the Johannine Christ does seem to differ radically from that of the Synoptic Jesus. In the Synoptic Gospels Jesus appears in the recognizable role of a Palestinian teacher, speaking in parables and in the easy language of the people, and working miracles of healing and of exorcism. In John there are few miracles, no exorcisms, and no parables—and the Christ who speaks does so in magisterial tones and in a language that is typical of the Johannine epistles as well as of the Gospel, but not at all of the Synoptic Gospels.

That this situation should have been characterized as a Johannine question involves in part a kind of prejudgment. There is, after all, no particular reason why John should be measured against the standard of the Synoptic Gospels rather than the other way round. In the past, however, it was often taken for granted that while the Synoptics had confined themselves more or less to the actual historical conditions of the life and teaching of Jesus, John had disregarded them in the interests of his advanced theology and had transmuted Jesus' words into the language of later Christianity. As already indicated, this simple view can no longer be maintained. Both in the Synoptics and in John, Jesus speaks as a Palestinian Jew, and while some explanation must be given of the respective emphases, neither is antecedently more or less "historical" than the other. The same kind of judgment must be made concerning the other discrepancies between John and the Synoptics.

It is far more likely, for example, that Jesus paid multiple visits to Jerusalem, as John tells the story, than that he should have come only the one time mentioned in the Synoptic outline. Here and elsewhere the kerygmatic framework adopted by the Synoptics has doubtless synthesized, telescoped, and assimilated the historical facts in the interest of a topical and logical rather than a chronological order. In one sense the Synoptics are "timeless": from them alone we could not determine whether Jesus' ministry lasted a year or several or perhaps only a few months. John, on the other hand, probably does intend to give us a chronology of the ministry, at least in a limited way. We must insist that it is only in a limited way, because for John as well as for the Synoptics chronology and such matters are always subordinated to deeper concerns. Once and for all, let it be noted that in arranging the Gospel passages as we have in this book, relating the Synoptic material to John and John to the Synoptics, we do not intend to make the chronology any more precise than the Gospels themselves intended. Sometimes it is altogether impossible to "harmonize" the two blocs of tradition—just as it is sometimes impossible to reconcile the Synoptics completely among themselves—for the very good reason that the materials with which we deal were not designed with any such end in view.

When all is said and done, the basic difference between John and the Synoptic Gospels is that while the latter are an outgrowth of the standard apostolic *kerygma* the Fourth Gospel has developed independently of it. This is not to say that it is unaware of the Synoptic tradition; on the contrary, it seems to presuppose it on any number of occasions. Whether there has been any dependence of the written Gospel of John on the written Synoptic Gospels may be disputed. Probably the majority view would have it that John has been written with advertence to the Gospel of Mark, but there does not appear to be any conclusive evidence to link it to the other Synoptics. The undoubted affinity of John for Luke, as was suggested above, may very well be accounted for by Luke's knowledge of the Johannine tradition.

Developed apart from the Synoptic outline and perspective, the Gospel of John is uniquely the witness of its apostolic author. It is the fruit of a lifetime of meditation on the enduring historical significance of Jesus' words and deeds in which the three Gospel "depths" of which we spoke above tend to merge and unite. In it we hear speaking at one and the same time the Jesus of history, the Jesus living in his Church through the grace and enlightenment of the Holy Spirit, and the Jesus known through his prophet John. No other Gospel so much repays careful reading as does this one. Its special characteristics we can best see in the commentary, but suffice it to say for the present that it was not for nothing that the early Fathers called this the "spiritual" Gospel and spoke of its author as the Theologian.

Roman   Having made some necessary observations on the nature of
Palestine   the literature with which we shall be concerned in this book,
              we should also say a few words about the world in which it
grew up and with which it deals. It was, of course, a Roman world. The Gospels emerged from important centers of the worldwide Roman empire: Ephesus, Antioch, Rome itself. They appeared in the Greek language which was official throughout the Empire. Their setting is Roman Palestine, a tiny and, from the Roman point of view, quite insignificant

outpost of this empire. They are at one and the same time, therefore, both the products of their age and in the most profound contradiction to it.

The Gospels testify to realities that were to have no part to play in the official Roman scheme of things for a couple of centuries. What that scheme of things had to do with the Gospel realities, we can readily see in the few scant references to Jesus which occur in contemporary non-Christian literature. The Jewish historian Flavius Josephus (A.D. 37–105 more or less) mentioned Jesus in his *Jewish Antiquities* (XVIII. 63 f.). Unfortunately, the text as we have it today has been tampered with by Christian interpolators; all that can be concluded with certainty is that Josephus knew of Jesus as a Jew put to death under Pontius Pilate from whom had derived "the race of Christians." The younger Pliny, writing in A.D. 112, noted merely that the Christians known to him worshiped Christ "as a God" (*Epistles* X. 96). Cornelius Tacitus (A.D. 54–119), recording the persecution of the Christians under Nero, knew that Christ had been put to death by Pilate during the reign of Tiberius (*Annals* XV. 44); Christianity itself Tacitus regarded as a "most mischievous superstition." Finally, Suetonius (A.D. 75–160) refers to Christ, if he refers to him at all, only as a name, the meaning of which he had misunderstood (*Life of Claudius* XXV. 4).

The map on page 12 will give us a picture of the Palestine that signified so little in Roman eyes. During the ministry of Jesus it was divided into two political units, each of which has a certain significance for the Gospel narrative. Judea and Samaria formed one unit which was ruled directly by a Roman governor whose headquarters were in Caesarea. The governor who has become best known in history because of his involvement in the crucifixion of Jesus was Pontius Pilate, who administered Roman rule from A.D. 26–36. It is customary to refer to these Roman governors as "the Procurators"; however, this title was not actually used till after Christ's death. In his own day, Pilate was styled "Prefect of Judea." Technically speaking, Judea was not important enough to be a full-fledged province in the Roman civil service. It was subject to the Legate of Syria, who was expected to render military help as needed. Practically, however, it ranked as an imperial (as distinct from a senatorial) province, that is, a district in which the populace was regarded as hostile and in which repressive measures could be taken with a minimum of formalities when rebellion was threatened.

Direct Roman involvement in Palestinian affairs dated from 63 B.C., when the Jewish commonwealth, torn by civil war resulting from rival claims to the throne and the high priesthood, had been annexed to the Province of Syria as a solution of *pax romana*. From 40–4 B.C. the entire land had been ruled by that extraordinary adventurer, half genius half madman, with whom we are so familiar from the story of Christ's birth,

Herod the Great. Herod, a non-Jew who had married into the royal Hasmonaean house whose intrigues had hastened the intervention of the Romans, obtained the title "king" from the Roman Senate. His kingdom embraced almost everything that appears on the map of Palestine except the Decapolis, a nearly totally pagan region that always remained directly subject to the Legate of Syria. On Herod's death, however, the kingdom was dismembered. Judea and Samaria, after a brief interlude, assumed the provincial status described above. The extreme northeastern portion (Ituraea, Trachonitis, etc.), also mainly pagan, came under the government of Philip, apparently the most capable of all Herod's sons. Like the Decapolis, this region has only a minor role to play in the Gospel story.

The other major political unit of Roman Palestine in the days of Jesus was made up of Galilee and Perea. Perea does not figure largely in the Gospels, but Galilee was Jesus' homeland, the scene of the greater part of his public ministry, and the region from which he drew his first disciples. After the death of Herod the Great, Galilee and Perea had fallen to the lot of another of his sons, Herod Antipas. Antipas, like Philip, was never permitted by the Romans to allow himself a more imposing title than "tetrarch" (originally, this referred to someone who ruled the fourth part of some province); however, popularly he was regarded as king and is so called in the Gospels.

Common subjection to the Legate of Syria and Roman standardization worked toward a sameness of political institutions throughout Palestine. The hated taxgathering system (the "publicans" of the Gospels), all-important to the Roman administration, was a continuous source of friction and a case of conscience for pious Jews (cf. Mt 22:15–22). By Roman lights, the Jews were treated leniently and given extraordinary privileges. They were not required to serve in the army, and officially every effort was made to respect their religious scruples. Within limits, they were permitted to govern themselves by their own laws. Nevertheless, Roman administration in this provincial outpost was inclined to be clumsy, inept, and corrupt, and the tension between Jew and Roman is very apparent in the Gospel story. The Roman governors continually intervened in the appointment and deposition of the high priests and in many other ways never permitted the Jews to forget that they were a subject people. Presaged by uprisings recorded in part by the New Testament, the endemic hatred of Roman rule finally led to the great revolt of A.D. 66, the end of which was the destruction of Herod's great temple and, eventually, of Jewish Palestine itself.

Jewish   From the Jewish point of view, the map of Palestine would
Palestine   have been drawn quite differently from the lines laid down
                   by the Romans. The chief city for the Jews was not, of

course, the administrative center of Caesarea, but Jerusalem, the ancient holy city of David and the site of Solomon's temple. The temple which now stood there was one of the wonders of the contemporary world, shrewdly built by the great Herod at the outset of his reign in order to assure Jewish allegiance. In Jerusalem sat the Sanhedrin, the great council of the Jewish nation and its highest court, presided over by the high priest and composed of members drawn from the chief priestly and lay families and from the scribal profession. Jerusalem, and Judea because of it, was the spiritual and intellectual heartland of Judaism, the goal of its pilgrimages and the norm of its observance even for the vastly greater number of Jews who lived outside Palestine, in the Diaspora.

In Jewish eyes, Samaria was no part of Judea but a foreign country inhabited by foreigners. In point of fact the Samaritans, descendants of northern Israelites who had intermarried with Gentile settlers in the land, were ethnically little different, if at all, from the Jews of Judea. Their religion, too, a selective form of Judaism, was probably closer in doctrine and practice to what would have been considered normative than was the religion of many Judean Jews. However, a long history of mutual antagonism and hatred sundered the two peoples utterly. (See Sir 50:25 f., where the Samaritans are equated with the Edomites and the Philistines: the Samaritans are "the degenerate folk who dwell in Shechem.") It was this Jewish attitude toward the Samaritans that contributes the special poignancy to Jesus' parable of "the good Samaritan."

Toward the Galileans, the Judeans adopted a somewhat different attitude. As L. E. Elliott-Binns has said, "The Jews [that is, the Judeans] hated the Samaritans; the Galileans they merely despised." Evidence of this Judean attitude toward Galileans can be seen in Jn 1:46, 7:52. The reasons for this feeling were manifold, but chiefly derived from the Galileans' involvement with the Gentiles. The very name of Galilee proclaimed this involvement: it was the "circuit [galil] of the Gentiles" (Is 8:23; Mt 4:15), surrounded by Gentiles and heavily infiltrated by them. Jews who lived in Galilee simply could not adopt the attitude of exclusion with regard to Gentiles and Gentile ways that was possible in Judea. Inevitably different customs and observances grew up, encouraged by Galilee's relative isolation from the Judean center. The educated Galilean Jew probably spoke the Greek of the Gentiles as well as Palestinian Aramaic. It has even been suggested, though with less probability, that Greek was more common than Aramaic as the language used by the Jews among themselves. There were, in any case, Greek-language synagogues, especially for those Jews who had come out of the Diaspora; there was even at least one of these in Jerusalem itself. For whatever causes, the Galileans spoke a dialect that readily distinguished them from the Judeans (cf. Mt 26:73).

Together with an openness toward religious doctrine and a lack of rigor in its observance the Galileans combined a fierce Jewish nationalism, not unusual in the provincial population of any ethnic group. Revolts against foreign domination were quite as likely to begin in Galilee as in Judea. The combination of these qualities could readily account for "sons of thunder" (Mk 3:17) whose laxity with regard to Jewish observances repeatedly scandalized the more literal-minded doctors of the Law.

Cutting across geographical differences were the "denominational" divergences that distinguished one Jew's religion from another. The reader may be initially surprised to learn of such differences—some of which were rather important—since the orthodox Judaism of post-Christian times has generally presented such a monolithic structure. For all practical purposes only one form of Judaism, that of the Pharisees, survived the Roman repressions of A.D. 70 and 135 that followed the major and final Jewish revolts in Palestine. In the time of Jesus, however, the religion of Judaism was by no means as standardized as it became through the talmudic legislation of Christian times.

In one sense of the word, it is probably not correct to regard Pharisaism as a denomination or sect. It was, as it remained after the destruction of Jerusalem, by and large the normative religion of most of Palestine and the Diaspora, the religion taught in the synagogues and professed by the greatest number of the scribes (who would later be known as the rabbis). It was, in broad outline, the religion as practiced by Jesus and the early Jewish Christians; St. Paul considered it a point of honor to identify himself as a Pharisee (Phil 3:5). Much of Jesus' teaching was echoed by the best of Pharisaical Judaism. It represented the progressive tradition of Old Testament religion, a religion of the spirit rather than of the letter, which allowed for development and accommodation. In practice, Pharisaism was normative to some extent even for those who rejected it in principle. The Jerusalem priesthood, for example, was obliged to follow the Pharisaical interpretation of the liturgical law.

Why is it that the Gospels so often give the impression that Jesus and the Pharisees were in essential opposition, if indeed he actually practiced Pharisaical religion? Several observations are in order. Firstly, when we say that Pharisaism was normative Judaism, we are speaking of it in its non-professional sense, as the normal development of Old Testament religion. Jesus, like the average Jew of his day, could practice this religion without being a professional Pharisee. The professional Pharisee, as a matter of fact, would not have conceded that the average Jew practiced his religion at all. Pharisaism in the professional sense descended to many particulars which were the practice of only a few: in this sense Pharisaism was, indeed, a faction. From the rest of the Jews, "this accursed crowd which knows not the Law" (Jn 7:49), the Pharisee considered himself separated by his superior knowledge and consequent observance ("Pharisee" probably means "separated"). Secondly, while

Pharisaism was born of a progressive tendency, it also had a built-in proclivity for the type of legalistic formalism with which it is frequently identified in the Gospels. The selfsame tradition that sought the spirit in the letter could, in the wrong hands, become a soulless literalism in its own right—conservatism is the liberalism of the past generation. It was this kind of Pharisaism that Christ condemned (cf. Mk 7:1–13). It is only fair to add that it was likewise condemned by some of the Pharisaical scribes who stood in the tradition of Hillel and Gamaliel, in whose school St. Paul studied (Acts 22:3). Finally, as we saw above in the discussion of form criticism, the Gospels had cause to lay stress on the opposition between Jesus and the leaders of Judaism rather than to emphasize their points of agreement.

The chief rivals to the Pharisees mentioned in the Gospels were the Sadducees; the meaning of this term is unknown, but it is usually thought to have had some relation to the Zadokite priesthood. The Sadducees were truly a sect who had very little following among the people but included most of the priestly aristocracy. They rejected such Pharisaical developments in doctrine as a belief in the resurrection of the body (probably also, therefore, a belief in personal immortality) and a world of angels and spirits (cf. Acts 23:8); like the Samaritans, they may have rejected as canonical Scripture anything beyond the Torah of Moses. In their legal interpretations they were more rigorous than the Pharisees, adhering to the letter of the law to the disregard of any subsequent developments or the need of adaptation. With this religious fundamentalism they combined a spirit of conciliation with the Romans that made their patriotism suspect in the eyes of many Jews. This latter attitude was doubtless dictated by their economic status more than by anything else. At all events, Sadduceeism did not possess the vigor to survive the fall of Jerusalem.

A third division of Jews which, curiously enough, is never mentioned in the Gospels—unless, indeed, it is taken for granted more often than we realize—until fairly recently was known only from the somewhat conflicting accounts of Josephus and Philo of Alexandria (approximately 20 B.C.–A.D. 45). This was the Essenes, a name for which no satisfactory explanation has yet been given. Because the sectaries of Qumran, the people who produced the so-called Dead Sea Scrolls, have been rather convincingly identified as Essenes, we now know a great deal more about the peculiarities of this sect.

In the commentary we shall have occasion to refer to the Qumran people and their literature, hence only a few general observations are necessary at this time. There seems to be no doubt that Essenian Judaism exercised some influence on the beginnings of Christianity, and it is even likely that there were disciples of Jesus who had first been Essenes. This is hardly surprising: those Jews who embraced Christianity could have come from Essenism as easily as from Pharisaism or another form of Judaism. Despite a number of incidental correspondences from this direction, however, it is certain that Jesus and the writers of the New Testament were far more indebted to normative Judaism than to Essenism.

The Essenes were a "withdrawal" sect: even those who did not, as the Qumran people did, live a quasi-monastic existence, considered themselves to be completely separated from conventional Jewish life. In some respects they appear to have been super-Pharisees, but in others they differed quite radically from the normal tradition of Judaism. They rejected the Jerusalem temple and followed their own liturgical calendar. Their religion was highly eschatological; they were expecting an imminent end of the world as we know it, and like all sects of their kind they regarded themselves as the only elect which would be spared in the general conflagration: they were the only true Israel. It is likely enough that there were other sects of the same kind throughout Palestine; the times, as we shall see, were ripe for them. The Essenes, too, were unable to survive when the Roman fist at last closed inexorably on Palestinian Jewry.

It was into this kind of world that the Gospels were born. They are at once a clarion of their age and the knell of the coming age that would transform it utterly.

2. THE WORD MADE FLESH

Jn 1:1–2   The Prologue to John, the passage which forms the subject matter of this chapter, is a formidable enough beginning for any study of the Gospels. Volumes have been written on it, and on individual parts of it, without pretending to do more than scratch the surface of its meaning.

It may be thought that its high theological content might require it to be deferred for later consideration, after some of the (deceptively) simpler presentations of the Synoptic Gospels. However, since the Gospels are an expression of Christian faith in Christ, it is well to begin where John did, with the origins of the Christ-event where Christian faith had learnt to place them, anterior even to the nativity stories recorded by Matthew and Luke. Though the doctrine of the pre-existence of Christ is never dealt with explicitly in the Synoptic Gospels, it was part of the faith that produced them; it is found in the writings of Paul, and enunciated by him in the words of even older Christian confessions (Phil 2:6–8; Col 1:15–17, etc.).

Is the Prologue of John itself such a confession, a hymn, possibly of liturgical origin, that has been used by the evangelist to introduce his Gospel? Many authors think so, for reasons that are deserving of consideration. Such a question we cannot and need not answer here, however. The Prologue is, in any case, an integral part of the Gospel, whatever may have been its ultimate origin. It is, in a way, a summary of the entire Gospel.

John writes *In the beginning*, making a pointed allusion to the first verse of Genesis: just as the Old Testament began with the story of God's creation of the universe and world of man, the Johannine version of the New Testament now begins to tell the story of the new creation that has taken place in Jesus Christ. (The concept of the redemptive Christ-event as a new creation was also a common Christian idea; it can be found explicit in 1 Cor 15:45–49, for example.) Jesus himself is the creative *Word* of God.

For the uniquely Johannine conception of Christ as the Word (*logos*) we probably do not have to go outside the thought forms of the Old

Testament, though *logos* also had an analogous usage in the popular
Hellenistic philosophy of the time. God's word is his utterance of himself
in power, manifestation, revelation. It is creative: "By the word of the
Lord the heavens were made" (Ps 33:6); similarly, in verse 3 John says
that without the Word nothing was made. In a pre-eminent way it is
through the prophets that God's word became known. Judaism exalted
the Torah as the word of God par excellence and Moses, therefore, as
the greatest of the prophets. Christ, however, has revealed God much more
excellently than Moses and the prophets (note vss. 17 f. and cf. Heb
1:1–4). This he has done because he himself is the very Word of God
indeed, God incarnate, manifest, visible (so also Col 1:15–20).

John says that in the beginning the Word already *was*. The evangelist
knew how to take full advantage of the popular Greek in which he
wrote, which was able to distinguish various aspects of being. Here and
elsewhere in the Prologue when referring to the Word he uses the imperfect tense, signifying continuous existence without reference to beginning or ending: the Word has the timelessness of God himself. On the
contrary, when he wants to speak of past events that have occurred at
determined times (as in vss. 3, 6, 14, creation, the appearance of the
Baptist, the incarnation), he uses the aorist tense. There was nothing
particularly startling about this language, as far as Jewish tradition was
concerned. The wisdom of God, identified with his word, had long been
personified and represented as present with God from the beginning of
creation (see, for example, Prov 3:19, 8:22–31). Neither, therefore, was
there anything extraordinary about speaking of the Word as *with God*,
or more accurately, *in God's presence* (literally, "towards God"). A
distinction is thereby drawn between the Word and the personal God
(determined by the definite article in the Greek). This would have been
perfectly comprehensible to a Jew but definitely puzzling to a pantheistic
Hellenist for whom *logos* meant simply a divine emanation.

The Word was God. Here, on the contrary, John says something that
the Hellenist would think he understood but which a Jew could hardly
say. Judaism could personify the wisdom or word of God and represent
it as the first of God's creatures, present with him from the beginning, but
it could not identify it with God. This its conception of monotheism
would not allow. Already, therefore, while using traditional language,
John has introduced uniquely Christian ideas that give new meaning to
the words with which he had to work. Here "God" is used predicatively,
without the article: the Word, whom he has just distinguished from the
Person of God, is nevertheless a divine being in his own right. We immediately see, therefore, that the Word of which he is speaking is a "he"
and not an "it."

Jn 1:3a   This being so, when he now speaks explicitly of the Word
            as creative, he says more than the traditional language of

itself might signify. As the following verses show, he is already associating in his mind the new creation of Christ with the first creation of all things. On the surface, he repeats the thought of Ben Sira: "At God's word were his works brought into being" (Sir 42:15); so also Is 48:13 (both texts merely paraphrase Gen 1:3). There is an even more striking parallel in one of the Qumran scrolls: "Through his knowledge all things have come to be, and everything that is is ordained by his thought; and without him nothing is made" (1 QS 11:11). The Word of John, however, is a Person of mind and will who has himself entered into the first creative act as surely as he did into the work of redemption. Nevertheless, John never explicitly calls Christ the Creator. Later Christian theology, too, while considering every external work of God as done by all three divine Persons, has continued the biblical tradition of "attributing" the work of creation to God the Father only.

The better punctuation of the text, as attested both by manuscript evidence and the earliest Christian tradition, is the following: "(3a) . . . without him nothing came to be. (3b) What came to be (4) in him was life . . ."

Jn 1:3b–5 This further statement in no way merely repeats the thought of the preceding. In the first place, John is now speaking of the life of men, something quite different from the mere existence of all things. Secondly, in the Johannine writings "life" never means simple existence. This is one of the key words of John's Gospel, a word by which he designates that gift of God by which he has brought man into his own sphere of existence, which a later theology would call "sanctifying grace."

What came to be in him was life. Some of the Greek manuscripts have *is life;* both readings can be defended. By some this is taken to mean that whatever came to be (in the context, only men are meant) found its life, and could find its life, in the Word only. This, of course, is certainly John's thought. However, it is probable that he means much more than this. The "what came to be" is the life itself, which in turn is *the light of men.* Just as John did not speak of the Word as Creator but rather as having a role in creation, so he does with regard to the communication of life to man. If the Word is God, as John has said, then of course he is also Author of this life as well as the means by which it is communicated. But John is not writing a treatise on the metaphysical nature of divine Persons. He is writing a Gospel, which is a history of salvation. And in the divine economy of salvation life "came to be" in Christ that he might dispense it to mankind: "As the Father has life in himself, so he has given to the Son to have life in himself" (Jn 5:26 f.; note also 3:35 f.). "I have life because of the Father," Jesus says, and correspondingly, whoever communicates with Christ "will have life because of me" (Jn 6:57). The New Testament consistently describes salvation as a work of God accomplished through Jesus Christ: it "attributes" it to God the Father working through the Son.

It will be observed that John makes no conscious effort to distinguish between the Word as timeless and pre-existent and as incarnate and encountered in history—this despite the fact that only in verse 14 does he refer explicitly to the incarnation. Some of what he says applies properly only to the one or the other condition, but it is we, not he, who feel the need to make the distinction. This is perfectly in line with the rest of New Testament christology, which is first and foremost a soteriology. That is to say, it deals with Christ in his existential character as divine Savior without attempting to isolate his divine nature for separate consideration. The time was as yet far distant when the theology of Christ's personality and the relation between his divine and human natures would have to be thoroughly elaborated in the Church, following on the christological heresies of the fourth and subsequent centuries.

"Light" is another favorite Johannine word. As the term itself might suggest, it means enlightenment: God's manifestation of himself to men. This it is, however, in no merely intellectual sense. Through his Word God manifests himself as he really is; as Jesus says, God's manifestation of himself consists in his coming and dwelling with the one whom he loves (Jn 14:22 f.). When John speaks, as he so often does, of our "knowing" God, he does not mean that we know something about God; he means that we know God himself, as a man knows his friend, as a husband knows his wife: there is a shared existence, a community of being. So much we understand by the life of grace. That is why life can be equated here with light. That is why primitive Christianity spoke of the baptism that summons men into the new life of God's grace an "enlightenment," a passing from darkness into light (see also 1 Pt 2:9).

The light shines in the darkness probably represents John's judgment on the entire history of God's revelation, not just the ministry of Jesus. "Darkness" is, obviously, the opposite of light. By this term John designates the world of man which is desperately in need of divine enlightenment. This world is not evil, for God loves it (Jn 3:16); it is only when men prefer their miserable state of darkness to the light that evil becomes manifest (Jn 3:19): then occurs "the power of darkness" (Lk 22:53), the reign of evil. Faith, the acceptance of God as he has revealed himself, casts out darkness (Jn 12:46). The light-darkness dichotomy, fairly common elsewhere in the New Testament, was also employed by the Qumran sectaries.

The final words of this section can be translated *the darkness did not comprehend it* or *the darkness did not overcome it*. If the first, the author thinks of the long history of revelation, culminating in Jesus

Christ, which has also been so often a history of rejection and unbelief. If the second, he testifies to the power of divine grace, continuing through the prophets to the One greater than the prophets. Or perhaps he intends the reader to take both meanings: multiple levels of meaning are far from unusual in John.

Jn 1:6–8   Almost casually, the person of John the Baptist is introduced into the text. John follows the standard Gospel outline to the extent of beginning with the ministry of the Baptist (vss. 19 ff.), and the fact that here and in verse 15 the Baptist is apparently intruded into this paean on the Word by the use of verses borrowed from the later narrative is evidence to many that the Prologue has been adapted by John from an earlier text (note how vs. 9 logically follows on vs. 5, and vs. 16 on vs. 14). This may be. However, it is also typical of John to interlock the various parts of his Gospel by anticipations and back-references.

This man came as a witness. "Witness" is another of John's key ideas, which we can better appreciate when it is formally introduced in the story of the ministry of the Baptist. It is well to note here, however, that by introducing at this time the idea of the Baptist as witness to the Word—the incarnate Word, of course—John confirms what was said above, that throughout this entire passage, and not just from verse 14 on, he is thinking of the Word both as eternally with God and as incarnate in the person of Christ. In insisting on the Baptist as a witness to the light and not the light itself, John reflects the mild but persistent "polemics" waged throughout the Gospels in respect to the Baptist. It is not that the Gospels intended to minimize his importance; as we shall see, this is far from the case. There were contemporary with the Church, however, various Baptist sects, composed of those who had taken the preaching of the kingdom by John the Baptist as itself the fulfillment of prophetic expectation rather than what the Baptist himself proclaimed it to be, the final prophetic voice heralding the fulfillment in Jesus Christ (see Acts 19:1–7). The Gospels sought to show this, therefore, from the Baptist's own life and words. Here we have another example of the formative influences that have been brought to bear on the Gospel materials.

Jn 1:9–13   John says of the Word that *he was the true light that enlightens every man.* All the way through this Gospel we hear this adjective "true." Jesus is the "true" vine, he gives "true" life, and so on. Probably this exemplifies the evangelist's ability to turn to good account for the mainly Gentile Christianity for which he wrote a usage that had been authentically Christ's. For the Jew, all that was "true" pertained pre-eminently to God (cf. Jn 7:28), and was thus distinguished from the "vanity" that is the lot of every merely human act or device (cf. Eccl 1:2–8 and *passim*). In the popular Hellenistic philosophy of the Roman world there was an analogous usage. The "true" designated the reality that was judged to be only partially reflected in what was visible and tangible in the world of man. The *coming into the world* of this verse probably goes with "the true light" rather than with "every man"; however, little difference is made in the sense of the passage in either case.

The "world" of which John speaks, as we noted above, is the world of man and his affairs, not of itself evil, but *de facto* prone to the control of darkness because of sin. As John has already intimated, the entire history of God's invasion of this world through his word has been one of man's refusal to know God: "know," we are reminded, is not merely to acknowledge theoretically, but to experience practically. St. Paul also indicts the world for refusing to acknowledge the God who had revealed himself to it by his creative word (Rom 1:18–23). By *his own* John singles out particularly the Old Testament people of God, Israel, whose fault was the greater for the special intimacy into which God had drawn it with himself especially through the prophetic word. Refusal to heed this word is the burden of the prophets' constant complaint against Israel (cf. Is 6:9 f.; Jer 1:18 f.; Ezek 2:3–6; Amos 4:6–11; Acts 7:51–53, etc.). The major theme of the entire first half of John's Gospel is that of the light shining in darkness and the rejection of Jesus the Word by his own.

Still, though unbelief has been far too often the rule, it was never total. At all times during the history of salvation there have been those who accepted God's word and thus were made the recipients of his extraordinary grace by which they were made *sons of God* (see Deut 14:1; Ex 4:22; Hos 1:10). So it has proved to be with the Word incarnate, and to this the Gospel is testimony. The Gospels and the rest of the New Testament use many different terms to express the mysterious and wonderful relationship with God into which man is brought through divine grace. John has already spoken of "life" and "light." Here he speaks of divine sonship, emphasizing in verse 13 that nothing less than a genuine rebirth of man is involved which cannot be effected by man's unaided power, generative or otherwise; the notion of this heavenly birth will be the special theme of John's chapter 3. He also says that this new birth takes place in *those who believe in his name*. Faith is the response to God revealing himself, the acceptance of his word. It is not merely a condition for the divine action to work in man; it is itself concretely the transforming power of God constituting men his children, since no one can believe unless he be drawn by God (Jn 6:44). In the New Testament faith hardly ever means belief in some*thing*; almost invariably it signifies belief in some*one*, namely God, the state of man's being which is both the result and the constitutive element of a total commitment of his person to the Other, a commitment in turn which implies a community of life with the Other. In Semitic usage the "name" is the person himself, the person, that is, as he can be known and experienced by others. The Jews often referred to God simply as "the Name."

John says he gave men *power to become sons of God*. The choice of words is not casual. John's is a Gospel of vitality, of dynamism. For all his stress on faith, one may be at first surprised to learn that the word "faith" never occurs in the Gospel of John. But again, this is a studied procedure. John always uses the verb, "believe," for he wants to insist that faith is an active thing that involves man's whole life and being, not simply a passive state of mind. Similarly Paul speaks of faith as a "work" (1 Thes 1:3). In the same way, to become a son of God is not just a once-for-all experience which man passively undergoes. It is a lifelong engagement on which he embarks through faith, which must continually find expression in his every thought and deed.

Jn 1:14   So habituated are Christians to the concept of the incarnation, it is difficult for them to appreciate how startling to men of the first Christian century, how shocking to their sensibilities, was John's climactic statement: *The Word became flesh*. Both to Jew and Gentile an assertion of this kind had to run the inevitable risk of being taken as patent and calculated absurdity, as in fact it has so often been taken by Jew and Gentile thereafter.

Latent in popular Hellenistic thought was the conviction that man's body, the flesh, was evil, entirely antithetic to anything divine. The Platonic aphorism is famous: *sōma sēma*, "the body is a prison." The real being of man was his spirit, which was encased in the flesh that restricted and shamed it. The Greeks burnt the bodies of the dead that the spirit might be fully and finally released from the imprisoning flesh. It might be thought paradoxical that men could think this way and yet so often adopt hedonism as their philosophy of life, making the pleasures of the flesh their paramount aim. The paradox, however, is only apparent—if the flesh were indeed opposed to man's "real" existence, what was done in the flesh could be considered morally irrelevant. This pernicious conception of man's corporeal nature entered Christianity early as a heresy (cf. 1 Cor 6:12–20) and has dogged its footsteps through all subsequent generations, sometimes appearing as a distorted and un-Christian approach to asceticism.

There was no room in the healthy materialism of Jewish thought for such ideas. As God's creation, the flesh was good. There precisely, however, was the rub: "flesh" implied all that was created, therefore passing and transitory, not antithetic to but certainly incompatible with the divine Creator. "All flesh is grass," wrote the prophet, thus characterizing the contingency of man. "Their glory is like the flower of the field. The grass withers, the flower wilts . . . but the word of our God stands forever" (Is 40:6–8). Here, as we readily see, the strongest possible contrast is drawn between flesh and the word of God. Yet John says that the Word became flesh. He has deliberately chosen the most uncompromising word that was available to him in order to express the reality of the incarnation. This is an habitual stress in the Gospels. The christological heresy that offered the greatest challenge to Christian orthodoxy in its earliest period was not denial of Christ's divinity; such a denial would be reserved for a later age, not for one in which "divine saviors" were commonplace. The danger was rather that of Docetism: the tendency to deny or at least to mitigate the reality of the humanity of Christ and all that it implied.

John's Gospel is apostolic testimony that the Word become flesh *dwelt among us*. This is another starkly realistic statement, the literal, or etymological meaning of which is: "he pitched his tent among us." It is not unlikely that John was thinking of the etymology, for the Greek verb (*skēnoun*) had long been used by preference as the equivalent of the Old Testament Hebrew expression (*šākan*) by which the presence of the Lord was designated, especially his presence in visible "glory" at the Tent of Meeting (cf. Ex 40:34–38). We have even more grounds for this understanding of John's meaning when we see that he goes on to say: *We saw his glory*. Throughout the Old Testament the "glory" of God refers especially to his visible presence, made manifest in smoke, fire, or some other medium. It refers as well and specifically to God's manifestation of his saving presence (Is 60:1; Hab 2:14; etc.). Under both these aspects this is also the meaning that John attaches to the word as it relates to Christ. We shall understand this better as we see the term in actual use throughout the Gospel. It will suffice to say now that by "glory" John means the entire Christ-event, in which the saving presence of God has been visibly manifested.

Glory of an only-begotten Son from the Father. This specification of the glory proper to the Word will be the principal theme of the second half of John's Gospel, beginning with chapter 13. Now that John has definitely spoken of the Word become flesh he abandons the more generic term and refers to him in his character in salvation history as Son; in verse 17 he will use for the first time his historical name. To speak of this glory as *rich in grace and truth* is to identify it further as the salvific work of God. "Grace and truth" represents the Old Testament hendiadys *ḥesed we'ĕmet* (see especially Ex 34:6, where the expression appears practically as a descriptive definition of God), the sense of which is "loving-kindness and constancy" or perhaps "utter steadfast love." This loving protection of a God faithful to his promises was, concretely, the salvation for which the Israelite looked: it was the grace of God's saving presence.

Jn 1:15–18   After another parenthetical reference to the witness of the Baptist, a text which we shall later see verbatim in its proper context, John continues and concludes his theological introduction. *Of his riches* of grace and truth *we have all received.* As before, John's treatment of the Word who is Son of God concentrates on his mission as Savior. *Grace after grace* doubtless means that the saving mission of Christ and the Christian life which is its result are grace-ful throughout: first, last, and always they are purely a divine gift. To the Jew the greatest of God's gifts was the Torah which epitomized his religion; here was, indeed, truth and salvation. Not to minimize the Old Testament revelation, but to put it in perspective, John says that *the Law was given through Moses,* but *grace and truth came through Jesus Christ.* The Law was grace and truth—John would hardly have denied this—but in the fullest sense, grace and truth are the exclusive revelation of Christ; similarly, the author of Heb 1:1–4 contrasts the diversity and fragmentation of prophetic revelation with the true image of God that has been seen in his Son.

Probably the same contrast is uppermost in John's mind when he adds that *no one has ever seen God.* Here the Old Testament tradition on which he depended was varied and seemingly contradictory. The Bible certainly does relate often enough that this or that person was granted a vision of God (see Ex 24:9–11, for example). The Jews of John's time, however, were sophisticated enough to understand these simple stories in the spirit in which they had been written. They knew that the God of heaven had nothing about him that was literally palpable to mortal eyes. Another of the naïve biblical stories tried to express this truth by the assertion that even Moses, who was closer to God than any other man and spoke to him "face to face" (Ex 33:11; Num 12:8; Deut 34:10), nevertheless was not permitted to see God's "glory" but only his "back" (Ex 33:18–23). Thus, though God has indeed made himself known, he stands *revealed,* in the prophets and especially in Moses—his moral will and nature, his words and deeds of love, mercy, fidelity, salvation—still, only in the Christ-event has this revelation become complete. Only one who is *in the bosom of the Father,* who himself lives and shares the divine life as no merely human prophet could, could be the instrument of this revelation. For he alone is *God the only-begotten* (this reading of the text is preferable to "the only-begotten Son" which appears in most of the manuscripts); in this Man alone has God appeared whole and entire, incarnate in his very flesh.

With this John brings his magnificent Prologue to a close. His Gospel is to be the record of how and in what ways the Only-begotten has revealed the glory of the saving God. In their own manner and after their own proper viewpoints, as we shall see, the Synoptic Gospels are also a record of this selfsame revelation. It is to them that we now turn.

3. THE TERM OF PROPHECY

Lk 1:1–4   From the sublimity of the Johannine prologue we now turn to the comparatively matter-of-fact prose of the Synoptic Gospels. Of the Synoptics, only Luke has given us an introduction to the Gospel message. In doing so, he conformed to the literary conventions of his time, which required a dedication and a statement of purpose. He also did it in the grand style: these verses are written not in the vulgar Greek that we otherwise expect in the Gospels, but rather in the language of the classical Greek authors.

Was *Theophilus* (God's friend) an historical personage, or is this simply Luke's name for the Christian reader for whom the Gospel was written? The same dedication appears at the beginning of the Acts of the Apostles, introducing the second volume of Luke's work in his tripartite view of the record of salvation history—the era of Israel (the Old Testament), the era of Jesus (the Gospel), the era of the Spirit (Acts). Most commentators seem to be of the mind that Theophilus was, indeed, a real person. The question is of no great importance, however, since in any case it is evident that Luke did not write for Theophilus alone, and Theophilus' condition is precisely that of the entire Christian world, ourselves included, which forms Luke's wider audience.

Luke, of course, did not invent the Gospel form which he used so effectively and artistically. Not only is it practically certain that he had the Gospel of Mark before him as he wrote, as we saw in Chapter 1 the Synoptic tradition which he mainly reproduces itself grew out of the *kerygma* of the primitive Church. Luke tells us this. He writes that Theophilus *may understand the certainty of the things in which you were catechized.* Luke's situation was that of Theophilus. He had received the same catechesis *regarding the things that have been brought to fulfillment among us,* that is, in the Church, from the same source of tradition: *as the original eyewitnesses and servants of the word handed them down to us.* Moreover, Luke takes his place within a succession of those who had attempted to articulate the Gospel message as he was now doing. *Many have undertaken to draw up an account,* he says. He does not tell us how many of these undertakings he regarded as successful or whether he made use of any or all of them in preparing his own Gospel.

He does tell us, however, at least some of the special qualities he ascribes to his Gospel, qualities which justify and even necessitate his taking pen in hand. For one thing, he has *followed up all things carefully from the very first*, verifying, checking, striving to make his Gospel as accurate and as instructive as possible. In Chapter 1, we discussed some of the means that were available to Luke to do this. Commentators would generally agree that he has succeeded admirably in this intention. Again, he has constructed his Gospel as an *orderly account*. By this he does not necessarily mean chronological order. In fact, as we have already seen, precise chronology is not a characteristic of the Gospels, for many reasons. An orderly account, rather, in Luke's sense is one that follows a logical pattern, a literary form, by which the writer functions not as a mere chronicler of events but as an interpreter of history, showing the relation of one fact to another, bringing out the inner meaning of events, a meaning that is seen through the eye of faith. One does not read very far in Luke's Gospel without perceiving the order that he has followed.

Lk 1:5–7 The beginning of Luke's order immediately becomes apparent in the passage that opens before us. In company with Matthew and in contrast to Mark and John, Luke prefaces to the Gospel proper—that is, the history of the ministry of salvation that begins with the preaching of John the Baptist—a section which we customarily regard as a narrative of Jesus' infancy. Actually, this is probably not too accurate a description of what Luke intended to give us. That is to say, it is doubtful that there existed in the Church of Luke's time a literary form that could properly be called "narrative of the Lord's birth and childhood," that there was, in other words, an interest in such biographical details for their own sake. It is true that such an interest did develop somewhat later on; it is very much reflected in the apocryphal gospels, the greater number of them of heretical origin, which are filled with biographical details, most of them legendary and some downright grotesque and pernicious, attempting to supply for the "deficiencies" of the canonical Gospels. The apostolic Church that produced the Gospel materials, however, hardly could afford the "luxury" of mere biography, even biography of Jesus. Its conservation of the tradition and its literary use of the tradition were strongly determined throughout by the practical demands of its life in the world, its pastoral ministry, catechetics, apologetics, polemics. Ordinarily only what was directly relevant to these ends passed into the *kerygma* and from the *kerygma* into the Gospel. We have already noted how that busy pastor St. Paul corroborates all this, how the Gospel that he preached in his letters has taken so little cog-

nizance of the earthly life of Jesus. There is something of a parallel in
the "holy places" of Palestine, the sites associated with this or that event
in the life of Jesus. For most of these there is no authentic tradition
that can be traced back beyond the fourth or fifth Christian century,
for the simple reason that the earliest Christian community there was
in no position to cherish these places and so establish a tradition.

This is not to say that Luke does not give us true information about
the birth of Christ or that this has nothing to do with his Gospel. Far
from it. Indeed, that is the point that we should now make: that for
both Matthew and Luke what we term their infancy narratives are in
actuality components in the strictest sense of the word of their record of
the Gospel, the good news of the salvation achieved in Jesus Christ and
perpetuated in his Church. They are not introductions to or preparations for the Gospel story as told by these two evangelists, but integral
parts of it. This is the main reason for the divergences between the two
narratives, quite apart from the fact that the data which the evangelists
share in common had reached them through different and independent
streams of tradition.

In Luke's Gospel the infancy narrative is an elaborate expansion of
the teaching common to all the Gospels, that the Baptist is the last
divinely sent prophetic witness to the coming Christ. There is a systematic paralleling throughout these two chapters between the Baptist and
Jesus, in which annunciation corresponds to annunciation, birth to birth,
hidden life to hidden life, and in which the Baptist gradually recedes
from prominence and Jesus comes to the fore (cf. Jn 3:30). Linking the
two parallel developments are the two mothers, their relationship and
association, and the prophetic theme is constantly maintained through
countless allusions to the Old Testament. The language also changes.
Beginning with 1:5 the classicism of the introduction is dropped
abruptly and Luke begins to write Greek that has a strong Semitic
flavor. The Semitisms, however, are not those of Palestinian Aramaic, as
in Mark and John, but biblical Hebrew. This fact has led many to the
conclusion that Luke's source for these chapters was a primitive Christian
composition in Hebrew, later translated into Greek. There is much to be
said for such a theory; Luke certainly did use sources, and the Qumran
literature has shown that Hebrew was still a living language, at least for
literary purposes, at the beginning of the Christian era. On the other
hand, however, Luke is a superb enough artist to have deliberately imitated here the "translation Greek" of the Septuagint, the Old Testament
of the nascent Church. John the Baptist is the "last man of the Old
Testament" (cf. Lk 7:28) who gives way to Jesus Christ, the "first man
of the New Testament."

Luke begins with lines reminiscent of 1 Sam 1:1 f., introducing a theme
that will be further pursued in these narratives. *Herod was king of Judea*

—the title conferred on him by the Roman Senate, understanding broadly all of Jewish Palestine—officially from 40 B.C. The character of this king, Idumaean and Arabian by birth, is known to us chiefly from the writings of Flavius Josephus and is corroborated by the picture drawn of him by Matthew; Luke, however, mentions him only to give a general chronological indication.

It will be noted that Luke stresses the completely priestly ancestry of John the Baptist. *Zechariah* was a priest of the Jerusalem temple, *of the division* of the priesthood *called after Abijah* (cf. 1 Chron 24:10), that is, belonging to the eighth of twenty-four divisions of the Jewish priesthood which officiated in turn at the temple. Traditionally, all these were descended from Aaron, the Mosaic high priest (cf. Ex 28:1 ff.). *Elizabeth*, too, was *of the daughters of Aaron*. John the Baptist, therefore, is eminently a priestly as well as a prophetic figure. In Jewish messianic thinking a priest often accompanied the Messiah as forerunner and anointer (cf. Zech 3:6–9, 4:1–3, 11–14; etc.).

Lk 1:8–12   John the Baptist was a child of promise born to aged parents, like Isaac (Gen 17:15–21), like Samson (Jgs 13:2–7), like Samuel (1 Sam 1:3–18). In this section Luke has already begun to employ a literary form which contributes a deep theological content to his narrative and which must by no means be overlooked through any misconception of the author as a "factual" historian. This form consists in the systematic exploitation of Old Testament stories, language, events, figures, all of which are woven into the tissue and fabric of which the Gospel account is composed. So systematic is the construction, we can take note only of the more important allusions. This literary form is sometimes called *midrash*, a late Jewish term for a scriptural commentary that draws out and applies to contemporary life the historical or moral implications of the sacred text. The second half of the Book of Wisdom (chs. 11–19) is a good example of *midrash*, where the author retells the Pentateuchal story of Israel's oppression in Egypt and the Exodus, systematically applying the older history to the circumstances of his own time, when God's people was once more being persecuted by Egyptians. This type of *midrash*, called by them *pesher*, was much in vogue among the people of Qumran. Strictly speaking, Luke is not so much commenting on the Old Testament as he is using it to clothe and describe New Testament events. *Midrash*, therefore, may not be the precise term for his literary form. In any case, it is an exemplification in narrative of the conviction that the events of the Old Testament foreshadowed those of the New (cf. 1 Cor 10:11), that the God who had revealed himself fully in Jesus Christ had not done so without showing himself in many types beforehand (cf. Heb 1:1 f.).

We should not misunderstand the purpose of this literary form, nor the intentions of those who have attempted to define it through their studies.

The agreement of the independent Gospels of Matthew and Luke testifies to the core of essential historical fact that had been handed down by the tradition. The no less obvious diversity between them indicates what pertains to literary artistry and interpretation. Most of what is contained in these chapters could have been described in a variety of other ways without impairing its historical affirmation in the least. Some of what is related is, in fact, ineffable and incapable of ever being adequately captured in human speech and narration. We have, for example, annunciations, revelations to men of the mind and intentions of God. How precisely do such things occur? Prophets and mystics through the centuries have complained over the impossibility of their explaining to others exactly what had been the circumstances of their experiences. Luke, or his source, has chosen to narrate them in a way that was meaningful to the Christians of the first century, in the terms of familiar Old Testament types. These stories are not the statistical reports of uncommitted observers but the interpretation known through faith and given in the language of faith to certain events that took place during the reign of the man whom history knows as Herod the Great. Apart from the Christian faith that perceived the true meaning of these events, they would have meant nothing to history.

One of the Old Testament types of which Luke has made considerable use in this section is the vision of the seventy weeks (of years) in the ninth chapter of the Book of Daniel. Zechariah was *officiating as priest before God* at the time of the annunciation of the Baptist's birth. It was *his lot to enter the temple of the Lord to burn incense.* The daily morning and evening sacrifices of animals were performed on the altar of holocausts in the temple courtyard, but the conclusion of the rite was the scattering of incense on the altar within the holy place of the temple, which only the officiating priest could enter. Even with the priesthood distributed into twenty-four divisions, they were in such numbers that the performance of this highly coveted function had to be determined by lot. Now it was also at the hour of the evening sacrifice that Daniel received his vision of the seventy weeks (Dan 9:21), and from Gabriel, the angel of Zechariah's vision (cf. Lk 1:19); nowhere else in the Bible is there mention of an angel Gabriel. Daniel's vision was an apocalyptic reinterpretation of Jeremiah's prophecy of the seventy years of exile (Jer 25:11, 29:10) uttered in 605 B.C.; according to Daniel the end of the exile would be really consummated after seventy *weeks* of years, that is, 490 years after Jeremiah's prophecy (for both Jeremiah and Daniel these numbers are schematic and approximative). Then would occur the banishment of iniquity, the beginning of the reign of righteousness, and the anointing of a Most Holy (Dan 9:24). For the author of Daniel, this meant the reconsecration of the temple in 165 B.C. (the age in which he was living), after the successful rebellion of Judah the Maccabee against the Seleucid king Antiochus IV Epiphanes who had erected there the "horrible abomination," the statue of Zeus Olympios (Dan 9:27; 2 Macc 6:2): the feast to commemorate this Dedication (cf. Jn 10:22), in Hebrew *Hanukkah*, is still celebrated by Jews to this day. It will be noted that Luke counts seventy weeks (490 days, cf. Lk 1:26, 56 f., 2:21 f.; Lev 12:2–6) from the annunciation of Gabriel to the presentation of Jesus in the temple: he knows of a Most Holy and of a reign of righteousness that far transcend anything Daniel dreamt of.

Luke is not simply being clever; by this device he begins to convey a profound theological teaching. What the temple of Jerusalem was, pre-eminently the house of God, Christ is in a far more excellent way. Jesus replaces the temple (cf. Jn 2:19–21, 4:20–24), Jesus and the Church which is the body of Christ (cf. 1 Cor 3:16 f.). This explains the significance of the temple in the Lucan outline: the Gospel which begins in the temple as a place of Jewish sacrifice ends in the temple that has become a place of Christian prayer (Lk 24:53); again, the Gospel of the Spirit, the Acts of the Apostles, shows the movement of Christianity from the temple (Acts 3:1) into the entire world which will henceforth be its home.

Lk 1:13–20 Not only does Luke parallel the Baptist with Jesus, for the reasons already indicated, he also parallels strikingly the details of the stories. The annunciations to Zechariah and Mary (cf. Lk 1:26–38) follow a common pattern. After the introduction of the persons involved there is the description of the appearance of the angel, an appearance which excites fear and awe. The angel immediately proceeds to words of comfort, then announces the coming birth and the name of the child together with the office that he will fill in the saving economy of God. To the objection that is now made by the recipient of the annunciation the angel replies with a reiteration that the divine power will effect what it has announced, and a probative sign is added (Zechariah's dumbness, Elizabeth's pregnancy as a sign to Mary).

The pattern has been modeled on the narratives of classic annunciations in the Old Testament: the birth of Isaac (Gen 17–18), the mission of Moses (Ex 3–4), the mission of Gideon (Jgs 6:11–24), the birth of Samson (Jgs 13). An examination of these Old Testament passages will make clear as well the provenance of some of the phraseology employed by the Gospel.

The name *John* (and also that of Jesus) was quite as common in those days as it is in these. The Bible, however, always takes careful note of the meaning of names, to which far more significance was attached by the ancients than by us. John (Hebrew *Yohanan*) means "Yahweh has bestowed grace": a name eminently suited to the precursor of the Lord. His prophetic character is now underlined. Like Jeremiah (cf. Jer 1:5)

he will be filled with a holy spirit from his mother's womb, given a
prophetic call even before his birth. Like Elijah he will be the messenger
of reconciliation (Mal 3:23 f., cf. 3:1). And like Samuel and Samson he
will be a perpetual Nazirite (cf. Num 6:1–8), consecrated to a penitential
life that will foreshadow the Life of sacrificial obedience by which the
world's salvation has been assured (cf. Phil 2:8–11).

Lk 1:21–25   Like others who have received the revelation of God,
                   Zechariah's eventual appearance was something of a con-
sternation to the people who awaited him (cf. Ex 32:1, 34:29 f.); they
recognized that something had taken place that was beyond their ken.
As officiating priest he was supposed to give the final benediction, which,
however, he could not do, but only *make signs to them.*

After the completion of the tour of duty of Zechariah's division, he
returned *to his own house* in the Judean highlands (cf. Lk 1:39). Tradition has usually and most consistently identified this site with Ain Karim,
a village in the southwestern suburb of Jerusalem. Elizabeth's reaction to
the long-hoped-for conception of a child was to echo the words of Rachel
(cf. Gen 30:23).

Lk 1:26–33   And now we read the beautiful story of the annunciation
                   to Mary, *in the sixth month* of Elizabeth's pregnancy.
This took place in a little *town of Galilee called Nazareth,* a village little
esteemed in a countryside that was little esteemed (see the remarks on
Galilee in Chapter 1). Nazareth is never mentioned in the Old Testament and very little outside it; even by the later Christians it was held
in little veneration until a relatively tardy period. Its sole claim to fame
in history is as the residence of the Holy Family.

In keeping with the marriage customs of the time, Mary was doubtless
a girl of some fourteen or fifteen at the time of the annunciation. Her
home was probably like most in this poor village, a cave dug into the side
of a hill with perhaps a small extension on the front. There would have
been a single door to the house, with a small opening on the side for
ventilation. Light came from the open door or from a lamp consisting
of a saucer of oil in which floated a wick. On the floor were perhaps a
few mats, perhaps not even that. The floor itself was simply clay beaten
hard by the many footsteps of the family.

Mary was *a virgin betrothed to a man named Joseph.* The virgin birth
of our Lord is one of the historical facts on which the independent narratives of Luke and Matthew are agreed. In view of what has already
been said of the literary form of these narratives it might be well to
note—even though in this book we are concerned with biblical exposi-
tion rather than the justification of Christian belief—that in their transmission of this tradition the evangelists have neither imitated nor even

paralleled any of the various wonder-legends that have become associated with the births of other famous men. Such parallels have often been claimed: Sargon of Akkad, Buddha, and the emperor Augustus are among the names most frequently cited. However, in the analysis, the Gospel story of divine annunciation accompanied by virginal conception remains unique. The chief inspiration for the narratives of both Matthew and Luke has been the Old Testament; but in the Old Testament, too, any real precedent for this account is entirely lacking.

Again in connection with the literary form in which Luke has clothed this narrative, it should be observed that he never really describes the vision of an angel, whatever have been the echoes of his story in Christian art. His emphasis is entirely on words of revelation. Mary is greeted in the language with which the prophets had apostrophized the eschatological Jerusalem about to receive its Redeemer (compare the words of the annunciation with Zeph 3:14–17; Zech 9:9 f.; Joel 2:21–27). Once more Luke is not merely playing with words: in his Gospel and in John's especially our Lady has a truly ecclesial character, herself the first of the redeemed figuring the whole people of God who are the recipients of God's beneficent grace and mercy. Hence the traditional translation *full of grace* (literally, "most favored one"), while it has taken on a depth of meaning for later Christian theology that transcends (without contradicting) the intention of the evangelist, nevertheless does accurately portray his thought. To the full, above and before all other creatures, has Mary been favored by God.

Jesus himself is designated as the Messiah of the Davidic line, one of the principal figures in which the salvation hopes of the Old Testament were crystallized; thus, as scion of *David his father*, he *shall be called Son of the Most High* (cf. 2 Sam 7:12–16; Pss 89:20–38, 132:11 f.). In verse 27 *of the house of David* doubtless refers to Joseph rather than to Mary, though Mary may also have been of Davidic descent as well as having some relationship to the priestly line of Aaron (vs. 36). Both Matthew and Luke trace Jesus' earthly ancestry through Joseph, his legal father, as a matter of course. Jesus' Davidic descent was part of the primitive Christian *kerygma* (cf. Rom 1:3), denoting one of the essential links in the continuity of salvation history. As will be seen, however, his fulfillment of the Davidic expectation was also uniquely his own.

Lk 1:34–38   Mary's question, unlike Zechariah's, does not express doubt, but it does reflect wonderment: *How will this be, since I do not know man?* Many have taken this to mean that Mary had already consecrated herself to a life of virginity, that her words indicate more than simply a present situation of fact. Otherwise, they say, her question would have been pointless, since in the normal course of events her marriage with Joseph would have soon been consummated and thus the child foretold by the angel would be conceived.

It is not, of course, impossible that our Lady should have resolved on a celibate life, unusual though this was in the Jewish tradition. Quite apart from the fact that she was something more than an "average" Jewish girl, celibacy was not without precedent among the Jews, even in Old Testament times (cf. Jer 16:2), and it was certainly practiced at the beginning of the Christian era by some of the Essenes. However, it is doubtful that any such conclusion can be drawn from Luke's narrative. In the pattern of the annunciation story the question is merely that of a virgin avowing her purity in the face of an enigmatic statement which implied that she would bear a child while she was yet unmarried. It serves to introduce the angelic explanation that the conception of the child will be virginal, achieved through the power of God and not of man.

In the angel's reply another Old Testament type is introduced to identify further Mary's character: she is a new Ark of the Covenant which God has made with his people (cf. Ex 25:10–16, 37:1–9). The Ark of the Covenant had been the abiding symbol of God's presence; in the Tent of Meeting and in Solomon's temple it was regarded as God's throne and footstool (cf. Is 6:1; Pss 99:5, 132:7; 1 Chron 28:2), the special residence of his "glory" (see above on Jn 1:14). As it once had done to the Ark (see Ex 40:34 f.), *the power of the Most High will overshadow* Mary. This parallels the words, *Holy Spirit will come upon you:* the creative spirit of God (Gen 1:2) will bring to pass what has been promised. As we shall see, Luke continues the theme of Mary the Ark of the Covenant in his story of her visitation of Elizabeth.

All good mariology, the biblical included, must be at the same time good christology: the mystery of the Mother of God is seen properly only when it is viewed as one aspect of the greater mystery of her Son as the saving power of God. If Mary is the Ark of the Covenant, the tabernacle of the divine presence, what of Jesus? He is this divine presence. *Therefore the Holy that is to be born shall be called Son of God.* Luke has, literally, "the holy thing to be born": there is an allusion to Dan 9:24 (see the comment above on vss. 8–12). In Jewish ears, "son of God" could have various particular meanings but always one central and pervading significance. The king of Israel was God's son (cf. 2 Sam 7:14) because he epitomized in his person the promised saving presence of God whose instrument he was, or was supposed to be. The Messiah, the eschatological king par excellence, would be son of God in this same way. All Israel, God's people chosen and saved by him, could be called "sons of the living God" (Hos 2:1), just as we have already seen John speak of all believers in the Word as God's sons (Jn 1:12).

In the context of this narrative, and even more in the full context of the Gospel, it is plain that Luke knows Jesus to be Son of God in a way that transcends all these others without contradicting them. Jesus himself, as we shall see, probably proclaimed himself as Son of God uniquely. The recognition of the full meaning of this proclamation, however, is part of the Easter and Pentecostal faith of the Church, enlightened by the Spirit which has also inspired the Gospels. It is no derogation from Mary's signal privileges, then, to conclude that she, too, at the time of the annunciation was unaware of the magnitude of what had been revealed to her. In this as in all else she is typical of the Church which first received the Word, then was led by the Spirit of God into the fullness of truth (Jn 16:13).

Mary's response was wholly in keeping with her character as model for all the faithful. *Behold the slave-girl of the Lord:* what she has always been she wills to continue to be, completely at the disposal of the divine pleasure wherever it may lead her. It is evidently Luke's meaning that at this moment the incarnation took place. This he describes as he does everything else, with the utmost delicacy and tact.

Lk 1:39–55 Elizabeth's pregnancy in advanced age had been offered to Mary as a sign of the divine power, and now *with haste* Mary goes *into the hill country* about Jerusalem, to the *town of Judah* where Zechariah and Elizabeth had their residence, to visit her favored kinswoman. Jesus has already begun his life pilgrimage that will end in Jerusalem. Also, the Precursor while yet unborn begins his work of announcing the Savior.

The stirring of a child within the womb is a normal enough occurrence, but to those deep in biblical history such things would be recognized as portents: Luke uses the same verb found in the description of a similar happening in Gen 25:22. Elizabeth was thereupon inspired to recognize Mary as the most favored of all women because of the child she was to bear, the identity of whom was made known to her. Elizabeth's salutation of Mary together with the angel's make up the first part of the Hail Mary! *How has this been granted to me that the mother of my Lord should come to me?* echoes the words of David to the Ark of the Lord, following which it remained in the house of Obed-edom for three months (2 Sam 6:9–11). *Blessed is she who has believed* praises Mary's unshakable trust in God and expresses Elizabeth's share in it.

Some manuscripts place the famous Magnificat which follows on Elizabeth's lips rather than Mary's. The reason for this is not hard to find. The resemblance of the Magnificat to the Song of Hannah (1 Sam 2:1–10) was not lost to early readers of the New Testament, and it is Elizabeth rather than Mary who is likened to Hannah in the Gospel. However, there is scarcely any doubt that the great majority of the manuscripts have correctly ascribed the words to Mary, as Luke intended. Luke's use of his Old Testament types is imaginative, never mechanical.

The canticles of the Gospel, here the Magnificat, the Benedictus in verses 68–79, the Nunc Dimittis in 2:29–32, somewhat parallel the sermons of Acts which are ascribed variously to Peter, Stephen, Paul, and others. They are, of course, free compositions of the author and his sources, employing the same vocabulary and style. No one has ever been under the illusion that they could have been drawn from the stenographic reports of eyewitnesses. Nevertheless, just as scholars will agree that the sermons of Acts in a general way authentically reflect the settings and personalities with which they are associated, something similar can be said of the canticles. They are in no way anachronistic, but rather highly accurate portrayals of the most elevated kind of Jewish messianic expectation, done exclusively in Old Testament terms. They are, in fact, mainly mosaics of Old Testament texts. The Magnificat itself has this character to a degree that almost amounts to a *tour de force*. If the reader would test this, let him read it in conjunction with the following texts, read in order: 1 Sam 2:1, 1:11; Gen 30:13; Deut 10:21; Pss 111:9, 103:17, 89:11; Job 12:19; 5:11; 1 Sam 2:7; Ps 107:9; Is 41:8; Ps 98:3; Mi 7:20; 2 Sam 22:51. As the Qumran literature has shown, impromptu compositions of this kind would have presented no difficulty to pious Jews immersed in the Old Testament.

The Magnificat is less a prayer than it is a meditation on the goodness of God and his saving deeds of mercy toward his people throughout history. There is very little of a personal note in it. However, the connection with Mary is definite enough. It is to *the lowly* and *the hungry* that the mercy of God has been shown; these were by now consecrated terms for the faithful clients of the Lord in whom the people of God could be epitomized (cf. Mt 5:3–10; Lk 6:20–26). Among these Mary takes a chief and culminating place: *he has regarded the lowliness of his handmaid. Henceforth,* with Elizabeth's salutation as the norm, *all generations will call me blessed.*

Lk 1:56–79   It is evidently Luke's thought that Mary remained with Elizabeth until the time of the Baptist's birth, even though he makes no mention of Mary in the succeeding narrative. It is in accordance with his notion of an "orderly account" to finish one story, once he has begun it, before embarking on another. The end of the story of the visitation is that after three months' time Mary *returned to her own house.*

After the birth of John the Baptist he was circumcised, in accordance with the Mosaic law, eight days later, at which time it was also customary to bestow on the child his name. *They were going to call him by his father's name:* this was not a common practice. It is not clear whether Elizabeth had learnt from Zechariah that his name should be John or whether she had arrived at it through independent inspiration. At any rate, Elizabeth's relatives and friends *all marveled* when Zechariah (who appears to have been struck deaf as well as dumb) confirmed her choice: either because of the amazing coincidence or because the parents were resolved on a name that was not "in the family." One gets the impression that the relatives and friends were disposed to be busybodies as well as goodhearted people rejoicing with the aged couple.

Zechariah's regaining his faculties was one more circumstance surrounding the birth of this child that convinced the neighbors that *the hand of the Lord was with him.* When Luke says that *all these things were spoken abroad in the hill country of Judea* and that *all who heard of them laid them up in their hearts,* he is doubtless indicating in a general way the source of his information and its reliability, in accord with his claim in his prologue. He makes similar statements later on concerning our Lady.

Zechariah's recovered speech is immediately put to inspired use in the utterance of the magnificent hymn we know as the Benedictus. Like the Magnificat, it has been woven out of Old Testament texts. The reader can "find" it in the following, read in order: Pss 41:14, 72:18, 106:48, 111:9, 132:17; Ezek 29:21; 1 Sam 2:10; Ps 106:10; Mi 7:20; Ps 106:45; Ex 2:24; Jer 11:5; Ps 105:8f.; Mal 3:1; Is 40:3, 42:7, 9:1; Ps 107:10. While the Magnificat extols the beneficent acts of God in history, however, the Benedictus tends to advert to the culmination of the divine plan in the present events. The *horn of salvation for us in the house of David his servant* refers, obviously, to the yet unborn Jesus, present, nevertheless, in the body of his mother who was doubtless standing by. Zechariah's own child is addressed as *prophet of the Most High,* as having the character of Elijah ascribed to him in the angelic annunciation.

Lk 1:80 Having paralleled the annunciations of the Baptist and of Jesus and now having told the story of the Baptist's birth and circumcision, Luke will proceed to the complementary history of the Lord's nativity which we shall consider in our next chapter. For the moment, however, he is done with the Baptist *until the day of his manifestation to Israel* (Lk 3:2 and parallels). Hence he speedily summarizes in a few short words roughly thirty years of the Precursor's childhood and manhood.

Luke says that *he was in the deserts.* What is meant is the wilderness of Judea between Jerusalem and the Dead Sea, from time immemorial and down to the present a desolate region chosen as a place of refuge by those who have withdrawn from the world for political or religious reasons. Because this is also the region of Qumran, in recent years there

has been a revival of an old theory concerning John the Baptist's penitential and meditative life of preparation, supposing it to have been
spent in the bosom of some group like the Essenes. While the question
cannot be settled definitely one way or the other, there is indeed something to be said for the idea that some of the contacts between Qumran
and the New Testament may be explained through the Baptist. We shall
see the further relevance of this hypothesis when we come to the history
of Jesus' first disciples.

Mt 1:18–25   We shall conclude this chapter with a consideration of
               Matthew's parallel to Luke's story of the annunciation:
here an annunciation made to Joseph. It will also be necessary to preface
some preliminary remarks on the Matthaean form of the infancy narrative.

Matthew's "Gospel of the Infancy," the first two chapters of his work,
is also very much an integral part of his whole Gospel, not something
that has just been added on. It is *the book of the origin of Jesus
Christ, the son of David, the son of Abraham* (Mt 1:1). Just as the
Gospel as a whole falls into five major divisions of narrative and discourse, so in the Gospel of the Infancy we have five distinct narratives
each built about a major prophetic text of the Old Testament. These
are the annunciation to Joseph (1:18–25), Jesus' birth in Bethlehem
(2:1–12), the flight into Egypt (2:13–15), the slaughter of the innocents
(2:16–18), and the residence of the Holy Family at Nazareth (2:19–23);
as will be seen, the genealogy with which the Gospel begins and which
we shall consider later in connection with Luke's genealogy of the Savior
is actually an introduction to the story of the annunciation to Joseph.
This technique of exploiting Old Testament prophecy is typically Matthaean, one of the distinctive characteristics of the First Gospel.

Matthew's Gospel is pre-eminently ecclesiological: its theme first and
foremost is the mystery of God's kingdom, first broached to Israel and
now realized in the Church revealed to the people of God through his
Messiah and chosen instrument Jesus Christ. The Gospel of the Infancy
genuinely introduces this great theme by showing how in the coming of
Jesus the history of Old Testament Israel has been epitomized. He who
is the beginning of the new Israel, of the Church, is also the fulfillment
and summation of all that has gone before. The promise was first given to
Abraham and achieved in his offspring Jesus (cf. Gal 3:15–18). Christ
who comes as a second—and a greater—Moses also figures in his own
life Israel's call from Egypt and its exile, along with its higher destiny to
be God's prophetic instrument for the salvation of the Gentiles.

Within their separate contexts, therefore, though following similar
methods, the infancy narratives of Matthew and Luke go their distinct
ways. They agree on the few basic affirmations about Jesus' conception

and birth that were part of the heritage of Christian faith, but they have been written from independent traditions that differed in many details. If they do not contradict each other, neither do they attempt to supplement each other, and for this reason there is some difficulty in reading them as one continuous narrative. Matthew's concern throughout is with Joseph rather than Mary. He does not, as Luke does, begin the story in Nazareth; rather, he seems to presuppose that Bethlehem was the home of Mary and Joseph and that only because of special circumstances after Jesus' birth did they take up residence in Galilee. Incidentals of this kind, however, hardly affect what the evangelists considered to be the substance of their message. Given their separate aims and origins, the two accounts doubtless have a higher degree of correspondence than would have been antecedently expected.

The origin of Jesus Christ was in this way. As Matthew begins Mary is already *with child by the Holy Spirit* and the fact is known to Joseph. Matthew, too, emphasizes that Mary was *betrothed to Joseph* and that this was *before they came together,* that is, before there had been any consummation of a marriage. The virginal conception, therefore, is just as plain in Matthew's account as it is in Luke's. It may be noted how Matthew speaks of Mary and Joseph as persons already well known to his readers, needing no introduction. The narrative is quite compact, wasting no time on superfluous details.

Was Joseph aware merely that Mary was pregnant, or did he already have an intimation—from Mary herself, perhaps—that her state was the result of a special grace of God? Here we are confronted by a much debated interpretation of the text. That Joseph was *a just man and unwilling to expose her* has been held to have as its obvious meaning that he suspected her, not unnaturally, of adultery. Though the two were not yet officially married, nevertheless an affianced bride was considered under Jewish law to have both the rights and duties of a wife, and therefore cohabitation with another man would bring with it all the penalties of adultery. Joseph, however, a kindly man, wished to spare Mary this obloquy, and therefore *he was minded to put her away privately,* simply to divorce her without giving any precise reason, as was possible according to contemporary Jewish practice (see on Mt 19:3–12).

This is a reasonable enough understanding of the text which may very well be correct. However, it is equally possible that it underestimates the fullness of Matthew's meaning, particularly the sense in which he speaks of Joseph as a "just" man. A just man, after all, was a man faithful to the law, and the law did not look kindly on a maiden who had betrayed her troth (cf. Deut 22:23 f.). If, then, it is Matthew's meaning that Joseph was unwilling to expose Mary to reproach *despite* his being a just man, he may be asking us to view the contemplated divorce in another light. In other words, Joseph recognizing the mystery of God

at work in Mary's life may have been intending to withdraw humbly from
the scene. In this case, the subsequent vision would have as its chief
purpose to inform him of the role he was intended to play as Mary's
husband and, as *son of David*, the legal father of the Savior.

At all events, *while thinking these things* it was revealed to Joseph
what he must do. As in Luke, the divine revelation takes the form of
an angelic appearance, but here (and in Mt 2:12 f., 19, 22; cf. also
27:19) the appearance occurs in a dream, another means of divine communication well known from the Old Testament (see especially Gen
15:12–16, 37:5–10; Num 12:6). Joseph was bidden to have no fear about
accepting Mary as his wife, since *what has been conceived in her is of
the Holy Spirit*. He is to be the father of this family, bestowing upon
the child his name. The name *Jesus* (Hebrew *yᵉhôšûaʿ*, later abbreviated
to *yēšûaʿ*) meant, effectively, "God saves." It was an extremely common name, both in the times of the Old Testament (Joshua, Jeshua)
and the New, but the Gospel does not hesitate to underline the relevance of its etymology in the present instance: *he will save his people
from their sins*.

Matthew invokes from Old Testament prophecy another name of equal
relevance: this Jesus of whose birth he is speaking is the *Immanuel* of
Is 7:14. This is the first of the Old Testament texts which he cites explicitly to indicate a foreshadowing pattern in the salvation history of
the past. The precise historical circumstances of Isaiah's prophecy need
not concern us here, as they did not concern Matthew. Isaiah had
spoken of the birth of a child as the sign of God's salvation, whose very
existence would be living evidence of God's saving presence: *'immānû
'ēl*, "God with us." Such is Jesus. Furthermore, in the Greek text of the
Old Testament which Matthew was using (though not in the original
Hebrew of Isaiah's prophecy) the mother of this child was called
parthénos, "virgin"—and Matthew, of course, was writing of a virgin
birth.

The episode is brought to a rapid conclusion. Whatever the state of
Joseph's mind had been, his course was now clear to him. *He took to
himself his wife:* Joseph concluded his betrothal with Mary by receiving
her into his home as his wife and acknowledging her child as his own.
The Gospel was not written to defend the Christian tradition of Mary's
perpetual virginity, but it certainly contains nothing that opposes it. *He
did not know her till she brought forth* her son is Matthew's final insistence on the virginal conception of Jesus; he does not necessarily imply subsequent marital relations between Joseph and Mary (see the similar uses of "till" in Mt 12:20, 13:33, 14:22, 16:28, 22:44, 24:39). Some
manuscripts (not the best ones) preface "firstborn" to "son" in this
passage: see on Lk 2:7.

4. JOY TO THE WORLD

Lk 2:1-7 We resume and conclude the infancy narrative by returning to Luke, the only evangelist who really tells the story of the nativity. He introduces this important event with another chronological indication. *Those days* refers, of course, to his previous indication (Lk 1:5), the time when Herod the Great was king (37-4 B.C.); Matthew also places the birth of Jesus within the reign of Herod. Luke now adds that these things took place during the lifetime of *Caesar Augustus* (30 B.C. to A.D. 14). Immediately we are made aware of the fact that our conventional reckoning of dates as B.C. and A.D., based on calculations made in the sixth Christian century, is in error by at least a few years. Jesus Christ was born sometime before 4 B.C.

Luke's further statistical information is subject to varying and uncertain interpretations owing to our lack of precise corroborative materials. The uncertainties concern minor matters of detail, but they do render an exact chronology impossible. There is no independent record that *a decree went forth . . . that a census of the whole world should be taken.* The "whole world" is the *oikoumenē*, the "inhabited earth," that is, the Roman empire. Various censuses, usually for taxation purposes, took place in the various parts of the Empire during the time of Augustus, involving both Roman citizens and those who were not. At one time or another, doubtless the whole *oikoumenē* was included in the census. Luke, of course, is interested in the census that affected Palestine; but it is in keeping with his universalistic interests to fit the birth of Jesus into a context in which the whole earth was involved.

Luke speaks of *this first census*, doubtless to distinguish it from another, well-known census which he mentions in Acts 5:37 (recorded also by Flavius Josephus), which took place in A.D. 6-7. It is only this second census, as a matter of fact, that is known to profane history as having taken place *while Quirinius was governor of Syria*. Publius Sulpicius Quirinius was certainly the Roman governor of Syria after A.D. 6. That he served a term as governor before 4 B.C. cannot be proved, but neither can it be disproved. In any case, Luke is mainly interested in connecting our Lord's birth with known persons and events rather than in supplying an exact chronology. It is known that the Romans undertook a census in Egypt every fourteen years. If this practice held true in the other Roman provinces, then presumably around 8 B.C. a census would have been taken in the province of Syria, under which Palestine would have been included. This is as close as we can come to assigning a date for the birth of Jesus.

All were going to register, each to his own city. This was certainly not the Roman method of taking a census, but again we are not entirely sure of the background of the text. It is likely enough that a Roman census of the Jews of Palestine would have been administered by Herod, and it is equally likely that it would have been done in the Jewish fashion, in the places of ancestral origin, since Rome was always willing to accommodate itself to its difficult Jewish subjects in matters that it did not consider essential. However, Luke's purpose here is to explain how it was that Jesus, of Galilean parentage, came to be born in Bethlehem, and on any accounting the census does not explain this, since Mary's presence would not have been required in any case. Joseph *was of the house and family of David;* Luke stresses Joseph's Davidic ancestry quite emphatically. We are half given the impression that the Holy Family had some connection with the city of David other than the casual one afforded by the census. It will be recalled that Matthew appears to take it for granted that Mary and Joseph were originally Judeans rather than Galileans. It is also to be noted that Luke still calls Mary Joseph's *betrothed* rather than his wife, though it is evident that the marriage spoken of in Mt 1:24 had by now taken place. This is Luke's delicate way of saying what Matthew said more bluntly in 1:25.

Equally delicate is Luke's description of our Lord's virginal birth, a description which stands in great contrast to the crudities of some of the apocryphal gospels. *The days of her delivery were fulfilled, and she brought forth a son, her firstborn.* "Firstborn" (Hebrew *bᵉkôr*, Greek *prōtotokos*) was a technical term for "the child who opens the womb" (cf. Ex 13:12–15). A "firstborn" might well be an only child: a funerary inscription from Egypt of the year 5 B.C.—almost precisely contemporary with the birth of the Savior—describes the virtues of a young Jewish mother who died giving birth to her *prōtotokos*. The firstborn had special privileges and was an object of predilection; thus Israel was called the Lord's "firstborn" (Ex 4:22). *She wrapped him round and laid him in a manger:* the manger, a wooden or stone trough for the feeding of animals, may have belonged to the shepherds who appear in the next episode; it seems to be presupposed that its location was already known to them (cf. vss. 12, 15 f.). Swept clean and lined with straw it would have made a comfortable if makeshift crib for a newborn child. That the manger was in a cave as the ancient Bethlehemite tradition maintains is not at all unlikely.

There was for them no place in the inn are words that have often been misunderstood. We need not think of stonyhearted innkeepers and townspeople turning away the Holy Family and refusing them hospitality. The text seems to suppose that Mary and Joseph had already been in Bethlehem for some days, and during this time they had probably stayed at the inn. The inn, the Palestinian *khan*, which would have been outside the city near the traveled roads, was simply an enclosure in which men and cattle were bedded down for the night. Privacy, always at a premium in the Near East, would have been impossible here. Luke is undoubtedly suggesting that Mary and Joseph deliberately chose a place of seclusion for the enactment of the mystery of the Lord's birth.

Lk 2:8–20   The familiar story of the shepherds is without analogy in the parallel history of the Baptist and it has no counterpart in Old Testament events or in "hero" legends; it is part of the Bethlehemite tradition of the humble birth of Christ. This event which had first been announced to one who called herself the lowly handmaid of the Lord is now first witnessed to by other humble folk, like those who will later hear the kingdom declared their own in Jesus' proclamation of the Gospel (cf. Lk 6:20).

The story conforms to the Lucan pattern: an angelic annunciation accompanied by an injunction not to fear is followed by an explanation and a sign. There is also a canticle which anticipates the later messianic acclaim of Jesus (cf. Lk 19:38), taken as usual from Old Testament phrases (cf. Ps 118:25; Is 57:19). *On earth peace:* "peace" inadequately translates a Semitic concept which really connotes wholeness, completion, at-one-ment with God. Concretely this happy state is now present in the babe of Bethlehem; similarly St. Paul calls Christ "our peace" (Eph 2:14). *Among men of good will:* a parallel expression in the Qumran literature confirms what was always the best understanding of these words, that the "good will" in question is God's. That is to say, it is through the gratuitous act of the divine mercy that this peace has been brought to men.

Two additional words in this passage are deserving of note. In verse 11 Jesus is called for the first time in the Gospel *Savior*, a term pre-eminently reserved in the Old Testament to the God of Israel. The angelic annunciation *I bring you good news* is the Greek verb corresponding to our word "Gospel." The shepherds respond to this proclamation by saying, literally, *Let us go . . . see this word which has come to pass*, and, as is the duty of all who receive the word, *they made known what had been told them*, in a sense becoming the first to preach the Gospel. Contrasting with the surprise of the villagers who heard the shepherds' testimony is the quiet Virgin who was *pondering these things in her heart.*

The episode of the shepherds who *were out in the fields in that same district* says nothing either for or against the tradition which makes December the month of the nativity. The climate of Bethlehem is temperate enough to allow for a very mild December. But in any case the traditional dating of Christmas, which probably cannot be traced back beyond the fourth Christian century, was doubtless arrived at on considerations other than those of the Gospel.

Mt 1:1–17   Before pursuing the infancy narratives to their conclusion,
Lk 3:23–38 it is appropriate at this point to consider the two earthly
                genealogies of Jesus which appear in the Gospels in Matthew as a preface to the story of his birth and in Luke as an insertion into the introductory part of the history of the public ministry.

The reader who approaches the genealogies for the first time is initially surprised to discover the many discrepancies between them. Matthew's is more typically Jewish in maintaining the descending order from father to son; Luke's, while not without precedent in the Old Testament, adopts the less usual procedure of working back through preceding generations. In keeping with his universalistic interpretation of the Gospel, Luke not surprisingly traces Jesus' ancestry all the way to human origins; Matthew, adhering more closely to the Gospel's Jewish beginnings, shows Jesus' descent from Abraham through the royal line of David. The most obvious difference, however, is in the genealogical names from David to Joseph, which follow two quite separate traditions, including even a discrepancy in the name of Joseph's father.

We have no way of reconciling the two genealogies completely, but there is no particular reason why we should try. To a considerable extent both are artificial. Even apart from the fact that no one could trace a person's ancestry back through seventy-five names to Adam, as Luke does, it will be noted that for the names prior to David he has simply reproduced the already artificial genealogies of the Old Testament. Matthew has three series of fourteen names. The fourteen he probably derived from 1 Chron 2:1–15, which already had counted fourteen generations from Abraham to David; fourteen is also the first multiple of seven, a number favored in Matthew, and is the sum of the numerical value of the Hebrew letters of David's name (*d-w-d*: vowels are not written in the Hebrew alphabet). In order to preserve symmetry he has omitted the names of three of the Davidic kings on whom he concentrates in his genealogy. In both lists the names subsequent to Zerubbabel are unknown to the Old Testament. Luke has given Joseph's Davidic lineage through a certain Heli, Matthew through a man named Jacob.

Both evangelists insist on what was part of the earliest Christian confession (cf. Rom 1:3), that through Joseph, his legal father, Jesus was truly of the Davidic descent in which the messianic expectation had been fixed. It would have been by no means unusual that a Jewish carpenter would be able to vindicate such an ancestry through family traditions. Such genealogies, however, were never complete and were subject to many variations.

We have seen the universalistic note of Luke's genealogy. In its own way, Matthew's is also universalistic. Contrary to Semitic custom, it includes the names of four women, the common denominator of whom seems to be that they were all Gentiles, non-Israelites who nevertheless became part of the history of the people of God even in Old Testament times.

Lk 2:21–24   Following the story of the shepherds, Luke concludes his narrative of the nativity by telling of two events which were of importance to him. *After eight days,* in accordance with the Mosaic law, occurred *his circumcision,* the rite by which a Jewish boy was accepted into the religious society of his people. Jesus, who was "born of a woman, born under the law" (Gal 4:4), became officially subject to the law of Moses by this rite. At the same time, as we have already noted in the parallel history of the Baptist, it was customary for the child to receive his name. It is doubtless the name-giving that was chiefly of interest to Luke.

The other event occurred thirty-three days later (cf. Lev 12:1–4): the end of the period of ritual uncleanness after childbirth and the time of the mother's ceremonial purification. Luke says curiously *the time of their purification.* The plural pronoun probably is used because, although the rite of purification involved Mary alone, occasion was taken at the same time to fulfill another law that did involve Jesus and which is the real subject of this passage: *they brought him to Jerusalem to present him to the Lord.* This presentation of Jesus—which did not have to be performed in the temple—was the "redemption" of the firstborn from the Lord by the payment of five silver shekels, say three dollars in our money (cf. Num 18:15 f.). Thus, though the purification was the occasion, and the sacrifice that is mentioned is that of the purificatory rite (cf. Lev 12:6–8), what is uppermost in Luke's mind is that Jesus ("Savior") the Redeemer now appears before the Lord himself redeemed: Daniel's prophecy of the seventy weeks has now been fulfilled in the consecration of a most holy (see above on Lk 1:8–12).

Lk 2:25–38   Accompanying this event, as was most fitting, were signs like those which accompanied Jesus' annunciation and birth. In the temple were two holy people who like Elizabeth and Zechariah, Mary and Joseph, represent the very best in the contemporary Jewish messianic expectation.

Simeon, for some reason, has often been represented in postbiblical tradition as a priest and an aged man. Luke says merely that he was *a just man and devout who was awaiting the consolation of Israel*. He was, in other words, like Mary one of the poor and humble of the Lord to whom prophecy had promised the messianic salvation (cf. Is 40:1, 49:13, 61:1 f., 66:13). This man, whom inspiration had first assured of a fulfillment of this hope in his own lifetime, was now inspired to discover its realization in the child in Mary's arms. His prayer of thanksgiving is reproduced in the canticle which we call the Nunc Dimittis, as usual an echo of prophetic themes whose universalism would have especially appealed to Luke (cf. Is 40:5, 52:10).

Simeon likewise has a prophetic blessing for Mary and her Child. It is the destiny of every prophetic word to be *a sign contradicted*. Jesus, the Word incarnate, will be no exception to this rule. Faith, the acceptance of the prophetic word of which he himself is the sign (cf. Mk 8:11 f.; Mt 16:1–4; Is 7:3–14, 8:14 f.), will determine in every case whether he shall be *for the fall or for the rise of many in Israel*. Broadly speaking, this is the teaching that is spelt out in the first half of John's Gospel. Simeon's word to Mary is also Johannine: *your own soul a sword shall pierce*. In the temple episode with which Luke will conclude his infancy narrative (Lk 2:41–52), Mary will receive a foretaste of the role which she is to play in the redemptive work of her Son. It will not be an easy role, for it will involve the same kind of renunciation of self and sacrificial obedience that are Christ's destiny. Not through the natural ties of motherhood but rather in her capacity as mother and model of the faithful will Mary accomplish what God has designed for her (see on Jn 2:1–11).

The *prophetess Anna* whom Luke introduces on this same occasion is described by him in some detail, but little is said of any prophetic function that she fulfilled. One of the devout of the Old Testament, she likewise foreshadowed the dedicated widows who were to become one of the institutions of the apostolic Church (cf. 1 Tim 5:3–8) *awaiting the redemption of Jerusalem.*

Lk 2:39–40   Having concluded his story of the nativity, Luke now takes the Holy Family back to their Galilean homeland; he has nothing further to relate concerning the circumstances of the Lord's birth. A final parallel to his story about the Precursor (cf. Lk 1:80) summarizes the "hidden life" of obscurity in which Jesus, too, was prepared for the day of his manifestation to Israel.

Mt 2:1–12   Matthew, however, who has even less to say about Jesus' actual birth than Luke does, resumes his infancy narrative at this point, *after Jesus had been born in Bethlehem of Judea in the days of King Herod*, with the well-known story of the coming of the Magi, an episode designed to feature the second of his prophetic texts concerning the Messiah (see above on Mt 1:18–25). As has already been seen, there is little use in trying to relate this event chronologically to what has been described in Luke's account. The two narratives have been prepared from altogether distinct traditions which grew up without reference to each other and in which such chronological considerations played no part. In the past, commentators have spent a great deal of time quite fruitlessly debating the precise sequence of events which, it was thought, was supposed by the combined Gospel story. What is now recognized as the proper study of the Gospel is to ascertain what each evangelist intended to contribute to its message through the use which he made of traditions which were independent of another's.

There can be no doubt as to what Matthew intended to bring out in the Magi story. His is a Gospel very much intended to speak to the existing Church, a Gentile Church which had transcended the privileges of the earthly Israel. The pagan Magi who have traveled from afar to seek out the awaited king stand in glaring contrast to the king and the wise of Jerusalem, all of whom are unaware of the great thing that has taken place among them and some of whom are made aware of it only to view it as an evil to be suppressed: truly, even from the very beginning Jesus "did not find faith like this in Israel" (see on Mt 8:5–13 and parallel). As before, the Gospel narrative includes many allusions to Old Testament prophecy and themes besides the one explicit citation of Mi 5:1 on the Bethlehemite origin of the Messiah. The theme of the Gentiles pilgriming to Jerusalem in the time of redemption is to be found in such passages as Is 60:6 and Ps 72:10 f. (a text which is doubtless responsible for the later Christian legend which transformed the Magi into kings). Possibly the star of the Magi is intended to evoke the star (*kôkāb*) from Jacob mentioned in the oracle of Balaam of Num 24:17: the secular messiah who led the second Jewish revolt against the Romans, which culminated in A.D. 135, was known popularly as Bar Kokeba, "son of the star." On the other hand, we may have to look no further for an explanation of the star than to the tradition of the Magi itself, since magi were astrologers. But above all, in this narrative the evangelist is thinking of Jesus in his character of a second and greater Moses—the Moses who like Jesus was born under a tyrannous king to the accompaniment of the slaying of innocents (Ex 1:15–22), who had to flee to a foreign land to save his life from the wrath of this king (Ex 2:15), the Moses who was born to be Israel's rescuer (Ex 2:10), its ruler and judge (Ex 2:14; cf. Acts 7:35).

Confronted by such a story as that of the Magi, the modern reader is likely to ask questions for which no answer is provided by the evangelist or the tradition on which he depended. *Magi from the east arrived in Jerusalem.* Elsewhere in the New Testament (e.g., Acts 13:6) a *magos* is a practitioner of occult arts, and the word is usually employed in a pejorative sense. Traditionally *magoi* were the astrologer priests of Persian Zoroastrianism, a monotheistic religion of sorts which had had some in-

fluence on the development of postexilic Judaism but which certainly had
little if any acquaintance with Palestinian Jewry and did not share its
messianic aspirations. That Persian priests should have been led by their
astronomical calculations to discern the birth of the Jewish Messiah and
that they should have journeyed from distant Persia to Herod's provincial
court in Jerusalem is unlikely in the extreme. Neither this fact, however,
nor the undeniably "midrashic" interpretation which the evangelist has
given to the story justifies any peremptory judgment concerning the
historicity of whatever real happening may lie behind the tradition. That
it is symbolic in much of its detail is undeniable, but it is equally undeniable that the Gospel traditions have not in principle been concocted
out of thin air. What is true is that in the form in which these traditions
have reached us they are no longer a legitimate object for the microscopic
investigation of historical criticism. Who the Magi really were, therefore,
and what were the precise circumstances of their relation to the birth of
the Savior are questions that cannot be answered from the Gospel sources,
the only sources that we possess.

King Herod was troubled, and all Jerusalem with him. This perturba-
tion, unwonted in those who should have been eagerly awaiting *the one
born King of the Jews*, anticipates the consternation of Jerusalem at
the time of Jesus' entry there as messianic king (cf. Mt 21:10). The
messianic text from Micah is cited by Matthew not in the restricted sense
of the original Hebrew prophecy, which was to celebrate the Ephrathite
clan of David chosen by the Lord to be his elect dynasty, but in the
sense of Christian fulfillment pointing to the Messiah's Davidic and
Bethlehemite origin. Herod's duplicity continues to contrast with the simple good faith of the Magi.

*The star went before them till it stopped over the place where the child
lay.* As it figures in the story the star of the Magi is obviously a divine
portent that can find no explanation in any of the normal manifestations
of celestial phenomena. *Entering the house*: in Matthew's Gospel there is
nothing of the tradition of Jesus' birth as a stranger in Bethlehem; as in
2:22 f., the evangelist takes it for granted that the Holy Family made their
dwelling there. *They worshiped him*: Matthew, of course, takes the
divine nature of Christ as part of the Gospel message. Whether he intends to suggest that the Magi acknowledged his divine as well as his royal
character is not certain, but it is likely enough that he did. The three *gifts
of gold, frankincense, and myrrh* have doubtless contributed to the idea
that there were three Magi. These were traditional gifts of homage (cf.
Ps 72:10, 11, 15; Is 60:6; Cant 3:6; Sir 24:20); there may be an echo of
the same idea in Jn 19:39.

Mt 2:13–15   In dreams the Lord both warns the Magi not to return to
                  the perfidious Herod with news of Christ's birth and com-

mands Joseph to take the child and his mother into Egypt away from his cruel power. There really would have been nothing too unusual about such a journey for Palestinian Jews. There were Jewish colonies throughout this nearby country, and Alexandria was one of the largest Jewish centers of the contemporary world.

Matthew, however, finds in this event a profound prophetic significance, on a par with Jesus' Bethlehemite origin. *Out of Egypt I called my son* were the words of the prophet Hosea (Hos 11:1) referring to Israel's election by God as concretely demonstrated in the exodus from Egypt by which it passed, under Moses, from slavery into freedom. It has been Jesus' destiny to be the Savior of the new Israel by becoming the firstborn of many brethren (cf. Col 1:18), reliving Israel's history in his own to bring that history to an even more glorious fulfillment. Israel was first God's son, and now his only Son has become one of Israel that all might be called sons of God.

Mt 2:16–18   Finding himself outwitted by the Magi, Herod reacts with all the ruthlessness by which he is notorious in profane history. Bethlehem and its environs, it is true, comprised only a small town, and the evangelist therefore represents the slaughter of the innocents as of perhaps a score of children rather than of the hundreds or thousands that became the theme of later artists and liturgists. But in any case it was a savage act worthy of the world which hates Christ, whose way is death in opposition to his way of life.

To accompany this account Matthew has chosen the most poignant of his prophetic texts, that of Jeremiah (Jer 31:15) on the occasion of the captivity and exile of northern Israel centuries before. Jeremiah had represented Rachel, the mother of Benjamin and Joseph (i.e., in popular thought, the people of Ephraim), rising from her grave at Ramah to weep over the plight of her descendants. In Matthew's time, as it is today, tradition had transferred the site of Rachel's tomb to the vicinity of Bethlehem (cf. Gen 35:19), and in this circumstance the evangelist found an even more appropriate cause for Rachel's weeping. But it is not of this coincidence alone that he takes note. Jeremiah's was a prophecy of salvation after tears, of redemption that would follow suffering, of return after exile and death.

Mt 2:19–23   The last of Matthew's prophetic texts that have provided the outline for his infancy narrative remains an enigma despite all the efforts that have been made to explain it. *He shall be called a Nazarene* is the customary translation, since it is evident enough that the evangelist intends to offer a providential accounting in prophecy for the fact that Jesus, born in Bethlehem, was nevertheless known as a Galilean from the town of Nazareth, where Mary and Joseph went after their return from Egypt. Luke was at pains to explain how Jesus came to

be born in Bethlehem in the first place, but Matthew, as he appears to
have no knowledge that the Holy Family originated in Nazareth, must explain why they did not return to Bethlehem. This was because of *Archelaus*, he says, who despite Jewish opposition was confirmed by the Romans
to succeed his father Herod in Judea after Herod's death in 4 B.C. Archelaus, who proved to be somewhat of a worse ruler than his father, if this
were conceivable, governed Judea—though not Galilee or Perea—until he
finally had to be removed in A.D. 6. The Holy Family, therefore, passed
into the territory of Herod Antipas, likewise a son of the great Herod,
but without his father's evil reputation. *Those who sought the child's life
are dead* reflects Matthew's consciousness of the parallel with Moses'
life (cf. Ex 4:19).

The word that Matthew actually uses is *nazōraios*, which does not at
first glance seem to be closely related to Nazareth; in point of fact, the
New Testament has another word, *nazarēnos*, which is a much more
obvious term for Nazarene. On the analogy with words like *pharisaios*
and *saddoukáios*, we would expect *nazōraios* to come out in English
something like Nazoree. It does not, because we know of no need for such
a word. Nevertheless, some scholars have thought that there was such a
title, of uncertain meaning, probably pejorative, applied by the Jews to
Christ and the first Christians. To this day, Jews refer to Jesus in Hebrew
as *Yešu han-nōṣrî* and to Christians as *han-nōṣrîm*. These terms are generally taken to mean "Nazarene(s)," but again this does not seem to
have been their original sense.

If there was such a contemptuous name given to Christ and the
Christians, it may be in this sense that Matthew connects it with prophecy, relating it to Nazareth by a play on words. Nazareth, we know, was
an insignificant village with a low reputation (cf. Jn 1:46). Jesus, the
Lord's Servant, was reputed by men as lowly and of no account, as had
been written in prophecy (cf. Is 52:13–53:6). But many other correspondences to the word have been sought in the Old Testament, such as the
neṣer (shoot) of Is 11:1, 60:21, etc., the *nōṣer* (guardian) of Is 27:3, etc.,
or the *nāzîr* (a consecrated person) of Jgs 13:5, etc. It would help, of course,
if we knew what prophetic passage Matthew had in mind. He speaks of
what was said by the prophets either, as St. Jerome thought, because he
refers to a general prophetic idea rather than to a specific prophecy, or
because he is invoking some non-canonical prophecy that is now unknown
to us. The mingling of canonical with apocryphal testimonial passages
appears in the literature of the Qumran sectaries.

Lk 2:41–52   On his final prophetic note, Matthew's Gospel of the Infancy concluded. Luke's infancy narrative, too, as we saw,
could very well have been completed with his final parallel (in Lk 2:39 f.)
linking the coming of the Savior with the Precursor, his summation of

the hidden life of Jesus at Nazareth. In a sense, the story with which Luke does choose to end his narrative appears both supplementary and anticlimactic, and bears a superficial resemblance to the apocryphal gospels which abound with wonderful stories about Jesus' boyhood. However, even if Luke has included the incident as an afterthought, it is his story throughout and he has thoroughly integrated it into his Gospel. As is apparent, it parallels and complements the story of Jesus' presentation in the temple.

His parents went every year to Jerusalem for the feast of the Passover. In these days of the Diaspora even pious Jews who lived afar were not expected to keep the three pilgrimage feasts in Jerusalem (Deut 16:16), but all who could would try to be present there for the Passover, commemorating the events of Israel's exodus from Egypt. At *twelve years of age* Jesus himself was not yet *bar mitzvah* and therefore not personally obliged to the Law in any case. The story that unfolds is perfectly comprehensible in itself. *Having completed the seven days* of the Passover observance, Mary and Joseph begin the return journey to Galilee, are separated from each other in caravan, and only when camp is made at the end of the first day's journey do they discover that Jesus is nowhere in the company. *After three days* would indicate the morning of the day following the one spent in the return to Jerusalem. Luke undoubtedly intends to evoke the memory of the resurrection of Jesus on the third day.

The scene of the finding of Jesus in the temple precincts evokes a picture familiar to travelers in the Near East: the informal schools conducted by masters with disciples at their feet, posing and answering questions. Mary's protestation is typically a mother's, in which relief is mingled with a touch of exasperation at finding him calmly attending the discussions of the rabbis while he had been frantically sought after. But it is now that she must begin to learn her destiny, foretold years ago by Simeon. *Your father and I have sought you,* she has said. Rather, replies Jesus, *why did you not know that I would be at my Father's?* He who was in one sense Jesus' father, and in a sense certainly not to be minimized, must nevertheless soon make way for Jesus' Father above all in the public life which this Son will lead as one of sacrificial obedience which will permit no interference from earthly ties. Joseph, as a matter of fact, now unobtrusively disappears from the Gospel story. Mary his mother will remain, but, as we shall see, the Gospel will be no less clear concerning the role in which providence has cast her. Not as Mary of Nazareth, wife of the carpenter and mother of a boy Jesus, but as the first of believers and exemplar of Christians will her life find its fulfillment, even as she has already been hailed as Daughter of Zion and Ark of the Covenant. Her greater unity with her Son will be achieved through the paradox of the separating sword of renunciation.

He was subject to them. Jesus' presence in the temple is a foreshadowing of his entire life, which is that of the obedient Servant of God who has come not to be ministered to but to minister to others; this chosen role is likewise exemplified in the "hidden life." At the close of this narrative Luke again reminds us of the parallel with the history of the Baptist by a summary statement very like that of verse 40.

5. A LIGHT BEGINS TO SHINE

Lk 3:1–2　　All the Gospels begin the story of the salvation wrought in
Jesus Christ by recalling the proclamation of the kingdom by
John the Baptist, the last in the long prophetic series that had testified
to the saving design of God. Only Luke, however, as is his wont (cf.
Lk 2:1 f.), has attempted to relate the kerygmatic history of the Gospel
to the world history into which the New Testament was born.

The fifteenth year of Tiberius Caesar, however, is not as precise an
indication as it might be, though Luke undoubtedly intended it to be
so. Tiberius became emperor in his own right in A.D. 14, on the death of
the emperor Augustus who was reigning at the time of Jesus' birth. He
had already been accepted by Augustus as co-ruler a couple of years before this, however. Presumably Luke is counting from the beginning of
Tiberius' separate reign. Presumably, too, he is counting by the Roman
method of reckoning regnal years. If these assumptions are correct, he
indicates a date sometime between October of A.D. 27 and September of
A.D. 28. This was the beginning of the Baptist's prophetic mission: *the
word of God came upon John, the son of Zechariah, in the desert;*
thus he resumes the story which he broke off in 1:80. It is the evident
sense of the Gospels that Jesus' own ministry did not begin long after
this.

A glance at the map of Palestine in Jesus' time will make clearer the
rest of the data that Luke gives. *Pontius Pilate was governor of Judea,*
which included Samaria, between A.D. 26–36, the fifth to serve in that
capacity after the removal of Herod's son Archelaus. The *Herod* who
was *tetrarch of Galilee* and Perea was Antipas, another of Herod's sons,
while still another, *Philip,* governed *Ituraea and Trachonitis,* the northern region of Herod's old kingdom, a region which scarcely enters into
the Gospel picture. In mentioning *Lysanias the tetrarch of Abilene,*
Luke was once thought to have made a serious historical blunder, since
the only Lysanias of that description then known had been put to death
by Mark Antony in 34 B.C. A contemporary inscription discovered and published in 1912, however, confirmed the existence of Luke's Lysanias.

Abilene does not figure in the Gospel; Luke merely notes Lysanias as a statistical fact, a ruler on a par with Antipas and Philip.

The high priesthood of Annas and Caiaphas does concern the Gospel record, and of course we shall meet these worthies again.

Lk 3:3–6   Matthew and Mark, who lack Luke's historical introduction
Mt 3:1–6   to the Gospel story, substitute for it in their own ways.
Mk 1:1–6   Matthew's *in those days* obviously has no reference to the
              infancy narrative which he has made the preface of his Gospel. The expression is merely conventional and somewhat mechanical, as are so many apparently statistical references in the Gospels. Mark, who is only now beginning his Gospel is, seemingly, the only evangelist to use that word for his work (of all the evangelists, only Mark and Matthew use the word *gospel* at all). Even here, however, Mark's emphasis is doubtless less on his narrative of the Gospel than on the fact of the Gospel itself, the good news of the salvation prophesied of old and now fulfilled in Jesus Christ. Similarly, his reference to *the beginning* may evoke the idea of new creation as well as entitle his work.

The Synoptic Gospels have a representation of the Baptist which partly agrees with the presentation of John and partly, as we shall see, is at variance with it. They all apply to him the words of Is 40:3, which spoke of the joyful news of coming salvation, the Lord again coming to visit his people after their exile and degradation. It is interesting to see how the several evangelists use the quotation. Mark prefaces to it lines that come from Ex 23:20 and Mal 3:1, all of which he includes as the words of *Isaiah the prophet*. One of the sources on which the evangelists drew— one of the Gospel "forms"—was testimonial collections, series of Old Testament texts of the same or similar purport which had been melded together and were cited only by a generic reference; this passage is far from being isolated in the Gospels. Matthew and Luke omit the expansion on the Isaian text here probably because they found it in a better context in the source they share independently of Mark and have therefore reproduced it elsewhere in their Gospels (Mt 11:10; Lk 7:27). Luke, on the other hand, extends the Isaian citation down to Is 40:5, undoubtedly because of the final words: *and all mankind shall see the salvation of God*; Luke rarely misses an opportunity to stress the universality of salvation.

Matthew and Mark also agree (Luke, however, does not) in recognizing in John the Baptist a second Elijah the prophet: it is for this reason that they note the Baptist's *garment of camel's hair and leather belt* (see 2 Kgs 1:8). Luke omits this description, as he does that of the Baptist's simple and penitential diet, probably because he felt that such references would be lost on his Gentile readers. *Locusts and wild honey*, that is, the sweet gums of various trees, are still eaten by the desert Arabs; the locusts are roasted and eaten whole or ground into a powder and mixed with other food.

John the Baptist was preaching a *baptism of repentance* in view of the imminent *kingdom of God* ("kingdom of heaven" in Matthew: a Jewish paraphrase). As such, he was continuing a venerable prophetic tradition. It is not merely that he spoke of the coming soon of what prophets had first enunciated and had become one of the favorite themes of later Judaism, God's definitive breaking into man's history, establishing for all time a reign in which his will would be as truly done on earth as it is in heaven. This expectation, sometimes expressed in nationalistic and particularistic terms, sometimes quite spiritually, was shared by many in Israel, and not only by withdrawal groups like the Essenes: the Gospels show here and elsewhere with what enthusiasm the Baptist's preaching had been received in Palestine. Far more important was it that John was preaching *metanoia*, the word that we translate "repentance," which means a change of mind and heart, conversion, a thoroughgoing revision of one's actions and attitudes to bring them into conformity with the will of God. This is what the prophets had preached as the condition of God's coming: for his kingdom God has need of men. This it is that leads to *the forgiveness of sins* and the beginning of the kingdom.

As the sign of this entry into a new way of life John baptized his disciples in water. Baptism was a rite not unknown to the Jews, and it is likely that it was practiced by the Qumran Jews in particular; at all events, its symbolism is obvious enough to explain its use by other religions which have no connection with Judaism or Christianity. Because of John's proximity to the New Testament, however, and because of the continuation that his practice was to find in the sacramental baptism of the Church, he has been remembered in Christian tradition as the Baptizer.

Mt 3:7–10 Matthew and Luke supplement Mark's account from an-
Lk 3:7–9   other source that they share in common, a passage which
               suggests some of the content of the Baptist's preaching. It further explains what was involved in the *metanoia* preached by John: it must be a soul-searching that results in total compliance with the grace of God, setting no reliance on any supposed automatic guarantees of race or formal religion. "He is not a Jew who is so outwardly . . . but who is so inwardly" (Rom 2:28 f.). This, too, was in the authentic prophetic tradition (cf. Jer 31:31–34, for example). *The axe is laid to the root of the trees* lends an expressive eschatological note to this preaching: the kingdom is near, and the time for repentance is short.

Brood of vipers is a surprisingly harsh judgment to encounter this early in the Gospel story, and for this reason many are of the opinion that the tradition on which Matthew and Luke depended has anticipated in the career of the Baptist a situation that better fits in the ministry of Jesus (cf. Mt 12:34, 23:33). It is a common tradition of the Gospels, however, that John who was popularly received as a prophet was regarded with cynical skepticism or feigned acceptance by many within the Jewish leadership (cf. Mk 11:30–32 and parallels). It is to these latter that these words were addressed, as is evident from Matthew's reference to *many of the Pharisees and Sadducees*—terms which themselves are doubtless excessively generic, as we shall see. It is Luke's casual *the crowds* which could give the impression, belied by his own context, that the Baptist's denunciation was a wholesale one. Elsewhere (cf. Lk 7:29 f.) he clearly makes the distinction just mentioned.

Lk 3:10–14   Luke himself now expands on the story from a source of his own to show the basic good will of "the crowds." This evangelist rarely misses an opportunity to "actualize" the Gospel story for his readers: what the Baptist indicated as the conditions necessary for reception of the kingdom could serve as guidelines for the members of the kingdom-Church.

The Baptist's injunctions reiterate the essentials of the prophetic conception of true religion: justice and charity proved by deeds (cf. Jas 1:27, 2:16 f.). *The taxgatherers* of our text were the famous "publicans," Jews who collected the taxes farmed out by the Roman authorities, men who were in an easy position for extortion and for victimizing their fellow Jews who excommunicated them for their service of a heathen oppressor. Probably in much the same position were the *soldiers*, military police in the hire of the Romans who in a police state could often wield a terrible and arbitrary power. Like the prophets and like Jesus himself (cf. Mt 22:15–22), John refrains from any sociological comment on these existing political institutions; his attention is wholly directed to the people who are involved in the institutions.

Lk 3:15   Luke alone of the Synoptic writers goes on to say that so
Jn 1:19–24   great was the enthusiasm that was engendered by the
                  Baptist's preaching, and so much in tune was his proclamation with popular anticipation, that the question began to be asked whether he might be the Messiah, the long awaited one who would redeem Israel for God. In this he agrees with John, who now begins his version of the Gospel story with the account of a mission to the Baptist from the Jewish leadership in Jerusalem.

This is John's witness. The significance of "witness" in the Fourth Gospel we have already seen anticipated in the Prologue, Jn 1:7, 15. The witness of the Baptist consists in testifying to what he, John, is not, then to what Jesus is; this witness to the truth of God's word will be continued throughout by the protagonists of the Gospel as the fulfillment of the prophetic witness of the Old Testament and the beginning of the new prophetic witness of the Church inspired by the Spirit of truth.

The Jews in John's Gospel usually designates the official leadership of Judaism in Jerusalem, though sometimes the term is more general or neutral. Because these persons, who historically were Jews, epitomize for John the unbelieving world which will not accept Christ, "the Jews" is more often than not a pejorative expression in the Fourth Gospel. It is not, however, a term of opprobrium in itself for an author who himself was doubtless a Jew. John says that the delegation to the Baptist was composed of *priests and Levites* (this combination only here in the Gospels), those who were empowered by the Mosaic law to judge in religious matters; in verse 24 he says they were *of the Pharisees*. The association of priests and Pharisees is unlikely, and the unlikelihood is only increased if we read in verse 24 with some manuscripts that the priests had been sent *by* the Pharisees. Either these terms are being used somewhat indifferently for readers for whom the exact distinctions in Judaism were no longer of concern, a situation which seems to be verified elsewhere in the Gospels, or, as is equally likely, John has summarized in one account various embassies that had gone out to the Baptist.

I am not the Messiah. Jesus' habitual identification of himself in John's Gospel is "I am," the full significance of which we shall see later; the Baptist's negative confession thus prepares the way for the revelation of the Word. *Elijah . . . I am not:* as we have already seen, Matthew and Mark see in John the Baptist a fulfillment of the Jewish expectation that the prophet Elijah would return to inaugurate the kingdom of God (Mal 3:23; Sir 48:4–12). The Baptist, however, refuses the identification. The Gospel of John, too, doubtless prefers to find the Elijah-figure realized in Jesus himself: this probably represents an earlier stage of Christian thinking, a vestige of which can also be found in the Synoptic tradition (see on Lk 7:11–17). Allied with this is the Baptist's denial that he is *the prophet*. The prophet in question is the eschatological prophet-like-Moses who appears in some Jewish messianic speculation, and sometimes identified with the eschatological Elijah, as the one sent by God to reveal the kingdom; the speculation resulted from a reinterpretation of Deut 18:18 concerning the prophetic succession in Israel. Throughout the New Testament, and especially in John's Gospel, the prophetic character of Jesus is stressed, often in connection with this messianic idea (cf. Jn 6:14, 7:40; Acts 7:37). The Baptist identifies himself only with the disembodied prophetic voice of Is 40:3, as already seen in the Synoptic Gospels.

Jn 1:25–27	Why, then, was John baptizing for the kingdom of God if,
Mk 1:7–8	seemingly, he had dissociated himself from any active
Mt 3:11–12	part in the kingdom? All the Gospels address themselves
Lk 3:16–17	to this question, which was obviously an important one for
	them. The Baptist had been an extremely popular

preacher who had attracted many disciples, and in the mind of many his relation to the Church was ambiguous or confused. In apostolic times there were groups which traced their origin to the Baptist, which however maintained their separate existence apart from the Christian community (cf. Acts 19:1–7). It was necessary to show from the Baptist's own testimony that his role had been fulfilled in immediately prophesying the Christ.

The Baptist characterizes himself with extreme humility in relation to the coming one, in whose presence he is not even worthy of the slave's task of removing his master's sandals. As for his baptism (mentioned by John only in vs. 33), it is only a foreshadowing of greater things to come. *He will baptize with Holy Spirit*: what John's baptism only announces will become a reality in the coming kingdom. The holy spirit of God as the principle of the divine power in its dealings with man (the prophetic spirit, etc.; cf. especially Is 11:2) was already a familiar concept from the Old Testament. Christian revelation was to make known the personality of the Spirit in a way as yet unknown by the Baptist. Matthew and Luke add *and with fire*. Fire, too, was a frequent Old Testament representation of the divine presence (Ex 3:2, 19:18; Ezek 1:4, etc.), and it was particularly associated with the coming of God's purificatory judgment (cf. Mal 3:2; Is 1:25; Zech 13:9). It is doubtless in this sense that fire is mentioned here, as is further exemplified in the figure of the *winnowing* that is soon to take place: the judgment and election of God that will come to term in the response evoked by the kingdom. The evangelists themselves doubtless expect their Christian readers to reflect even more concretely on the sacramental baptism of the Church and the Pentecostal fire that had launched it in the world as the continuing presence of the Spirit.

Lk 3:18–20   Luke alone now proceeds to do something that initially seems quite strange and unworkmanlike, interrupting the flow of the Gospel narrative. Before going on with the story, he gives in summary form the account found elsewhere in Matthew and Mark (Mt 14:3–5; Mk 6:17–20) of the Baptist's imprisonment by Herod Antipas. This, however, is Luke's method: he likes to finish a story once he has begun it (cf. also Lk 1:80, 2:40, 52). Having given samples of the Baptist's preaching, he states that it continued for some time, and then explains what brought it to a halt.

Lk 3:21–22   All the Gospels knew as an historical fact that Jesus had
Mk 1:9–11   received baptism at the hands of John the Baptist; even
Mt 3:13–17   John, who omits this narrative for his own reasons, was
                         aware that it had taken place. Whereas Mark simply tells the story as a matter of fact, however, the later Gospels seem to be sensitive to its implications. Why should he who was sinless have sub-

mitted to a baptism of repentance for the forgiveness of sins? Luke hurriedly deals with the actual baptism almost as an aside, using only three words, and devotes his attention to what follows. Matthew shows the most concern. Not only has he introduced a dialogue between Jesus and the Baptist that explained the proceedings, probably for the same reason in his earlier description of the Baptist's baptism he did not characterize it, as did Mark and Luke, as one "of repentance for the forgiveness of sins" (compare Mt 3:1 f. with Mk 1:4 and Lk 3:3).

Mark, serenely unconcerned with the tradition he was reporting, also makes no effort to show any further connection between Jesus and the Baptist; he now without further ado introduces Jesus for the first time (according to Lk 3:23 he was "about thirty years of age") *coming from Nazareth of Galilee to be baptized by John in the Jordan.* In Mark there is no testimony of the Baptist that Jesus was the one for whose coming he had been preparing. Neither does such a testimony appear in Luke, though Luke has shown very well in his Gospel of the Infancy the intimate association that he ascribes to Jesus and the Baptist; he is the only evangelist who tells us that the two were blood relatives. Perhaps by adding "bodily" to his description of the descent of the Holy Spirit upon Jesus (vs. 22), Luke intends to suggest that the vision was also perceptible to the Baptist and therefore a subject for his testimony. To this extent he would be in line with the more explicit portrayal of John's Gospel. Matthew may have a similar intention in changing the declaration of the heavenly voice from the second to the third person (vs. 17, "This is my beloved Son"); and certainly the dialogue between the Baptist and Jesus presupposes some understanding on the former's part of the latter's character.

At first glance Jesus' reassurance to the humble Baptist protesting the incongruity of this baptism does not explain a great deal. *It is proper for us to fulfill all justice* means little more than "it is necessary to do God's will"; by "justice" (cf. also Mt 5:6, 10, 20, 6:1, 33, 21:32) is meant the rightdoing which consists in submission to and furtherance of the will of God. An examination of the details of the theophany which follows, however, explains the meaning further. Rising from the water of the baptism in which he had humbled himself, Jesus sees *the heavens opened above him* (Mark says he saw them "split open") and *the Spirit of God descending as a dove upon him,* and in this moment he is proclaimed the Servant of the Lord. The theophany, therefore, which doubtless had a trinitarian meaning for the evangelists, is also a portrayal of the doctrine contained in the ancient christological hymn in Phil 2:6–11. In a fashion it sums up the whole significance of Jesus' life, a life of abasement from which emerges a glorified Savior: cf. Lk 12:50, etc., in which Jesus refers to his sacrificial death as his "baptism." *You are my beloved son, with whom I am well pleased* evokes most clearly

the Servant canticles of Is 42:1, 44:2. An important variant in the text
of Luke replaces these words with those of Ps 2:7: a more "routine"
messianic text.

In the intention of the Gospels this scene represents the divine proclamation of Jesus' salvific character, and, with the qualifications noted
above, it is to be noted that it is a proclamation made to Jesus himself.
The Gospels do not concern themselves with the question of a prior
"messianic consciousness" on his part, though perhaps passages like
Lk 2:40, 49, 52 are intended as hints in that direction.

Mk 1:12–13   The Synoptic Gospels follow the story of Jesus' baptism
Lk 4:1–2   with an account of his temptation in the wilderness
Mt 4:1–2   (Luke inserts between the two his version of Jesus'
              genealogy, which we have already seen). Probably there
was a catechetical purpose in this ordering of events: the newly baptized
Christian would be reminded that, despite the presence of the Spirit
which he had received, he was still subject to the wiles of Satan in the
wilderness of this world. There is also an evocation of the salvation history
of the Old Testament: the forty years of desert wandering during which
Israel, after passing through the waters of liberation (Ex 14:19–31), was
prepared to receive the kingdom which the Lord had promised it. It
may be for this reason that Mark notes that Jesus was *with the wild beasts*
(cf. Num 21:6–9; Deut 8:15).

Above all, however, the evangelists see here the beginning of Jesus'
prophetic role, the activity of a man *filled with Holy Spirit*—Mark says
expressively that *the Spirit drove him into the desert*. The narrative of
the forty days fast recalls the history of the prophet Elijah, as does
Mark's statement that *the angels ministered to him* (cf. 1 Kgs 19:4–8).

Lk 4:3–13   Moreover, in the extended narrative of the temptation
Mt 4:3–11   contained in Matthew and Luke we are given a much
              deeper insight into the kind of prophet Jesus is to be,
how, in other words, he will reveal God. The narrative has been drawn by
these evangelists from a common source and slightly modified by each; the
most obvious change is Luke's revision of the order of events, a device
which permits him to give his customary emphasis to the Jerusalem temple
(see on Lk 1:8–12). It is a masterpiece of biblical storytelling consisting
in a deft use of allusion in which far more is implied than appears on
the surface. Again Jesus relives the experience of Israel, but whereas Israel
succumbed to temptation in the desert, he triumphs over it. Undoubtedly
this is the dramatization of spiritual experiences at various times and
places to which Jesus, as one of us, was always subject (Heb 2:18,
4:15); the Gospels themselves give hints of other such occasions. What
was offered to Jesus, and what he emphatically rejected, was the opportunity to become a Jewish Messiah in the vulgar sense.

The note that *he was hungry* after his fast serves to introduce the first phase of the temptation: *If you are the Son of God, command these stones to become bread.* Similarly in the wilderness Israel had been tempted through hunger and had given way to the temptation, rebelling against the divine will (Num 11:5–20). Jesus has just been declared God's Son: may not God's Son exercise his right to be fed by the use of divine power? Miraculous abundance of food was one of the characteristics popularly ascribed to the messianic age. Jesus counters with the words of Deut 8:3, referring to the lesson that Israel should have learnt from its hunger in the desert but had not. His appearance in the world as God's Son is not for his personal advantage but for obedient service in God's designs on his people (cf. Jn 4:34).

The tempter returns to the attack, this time showing that he too can cite the Scripture (Ps 91:11 f.). Belief in the protecting agency of angels was widespread, and who should have a better right to this protection than the Son of God? To test this, why should Jesus not cast himself from the highest pinnacle of the temple compound so that all Jerusalem might see how God takes care of his Son? It was frequently believed that the Messiah would perform all kinds of wonders like this. Again Jesus cites Deuteronomy, and again in reference to a failing of Israel (Deut 6:16). Not even the Son of God—or, especially not the Son of God—can presume to act as an autonomous agent and continue to rely on the divine protection. Divine protection and obedience to the divine will go hand in hand.

The final presentation of the temptation is the most significant. *All these [kingdoms of the world] I will give you if you fall down and do me homage.* We must not, of course, see in this an invitation to a crude diabolism. Rather, Jesus is being confronted with the option of pursuing his ends by the use of political power, in the manner that the Jewish Messiah was expected to; this is precisely the temptation which Jn 6:15 says was offered to Jesus by the enthusiastic crowds. Satan is the ruler of this world (Jn 12:31; cf. vs. 6 in Luke), not in the sense that the world is irremediably evil, but in the sense that by sin the world and its ways have become subject to his direction. Whoever chooses as his own the route of worldly wisdom to the ends foreordained by God has thereby chosen the false gods of this world, as Paul protested to the Corinthians (cf. 1 Cor 2:6–16). What Israel had not always succeeded in avoiding, and what many Christians at various times have found an irresistible temptation, Jesus utterly rejects as a satanic intimation, citing Deuteronomy for the third and final time: *the Lord your God shall you adore and him only shall you serve* (Deut 5:7–9, 6:13, 10:20).

Matthew concludes his narrative by repeating Mark's words about the ministering angels. More significantly, perhaps, Luke says that *the devil departed from him till a more opportune time.* It is not of the human condition to be forever free of temptation.

Jn 1:28–34   The Synoptic Gospels now begin their second major division, the story of the Galilean ministry. John, too, as we shall soon see, also takes Jesus into Galilee, but with a quite different version of the events; the points of contact between the two traditions become very rare indeed. It is impossible to work out a convincing harmonization from the standpoint of chronology, and chronology is far from being the only note of discord. While nothing is ever said in either tradition that excludes the other as an impossibility, neither one has supplied us with sufficient statistical data to make a positive conciliation possible. Each will have to be examined separately for its own particular contributions.

As he often does, John makes more precise something that is said in more general terms in the Synoptic Gospels: *These things took place in Bethany beyond the Jordan where John was baptizing;* the site of this Bethany, however, is otherwise unknown. *The following day.* John says nothing of the baptism and temptation of Jesus. Rather, he continues and concludes the theme he has begun, of the witness of the Baptist to the Word. Just as he began his Gospel with a treatment of the creative Word of God in evident allusion to the Genesis creation story (see Chapter 2), he now commences an artificial seven-day unfolding of the new creation, culminating in 2:11 with the first manifestation of Jesus' "glory" (see on Jn 1:14). The seven-day sequence, counting from the beginning of the Baptist's witness, can be seen indicated in 1:29, 35, 40–42, 43, 2:1. That 2:1 introduces something that takes place "on the third day" is additionally significant, recalling the resurrection through which Christ became "life-giving Spirit" (1 Cor 15:45).

The artificiality of "the next day" immediately becomes apparent. Though John does not mention Jesus' baptism in so many words, he evidently supposes it, for the Baptist's testimony, previously negative and generic, is now positive and precise in virtue of a revelation given him at that time. He can now point to Jesus as *the lamb of God who takes away the world's sin.* From what we know of the Gospels, there can hardly be any doubt that the evangelist understands, and expects his readers to understand, a reference in these words to the suffering Servant of the Lord of Is 53:7–12. From what we otherwise know of the Baptist, however, it would be difficult to believe that he could have had in mind at this time a notion of the redemptive value of the sacrificial life of Christ (see on Mt 11:1–6; Lk 7:18–23). Nevertheless, he could have had a revelation of Jesus' character as God's Servant, in the same sense that we find it revealed in the Synoptic story of the baptism, namely the figure of Is 42:1 ff. upon whom the Lord has put his Spirit (cf. vs. 32

below) and who will "establish justice in the earth." This is rendered the more probable when it is realized that in the Aramaic which the Baptist spoke the same expression means "lamb of God" and "servant of God."

But the Baptist also says of Jesus that *he existed before me.* Does this not presuppose a knowledge of the fullness of Jesus' character, the pre-existent Word of God? For the evangelist again, that is doubtless what these words signify. The Baptist, however, if he thought of this Person as a returned Elijah (see above on vs. 21), could have intended something much more prosaic. The Baptist proceeds to explain that this knowledge had been revealed to him through a prearranged sign, verified at the time of Jesus' baptism (already intimated, we have seen, in Matthew's version of the story). *The Spirit descended and remained upon him* (Is 42:1), and thus he recognized in him *God's chosen one* (this is the better reading of the manuscripts): another reference to Is 42:1.

Jn 1:35–42   From the witness of the Baptist the Fourth Gospel now turns to that of Jesus' first disciples, whom we discover to have been first the disciples of John the Baptist. There is nothing of this in the Synoptic Gospels, which place the call of these same disciples in Galilee rather than Judea. It is most likely that in this instance John's version of the events is to be preferred as closest to the historical happenings. It is antecedently likely, given the common tradition of the association of Jesus and the Baptist, that there would have been some such connection as this rising from the earliest sources of the tradition. It has been suggested, too, that in this fact we may have an explanation of the influence, linguistic and otherwise, that seems to have been exercised on the Gospel tradition by a Judean group like that of Qumran. From where John was baptizing by the Jordan it was only a few miles to Qumran; and, according to Luke, his entire youth had been spent in this neighborhood. The suggestion is not at all unreasonable that there was some connection between the Baptist who preached the coming kingdom of God and the Essene community which had retired to the same desert in which he preached to prepare for the kingdom's imminent arrival. If some of Jesus' first disciples came to him from the Baptist, the route of Qumran influence into the formation of the New Testament tradition should not be too hard to trace.

The first two disciples are introduced to Jesus by the Baptist himself, repeating the designation he made in verse 29; they are *Andrew the brother of Simon Peter* (the two are usually mentioned together in the Synoptic Gospels) and an unnamed disciple who may himself be the John of the Fourth Gospel. A progressive development is shown in the recognition of the disciples, who first give Jesus the courtesy title *Rabbi,* then, after spending the day and night with him, name him *Messiah.* The reference to *the tenth hour,* that is, late afternoon, is doubtless intended to situate the subsequent action on the following day; it is even likely that verse 41 originally read "early next morning" (*prōi*) rather than "first of all" (*prōton*).

The special importance of Peter among the original group of disciples is brought out by the change of his name, a sign of entry into a new way of life (cf. Apo 3:12). *Cephas* is the Grecianized form of the Aramaic *kêphā*, "rock," which has also been translated by the Greek word *petros*=our "Peter." Mk 3:16 also notes that Jesus made this change of names, while Mt 16:18 associates it with Peter's great confession (the equivalent of this appears in Jn 6:68 f.) and his being accorded primatial status (cf. Jn 21:15–19). Again it is probable that John retains a more accurate historical recollection of events that happened separately and that Matthew's version has put them together for topical reasons.

Jn 1:43–51   As already noted, John's chronology is symbolic, and it is not certain whether he intends to situate this entire scene in Judea. It is likely enough that *Philip*, at least, is presented by him as another disciple of the Baptist; *Nathanael*, however, may have been found by Philip in Galilee. *Bethsaida*, here called Galilean, was technically in the adjoining territory of Gaulanitis; for some reason John says that it was *the city of Andrew and Peter*, though the Synoptic Gospels identify them as residents of Capernaum. Nathanael (the name is found only in John) is usually identified with the Bartholomew of the Synoptic Gospels, but the equation is not certain.

The witness to Jesus' character continues to become more precise. Philip speaks to Nathanael of *him of whom Moses wrote in the Law and the prophets as well*, that is, the eschatological prophet of Deut 18:18 and the Davidic Messiah. Nathanael, despite his initial skepticism —*what good can possibly come from Nazareth?* indicates both the insignificance of Nazareth and a Galilean inferiority complex concerning God's salvific plans (cf. Jn 7:41)—concedes, on the basis of Jesus' prophetic knowledge of some fact otherwise known only to himself, that he must indeed be *the Son of God*, the Messiah (Jn 11:27; cf. 2 Sam 7:14; Pss 2:7, 89:26 ff.), *the king of Israel* (Jn 12:13; cf. Zeph 3:15). But this is not enough, says Jesus; Nathanael will yet see *far greater things* as the object of his faith, and in these know Jesus as he truly is.

The far greater things which Nathanael will see are already intimated in the name given him by Christ, the *true Israelite*: by popular etymology "Israel" was taken to mean "one who sees God." Unlike the original guileful Israel (Jacob) who also saw God (Gen 28:10–17), Nathanael is *without guile. You shall see heaven opened and the angels of God ascending and descending upon the Son of Man*: referring to Jacob's vision, Jesus says that the true Israelite will see the far greater thing of the divine presence made manifest in himself (cf. Jn 1:14, 2:11). The Son of Man, in John as in the Synoptic Gospels, is the title which

Jesus uses by preference for himself. Its full implications we shall see as the Gospel story progresses.

It is quite evident that here as elsewhere there is a marked difference between the Johannine portrayal of Christ and the Synoptics' representation of a Jesus reticent in the extreme concerning his messianic character. From a strictly historical point of view, there is no doubt that we must prefer the Synoptic picture of a gradual and implied revelation. Whereas Peter's confession of Jesus' messiahship comes as a grand climax in Mark's Gospel to a slow and patient awakening of faith (Mk 8:27–30), in these few verses of John's first chapter virtually every messianic title has already been applied to Jesus and taken almost as a matter of course! But John, who presupposes the Synoptic tradition, likewise takes the fullness of Christian faith in Jesus for granted. His purpose in retelling the Gospel story is to bring out its implications for the Christian here and now. We see this immediately in the next episode in which he shows how the disciples, true Israelites all, actually beheld the glory of the Word made man.

Jn 2:1–11   *On the third day* (see above on vs. 29) after Jesus' promise to Nathanael we find him at *a wedding feast in Cana of Galilee* (probably the present-day Khirbet Qana, a ruin nearby the village of Kefr Kenna, the "traditional" site of Cana). Despite the Synoptics' interest in the Galilean ministry, neither this event nor Cana itself is ever mentioned in the other Gospels. Such a story as this, however, would not have been easily adaptable to the kerygmatic outline which lies behind the Synoptic Gospels, whereas it is eminently suited to the symbolic treatment in which John delights. In it John has found an illustration of one of his favorite themes: the presence of the historical Christ in the faith of the Church. The story also establishes a pattern which John repeats often in his Gospel.

The mother of Jesus was there. As becomes quickly apparent, the mother of Jesus who is mentioned by John always in this way, has a spiritual as well as an historical significance in the Fourth Gospel paralleling the portrayal of Mary in Luke's Gospel of the Infancy; her other most significant appearance is in Jn 19:25–28 at the end of Jesus' public life. In this episode she assumes a dominant role as the member of the family who had been primarily invited, presumably as having some special connection with the anonymous wedding couple. Jesus' *disciples* evidently include the five thus far mentioned and possibly others; there is no further explanation in John concerning the gathering of the remainder of the Twelve (Jn 6:67). The story that unfolds involves all of these as principals.

Mary's simple statement, *they have no wine*, is the equivalent of a request, as is shown by her subsequent instructions to the servants. *What*

to me and to you?, to cite the Lord's reply quite literally, is a biblical
idiom (cf. Jgs 11:12; 2 Sam 16:10; 1 Kgs 17:18; 2 Kgs 3:3; 2 Chron
35:21; Mk 5:7) which verbally is a rejection of Mary's request on the
grounds that she has no claim on Jesus. The sense in which it is and
is not a rejection in fact is made plain in the continuation of the story.
Pertinent here is the title of address, *woman*, and Jesus' explanation
that *my hour has not yet come*.

To insist, as is often done, that "woman" was an ordinary term of
address implying neither coldness nor disrespect (cf. Jn 4:21), is valid
but somewhat pointless. It is worse than pointless to paraphrase it, as
some translations have done, with some such expression as "mother." It
is precisely not as his mother, in the merely natural sense of the word,
that Jesus now speaks to Mary. The unusual title cannot be dissociated
from its other appearance in Jn 19:25–28, where it becomes even more
apparent that for John, just as for Luke, Mary is a figure of the whole
people of God, the Church. As such she is the woman, the new Eve,
mother of all the living (Gen 3:20; cf. Apo 12:1–6). She has this character, however, only in virtue of her Son who has come to bring new
life, and he is only now beginning his work. In John, the "hour" of
Jesus refers to his glorification, that is, to his salvific death and resurrection (cf. Jn 7:30, 8:20, 12:23, 27, 13:1, 17:1). Until this work is
accomplished, the woman has no title to what she requests. Nor may
she request it under another title. Simeon had already spoken to her of
the role in which she had been cast in the history of salvation, a providential role quite transcending the ties of natural relationship (Lk 2:35;
see also on Lk 2:49 and Mk 3:31–35 and parallels).

Nevertheless, the hour which has not yet come can be anticipated in
Jesus' "signs." *Do whatever he commands you to do*: Mary's instruction
shows that she has understood Jesus' intention; John expects his readers
to recognize such implications without being told. The rest of the story
mainly consists of lifelike detail, though John also intends us to take a
second look at some of what he says. The *six stone water jars* dramatize
the magnitude of Jesus' act: the amount of liquid involved would have
been in the neighborhood of 150 gallons! That they were there *for the
Jewish purifications*, that is, the ritual washings to which the Jews were
attentive before and after meals, both explains the presence of such a
large quantity of water and forms part of the Johannine pattern in these
stories. Time after time in the narratives that follow some life-medium
(frequently enough water) or some other good identified with Judaism
is seen to be replaced with a better good that comes from Jesus, who is
life in truth. The familiarity with which *the headwaiter* addresses the
bridegroom in the denouement of the story suggests that the custom was
being followed of electing one of the invited guests to serve as the
master of the banquet.

This Jesus did as the first of his signs. For John the "signs" are pre-eminently those things which Jesus did—or rather, which he now does—in which the eye of faith may perceive the saving act of God, in which he is, therefore, pre-eminently the Word of God. Thus John says that *he revealed his glory.* The continuing episodes of this Gospel detail many similar signs. *His disciples believed in him:* Jesus has now fulfilled his promise to Nathanael, though as yet admittedly in an obscure way. The story of the "new creation" has concluded with a wonder of creation that will in turn be the beginning of a series of life-giving acts in which the Life of the world reveals himself as an object of faith greater than anything the Old Testament could encompass. With the same eye of faith, John suggests to his Christian reader, this same glory is yet to be seen in the Church, in the signs by which the life-giving Christ continues his saving work. There can hardly be any doubt that in telling the story of the water made wine John intends for us to recognize in a special way the significance of the sacrament of the Eucharist.

6. LIVING WATER

Jn 2:12   In this chapter we shall mainly pursue John's Gospel, see-
              ing how some of the themes which he has once begun to
draw out continue to be reasserted. John makes only a cursory mention
of Jesus' stay in Capernaum, agreeing with the Synoptic Gospels to the
extent that the ministry there was of brief duration. However, there is a
Synoptic emphasis on Capernaum that is quite lacking in John, as we
shall see. If the shortest reading in the manuscripts of this text is the
original one, Jesus' companions at this time are listed merely as *his
mother and his brethren*. In this case, "brethren" would doubtless refer
to his disciples rather than, as later and usually in the Gospels (Jn 7:3,
etc.), to the members of his family.

Jn 2:13–17   John immediately takes Jesus back to Jerusalem on the
Mt 21:12–13   occasion of a *Jewish Passover*. The festivals of Judaism
Mk 11:15–17   are emphasized by John as part of his way of showing
Lk 19:45–46   how Jesus has fulfilled the hopes of which they were
                  the sign. This is only the first of several Passovers which
John places within the period of Jesus' public life. The following episode
is also recorded by the Synoptic Gospels as taking place at a Passover
season, the only Passover with which they deal, at the end rather than
at the beginning of Jesus' ministry; and even then, the Synoptics do
not agree on which day of the week the event took place. The chronology
is obviously not to be pressed on either side; if a point had to be made
of it, we would probably have to agree that the Synoptics' is more likely.
We treat the matter now, however, because of the close relation it has
to John's theological development.

The versions of the story, of which Luke's is by far the briefest, agree
on the essentials. *Entering the temple*, that is, the outer courtyards surrounding the holy places, Jesus drives out of the precincts the buyers and
sellers of the animals used in sacrifice and the animals themselves (John
alone speaks of him using a *whip of cords*); he also overturns the bank-
ing tables used by the money-changers. The animals, of course, were
bought and sold for the convenience of pilgrims, who could hardly have

been expected to bring them along with them. Similarly, money-changing
was a necessity for foreigners as well as to provide acceptable, "non-
idolatrous" money, money that did not bear pagan inscriptions or images.
Though there may have been some incidental chicanery involved in all
this, still the enterprises of themselves were perfectly legitimate. To what,
then, was Jesus objecting?

The answer is given in his accusation, given by the Synoptics as *you
have made it*, the temple, *a robbers' den*. This is a citation of Jer 7:11,
just as his preceding words concerning the temple as *a house of prayer*
are a citation of Is 56:7; Jesus is not, therefore, necessarily passing judgment on the personal honesty of those whom he was confronting, but
he is repeating a prophetic judgment on the inviolable sanctity of God's
house. The sense of his gesture becomes more explicit in the Johannine
version of his command: *Don't turn my Father's house into a market
place*. Jewish custom forbade the use of the temple grounds for profane
purposes, even for such an innocent one as a convenient meeting place
for friends. The custom was now being flagrantly violated. Consistent
with his action in expelling the buyers and sellers, according to Mark
Jesus *would not allow anyone to carry anything through the sacred place*,
to use it, in other words, as a shortcut from one place to another.

Jesus' action was understood by his disciples as a sign of messianic
fulfillment (cf. Zech 14:21), and according to John they applied to him
in this connection the words of Ps 69:10, a psalm used very often in
the New Testament in a messianic sense. His zeal for the holiness of
the temple contrasted strongly with the laxity of the temple personnel,
in whose charge the temple was. This episode is at least a partial explanation of the hostility shown to Jesus by the Jerusalem priesthood.

Jn 2:18–22   Representatives of this group, as usual called by John
simply *the Jews*, now come forward to demand by what
authority he has done what they have neglected to do. They ask for
a sign: this demand for a supernatural intervention was constantly being
made of Jesus (cf. Mk 8:11, etc.), who consistently refused to comply
with it. His signs were never given indiscriminately or for the ill-disposed;
they were signs of faith, to awaken it or to deepen it. This is brought
out by John, who now indicates the full significance that he saw in the
episode he has just related: *Destroy this temple and in three days I
will raise it up . . . he spoke of the temple of his body*. The resurrection
is the great and adequate sign for all believers. The temple, holy though
it was, has now been replaced by a holier temple, the resurrected Christ,
and by the Church which is his resurrected body.

The Jews, not unnaturally, take these words in another sense (cf. Mt
26:61 and parallels); Jesus did, as a matter of fact, foretell the destruction
of the Jerusalem temple (cf. Mk 13:2). *Forty-six years*: the temple was

begun, according to Josephus, in the eighteenth year of Herod's reign (that is, in 20 or 19 B.C., according to our reckoning); thus the date indicated for this passage is sometime in A.D. 28. The temple was still in the process of building during the lifetime of Jesus and was completed only a few years before its destruction by the Romans in A.D. 70.

Jn 2:23–25   In the following summary statement that forms the transition to the story of Nicodemus, John shows that he presupposes a knowledge of the Synoptic tradition with its stress on the many miracles of Jesus' ministry. Correspondingly, *the signs* of verse 23 does not appear precisely in its Johannine sense. Jesus, knowing man better than any other man could know, put little reliance on the incipient faith awakened by enthusiasm over his miracles ("signs" in the Synoptic Gospels). It could, it is true, develop into a true knowledge of God in Christ, as would be exemplified in the case of Nicodemus. Too often, however, it would prove to be a hindrance rather than an aid to this knowledge (cf. Jn 6:2, 60).

Jn 3:1–13   Nicodemus was one of those who were attracted by the works which Jesus was performing. As a Pharisee, a member of the Sanhedrin, the high court of seventy-two which formed the supreme governing body of the Jews, and a rabbi, he represents to John the very essence of Judaism, and thus affords the evangelist with another opportunity to show how Jesus has brought in reality what the old dispensation could but promise. Though the circumstances of his visit in the face of official opposition to Jesus explain naturally enough why he would have come secretly *at night,* John probably notes this in an additional meaning: Nicodemus comes from the darkness (cf. Jn 1:5) to Jesus the light, while later Judas will desert him for the darkness (cf. Jn 13:30).

Nicodemus addresses Jesus as *Rabbi,* the title first used by the disciples when he began to reveal himself to them (Jn 1:38). As he had done in their case, Jesus proceeds to offer Nicodemus a challenge to faith far beyond anything he had imagined. *Unless a man be born from above he cannot see the kingdom of God:* the kingdom of God is not to be perceived merely in the marvels that have attracted Nicodemus' attention; it is to be found only in a spiritual regeneration (cf. Jn 1:12 f.). The word translated "from above" can also mean "anew"; the ambiguity permits Nicodemus to take a literalist surface meaning: *How can a man who is old be born again?* It is part of the artistic arrangement of the Johannine dialogues and discourses that double meanings and initial misunderstandings lead to a deeper exploration of Christ's teaching.

Jesus proceeds to explain the nature of the rebirth about which he is speaking. It is spiritual rather than natural. In speaking of "flesh" and "spirit" he builds on concepts familiar to Judaism from the Old Testament: it is this that gives point to his words of rebuke in verse 10. Both flesh and spirit relate to life, but whereas flesh represents all that is transitory about life, as we have seen (see on Jn 1:14), spirit is the God-given force by which alone life is possible (cf. Gen 2:7; Job 10:9-12, 33:4; Ezek 37:8-14). Furthermore, the vital activity of spirit appears under various forms and in varying degrees: there is a spirit-life which altogether transcends the normal. Thus the prophet is a "man of the spirit" par excellence (cf. Hos 9:7); thus, too, the messianic leader would possess the spirit in a pre-eminent way (cf. Is 11:1-3), and the messianic times would be characterized by an extraordinary outpouring of spirit (cf. Ezek 36: 27; Joel 3:1 f., and Acts 2:16-21).

The spirit blows where it will. Jesus employs a play on words (in Aramaic and Greek the same word "spirit"="breath"="wind") to serve as an analogy. Just as the wind cannot be seen but only perceived in its effects, so it is with the new spiritual birth of which he has been speaking; it is imperceptible to fleshly eyes. That Nicodemus, though *a master in Israel,* cannot understand the relatively *earthly things* that Jesus has said to him, shows his incapacity at the present to receive the *heavenly things* which are involved in the acceptance of Christ in true faith. As yet Nicodemus has not recognized in Jesus *the Son of Man,* who alone can reveal the heavenly God as he truly is. *We speak of what we know:* Jesus, representing the true Israel, contrasts his word with the inadequacy of the knowledge of the Israel for which Nicodemus spoke (vs. 2).

In verse 5 John quotes Jesus as saying that this new birth comes through *water and spirit.* Such words could have been used to Nicodemus, who would have been expected to understand them in terms of a ceremonial baptism like that of John the Baptist, which in fact the evangelist associates with Jesus in the later verses 22-30. However, it is likely that John, who thinks of the Spirit of Jesus' discourse as the divine power animating the Church and evidenced in Christian life, has added the reference to water as a reminder of sacramental baptism. Doubtless, too, the "we" of verse 11 represents the Christian testimony of the evangelist joined to that of Jesus. It is usual in these Johannine discourses for dialogue to merge into monologue, and for the words of Jesus to become those of John. The evangelist's testimony, after all, is to the revelation of Jesus as he himself has come to know it through the continuing enlightenment of the Spirit.

Jn 3:14-21   Nicodemus has now disappeared from the scene entirely, and the Gospel continues to explain in greater detail what is the basis of the spiritual life to be revealed in the Son of Man. It is his redemptive death and resurrection. Alluding to the story of Num 21:4-9 (cf. Wis 16:6 f.), the Gospel states that *the Son of Man must also be raised up* if man is to be brought into the heavenly realm of the life of the Spirit. To be "raised up" for John is for Jesus to be "glorified" (both terms are used of the Servant of the Lord in Is 52:13), and the sense is of both the physical raising of Christ on the cross and his ascent to the Father as Lord and Savior. It is in this character that *everyone who believes in him will have eternal life.*

In turn, the exaltation of Christ, the consummation of his sacrificial life of obedience, is a sign to man of the divine love and will to save. *God so loved the world:* the world, though it is the arena in which evil too often prevails, is itself not evil but the object of God's saving love. This love has been shown to its full extent in God's sending his *only Son.* The Son has not been sent, in turn, *to judge the world:* not, as one popular idea of the Messiah would have had it, did the Son come crushing God's enemies and scourging mankind, but rather revealing in himself the loving God as the object of the world's faith. Faith brings salvation, but on the contrary willful unbelief is its own condemnation, because it rejects the only source of salvation. If the world as such has, indeed, been judged, it is because *men loved the darkness rather than the light:* here John anticipates his summation of the first part of his Gospel (Jn 12:37ff., cf. also 1:5, 9f.). The language of this section has numerous affinities with that of the Qumran literature.

Jn 3:22–30   John continues with a story that is thematically parallel to the story of Nicodemus in verses 1–13, just as the meditation which follows in verses 31–36 corresponds to the one we have just seen in verses 14–21. The parallel serves to confirm the view we have taken of the meaning of the Nicodemus episode for John and also further explains why John omitted any direct mention of Jesus' baptism at the hands of John the Baptist (see above on Lk 3:21f. and parallels).

After these things, Jesus and his disciples came into the land of Judea. In the present context, this would mean that Jesus left Jerusalem and went into the Judean countryside. However, since this passage is in its present place for thematic rather than chronological reasons, the historical antecedent is unknown and may well have been some phase of the Galilean ministry. *He was baptizing:* John, or the editor of his Gospel, specifies in Jn 4:2 that it was not Jesus himself but his disciples who were doing the baptizing. This baptism was obviously not the sacramental baptism of the Church by which the Spirit is given after the glorification of Christ (cf. Jn 7:39), but a continuation of the baptism of John the Baptist in preparation for the coming of the kingdom; the Synoptic Gospels also represent Jesus' initial preaching of the kingdom as a continuation of the ministry of the Baptist (see below on Mk 1:15). Nevertheless, this event is for John a "sign": a baptism associated with Jesus is here set in opposition to the baptism of John the Baptist and shown to be what has replaced it in the progress of the history of salvation. It would have obscured and interfered with John's thematic treatment had he interrupted it to describe the Baptist's baptism being administered to Jesus.

The location of *Aenon near Salim* where *John was also baptizing* is not certain but is usually thought to have been in northern Samaria. A dispute between the disciples of the Baptist and some unnamed Jew *over purification,* presumably the Jewish purificatory rites (cf. Jn 2:6), furnishes the occasion for the Baptist to complete his testimony to Jesus; the nature of the controversy is not explained and was, of course, irrelevant in view of the greater issues involved. Somehow Jesus' name was brought into the conversation, and the disciples discovered and reported to their master that his renown was now exceeding the Baptist's. The latter's response is to repeat his earlier protestation that he is not the Messiah but only the one who makes a way for him. He stands in the position of *the friend of the bridegroom,* the best man at the wedding who arranged the marriage not for his own but for the bridegroom's sake. His final words sum up his foreordained purpose in relation to Jesus: *he must increase and I must decrease.*

The evangelist notes that *John had not yet been put in prison.* Luke, as we have seen (Lk 3:19 f.), has already described the Baptist's imprisonment. The other two Gospels have completed the story of John the Baptist later on in their chronicle.

Jn 3:31–36   John's commentary which follows both continues and parallels his observations in verses 14–21 above. Again he contrasts with "earthly" knowledge the heavenly truths that have been made known in Christian revelation. Again he marvels over the spectacle of unbelief. *He who receives his witness has set his seal on this, that God is true:* just as Christ is witness to the truth of God, God is witness to the truth of his testimony (cf. Jn 6:27). *Not by measure does he give the Spirit:* prophets like John the Baptist, the last of a long line, had truly possessed the Spirit of God, but the fullness of prophecy has come only in the revelation of the Son (cf. Jn 1:17 f.; Heb 1:1 f.). Again the explanation of salvation is found in the overflowing of divine love.

Jn 4:1–3   Though as usual chronology is not a primary consideration
Mt 4:12   in the development of the Gospel, it is likely that John in-
Mk 1:14   tends to situate the following story in the period with which
Lk 4:14a   the Synoptic Gospels begin their history of the Galilean min-
istry, after the arrest of John the Baptist by Herod Antipas. The same Judean leadership which had looked upon the Baptist's preaching with suspicion, to say the least (cf. Mt 21:25 ff. and parallels), was now turning its hostile attention toward the man who was continuing that

preaching and with even greater popular success. For this reason Jesus
left Judea and returned to Galilee.

Jn 4:4–19   *He had to pass through Samaria.* This was to follow the
               most direct route, a three days' journey, between Jerusalem
and Galilee. Jews very often lengthened the trip in order to bypass
Samaria, however, because of the hostility of the Samaritan population
(see page 33 and cf. Lk 9:52 f.). The Synoptic Gospels have nothing
about any contacts between Jesus and Samaritans, though Luke records
that he spoke favorably of them on occasion (cf. Lk 10:29–37); in
apostolic times the Samaritans received the Gospel of Christianity with
enthusiasm (cf. Acts 8:1–25). The *Sychar* of John's text may be the
modern village of Askar, nearby the ancient Shechem, where was *the
field which Jacob gave to his son Joseph* (cf. Gen 33:19, 48:22). The
location of *Jacob's well* where Jesus sat to rest is, in any case, well known:
it still exists midway between Shechem and Askar. John notices these
details because they are to play a part in his story. The disciples left
Jesus at the well and went into the town to buy food, since *it was
about the sixth hour,* that is, noon.

This story continues John's thematic pattern and the structure of the
Johannine discourses. The woman's misunderstandings permit the deeper
sense of Jesus' words to be progressively emphasized, and correspondingly
she is offered the opportunity to recognize in him an ever more important figure of faith. Once again a life-giving element associated with
Judaism—water, as it happens—is seen to be only a faint reflection of
the reality that is to be possessed in Christ.

How is it that you, a Jew, ask a drink of me, a Samaritan woman?
expresses surprise twofold. Strict Jews would not associate with the "unclean" Samaritans, much less accept food or drink from them. Neither
would they be seen conversing with women: a rabbi would not speak
in public even with his own wife. While both John and the Synoptic
Gospels show that Jesus was, in general, faithful to the law and customs
of his people, they also bring out plainly that there was nothing fanatical or merely legalistic in his observance. Jesus immediately points out
that the true *gift of God* with which he is concerned is not the water
which he has asked her to give him, but the gift of himself which is
being offered to her. *Living water,* like the "rebirth" of which he spoke
to Nicodemus, is deliberately ambiguous. The surface meaning, taken by
the woman, is the running water of a river or spring. In its figurative
sense the expression comes from the Old Testament (for example, Jer
2:13; Zech 14:8) and signifies divine life and grace.

Ironically, the woman asks if Jesus pretends to be *greater than our
father Jacob who gave us the well.* The question serves the double purpose of identifying the "water of Judaism" that is being contrasted with

Christ and of contributing to the "Johannine irony," that is, to the pattern of John's Gospel in which people so often assert in a superficial
way what is true in a much more profound sense. Ironical, too, is the
term by which she first addresses him. On her lips the title *kyrie* meant
nothing more than *sir*, a respectful but ordinary form of address. It
is also, however, the word by which Christians testified to their faith in
their risen Lord (Phil 2:9–11). It is this word which, still uncomprehend-
ing, she uses after he has explained that the "water" which he will give
not only sustains life but is itself the very source of everlasting life. This
water, of course, is Jesus himself. John also would expect his Christian
reader to think of baptism, which has already been brought in so often
in these early chapters of his Gospel, truly the water which gives life.

As he had done before in the conversation with Nathanael, Jesus now
introduces an apparently irrelevant topic whose purpose is to show that
he is possessed of a mysterious and superhuman knowledge: *call your
husband*. The woman did not expect to have the literal truth of her
reply revealed so bluntly; doubtless she answered as she did simply to
put an end to a somewhat strange and potentially embarrassing conversation. Now she begins to realize that this is no ordinary Jew talking
to her; she confesses that he must be *a prophet*.

Jn 4:20–38   A prophet indeed Jesus is, but in a way that far transcends her present understanding. She puts to him an
implied question, in keeping with later Jewish thinking on the role of
prophecy, namely, that it would intervene to solve disputed questions
in the matter of law and observance (cf. 1 Macc 4:46). According to
Samaritan tradition, *our fathers worshiped on this mountain* of Gerizim
at whose foot this conversation was taking place; the Samaritan temple
which had once stood there had been destroyed more than a century
previously, but the site was still a place of worship as it is to this day
for the tiny Samaritan community that has survived in Palestine. The
Jews, on the contrary, held that only in Jerusalem could acceptable sacrifice be offered. The resultant controversy between Jew and Samaritan
was only one of the issues on which they were bitterly divided. Jesus
answers the question, at the same time pointing out how irrelevant it
already is in the divine scheme of things. *Salvation is from the Jews*, not
the Samaritans: the one who speaks to her is this salvation in very fact.
And now that salvation has come, neither Jerusalem nor Gerizim will
matter to the God who must be worshiped *in spirit and in truth* (see
on Jn 1:17 f.).

In rejoinder, the woman expresses her belief in the coming of *Messiah*
who will fulfill the hopes of Jew and Samaritan alike. As we have already
seen before, in John's Gospel Jesus accepts this title freely (cf. Jn
1:43–51). However, his words as reported by John contain a further

subtlety: *I who am speaking to you, I am* is the self-identification of the God of Israel according to Is 52:6. Furthermore, it is possible that the messianic expectation of the Samaritans—something about which very little is known, though it most likely was developed from the prophetic idea of Deut 18:18—was such that Jesus could more readily associate himself with it than he could with the nationalistic concepts current in Galilee and Judea.

The rest of the story is acted out in two concurrent scenes. The woman hurries away to her townsfolk to bear to them the message of Philip (cf. Jn 1:45 f.), in her haste *leaving behind her water jug:* John may be insinuating that she had no further use for it, now that she had found the source of living water. Meanwhile the disciples, surprised at finding the Master conversing with a woman but being too well trained to interrogate him about it, now urge him to take the food they had gone to procure. *My food is to do the will of him who sent me and to accomplish his work* sums up the entire life of Jesus. His additional words on the harvest already prepared in Samaria, a harvest they are to reap where they have not sown, doubtless refer to the phenomenal success of the apostolic preaching of Christianity among the Samaritans (Acts 8:4–25).

Jn 4:39–42   The Samaritans fully satisfy the Johannine ideal of the true believer. Having been attracted at first by the woman's report of one who did wonders, they at length come to believe simply because of Jesus' word (cf. Jn 8:30, 10:38), the word of life. *We have heard and we know* (cf. Jn 3:11) *that he is truly the Savior of the world:* doubtless this title, an usual one signifying something far greater than the Jewish Messiah (cf. 1 Jn 4:14), is used in recognition of Jesus' transcending racial and national barriers in bringing to them the message of God's salvation.

Jn 4:43–45   After this Samaritan interlude, John brings Jesus into
Lk 4:14b–15   Galilee (cf. vs. 3 above), where he records that he received an enthusiastic reception for the same reason that Jesus had achieved acclaim in Jerusalem and Judea (cf. Jn 2:23–25, 3:2). Luke also mentions the popular enthusiasm that accompanied the beginning of the Galilean ministry.

Somewhat curiously at first glance, John quotes here of Jesus a saying also ascribed to him in the Synoptic tradition (cf. Mk 6:4 and parallels). Since he has just represented Jesus as leaving Judea to avoid unwelcome attention and goes on to say that the Galileans received him willingly, some have concluded that for John Jesus' *own country* was Judea rather than Galilee. This, however, does not seem to have been the case. Rather, John is probably giving here a parenthetical judgment that applies to the ministry in Galilee as a whole, a judgment in which the Synoptic

Gospels concur, as we shall see. In just a moment we shall see Luke doing something very similar to this in his Gospel.

Jn 4:46–54 John, who as we know devotes very little space to the Galilean ministry, takes this occasion to continue his portrayal of the "signs" of Jesus by returning us immediately to Cana which, he reminds us both at the beginning and the end of the following story, was the scene of Jesus' first "sign" (Jn 2:1–11).

The story itself is probably the Johannine version of one that is told under a somewhat different form in Mt 8:5–13 and Lk 7:1–10. Not only the variations inevitably produced through oral transmission, but also the particular emphases of the several Gospels into which these episodes have been fitted, explain the considerable differences with which what was originally the same story can be described in our texts. In this instance the differences are wide enough to demand our separate reading.

As John tells the story, while Jesus was tarrying in Cana—we might think of him visiting in the home of Nathanael—a certain *royal official whose son was ill* came to him from nearby Capernaum. The "royal official" would have been some kind of employee of Herod Antipas; Antipas, we have noted, was not officially styled king and therefore had no royal service, but popularly he was accorded the trappings of kingship. Like Nicodemus and the Samaritans, this man is first attracted to Jesus by the wonders that are being ascribed to him, but in his need and under the guidance of Jesus he ends by putting his faith in the Master's word alone. As in the first "sign," Jesus' initial reply appears to be a refusal, which however only serves to differentiate and underline the meaning of the sign. Again life is bestowed through the creative and saving Word of God. In the denouement of the story the proper relation of faith and miracles is to be seen: the official who had believed before the miracle was accomplished now finds in the work a sign by which his faith may be deepened and explained (cf. Jn 20:30 f.).

Mk 1:15 We now take leave of the Gospel of John for a while
Mt 4:13–17 and enter into the Galilean world of the Synoptic Gospels as they begin to unfold their version of Jesus' public ministry. Matthew and Mark mark the continuity between the Baptist and Jesus by showing the latter preaching John's message without essential change: *repent, for the kingdom of God is at hand. Believe in the Gospel,* adds Mark, that is, in the message of coming judgment and salvation.

Matthew, as is his custom, has taken occasion from the beginning of the Galilean ministry to find a fulfillment of ancient prophecy (cf. Is 8:23–9:1). *The land of Zebulun and the land of Naphtali* in northern Israel, the *Galilee of the Gentiles* (literally, in Hebrew *galil*=district, called "of the Gentiles" because it was so heavily populated with pagans)

had been the first of the promised land to bear the brunt of foreign invasion, itself a fulfillment of prophecy as the divine punishment visited
on Israel for its sins. Isaiah had seen a vision of restoration of this land
in the reign of a messianic king (9:5 f.), and now indeed, says Matthew,
light has begun to shine on them.

Lk 4:16–22a   Matthew and Luke begin the narrative of the Galilean
                    ministry in Nazareth, the city of Jesus' youth; Mark has
no such geographical precision. Luke, for his part, has filled out the bare
mention of Nazareth with an example of Jesus' method of teaching in
the Galilean synagogues which he noted in the preceding verse 15.
Actually, he has done much more than this. As we have already seen
more than once, Luke likes to finish a story once he has begun it. Thus
here, once having shown Jesus teaching in Nazareth, he continues down
through verse 30 to describe what was the end result of Jesus' preaching
at Nazareth, namely, rejection by his own townspeople. In this way he
has begun his history of the Galilean ministry with a summation somewhat like that of Jn 4:44. Because the continuation of the story finds
a more logical place later on where it is paralleled by Matthew and
Mark and appears this early in Luke only through a peculiarity of narrative technique and not as part of his Gospel structure, we shall defer it
for the moment. The beginning of the story deserves attention in its
own right as illustrating the teaching method of Jesus.

*He entered the synagogue on the Sabbath day according to his custom
and stood up to read.* The synagogue order of service, which included
a reading from the Law, another from the Prophets, an interpretation
(that is, a translation from the Hebrew), and a sermon, was not otherwise rigidly determined. Any male from the congregation could be invited to take these parts, and it was customary to extend the honor to
distinguished visitors; the synagogue was, and is, essentially lay-directed.
In the present story, which is possibly a synthesis of various like occurrences, Jesus appears to be assuming the role of reader and interpreter
as well as that of preacher. It is presupposed that he was already well
known as a teacher, but it also appears that this was his first sermon
at Nazareth. Having been handed the scroll of the prophetic writings,
he found the passage of Is 61:1 f., either because this was the reading
assigned for that day or because the choice of reading had been left to
him. Since the text is cited rather freely and has also been combined
with Is 58:6, Luke probably intends us to understand the latter alternative: the evangelist has put together various passages which together express in prophetic language Jesus' concept of his mission.

Taking his seat, Jesus proceeded to give a homily on the text, applying
its living word to himself and his appearance before Israel. He identifies
himself with the prophetic proclamation of salvation with which the

Isaian text was concerned, in a way that is consistent both with what the Synoptic Gospels have thus far said of his message and with what they, especially Luke, will show of its development in the Galilean ministry. *They bore witness to him and marveled at the pleasing words that flowed from his mouth:* Jesus' message was one of joy and good news, which struck a responsive chord in the hearts of the poor and oppressed of Galilee. Time alone would show whether the witness which they were now eager to give would endure. For the time being, at least, Jesus enjoyed popularity in his homeland.

7. ACCLAIM IN GALILEE

Lk 4:31   As we saw in the last chapter, Matthew and Luke begin
Mk 1:16–21   their story of the Galilean ministry at Nazareth, the
Mt 4:18–22   town where Jesus had spent his childhood and youth
and by whose name he became familiarly known as the
Nazarene. From Nazareth they take us to Capernaum, and Capernaum
is also the first place in Galilee that is mentioned by Mark. We are left
to imagine the circumstances that prompted Jesus to make this city the
center of his Galilean activity; the attentive reader of Mark's Gospel will
note how persistently it features "the house" in Capernaum, the house,
that is, of Simon Peter, the eyewitness who traditionally stands behind
this Gospel. At Capernaum, too, Jesus taught in the synagogue, as was
his custom throughout Galilee.

It is here that Mark, and Matthew following him, places the call of
Jesus' first disciples. We have already seen that in John's Gospel a quite
different picture is drawn of the same event, in which at least two of
the same disciples are involved (see Jn 1:35–42). We do not have the
means of harmonizing these separate versions which have been handed
down by traditions independent of each other. We can at least maintain, however, that they presuppose historical facts that are not mutually
incompatible. It is likely enough, as John told the story, that Jesus met
his first disciples through John the Baptist; as a matter of fact, this
present story makes better sense if it is assumed that the disciples were
not now meeting Jesus for the first time. The Synoptic account, for its
part, reads very much like the factual account of someone who had seen
these things happen. We should remember, too, that John is well aware
that these disciples were Galileans and not Judeans.

The sea of Galilee is the name used by Mark and Mattew to refer
to what Luke calls *the lake of Gennesaret* and John *the sea of Tiberias*;
it is a fresh-water lake some thirteen miles north and south and about
seven east and west in what is easily the most attractive part of
Galilee. *Simon and his brother Andrew* have already been introduced
by John's Gospel. The Greek of the Gospel makes it clear that they were
fishing with the circular throw-nets still used by the Arab fishermen of

the region. *Fishers of men* was an expression already used in the Old Testament (Jer 16:16), there, however, in connection with divine judgment rather than salvation. *James and John, the sons of Zebedee,* who were *mending their nets,* according to Lk 5:7 were Peter's partners in fishing. Mark's mention of *the hired men* left in the boat with Zebedee might suggest that this group had made something of a success of their business.

Mk 1:22–28   Referring to Jesus' synagogue teaching, Mark and Luke
Lk 4:32–37   note the pleased surprise of the people at *the authority*
with which it was presented. This undoubtedly means the authentic voice of prophecy that could be discerned in what Jesus was saying, as contrasted with the traditionalist and repetitive doctrine of *the scribes.* This contrast, and the tensions it aroused, would eventually cost Jesus his forum in the synagogues. Matthew has appropriately transferred these lines to the end of the Sermon on the Mount in which he has preserved a master summation of Jesus' teaching (cf. Mt 7:28 f.).

In this and the following little section Mark has constructed what might be called "a typical day in the Galilean ministry," featuring a typical exorcism and a typical healing miracle followed by a summary. This construction has been followed by Luke but not by Matthew. Matthew, somewhat surprisingly, omits the story of the exorcism entirely; we shall have to see if we can discover the reason for this later on.

The New Testament world accepted demonic possession as a matter of fact, and the Synoptic Gospels relate numerous exorcisms performed by Jesus and presuppose that exorcism was practiced successfully by other people as well. We are not faithful to the Gospel message if we do not take it as seriously in this respect as we do in all others. While it is true that in certain instances which we shall have occasion to note the Gospel may attribute to "a spirit" some affliction which nowadays we would classify more prosaically as epilepsy or insanity (and we should remember that well into the Middle Ages and beyond insane people were commonly regarded as diabolically possessed), there can be no doubt that in the generality of cases the Gospel is speaking of the real exorcism of real devils. This fact causes difficulty for many present-day readers of the New Testament who are embarrassed to find a book which otherwise corresponds so closely to human experience entering in this respect into a world which sometimes seems to them alien and mythical. They may even suspect that to some extent it was an embarrassment to the evangelists themselves. It has often been noted that while John's Gospel is well aware of the many miracles ascribed to Jesus in the Synoptic tradition, it actually describes a mere handful of these on its own, limiting itself to those which it regards pre-eminently as "signs," and mentions no exorcisms at all.

However, it must not be thought that in any case do the Gospels deal with miracles for their own sake. Wonder stories were the order of the day, and in making use of them the Gospels have been quite sober and restrained by contemporary standards. Merely to assert that Jesus was a wonder-worker would have meant little to those who first heard or read the Gospel, since even more wonderful works were attributed to many others of the past and present and were commonly accepted as true. Even though they are not signs precisely in the Johannine sense, for the Synoptic Gospels the miracles and exorcisms of Jesus are nevertheless signs. They are signs of what Jesus was proclaiming: the breaking in of God's kingdom and saving power, the destruction of the reign of evil. This is why, explicitly or implicitly, these works are always premised on faith in the divine power revealed in Jesus. In an age which thought of evil as personal and experienced it as personal, the exorcisms of the Gospels play a role that is altogether proportionate. The same saving power of God is exercised in our own world in more impersonal ways, but the devils it exorcises are no less real.

The meaning we have just assigned to the exorcisms is clearly brought out in the words of *the unclean spirit* of this story. *What to us and to you* (see on Jn 2:4) points to the essential opposition that exists between the demonic order and *the holy one of God* who has come to put an end to its power. The bystanders understand this. *They were all amazed,* not simply at the sight of an exorcism, but at the power of Jesus' word, which alone sufficed to destroy the reign of Satan. This itself was a *new teaching,* a new *word* as Luke quotes them as saying, a further revelation of whom God had sent among them.

In the imposition of silence which Jesus places upon the unclean spirit in this story we have the beginning of what has been called "the messianic secret," a characteristic of Mark's Gospel which has been partially carried over into Matthew and Luke. Persistently throughout the Gospel story we find Jesus being named by one or another title, usually a messianic title in some sense, usually by the demons but sometimes by others as well, and just as persistently Jesus refuses to allow the title to be heard. Corresponding to this is Jesus' frequent injunction to those who have experienced the works of his saving power that they keep silence about what they have witnessed. Never once in the Synoptic Gospels does Jesus designate himself Messiah or use the equivalent title Son of David, and never once does he in any clear and unambiguous way accept this designation from others. We have seen that in this respect among so many others the Fourth Gospel is markedly different from the Synoptics.

The term "messianic secret" was first applied to Mark's Gospel by those who felt it was a technique by which the evangelist had explained away an embarrassment of primitive Christianity: by this fictional device the apostolic Church was justified in hailing as Messiah one who was known to have never proclaimed himself Messiah in his own lifetime. Today very few would try to support this thesis. It would, for one thing, leave unexplained the Church's designation of Jesus as Messiah in the first place, to say nothing of the fact that without a messianic claim of some kind on Jesus' part it is impossible to account for his crucifixion. Rather, it would appear that the messianic secret is part of the authentic history of Jesus, though it is easily admissible that Mark has schematized the history in preparing his Gospel. The messianic secret finds its logical explanation in the unique interpretation which Jesus gave to messianism and accepted it as an identification of himself. It was an interpretation so unique as to preclude the possibility of its being expressed simply in terms of Jewish expectation, let alone in terms originated by the powers of this world inimical to the kingdom of God (see above on Lk 4:3–13 and parallel). If we read the Johannine discourses sympathetically with this Synoptic viewpoint in mind, it is not hard to see that in their own way they try to make a point that is rather analogous.

Mk 1:29–31   Mark and Luke now proceed to tell the story of a typical
Lk 4:38–39   healing miracle—typical, though the case itself was a
Mt 8:14–15   special one which has left its mark on the Gospel trans-
              mission, particularly in the vivid form in which Mark
has preserved it. Matthew briefly parallels the same story and also locates it at Capernaum; it occurs, however, at a later stage in his Gospel because of his insertion of the lengthy Sermon on the Mount which we shall begin to consider in our next chapter.

Immediately on leaving the synagogue they entered the house of Simon and Andrew together with James and John. It has been remarked that this somewhat awkward sentence betrays its first-person origin—"we entered our own house in the company of James and John." The mention of *Simon's mother-in-law* is one of the very few in the New Testament which take cognizance of the family affairs of Jesus' immediate disciples (cf. 1 Cor 9:5). The story probably intends to say that her fever (Luke uses a proper medical term to describe the affliction) came as a surprise to the disciples, who had brought their Master home doubtless to take food. Matthew and Mark say that Jesus touched the woman's hand, Luke adds that he "rebuked" the fever. That she was able immediately to rise and *wait on them* dramatizes the effectiveness of the cure. It is to be noted that this is the first time that Simon Peter appears in Luke's Gospel where, however, he is named without explanation as already well known to the reader.

Mk 1:32–34   The "typical day" ends with a reference to many cures
Lk 4:40–41   and exorcisms on this memorable day in Capernaum. As
Mt 8:16–17   this was a Sabbath day, there is a special relevance to the
              note that these took place *in the evening,* when journeys

could be taken and burdens carried without violation of the law of rest. Again Mark's version is the most natural and vivid with its picture of the townsfolk *crowded about the door* of Peter's house. Matthew says that *he cured them all* whereas Mark has "many," but doubtless the meaning is the same (Mark means, in other words, that they were many and that he cured them). Matthew also finds in these events another prophetic fulfillment which is implicit in other descriptions of healing miracles: they are signs of the spiritual healing wrought through the humble sacrifice of the Servant of the Lord (Is 53:4). To Mark's reiteration that Jesus *forbade the demons to speak because they knew him*, that is, they would have identified him as the Jewish Messiah, Luke adds a more explicit designation by the demons which Mark has reserved for his summary description in 3:11.

Mk 1:35–39   The following episode is also intimately connected with
Lk 4:42–44   the preceding by Mark and Luke; it is omitted by Matthew. *In the morning at an early hour while it was still night* again strikingly evokes the memory of an eyewitness, suggesting Peter's surprise and dismay at finding Jesus gone; Luke's paraphrase is in better Greek, but his account is pallid by comparison. Jesus *had gone away to a secluded spot where he was at prayer*; but Peter and his companions (Luke again says simply "the crowds") *tracked him down*, in Mark's graphic phrase, certain that they are bringing him welcome news that will persuade him to return quickly: *Everyone is looking for you*. Thus ingenuously presented we see in fine relief the contrast between the good-willed but naïve enthusiasm of those for whom the kingdom of God has already come in power and the meditative Christ who knows how far from realization is the work he has come to do. There is an apparent variation in the conclusion of the story as told by Luke: the best reading of the text is that *he was preaching in the synagogues of Judea* rather than of Galilee. However, the difference is probably only apparent, since Luke sometimes uses "Judea" to mean "Jewish land" in general, that is, Palestine (cf. Lk 23:5; Acts 10:37, etc.).

Lk 5:1–11   It is at this point that Luke has inserted his own version
           of the call of the first disciples, a version that differs in certain obvious respects from that of Matthew and Mark. In it Peter is featured almost to the exclusion of the others, and a wonder is related of which we did not hear before. There would seem to be no doubt, however, that the stories go back to the same event. Luke has preserved this independent variant of the tradition and placed it here seemingly because he intends it to be the beginning of a unit developing the theme of the calling of the Twelve concluded in Lk 6:16.

In this story the fishermen are *washing their nets* rather than drying them. Jesus' expedient of avoiding the press of the crowds by teaching from the boat is also related in Mk 4:1 f. and was probably a practice that he adopted often. The Sea of Galilee abounds in fish, so that it is not the size of the catch, though this was remarkable, but the extraordinary knowledge of Jesus that is seen as a wonder. Peter has begun by calling Jesus *Master* (*epistatēs*, a word found only in Luke): here not "teacher," as in the parallels, but rather "leader," one whose business it is to command. At the sign of the Lord's power he realizes that even this was an inadequate designation and is struck with chagrin at the contrast with his own human frailty. Luke concludes the story by saying that *they left everything and followed him.* These disciples were only fishermen, it is true, whose way of life was at best precarious. However, they gave up everything they had, and no man can give up more than this.

Mk 1:40–45   Luke now rejoins Mark to tell the story of the cleansing
Lk 5:12–16   of a leper; both of the evangelists locate the story in the
Mt 8:1–4   context of Jesus' circuit of the Galilean cities after his
               departure from Capernaum. Matthew has his own brief
parallel to the story which, however, he has attached immediately to the Sermon on the Mount as its sequel, doubtless in order to bring out how Jesus' authority in word (cf. Mt 7:29) was also an authority of action.

"Leprosy" is used in the Bible to refer to a variety of skin diseases, none of which may have been precisely what we understand as leprosy; this does not lessen the fact, however, that the diseases were loathsome and painful, and often incurable. In those days of primitive hygiene and lack of resources against contagion, the law perforce adopted a harsh attitude toward lepers. They were forced to live apart, not to enter cities, and to warn away any who would come near them. The leper in this story had violated the law by entering a town, a sign of the faith that drove him on and which is implicit in his dignified statement: *If you will, you can cleanse me.* Equally remarkable is the gesture of Jesus: *stretching forth his hand, he touched him.* It was the simple word of the Lord which healed the man; the touch was a sign of sheer compassion. Jesus' injunction to the man to *show yourself to the priest* and perform the ritual sacrifices (cf. Lev 14:2–32), while consistent with his own obedience to the Law of Moses, was also a necessity if the cure was to be officially certified and the restored leper once more admitted into society.

Mark's version of the story contains some important notes that have disappeared in the parallels. The best reading of the text has it that Jesus *was angry* as he stretched forth his hand. (Most of the manuscripts have instead that he "was filled with compassion"; but this reading seems to be an obvious change made by early copyists who were unable to find a cause for the Lord's anger.) At what was Jesus angry? Possibly at the violation of the Mosaic law, which he revered as the revealed will of God. More likely, however, is it that it is the same emotion that is implied in verse 43, a verse extremely difficult to translate which suggests that Jesus' command to the former leper was accompanied by an inarticulate indignation (the same verb is used to express his reaction to Lazarus' death in Jn 11:33, 38). It is the presence of evil itself which angers Jesus, evil manifest in its works of human suffering and death. He was no clockwork faith-healer unconcernedly scattering miracles in his wake, but a man committed to a life-and-death struggle in which he was deeply and emotionally involved. Mark's Gospel is testimony to an aspect of the personality of Jesus the God-Man which we ignore or gloss over only to our loss.

The messianic secret is continued in Jesus' command that the man he had healed was to *say nothing to anyone*. As was so often the case, the command went unheeded. The Gospels speak again of the enthusiasm over Jesus that spread throughout Galilee, and it is this background that provides the setting for the following episodes.

Mk 2:1–12   Having described somewhat the popular success that had
Lk 5:17–26   followed Jesus' progress through Galilee, Mark now be-
Mt 9:1–8   gins to indicate where the opposition to Jesus lay. The
scene is again Capernaum. The evangelist has joined together five conflict narratives, most of them also pronouncement stories featuring the Lord's teaching on one or another point, which bring out the hostility which Jesus had aroused on the part of some of the elements in official Judaism. In this topical arrangement Mark has been closely followed by Luke. Matthew, who as we have seen pursues a distinct outline of his own, has divided the series into two sections and inserted them elsewhere in his Gospel.

In Chapter 1 we commented briefly on the role that the conflict story served in the development of the Gospel material. These narratives—we will easily note that they are somewhat standardized, reduced to bare essentials, and consequently lacking in some of the freshness of the eyewitness recollections that Mark has recorded thus far—are reflections of the preoccupations of a Church that preserved them primarily for their catechetical values, the solutions they offered to problems that beset nascent Christianity during the formative period of the Church. We should try to discern those preoccupations as we study them, in addition to recognizing the role the stories play in the life of Jesus and in the written Gospel.

The introduction to the story in Mark's Gospel may have been taken from the evangelist's eyewitness source rather than from the ecclesiastical tradition on which the stories mainly depend. It depicts a realistic picture taken from Palestinian life which has been refracted by Luke and omitted by Matthew. After his tour of Galilean cities Jesus is again *at home* in Capernaum, presumably in Peter's house, with the crowds pressing about the door as before while *he preached the word to them*. It is this situation that explains what occurred with the paralytic man. He was being *carried by four*, one at each corner of the light mattress or mat that was *the bed* of the poor man: Matthew and Luke substitute a more elegant Greek word for "bed" than the common term used by Mark. Finding the doorway impossibly blocked, the paralytic's friends hoisted him to the low roof of the house, *made an opening*, then handed him down to Jesus still on his pallet. This was not quite as spectacular a thing as it might seem to us: the roof of a Palestinian house would ordinarily have been of beaten earth and twigs or loose flat stones easily displaced. Luke, paraphrasing the account for readers familiar with the more formal architecture of the Mediterranean world, speaks of them going *through the tiles*—rather a different kind of project! At any rate, their action was dictated by a single-minded faith that could not but please Jesus.

Instead of a word of healing, however, Jesus tells the man that his sins are forgiven. This does not mean, certainly, that Jesus shared the naïve conception of physical suffering as a personal retribution meted out for specific sins (cf. Jn 9:2 f.); he did, however, see a radical connection between physical and moral evil, and it is this connection that constitutes the healing miracles as signs of the saving presence of God. Thus he goes to the root of the matter in saying, *Your sins are forgiven*.

Matthew and Mark speak of *the scribes* as the opponents of Jesus on this occasion; Luke refers to *the scribes and the Pharisees*. In context the same persons are meant: it was the scribes or rabbis, the "professional" Pharisees, whose sense of orthodoxy was offended by Jesus' teaching. In view of the role of the conflict stories in the catechesis of the apostolic Church, specific names for the various elements of official Judaism sometimes tend to be used indiscriminately. The scribes accuse Jesus of *blaspheming* by arrogating to himself a power which belongs to God alone, the power to forgive sins. Jesus' sign, therefore, must be understood as a demonstration that he truly possesses this power, not that he is merely declaring that God has already forgiven the man. On the other hand, it is not precisely correct to see in it a proof of his divinity: this would be to accede to the scribes' position rather than to refute it. The function of the sign is to show that he, the man whom they all knew, rightly exercised a divine prerogative. This is the meaning the story had in the Church's tradition, as is brought out in the conclusion which Matthew has substituted for the rather conventional ending in the parallels: *the crowds gave glory to God who had given such power to men*. In Matthew's Gospel this episode is part of a section in which the powers and prerogatives of the Church are shown to be extensions of the powers and prerogatives of Christ. *Which is easier to say*: paradoxically, the more difficult thing, the pardon, is proved by something that is relatively easy, simply because the latter is palpable and evident to all in its effects.

In this passage, and habitually in all of the Gospels, Jesus refers to himself as *the Son of Man*. The meaning of no other New Testament title has been more hotly debated, and it is probable enough that it sometimes means more than one thing in various contexts. In the present episodes, for example, it is likely that the etymological sense is often being stressed (Aramaic *bar nasha*=Man, with an emphasis on the human estate). As a title, it certainly cannot be separated from the description in Dan 7:13 f. in which the eschatological Israel is represented as "one like a son of man" who has "received dominion, glory, and kingship . . . his dominion is an everlasting dominion that shall not be taken away, his kingship shall not be destroyed." In many passages of the Synoptic Gospels Jesus speaks of the Son of Man as the eschatological judge and savior, and it is reasonable to conclude that he has concretized in himself this figure of the redeemed and redeeming Israel, especially, as we shall see, when this figure had been uniquely combined by himself with the even more significant one of the Servant of the Lord. In John's Gospel, where eschatology is more often than not presented as "realized" here and now, the Son of Man has this especial significance. It is also possible, though this is uncertain, that Son of Man had a messianic meaning for at least some Jews. It is equally possible that behind the Son of Man figure in the Book of Daniel and other Jewish apocalyptic thinking there may lie a concept shared with other Near Eastern peoples of a primordial Man, first-created of God and principle of all life. At all events, the Son of Man seems to be integral to the kingdom of God as it was preached by Jesus. In Mark's Gospel especially, the title is seen to be part of the messianic secret: it was distinctive and calculated to excite interest, bound up with Israelite soteriology yet not associated with a particularist messianism, and above all capable of being filled with a new content by Jesus who made it his own.

Mk 2:13–17   The second conflict story is introduced by Jesus' call of
Lk 5:27–32   another disciple, named *Levi* by Luke, *Levi* [the son]
Mt 9:9–13   of *Alphaeus* by Mark, and *Matthew* by Matthew. All
               three evangelists later on list a Matthew, but no Levi, as one of the Twelve, the apostle which tradition has associated with the authorship of the First Gospel. Double names were not uncommon; however, the fact that Luke and Mark know this man only as Levi may well indicate that they were unaware of his identification with the Matthew of the Twelve. He was *sitting in his toll booth,* evidently a collector of taxes and tolls in the employ of Herod Antipas at the border city of Capernaum. As such, he was not one of the "publicans," the tax-gatherers for the Romans, but in Jewish eyes he undoubtedly belonged to

the same social class. His occupation was probably quite lucrative, and thus his decision to follow Jesus involved a greater sacrifice in some respects than that of the earlier disciples who, after all, could go back to fishing at any time. It is Luke who notes that *he left everything*.

Levi gave a banquet to which he invited his friends, and the friends of such a man in such a line of business were inevitably "not the best kind of people." Those who are called *sinners* were not primarily loose-livers or notorious scofflaws, however, though to be sure some of these may also have been present. To the scribes—Matthew and Luke again have *Pharisees*, while Mark with closer accuracy writes *the scribes of the Pharisees* —they were "sinners" who could or would not keep the Law according to the scribal interpretation: it is little exaggeration to say that in this category were included most of the people who were not scribes (cf. Jn 7:49). Those, for example, who had to deal with Gentiles in their business of making a living were habitually unclean according to the scribal idea of legal purity. Hardly anyone but a professional student of the Law could master the casuistry and traditional lore that were involved in the strict practice of scribal Judaism. The uninstructed and non-practicing masses of a formally Catholic country today, or the unchurched majority of any major city, would correspond almost exactly to the "sinners" of the Gospel.

The text does not say that the scribes were present at Levi's banquet, though they easily could have been, given the informality of Oriental meals. Their objection was made to a known and habitual practice of the Lord. His answer was, of course, a norm of action for the Church of all time. *It is not the healthy who need a physician, but the sick*: it is the business of Christ, and of Christ's Church, to seek out those whom a complacent society might regard as its offscourings. There is no sentimentality or false mystique about the basic goodness of the common man in Jesus' words: he recognizes that they are indeed sick, whatever they may think of themselves, just as by the same token "the healthy" may not actually be in such good health as they imagine. In precisely the same vein he says, *I have not come to call the just, but sinners*. For good measure, Matthew quotes the Lord as employing a rabbinic formula to explain to the rabbis of the Law how his conduct exemplifies the spirit of Hos 6:6 and is therefore a prophetic condemnation of their own attitudes: *Go and learn what this means, "I desire mercy, and not sacrifice."* The scribes used external conformity to the Law as the criterion and checklist to determine who was the just man and who the sinner. Jesus did not deny for a moment that externals are a powerful index to a man's soul; this is a consistent biblical teaching (cf. Mt 7:15 f.; Jas 2:14–17, etc.). But externals, especially carefully selected externals, have a way of becoming religion itself instead of remaining its flower and fruit. Formalism is the temptation of the righteous, and the means by which they become self-righteous.

Mk 2:18–22   It is fairly easy to see the meaning that the following
Lk 5:33–39   episode had in the catechesis of the apostolic Church.
Mt 9:14–17   By means of it the Church both justified its practice of
fasting by a saying of the Lord and also defined the spirit which differentiated Christian fasting from every other kind. The event that is presupposed could have occurred virtually anytime during Jesus' public life, though it seems to be from a time after the Baptist's removal from the scene. Luke simply connects it with the preceding passage, though Mark does not. Matthew has the Baptist's disciples themselves pose the question, while in Mark it is simply "they" who ask Jesus.

The situation seems to have been this. The Baptist and his followers imitated the Pharisees in the practice of periodic fasts over and above the one fast that was prescribed by the Law for the solemn Day of Atonement. Mark's expression *the disciples of the Pharisees* is somewhat puzzling, but he appears to mean nothing more or less than those who subscribed to the Pharisaical interpretation of Judaism. In this respect at least Jesus deviated from Pharisaical practice, and his disciples naturally with him. Moreover, he justified his contrary practice not on the score that such fasting was at best optional but on the radical significance that fasting must have if it is to be more than an empty observance. *The sons of the bridegroom* is a Semitic expression meaning the friends and companions of a bridegroom at his wedding feast. A wedding feast is no place for fasting, obviously. But it is precisely a wedding feast that they are celebrating who recognize in Jesus, however imperfectly as yet (cf. Jn 3:25–30), the bridegroom of the messianic kingdom. Therefore they should take no part in the fasts of those who do not recognize this kingdom, whose fasting is a penitential preparation for a kingdom to which they still look in the future. *The days will come when the bridegroom is taken away from them*: this is a veiled reference to his death. There is a fasting proper to Christians which, however, finds it motivation in the Christian event itself and not in its Jewish heritage. Christian fasting has its explanation in the new revelation of the mystery of the Cross.

Concluding this episode Mark (or the catechesis on which he drew) has quoted two little parables of the Lord, both of which illustrate the impossibility of effectively combining incompatibles. In context, of course, the incompatibles are Judaism and Christianity: now recognized as such by a Church that had gone through the painful experience of the Judaizing crisis. *Raw cloth* is no good to patch *an old garment* because the inevitable shrinkage that it will undergo will result in a greater rent than before. *New wine* still undergoing fermentation cannot be contained in *old wineskins* weakened with age and transport. It is interesting to note Luke's paraphrase of the first parable, which underlines the folly by having the patch torn from a new garment. Luke also adds a third parable which, from another standpoint, teaches the same lesson. A man used to good *old wine* can hardly be persuaded to drink raw new wine along with it: the two do not mix. These examples, incidentally, effectively show the difference between a parable and an allegory, a distinction whose importance we shall see later.

Mk 2:23–28   The final two conflict stories revolve about the question
Lk 6:1–5   of the Sabbath. While Mark and Luke keep them within
Mt 12:1–8   the context of the first part of the Galilean ministry,
              Matthew has reserved them for a later period in his
Gospel where he treats of the opposition to Jesus in a way proper to himself. These stories point up the almost superstitious reverence in which the Sabbath was held by the Jews. It would, indeed, be difficult to exaggerate the importance of this observance in the Jewish mind; we must remember that it was by the Sabbath above all that the Jew distinguished himself externally from the sea of paganism that surrounded him, and therefore quite apart from its religious value as honoring the Creator God it had an emotional claim on him that some other laws and customs did not. By the same token, it was over the Sabbath that early Jewish Christianity came into easy conflict with non-Christian Judaism, and this explains the popularity of this kind of story in the Gospels.

His disciples began to pluck ears of grain; Luke adds that *they were rubbing them in their hands.* It was to this that the Pharisees objected. The Law did not forbid eating from a neighbor's field (Deut 23:26), but it did forbid harvesting on the Sabbath (Ex 34:21). In the strict Pharisaical view, what the disciples were doing constituted harvesting; it was one of the thirty-nine works which the rabbis counted as violations of the Sabbath. Even to discuss business or to plan one's work for the morrow was forbidden. It is only just to add, however, that while rabbinical opinions could be cited that were even narrower than the one ascribed to the Pharisees in this story, there were always other rabbis who followed a more liberal view.

Dealing with rabbis, Jesus uses rabbinical argumentation, which is argument from precedent. *Have you never read what David did* refers to the story in 1 Sam 21:1–6. When David was in danger of his life from King Saul he begged food of the priest Ahimelech (Mark has "when Abiathar was high priest," associating the story with Ahimelech's far more famous son whose priesthood was identified with David's reign); Ahimelech, having nothing else to offer him, gave him the showbread of the sanctuary (cf. Lev 24:5–9), which ordinarily was reserved for sacred purposes alone. The lesson is obvious: human need takes precedence over ritual law. The other precedent given by Matthew is to the same effect: *on the*

Sabbath the priests in the temple profane the Sabbath. What would normally be considered work violating the Sabbath is considered lawful for the priests because it is necessary to fulfill duties more pressing than the Sabbath law. *A greater than the temple is here:* this statement probably is in tune with the final sentence cited by all the evangelists, that the Son of Man is lord of the Sabbath in virtue of his character as fulfillment of what the temple had only imperfectly represented (so also Jn 2:19–21). It is also possible, however, that it echoes in other language the principle cited by Mark: *the Sabbath was made for man and not man for the Sabbath.* The rabbis themselves cited such a principle as this in justifying work on the Sabbath that was necessary to save a man's life. Jesus takes it much farther, however, in insisting that the human condition as such, not just its preservation under extraordinary circumstances, takes precedence over every ritual law however holy. Matthew again cites Hos 6:6 in much the same sense as before: if the Pharisees would be truly religious, they would judge the disciples not by the letter of a law but by their adherence to its spirit.

Thus the Son of Man is Lord even of the Sabbath! Luke puts these words in the mouth of Christ, but this is not evident from Matthew and even less so from Mark. It is likely that the statement was originally a Christian comment on the foregoing episode (which, after all, is not about abolition of the Sabbath but about its proper observance), a comment recognizing in the risen Lord of the Church the one who had replaced the Sabbath of the Jews. It is still possible, however, that this is a saying of Jesus playing on the ambiguity of the Aramaic *bar nasha=* "son of man"="man": man himself is superior to the Sabbath.

Mk 3:1–5   The second story involving the Sabbath also describes
Lk 6:6–10   a healing miracle and leads to a further pronouncement
Mt 12:9–13   of Jesus. Luke says that it took place *on another Sab-
                bath,* which has led to a curious reading that appears in most of the manuscripts of Lk 6:1: "on the second first Sabbath." Probably an ancient copyist inserted "first" in this verse in view of Lk 6:6, while another corrected it to "second" because of Lk 4:31; eventually both words got into the text which then made very little sense but was able to inspire some interesting commentary at times.

In this story only Luke specifies from the outset that a conflict is joined with *the scribes and Pharisees;* only at the conclusion of the story do Matthew and Mark agree that it was indeed these who were watching Jesus *that they might accuse him* of Sabbath violation. The man *who had a withered hand,* possibly a victim of infantile paralysis, afforded Jesus with the occasion of testifying to the word of God in the face of the hostility that surrounded him. The rabbis would concede that what was necessary to save a human life could be done on the Sabbath, but that any healing or medication that could be put off was forbidden. Again Jesus establishes a principle on a quite different plane of thought. *Is it lawful on the Sabbath to do good or to do evil, to save a life or to kill it?* Once more he asks that a judgment be made not out of the casuistry involved in considering a law as an absolute in itself, but rather from an enquiry into the meaning of law as the communication of the will of a merciful and beneficent God. Within such a context, does every act of man blur into the one concept of "forbidden work"? Or is it not relevant to ask whether such and such an act furthers the same purpose for which the law was given, while another does not? Does the God who established the Sabbath to help rather than to harm man intend that it should be the occasion of suffering and pain?

Jesus' plea for mercy rather than sacrifice is greeted with a sullen silence. Mark says that *he looked round at them with anger,* and understandably so. Grieving as well as angry, he quickly brings the episode to a close. *Stretch forth your hand!* This was his answer to his own question and his witness to their small-minded vision of God.

Matthew has drawn on a source also known to Luke (see on Lk 14:1–6) to add to this story another precedent used by the Lord, this time taken from rabbinical casuistry concerning the Sabbath law. If a man's *one sheep,* his only property, were to be in danger of loss by falling into a pit, he could save its life without violating the Sabbath. But *of how much more value is a man than a sheep!* Yes, the rabbis might answer, but rescuing the sheep constituted an emergency, whereas the healing of a man could be deferred. Yet they do not answer, and with cause. Such an answer would imply that their concern for a man's property—for the concession was obviously not made out of consideration for the sheep—outweighed their concern for the man himself. It is interesting to note that Jesus' argument could not have been used against some of the Jews of his time, who were more consistent, and also more rigorous, than the rabbis with whom he was speaking. The so-called "Zadokite Document," the sectarian rule of a group pertaining to if not actually identified with the Jewish sect of Qumran, contains this specific regulation: "No one is to foal a beast on the Sabbath day. Even if she drop her young into a cistern or a pit, he is not to lift it out on the Sabbath."

Mk 3:6　　And so, the Gospels now tell us, Jesus' enemies found a
Lk 6:11　　common cause in their opposition to the new Teacher of
Mt 12:14　　Galilee. Mark says that these Pharisees *took counsel with the Herodians.* The Herodians were the Jewish supporters of the house of the Herods, in this case those who were influential with the tetrarch Herod Antipas. Since they undoubtedly shared in the pagan atmosphere that pervaded Herod's court, for the Pharisees to seek their advice was tantamount to consorting with publicans and sinners. Stranger

alliances than this, however, have been made against a common peril. We
are not told that the Herodians themselves had anything against Jesus.
Their influence might be used, nevertheless, to induce Antipas to deal
with Jesus as he had already dealt with John the Baptist.

Mk 3:7–12   To counterbalance this picture of implacable hostility,
Mt 12:15–21   Mark now presents a summary statement on the phe-
Mt 4:23–25   nomenal success of Jesus' preaching, a description with
                  which he introduces his main treatment of the Galilean
ministry. Luke reproduces this Marcan material: he has already used part
of it earlier in his Gospel (see Lk 4:40 f. paralleling Mk 1:32–34 above),
and he will use the remainder to introduce his equivalent of the Sermon
on the Mount which we shall see in our next chapter. Matthew's parallels,
which we consider here, are somewhat similar. Partly he has imitated
Mark's summary statement in the three verses he has placed immediately
before the Sermon on the Mount, the great discourse in which he has
epitomized the height of the Galilean ministry. He has made use of a
like summary to conclude his version of the two Sabbath controversies
we have just seen, which as we know he has located in a different part of
his Gospel in pursuit of his own theological outline.

What all these summaries conspire to produce is a single effect: the
fame of Jesus, largely premised on the signs of his healing miracles and
exorcisms, was now becoming widespread not only among the Jews of
Galilee and Judea but also among those of the immediate Diaspora of
the neighboring territories of the north and south and east. The cries of
the demons, *You are the Son of God*, whose testimony Jesus continually
refuses to accept, have probably been rephrased in the Gospel in the
light of Christian faith (so also Mk 5:7; compare Mk 15:39 and Mt 27:54
with Lk 23:47).

Matthew's contribution to these passages is, as usual, a citation of Old
Testament prophecy (Is 42:1–4) which he finds fulfilled in these events.
The true Servant of God who by the evangelist's time has fulfilled the
earnest of these former days in order to *proclaim justice to the nations*,
pursues his spiritual destiny in the quiet assurance of the power of God,
without the stridency of any compelling propaganda or the triumphalism
of a King Messiah: this is Matthew's explanation of the "messianic secret." It is the lengthiest quotation of the Old Testament in the First
Gospel.

Mk 3:13–19   One final detail completes this picture of Galilean suc-
Lk 6:12–16   cess and enthusiasm: the choice by Jesus of the twelve
Mt 10:1–4   special disciples called by the evangelists apostles (but
                  rarely, except by Luke), and whom we tend to think of
as *the* apostles on whom the Church was founded (Eph 2:20). Certainly
the Gospels, all of which in varying degrees have in mind the interests of

the existing Church for which they were written, treat the selection of the
Twelve as an event of special importance, over and above the call of
the disciples already described. Both Mark and Luke say that the designation of the Twelve took place on *the mountain*, evoking a theme which
repeatedly occurs in the Gospels and which is doubtless intended to recall the decisive events in Old Testament history when the word of God
came to Moses (Ex 24:12–18) or Elijah (1 Kgs 19:8 ff.) on "the mountain
of God." Luke adds that *he continued in prayer to God all night*: a note
which he often prefaces to acts that are of especial significance in the
life of Jesus. Mark and Matthew say that Jesus *gave authority* to the
Twelve such as he himself possessed, and in the Acts of the Apostles Luke
habitually shows various ones of the Twelve, and especially Peter, standing in relation to the early Christian community precisely as Jesus had
stood in relation to his contemporaries. There can be little doubt, therefore, that the Church which produced the New Testament looked on the
apostolic Twelve as its link with Jesus, just as there can be little doubt
that Jesus chose the symbolic number twelve in relation to a new era in
the salvation history of Israel (cf. Mt 19:28; Lk 22:30).

However, if the New Testament manifests great interest in the Twelve
as an apostolic college, the same can hardly be said for its concern with
them as individuals save in a few instances. This becomes evident, first
of all, when we compare the lists of the Twelve as they appear in the
Synoptic tradition, including the second list given by Luke in Acts 1:13:

Mark	Luke	Acts	Matthew
Simon Peter	Simon Peter	Peter	Simon Peter
James ⎫	Andrew his brother	John	Andrew his brother
and ⎬ of Zebedee			
John ⎭	James	James	James ⎫
			and ⎬ of Zebedee
			John ⎭
Andrew	John	Andrew	
Philip	Philip	Philip	Philip
Bartholomew	Bartholomew	Thomas	Bartholomew
Matthew	Matthew	Bartholomew	Thomas
Thomas	Thomas	Matthew	Matthew
			the publican
James of Alphaeus	James of Alphaeus	James of Alphaeus	James of Alphaeus
Thaddaeus	Simon the Zealot	Simon the Zealot	Thaddaeus
Simon	Judas of James	Judas of James	Simon
the Cananaean			the Cananaean
Judas Iscariot	Judas Iscariot		Judas Iscariot

The lists, we see, are fairly stylized. They follow a tradition which had
divided the names into three series of four, in which Peter always appeared first, Judas Iscariot always last, the second and third quartets were
always headed by Philip and James of Alphaeus respectively, and the
rest of the names had no particular place of order.

Furthermore, while the lists do, by and large, refer to the same persons, there are also some discrepancies. We have already seen (above on Mk 2:13–17 and parallels) that it is probable that Mark and Luke did not identify "Levi the taxgatherer" with Matthew the apostle, as Matthew definitely does; Mark spoke of him as "Levi of Alphaeus," but the only "of Alphaeus" in the lists of the Twelve is the second James. Simon the Cananaean and Simon the Zealot are the same person: "zealot" is simply Luke's correct translation of a Semitic term (Aramaic *qan'ānā*) used to characterize members of a politico-religious party which in later times spearheaded a fanatical resistance to Roman rule in Palestine. But it is by no means certain that the Thaddaeus of Mark and Matthew was known to be the same as the Judas (whom we usually call Jude) of James listed by Luke. (To complicate the matter further, some of the Greek manuscripts of Mark and Matthew have the name Lebbaeus instead of Thaddaeus.) John, though he also speaks of the Twelve (Jn 6:70), never gives us a list of them. As we have seen, he mentions by name Peter, Andrew, Philip, and Nathanael; he also includes in his Gospel the names of Thomas and Judas Iscariot, and at various times he presupposes the presence of one or more unnamed members of the Twelve. His Nathanael appears nowhere in the Synoptic lists; if he is to be identified with anyone there, the most likely candidate is Bartholomew (Aramaic *bar tolmai*= son of Tolmai, a "family" name).

All of this suggests that while the institution of the Twelve was of the utmost importance to the New Testament Church, it was with the institution rather than with the personalities of the apostolic college that the tradition was concerned. Aside from Peter and the sons of Zebedee and, of course, Judas Iscariot, the members of the Twelve rarely appear as distinct personalities in the Gospels. This is not as surprising as it might at first appear. The Church of the New Testament, after all, was interested in those aspects of the tradition which vitally affected it, and it was the apostleship itself rather than its original components that was of the most concern to a Gentile Church remote from Palestine. We have no authentic information about the activity of most of the Twelve after the first days of the Church in Jerusalem, but it is likely enough that they remained identified with Jewish Christianity, particularly, perhaps, with the Galilean Christianity about which we know practically nothing. By the time the Gospels were written this Christianity had all but disappeared. Meanwhile the apostleship had broadened, and other apostles like Paul and Barnabas had opened up a new age for the Church of which the Gospels are a product.

Apostle means "one who is sent," even as Jesus is shown in these passages to commission the Twelve to go forth and speak in his name. The title, as well as the office, therefore, doubtless derives from the Lord. Two other terms here may need explanation. Mark says that Jesus nick-

named the sons of Zebedee *Boanerges, that is, "sons of thunder."* Behind
the word which Mark transliterates as "Boanerges," scholars have suggested there may lie a Hebrew *bnê rogez* or *bnê regesh,* either of which
roughly (but only roughly) can mean "sons of thunder." But what does
"thunder" mean in this connection? Perhaps Lk 9:54 gives some kind of
indication. Or perhaps Mark, not knowing the origin of the nickname,
found a popular etymology in the Greek word for "thunder" (*brontēs*).
Iscariot, applied to Judas the betrayer by all the evangelists without explanation, remains a puzzler. It is usually understood as representing the
Hebrew *ish qerioth,* that is, "the man from Kerioth" (a Judahite city
mentioned in Jos 15:25). This is not very satisfactory, but it is equi-
probable with any other alternative that has been proposed. Obscurities
of this kind testify to the antiquity of the tradition on which the Gospels
drew.

8. THE KEYS OF THE KINGDOM

Mt 5:1–2   In the foregoing chapters we have somewhat tended to
Lk 6:17–20a   slight Matthew, bringing in his parallels to the Marcan
or Lucan material to the disregard of his own way of
arranging things. This has been done out of practical necessity in view of
the limits that we have set on ourselves in reading the Gospels in harmony, for the reversal of the process would have made the more or less
common order of Mark and Luke incomprehensible. Now, however, Matthew comes into his own as we begin to study one of the chief contributions he has made to the Gospel story, which is, as a matter of fact,
probably the most famous passage in all Christian literature, the Sermon
on the Mount.

We speak of it as the Sermon on the Mount because that is what
Matthew called it, utilizing the symbol of *the mountain* which we have
already noted above in Mark and Luke (see on Mk 3:13–19; Lk 6:12–16).
Matthew makes a point of the mountain because for him Jesus is a new
and greater Moses proclaiming a new and greater law from the source of
divine revelation. The Sermon is the first of the five lengthy discourses
in which Matthew has mainly summarized the teaching of Jesus; he has
placed it appropriately in the midst of the Galilean enthusiasm over
Jesus' initial preaching of the kingdom because it epitomizes the spirit of
the kingdom as Matthew knew it to have been realized in the Church.
Luke, who has a much shorter version of what was undoubtedly the
same sermon, states more matter-of-factly (and more realistically) that
Jesus addressed the crowds on *a level place*. Luke's purpose in repro-
ducing the discourse is not so programmatic as Matthew's. Having described Jesus' choice of the Twelve, he used his own account of the
Galilean acceptance of Jesus (see on Mk 3:7–12 and Mt 4:23–25 above)
as a preface to the sermon as Jesus' proclamation of the kingdom to the
Twelve and to the multitudes. In these latter he sees "the poor of the
Lord" who now have the Gospel preached to them (cf. Lk 4:18).

That Matthew and Luke found the record of this sermon in the common source they have used independently of Mark seems to be evident
enough, despite the difference in length (one hundred and nine verses

in Matthew against thirty in Luke) and purpose with which it appears
in the two Gospels. Neither version pretends, of course, to be a stenographic account of any single sermon preached by our Lord: in both cases
the sermon has been adapted to the Gospel. It is equally certain that
Matthew, who has done the most with the sermon, has also introduced
far more changes than Luke. He has imposed on it a rigid outline more
appropriate to a literary composition than to oral delivery, and into this
outline he has fitted various sayings of the Lord which often appear elsewhere in the other Gospels (and, for that matter, which sometimes appear
elsewhere in his own Gospel as well). The original moment of the sermon
is usually more perceptible in Luke than in Matthew, in view of the
sense in which it figures in these two Gospels; however, all Christian
history is testimony to the success of Matthew in synthesizing its perennial
significance for all Christians of all time. That the Sermon on the Mount
is only one of the five discourses of Christ in Matthew's Gospel should
warn us that in the intention of the evangelist it is not all of Christian
teaching. It has, for all that, captured the heart and spirit of Christianity
in a way that nothing else ever has.

Mt 5:3–12   The differences between Matthew's and Luke's versions
Lk 6:20b–23   of the Sermon appear immediately from the first words,
                    in the Beatitudes with which it begins. In Matthew's
Gospel there are eight Beatitudes (originally, perhaps only seven), and in
Luke's four; in the first instance they have been put in the third person
and have a wider application, in the other they have the form of direct
address. In both Gospels, however, it is important to observe, the Beatitudes and the rest of the Sermon are addressed to Jesus' *disciples*
(Mt 5:1b–2; Lk 6:20a): the Sermon on the Mount is not a collection
of idealistic poetry but a proclamation of Christian values and (especially
in Matthew) a realistic exhortation to a standard of virtue that is possible
only through the power given by the Spirit of God.

A beatitude, translated *blessed* . . . or *happy* . . . , is a fairly common
literary form in both the Old and the New Testaments (cf. Pss 2:12,
33:12, 40:5; Mt 11:6; Lk 1:45, etc.). Almost invariably it involves the
possession of a present good, which in turn, explicitly or implicitly, is the
earnest of an even greater good to come. The Gospel Beatitudes are
eschatological: they look forward to a blessedness that is to come, a
consummation of the divine plan of salvation. However, they find the
beginning of this same blessedness in the here-and-now situation that is
the result of Jesus' coming and his saving word. They are, therefore, a
combination of "final" and "realized" eschatology.

Blessed are the poor in spirit is Matthew's equivalent of Luke's *Blessed
are* [you] *poor*. The two do, in fact, mean much the same thing, though
Luke has preserved the form of proclamation to a distinct audience which

was, in point of fact, poor; the entire first generation of Christianity drew
its membership basically from the economically and socially underprivi-
leged, like the Galilean peasantry. Nevertheless, Luke is not saying that
there is anything blessed or happy about belonging to the social class of
the poor—the idealization of the sturdy virtues of the poor, a romantic
notion devised by comfortable philosophers who have never experienced
the degrading effects of an unwanted, grinding poverty, is not an error
propagated by the Bible. Poverty of itself is not blessed, though one may
be blessed for voluntarily embracing it: in which case it is his motive that
makes him blessed. Neither, of course, is Luke speaking of this voluntary
poverty that was later to be made the object of one of the three vows of
Christian perfection, taken as a means of imitating more literally the
penitential life of Jesus. He is not speaking of it directly, that is, though
he does include the idea: some of those to whom Jesus was proclaiming
his kingdom had, in fact, literally made themselves poor for his sake (Levi,
for example, Lk 5:28). What he is saying is: Blessed are you, my disciples, who are poor. The blessedness comes from discipleship, but in their
poverty they fulfill an eschatological promise. From Old Testament times,
because of a long history of social oppression and injustice, the poor, the
anawim, represented above all those who, having no worldly means of
their own to fight the battle of life, placed their whole reliance on God and
his vindication. When a person wished to give himself a special title to
God's saving help, he called himself a poor man (cf. Ps 40:18). At long
last, says Luke, the cry of the poor through the ages has been heard: *yours
is the kingdom of God.*

Hence the meaning of Matthew's paraphrase. To be poor in spirit is not
precisely or simply to have the spirit of poverty, but to have the spirit—
that is, the mind, the attitude of being—of the *anawim*, to be conscious
of standing before God always naked and defenseless, trusting in him and
him alone. It is no less than this that Matthew lays down as the indispensable quality of a Christian. It is a quality far more easily asserted than
lived, and far more embracing than to be, or to think that we are, "detached" from worldly goods.

The next two verses of Matthew's Gospel appear in reverse order in
many of the Greek manuscripts. In fact, since *Blessed are the meek, for
they shall inherit the land* is a citation of Ps 37:11, it is believed by many
that this verse is an ancient interpolation into Matthew's text, introduced
as a commentary on the first Beatitude. If this view is correct, the primitive
number of Matthew's Beatitudes would be reduced to a symbolic seven,
corresponding to patterns found elsewhere in his Gospel. Whether or not
this is the case, it is true at all events that there is little if any difference
in meaning between the two Beatitudes. "Meek," though traditional, has
never been too accurate a rendering of what is meant by the operative
word here. The "meek" are also the *anawim*, patiently enduring what must

be endured in their confident expectation of God's justice. The "land" is a reference to Palestine as the land of God's promise; already in Old Testament times (the psalmist of Ps 37:11; cf. also Ps 25:13; Is 57:13, 60:21, 65:9) the original inheritance of the promised land by Israel was seen as a type of the eschatological kingdom of God, as it is also in the New Testament (see Heb 4:1–13).

The next two Beatitudes, found both in Matthew and in Luke though in a different order, likewise constitute a commentary on the first. *Blessed are you that hunger now*, Luke quotes the Lord who was speaking to people who were physically hungry. Matthew translates this as *those who hunger and thirst for* God's vindicating *justice*: not in any selfish spirit, but that God's sovereign will be done (cf. Pss 36:11, 40:11, 85:11). These *shall be satisfied* in the kingdom of God wherein every desire for what is right and just will be fulfilled. Similarly, Luke's *you who weep now* but who *shall laugh* is rendered by Matthew as *they who mourn . . . shall be consoled*. The causes of the *anawim*'s mourning were many. The end of this mourning, as had long ago been prophesied, was in the consolation that Israel would find in the establishment of God's kingdom through the ministry of his Servant (cf. Is 40:1 ff., 61:1–3, etc.).

From the more or less passive qualities of the *anawim* Matthew passes to quite active attributes in the three following Beatitudes which he alone reproduces. *Blessed are the merciful* enshrines a cherished Old Testament idea: that the principle by which God has joined man to himself and by which in turn man preserves his union with God and with his fellows is the single one of loving-kindness, covenant fidelity. It is this concept (*ḥesed*), especially beloved of the prophets, that defines the meaning of the "mercy" which God prefers to sacrifice (Hos 6:6; see on Mt 9:13 and 12:7 above). The corporal and spiritual "works of mercy" of traditional piety fit precisely within this concept, faithfully echoing the biblical doctrine that man's service to man is the measure of his loyalty to God. *They shall obtain mercy*: the *ḥasîd*, the man of *ḥesed*, is already blessed in the possession of God's gift which he shares with others, and this blessedness is the token of the final mercy that he will obtain from God.

Pure of heart is another expression that we habitually somewhat mistranslate, which at least can give an erroneous impression owing to differences of idiom. "Pure" is used here in the same sense in which we might speak of "a lie, pure and simple," that is, whole, integral, entire; and "heart" for the Semite is not pre-eminently a metaphor for man's emotional life but rather a surrogate for his entire self: a man *thinks* in his heart (Gen 8:21; Eccl 8:5, etc.). What we should understand by the pure of heart, therefore, is the "simple," in the best sense of this often misused word (see also Mt 6:22–24, 10:16). These *shall see God*: see above on Jn 1:15–18. The vision of God which they have through faith in this life is in all substance the eschatological vision of God (cf. Jn 14:9; 1 Cor 13:12).

Somewhat surprisingly, the word *peacemakers* appears nowhere else in biblical literature, though the idea is an ancient one. "Peace" (*shalom*) was a sacred word for the Semite, denoting a positive state of wholeness and productivity rather than the merely negative absence of hostilities that we sometimes tend to associate with it; "peace" was the greeting by which he announced his benign intentions toward man. It is no wonder, then, that unending peace and the kingdom of God become identified (Is 9:6). In Eph 2:14 Paul speaks of Christ concretely as "our peace." Those who in their lives and works further this peace of God, in the last day *shall be called God's children*, for this they have been all along (cf. 1 Jn 3:1).

Matthew and Luke come together again for the final Beatitude. It is, in a way, a summation of all that have gone before, and seemingly Matthew signals this fact by ending it with an "inclusion," a repetition of the promise of the first Beatitude: *theirs is the kingdom of heaven. Those who are persecuted for the sake of justice*, Matthew further explains, are those persecuted *on account of me*, and Luke, *on account of the Son of Man*. The "justice" in question, therefore, means here what it ordinarily means in Matthew's Gospel: the way of salvation as it has been revealed by God in Jesus Christ. This use of the word justice, to signify the true way of life made known by God, is peculiarly associated with the prophetic vocabulary of the Old Testament. Fittingly, therefore, the Christian who undergoes persecutions and indignities for the cause of his religion is likened to the prophets and promised a "prophet's reward" (cf. Mt 10:41). The Church of the New Testament was fully persuaded that the patient and joyful endurance of persecution was a sign of its prophetic character willed by God (cf. 1 Thes 1:4 ff.; 2 Thes 1:4 ff.).

Lk 6:24–26   In his commentary on the final Beatitude, Matthew adopts the direct address of the original sermon form. Luke, who has preserved this form all along, now has a proper contribution to make in the "woes" that accompany and complement the four Beatitudes of his version of the Sermon. The woes need not have been addressed to any specific persons in the crowds which had flocked to hear Jesus; they are apostrophes directed in traditional fashion against those who represent the exact opposite of the *anawim* (cf. Is 65:11–16). As is evident, they simply reverse the blessings of the Beatitudes, and they should be understood in this sense. While primitive Christianity counted in its membership few persons of influence or wealth and, like the *anawim* of the Old Testament, could almost without qualification identify the rich as its enemies (cf. Jas 5:1–6), the Gospels never make the mistake of finding evil in things rather than in people. They are agreed, however, and Luke above all makes a point of it (cf. Lk 12:16–21, 16:19–30), that the wealthy man far too easily misses the purpose of his existence simply through his pursuit of "the good life," just as the good esteem of men far too often can be a sign that one has never risen above the aspirations of this world (cf. Jn 15:19; Jas 4:4). *The false prophets* are those who confused their own hopes and dreams with the word of God. They told complacent or evil men what they wanted to hear (cf. 1 Kgs 22:1–28; Jer 27–28, etc.), and thus won their praise.

Mt 5:13–16   Matthew himself continues the Beatitudes by appending to them two little parables of the Lord which further define the character of the true disciple of Jesus. The same sayings of Christ we shall meet in other contexts in the Gospels of Luke and Mark; there are also some echoes in the Gospel of John. Because the specific context can mean a different application of the saying and therefore a different interpretation in the concrete, it is necessary to see each passage as it occurs in the Gospels. It is the proper function of authorship, of course, that each evangelist should have made the words of the Lord his own and have integrated them into the form and design of the Gospel that is peculiarly his; in the strictest possible sense, too, it is in this dimension that we read the teaching of Christ as inspired Scripture. In some instances we have good reason to believe that the evangelists drew on collections of the Lord's sayings which had preserved his words without reference to their original historical contexts; they consequently fitted these into their narratives in various applications.

The reason for the association of *salt* and *light* is obvious: both are necessities for life. The Christian character has profound significance not only for God and the Christian himself, but also for the entire world. As of old God chose Israel to be a light to the nations, so it is with the Church: *a city set on a hill which cannot be hid.* By mirroring in their lives the Christian virtues and testifying to the salvation wrought in Christ, the followers of Jesus "salt" the world, functioning for its life as salt functions in flavoring and preserving food. They give light to the world by their *good works*, compelling men to *give glory to the Father* whose grace has made such things possible. This is Matthew's expression of the idea of "witness" which is so prominent in the Gospels of Luke and John. It explains the warnings and injunctions here attached to the parables which themselves take the form of parables, borrowing their analogies from everyday Palestinian life. The salt that was in common use was often imperfectly refined and chemically impure; it could lose its saltiness and therefore its value. The Palestinian house would ordinarily be illuminated by a single lamp, often enough a mere saucer of oil in which floated a lighted wick; if such a lamp was to do its job properly it had to be set in the clear, on a stand from which it could cast its light unimpeded. What is involved in Christian witness, in other words, is simply that the Christian be truly himself, that he always act precisely as his Master has intended him to act. This is far removed, of course, both from an ostentatious parading of good works that gives witness to the worker rather than to God, and from the self-conscious compulsion to "give good example" that often distorts Christian witness into playacting.

Mt 5:17–20   Having set forth the Christian's duty to testify to God through his good works, Matthew now explains in the Lord's words what is the distinctive nature of the Christian righteousness that offers this testimony. It is characteristic of this Gospel that such a definition would be made in terms of its relation to Jewish law and practice; however, it would also have been inevitable that Jesus himself would have chosen these terms. The introductory principle is stated in a passage that is entirely proper to Matthew, with the exception of one verse that is found in a different context in Lk 16:17.

Do not think I have come to abolish the Law and the prophets. Probably no other verse of Matthew's Gospel has caused more controversy than this. "The Law and the prophets" is contemporary Jewish language for "the Bible," or in Christian language, "the Old Testament." In context, there can be no doubt that what is meant is the revealed will of God as set forth in the Old Testament, specifically in the Law of Moses: in Jewish thinking the prophets of the Old Testament functioned preeminently as interpreters of the Law. Jesus seems to be saying, then, that the Old Testament law remains forever in effect: *till heaven and earth pass away* is doubtless popular idiom for "never." The rest of the text appears to bear this impression out. Jesus insists that *not one iota, not one "horn" will disappear from the Law,* that is, not one *yod,* the smallest letter of the Hebrew alphabet, which was sometimes written as a simple dot, and not one *qots:* the little protuberance that distinguishes, for example, the letter ב (*b*) from the letter כ (*k*). *Till all things come about:* again, the meaning is probably "till the end of time," ascribing a practical perpetuity to the Law. He goes on to say that whoever disregards *one of the least of these commandments* (the rabbis distinguished between the "light" and the "heavy" precepts of the Law) will be excluded from the kingdom of God. And so on. Yet the New Testament—with Matthew's Gospel very much included!—is at one in the conviction that the Mosaic law has been superseded by the law of Christ, that Christians are entirely free of its precepts.

That Jesus himself said these words, or words very much like them, there can be no doubt. They constitute the kind of defense that he would have inevitably been called upon to make in his controversies with the rabbis. They are consistent with his own practice as we see it reflected in the Gospel stories, which portray him as keeping the Law faithfully, though without fanaticism or literalism. It is not surprising, therefore, that some interpreters imagine the original context of these lines to have been other than that of Matthew's Sermon, on some occasion, for example, when in hyperbolic Oriental language Jesus was expressing his here-and-now teaching on fidelity to the Law which had been called into question. Or, if Matthew's context is to be preserved, they understand the passing away of heaven and earth, etc., to refer to the old era which Christ was bringing to an end and which ceased to be with his death, resurrection, and the emergence of the Church: Jesus taught the permanence of the Mosaic law, in other words, but only for his own lifetime.

Neither of these explanations is particularly convincing, and certainly neither of them gets at what Matthew means by these sayings in his context, the only context in which we possess them. Neither is the solution to be found in applying Jesus' words only to a part of the Mosaic law, as though he were speaking of the permanence of its moral prescriptions and keeping silence about the rest. Neither Jesus nor Matthew, neither the New Testament nor the Old Testament, would have made any distinction between the commandments of the Law, moral, ritual, or otherwise: all of them were equally the expressed will of God.

Rather, we must first see carefully what "the Law and the prophets" signifies in Matthew's Gospel, then understand in this light what it is for Jesus to fulfill this law. "The Law and the prophets" is the Old Testament revelation expressed in law, to be sure, but by no means the letter of any law. It is, instead, the divine word itself as revealed by the Law and the prophets but transcending their imperfect utterance. The Golden Rule, the law of universal love: these are "the Law and the prophets" (Mt 7:12, 22:40). They convey the spirit of the Law of God, in other words. But taken at the letter only, obviously they are not simply convertible with God's revealed will; neither is any letter of the legal or prophetical books of the Old Testament, nor all of them put together. The God who once revealed himself in law and prophecy has now made himself known by a Son who is the stamp of his very being (Heb 1:1–3). Christ fulfills the Law not by transmitting another law to replace it but by revealing a vision of God at which the letter of the ancient law could only hint. Christ himself is the new law, and it is the life of Christ that the Christian must lead. Thus we see the meaning of the *righteousness exceeding that of the scribes and Pharisees:* not only quantitatively but also qualitatively the Christian must lead a life of obedience to God's will which surpasses the legal piety of the Old Testament.

Faithful to the Law, Jesus nevertheless taught that true fidelity to the Law as will of God sometimes entailed the disregard of the Law's letter; we have seen this borne out in the conflict stories of our preceding chapter. The lesson of his life is the exact opposite of legalism. The apostolic Church learnt this lesson well and found true precedents in Jesus' life and teaching when, with the guidance of the Spirit of God, it recognized that the Mosaic prescriptions were only a vanished shadow of a substance now possessed in Christ (cf. Col 2:16 f.).

Mt 5:21–26   Matthew proceeds to illustrate what is meant by a righteousness that exceeds that of the scribes and Pharisees by a series of six contrasts which have as their point of departure an enunciation of the Mosaic law. These will be correctly understood only when it is recognized that they do not attempt to pit one law against another; rather, they show how a sovereign and divine good once expressed in the Law—and expressed well, for that matter—must now be pursued in a personal dimension that escapes the confines of law. For the most part these contrasts are proper to Matthew, but one of them is paralleled by Luke and occasional verses are found elsewhere in the other Gospels.

You have heard. In the situation of Jesus' Sermon, those addressed would not be such as had read the Law themselves, but who had heard it read and taught in the synagogues. *It was said to the ancients:* thus it was revealed to the original recipients of the Law. *You shall not kill:* the contrast begins with a citation of one of the Ten Commandments (Ex 20:13; Deut 5:17), but equally important is the reference to *the judgment* that is to be exercised against those guilty of bloodshed (Ex 21:12; Deut 17:8). In banishing uncontrolled blood vengeance as the sanction against murder and substituting for it the judicial processes of civilized society, the Law of Moses was eminently the word of God for Israel. *But I say to you:* Jesus consciously sets forth his word as revelation, on the plane of what was "said" before. Not, however, to oppose revelation to revelation or to contradict the spirit of the Law: the rabbis, too, understood that hatred and contempt of one's fellow man were implicitly forbidden by this commandment. It is precisely the spirit of the Law—"the Law and the prophets" as we have defined it—that constitutes the way of life in the kingdom of God, rather than the letter of any law. Hence Jesus' teaching, though phrased in the juridic terms of the parallel which illustrates it, obviously has nothing to do with law in the accepted sense of the word: *judgment, the council* (the Sanhedrin), *gehenna* do not determine actual legal penalties for specific violations of law, but simply emphasize the malice of hatred which is every bit as bad as murder. Similarly, no "degrees" of malice are here being expressed in exclusive terms: *raca* (which means something like "blockhead") and *you fool* are random examples of the unwholesome kind of anger which is alien to the Christian spirit.

Two little parables have been joined to this pronouncement to underscore its positive implications. Both parables bring out the primacy of fraternal charity in the Christian life, though with somewhat different emphases. In the first place, reconciliation with one's neighbor is seen as the touchstone of one's good relations with God, which are signified by external worship but not replaced by it. Secondly, the time for reconciliation is now; there is an eschatological urgency to Christian charity, which on no account can be deferred. *You will not be released until you have paid:* this clause has nothing to do with regard to eschatological punishment but is a parabolic detail. The comparison is being drawn between the urgency of fraternal harmony and the practicality of settling a debt out of court rather than by awaiting the process of law, which according to the customs of the times included the possibility of a debtor's prison till the debt was paid. The Christian is being reminded of God's coming judgment, it is true, but nothing is implied concerning the nature of the judgment itself or its penalties.

Mt 5:27–30   The second contrast also begins with one of the commandments of the Decalogue, the prohibition of adultery (Ex 20:14; Deut 5:18). Though the letter of this law was originally concerned exclusively with the rights of possession and the stability of the family and of society which are jeopardized through adultery, the Jews knew that in keeping with its spirit lustful desires and intentions were also contrary to the will of God. Again it is in this spirit that Jesus roots his "new law." *He has already committed adultery with her in his heart:* in Semitic thought, the "heart" of man is man himself in his inmost being. Here, then, is wherein sin really consists. If sin is an act of alienation, it has already taken place when man has willed the alienation of himself from God or his fellows. "Am I my brother's keeper?" (Gen 4:9) gave verbal expression to a sin whose outward expression was the first murder.

Matthew quotes the Lord as employing two hyperbolic examples which dwell on the power of sin to destroy man and what man must do to avoid such a destruction at all costs. *If your right eye . . . your right hand,* if any part of man however noble and necessary, if any thing however precious, would lead him to sin, it must be ruthlessly cast aside rather than that the whole man should perish. Spiritual writers customarily cite this passage in warning against the "occasions" of sin, that is, objects that are not sinful in themselves but owing to circumstances can lead to sin.

In these and the preceding verses we find our first Gospel references to *gehenna.* Gehenna was originally the Hebrew *gê hinnom,* "the valley of (the sons of) Hinnom" to the south of Jerusalem, which doubtless derived its name from the tribe or clan which had inhabited it. It acquired an unsavory reputation owing to its use as a place of human sacrifice during the time of the kings (2 Kgs 23:10), and later it became a charnel and a refuse dump (Jer 7:32), a scene of fire and corruption. In Jewish literature and in the New Testament the name has been applied to the place of eternal perdition, the abode of the evil dead, thus "hell" as we now customarily use this English word.

Mt 5:31-32   Another prescription of the Mosaic law which marked its enlightened legislation as a blessing given to the Old Testament people of God was its regulation of divorce (Deut 24:1-4). Divorce itself was an institution taken for granted by the people of Israel in company with all others of their time, members of societies whose primary concern was for the survival of the race and the prerogatives of the males who perpetuated it and gave it their names. The same considerations justified polygamy and weighted the scales against a recognition of women's rights over against those of men. What the Law did was to insist that when a man decided to divorce his wife—there was, of course, no thought that a woman could divorce her husband!—he must *give her a certificate of divorce*. This was for her protection, lest she be later accused of adultery when she was married to another man. The dominant male, in other words, though his right to divorce went unquestioned, was not allowed to have it all his way. In some fashion the rights of woman and her dignity were being recognized. This was the spirit of the Law.

And it is this spirit that continues as the law of Christians. As we shall see elsewhere (on Mt 19:3-9 and parallels), in his teaching on marriage Jesus goes behind the letter of the Mosaic law and insists that it is the Creator's will that it be a monogamous and indissoluble union. The Old Testament had recognized this view of marriage as an ideal, but had never implemented it legally. Now a new voice of revelation makes the ideal a reality. Henceforth not merely an irregular divorce, but any divorce, will constitute a remarried woman an adulteress, for marriage is once and for all.

Matthew tempers the proclamation of the abolition of divorce with the well-known clause: *except in the case of immorality*. An equivalent clause appears in Matthew's version of the Lord's later *ex professo* pronouncement on marriage and divorce, and we shall see its meaning there.

Mt 5:33-37   The fourth contrast Jesus draws not merely with the letter of the Law requiring fidelity to oaths sworn in the name of God (cf. Ex 20:7; Lev 19:12; Num 30:3; Deut 5:11) but also with certain casuistic practices by which the spirit of the Law was violated. The Jews, out of reverence and to avoid taking the name of God "in vain," would customarily substitute various equivalent expressions for it: thus, habitually, "kingdom of heaven" rather than "kingdom of God" in Matthew's Gospel. A man would swear, then, *by heaven*, meaning by God, or *by Jerusalem*, the holy city, or even avoid sacred connotations altogether, swearing *by the earth* or by his own honor. Hence arose many fine legal distinctions concerning the relative value and obligation of oaths sworn in this or that way. Jesus rejects this casuistry. An oath is an oath; by whatever formula, the purpose of an oath is to call into witness the God of all truth who cannot be distinguished in any way.

The spirit of the Law was to honor the sacred character of the plighted word. This spirit should prevail in the kingdom of God, Jesus goes on to say, in a Christian speech that is its own guarantee. *Swear not at all:* this is not a divine law prohibiting legitimate authority from requiring oaths or forbidding Christians to satisfy its requirements; it is a call to a higher recognition of what the Old Testament had already sensed (cf. Sir 23:9–11), that oaths are at best a compromise with a sinful and disordered world, that in the society of man as willed by God they have no part to play. That is why Jesus says that beyond the Christian's simple "yes" or "no" (cf. Jas 5:12) *anything more than these comes from evil* (or, *from the evil one*): it acquiesces in a condition of human intercourse that has been made necessary by sin and evil.

Mt 5:38–42   *An eye for an eye and a tooth for a tooth* expresses the
Lk 6:29–30   so-called law of talion or exact compensation repeatedly
                stated in the Law of Moses (cf. Ex 21:24; Lev 24:20;
Deut 19:21). Apparently harsh in its positive formulation, it was in reality a law of mercy shared by all civilized peoples of antiquity. Its sense was *only* an eye for an eye, *only* a tooth for a tooth, thus insisting on the principle of strict justice in human affairs and excluding what would otherwise have been unrestricted private vengeance. It is by the law of talion, of course, that society is governed today, and indeed it would be difficult to imagine how it could be otherwise. Justice must be at the basis of every genuine law, and without law society cannot survive. Neither the Jews nor the modern state which governs by law, nor the Old Testament itself, for that matter, have interpreted talion as a perpetuation of literal eye-gouging or the knocking out of teeth. Talion merely insists on proportionate indemnification, proportionate and not disproportionate reciprocity under law.

And with this there can be no quarrel: it is doubtless as enlightened a legal principle as we shall ever have. Yet here precisely can it be seen perhaps best of all why the letter of even the very best of laws is a letter that kills. It kills because man cannot live by law alone, not even by the very best of laws. Man is well advised to obey the law, which is a lamp to his feet (Ps 119:105). But this does not give him life. What gives him life, and what makes meaningful his submission to law, cannot itself be formulated as law, even though, paradoxically, Paul can call it "the law of the Spirit of life in Christ Jesus" which has set him free from law (Rom 8:2), even though, as we have seen, Matthew can think of it as "the Law and the prophets" or simply "the Law."

Not to the judge or jury whose duty it is to vindicate the rights of the injured, but to the injured person himself, Jesus says, *do not resist the evil man.* The "evil man," in context, is the man who inflicts an evil upon another: whether he does so from evil or good intentions is immaterial to the situation. Jesus gives four examples to illustrate his meaning—a blow on the face, a lawsuit, guidance or carterage levied by the military police, even robbery or extortion—all of which add up to the same injunction: do not insist upon redress, upon your rights, but yield even beyond what may be demanded by circumstances. Luke parallels Matthew in recalling three of these examples from his version of the same Sermon; in his Gospel, however, which omits Matthew's lengthy development of the nature of Christian righteousness in relation to the Mosaic law, they appear as illustrations of the radical law of Christian love with which Matthew deals in his final contrast.

As the Lord's words are not laws in the accepted sense of the word, it is obvious that they lay down no absolute rules to govern Christian conduct in every conceivable case. The Christian must submit himself to the guidance of the Spirit and a rightly formed conscience, that he may be prepared to do the right thing at the right time. Love does not conflict with justice; it always satisfies justice even if it goes beyond its demands. But it should be insisted upon that Jesus' teaching is in no way the assertion of an unrealizable ideal, as though the ideal itself were its sole justification for being uttered. It is altogether practical, from the standpoint of human society itself. There are numerous contemporary evidences of this. If everyone were to insist at all times on an exact retribution for every injury, if violence were continually to be opposed to violence, the fruit would be endless enmity and hostility which would render the society of man impossible and choke off the growth of the human spirit. Love, however, is as contagious as hate. There must be, if an order of justice is ever to be established, the prophetic figure who takes the first step by foregoing his own rights to redress, who witnesses to the power of love over hatred and fear, who wins for society as a whole what he does not demand for himself. And if this is true for the human estate as such, it must be true above all for the Church whose mission it is to stand before the world as the prophetic figure of what God wills the world to be.

Mt 5:43–45   Matthew draws his final contrast between Law and
Lk 6:27–28, 31   law leading from the concept of love, which as we
                 have already noted is basic to what has been enunciated in the foregoing. *You shall love your neighbor* are the words of Lev 19:18. Nowhere in the Mosaic law, it is true, do we ever find anything like *you shall hate your enemy*. It might be thought, however, that by omission the Law had at least left itself open to such an interpretation through its silence on the question: who is my neighbor? (cf. Lk 10:25–37). Semitic thought expresses itself in black and white, not in greys, and it makes an easy semantic transition from "not love" or "less love" to "hate" (cf. Lk 14:26). Moreover, in context the "enemy" does not refer so much to personal as to official hostility, to the enemies of the

state and of religion, therefore, to the persecutors of the Church. Sentiments that a man might feel ashamed to acknowledge concerning another individual human being personally hostile to him, he often expresses even proudly when they can be directed against "the enemy" of his race, his nation, his religion—we do not have to go back to the Jews of the first Christian century to verify the truth of this. But as far as the contemporary scene of the Gospel is concerned, we may have an idea of what Jesus was talking about in certain of the Psalms whose language we find somewhat embarrassing in this respect (cf. Pss 58:7–12, 137:7–9, etc.). The Qumran sectaries acknowledged as an obligation correlative to the love of God and his friends, "to hate all the children of darkness, each according to the measure of his guilt, which God will ultimately requite."

The spirit of the law of love was to reverence the human dignity that is the creation of God, to recognize in every man the divine image (Gen 1:26 f.) and to find joy and peace in the one human family. The letter of the Mosaic law had expressed this spirit not only by enjoining love of one's fellow Israelite, but also, under certain conditions at least, love of the foreigner: this in an age when "foreigner" and "enemy" were often synonymous (in some languages the two words are the same). Now Jesus expresses this spirit in Christian terms. Love must be universal because God has now shown the family of his fatherhood, radically or potentially already present in the creation of mankind itself, restricted no longer to a particular people or nation but extended to its full potential in the Church. The Christian must love his fellow Christian for what he is, and he must love every other man for what he should be: for what, in God's intention, he already is as well.

That which is new about the Christian dimension of love is that it does not judge men by its concept of neighbor but rather adjusts its concept of neighbor to fit man. In this it is urged to find its example in God himself, *who makes his sun rise on the evil and the good* indifferently, *and rains on the righteous and the unrighteous.* It is not, obviously, that there is no difference between good and evil, or that the Christian is supposed to pretend to like evil things that are done to him. It is simply that such considerations are irrelevant to love, which must disregard them. That these considerations have a habit of getting in the way of love is to put the situation mildly. The Gospels have intentionally set the duty of Christian love within the context of its severest test and proof. In doing so they have left us in no doubt that it is a hard and demanding way of life having nothing to do with sentimentality or an ingenuous romanticism. One can easily persuade himself that he loves "mankind," which he has never encountered except as an abstraction of his mind. It is a different matter entirely to love a person who has made himself known in ways that are altogether unlovable.

Because the measure of love is man himself and not man's often un-

lovable ways, Luke has appropriately inserted here his version of the
Golden Rule that Matthew has put later in the Sermon (Mt 7:12).
The man we know best of all is the one who is our self. If in this sense
we make ourselves the norm of our conduct toward others, we shall be
following the way of love. Love shows itself above all in seeking the good
of the loved one. The good that we would have others to do for our self
that is known to us but perhaps hidden from them is the norm of what
we must do for these other selves which are often hidden from us by intent
or by circumstance.

Mt 5:46–48   The final words of the evangelists on the subject of
Lk 6:32–36   Christian love insist once again on its disinterestedness
               and universality. In love itself there is nothing extraor-
dinary. Everyone finds it easy to love his own, to reciprocate love: everyone, says Matthew, in words originally intended for Jews, *taxgatherers*
and *Gentiles* not excepted; Luke translates *sinners* as a "Gentile" equivalent. To love in this fashion is only natural, certainly, but it does not
transcend the capabilities of a sinful, imperfect world. It has no dynamic
power to advance the human spirit. To be *merciful* as God is merciful,
on the other hand, to be *kind to the ungrateful and the selfish*, is to rise
above the static condition of sinful man and to enter into the perfection
of God and his kingdom. It is to offer to man a vision of himself and his
worth as they are known and loved by God, who knows man as even man
cannot know himself.

9. TREASURE IN HEAVEN

Mt 6:1–4   As we begin the second part of the Sermon on the Mount we are still under Matthew's guidance. Just as Luke did not attempt anything like Matthew's detailed analysis of Christian righteousness in terms of its contrasts with the Law of Moses, neither has he any parallel to this next section in which Christian piety is outlined against the backdrop of certain contemporary Palestinian practices. As is immediately seen, whereas Matthew's previous chapter dealt with the spirit of Christianity as expressed in some of its guiding principles for life, this chapter begins by considering some of the specifically religious observances that also manifest its peculiar spirit. A general principle is first asserted, which is then illustrated by three examples.

The general principle is to *beware of practicing your religion before men in order to be seen by them.* What is understood here as "religion" is denoted by the same word ("justice" or "righteousness") which Matthew used above in relation to the total moral and social life of the Christian; here its application is to works done in the explicit name of religion. Obviously this principle does not contradict what was said in Mt 5:16. A truly Christian life is by its nature a public affair which men can and will see. The point made here, however, is that it must be a life lived for God, and for God in man, seeking the approval of God and not of man.

The first example that illustrates this principle has an easy application to religion as we know it today. To *give alms* is, literally, to "do mercy": as we have seen above (on Mt 5:3–12), "mercy" is one of those qualities in which man best achieves the end of religion, which is to become God-like. In this concrete and practical sense we take it for granted that "mercy" (*eleēmosynē*) and "charity" are pre-eminently works of religion; this is part of our Jewish heritage and does it honor. If, on the other hand, "eleemosynary" sometimes evokes an image of something less than disinterested and reciprocated kindness, if we tend to call Christian love by some word other than "charity" in order to avoid misunderstandings, it is partly because of what is being described in these Gospel verses. Man, who is incurably nominalist, sincerely believes that beautiful words ennoble his deeds. This we should carefully bear in mind. The *hypocrites* of these passages were not persons who consciously led double lives; they were, as they thought, devoutly religious people.

Having a trumpet blown in synagogues and streets probably is to be taken at the letter. Collections for the poor, which were efficiently organized in Jewish Palestine, were announced by the sounding of a trumpet. The temptations that this offered for conspicuous giving may be imagined when we consider that it was the equivalent of all that our modern organized charities can do to set forth the solid advantages of good-doing. *Let not your left hand know what your right hand is doing* is a graphic way of saying that almsgiving should be *in secret*. It is not, quite evidently, that a point should be made of secrecy, which is often, like the celebrity *incognito*, the surest way of attracting attention. Rather, it is one's motive that should be secret, hidden both from man and from oneself. Almsgiving should be for God and the sake of his poor, and neither to excite the admiration of others nor to induce a feeling of euphoria and self-satisafction.

Mt 6:5–8   The second example of pure religion has to do with prayer.
             If the conspicuous doing of good deeds is a perennial temptation offered to religion, conspicuous praying—and it is about conspicuous praying that these verses are concerned first of all—holds an even more obvious peril, where religion's interest is quite vested. The peril increases in proportion to the public rather than the personal character of the prayer, it seems. A man who would quite rightly be ashamed to pray openly merely to impress another human being with his godliness, nevertheless often feels compelled to make a public display of the prayer of the godly community with which he identifies himself. This is one aspect of what we have recently learnt to call triumphalism, which appears to be the manifestation of a basic insecurity in regard to spiritual realities, seeking reassurance about these by appeal to what the world recognizes as evidences of success. Jesus' contemporaries found occasion for their triumphalism in prayer where they found it for obvious almsgiving, *in synagogues and on street corners*. By the same token, Jesus was not condemning prayer in common any more than he was condemning alms or synagogues (cf. Mt 18:20). The *room* in which one prays to God *in secret* does not necessarily shut out others to pray to God in secret; it shuts out those whom we would have admire our piety.

Jesus also says that in prayer we must *not babble like the Gentiles*. The Greek verb found in this verse appears to have been coined by Matthew from an Aramaic expression meaning, roughly, "speak nothing at great length." Probably the Gentiles acquired a reputation for windy prayers with the Jews owing to the multiple names and attributions under which they invoked Deity. Jesus is also doubtless thinking of the lengthy pagan formulas to whose mechanical repetition a quasi-magical efficacy was often attached. However, his emphasis is on the quality of prayer rather than its quantity: *your Father knows what you need before you ask him.* The Christian who knows through Christ that God is his loving Father stands already in that serene relation to him that is prayer itself and that renders superfluous the elaborate honorifics which the pagans felt it necessary to bring to the objects of their worship.

At this appropriate place Matthew has introduced that ideal example of Christian prayer which is ascribed to the Lord himself and which has always been a feature of the Christian liturgy (Mt 6:9–15; Lk 11:1–4). This prayer, the Our Father, exists in a shorter form in Luke's Gospel, but in a different context, where it will be more convenient for us to examine it (see below, page 232 f.). Appropriate though its insertion may be at this point, it also interrupts the structural pattern into which Matthew has cast the Sermon on the Mount, which now sets forth the third and last of the Lord's examples of sincerity in religious practice.

Mt 6:16–18   Fasting, as we have seen (above on Mk 2:18–22 and parallels), was a religious observance taken for granted both by the Jews who first heard the Sermon on the Mount and by the Christian Church for which Matthew wrote his Gospel. Whereas in the earlier catechetical passage (placed later on, as it happens, by Matthew) the Gospel was concerned with the difference in meaning between specifically Jewish and specifically Christian fasting, here the purpose is, as above, to warn of the dangers to religious simplicity that lurk in any work for God that is performed under the eyes of men.

The fasting with which the first-century Church was acquainted was, externally at least, a complete and thoroughgoing act of penance. The oil which the Oriental considered so necessary to keep his head clean and fresh was laid aside. The hair was left uncombed and the face went unwashed. The feet were left bare against the cruelty of makeshift roads and paths. The whole man, in other words, was engaged in the fast—or so it would seem outwardly—and not just the control of his appetite. This, of course, was as it should be, provided that the whole man was so engaged inwardly as well. The occasions were all present, however, for the same conscious or unconscious hypocrisy which could vitiate almsgiving or prayer. Jesus does not reject the externals of fasting so much as he inculcates the motive with which they must be used, visible only to *your Father who sees in secret.* The Christian must not *go about looking dismal* for the edification of man, himself included. Though many religious people cannot be persuaded of this, such practices, which try to employ religion as a lever and a tool foreign to its avowed purpose, ultimately repel rather than attract; men can ordinarily discern very well what has been staged for their benefit and what they have merely been allowed to see.

Mt 6:19–21   From this point down to nearly the end of the Sermon on
                  the Mount, Matthew's arranging hand becomes particu-
larly evident. Almost every verse is paralleled elsewhere in the Gospels,
usually by Luke, but usually also not in the context of this Sermon. We
shall have to see most of the parallels in their own proper context and
content ourselves for the present with seeing to what ends Matthew has
disposed the material. Opinions differ as to how he intended the remaining outline of the Sermon to be read. The simple and seemingly satisfactory solution that is followed here is that in Mt 6:19–7:12 the evangelist has gathered together various sayings of the Lord to make up seven
pronouncements on the spirit with which the Christian should approach
this or that aspect of life. Needless to say, some of these concerns over-
lap and no attempt should be made to draw a hard and fast distinction
between them.

The first pronouncement, on true riches, follows easily from the preceding section on right motives. The man who has it as his single-minded
rule to please God rather than men will readily understand that it is
treasures in heaven that he must seek, that is, the good will and rewards
of God, rather than earthly riches. We are reminded, first of all, that
while the latter are fleeting, the former remain forever. *Moth and rust*
are not mere figures of speech as applied to worldly wealth: in the
world of the Gospel money was not counted in stock shares or banknotes
but in rich stuffs, metals, and the like. The important thing is, however,
that *where your treasure is, there your heart is also.* The principle is as
applicable to a pauper as to a millionaire. Even if a man dies poor, he
may have spent his life coveting what the world has to offer. There his
heart has been, and there it will remain for what it is worth to him.

Mt 6:22–23   The following two verses, which Luke interprets in quite
                  a different way (Lk 11:34f.), are somewhat perplexing
in their Matthaean context. Doubtless they were, or were built upon, a
popular parable of the time that was useful in various applications. It is, at
any rate, entirely Semitic in its inspiration.

The preceding verses spoke of the heart of man. Now we hear that *the
eye is the lamp of the body.* This seems to offer us a clue to the connection of thought intended by Matthew. Through the eye light is brought
into a man: thus the Semites thought of the process of seeing. *If the eye
is evil,* that is, if it is unsound, blind, or failing, then the light cannot
penetrate and the *whole body will be full of darkness.* A man's eye, then,
has much the same relevance here to his body—his person—as does his
heart. If it is fixed on God, the source of all light, then all will be as it
should be. If it is not, then what would normally be *light in you,* as coming through the eye, will in actuality be *great darkness.*

Mt 6:24   The theme of divided allegiance in man, or potentially di-
               vided allegiance, with heavenly and earthly riches suggested

as the souce of division, leads to the third pronouncement: *You cannot serve God and mammon.* The principle is illustrated by a parable, *no man can serve two masters,* whose truth, and its consequences, are immediately evident to anyone who has had to try to do so. (On the Semitic dichotomy "love" and "hate," see on Mt 5:43 above.) It is possible that Matthew presupposes the etymological meaning of mammon. This word, which in popular speech meant simply money or capital, appears to have been derived from the same root from which Hebrew took its words for "faith" and "trust" (compare the analogous development of "trust" in a financial sense in English). At any rate, as summing up all that can inspire confidence in this world, "mammon" admirably contradicts the God in whom the poor of the Gospel must place their trust.

Mt 6:25–34   The fourth pronouncement, an extended discourse on
Lk 12:22–31   trust in God, also follows quite naturally in this context. That Luke has reproduced elsewhere the same discourse differing in no point of substance shows that the two evangelists have made use of a common traditional catechesis. Though the Lucan context differs from Matthew's, the teaching of the discourse is so similar in the two Gospels that we can take the passages together.

As they appear in Matthew's Gospel these words are among the best known of the Sermon on the Mount; they are also among the most frequently misunderstood. On occasion they have been invoked to justify a quietistic waiting on divine providence, or, in more profane and prosaic terminology, shiftlessness. They have been praised, chiefly on account of the parables of the birds and the flowers of the field, as a kind of poetic idealization of a life that has never been and cannot be on this world, but which is beautiful to contemplate—from a distance. Above all, they have been most often quoted in indictment of a social or economic class by members of a conflicting and corresponding class which apparently believed they were written for its vindication. The discourse has nothing to do with any of this.

The first point to note about it is that it is addressed to everyman. *Food* and *clothing*: are there any goods of man more basic than these? Everyone sitting before Jesus as he taught, everyone who has subsequently read his words or heard them preached, has had these two concerns constantly in his mind throughout life. And it is of these that Jesus says *do not be anxious.* Not to be anxious is not to have no care. Not to be anxious is to care very much, but to care in measure and in faith. Has not God given the greatest gift, which is life itself? And if so, then may he not be trusted to provide what is necessary for life? The Gospel does not oppose prudent planning and discretion. What it rejects utterly is the kind of planning that dispenses with providence, the quest for a security that would make faith superfluous.

It is this principle that is illustrated by the parable of *the birds of the air* (Luke has *the ravens,* possibly in allusion to Ps 147:9). The point is not that the birds do no work but that they go about their daily rounds without anxiety for the morrow. What the birds do instinctively man should do of set purpose, if he truly believes that the God who cares for these least of his creatures cares even more for him whom he made in his image and likeness. Decent care is one thing, anxiety another. *Who by being anxious can add one measure to his lifespan?* Contrary to an impression carefully cultivated by propagandists of various kinds, no one can assure himself of even an additional moment of existence by eating and drinking the right things at the right time or by taking any amount of therapeutic precautions. These may all be helpful in their way, but their way does not afford a mastery over the life which is in the hands of God. The Christian life from beginning to end is, or ought to be, an act of faith in the Author of life. It is this faith that gives, or should give, a distinct dynamism to the life of the Christian, who begins works whose end he can never see, who often finds his Christian duty to lie precisely in the direction of what the world knows as folly.

The lilies of the field of which the second parable speaks are not the tall, stately flowers of classic beauty with which we are familiar. They are the tiny wild flowers and scarlet anemones that dot the hills and fields of Palestine in the spring, contributing to the land a gaudiness that explains the comparison to the robes of an Oriental monarch like Solomon. They have but a brief life in the thin soil, after which along with the other grasses they are *thrown into the oven* as fuel in lieu of wood, which is ordinarily scarce and precious. Their very transitoriness adds to the force of the example. If God is so solicitous for such things, how much more will he be for his children? The conclusion, then: live not as *Gentiles* ("the nations"; Luke, deferring to the Gentile origin of his readers, has *the nations of the world*), that is, in Jewish thought, those who have no belief in a personal God of providence, who think, or who act as though they think, that man has been put into the world simply to exist and survive, to feed, to sleep, to propagate, and to die. Live rather for God's kingdom, and trust him for what else is necessary. The Christian's day-by-day task, Matthew adds (vs. 34), is responsibility enough without worry over the future.

Mt 7:1–5   If the first four pronouncements of this series were fairly
Lk 6:37–42   logically connected, the final three appear to be rather disparate. They are bound together, however, and also tied to the preceding by their common concern over certain definite Christian attitudes. The first of them is paralleled by Luke in his version of the great Sermon, and here, interestingly enough and quite by exception, it is Luke rather than Matthew who has expanded the text by borrowing from other parts of the Gospel.

Judge not that you be not judged, says Matthew. Luke has it, *and you
will not be judged.* The variance seems to be slight, but when the two
are read in separate context it is seen to be more significant. There is a
finality, a once-for-all note in Matthew's text that is lacking in Luke's.
Judgment, says Matthew—and in his Gospel "judgment" almost invariably means the judgment of condemnation—is the prerogative of
God. Take from God this prerogative, and you call down upon yourself
God's judgment. It is as simple as that. Instructions of this kind were
especially relevant in the eschatologically minded community of primitive
Christianity.

Luke sees these words rather as part of the Lord's teaching on Christian
love, with positive as well as negative implications. The *measure* of the
forgiving disposition one manifests toward others is the measure by which
one asks to be forgiven by God—except that God, who gives without
measure (cf. Jn 3:34), will recompense such a man far beyond his deserts.
Luke compares God, or those whom God uses as the instruments of his
beneficence, to a generous, honest merchant who pours out without stint
the grains he sells in the market place.

Luke also introduces two parables (used otherwise by Matthew, the
second by John as well) to lead into the second lesson of this passage,
which deals with the judgment of others that often masquerades as
fraternal correction. *Can a blind man lead a blind man?* He can, of
course, but with obviously disastrous results. Anyone who has been witness
to the casual ways of the Palestinian in respect to unfenced cisterns, wells,
quarries, and, nowadays, excavations in the middle of concrete footpaths,
will know what the Gospel is talking about. *No disciple is above his
teacher:* no one can teach more than he knows, and thus his student
when fully taught will be like his teacher at best. All this is to say what
the Lord's proverb quoted by both Matthew and Luke puts so graphically:
before setting oneself up as an example to others, judging and correcting
them, one must set his own house in order. Otherwise such correction is
only presumption and hypocrisy. With typical Oriental hyperbole the
proverb pictures the hypocrite of this kind offering to remove a splinter
from his neighbor's eye while his view is blocked by a whole log of wood
lodged in his own eye.

In Matthew's purview of wholly negative judgment, the injunction to
cast the log from your own eye is doubtless ironical. No man will ever be
in a position to judge his fellow as Matthew understands judgment without condemning himself once and for all. Luke, in his context of fraternal
charity, does envision a judgment that works to the benefit of the neighbor. He does not mean, of course, that correction can be given only by
the perfect. For Luke the log that must be cast from the eye is the evil
to which a man is blind, or which he excuses in himself while condemning
it in others. It is this that constitutes his judgment hypocrisy.

Mt 7:6   The connection which Matthew intended this present verse to
              have with the preceding or the following context is not too
clear. Was he thinking of judgment here as Luke does, that is, in terms
of fraternal correction, and applying the Lord's saying to the situation in
the sense of Prov 9:7: "He who corrects an arrogant man earns insult"?
Verbally, the saying means that holy things should not be exposed to
the contempt or the disinterest of those who will not or cannot properly
appreciate them. It is probably a proverb reflecting Jewish usage, in
which *dogs* and *pigs* signified Gentiles. (Not necessarily intended as an
evaluative judgment; it was simply that, like the Gentiles, dogs and pigs
were ritually "unclean" according to the Law of Moses.) The first- or
second-century Christian writing known as the Didache cited these words
of Jesus as requiring the withholding of the Eucharist from the unbap-
tized. We understand them rightly, too, when we recognize that unbelievers have a right not to be annoyed by the public display of what may
be quite sacred to us and equally meaningless to them.

Mt 7:7–11   Appropriately enough, Matthew concludes his series of
Lk 11:9–13   seven pronouncements with these words on the power
                  of Christian prayer. Luke has the same passage almost
verbatim with this, but in an entirely different context where it is attached to a parable which he alone relates. Since the context hardly
affects interpretation in this case, we can take the two Gospel pericopes
together.

The theme of the efficacy of prayer is common in the Gospels. Prayer
will be answered, says the Lord, not simply because it is persistent,
though his exhortation is to perseverance in prayer, but because God is
our *heavenly Father*. He is this, of course, because we have been
constituted his children through Christ. By the same token, we have no
right to expect an answer to our prayer if we are not living as his children,
for in such a condition we are refusing to acknowledge his fatherhood.
There is, therefore, no automatic or guaranteed prayer on which we can
depend apart from the grace of Christ. Our Christian life must be our
prayer.

The passage uses several parables to illustrate a fortiori the confidence
that may be reposed in God's willingness to answer prayer. Who, if his
son calls to him for something to eat, will give the child instead a useless
or harmful thing—a stone in place of bread, a viper instead of a fish? No
true father would do such a thing. If human beings, then, sinful as they
are, act thus toward those whom they love, how much more will the good
God *give what is good to those who keep asking him.*

Luke also asks, what father would give his child a scorpion in place of
an egg? The parallel is somewhat curious: while there is some superficial
resemblance between a stone and the flat, round loaves of the Near East,

and between some snakes and some fishes, there seems to be none between an egg and a scorpion. Probably all these examples were taken from contemporary proverbs. Luke's other variant is rather more important: *the heavenly Father will give Holy Spirit to those who keep asking him*. He has taken occasion to emphasize the most precious of God's gifts to his children, the motive and end of all the rest.

Mt 7:12   It is at this point, less appropriate perhaps than that chosen by Luke (above Lk 6:31), that Matthew has quoted the teaching of the Lord that we know familiarly as the Golden Rule. He has placed it here, it seems, because he sees in it a summation of all that has gone before—thus he calls it *the Law and the prophets* (see above on Mt 5:17-20)—and in Matthew's mind the instructional part of the Sermon on the Mount is now being brought to a conclusion. What will follow this, to end the Sermon, is a series of four combined exhortations-warnings which invite the Christian to recognize the seriousness of his commitment to Christ's message.

The Golden Rule has precedents in the Old Testament (cf. Tob 4:15) and in Jewish teaching before Christ. The formulation of the great Rabbi Hillel (about 20 B.C.) is most famous: "Do to no one else what is displeasing to you; this is the whole Law, and everything else is commentary." The Jewish examples are negative in expression whereas Jesus' pronouncement is positive. It has sometimes been objected that the very positive character of the Golden Rule turns it into an idealism that is unworkable in practice. Others, quite to the contrary, have protested at its lack of idealism since it invites a man to use himself as a norm of moral conduct. To deal with the second objection first, we should observe that the Golden Rule requires that we do to others as we would *want* them to do to us, not as we necessarily expect it to be done or as it has been or is being done. The self, therefore, is the norm of no one's conduct except one's own, and that only to the extent that it is the norm of the human condition—the only norm, as it happens, that is valid for every man. It is in this sense that charity begins at home (see above on Mt 5:43-45 and parallel). As for the rest of it, it is true enough that the Golden Rule can easily come into conflict with the enlightened self-interest that is the dictate of the natural law. The law of Jesus frankly demands a standard of conduct that transcends what may be normally expected of man because it is addressed to man as possessing the more than normal fullness of life which is the gift of the Spirit of God. That man can and does possess this life and live in accordance with it has been proved by the example of countless Christians. That not all Christians live to its fullness the life that has been given to them, that even the majority does not, is a statistical fact that cannot be denied.

Mt 7:13–14   Terminating the Sermon on the Mount, Matthew lists four exhortations of the Lord which offer some kind of commentary on what we have just been discussing. If Christians are not invariably what their calling professes them to be, this may be laid to their not having heeded Jesus' warnings implicit in these final statements on the kingdom of God.

The doctrine of "the two ways" is ancient in religious thought; it is found in the Old Testament (e.g., in Ps 1), at Qumran, frequently in the New Testament and with other early Christian writers, and in various pagan religions as well. As expressed here in Jesus' words Matthew has applied it to the teaching of the Sermon on the Mount; later on we shall see Luke employing it in a quite different context (see on Lk 13:22–25). Here its purpose is to insist on the great difficulty of the Christian way in contrast to the way which man is more naturally disposed to take. It is a way that one must *seek in order to enter*: to find it he will do well to rely on no help of man but follow Jesus only.

The passage is a parable and must be interpreted as such. The narrow gates of a city were little used, while the larger ones would naturally attract the greater traffic. In the same way, a narrow lane is not as well traveled as are the main highways. This is the basis of the comparison which Jesus intends: one way is enticing, the other is not. There is no judgment passed on how many do, in fact, find *the gate that leads to life* and how many do not. Neither are we told how many continue on *the rough road* once they have found it.

Mt 7:15–20   The second exhortation is a warning against *false prophets*. There would seem to be no doubt that by *wolves in sheep's clothing* Matthew understands false teachers within the Church itself. As the New Testament makes very plain, heresy has plagued the Church from the very beginning. The malice of heresy is not that it manifests an independence of mind—independence of mind may or may not be admirable depending on a variety of circumstances—but that it peddles falsely as the word of God precisely that from which the word of God has come to save us: the hopelessness and inadequacy of the unregenerate human condition. Like the false prophets of the Old Testament who prophesied the thoughts of their own hearts rather than God's (cf. Ezek 13:2), the false teacher may have honestly confused his own imaginings with the will of God. His sincerity, however, does not make his doctrine the less pernicious.

By their fruits you will know them. Matthew applies the parable of the fruit trees (see above on Mt 3:7–10 and parallel) as a test of prophecy. Some of the worst heresies—Gnosticism, Jansenism, Quietism, for example—have been proposed as superior kinds of Christianity. They were rightly judged not by their claims but by their effects, which were to distort the image of God in human lives, to substitute pride for piety, and to make Christian charity the bond of a sect. Other heresies would distort Christianity in other directions, converting the Gospel into a pious Stoicism, equating it with bourgeois respectability, with tribalism, with the good life, or any number of alien philosophies. Jesus' words are addressed to every Christian, who must have a sound eye and ear for the Gospel and be able to detect false notes and discern bad fruits from good. These he acquires in a true and prayerful life of the Spirit in which he knows God. Relatively few false prophets will ever be formally condemned by the Church as heretics. The purity of the Gospel is every Christian's responsibility.

Lk 6:43–45 Luke has used this same parable, also as part of the conclusion of his version of the Sermon, but his application of it is quite different. In his Gospel the parable is a continuation of the teaching on true fraternal correction (see on Lk 6:37–42 above), and therefore offers the would-be judge of others a criterion by which he may gauge his worthiness to act as reformer. In the same spirit he adds (vs. 45) a saying on the necessity of making *the mouth* (what a man says) agree with *the heart* (what a man is). Matthew has this same combination of sayings in a later and different context (see below on Mt 12:33–37).

Mt 7:21–23 It is easy to see how the following verses in Matthew's
Lk 6:46 Gospel relate to what has just gone before. If the Christian must be on his guard against false prophets, there is an even more insidious enemy that may be lurking within his own person. It is so easy to deceive oneself with good intentions and brave words. The Lord whose name may come so readily to our lips will never be deceived, however. Matthew puts this saying in the context of eschatological judgment, and there is a chilling finality to the words *I never knew you*. It is not merely that faith must be proved by good works; what gives the appearance of being such works can also be illusory. Paul speaks of a faith such as can remove mountains, yet leave its possessor as nothing in the sight of God (1 Cor 13:2). The only works that count for a man are the works that come from his heart, that show what he truly is as a Christian: this is what it is to do *the will of my Father*. A man may have worked miracles in Christ's name and have been the instrument of grace for many others. But he may have been only a channel for a divine power that has never touched him personally. Only through the opening of his own heart will God's grace have flowed into his own life to bring forth the good fruits that mark him as a true Christian.

Luke begins his peroration on the Sermon with a verse that is substantially in the words and spirit of Mt 7:21. He has a parallel to the remainder of Matthew's text in a later, also eschatological, context (cf. Lk 13:26 f.).

Mt 7:24–27 Both Matthew and Luke conclude the Sermon on the
Lk 6:47–49 Mount with the Lord's parable of "the two houses." It is
interesting to see how each has made use of it. Matthew contrasts the *house built on rock* with that constructed *on sandy ground.* This version presupposes the simple conditions of Palestinian living. It was and is vital to the Palestinian peasant that he set up his dwelling near the precious water supplies, such as are the wadies, the water courses which for most of the year are only trickling streams or dry sandy soil. The temptation is to build on the level wady bed rather than to seek the higher rocky ground. In the rainy season, however, the wadies can become torrents within a moment; even seasoned travelers in the Near East have been overtaken by disaster in these flash floods. Luke has cast the parable in a less regional setting, drawing the contrast between houses provided and unprovided with deep, firm foundations.

The meaning of the parable, in any case, is not too difficult to see. It is easy enough to hear the Lord's words and to admire them: even unbelievers frequently do this. It is another thing to take them into our hearts and make them part of our lives. But if we do not do so, we deserve to be compared with the foolish builder of the parable. Unlike the unbelievers, we have committed ourselves to these words and we shall be judged by them. What should have been for us the source of life, therefore, can easily become the occasion of our destruction. As one commentator on Luke has put it: "The audience are left with the crash of the unreal disciple's house sounding in their ears."

Mt 7:28–29 Matthew concludes the Sermon on the Mount with a
formulaic statement which he repeats almost identically when ending each of the five major discourses which determine the outline of his Gospel (cf. Mt 11:1, 13:53, 19:1, 26:1). In turn, this formula is reminiscent of that used to terminate the discourses of Moses in the Book of Deuteronomy (cf. 31:1). In this instance the evangelist has fittingly incorporated into his summary statement the words used earlier by Mark in connection with Jesus' teaching in the synagogues, concerning the contrast remarked by the people in comparing it with the ordinary teaching of their rabbis (see above on Mk 1:22 and Lk 4:32).

10. PARABLES OF THE KINGDOM

Lk 7:1–10 Both Luke and Matthew follow the Sermon on the Mount
Mt 8:5–13 with the story of a healing in Capernaum (Matthew, however, having prefaced to it another healing story which we
have already seen on page 105 when dealing with Mk 1:40–45 and its
parallels). From now on, as will soon be made evident, Matthew and
Luke tend to draw wider and wider apart in the separate use they have
made of the Gospel material they share supplementary to Mark. For a
variety of reasons we have chosen usually to follow Luke's order rather
than Matthew's, but we shall also try to remind ourselves as we go along
of what distinct purposes Matthew had in mind in his ordering of events.
Just as the Sermon on the Mount, the first of the great discourses, was in
some measure prepared for by the narrative of Mt 1–4, the text of Mt 8–9
leads into the missionary discourse of Mt 10: in these chapters Matthew
thinks of Jesus as exemplifying in his words and deeds the spirit of the
instruction he will give to his disciples in the second discourse. In like
manner, Mt 11–12, some of which we have already seen paralleling the
conflict stories of Mark and Luke, are the introduction to the parables of
Mt 13, which Matthew has constituted the third of the Lord's discourses
by which he seeks to explore the mystery of faith and unbelief. Luke's
order does not, in this respect, have these complications. Basically he has
followed and will continue to follow Mark's story of the Galilean ministry,
though for the moment he is drawing on a source that was not used by the
Second Gospel.

As we have noted above (on Jn 4:46–54), the story that we find before
us in all likelihood goes back to the same event that gave rise to the somewhat different story found in the Fourth Gospel. It is not at all difficult to
understand why the story in its present form should have had great appeal
for Matthew and Luke. The man who figures most prominently in the
episode is a Gentile; not only that, but of him the Lord said *I have found
no Israelite with faith like this!* It was to precedents like this that the
Gentile churches of Matthew and Luke could appeal when they set the
events of Jesus' life in relation to the existing Christian condition. Though
in his earthly ministry Christ had confined his preaching to the people of

Israel, there was inherent in his proclamation a concept of universal salvation that made the post-resurrection mission of the Church to the Gentiles a logical development divinely willed. Matthew would go even further than this (cf. vss. 11 f.); in his view the Church signifies not only that the privileges of Israel have been extended to the Gentiles, but that a new elect people has replaced the old (cf. Mt 21:43).

There remain some differences in the story as it appears in Matthew and in Luke. Both Gospels speak of the man as *a centurion*, not, presumably, as the commander of a hundred men within a Roman legion, but as an officer in the service of Herod Antipas, who doubtless organized his civil and military forces on the Roman pattern. In Luke's account the centurion never speaks to Jesus directly but only through emissaries, first a group of the Jewish city-fathers, then some of his own friends. This doubtless tells us something of the man's character and also his status. The Jews say that *he loves our nation and he built our synagogue for us*. Probably, therefore, he was not a proselyte, a convert to Judaism, but like many of his contemporaries a good pagan who felt drawn to the Jews through similar convictions about the nature of God and the moral law. Luke takes for granted that the centurion's solicitude was over one of his slaves (*doulos*), which in itself was somewhat extraordinary. From Matthew we might gather that it was the centurion's son who was ill (*pais*= boy but also servant; Luke has *pais* in vs. 7).

According to the usual interpretation of the Law, a Jew would become legally unclean from association with a Gentile in his home. The Jewish elders were apparently disturbed by no scruples in this regard, nor was Jesus, but the centurion shows extreme delicacy, professing himself *not worthy* that Jesus should come to his house. Such delicacy, in turn, accompanies a faith in Jesus' serene *authority* which requires no bodily presence to work its will. It is this quality of faith that earns Jesus' accolade.

Lk 7:11–17   Matthew continues the preceding story with two passages concerning Jesus' works of healing which we have already seen above in other contexts. Luke's sequel is this story of the raising to life of a widow's son, another wonder which Jesus performs merely by his word. This is the first Gospel passage we have encountered which actually describes the restoration of life to a dead person, and it is given to us by Luke only; however, all four Gospels contain similar stories and the fact itself was taken for granted by the New Testament and the rest of early Christianity. It is not by chance that in this account Luke for the first time calls Jesus *the Lord*, the name by which the apostolic Church acknowledged Christ as divine Savior, the conqueror of death and giver of life (cf. Phil 2:9 f.).

Nain (Hebrew *na'im*, fair; modern Arabic *nēn*) is today a rather squalid Muslim village of some two hundred souls, in the plains near Nazareth. It is possible that it may have been a larger town in New Testament times:

the site has never been excavated archaeologically. By established custom burials took place outside the town walls; thus Jesus, *his disciples,* and the *great crowd with him* met this funeral cortege just as it was passing out through the town gate on the way to the burial ground. Luke's story contains a large number of incidental details that point to the human interest he found in this event. Most important to him, however, is its prophetic significance: *God has visited his people* (cf. Lk 1:68). *He gave him to his mother* evokes the memory of the great prophets Elijah and Elisha (cf. 1 Kgs 17:23; 2 Kgs 4:36) to whom similar wonders were ascribed in this Galilean region. Hence the acclaim of the people: A *great prophet has risen among us!*

Lk 7:18–23   Luke takes occasion from the widespread attention which
Mt 11:2–6   Jesus had attracted through works like the one just de-
                  scribed (vs. 17) to introduce the story of the Baptist's query which he shares with Matthew. Though Matthew has placed his briefer version of the story elsewhere in his Gospel, the context is really much the same: *John in prison heard about Jesus' works.* Luke has already mentioned the Baptist's imprisonment (Lk 3:20); Matthew, who will explain the circumstances later (Mt 14:3 ff.), previously said only that John had been arrested (Mt 4:12). That the Baptist, though in prison, could maintain contact with the outside world and send messages through his disciples is in keeping with what we are otherwise told in the New Testament about the normal conditions of imprisonment.

There can hardly be any doubt that both Matthew and Luke believed that the Baptist had already designated Jesus as the awaited Messiah (see above on Lk 3:21–22 and parallels). Nevertheless, it seems to be evident enough that the Baptist here was asking a real question, and on his own behalf: *Are you he who comes*—the Messiah—*or shall we look for someone else?* If the question is somewhat puzzling, Jesus' answer appears to be more so. It was the works of Jesus which occasioned the question in the first place, yet it is only to the works that Jesus points (with the implied reference to messianic texts like Is 26:19, 29:18 f., 35:5 f., and especially 61:1: the Servant of the Lord) by way of reply, telling the disciples to *tell John what you hear and see.* What are we to make of all this?

Seemingly we are confronted again by the disparity of Jewish and Christian thought concerning messianism. The Baptist believed Jesus to be the Messiah: his works proved that he was. But this being the case, why was he, John, languishing in prison while tyrants like Antipas still lived in security? When would the messianic kingdom be inaugurated as it should, in a burst of power and with the terrible might of the wrath of God, crushing all opposition and establishing right for ever? The Baptist's question, then, came to this: Since you are the Messiah, why are you not acting like the Messiah?

To such a question Jesus could reply only as he did. The signs of the messianic era which the Baptist has recognized are not a prelude to something else that is to come: they are a proclamation of the kingdom as it is, a kingdom which triumphs not by crushing its opposition but by submitting to it, a kingdom whose principal figure is one who is Servant of all. Though John the Baptist does not yet realize this, he himself has already begun the final course of a life which, like Jesus' own, will be a testimony to the kingdom as it really is. Faith in Jesus' word alone can extract meaning from such a life. Therefore, *blessed is he who is not scandalized in me.*

Lk 7:24–35   Both Luke and Matthew continue the preceding episode
Mt 11:7–19   with the testimony of Jesus to the Baptist. It is quite
                 evident that for this testimony they have depended upon
a traditional source elaborated in the apostolic Church; however, there is every reason to suppose that it goes back to an authentic setting in the life of Jesus, who must have been called upon more than once to declare himself in relation to the Baptist.

Jesus offers his testimony by asking the crowds to offer their own: it is their testimony which he accepts. Why had they sought John out? Because he was just like any other weak and fickle human being, *a reed shaken by the wind?* Obviously not. Because he was *someone luxuriously clad:* pre-eminent among men according to the standards by which the world recognizes pre-eminence? Hardly; such people were rather those who were now persecuting the Baptist. A *prophet,* then? *Yes, and more than a prophet!* Here in Matthew and Luke are cited the words of Ex 23:20 and Mal 3:1 which in Mk 1:2 were joined to the Isaian passage which all the evangelists use to identify the Baptist in his relation to Jesus and his kingdom (see above on Lk 3:3–6 and parallels). It is this, in fact, that finally determines the greatness of the Baptist: he is the greatest of the prophets, and no man is greater than he, because of his immediate proximity to the kingdom which he announced. By the same token, *the least in the kingdom is greater than he.* This is stated not to disparage the person of the Baptist but to further define his position in the history of salvation. *All the prophets and the Law delivered their message until John:* the Baptist is the last of a most distinguished prophetic line, but he remains within that line. As a child of grace, John of course shares in the New Testament just as did all the other holy people of the Old Testament; but he has not been destined to take an active part in the kingdom which he prophesied. His glory, says Matthew, is to have been *Elijah* the precursor (again see on Lk 3:3–6 and parallels). Luke omits this reference, since immediately before he has represented Elijah as a type not of the Baptist but of Jesus himself (see above on Lk 7:11–17).

It is probably best to take verse 12 in Matthew's text as a parenthetical remark suggested to the evangelist because of its topical connection with

John and the kingdom. Much the same words appear elsewhere in Lk 16:16, but probably in a quite different sense. Matthew seems to be alluding here to real violence directed against the kingdom since the time of the Baptist: either persecutions directed against the Church, or Jewish attempts to establish a political kingdom by military force in Roman Palestine, or something similar. The meaning is far from clear.

Luke also encloses a parenthetical remark in verses 29 f. All the Gospels make the point from time to time that while the religious and political leadership of the people tended to be lukewarm or actively hostile toward both Jesus and the Baptist, the people as such were disposed to receive them.

Yet in the long run the leadership won out, as it has a way of doing, just as popular enthusiasm has a way of waning. Jesus came unto his own and his own did not receive him, as he knew they would not. The parable with which the two evangelists conclude this passage does not deal with the rejection of Jesus by the Jews as an issue of polemics—it is really incidental that *this generation* happened to be Jews. The parable is the story of everyman to the extent that he remains a part of this generation, a child of this world which blinds itself to the light of the word when the word will not conform to its tastes. This generation, says the Lord, is like wayward children who demand that everyone adjust to their mood of the moment. John the Baptist came among them leading an austere life and preaching repentance: they would have none of this. *He has a demon:* he is a fanatic! Jesus, on the contrary, though closely associated with the Baptist, exercised perforce a quite different kind of ministry, living not in solitude but in normal fashion among normal people, seeking out those who needed him the most. What laxity! Living in pleasure and with low company!

Wisdom is vindicated by her works, says Matthew. The wisdom of God's word (cf. 1 Cor 1:21) as manifested in the Baptist and in Jesus, cannot be, as this generation would have it, at one and the same time too narrow and too free. It is the world that is wrong, not wisdom. Had the world been able to read the signs of the times (cf. Lk 12:54–56), it would have seen the meaning both of the Baptist's penitential preaching and the joyous proclamation of Jesus. *Wisdom is vindicated by all who are her children,* says Luke. The faithful few who know how to discern wisdom in what is foolishness to men are wisdom's children (cf. 1 Cor 1:22–25).

Lk 7:36–50   Matthew continues in his Gospel with Jesus' lament over the cities of Galilee, a passage which fits in very well in this context of faith and unbelief, which however we shall see later on (see below on Lk 10:13–16). Luke gives us in this place a story reported only by him, doubtless intended to illustrate the way in which God's wisdom can find its children in quite unlikely places.

The scene which Luke describes is very similar to a later one set in relation to the narrative of Jesus' passion and death by both John and the Synoptic Gospels (Mt 26:6–13; Mk 14:3–9; Jn 12:1–8); so similar is it, in fact, that Luke, who as we know avoids even apparent repetitions, has omitted the second episode in telling his Gospel. The two stories are quite distinct, however, with different principals and different purposes in different locales. Because of their fundamental resemblance—the action of a woman concerning our Lord at a banquet—it appears that in oral transmission details from the two stories have become intermingled, with the result that they are now even more similar than they originally were. The name "Simon," for example, which appears quite unheralded in verse 40, has doubtless been borrowed from the second event, which according to Matthew and Mark took place in the house of "Simon the leper." The anointing of Jesus, too, which in the present story is something of an anomaly, may be an intrusion from the later setting in which an anointing is the whole point of the account. As will be seen, the influence has been reciprocal, and some of the particulars of the other story as it now appears in the Gospels undoubtedly owe their origin to this tradition preserved by Luke.

It is not entirely clear why *one of the Pharisees asked* Jesus *to eat with him*. Possibly he had been included in a general invitation to a banquet, for curiosity's sake; while the Pharisee does not appear to have been particularly hostile toward Jesus, neither did he treat him as an honored guest. *There was a certain woman in the city, a sinner*: the meaning is that she was a notorious sinner, doubtless a prostitute. She had recently repented, as the story will show, but either this was as yet unknown or, as so often happens, her life had already acquired for her a permanent reputation as far as respectable society was concerned. Undoubtedly she was an intruder in the house, but as we have already seen Palestinian gatherings were semi-private at best. Learning that Jesus was present at the meal, *she stood behind him at his feet*. The Jews of Palestine often adopted the Roman custom in taking food: reclining on mats surrounding a low table (one side of which was kept free for the waiters), leaning on the left arm and eating with the right hand. Thus a person's feet would be behind him; the sandals were also removed at meals.

It is likely enough that the woman came with nothing more definite in mind than to see Jesus, to be close to him. Overcome with emotion, however, she kneels at his feet, weeping. Her tears fall upon his feet and, in the most natural way possible, she looses her hair and uses it to blot away her tears. As we suggested above, the detail of the ointment and her anointing of Jesus' feet are best explained as intrusions from another story. Anointing the head was customary (see vs. 46), but there was no purpose or precedent for anointing the feet. The Pharisee, in any case, was scandalized at this public display and contemptuous of Jesus for permitting himself to be made the object of it by such a person.

The lesson of the Lord's parable, quite plainly, is: he who is forgiven much, loves much, while *he who is forgiven little, loves little.* He contrasts the mean spirit shown by the Pharisee in his minimal hospitality with the exuberant manifestation of the woman's love. The Pharisee had little love in his make-up because he was not conscious of having been loved; he had not experienced the incredible mercy of God's forgiveness because he did not know that he had done much to need forgiveness. The woman knew all that the Pharisee did not. She had repented of her evil life, doubtless as the result of Jesus' preaching. Her faith had saved her (vs. 50). Aware of the divine love that had been shown her, she loved much in return. It was *because of this,* Jesus said, *because she has loved much,* that he can confirm with all authority that *her sins, many as they are, have been forgiven her.* The parable has a great deal to tell us about the nature of love as Jesus understood it.

Lk 8:1–3   Having related one woman's story which obviously meant much to him, Luke now mentions several other women who, like this woman, had been the beneficiaries of Jesus' healing ministry. It is one of Luke's engaging qualities that he has striven to give women their proper place of prominence in his Gospel set in the man's world of Palestinian Judaism. This apparently summary statement that Luke has given us is actually of some importance in explaining how Jesus and his little band of disciples were maintained in their preaching activity through the support of several well-to-do women. *Mary* was *called Magdalene* presumably because she was a native of Magdala on the west shore of the Sea of Galilee; this city is today only a ruin. Luke introduces her here apparently for the first time, and there is no reason to suppose that she was the unnamed woman of the preceding episode, though popular tradition has made this association. There is no reason, as a matter of fact, to think that the Magdalene had ever been a notorious sinner: *from whom seven demons had gone out* need be nothing more than the Gospel's way of saying that she had suffered from some extraordinary mental or physical illness. We know nothing further about *Joanna, the wife of Chuza, Herod's steward.* Chuza could have been in either the civil service or the private employ of Antipas. Neither do we have any further information about the *Susanna* whom Luke mentions, though he speaks of her as someone with whom his readers would be presumed to be familiar.

Mk 3:20–21   After our lengthy excursion into the Gospel story that is proper to Matthew and Luke we now return to the story of the Galilean ministry as it was disposed by Mark. This present little section has the distinction of being one of the very few Marcan passages that have been utilized neither by Matthew nor by Luke. The reason that they have omitted it seems to be quite evident: despite its brevity, it raises more questions than it offers explanations, and the two later evangelists did not want to bother with its problems.

Mark says, not in connection with any specific context (having just given his list of the Twelve), that Jesus *came home:* Capernaum is doubtless meant. As before, the news is quickly spread abroad and almost immediately an enthusiastic crowd has gathered about the door of the house, jostling, questioning, and merely getting in the way of Jesus and his disciples, *so that they were not even able to get a bite to eat. Hearing of this,* we are told, *his own people went out.* Who are "his own people" (literally *hoi par' autou*=those on his side)? It is generally taken for granted that they were the close relatives of Jesus who appear in the next passage that we shall consider (Mk 3:31–35 and parallels). This assumption is probably quite correct; it should be observed, however, that it is not entirely certain, for the expression can mean other things. They went out, the text says, *to take charge of him.* Or should it be read, to take charge of *it,* that is, of the crowd? Either reading is possible from the Greek. Assuming, again, that Jesus is meant, the sense seems to be that his relatives, disturbed by the notoriety which he was attracting to himself and doubtless out of sympathy with it (cf. Jn 7:5), were resolved to draw him back into the family seclusion: he was becoming an embarrassment to them. *For they said* [or, "it was being said"?], *"He is out of his mind"* [preferable to "it"=the crowd again, which could have been out of "its" mind]. The allegation is not of insanity, precisely, but of fanaticism, lack of balance.

The function that Mark intended this somewhat obscure passage to serve in his Gospel is itself not too clear. Presumably he intended it to parallel what he has immediately following: the incredulity of Jesus' own family more than matched by the malicious charges of the scribes. At any rate, there is no sequel, and we hear no more about what Jesus' "own people" did or intended to do. The encounter with the scribes we shall see later on in a better context.

Mk 3:31–35   It is probable that Mark associated *the brothers* of Jesus
Mt 12:46–50   who appear in this next passage with "his own people"
Lk 8:19–21   of the preceding. Both he and Matthew have put the
                 story immediately before the "day of parables" in
which the Lord speaks at length on the mystery of the kingdom of God; Luke has put it immediately after. The situation is not incidental: Jesus' doctrine of a kingdom that takes precedence over every earthly tie (cf. Mt 8:21 f., 10:37) is being illustrated in his own life.

Jesus' teaching is perfectly straightforward and clear. He has come to establish a family of faith (cf. Rom 8:29), and they make up this family who *do the will of God* as he does it. This is a common New Testament teaching (cf. Jn 15:14); from the Pauline epistles and the Acts of the Apostles we know that "brother" was the customary title by which the early Christians recognized one another, a usage which continued an Old Testament precedent. Neither Jesus nor the early Christians thereby minimized natural relationships (even though Luke has considerably toned down Jesus' "rejection" of his family in this passage for fear that it might be misunderstood); it was merely a question of establishing priorities.

Who were those whom this Gospel story names the brothers and sisters of Jesus? For insisting that they were cousins or at any rate something other than uterine brothers and sisters Catholic interpreters have sometimes been charged with departing from the plain sense of Scripture merely to uphold the Church's belief in the permanent virginity of Mary. It is true that Catholic interpretation has been colored by this belief, but it is equally true that the ancient tradition on which the belief rests cannot simply be disregarded in the interpretation of the New Testament. It would be hard to see how the tradition could ever have developed had it been thought that any scriptural passage opposed it. As a matter of fact, the early Church appears to have been fairly of one mind on this subject, with Tertullian in the third century forming a singular exception following his lapse into heresy. The Gospel and other New Testament references to Jesus' brothers presuppose Semitic usage, which makes "brother" do for half brothers (Gen 37:16), nephews (Gen 13:8), cousins-german (1 Chron 23:22), more remote cousins (Lev 10:4), and relatives in general (2 Kgs 10:13). Later we shall see that at least some of those whom it calls Jesus' brothers the Gospel itself explicitly states were sons of another woman than Mary the mother of Jesus.

Mk 4:1-9   A matter of much more absorbing interest to the Gospels
Mt 13:1-9   is now introduced to us by the common Synoptic account
Lk 8:4-8   of the parable of the sower. We have already seen a considerable number of parables in what the Gospels have given us of Jesus' teaching, so much so that we hardly need to be told now that parables were a predominant feature of his preaching in Galilee. It is now, however, that the Synoptic Gospels choose to take up Jesus' parabolic teaching *ex professo*. This is particularly the case in Matthew's Gospel, which has taken up Mark's "day of parables" and expanded it to the symbolic number of seven parables, converting it into the third of the major discourses of Jesus which constitute the outline of the First Gospel.

There was, of course, nothing particularly original about Jesus' teaching in parables. Parables have been in use among almost all peoples from time immemorial. They have been particularly popular with Orientals, who like to use their imaginations as well as their minds in learning and in teaching. The Old Testament is filled with parables of various kinds, which is one reason for the fact that it is such enduring literature. Parables were a common teaching form for the rabbis of Jesus' day, and in his lavish use of parables therefore our Lord was simply adopting, as a good teacher should, an instructional method with which his hearers were quite familiar.

It may be helpful to distinguish the different kinds of parable which we encounter in the Gospels. The simplest form is the *parabolic saying*, which may be what we would ordinarily call in English a proverb, a simile, or a metaphor. Essentially this is to talk in pictures: "You are the light of the world"; "You cannot put a new patch on an old garment." What may be termed the *parable* proper is the immediate development of this, a figure of speech that makes its point through the short description of some action or fact. The parable of the sower is a parable in this sense. Finally, we have the *parabolic story*, a further enlargement in which the parable becomes a complete short story with a cast of characters and a finished action: we think immediately of the good Samaritan or the prodigal son. To all of these we give the name parable in a general way, for they have in common what is essential to a parable: to teach something by comparing it with something else. The "something else" is invariably a familiar reality, in the light of which the hearer of the parable is invited to take a closer look at the something new that he is being taught.

Ordinarily the parable is content with performing its essential function of making a simple comparison: it has one point to make, and one only. Especially in its developed forms, however, the parable easily verges upon *allegory*, from which nevertheless it should be firmly distinguished. An allegory is a sustained metaphor, in which a whole series of details is systematically related to the details of another reality. The Johannine figure of the true vine and its branches has the character of an allegory: Christ corresponds to the vinestock, his disciples to the branches of the vine, God to the vinedresser, and so forth. Like the parable, the allegory can be either quite simple or very involved, depending on the degree to which it is developed. A modern work like *Lord of the Flies* is a good example of the artistic use of complicated allegory.

The parable sometimes verges on allegory, we have said. In other words, we do not exclude the possibility that some of the Gospel parables may occasionally go beyond the one point proper to the parabolic comparison and make other points as well. That is to say, the parable may at times contain allegorical elements. This is definitely not the rule, however. In the well-known parable of the good Samaritan, for example, it is pointless to ask for the "meaning" of details like the road to Jericho, the inn, the innkeeper, the oil and wine, and the rest. Such details are present merely to make up a vivid and interesting story, merely to constitute the parable in the first place. They have no allegorical significance beyond the single message of the parable, which is that everyman, however separated by race or nation or religion, is everyman's neighbor. It is essential to recognize this difference between parable and allegory, for otherwise it is very easy to misread the parables and understand them in ways quite foreign to their original intention. When the Lord says that the way to destruction is wide and well traveled, he is speaking a parable, not an allegory (see above on Mt 7:13 f.). He is saying that the road to hell is as easy to find as a busy public highway; he makes no pronouncement concerning the number of those who actually travel this road. If the Lord's sayings in Mk 2:21 f. and parallels were allegories rather than parables, we would have to conclude that they were unhappily stated, since each of them concerns a good thing that is old being spoilt by something new—and *ex hypothesi* the latter would be his own new teaching. As parables, however, the sayings do not intend to establish any such relationship. They merely illustrate the principle that the new and the old cannot be mixed.

The allegorical potential within the parables, it should be added, has sometimes been exploited by the Church or by the evangelist in adapting their teaching to situations other than the original ones in which they were uttered. We shall see an instance of this in a moment. We have already observed how certain of the parables appear in different contexts in the several Gospels, where they invariably take on different shades of meaning. The evangelists also have a tendency to connect in topical or logical grounds parables that originally had a separate existence. In practice we must first of all interpret the parables as we find them in the Gospels, whatever may have been their historical context in Jesus' preaching. This is, after all, to get at the inspired meaning of the Scripture. In some instances, however, by comparison of one Gospel with another, by taking into consideration the known tendencies of this or that evangelist, or simply by scrutinizing the parable itself independently of its present context, we may with greater or less probability reconstruct the process by which the parables have passed from their existential situation in Jesus' proclamation of the kingdom into the existential situation of the Gospel teaching.

Let us test this assertion by considering the parable of the sower apart from the explanation that is later given to it. *The sower went out to sow:* Jesus takes a familiar picture from Palestinian life. Farming methods in the Near East were and are crude and prodigal. Having broken the soil by perfunctory plowing, the sower simply walked through the field scattering seed on either side by the handful. He did not expect all of it to take root. Some would inevitably fall on the beaten path instead of the plowed area and thus remain on the surface to be trampled on or eaten by birds. Some would be scattered in areas where there is only a thin layer of soil over bedrock: this is the geological description of much of the land of Palestine. In such ground the rain does not seep away so quickly and the excess moisture would cause the seed to germinate immediately and begin to grow. But it would be a premature growth that could not last; the sun and the plant's lack of roots would soon finish it off. Still other seed would fall among thorns, which rob the soil of its nourishment and choke off the growth of the grain. Finally the rest of the seed— the bulk of it, let us hope—would fall where the sower wanted it to fall, in his good ground where it would prosper in varying degrees.

He who has ears, let him hear! Thus the Lord issues his challenge to understanding. But what was his meaning? In the circumstances of the Galilean preaching, seemingly he intends the parable to illustrate how the kingdom was being proclaimed. It would—it already had—encountered much opposition and much indifference. Nevertheless, now was the one and only time of sowing in view of the anticipated harvest. Now, therefore, was the one and only time for decision: a second chance would not be offered. The parable is an eschatological summons to heed the all-powerful word of God which can, if men will but permit it, produce fruit *thirty, or sixty, or a hundred for one.*

Mk 4:10–12 Following Mark, all the Synoptic Gospels here insert an
Mt 13:10–17 explanation of Jesus' use of parables in answer to a
Lk 8:9–10 question of the disciples. It may well be, as many scholars suspect, that this explanation had originally to do with all Jesus' teaching, not his parables exclusively; even if this is so, however, it has been most aptly applied to the parabolic teaching because of the inherent obscurity of the parable as a literary form. What is unfortunate, nevertheless, is that these verses have sometimes been interpreted as meaning that Jesus used parables as a deliberate means of hiding his teaching from the multitudes. This certainly cannot be the sense of the Gospels. Parables were not intended to conceal meaning but to clarify it. Their obscurities, which were only relative, were not designed to make them pointless riddles but to challenge the hearer to penetrate more deeply into the realities which they signified, just as the apparent absurdity of a paradox challenges us to examine more closely the truth it expresses in an unusual way.

Still, as the evangelists knew full well, Jesus' teaching, however much he had intended it for all, had been widely disbelieved and unheeded. What was the providential explanation of this fact? *To you,* says Jesus, that is, to his disciples who have believed him, *has been given the mystery of the kingdom of God; but to those outside* the community of faith, *everything appears in parables.* This statement evidently depends on the material meaning of the word "parable"—that is, roundabout speech, enigma, riddle. He says, then, first of all, that the same word which was light and truth for those who would believe could merely increase the darkness for those who would not see. This, as we know, is a common affirmation of the New Testament (cf. Jn 9:39). Matthew, who says the same thing more simply, adds (in vs. 12) a saying which Mark and Luke reproduce further on. His meaning is doubtless eschatological: the present loss or gain represented by unbelief or faith points to the eternal loss or gain that will follow in the final judgment.

But Mark and Luke go on to record the Lord as saying that he teaches in parables precisely *in order that* those destined not to believe *may look but not see, hear but not understand,* and so on. It is these words that cause most of the difficulty with this passage. Matthew may have been sensitive to the difficulty when he changed Mark's "in order that" to "because": the Lord conceals his teaching in parables *because* the people look but do not see, etc. It is doubtful, however, whether this alteration really changes Mark's meaning, particularly since Matthew, as is his custom, takes the opportunity to cite in full the "offending" passage from Is 6:9f. that is implicit in the texts of Mark and Luke. Is Jesus saying then, after all, that his teaching is a deliberate source of confusion to those who lack faith?

Rather, we must understand the evangelists as finding a prophetic precedent for the present events in Israel's past and as citing the Old Testament in this spirit. God had commanded Isaiah: "Go and say to this people: 'Listen carefully, but you shall not understand! Look intently, but you shall know nothing!' You are to make the heart of this people sluggish, to dull their ears and close their eyes. Else their eyes will see, their ears hear, their heart understand, and they will turn and be healed." It was not that he willed Isaiah's preaching to have these results, but that he knew that it would. He willed the repentance that Isaiah's words would never effect, yet his mercy compelled him to offer grace in the full knowledge that it would be rejected. Even so, the Gospels tell us, what happened in Isaiah's time was now being repeated when one greater than all the prophets preached the fulfillment of all prophecy. Again the intention was otherwise, and again the result was the same.

Matthew concludes this section by appending a saying of Jesus for which Luke has found an even better context in another part of his Gospel (cf. Lk 10:23f.). Here the blessedness of the believing disciples is contrasted with the sad state of those who look but do not see, listen but do not understand.

Mk 4:13–20 Mt 13:18–23 Lk 8:11–15	Faithful to his principle that the Lord explained all things to his disciples (Mk 4:34), Mark, and the other Synoptists with him, has inserted at this point an explanation of the parable of the sower. When it is read

attentively, however, it speedily becomes evident that it is not so much an explanation of the parable as it is an adaptation of it to somewhat different purposes. Though the explanation begins with the assertion that *the seed is the word*, almost immediately it becomes instead the different kinds of men who receive the word. Various of the details of the parable have now been allegorized: the birds of the air, for example, appear as Satan, the tempter. No longer is it a question of the triumph of the kingdom over every opposition, of faith versus unbelief, but rather of various depths of faith and of the vicissitudes to which faith is subject.

The conclusion appears to be irresistible that this is an explanation given to the parable by the apostolic Church at a time when the conditions that it presupposes—persecutions, for example, and the lure of wealth—had become sources of danger to the fervor of Christian faith. The language and style of the passage confirm this conclusion. By no means, however, is its value thereby lessened at all. Quite to the contrary, it is a precious testimony to the way in which the word of the Lord remained living in his Church and was recognized as relevant to the present and future as well as the past.

Mk 4:21–25   Mark continues his treatment of the parables, and Luke
Lk 8:16–18   concludes his, with a series of the Lord's sayings that
                had evidently been composed into a unit by one of the
oral or written sources of tradition upon which the written Gospels depend. In Mark the schematic memory device by which the sayings were linked together has also been preserved:

verse 21: And he said to them . . .	(a) saying about the lamp and lampstand
verse 22: For . . .	(b) saying about the hidden thing
verse 24: And he said to them . . .	(c) saying about measure for measure
verse 25: For . . .	(d) saying about haves and have-nots

Luke's version of this collection seems to be a summary of Mark's; among other things, (c) has been truncated. Luke also has (a), (b), (c), and (d) as individual units distributed throughout his Gospel (Lk 6:38, 11:33, 12:2, 19:26). Matthew, too, who does not reproduce the present series (though we just saw him use [d] in Mt 13:12 above), likewise has his own, and different, distribution of (a), (b), (c), and (d) a second time (Mt 5:15, 7:2, 10:26, 25:29). Both Matthew and Luke brought (c) into the context of the Sermon on the Mount, but each gave it a different application.

What is the meaning of the series in this context? Because of the artificial connection of ideas, the evangelists' intention is not too clear. Possibly it is this: If there is at present any obscurity about Jesus' teaching, it is not for the purpose of keeping mankind forever in the dark. It will be the function of his disciples to explain his teaching. Therefore they must understand it in all its depth. Continual application will deepen their understanding, but neglect of it will cause them to lose what they thought they possessed. Even they can prove to be the rocky ground where the seed of faith has been unable to grow.

Mk 4:26–29 The common theme of sowing has induced Mark to continue his "day of parables" with this one concerning the seed which grows of itself. Luke has finished with parables for the moment, but it is somewhat curious that Matthew, the great collector of parables, should have passed this one by. Perhaps it was because his concern throughout is with the part played by the believer in the furthering of the kingdom, and this parable was not easily adaptable to such a viewpoint.

The parable, in fact, is wholly taken up with the idea that the kingdom is the work of God and not of man. Just as the seed contains within itself an inner power that governs its life and growth, so the kingdom possesses its own dynamics beyond the sufferance or control of man. Of course, what is not said in the parable should not be pressed for implications that it does not intend. Man's part in the kingdom is not merely passive. The point is, however, that the kingdom is proof against both its enemies and friends alike, who cannot divert it from the "harvest" intended by God (Mark quotes Joel 4:13) either by malice or by well-intentioned bungling. The message is not insignificant for Christian faith and hope.

Mt 13:24–30 A message of equal significance is conveyed by this next parable related by Matthew only, again connected with the preceding by the figure of sowing. Here we see a wealthy farmer *sowing good seed in his field* and then entrusting it to the care of his servants. *While they were asleep,* however, *his enemy came* and oversowed the same field, this time with weeds, called *zizania* in the Gospel, a particular kind of grass that looks very much like wheat until it has fully developed. Such stories of revenge were well known in the East, where the desire to get even might lie hidden for long years awaiting a suitable opportunity to repay with interest.

In this story the master restrains the impatient zeal of his slaves, who are all for rooting out the weeds immediately even at the expense of losing the wheat. Rather, the time of harvest must be awaited. The lesson seems to be clear. The coming of the kingdom has not meant an automatic triumph of good over evil. The same field in which the seed of the word has been planted has also been sown with weeds. The time of God's eschatological judgment must be awaited with patience. And with faith. Good men are always subject to the temptation to despair over the apparent permanence of evil.

Mt 13:31–32   Though Matthew has put the preceding parable in the
Mk 4:30–32   context of Jesus' instruction of his disciples, it is very
Lk 13:18–19   likely that it was originally a response to his adversaries.
It answers the objection: If the kingdom has really
come, why has nothing happened? why do the evil yet prosper? The
same judgment may be made concerning the following two parables,
both of which Luke has placed, doubtless quite rightly, in relation to
one of the Lord's controversies with the Jewish leadership in the synagogues.

What could be less like the kingdom of God as men had fondly
anticipated it than the tiny band of Jesus' followers, disreputable, most
of them, in the eyes of the world? It is precisely for this reason, Jesus
replies, that the kingdom of God is *like a mustard seed*, the smallest
seed known to a Palestinian farmer, which quite marvelously in a short
period of growth is transformed into a veritable tree. The evangelists
would have especial cause to recall this parable, they who had seen the
Church develop in a short lifetime from a peculiarly Jewish institution
into a movement in which men of all nations were finding a home.
To call the mustard plant *a tree* (Matthew and Luke; Mark, more
realistically, *the largest of the bushes*) is not too great an exaggeration,
since it sometimes grows to a height of ten or twelve feet; however,
there is an allusion here to an Old Testament figure of worldwide empire (cf. Dan 4:9, 18; Ezek 17:22 f., 31:6).

Mt 13:33   Much the same lesson is taught in the parable of *the*
Lk 13:20–21   *leaven*, omitted by Mark. The mysterious action of
yeast, quietly and inexorably transforming the dough
in which it has been *hidden*, was another familiar analogy to illustrate
how the kingdom, tiny though it was, could eventually entirely overcome
its hostile environment. The unrealistically large amount of flour that
appears in the parable—*three measures* are well over a bushel, or something like three dozen gallons—serves to emphasize the point uncom-
promisingly.

Mk 4:33–34   Mark concludes his "day of parables" with a summary
Mt 13:34–35   statement. Because, as we have seen, Mark relates
Jesus' parabolic teaching to the "messianic secret" by
which he revealed himself only by degrees, he makes a point that this
method taught the people *in a way they could understand*, while *privately
he explained everything to his disciples*. Matthew follows Mark in the
summary statement, and characteristically he finds an Old Testament
(that is, "prophetic") precedent for the parabolic teaching in the words
of Ps 78:2.

Mt 13:36–43   Matthew, however, unlike Mark, has not yet done with
Jesus' parables of the kingdom. What follows is entirely
proper to his Gospel, and he has further separated it from what has
gone before by noting that it was a private instruction to the disciples,
in the house away from the crowds.

Matthew begins with an explanation of the parable of the weeds
(vss. 24–30 above), the only other passage in the Gospels like the explanation that was given to the parable of the sower. This second explanation has the character of the first: it is a later application of the
parable made by the Church. The parable, first of all, has been allegorized, though without any appreciable change in meaning thereby.
The perspective of the final judgment remains paramount. What seems
to have been changed, however, is the precise effect of God's judgment
on the kingdom: it is now a purification *gathering from his kingdom
all stumbling blocks and evildoers*. The evil over which the kingdom
triumphs, in other words, is internal to it as well as external. In keeping
with this, a distinction seems to be made between the kingdom of the
Son of Man in verse 41 (the Church on earth?) and the kingdom of
the Father in verse 43 (the eschatological kingdom?): compare 1 Cor
15:24. The lesson of this extension of the parable is quite as important
as that of the parable itself. If good men are tempted to despair over
the perdurance of evil, the temptation is the greater when evil is found
in the very temple of God. However, the point previously made remains
valid: a premature weeding would destroy the kingdom and nullify its
redeeming power.

Mt 13:44–46   Matthew has just been speaking of the kingdom under
the figure of seed sown in a field. It may be the tenuous connection formed by the word "field" that caused him to introduce
here the double parable that begins with the kingdom as *a treasure
hidden in a field*. Be that as it may, the point that is made by these two
little parables is quite a different one: that no sacrifice is too great in
order to acquire a place in God's kingdom. The relevance of this teaching both to our Lord's preaching and to the catechesis of the Church is
obvious.

The idea of a treasure trove is exciting under any circumstances, but
it could especially quicken the imagination in Palestine, where the civili-
zations of thousands of years lie below the surface of the ground, and a
man with a plow may easily turn up a treasure in a field. Treasure found
in this way belonged by law to the owner of the field: the parable presupposes that the man who found it was a sharecropper. In this instance the kingdom is figured as presented as it were by chance; in the
parable of the *merchant's search for fine pearls* it is represented as the

object of a lifelong quest. Both kinds of men find their way into the kingdom, and both have a common duty once they have found it.

Mt 13:47–50   Matthew's final parable continues the thought expressed by the parable of the weeds and especially by the explanation given to that parable. It is aptly situated in a context of instruction of Jesus' disciples, for it gives an answer to a question that would most naturally have been asked by those whom he had destined to be fishers of men. To whom must the kingdom be offered? Jesus' reply is that they must fish as with *a dragnet*, which is indifferent to its catch, dredging up in its path *things of every kind* (and not fish only). The sorting out will be left to God and his angels of judgment. Meanwhile, the Church can no more dissociate herself from sinners than could Jesus depart from the company of taxgatherers and prostitutes that gained him a bad reputation in certain quarters. It is to make sinners into saints that the kingdom is preached.

Mt 13:51–53   Matthew concludes the parabolic discourse with a saying of the Lord that is a little parable in itself. To Jesus' question whether his disciples have understood the mystery of the kingdom of God their answer was a perhaps overconfident yes. On this assumption, then, he continues, *every scribe who has become a student of the kingdom of heaven is like the head of a house who can bring out of his storeroom both new things and old.* Just as a prudent householder knows what he has on hand and has seen to it that he has on hand the necessary provisions that must be acquired from time to time if he is to be a generous and capable host, so has the new "scribe" that has risen in Israel learnt to perform his task with equal efficiency. He has become a student of the kingdom as the scribes of Judaism were students of the Law. As there is a Christian interpretation of the Law that illuminates the old figures with new light (see Chapter 8, and especially on Mt 5:17–20), so is it with the Christian understanding of the kingdom of God. There is no doubt that the evangelist considers himself to be such a Christian scribe, and his Gospel to be this new kind of scribal instruction.

The "day of parables" ends with the conventional formula with which Matthew has concluded each of Jesus' major discourses (see above on Mt 7:28 f.).

11. REJECTION IN GALILEE

Mk 4:35–41   After the parables, Mark and Luke now resume their
Lk 8:22–25   story of the Galilean ministry. We rejoin Matthew,
Mt 8:18, 23–27   too, at the stage in his Gospel in which he is de-
                   veloping the picture of Jesus the model of mission-
aries, preparatory to the missionary discourse which the Lord gives to his
disciples in chapter 10. Matthew, as we have seen and shall continue to
see, is by far the most independent of the Synoptic Gospels in his ordering
of the traditional material.

For an undisclosed reason, Jesus decides to cross to the other side of
the Sea of Galilee, apparently using Peter's boat. Other boats also accompanied him, but presumably they turned back in the storm that
ensued. As usual, Mark has the most vivid and lifelike account of what
happens, giving evidence of dependence on an eyewitness. The sudden
squall (so Mark and Luke; Matthew uses a word that properly means a
much greater cataclysm) is not extraordinary. The Sea of Galilee, about
685 feet below sea level, is surrounded by mountains almost on all sides.
Particularly at night (*as evening drew on*) a storm can quickly develop:
as warm air from around the sea rises, cool air rushes down from the
mountains to take its place, often causing a violent wind. At the northern
end of the sea there are valleys to the east and west which help to
funnel the wind over the water. Within the matter of a half hour the
normally glassy surface can be transformed into chopping waves of seven
or eight feet, more than enough to be a danger to light fishing craft.

The scene in the boat as it begins to ship water is one of the Gospel's
best efforts at portraying both the essential humanity of Jesus and those
qualities that caused other men to recognize in him that which transcended their human estate (Matthew brings this out in verse 27, saying
that *the men marveled*). Jesus was asleep in all confidence, and doubtless
honest bone-weariness from his labors, on *a cushion*, probably a wooden
or leathern seat in the boat that doubled for this purpose. Mark's record
of the disciples' appeal for help includes the tone of exasperation uttered by men in straits for which they hold Jesus responsible: *Master,*

do you not even care that we are perishing? Matthew's, on the other hand, echoes the cry of liturgical prayer: *Save, Lord!*

There is no doubt that the Gospels recognize in Jesus' quieting of the storm an exercise of the same kind of power by which he cast out Satan and worked miracles of healing (Mk 4:39 quotes him as using the same command to the sea that is addressed to the demon in Mk 1:25). "Nature" miracles of this kind no less than the healing miracles pointed to the inbreaking of God's kingdom, a restoration of order which is the essence of the biblical idea of creation, and a subjection of all things to the rule of God and his Messiah. Such was the interpretation of the primitive Church, based on the evidence of competent witnesses. The witnesses themselves, in this passage under discussion, had not yet reached this interpretation, but their wonderment at what they had seen led them in its direction.

Mk 5:1–20 After the storm on the lake, according to all the Synoptic
Lk 8:26–39 Gospels, Jesus and his disciples *came to the other shore;*
Mt 8:28–34 Luke adds *opposite Galilee,* for technically they were
     now in the territory of the Decapolis. Mark and Luke (according to the evidence of the best manuscripts) call this *the land of the Gerasenes,* which is the first of the difficulties presented by this story. The story presupposes a site by the shore, but Gerasa, the modern Jerash, is some thirty miles away to the southeast. Matthew (in the best manuscripts) revises Mark's geography to read *the land of the Gadarenes,* but this is no real help: Gadara is still a good six miles from the shore. A variant in the manuscripts of all three Gospels, but especially of Luke, reads *the land of the Gergesenes;* it is now generally agreed that this is the result of a "correction" supplied to the text by Origen in the third century, who was thinking of the Girgashites (in Greek, Gergesites) of the Old Testament (cf. Gen 10:16, 15:21; Deut 7:1; Jos 3:10, 24:12). There are other variants as well, all of which show that the geographical difficulty was recognized almost from the very beginning, by apparently everyone except Mark. It is likely enough that Mark, whose knowledge of and interest in northern Palestinian geography is rather casual, intended merely a generic reference to the Decapolis, of which Gerasa was a prominent town best known to him. However, there is a site on the eastern shore of the Sea of Galilee almost directly across from Magdala which seems to fit most of the requirements of the story. Here the bank is narrow and there is a precipice, while the mountainside contains natural caves, the customary location of *the tombs* presupposed by the Gospels. There is also a ruined village nearby which existed in Jesus' time; today it is called Kursi, but in Aramaic this would have been Kersa or Gersa. The similarity in names is at least suggestive.

An obvious discrepancy between the Gospel accounts that immediately springs to the eye is the number of demoniacs that are featured: one by Mark and Luke, two by Matthew. It might be easy to think of Mark and Luke passing over a second man without mention, since the person about whom they do speak became well known to the infant Church as a kind of pre-Christian evangelist of Christ to the Decapolis. Mark's story especially leaves us in no doubt that this is no routine recital but a documented history of a well-known event involving a well-known person. On the other hand, however, Matthew, or the tradition on which he depended, shows a strong favoritism for two's. The two of this present story may represent his way of catching up on or summarizing the Gospel narrative. As we saw, he omitted the story of the possessed man given in Mk 1:23–28; perhaps for this reason, therefore, he now adds another demoniac to the one which he found in Mark's Gerasene account. In a quite similar way, as we shall see later on, Matthew (in 20:30) speaks of two blind men to Mark's one, having omitted an earlier story about a blind man described in Mk 8:22–26. In Mt 26:60 it is only Matthew who makes a point of there being *two* witnesses at Jesus' trial. And there are other instances. It may be that the fondness for two's has something to do with the requirement of the Mosaic law for valid testimony (Num 35:30; Deut 19:15; cf. Jn 8:17 and Mt 18:16), or it may be due simply to the vagaries of the oral tradition on which the evangelists depend.

This story at one and the same time is unique in the Gospels and also partakes of characteristics common to other descriptions of exorcisms. As before, the demons call Jesus by name, simultaneously recognizing his authority with God and fearing it; one present-day commentator has observed that "these conceptions are perhaps less contrary to today's psychiatry than they would have been fifty or sixty years ago." Through the mouth of the insane man whose frenzies are so graphically depicted by Mark, an appeal is made by the forces of evil that Jesus *torment them not.* Matthew speaks of a torment *before the time* and *here,* in the Decapolis, introducing an eschatological note and taking cognizance of Jesus' activity in a pagan land. On Jesus' enquiring the man's name (to know another's name, according to universal ancient belief, is to possess some power over that person), according to Mark and Luke he identifies himself as *Legion,* a term borrowed from the Roman military unit composed of something over six thousand men. This can be taken either as demoniacal arrogance and boasting or as a cry of anguish wrung from the demoniac himself, recognizing the turmoil within his person. At all events, the exorcism follows in any case.

It is the circumstance of the exorcism involving the *herd of swine—* another indication that this event took place among Gentiles—that has always occasioned the greatest difficulty in this story. What was the purpose of this gesture? As far as the fact itself is concerned, it would not be contrary to the reality of the Gospel account to imagine the swine's headlong flight as caused by the paroxysms that usually accompanied exorcism. It was, certainly, an effective way of dramatizing the deliverance that had taken place. In the conversation between Legion and Jesus, however, the Gospels doubtless indicate their interpretation of what happened. Mark says that the demons asked not to be sent *out of the country*: another ancient belief put territorial limits on demoniacal activity; Luke has it that they asked not to be cast *into the abyss*. Probably Mark and Luke agree with Matthew, then, in understanding the episode of the Gerasene/Gadarene swine as exemplifying the preliminary character of Jesus' onslaught against Satan in the exorcisms of his public life. The exorcisms were evidence that the kingdom had indeed come, but the final banishment of the forces of evil would take place only in the eschatological age brought in by the redemptive death and resurrection of Christ.

Luke and Mark conclude the story by adding various details about the man who had been exorcised, who was instructed to make known what the power of God had effected for him. Matthew omits these details but joins the other Gospels in remarking how the inhabitants besought Jesus *to depart from them*. This doubtless speaks volumes about the hierarchy of values cherished in rural Gentile society. Understandably awe-struck by what had occurred, they nevertheless could not bother to discover whether this man's mysterious power was destined for their good or their ill. They could only see in Jesus a threat to their settled way of life. Their pigs were more important to them than the life of the spirit.

Mk 5:21–43   Mark and Luke continue the story with two connected
Lk 8:40–56   miracle events that are set in Capernaum; Matthew has
Mt 9:18–26   the same narrative, before which, however, he inserts
             three passages that we have already seen above in parallel. As usual, Mark's is the lengthy, detailed account which in this instance is abbreviated by Luke and condensed even more by Matthew.

Jairus, unnamed by Matthew, was doubtless quite a distinguished person, and thus his humble mien in Jesus' presence testifies to his sincerity and the urgency of his appeal. He is called *a ruler* by Matthew and identified by Mark and Luke as *one of the leaders of the synagogue*. The leaders of the synagogue were the lay officials who not only determined the order of its services (see above on Lk 4:16–22a) but exercised other functions of prestige in Jewish society. Jairus' prominence undoubtedly accounted for the *great crowd* which accompanied Jesus and his disciples responding to his request. In Matthew's Gospel, Jairus' request is from the beginning for a restoration of life: this is the only such miracle recorded by Matthew. Also Matthew notes that Jesus *rose* to accompany

Jairus: the First Gospel has Jesus at table in the house of Levi at this juncture (cf. 9:10) rather than just having recrossed the Sea of Galilee.

The story of the healing of the *woman afflicted with a flow of blood for twelve years* is drastically reduced to a few lines by Matthew, but Luke's and especially Mark's accounts contain various items of interest that should by no means by overlooked. For one thing, whereas Mark offers a fairly testy commentary on Near Eastern medicine to which his own experience might have contributed—*having suffered much from many doctors and spent all she had, and having got no better but rather become worse*—Luke says instead that *she had not been able to be healed by anyone* (the *having spent all her means on doctors* of some Lucan manuscripts is probably a harmonizing addition to the text). A touch of this kind leads us to suspect that Col 4:14 should be taken at the letter and that Luke was using a euphemism dictated by the code of medical ethics. Far more important, however, are the reactions of Jesus to the woman's approach, particularly as related by Mark.

The woman believed that she would be healed *merely by touching his garment*; Luke and Matthew speak of *the tassel of his garment*, referring to the Jewish practice prescribed by Num 15:38 f. and Deut 22:12. This was not necessarily superstitious in intent. Jesus said that it was the woman's faith that saved her, and the desire to achieve physical contact with the object of one's faith is not unsound. Her touch was covert because legally she was unclean (cf. Lev 15:25-27; Num 19:11). Jesus' question and Mark's notation that *he was looking about in the crowd* indicate a genuine search for information, not playacting. Similarly, Peter's and the other disciples' somewhat exasperated reactions, pointing to the jostling and milling crowd surrounding Jesus, suggest accurate historical recollection rather than dramatic invention. Mark's explanation is that *he perceived that the power which proceeded from him had gone forth*. All of this adds up to a primitive and perhaps ingenuous appreciation of Jesus' consciousness of his role as the instrument of God's healing power, toned down or omitted in the parallels, but all the more valuable for these reasons. This is a passage that must be taken into firm consideration whenever it is a question of determining the extent to which the expression "emptying" in Phil 2:7 means precisely what it says. Jesus partook of our human condition wholly and exactly. The Gospel insists, at the same time, that he was an active cause and not merely a passive occasion of the divine power operating in and through him.

Faith had cured the woman and would save Jairus' daughter. Jesus told the distraught father to disregard the message of death and to *believe* (in Mark, *continue to believe*). Disregarding also the professional mourners (cf. 2 Chron 35:25; Jer 9:16 f.) and others present who greeted with mocking skepticism his assertion that the girl was *not dead but asleep* (cf. Jn 11:11), he entered her chamber, taking with him her parents and three of his disciples, Peter and the two brothers James and John. These three form a select group within the Twelve, which on more than one occasion is accorded an extraordinary witness to his works. Mark recalls the Aramaic words of Jesus' command to the girl, paraphrased by Luke and omitted by Matthew. Literally, *talitha kum* means "little girl, get up." The noun is the feminine form of *talya*, a word which in Aramaic signifies "lamb," "child," or "servant" (cf. Jn 1:28–34; cf. also the ambiguity of *pais* in Mt 8:5–13). A great number of manuscripts of Mark have *talitha kumi*, which is "better" Aramaic, and for that reason evidently an elegant scribal correction of the original text. Mark and Luke conclude the story with Jesus' usual injunction to keep the matter quiet for the preservation of the "messianic secret" (a motive that did not obtain in pagan Gerasa/Gadara).

Mk 6:1–6a   Pursuing Mark's chronicle, we now come to a passage
Mt 13:54–58   which intentionally achieves a climax in the Second
Lk 4:22b–30   Gospel: the rejection of Jesus by the people of Nazareth
                     and the beginning of the end of the Galilean ministry. Though Matthew's order of events is different, he too has placed his parallel version in somewhat the same position in his Gospel. It follows there the "day of parables" and begins the narrative section leading into the fourth of Jesus' major discourses (ch. 18), a section in which we see the Lord concentrating more and more on the instruction of his disciples and more or less resigned to continued rejection by people and leaders alike. Luke, as we remember, has an entirely different sequence for this episode, having set it at the beginning of the Galilean ministry (see above in Chapter 6).

Luke (in 4:16–22a) has described for us the synagogue procedure presupposed by Mark and Matthew as they open their accounts. Jesus' teaching on this day was the culmination of many words and works which his compatriots had witnessed or about which they had been told. *Where did he get all this?* Such questions as Mark and Matthew quote could have been asked in honest admiration, as is certainly the reaction depicted in Lk 4:22a. Do the Marcan and Matthaean versions of this story come, like the Lucan, from a fusion of experiences at Nazareth, friendly as well as hostile? This may be. Whatever the original import of the questions, however, as they now stand the evangelists intend to show them as hostile, the accent resting on the repeated deprecatory *where*. For the Nazarethites are about to illustrate the principle of human nature expressed in a thousand proverbs and by Jesus in the saying earlier ascribed to him by Jn 4:44 and now by the Synoptics: *a prophet does not go unhonored except in his native country*. Familiarity, which breeds contempt, is also an obstacle to faith. The people of Nazareth already knew too much about Jesus, or thought they knew, even to believe their own eyes and ears which told them that he was more than they could ever know.

Luke has the Nazarethites identify Jesus as *the son of Joseph*, Matthew as *the carpenter's son whose mother's name is Mary*. Both these versions employ routine language. Much more unusual is Mark's (according to the best manuscripts) *the carpenter, Mary's son*. The supposition, here and elsewhere in the Gospels, seems to be that Joseph is dead, and it is only to be imagined that in Nazareth Jesus would have been associated with his father's craft both in fact and in the mind of the people. What is completely extraordinary is that a man should be called by his mother's name: in Jewish mouths this would imply a reflection on his legitimacy, which does not appear to be the intention of the text. It is probable, therefore, that this is Mark's title for Jesus and, if so, perhaps an indication of his acceptance of the tradition of Jesus' virgin birth explicitly affirmed elsewhere by Matthew and Luke.

Matthew and Mark quote the Nazarethites as citing in evidence against Jesus apparently all the closest of his relatives they can name: his father and mother, *his brothers*, four of whom are named, *and his sisters, all of whom are here with us*—the last, seemingly a larger group, would represent Jesus' women relatives who had married into various families of Nazareth. Of the four brothers mentioned, *James, Joseph* (in Mark, *Joses*), *Judas, and Simon*, at least the first two are elsewhere identified as sons of another woman than the mother of Jesus (Mk 15:40, 47; Mt 27:56). If the James of this list was the "other" James among the Twelve, he was the son of a man named Alphaeus (Mt 10:3 and parallels). If the Judas of the list is the person to whom tradition ascribes the Epistle of Jude, the Scripture makes him a brother of this same James (Jude 1).

Because of their lack of faith, say Mark and Matthew, Jesus *could not work any miracle there*. This is, as Mark shows, one of the Semitic "relative absolutes": he did heal a few sick people. Nazareth stands as typical of the barrenness of unbelief. Luke underlines this while showing its pettiness and pointlessness as well, possibly combining events from yet other encounters of Jesus in this city. *Doctor, heal yourself!* is perhaps a petulant and mocking retort inspired by Is 61:1 which Jesus had cited. The Nazarethites apparently reproached Jesus for making Capernaum rather than Nazareth the center of his ministry in Galilee. He replied by reminding them of *Elijah and the widow of Zarephath* (cf. 1 Kgs 17) and *Elisha and Naaman the Syrian*: great prophetic figures often rejected by their own people, whose great works were expended not on Israel but on Gentiles with whom they found faith. It is Luke, too, who relates—somewhat unusually for him—the violent reaction of Jesus' compatriots who tried, or at least strongly desired, to lynch him.

Mk 6:6b–13   It is necessary again to do considerable vio-
Lk 9:1–6   lence to the order of Matthew's Gospel simply
Mt 9:35, 10:7–11, 14   to keep it in parallel with the less complicated
                              disposition of Mark and Luke. The passage
that we have before us Matthew has incorporated into the second of the
major discourses which set forth the teaching of Jesus; it is even necessary, therefore, to break up one of the cherished five instructions to
maintain our parallel. The narrative nucleus common to the three Gospels
and occurring roughly in the same "chronology" justifies this procedure,
however, and we can extract it from the Matthaean heart of the discourse
which we reserve for later treatment. This is admittedly not an ideal
way to approach the several Gospels, but then again we have already
settled for something less than the ideal.

The parallels in Matthew and Luke, who have worked from independent sources, help to explain the importance of this development in
Mark. The crisis pointed up by the rejection at Nazareth continues.
There is a strong note of urgency and of working against time in Jesus'
tour of *all the towns and villages, teaching in their synagogues and proclaiming the good news of the kingdom, healing every disease and every
sickness.* We have the impression that Jesus appreciates as never before
the immensity of the task with which he is challenged and the odds
against his succeeding.

It is in this light that we should understand his missioning of the
Twelve. This was no long-range plan for providing a succession to himself, despite the fact that Matthew has made it the precedent for such
an idea of the apostolate in his Gospel. Rather, it was a practical measure
dictated by a present need. The Twelve could be his presence in many
places at one time in proclaiming the kingdom here and now. Hence they
were empowered to do precisely what he was doing: to preach, to heal,
to exorcise—the signs of the advent of the kingdom of God.

In keeping with the urgency of their mission are the practical instructions given them for their conduct on the road. They should go *two by
two*, says Mark; this was a Jewish custom (cf. Lk 7:18; Jn 1:37), not
mentioned here by Matthew or Luke (but cf. Lk 10:1). They were,
further, to live strictly off the land, like an invading army, and to carry
with them, practically speaking, only the clothes on their backs. Some of
the details here are spelt out differently by Mark (*take a staff, wear
sandals*) and Matthew and Luke (*no staff, no sandals*), but the spirit is
the same; it is doubtless impossible, and in any case inconsequential, to
decide which version of the Lord's injunction is the more "primitive."
The mission of the Twelve constituted them what Jesus himself had become, an itinerant preacher of the kingdom. The urgency of their mission
is also communicated in his instruction to *shake the dust from your feet*
of any town or village that would not receive them. This expressive ges-

ture was intended to be a sermon in itself, to indicate that the inhabitants were taking upon themselves the consequences of a spiritual attitude that marked their land as heathen and unclean.

Describing the beginning of the mission of the Twelve, Mark alone adds the detail that they were *anointing sick people with oil*. The use of oil in healing was contemporary practice (cf. Lk 10:34) and had a religious significance in the apostolic Church (cf. Jas 5:14). It is not impossible, therefore, that Mark both recalls a factual occurrence and insinuates an apostolic precedent for one of the rites of the Church with which he was familiar.

Mk 6:14–29   It is somewhat extraordinary that Mark, usually so single-
Lk 9:7–9   minded in his choice of material to make up the Gospel
Mt 14:1–12   of Jesus Christ, should have devoted the attention that
he has to the story of the Baptist's execution, a story that involves Jesus neither directly nor indirectly. The explanation is partly that Mark, who is a stickler for detail, needed the story to supply the background for Herod's superstitious fear related by the evangelist in the verses that now constitute its prologue—verses which do involve Jesus very much. Also, the story provides an artificial time lag to separate the account of the mission of the Twelve from that of their return immediately after. Matthew has given one of his customary summaries of the story, placing it topically in relation to Jesus' rejection at Nazareth. Luke has retained only the prologue. The execution itself is the kind of motif that he avoids; besides, he had already said about it as much as he felt it necessary to say earlier in his own way (see above on Lk 3:18–20).

The tradition relates that *Herod the king* (Luke and Matthew more accurately refer to Antipas as *the tetrarch*) was disposed to credit the popular, and singularly uninformed, opinion that Jesus was *John the Baptist raised from the dead*. Apparently one amateur accounting for Jesus' miraculous powers was that they were the new manifestation of the famous preacher whose earlier ministry had not been accompanied by miraculous signs (cf. Jn 10:41). Herod's information doubtless came from his courtiers, lax Jews who had heard of Jesus with amused disinterest and followed his career by hearsay here and there. Herod had thought to rid himself of the troublesome Baptist, and now, here was the trouble all over again! Others were speaking of Jesus as *Elijah* or another *prophet like one of the prophets* of old (see above on Jn 1:19–24). Luke alone adds that Herod *kept seeking to see* Jesus, and later Luke alone will record the gratification of his wish (cf. Lk 23:8).

The story of the Baptist's execution by Herod Antipas is one of the few instances of a Gospel account which is paralleled in profane history (chiefly by Flavius Josephus in his *Antiquities* XVIII. 116–19). The two histories do not agree in all details but rather complement one another.

Antipas *imprisoned John on account of Herodias, his brother Philip's wife.* In the Gospel the explanation of this is that the Baptist was denouncing the tetrarch for the violation of the Mosaic law (Lev 18:16, 20:21). Antipas had taken as his wife Herodias, his niece as well as his brother's wife, a woman of about thirty-five who had already borne her husband a daughter, the girl who figures in the Gospel story and whose name was Salome. Herodias had repudiated her husband by a divorce recognized in Rome but not in Jewish law. Salome, as it happened, later married her uncle, Antipas' brother, the tetrarch Philip. It may be that the Gospel has followed a tradition which had confused the names of Salome's husband and Herodias' (who is not otherwise known in profane history except as "Herod"); given this incestuous entanglement, confusion is hardly surprising.

To marry Herodias, Antipas had repudiated his first wife, the daughter of the Nabataean king Aretas, who in revenge eventually gathered an army and defeated Antipas. It is in this context that Josephus explains the Baptist's execution, as a political measure taken by Antipas against a man whom he feared as too popular with the masses and therefore a potential leader of rebellion against his rule. Though Mark says nothing of this and speaks instead of a *birthday banquet* at which Antipas was persuaded to kill John, the military and political background explains the presence of the *military officers and leading men of Galilee* which he notes; the scene, according to Josephus, was Antipas' palace at Machaerus in Perea, on the Nabataean frontier. Neither Josephus nor the Gospel provides us with any information on the time of this event in relation to the ministry of Jesus.

Extrabiblical history contains nothing as interesting as the Gospel story of Salome's dance, to say nothing of the Freudian paraphrase by Oscar Wilde, who unfortunately erred in several points of fact, including the timely demise of the cold-blooded young murderess. The biblical tradition rings true, however, in any number of details. The moral swampland of the Herodian family has not been exaggerated, nor has the complicated character of Antipas been caricatured, a man who was hagridden in more than a single sense.

Mk 6:30–33   Only Matthew connects what follows with the execution
Lk 9:10–11   of the Baptist: Jesus' withdrawal *by boat to a deserted*
Mt 14:13   *place* was, in his mind, a prudent removal from the ter-
Jn 6:1–4   ritory of Herod Antipas. Mark and Luke, however, un-
              derstand it as a retreat for the twelve *apostles* (who,
incidentally, are given this name in this passage) after their arduous mission tour. Luke specifies the place to which they withdrew as near the *city called Bethsaida* Julias, in the territory of the tetrarch Philip, the birthplace of Peter and Andrew (Jn 1:44). Mark explains that the

crowds which, despite Jesus' intentions, *assembled there before them* were Galileans who had seen them depart and had followed them by foot on the shore. John, whom at long last we rejoin in these parallels, tells us nothing contrary to any of this; we shall discuss the Johannine "chronology" later. He indicates that the gathering was due to Jesus' reputation for miracles: as both he and the Synoptics have shown many times, this was not invariably a good sign. John locates the scene that is about to ensue *on the mountain,* a determination that is unparalleled here by the Synoptics (but paralleled in Mt 15:29); see on Mk 3:13–19; Lk 6:12–16; Mt 5:1 f. John adds that *the Jewish feast of Passover was near.* He does this for a theological purpose, since he has in mind the Christian passover figured for him in the miracle of the loaves; however, the Synoptic story also presupposes quite incidentally that it was spring (cf. Mk 6:39).

Mk 6:34–44   The miracle of the loaves, the only miracle story found
Lk 9:12–17   in all four of the Gospels, raises innumerable questions.
Mt 14:14–21   The question that most naturally comes to the mind of
Jn 6:5–15   twentieth-century man, or at least of most twentieth-
               century men, probably is: What actually happened?
This is not a question to divide the believer from the unbeliever, but one which the believer can also ask. We frequently speak of this event as a "multiplication of loaves," but the Gospels do not call it that. "Multiplication of loaves" is an interpretation of the event—a rationalistic interpretation, if you will—made by one who accepts it as a miracle. It may be, and probably is, the correct interpretation, but an interpretation it is in any case. If we ask, "How otherwise could five thousand people be fed with five loaves and two dried fish, and fragments be gathered into twelve baskets, than by a miraculous multiplication of food?" we ask a legitimate question; but we imply the same rationalist principle that accounts for the hundreds of alternative solutions that have been proposed by those who believe that miracles do not (not necessarily cannot) happen. Let us leave the matter there. Everyone is free to speculate, but speculation begins where the Gospel leaves off. It is sufficient for our purposes simply to see what the Gospel has said. The Gospel has told us what happened, but not how. It will have to be added, however, that what happened, as the Gospels tell it, was something indeed miraculous, and any explanation that does not do justice to this fact is not faithful to the biblical record.

The next question may be easier to answer: What did the miracle signify in the life of Jesus? Matthew and Mark tell us explicitly that it was a work of *compassion,* because Jesus saw that the people were *like sheep with no shepherd.* John especially brings out the disparate character of the crowds who witnessed and participated in the act of Jesus. Jesus' solicitude was not simply for the people's material hunger, but to represent to them the kingdom of God which could, if they would allow it, assuage their often unfelt hunger for the things of the spirit. For Jesus the miracle of the loaves anticipates the eschatological messianic banquet (see below on Lk 14:15–24; cf. Mk 14:25 and parallels; see also Apo 19:9). It is a parable in action of the kingdom, the merciful dragnet of God drawing into itself things of every kind (see above on Mt 13:47–50).

It is this significance which the Gospels develop in interpreting the miracle as a foreshadowing of the Eucharist, the messianic banquet of the Church. The Synoptics describe Jesus' actions in terms that are allusively liturgical: *he took . . . looked up to heaven, blessed, and broke . . .* (cf. Acts 2:42). John does not have this much detail, but on the other hand his word for "blessed" (*eucharistēsas*) is more suggestive than the Synoptics' (the same word is used in 1 Cor 11:23, in Paul's account of the institution of the Eucharist, and by Mk 8:6 and Mt 15:36 in the doublet narrative of the loaves which we shall consider later). While the Synoptics say that Jesus gave the blessed food to the disciples who in turn gave it to the people, a perfectly natural detail when we think of the logistical problems involved in feeding a crowd of five thousand people, John's omission of the detail may well be deliberate in view of the circumstances of the Last Supper. In John the gathering (*synaxis*) of the fragments, noted by all the Gospels, is given as a command of Christ. The Didache uses this term for the gathering of the Eucharistic bread, and it likewise uses the same word (*klasmata*) for the Eucharistic bread that is found in all four Gospels to designate the fragments of the loaves of this story.

Mark and John especially have distinctive details to contribute that make this something quite different from a stylized tale of wonders. The somewhat querulous retort made by the disciples to the Lord's initial command to feed the people in Mark sounds like a conversation taken from life. In John it is turned into an interrogation to test Philip's faith made by a Master who is in complete control of the situation; it is likewise a continuation of the Mosaic theme (cf. Num 11:13, 22). The apostle Andrew in John's account emerges from the anonymity that generally surrounds most of the Twelve in the Gospels. He finds a boy, presumably a hawker of food, who provides the *five loaves*—John alone tells us they were *barley loaves*, the bread of the poor—*and two fish*—John alone tells us they were *dried fish*, though in any case we should doubtless have presumed this. Perhaps the most delightful descriptive detail of all is Mark's *they sat down, flower beds here and flower beds there, in hundreds and fifties*, which paints for us a vivid picture of the gay bright colors of Oriental dress clashing with the green of the hillslope.

A much more important contribution, from the standpoint of the Gospel history, is that made by John in his final two verses. In the sign which they have experienced the crowds recognize in Jesus the prophet-like-

Moses of Deut 18:18 (see above on Jn 1:19–24). So much to the good. But their enthusiasm is deceived and misguided. John has the same view of this period of the Galilean ministry as do the Synoptics: in various ways, but in every genuine sense of his mission as he conceived it, Jesus is being rejected. *They were about to come and forcibly make him king,* their Jewish Messiah (see above on Lk 4:3–13 and parallel). Therefore *he fled back to the mountain alone.* The "alone" hangs impressively in the air. What of the faithful Twelve?

Mk 6:45–46   The answer to this question seems to be given us by
Mt 14:22–23a   Matthew and Mark when they continue their chronicle
Jn 6:16–17a   stating that Jesus *forced his disciples to get into the*
               boat and precede him to the other shore of the Sea of
Galilee. (Mark adds *toward Bethsaida,* precisely where, according to Luke at least, they already were! All in all, it seems we must conclude that for Mark Bethsaida, like Gerasa, was merely a name he had heard, and that he had only the vaguest notion of its situation. To imagine another Bethsaida on the western shore is quite unnecessary.) Though the Synoptic Gospels said nothing of the attempt of the crowds to make Jesus king, they appear to know something of what happened, and they appear to recognize that the Twelve were also involved in it. It is really not surprising that the disciples, too, should have caught the messianic fever of the multitudes, and that Jesus quickly had to separate the one group from the other and himself from both. How prudent this was, would appear on the morrow.

At all events, Jesus was quite alone as he prayed in the hills near Bethsaida that night after the miracle of the loaves.

12. THE BREAD OF LIFE

Mk 6:47–52   This chapter begins, as did the last, with a storm on
Mt 14:23b–33   the Sea of Galilee. The passage before us, small
Jn 6:17b–21   though it is, has stirred up storms of its own. No other
               miracle story of the Gospels has been more questioned
than this one. The issue is not the possibility of miracles: for those for
whom all miracles are alike impossible, this miracle story is hardly different from any other. It is, rather, those who are unembarrassed by miracles in principle and who believe in the Gospel miracles specifically who
experience difficulty with this one. Many Christian commentators, some
Catholics included, prefer to understand this episode as a symbolic narrative, a parable constructed in Christian tradition, rather than as a record
of sober historical fact. They would not thereby necessarily insist that it
is purely symbolic, that there was no historical event at all that could
underlie it.

Why is this story so much different from the other miracle stories of
the Gospel? For one thing, unlike Jesus' other miracles, this one does not
seem to go anywhere. Jesus did not work miracles for their own sake,
but to reveal himself in response to faith, to proclaim the inbreaking of
the kingdom of God over death and evil and sin, to save men. In this
instance Jesus did not save the disciples from any peril to their life: the
storm, which is hardly mentioned by John, was merely tossing them about
a bit and delaying their progress. Secondly, what are we to make of
Mark's statement that *he was going to pass them by?* This makes admirable sense as a narrative device to elicit a response from the disciples, but
it is more difficult to explain historically. The same may be said of the
disciples' mistaking Jesus for *a ghost* (Matthew and Mark), a detail con-
sonant with a story of men seeing a figure *walking on the sea* from their
boat far out on the water (*twenty-five or thirty stadia* from land, says
John, or about two and a half miles) in the middle of the night *around
the fourth watch* (after three in the morning). At all events, whether the
story is to be taken as a parable or as factual reporting, there is no doubt
that it is concerned with a miraculous power that is ascribed to Jesus and
recognized as such. It is not a story that grew out of some misunderstand-

ing or exaggeration—the disciples mistakenly observing Jesus wading in the water near the shore, for example. Such an interpretation would submit the Gospels to a childish rationalism of which they are undeserving.

The three evangelists who have reproduced this story have done so apparently for three distinct purposes. Mark's intention seems to be summed up in his final verse. *They were astounded*, he says, now that they had seen Jesus walking on the waters, *for they had not understood about the loaves*; and the reason for this was that *their minds were completely blinded*. Their blindness, Mark suggests, was not malicious, but due simply to a lack of sight that had not yet been awakened by faith. They had witnessed the miracle of the loaves with little more, if any, understanding than was evinced by the crowds of whom John spoke in 6:14 f. Mark does not necessarily say that Jesus' walking on the water helped them to a better understanding, merely that it added to their astonishment. Miracles, this seems to be the point, do not direct and determine faith, but rather they are defined and determined by it.

Matthew, for his part, introduces the story of Peter also walking upon the water, but only for a while and only to underscore the vast gulf that separates his human powers from those of the Master who sustains him. It is doubtless this spectacle above all that persuades the disciples, according to Matthew, to confess of Jesus, *Truly you are Son of God!* Strictly speaking, this is, of course, the confession of full Christian faith. Whatever meaning Matthew intended it to have at this point, it is in some sense an anticipation of Peter's confession on behalf of the disciples in Mt 16:13-20. Correspondingly, this latter passage by no means has the climactic function that the parallel Mk 8:27-30 does for the Second Gospel.

According to John also the disciples confess Christ, but later (cf. 6:68 f. below). For John the walking on the water is one of Jesus' seven "signs," as was the miracle of the loaves (see above on 2:1-11), the full meaning of which is brought out in the lengthy discourse that follows. John undoubtedly sees a theophany in Jesus' appearance on the water and his identification of himself as *I am* (vs. 20, *egō eimi*: the ineffable name of Yahweh as translated by the Septuagint in Ex 3:14). The Synoptics have the same expression, but doubtless in the conventional meaning, "It is I." In the next verse John observes that the Lord thus revealed (cf. the imagery of Pss 29:3, 10, 46:2-4, etc.) the disciples *wanted therefore to take into the boat* (contrast the Synoptics).

Mk 6:53–56   We have been without the help of Luke in the preced-
Mt 14:34–36   ing passage, though we have had and continue to have
Jn 6:22–25   an unexpected parallel in John. The episode of Jesus' walking on the water marks the beginning of Luke's

"great omission" of Marcan material (Mk 6:45–8:26 is without Lucan parallels), which is something of an anomaly when we take into consideration Luke's fairly consistent adherence to Mark both before and after the omission. From this fact some have theorized that the edition of Mark used by Luke did not contain the omitted portions, but this seems unlikely. Rather, it is probable that most of the "great omission" was made by Luke on principle, together with some contiguous passages that went along as a matter of course. The story we have just concluded, for example, he probably left out for some of the reasons we noted on beginning this chapter. It is not Luke's way to introduce passages, or even verses, that could cause difficulty for his readers.

It is Matthew, Mark, and John, therefore, who now return us to Galilee. While the Synoptics offer a summary description of Jesus' healing ministry in the region of Gennesaret, however, John is busied with the crowds of yesterday, who eventually make their way to Capernaum. It is important to John that it should be those who witnessed the miracle of the loaves—not all five thousand, of course—who engage in the dialogue that ensues. Gennesaret is the fertile plain, only a few miles long, that borders the Sea of Galilee south of Capernaum.

There is no Synoptic parallel to the Johannine Eucharistic discourse that now begins. As we know by now, John's Gospel represents the ultimate development of a tendency, the opposite end of which is Mark with Matthew forming an intermediate stage, to portray the revelation of God in Christ less in action than in extended doctrine, the fruit of a long generation of Christian meditation and enlightenment in the Spirit. The present discourse is very much like the preceding ones in John. It begins with a question which is answered ironically in the development of the discourse: not how Jesus came to be in Capernaum is the vital issue, but whence he came to them as Bread of Life. The people address him as *Rabbi*, just as did Jesus' first disciples (Jn 1:38) and Nicodemus (Jn 3:2) at the beginnings of their encounters with him.

Jn 6:26–51a   Their curiosity about the way of his coming to Capernaum is symptomatic of their material thinking. Just as the woman at the well could think first of all only of natural water (Jn 4:15), they have been thinking only of the material bread with which he has fed them. *Not because you have seen signs*: the signs (in the Johannine sense) were there, but they have not recognized them. He therefore bids them raise their minds to higher things. Just as they must *labor* for their daily bread, so must they for *the food which endures unto eternal life*. The revelation of God as "bread" or "food" was a recognized Jewish figure.

Labor? What work must they do to perform *the works of God*? Their question seems to presuppose another misunderstanding: they are taking his meaning to be that there is something they can do which will provide them with a miraculously eternal bread. Jesus' reply is that the bread of which he speaks God gives to him who has *faith in him whom he sent*: the labor of which he has spoken involves the total submission of self to the Word of God in Christ. Persisting in their superficiality and understanding by faith merely human credibility, they ask, and not too politely, *what sign* he has to offer, at the same time minimizing the miracle of the loaves—the sign which yesterday had moved them to want to proclaim him king! Jesus, after all, had but fed them with earthly bread, whereas in the days of Moses *he gave them bread from heaven to eat* (Neh 9:15).

Not so, replies Jesus. First of all, it was not Moses but God who fed Israel with the manna. Secondly, the manna was heavenly bread only after a fashion. Only the Father now gives *true* bread from heaven (see above on Jn 1:9–13). This bread, which truly *comes down from heaven*, does not merely sustain life but *gives life to the world*. At this point the people reiterate the petition of the woman at the well (Jn 4:15); they recognize, at least, that he is speaking of something of which he alone is the source. This bread he now identifies with himself: *I am the bread of life*. This is the first of a series in John's Gospel (cf. also 8:12, 10:7, 9, 10:11, 14, 11:25, 14:6, 15:1, 5) in which Jesus employs the "I am" of Old Testament revelation (cf. especially Is 43:10, 46:4, 51:12) in connection with the New Testament kingdom as realized in himself. We have already seen the Synoptic Gospels' view of the miracle of the loaves as an enacted "parable of the kingdom" (see above on Mk 6:34–44 and parallels). In John's Gospel, which contains no parables, various of the themes of the parables of the kingdom are personified in Christ, who is for the evangelist the glorified Christ identical with his Church. *You have seen me,* Jesus continues, *yet you have not believed*. Their unbelief is culpable and evidence that they have not received and acted on the grace of God. Christ has come into the world precisely to be the instrument of God's grace, to do his will, that men might have eternal life and rise with the just *on the last day*.

The hostility of the crowds, latent up to this point, from verse 41 on becomes overt. Perhaps for this reason John now refers to them as *the Jews*, the term which he so often uses for the unbelieving Palestinian "world" of Jesus' own time (see above on Jn 1:9–13). Like their ancestors of the time of Moses, they *grumbled* at what they had received (cf. Ex 16:2, 8 f.). They reject Jesus' prophetic word for the same reason alleged by the Synoptic Gospels in relation to the incident at Nazareth seen in our last chapter: this is the Johannine parallel to Mk 6:1–6a and parallels above. Jesus' response to this challenge is mainly to reiterate what he has said previously, in addition to quoting Is 54:13. *Not that anyone has ever seen the Father*: see above on Jn 1:18.

Jn 6:51b–59   This little section forms the properly Eucharistic part of
Jesus' discourse: *The bread which I shall give is my
flesh for the life of the world.* Up to this point it has been a question
of a bread of life=Christ which God gives=reveals to men; now it is
Christ who gives this bread=his flesh=himself. The change of direction
as well as of intent legitimately raises the question whether these verses
are original to the discourse or are an insertion into it. There is no
reason at all, however, to doubt that they are original to John's Gospel.
This discourse, like others in the Gospel, has been composed of parallel
strands of Jesus' teaching in the Johannine tradition; the composition
was not necessarily made all at one time. The Eucharistic doctrine itself
is perfectly in keeping with John's other sacramental interests. Here the
Eucharist is connected with the redemptive life and death of Jesus as
is done later by the Synoptic Gospels and also by Paul (cf. 1 Cor
11:24).

John's Eucharistic word is "flesh" (*sarx*), whereas in Paul and the
Synoptic Gospels it is the "body" (*sōma*) of Christ; in the early patristic
Church both terms were used indifferently. The Johannine formula is
probably closer to the Semitic expression employed by Jesus. For the
significance of "flesh," see above on Jn 1:14 in Chapter 2.

The interchange between Jesus and his listeners continues in the
Johannine pattern. Like Nicodemus (Jn 3:4) and the woman at the
well (Jn 4:11), the Jews tend to take Jesus' statement in a crudely material sense. They would not have been encouraged to understand it
merely as a figure of speech: in Hebrew "to eat someone's flesh"="to
slander," "backbite" (so in Ps 27:2; a similar expression is found in
Aramaic in Dan 3:8). Neither is Jesus' meaning figurative, though it is
spiritual. Six times over he repeats his previous assertion, that to have
eternal life it is necessary to eat his flesh and drink his blood. "Flesh
and blood" is the common Semitic way of referring to the whole person.
Through the Eucharist the Christian is made to share in the life of
Christ, which is in turn the life which the Son shares with the Father.
I live because of the Father: as usual, the divine life of Christ is not
considered as isolated in itself apart from the economy of salvation, in
which *the living Father sent* the Son into the world. *This is the bread:*
thus the connection is made with the preceding part of the discourse.
It is part of the technique of John's Gospel, therefore, that the bread
which is Christ of the preceding verses could have been intended in a
twofold sense all along, referring also to the Eucharistic bread in which
Christ is present to the Church.

These things he said in a synagogue instruction at Capernaum. Inserted
at this point, perhaps this is a further indication of the composite character of the discourse. The notation probably applies more to verses
26–51a, however, than to this present section which sounds like an

instruction to a relatively restricted group of disciples (cf. the following verses). For the Capernaum setting, cf. verses 24 f. above.

Jn 6:60–66   *Many of his disciples* is the final designation of the crowd —in a synagogue instruction no more than a few hundred could have been involved—which just a moment ago were called "the Jews." Again we are persuaded that the discourse is composite. Furthermore, in the original intent of the passage it would appear that the *hard saying* which they refuse to hear was that uttered in the first part of the discourse rather than in that pertaining to the Eucharist. This makes relevant Jesus' question in verse 62 which corresponds to his dialogue with Nathanael (Jn 1:50 f.) and Nicodemus (Jn 3:12): the Eucharist is precisely one of those mysteries which they could not be expected to understand who were incapable of believing the "lesser" truth that Jesus is the bread of life come down from heaven (vs. 41). As he had once before to Nicodemus (cf. Jn 3:6–8), Jesus insists on the grace of God and the need of the Spirit's presence for the realization of spiritual things. *The flesh is of no value:* this is not a reference to his own flesh of which he spoke in the Eucharistic section, but to the incapacity of unaided human understanding (cf. Jn 1:14, 3:6); here we have a Johannine parallel to Mt 16:17 (see below). This rejection of Christ by those who had first been his disciples anticipates the summary statement of Jn 12:37 ff., and corresponds to the Synoptic evaluation of the Galilean ministry found in Mt 11:20–24 and parallel.

Jn 6:67–71   The confession made by Peter in the name of the Twelve, here in contrast to the rejection of Jesus by many of his disciples, is the equivalent in John's Gospel of the Synoptic scene in Mk 8:27–30 and parallels. This is the first time that John has taken explicit note of the Twelve.

Jesus asks if they, too, *want* to leave him: there is doubtless a deliberate allusion to the conclusion of the story in Jn 6:17b–21 seen above. Peter's confession of Jesus as the one who has *the words of eternal life* and whom they have come to know as *God's Holy One*, therefore, points to the walking on the water as a Johannine "sign" just as the preceding discourse pointed to the miracle of the loaves. In both these works Jesus revealed his glory, the saving presence of God. Jesus repeats (cf. vss. 37, 44, 63, 65) that their faith, by which they can truly see what was in the signs, has been made possible by divine election (cf. again Mt 16:17). *But one of you is a devil:* here the reference is interpreted by the evangelist as made to Judas Iscariot, the betrayer (cf. Jn 13:2). In the aftermath of Peter's confession in the Synoptic version (Mk 8:31–33 and parallels), it is Peter himself who was called "Satan" by the Lord, though in a quite different sense.

Jn 5:1   The fifth chapter of John's Gospel describes a visit by Jesus to
Jerusalem (ignored, as usual, by the Synoptic tradition) which
interrupted the Galilean ministry, the second such visit recorded by the
evangelist (cf. 2:13 ff.). The visit took place on the occasion of *a Jewish
feast*. It would be most convenient were John's fifth and sixth chapters
reversed—the order, indeed, in which we are treating them here!—for
then it would be easy to identify the feast with the Passover (the
second Passover brought into connection with Jesus' public life by John)
which according to Jn 6:4 above was "near." Unfortunately, there is no
textual evidence to indicate that these chapters were ever in any order
other than the one in which they now appear. In any case, it is extremely doubtful that a chronological concern of this kind would have
mattered much to John. He has not determined the feast in this instance (the scribes of various manuscripts determined it in differing ways,
however) because the precise occasion was irrelevant to his purpose.
Neither has he bothered to insert this chapter into any satisfactory se-
quential framework whether geographical or temporal. In Jn 6:1, as we
have already seen, Jesus is presumed to be in Galilee, yet 5:47 leaves
him in Jerusalem; furthermore, while chapter 4 is wholly taken up with
Jesus' departure from Judea and journey to Galilee, 5:1 returns him
immediately to Jerusalem. In exactly the same way, Jn 6:71 concludes
in Capernaum, but the very next verse beginning chapter 7 appears to
be at pains to explain Jesus' presence in Galilee rather than Judea.

Since John has not much cared where this story should be set within
the Gospel chronicle, it is of no great consequence that we should reverse the order of his chapters here. This we do simply for the convenience of our treatment in this book, the more readily to bring John
into harmony with the Synoptic order. Nothing further than this is implied or intended. For John and for us it is the story itself that matters.
Its purpose is to set forth another of Jesus' "signs."

Jn 5:2–15   *In Jerusalem*, says John, *there is at the Sheep* [Gate] *a
pool*. It is well to note that, however potentially symbolic
John may have found this story, it is also filled with quite factual and
even prosaic details. The Sheep Gate (cf. Neh 3:1, 12:39), to the northeast of the temple area, was unused in Jesus' time, but it had given its
name to the area even as names like the Bowery and Bowling Green
linger on today. The pool, if it is to be identified with the large double
cistern beneath the present-day Church of St. Anne in Jerusalem, did indeed as John goes on to say have *five porches*. As archaeological exploration has verified, four of the porches surrounded it in a rectangle
and it was bisected by a fifth. If the setting of this story is matter-of-fact,
so also are the persons who figure in it. The unnamed man who is

healed by the Lord appears to have been taken from a rather ordinary and routine life and hardly made to order for the occasion.

The pool was *called in Hebrew* (read "Aramaic") *Bethesda* (other manuscript readings are "Bethsaida," "Beth-zatha," etc.). The name "Bethesda" may have found confirmation in the nomenclature recorded on a copper scroll discovered in the third cave at Qumran. Whatever its name was, John's purpose in citing its "Hebrew" connections was doubtless to characterize the pool as the "water of Judaism" (as before in Jn 2:6, 4:12). Once again a salvation that Judaism had been powerless to effect will become reality merely through the word of Christ.

Curative powers, at least in the popular estimation, were attached to the water of this pool: the idea that the waters of certain regions are medicinal for bathing or drinking is still widespread today and is zealously encouraged by local chambers of commerce, with or without the support of medical opinion. In this instance, the water was thought to be efficacious when it *bubbled* (vs. 7); presumably what is meant is the periodical refreshing of the pool from the ground drainage or the spring which fed it. It may well have been that in the popular mind this phenomenon was ascribed to supernatural activity, as is asserted in the addition to the text found in verses 3b–4: ". . . waiting for the moving of the water. For an angel of the Lord went down into the pool from time to time and stirred up the water; and whoever was first to step in after the stirring of the water was healed, no matter what disease he had." These verses, un-Johannine in language, are missing in the best Greek manuscripts and undoubtedly are an explanatory gloss inserted by an imaginative scribe at some early time. We are left to imagine the impact that would have been made on history had there really been a pool with such powers, performing miracles by the clock day in and day out year after year.

The authentic text does not assert that anyone was actually healed at the pool, only that it was thought to have healing power. This gives added significance to Jesus' question: *Do you want to get well?* In place of a faint hope, perhaps grounded on scanty evidence if any at all, he offers an immediate certainty. The man's reply indicates that only a few, or perhaps only one person, could enter the pool at the time of the water's bubbling. The limitation may have been imposed by the smallness of the area, but more likely it was a rule established for the sake of preserving order at the pool.

Now that day was a Sabbath. Jesus' healing activity provokes a controversy over the Sabbath law, as in the Synoptic Gospels (see above on Mk 3:1–5 and parallels). The immediate issue was the man's carrying his pallet, against which specifically there was a rabbinical prohibition. The Gospel story supposes that in ordinary circumstances he would have followed rabbinical interpretation of the Law as a matter of course, but he argues reasonably enough that if Jesus was powerful enough to heal him his authority must also extend to determining what was lawful for the Sabbath. The man's character does not clearly emerge from this story. Seemingly he was little affected by what had been done to him. His reporting of Jesus to *the Jews* was probably not malicious but neither did it show great awareness of what was happening round him in Jerusalem. Jesus had to seek him out *in the temple* area on a later occasion, and there is no indication that his identification of *the man who made me well* was ever pursued on any more personal basis than this casual encounter in a public place. *Sin no more*: Jesus did not make a direct correlation between sickness and personal sin (cf. Jn 9:3); he was warning the man against the *worse thing* than physical illness that could befall him, namely the judgment of God.

Jn 5:16–30   John does not insinuate that the discourse which he has attached to the preceding story is all of one piece or that it was uttered on any single occasion. It is incident to *such things* as Jesus *was doing on the Sabbath*, for which cause *the Jews were persecuting* him: the imperfect tense in both verbs points to a repeated and continued activity. The Sabbath controversy is soon left behind in a development of majestic themes that mark this as one of the most important of the Johannine discourses.

My Father is still working, and I work as well. The implications of this pregnant assertion are immediately drawn out in the following verse. What Jesus was saying, first of all, was the truism accepted by all, that despite the anthropomorphism of Gen 2:2 f. by which the Sabbath law was motivated in the Priestly creation story, the activity of God was never at an end and never interrupted: how else could new life come into being and the world continue to exist? But Jesus' invocation of the divine example as precedent for his own action together with his persistent and exclusive reference to God as "my" Father (cf. vs. 18: *he called God his own father*) certainly did imply that he was *making himself the equal of God*. In the Synoptic Gospels also there are various indications that Jesus spoke of himself as Son of God in a unique sense and addressed the Father with an intimacy that others would not dare to use (for example, see below on Lk 10:21 f. and parallel). The present Johannine passage is, therefore, the equivalent of the Synoptic teaching on the Son of Man as Lord of the Sabbath (see above on Mk 2:23–28 and parallels).

Neither do the following verses mitigate this claim, though they might appear to on the surface. *The Son can do nothing on his own* is not said to imply the inferiority of one person to another but to express a functional relationship of persons in regard to their common work. Not only does the Son work *as* the Father works, he also works *what* the Father

works: their work is one and the same. The work in question is that
of the divine economy of salvation. In this economy the function of the
Son is to perform the will of the Father (cf. Jn 4:34 above). Doing
the will of the Father, Jesus shows forth a community of divine action
and of divine *love*, of which he is God's revelation to the world (cf. Jn
3:16, 35 above).

Two works in particular which are distinctively God's are exercised
by the Son in his ministry, and by the Christ who continues to live in
his Church: these are the *greater* works which Jesus will show, greater,
for example, than the healing of the man at the pool. First, *he gives life*,
he raises the dead to life. Secondly, he judges man, for *the Father . . .
has given all judgment to the Son*. While the eschatological resurrection
and judgment are not ignored, it is on the here-and-now realization of
what eschatology has in store that the emphasis is laid, for *the hour is
not only coming, it now is*. By faith in Christ, the Word of God in the
world, man passes from death to life eternal—the life of grace which is
the earnest and principle of the life of glory—and is acquitted of the
judgment of God. It is in Christ that man finds God and in him alone.
The divine life which the Father *has in himself* he has given to man
through the *Son of Man*, by sending him into the world as its life-giver
and judge. Jesus' part in this work of God, and the guarantee of its
efficacy, is the perfect harmony of his will with the Father's.

Jn 5:31–47   John concludes this discourse by reverting to a favorite
                   theme, that of *witness* (see above on Jn 1:6–8 and
1:19–24). Jesus recognizes in connection with the claims he has been
making the validity of the universally accepted legal principle that a
man's testimony in his own interest *is not true*, that is, it is juridically
valueless without corroboration. But he does have his corroborating witnesses. There is, first of all, *John* the Baptist, to whom the Jews had
sent (cf. Jn 1:19–24). As the Baptist had witnessed to him, so Jesus
witnesses to the Baptist (cf. Lk 7:24–35 and parallel above). *He was a
lamp* (cf. Ps 132:17) shining before the true Light (cf. Jn 1:6–8),
and by the Jews themselves he had been received as a prophet. Therefore his witness should be relevant in the present case. For his own part,
however, Jesus needs no *testimony of man*, for he has *a testimony greater
than John's*.

The ultimate witness to which Jesus appeals to testify that he does
the works of God are *the works* themselves! The argument, however, is
not circular, for he does not mean by "works" merely the verifiable deeds
that he has performed, but rather experienced events in which God
speaks and appears to him who has the ears and eyes of faith. His reproach to the Jews is that *you have neither heard his voice nor seen his
form* (an echo of Num 12:8). Because of their unwillingness to believe,

to be open to the voice of God, they do not have *his word* (*logon*) *abiding* (*menonta*) in them: unlike Jesus' true disciples who from the beginning took up their abode with the Word (Jn 1:39: *emeinan*) and who continually abide in him as he does in them (Jn 15:4: *menēte*). Deaf as they are to Jesus' prophetic word, they are equally deaf to the prophetic word of *Moses* in *the scriptures*, Moses *who wrote of me* (probably Deut 18:18 is meant; see above on Jn 1:19–24), whose teaching they fondly believe they are following. Therefore Moses will witness against them before God.

In these final verses the Gospel adverts to the specific question of Jewish unbelief, a posture and a fact to which the early Church was quite sensitive (cf. Rom 9–11). Despite his habitual references to "the Jews," John is not really as often concerned with this question as might appear. Frequently enough he is thinking in broader terms, of the unbelieving world of his own as well as of Jesus' times to which the Word of the Gospel continues to come in vain (Jn 1:10 f.), and it is only because of the historical circumstances of Jesus' life that he identifies this world as "the Jews." Here, however, the Jewish rejection of Jesus is contrasted with the acceptance of *another who comes in his own name*: doubtless a reference to the series of political messiahs (cf. Acts 5:35–37) whose leadership eventually led to rebellion against Rome and Roman vengeance on Palestine (cf. also Mk 13:6, 22 and parallels below). John's verdict on Jewish incredulity is essentially the same as the more general verdict he has passed on the unbelieving world at the end of his "book of signs" (see on Jn 12:37–50 below). St. Paul has dealt with the same question with somewhat greater sympathy and with a broader outlook on the providential designs of God.

Jn 7:1   Jesus' discourse ended, John has no further interest in the
Mk 7:1–13   situation that gave rise to it. Whatever is to be said of
Mt 15:1–9   the sequence of the text according to the evangelist's in-
                  tention, however, the first verse of Jn 7 provides a logical
sequel to what we have just seen above (cf. Jn 5:18). This verse takes us back to Galilee, where we rejoin the Synoptic tradition according to Mark and Matthew. The section before us is part of Luke's "great omission." The Jewishness of its subject matter, which Mark is at some pains to elucidate for his Gentile readers, may offer a sufficient explanation why Luke left it out. There is something similar, though not the same, in Lk 11:37–41.

We have here a typical conflict story which could have taken place at any time in the Lord's ministry. Jesus' adversaries in this instance seem to have been some local *Pharisees* of Galilee apparently egged on by *certain scribes who came from Jerusalem* (Matthew's summary makes both scribes and Pharisees Jerusalemites). The issue this time was not the interpretation and practice of the Law itself but *the tradition of the ancients,* the extension of the Law by custom to analogous observances which were sometimes regarded as having greater binding force than the written Law. Jewish practice was much divided concerning these observances. The professional Pharisee followed them as a matter of principle. The Sadducees firmly rejected them on the same principle. The ordinary Jew probably kept as many of them as he conveniently could, and the Judeans were in all likelihood more scrupulous on the point than the Galileans.

Jesus' attitude was also one of principle, neither mere acquiescence nor casual disregard. In respect to traditionary interpretation of the Law he agreed with the Pharisees: only in such an acceptation could the Law remain a living word and not become a fossilized letter. But the tradition had to get at the heart and spirit of the Law and serve these if it was to have any genuine religious significance. If, on the contrary, it became a law unto itself subject to no further interpretation it could easily end by destroying the Law it professed to explain (see above on Mk 2:23–28 and parallels). It was then only the *precepts of men* about which Is 29:13 had spoken, human observances which were no help but a positive hindrance to the true service of God.

So it was with the many Jewish purifications (cf. Jn 2:6), originally rites connected with the sacrificial liturgy which had now been extended by custom to the circumstances of everyday life, sometimes occasioning much hardship by disregarding the realities of existence in water-shy Palestine. It was not that the washings were a bad thing; religiously they were indifferent. What was bad was the encouragement given by such formal practices to the notion that they did, indeed, constitute a man's religion. They could so easily get in the way of his real religious duties. Just as it has not been unknown for a Christian to be more readily identified by his Friday diet than by his attention to the Sermon on the Mount, it was easier for a Jew to verify that he had indeed washed his hands to the elbow than that he had loved the Lord his God with his whole heart and his neighbor as himself.

It is under this aspect that Jesus speaks harshly of the Pharisaical traditions. Too easily could they *nullify God's word.* A particularly flagrant example of this he finds in the extension of *korban* permitted by some rabbis as a legal subterfuge by which a man might evade sacred duties, all in the name of piety. *Korban* was everything consecrated to God, which could not be put to profane use (in Mt 27:6 the temple treasury is called the *korbanas*). Mean-spirited men could release themselves from their natural obligations to support even their parents by declaring all their goods *korban.* Whether or not the "consecrated" wealth actually ever made its way into the coffers of religion might, of course, be another question. Whether or not it did was immaterial to Jesus. That this kind

of shoddy transaction could be condoned by the same persons who professed shock at unwashed hands, this was the insufferable hypocrisy which
revolted him.

Mk 7:14–23   The pronouncements that follow may have originally
Mt 15:10–20   belonged to other contexts. Their use here, however,
                        helps explain the interest taken by the early Church in
stories like the one we have just read. The Church had to be concerned
from the very beginning with the twin perils that are the standing temptation offered to every religion and every religious person: to conceive
of righteousness as a legalistic science, and to confuse religion with its
externals. That Judaism had sometimes given in to the temptation was
a cautionary example to Christians, an example, of course, which Christians have not always heeded.

Jesus' teaching is now addressed to the Galilean *crowd* rather than to
the scribes and Pharisees. He had, as we know, no illusions about these
people, who were as capable as any others of closing their minds to
truth. According to Matthew, who reports the disciples' concern over the
disgruntlement of the Pharisees, in this very passage Jesus speaks of the
Galileans as *blind men* led by these *blind guides* (the parable found in
Lk 6:39 above). Whatever their shortcomings, however, in this as in
other matters they deserved better leaders than they had had. As for the
Pharisees, Jesus denies that they are God's *planting* of which Is 60:21
had prophesied and insists that they *shall be rooted up*: a word whose
fulfillment Matthew recognized in the supplanting of the Synagogue by
the Church.

The Pharisees were scandalized because Jesus told the Galileans that
*nothing that enters a man from outside can make him unclean; it is
what comes from out of a man that makes him unclean.* It is not hard
to see why they took offense, for this little statement is one of the most
revolutionary utterances ascribed to Jesus in the context of contemporary
Judaism. It is not merely that he is teaching the priority of the interior
over the exterior in religion: the prophets of the Old Testament, the
Law itself, as well as rabbinical Judaism had already affirmed this principle. He addresses himself, rather, to the source of uncleanness, whether
moral or otherwise, and finds that it is entirely internal to man and in
no wise brought to him by things or persons from without. Radically,
this principle struck at the very existence of the legal and ritual purity
inculcated by the Mosaic law (especially the laws codified in the "Law
of Holiness," Lev 17–26, but also other precepts scattered throughout the
Pentateuch, as Lev 11 and Deut 14:1–21). Foods that from time immemorial had been avoided for various reasons the Law classified as "unclean" in order to give visual expression to the true and spiritual purity
that should characterize a people consecrated to God. There was, there-

fore, no fetishism involved in the kosher laws, nor did the best rabbinic teaching fail to bring this out. Nevertheless, until Jesus no rabbi had yet suggested the provisional character of the laws as such, as far as the letter of their observance was concerned. It is precisely this that Jesus did suggest, as the evangelists make quite clear.

Under other historical circumstances, it might have been that Judaism itself would have arrived at a similar conclusion, as some modern Judaism has done. There was from ancient times a strong prophetic tradition that pointed in that direction. Nevertheless, all the influences brought to bear on postexilic Judaism had determined it otherwise, interpreting the laws more rather than less rigidly and adding to them all kinds of extensions. Even Jesus, as far as we can tell, never carried out his own principle to the extent of actually disregarding the letter of the ancient laws. He did, as we know, interpret them more liberally than suited the taste of other rabbis. He refused to accept the traditions that had enlarged their compass and rigidified them. He did many things and consorted with many people that a narrower view of the Law called "unclean." It was the precedent of his life and his teaching alike that eventually led the Church, not without agonized hesitations (cf. Acts 10:9–16, 28, 15:1–21, 21:20–26; Gal 2, etc.), to follow his principle to its inevitable conclusions under the guidance of his Spirit.

These conclusions are presupposed by the evangelists when they report Jesus' explanation of his saying—actually, he paraphrases it with another parable—given to *his disciples* (in Matthew, Peter asks the question) privately *in the house* (cf. Mk 4:34). That the conclusions have been drawn is more obvious in Mark than it is in Matthew: Matthew's stand on the Mosaic law has been made quite definite in the Sermon on the Mount. In Mark, the last three words of verse 18 f. are almost certainly to be read as the evangelist's commentary: *He said to them, ". . . ," cleansing all foods.* What remained obscure to the disciples in Jesus' lifetime was now clear to the Church of the Gospels. The impressive list of vices that concludes the passage is Pauline in vocabulary and technique, and confirms what we have already judged to be the fact, that we have been reading a catechesis of the apostolic Church.

13. UPON THIS ROCK

Mk 7:24–30   For all practical purposes Mark has now ended his story
Mt 15:21–28   of the Galilean ministry as he takes the Lord up into
the land of Phoenicia, the pagan *district of Tyre and
Sidon* that bordered on Palestine. Even though he will show Jesus re-en-
tering Galilee once or twice, there will hardly be any more question of a
"ministry" there. The proclamation of the kingdom, Mark seems to be
saying, has now been made, and for better or for worse the Galileans
have heard the word preached to them. Later on (see on Lk 10:13–16
and parallel below) the other Synoptic Gospels will offer a more dramatic judgment on the Galilean ministry (Matthew has, in fact, already
anticipated it in his Gospel). From now on Jesus is seen more and more
in the intimate company of his chosen disciples, secluded from the
public gaze or at least seeking seclusion, forming and instructing the little band that had heeded his call. Though we know that too great a
point is not to be made of the kerygmatic outline of the Gospels, there
is no reason to think that this phase of it does not correspond to an
historical reality in Jesus' life.

Such a development also suits the purposes of Matthew, who is preparing for Jesus' discourse on the community life of the Church in chapter
18. The present story is obviously much to his liking, insinuating, as it
does, that the mission of salvation to the Gentiles began in the Lord's
own life. At the same time, the passage strikes the "Jewish" tone that we
so often hear in the First Gospel: the woman's prayer is heard only after
she has acknowledged the priority and privileges of Israel. It may be for
this reason that Luke, who has co-ordinated his ecumenism better than
either Mark or Matthew, has seen fit to omit the story.

Jesus' fame had crossed the border ahead of him into Phoenicia. Mark
sets the scene in *a house,* but Matthew, who appears to have drawn on
an additional source, has the woman following Jesus about the countryside. Matthew calls her by the ancient Semitic term *Canaanite,* while to
Mark she is a *Syrophoenician,* the word used by Greek writers to distinguish the Phoenicians of the Syrian coast from those of northern
Africa, the Carthaginians. The parable which provides the basis for the

interchange between Jesus and the woman, and which the latter cleverly turns to her advantage, probably makes an allusion to the eschatological messianic banquet (cf. Lk 14:15), but the main point is the distinction made between *the children* for whom the meal has been prepared, that is the Jews, and *the dogs* which at best are present on sufferance. Gentiles were sometimes called "dogs" by the Jews (see above on Mt 7:6); the Gospel softens the expression somewhat by using a diminutive form, thus "whelps" rather than the rangy curs that one would kick aside in the Near Eastern bazaars. The woman's witty solution, that even the dogs may expect the table scraps, somewhat resembles Paul's idea expressed by another figure in Rom 11:17.

The vivid personality of the woman in the story, along with some of its details which a Gentile Church could assimilate without finding altogether palatable, argue alike for its antiquity and its dependence on authentic recollection.

Mk 7:31–37   A glance at the map of northern Palestine should con-
Mt 15:29–31   vince the reader that in verse 31 Mark is either display-
ing his quite vague grasp of the regional geography, something we have had reason to suspect before, or he is describing a most circuitous route—New York to Washington, say, by way of Montreal and St. Louis—which Jesus took for some undisclosed reason. Matthew passes over the route, but along with Mark brings Jesus *to the sea of Galilee*. Both evangelists seem to suppose that the locale was outside of Galilee, somewhere in the pagan territory on the eastern shore (cf. vs. 31 in Matthew: the people *glorified the God of Israel* whom they have had revealed to them for the first time, presumably). Matthew also notes that *he went up on the mountain* (see on Mk 3:13–19; Lk 6:12–16; Mt 5:1 f.), making a point of it probably in view of the story that he is to tell next.

While Matthew contents himself here with a summary statement on Jesus' healing, Mark describes in some detail the cure of *a man who was deaf and had an impediment in his speech*. The sacramental gestures of the Lord on this occasion were not lost on the Church, which at a very early time incorporated them into its ritual of baptism, the sacrament by which the Christian's senses are opened to the word of God. Mark also has it that Jesus *groaned* preparatory to effecting the man's cure: quite likely this corresponds to other of his expressions of emotion on similar occasions (see above on Mk 1:40–45). In verse 36 the imposition of the "messianic secret" (see above on Mk 1:22–28) should not really have applied in this pagan land. It is possible that by now such conclusions to Jesus' miracle stories have become reflex and somewhat stereotyped for Mark. It is also possible that the story originally had a setting elsewhere in the Galilean ministry.

Mk 8:1–10   There seems to be no really convincing alternative to
Mt 15:32–39   the prevailing scholarly view, that the story of the feed-
                   ing of the four thousand is a doublet, that is, a variant
form in the tradition, of the story of the feeding of the five thousand
which we saw in Chapter 11 (see above on Mk 6:34–44 and parallels).
There are, it is true, various differences of detail between the two stories
—without these, doublets could hardly arise—but they are all of such a
kind as naturally develop in oral transmission. In every essential, on the
other hand, the two stories are the same. Mark, followed by Matthew,
has repeated in another setting what was originally the same account of
the miracle of the loaves. John has only the former story, though in any
case it is by exception that he parallels the Synoptic Gospels. Neither
has Luke repeated it. Even did it not figure in his "great omission" (see
above on Mk 6:53–56 and parallels), he would doubtless have followed
his usual practice of omitting even apparent repetitions.

The message of the two narratives, trivial emphases apart, appears to
be identical. Why, then, did Mark and Matthew retell the story, since
they were as well aware as we of its repetitive character? For one thing,
the event had come down to them in two variant forms, and they respected all the material that tradition had given them. Doublets are a
commonplace in Old Testament history, and they posed few problems
to biblical writers who were little bothered with questions of relative
chronology and statistical detail. Matthew in particular repeats himself
more than once: in just a moment we shall see another instance of this.
Secondly, this story was especially prized because of its sacramental overtones which we have already noted. Finally, it is likely that the evangelists
were pleased at the chance to relate in a Gentile setting such a work as
had once been performed on behalf of the Jews of Galilee.

The ending of the story poses a geographical problem that still awaits
solution. Both Matthew and Mark presuppose Galilee as the scene of
the next brief episode. Mark says that Jesus *got into the boat with his
disciples and went to the district of Dalmanutha.* No such place is known,
unfortunately. If Mark is something less than an expert on Galilean
nomenclature, however, in this instance Matthew, who revises him, affords us no better help. It was *the region of Magadan,* he says. Magadan
is equally unknown.

Mk 8:11–12   Back in Galilee—again, from the standpoint of any
Mt 16:1–4   genuine chronology, this passage must be timeless—Jesus
Lk 12:54–56   is asked by the Jewish leaders for *a sign from heaven* (cf.
                   Jn 6:30). Mark says that the Pharisees made this de-
mand, while Matthew says it was the Pharisees and Sadducees. The
combination of Pharisees and Sadducees acting in concert is historically
unlikely, and it is probable that for Matthew in this context these are

little more than traditional names. In the parallel Lk 11:16 which we shall see later it was simply "some of the people" who asked for the sign.

The sign for which Jesus was asked was the very thing he could not and would not give. His miracles were not available on call, but were true signs of the inbreaking of the kingdom as he had proclaimed it. Such witness as he could give was palpable only to a genuine faith (see above on Jn 5:31–47). They were not asking for a sign of the kingdom but for a sign that would confirm their own aspirations for the kingdom, their attempt to dictate to God the terms on which they would accept his dispensation. Before *this* unbelieving *generation* Jesus *groaned in spirit* (see above on Mk 7:31–37). To it *no sign will be given.*

Except the sign of Jonah, Matthew adds in eloquent paraphrase. Jonah, an historical prophet (2 Kgs 14:25) known, however, only from the seriocomic story in the Old Testament book that bears his name, in a sense epitomizes all prophecy. Jonah of the paradoxes, a nationalistic prophet sent to preach to Gentiles, cast away by men and brought back from death to proclaim a doom that proved in reality to be the salvation of a great city, who fled from the very word of God with which he was charged and who understood its fulfillment last of all men—Jonah stands as a sign of God's mysterious ways that confound the wisdom of men. A generation that is *evil and adulterous,* that is, faithless, unbelieving (cf. Is 57:3; Ezek 23:27, etc.), could understand Jesus no more than it could Jonah.

In verses 2b–3 Matthew, or someone who has expanded his text, has inserted a proverb which in a variant form Luke also has in a similar context. The proverb builds on the idea of "heavenly" signs and contrasts the ability of those who can read *the signs of the times* in a banal sense with their complete blindness to them in the one sense that ultimately matters.

Mt 12:38–42   *The sign of Jonah the prophet* has already appeared in
Lk 11:29–32   Matthew's Gospel, practically in the same words, of-
               fered in response to a challenge of *certain of the scribes and Pharisees;* in Luke's parallel, it is again *the crowds* who are addressed.

Here there is an expansion on the figure of Jonah as a type of Christ. *Just as Jonah was in the belly of the sea monster three days and three nights* (cf. Jon 2:1), *so the Son of Man will be in the heart of the earth three days and three nights.* This seems to refer to the mortal peril in which Jesus must carry out his prophetic witness, similar to that of Jonah, and even to the death that he will eventually undergo: all the evangelists testify that Jesus prophesied his death. Does it also allude to his resurrection? This may be. Luke's parallel is: *As Jonah became a sign to the men of Nineveh, so will the Son of Man be to this generation.* Jonah did, it is true, come before the men of Nineveh as one who had been brought back from certain death, yet it was not precisely in this fashion that he was a "sign" to them. Luke does not necessarily mean to say more than that Jesus comes before his generation as Jonah came before his, as a prophet, equipped with no further credentials than the word of God. Neither, therefore, does Matthew necessarily see in Jonah a pre-figurement of the resurrection. The primitive Christian formula for the resurrection is habitually "on the third day" (Mt 16:21, 17:23, 20:19, 27:64; Lk 9:22, 18:23, 24:7, 21, 46; Jn 2:1 [!]; Acts 10:40; 1 Cor 15:4) or, more rarely, "after three days" (Mt 9:31; Mk 14:58, etc.), neither of which expressions is really the equivalent of "three days and three nights."

Whether or not Jonah's deliverance figured in the thought of Jesus or of the New Testament as a type of the resurrection, it may be as well to observe at this point that no change is thereby effected in our judgment of the Book of Jonah, which is a work of didactic fiction. The New Testa-ment use of Old Testament types is theological and symbolical, not his-torico-critical.

Both Matthew and Luke exploit a further detail from the Jonah story: the conversion of Nineveh—Gentiles!—at the preaching of an Israelite prophet (Jon 3:5–10), an object lesson to this unbelieving generation that has heard and not heeded a prophet *greater than Jonah*. In like man-ner, the Queen of Sheba who once traveled from far-off Arabia to seek the wisdom of God incarnated in Solomon (1 Kgs 10:1–10) is a rebuke from Israel's history to those Israelites who have now spurned *one greater than Solomon*.

Mk 8:13–21   Rejoining Mark's chronicle, which is still being followed
Mt 16:5–12   by Matthew, we find the Lord and his disciples once
Lk 12:1   again in their boat, departing from Galilee almost as
             soon as they had come. Luke does not parallel this story,
but he has reproduced its key statement in another context where he has gathered various sayings of Jesus.

As Mark and Matthew tell the story, it takes on some of the elements of a Johannine discourse. The disciples react with surprising obtuseness when Jesus warns them against *the leaven of the Pharisees, which is hypocrisy*, Luke explains. Matthew has *the leaven of the Pharisees and Sadducees* (cf. Mt 16:1 above), while Mark adds *and the leaven of Herod*, doubtless with reference to the land of Dalmanutha/Magadan which they had just quitted. Leaven or yeast as a figure for doctrine, whether good or bad, fermenting in men's minds and determining their whole being and action, was well established in Jewish symbolic thought (see above on Mt 13:33). Nevertheless, according to Mark the Lord was forced to apply to his disciples on this occasion the same words he had previously spoken of the unheeding crowds who stood disbelieving before his parables (see above on Mk 4:10–12 and parallels).

In this story the evangelists seem to be making a catechetical point that transcends the saying about leaven. Even Jesus' disciples did not always comprehend the real meaning of his signs, a fact the Gospels themselves can obscure for us simply because they have been written in the light of a later Pentecostal faith. This point the story makes well by showing the disciples entirely consumed by trivialities while Jesus must patiently catechize them concerning the superficial details of the miracle of the loaves, which they had not understood (cf. Mk 6:52). The story in its present form presupposes the separation of the two versions of the miracle story in the tradition. This lesson was a useful one for the Church of the Gospels, which also counted members who did not properly appreciate the enduring Christian mysteries to which such miracles had testified (cf. 1 Cor 11:20–22, 27–29).

Mk 8:22–26   It is probably not by accident that Mark locates this next event, omitted this time even by Matthew, at *Bethsaida*, the site of the first miracle of the loaves. Blindness, he tells us, however hopeless it may appear is always curable. The story has some resemblance to the one found above in Mk 7:31–37, but its right to a place of its own in the tradition is assured. In particular, the man's comparison of the people whom he sees, apparently for the first time, to *walking trees* sounds like the uncontrived detail of a remembered and moving experience. On the other hand, Jesus' elaborate efforts to preserve secrecy may indicate an original setting in the Galilean ministry.

Mk 8:27–30   This next passage is a watershed dividing the flow of
Mt 16:13–20   Mark's Gospel. With the confession of Peter a climax is
Lk 9:18–21   reached, the "messianic secret" is broken once for all, and from now on the Gospel prepares us for Jesus' passion and death. Matthew, for whom the event does not have precisely the same significance, nevertheless has made an even greater thing of it in his own way for the special ends of his Gospel. Even Luke breaks his silence at this point to rejoin the kerygmatic outline of Mark. John, as we have seen, has his own version of a Petrine confession of Jesus (see above on Jn 6:67–71).

From Bethsaida, Mark supposes that Jesus and the disciples journeyed north, following the Jordan to its sources in *the environs* (Mark: *the villages*) *of Caesarea Philippi*. Caesarea Philippi, so called to distinguish it from the Caesarea of Palestine which was the residence of the Roman governor of Judea, had been recently rebuilt by the tetrarch Philip and named for the Roman emperor. Situated in the southern foothills of snow-covered Mount Hermon which rose majestically before them, it was and is a place of great natural beauty. It was undoubtedly for solitude and retreat that Jesus had brought his disciples here, and it is unlikely that they entered the pagan city itself. Luke says nothing about the place (the last event that he described was the miracle of the loaves at Bethsaida), but he notes, as he often does, that the Lord was at prayer before the important interchange that was to follow.

It was *while they were on the way* that Jesus for the first time put to them the question, *Who do men* (Luke: *the crowds*) *say that I am?* Their answers fairly correspond to the rumors and popular reports noted already on another occasion (see above on Mk 6:14–29 and parallels). Matthew alone has the name of *Jeremiah*, possibly because of the many late Jewish legends that surrounded the life of this great prophet (cf. 2 Macc 2:1–8, 15:13–16; however, 4 Ezra [2 Esdras] 2:17 ff. is a Christian interpolation inspired by Mt 16:14), possibly because the resemblance between the two prophetic figures was already remarked in Jesus' lifetime. It is initially surprising that no mention is made of the title Messiah, though this had most certainly been connected with Jesus on more than one occasion. Apparently the disciples withhold this word deliberately in order not to mingle popular ideas with their own belief, recognizing what the Lord was about to ask of them.

In all three Gospels *Peter* speaks, in his own name and that of the Twelve, the conviction at which they had arrived through reflection and observation. *You are the Messiah* is doubtless the primitive form of the confession, as found in Mark. Luke's *the Messiah of God* is synonymous with this. Matthew's addition *the Son of the living God* contributes a certain verbal solemnity but does not alter the sense. "Sons of the living God" was a title used by the prophet Hosea (2:1) for the eschatological Israel, a text quoted by Paul in Rom 9:26; its use here is doubtless in the same sense, that is, applicable pre-eminently to the Messiah of Israel. Messiah meant a variety of particular things to many people, for as we have seen the Jewish messianic expectation was complex and nuanced. What Peter may have meant by it we do not know in details, but it is evident that by using the title at all he intended to sum up in Jesus the realization of Israel's salvation-hope.

Did Jesus accept this designation as an accurate description of his role in salvation history? From Matthew (vs. 20) it would appear that he did, but Mark and Luke by no means permit us to give such a univocal answer. In these Gospels Jesus neither accepts nor rejects Peter's words, but immediately *ordered them not to tell anyone about him.* Furthermore, though we have described this passage as the ending of Mark's "messianic secret," it might be more accurate to say that it is the beginning of the process by which Jesus himself reveals a concept of messiahship that had not been grasped by Peter (see on Mk 8:31–33 and parallel below). It is impossible, therefore, to give a simple answer of yes or no to the question. It would seem that Jesus did accept the title in the spirit in which it was offered, but with some important reservations. This may become clearer from an examination of Matthew's major addition to the text, Jesus' conferring on Peter of primacy in his Church.

We call this an addition not to imply that Matthew made it up, but to acknowledge that it originally pertained to another historical context. Matthew's is not the only Gospel in which a primacy is ascribed to Peter. Luke has something very similar, which, however, he has placed amidst the events of the Lord's passion (Lk 22:31 f.); in John's Gospel it is by the resurrected Christ that Peter is singled out as the shepherd of his brethren (Jn 21:15–19). The variety and independence of the Gospel testimony persuade us of its objectivity. Most scholars would have no difficulty in accepting the fact that Jesus once said to Peter what we read in Mt 16:17–19, or something very like it. But not, apparently, on this precise occasion. Matthew, as he has done so often, has arranged his material topically, joining his tradition of Petrine primacy to the Marcan story of Peter's confession just as he has also chosen to narrate at this point the change of Peter's name, another development brought into various contexts by the other Gospels (cf. Mk 3:16; Lk 6:14; Jn 1:42).

When we recognize the nature of Matthew's parallel to the story of Peter's confession, its individual parts fall into place and make sense. We may recall that he has already shown the disciples confessing Jesus with a title more significant than that of Peter's "Messiah" (see on Mt 14:23b–33 above). Similarly, in Matthew's Gospel alone the Lord asks his disciples on this occasion, "Who do men say that *the Son of Man* is?," again already implying something more exalted than the comparatively prosaic "Messiah" elicited in the confession. While he has not verbally altered the terms of Peter's confession, therefore, not even by adding "the Son of the living God," he undoubtedly expects us to see in it not the still obscure affirmation of the disciples' pre-resurrection experience of Jesus, but the fullness of meaning which Peter, the disciples, and the entire Church later attached to the title *Christ* when confessing their resurrected Lord and Savior (cf. Acts 2:36).

It is for this reason that in Matthew's Gospel Peter's confession is ascribed to divine revelation: *flesh and blood have not revealed this to you, but my heavenly Father.* It is this confession of Christian faith which evokes Jesus' reciprocal testimony to Peter, for it is only within the ambit of Christian faith that Peter can exercise the role which Jesus assigns to him. *Therefore I say to you:* Peter has named Christ, and now Christ names Peter. If Matthew had written as Mark does, he would now have: *You are Cephas, which means Peter,* or, *which means Rock.* There is no doubt whatever that Jesus gave to his disciple Simon bar Jona ("son of John," according to Jn 1:42) the Aramaic name *kêphā* (see above on Jn 1:35–42), the name by which he was commonly known in the apostolic Church (cf. 1 Cor 1:12, 3:22, 9:5, 15:5; Gal 1:18, 2:9, 11, 14). The Greek *petros*, whence our "Peter," is a translation of this word, which means "rock." The word provides Jesus with the figure by which he designates Peter as the foundation of his messianic community: *upon this rock I shall build my Church.* The verb is in the future tense, for the Church comes into being only in the apostolic age following the resurrection and the gift of the Spirit. How Peter served as the rock of the apostolic community has been portrayed best of all by Luke in the first part of his Acts of the Apostles.

Only once again, and again by Matthew (18:17), is the word "church" (*ekklēsia*) used in the Gospels. Statistically in the New Testament it is eminently a Pauline word, and therefore many scholars have doubted that it or its Aramaic equivalent could actually have been used by Jesus. There appears to be no reason, however, why Jesus could not have said precisely what Matthew reports him as saying. In the Septuagint Old Testament *ekklēsia* is a common word, ordinarily the translation of the Hebrew *qāhāl*, the term which designates Israel as the congregation or community of the Lord (Deut 23:2, etc.). "The *qāhāl* of God" is one of the titles by which the eschatological Jewish community of Qumran identified itself. That Jesus, who had already begun to gather about him the messianic community which accepted his proclamation of the kingdom, should have provided for its continuance in the Church that would survive his death, is altogether reasonable. The occasion of this action, however, as we have already suggested, was probably more intimately connected with the time of his passion, death, and resurrection than this relatively remote period of Caesarea Philippi.

Against this Church, Jesus adds, *the gates of hell shall not prevail.* "Hell" here is not *gehenna* but *hadēs,* ordinarily the equivalent of the Hebrew *sheol*=death in a purely "neutral" sense as opposed to life (cf. Apo 1:18, 6:8, 20:13 f.), not the place of punishment of the evil dead (though in Lk 16:23 *hadēs* is represented as a place of torment, as is *sheol* in the Psalms of Solomon, a Jewish apocryphal work of the first century B.C.). Death is figured here as a city with gates, just as the Church is, "built" on a rock. The gates of an ancient city were its stronghold both for defence and offence. Death and the Church are thus seen as two warring cities, and victory is assured to the Church. In the biblical view death was never something merely natural as the inevitable lot of man—the pagan idea— but as evidence of the power of Satan (cf. Heb 2:14), the reign of sin and evil inimical to life and truth (cf. 1 Cor 15:26; Apo 6:8, 20:13 f.). Against all of this the power of the Church will be proof.

Still using the same figure, Jesus promises to Peter *the keys of the kingdom of heaven.* He who had the keys of a city controlled it as its head and ruler (cf. Is 22:22). The effect of Peter's rule will be to give men access to God's kingdom, in contrast to the teaching of the scribes and Pharisees (cf. Mt 23:13). How this rule will be exercised is expressed in the terms *binding and loosing.* This was a rabbinical legal formula meaning to declare with authority what was or was not of obligation. Peter's decisions as ruler over the Church of God will be ratified by God himself. The early Church was conscious that it survived as a result of these decisions, living by the teaching of the apostles under the headship of Peter (cf. Acts 2:42). In Mt 18:18 (the Johannine parallel is Jn 20:22 f.) this power of binding and loosing, shared by all the apostles, is more specifically defined in the jurisdiction of the Church over the forgiveness of sin.

Mk 8:31–33   It is important to recognize how closely in the mind of
Mt 16:21–23   the evangelists the following passage is connected with
Lk 9:22   Peter's confession. Even Luke, who delicately omits in
                this instance the continued interchange between Jesus
and Peter, brings out the connection by making verse 22 a part of the same sentence as verse 21. The disciples had confessed, in the person of Peter, Jesus' messiahship, but now Jesus himself completes the confession by defining the terms of his messiahship as known only to him and the Father. Accordingly, he applies to himself the title *Son of Man* (Matthew has already used it above) which he preferred to any other as most accurately defining his character. This is the first of three Synoptic passages in which the Lord unequivocally speaks of his suffering, death, and resurrection. The Son of Man *must* undergo these things by the divine decree; the *elders, chief priests, and scribes* designate the three divisions of the Sanhedrin. As already noted (above on Mt 12:38–42 and parallel), that Jesus foresaw his death and even his resurrection, which in Jewish concepts would be an inevitable corollary, as entailed in the messianic destiny he had been given to perform, is part of the consistent testimony of the Gospels and is by no means hard to credit. Accounts such as the present one, however, which have been written in the light of subsequent fulfillment, have almost certainly made explicit what was at the time understood far more obscurely by men who had not yet taken in the theology of the cross. Otherwise, much of what appears in the ensuing pages of the Gospel would be incomprehensible.

Peter's reaction to the Lord's words shows, in fact, how little as yet the fullness of Jesus' messiahship was appreciated by his own disciples. He *took him aside:* Peter's attitude is one of genial condescension, an attempt to raise the sagging spirits of his Master who is taking a far too pessimistic view of his prospects. Jesus' reaction in turn was a violent one: *he turned on* Peter in the presence of the other disciples. Without realizing it, Peter was playing the part of *Satan* (see above on Lk 4:3–13 and parallel), tempting him to follow the easy, human path of an earthly messiah rather than to adhere to the lonely course on which he had set himself, the course of total sacrifice of self. How little Peter still knew of his Master, and to what he had committed himself in becoming his disciple!

Mk 8:34–9:1   It is about the consequences of discipleship that Jesus
Mt 16:24–28   now begins to speak, in a series of sayings which have
Lk 9:23–27   been assembled doubtless from various periods in his
               life and appropriately attached to this context in which
the doctrine of the cross has been broached for the first time. Evidences of
editorial work are not lacking, including Mark's curious reference to *the
crowd*, which is out of place here and obviously earlier belonged to another
context.

The first saying has a greater immediacy to the life of Jesus as it appears
in Matthew and Mark than in its Lucan version. *Take up his cross* Jesus
probably intended to be understood most literally. It is by no means
necessary to suppose that the Gospel tradition has paraphrased his original
utterance in view of its knowledge of his crucifixion. It is probably safe to
say that everyone of his hearers had seen more than once the terrible sight
of a convicted criminal being driven along by whips, naked and covered
with blood, a beam of wood lashed to his shoulders, on his way to the
place of his execution. The Romans had made crucifixion a familiar occurrence in Palestine. If Jesus foresaw that his course was leading to his
death, he would naturally have thought of a death by crucifixion. And this
was what they must also expect who would heed his invitation to *follow
me*. On the other hand, *take up his cross daily* in Luke indicates an
adaptation of the saying to the continued perils and sacrifices of Christian
living (cf. 1 Cor 15:31) rather than an immediate summons to martyrdom.

The second saying, which Matthew and Luke repeat here in Mark's
version, they also have reproduced elsewhere (along with a variant version
of the first saying) from the source they share that is independent of Mark
(cf. Mt 10:38 f.; Lk 14:27, 17:33); it is also found in Jn 12:25 where we
shall see it later in context. It is, therefore, certainly one of the best attested of Jesus' teachings. In context it continues the thought of following
Jesus in the face of death and plays on the multiple sense of the word
psychē (the Hebrew *nephesh*), that is, the soul or self as it refers simply
to sentient existence on the one hand, and as it is destined for eternal life
on the other. A man may refuse Jesus' call to follow him thinking
thereby to save his life, yet by that very concern for self-preservation he
may lose his share in the only life that counts. To be willing to throw one's
life away, paradoxically, is the way into eternal life. *What would be man's
profit*, the Gospel adds, *were he to gain even the whole world, yet forfeit
his life?* When the Son of Man comes into his eschatological kingdom, it
will be made apparent who has really preserved his life and who has in
reality thrown it away.

The passage concludes with a final saying that has little to do with the
context but has been brought in because of its topical connection with
the kingdom of God. It is one of the most perplexing and debated of the

sayings ascribed to Jesus in the Synoptic Gospels—and, because of its difficulties, doubtless one of the most authentic. Because in it Jesus appears to entertain an eschatological view that did not correspond with the subsequent development of the Church, it has raised all sorts of questions concerning the limitations placed on his knowledge of such events (see below on Mk 13:28–32 and parallels). *Those standing here* would almost certainly have understood him to be speaking of the final judgment of God and the consummation of this order. The Gospel tradition has interpreted such sayings of Jesus in various ways, all of them, as we shall see, having some foundation in his other words and teaching. At least a provisional fulfillment of the coming of the kingdom they have seen in the story of the transfiguration that immediately follows.

Mk 9:2–10   If the preceding saying is perplexing to the commentator,
Mt 17:1–9   even more perplexing is the story that follows it. The story
Lk 9:28–36   of the transfiguration fits so strangely into the picture of
              Jesus' public life and is filled with so many symbolic de-
tails, by many it has been thought to be either a displaced resurrection-narrative or a parabolic portrayal of the spiritual realities which were hidden by the incarnation and perceptible only to the eyes of faith (cf. Jn 1:14). It may be doubted, however, whether either of these explanations completely accounts for the story of the transfiguration, which was assumed by the apostolic Church to have historical value in its own right (cf. 2 Pt 1:16–18). Whatever may have been the exact circumstances of the event, however, there is no doubt that as the story appears in the Gospels it has an artistic relationship to its surrounding context. It is, for one thing, the completion of the story of Peter's confession. This is the reason for the chronological indication, *after six days* in Matthew and Mark, *about eight days* in Luke, or as we would say, "a week later"—a virtually unprecedented agreement among authors who are usually notoriously indifferent to such matters. Peter's confession and its sequel, Jesus' prediction of his passion and its consequences for his disciples, form a unit with the transfiguration to set forth in all its fullness what the Synoptic Gospels want to say of the historical Jesus as the Christ.

Jesus takes with him the favored disciples *Peter, James, and John,* the same three who will witness his agony in the garden (see below on Mk 14:32b–42 and parallels); in several ways the Gospels associate these two episodes in which such seemingly conflicting sides of Jesus' person became manifest. Matthew and Mark locate the scene on *a high mountain,* while Luke says that *he went up on the mountain to pray.* It is Luke's practice to mention the Savior's prayer on important occasions; here, however, he makes a point of the prayer as part of the event itself, for it was *as he was praying* that Jesus was transfigured. Luke follows an independent source in his description of the transfiguration, and it is likely that this detail has something to say as regards the historicity of the event, that it may have been the consequence of ecstatic prayer. Luke alone also recounts that the disciples shook themselves awake from a heavy sleep as the vision opened before them (vs. 32), a thing which might suggest a psychological conditioning for this spiritual experience. Because of the connection of this story with Caesarea Philippi, it has often been suggested that the high mountain was nearby Hermon. The next events described by the Gospels, however, occurred in Galilee (cf. Mk 9:30), and therefore most early commentators identified the site with Mount Tabor. It should be evident, in any case, that it is impossible to extract a geography of the transfiguration from the Gospels.

The transfiguration, according to the Gospels, consisted in a change of Jesus' bodily appearance and an accompanying resplendence of his clothing. The verb used by Matthew and Mark which we translate "transfigure" (*metamorphoō*) is found elsewhere in the New Testament only in Rom 12:2 and 2 Cor 3:18 where it designates the spiritual transformation of the Christian through grace. The connection of these passages is more than verbal. The transfiguration was a visible anticipation of the eschatological *glory* (the word used by Luke in vss. 31 f. and by Paul in 2 Cor 3:18) of the Son of Man (cf. Mk 8:38 and parallels), even as the life of grace is an invisible anticipation of the eschatological glory of the children of God. In keeping with this understanding of the event is the appearance of *Moses and Elijah.* As we know (see above on Jn 1:19-24), in Jewish eyes these were eschatological messianic figures: in a sense they sum up all of Old Testament expectation, the Law and the Prophets. Matthew and Mark leave us to imagine about what they were *conversing with Jesus.* Luke, however, says that they *spoke of his departure* (*exodos*) *which he was about to accomplish in Jerusalem.* The glorification of the Son of Man is to be achieved through the willing obedience of the Servant of the Lord, not through the triumphant messianism of popular and nationalistic thought.

This message, too, is brought out in what follows. Of Peter's excited proposal that they build *three tents,* Mark observes that *he did not know what to say.* This can be taken two ways. Peter was understandably confused, and therefore his words need not be taken too seriously. On the other hand, it was the wrong thing that he said, for he was seeking to prolong the present glory by ignoring the means by which it was to be made possible, just as he had at the time of his confession of Jesus' messiahship. Doubtless there is an allusion to the eschatological Feast of Booths (Tabernacles or Tents): this joyous feast, in which ancient Israel had celebrated the kingship of Yahweh, in late Jewish prophecy had come to signify the consummation of the messianic age (cf. Zech 14:16-19), and thus its annual observance was particularly a time of messianic excitement (cf. Jn 7:2 ff.). Rather than with Peter's tents, however, the three eschatological figures are covered with a *cloud* of theophany (cf. Ex 24:15, 40:35; Num 9:18), and as before at Jesus' baptism the heavenly voice proclaims him Servant of the Lord (see above on Lk 3:21–22 and parallels). Matthew and Mark have, as in the story of the baptism, *my beloved Son.* The best manuscripts of Luke read *my chosen Son,* which contains an additional allusion to Is 42:1. *Hear him* is new: it undoubtedly refers to the injunction of Deut 18:15.

Jesus' command that they should say nothing of this vision *until the Son of Man had risen from the dead* underlines the anticipatory character of the transfiguration. Mark also takes the occasion to note the puzzlement of the disciples over the very idea of resurrection, another reminder that we are viewing the Gospel story through the refracted light of post-resurrection faith and understanding.

Mk 9:11–13   Mark and Matthew conclude the story of the transfig-
Mt 17:10–13   uration with a conversation between Jesus and the dis-
              ciples concerning the rabbinical opinion that Elijah
would return, according to the prophecy in Mal 3:23 f., to prepare the way for the Messiah; Luke, who likes to think of Jesus as himself taking the role of Elijah the reconciler, has omitted this passage.

Elijah had just been seen together with Jesus. How, then, could it be said that *Elijah must come first?* Jesus' reply is that Elijah has, indeed, come first, in the person of John the Baptist. More importantly, he came as a real prefigurement of the Messiah revealed in Jesus, for just as *it is written of the Son of Man* / Servant of the Lord that he *must suffer many things and be despised,* so it had been with the Baptist. The Baptist, too, *they treated as they willed, as it was written of* Elijah long ago (cf. 1 Kgs 19:2, 10).

14. YET A LITTLE WHILE

Mk 9:14–29 The episode with which we begin appears to presup-
Mt 17:14–21 pose the Galilean ministry, especially if by *scribes* Mark
Lk 9:37–43a means here what he usually does. The *amazement* of
the crowd at the sight of Jesus does not necessarily look
back to the transfiguration, as though it saw some traces of what the
three disciples had seen on the mountain, but can be explained by the
tension and excitement that had built up before his sudden and unexpected appearance. The failure of Jesus' disciples to cure the afflicted boy
had provoked a heated controversy, doubtless over Jesus himself, who
now arrived at the psychological moment. The atmosphere of skepticism
and unbelief which surrounds the scene, and which Jesus sees as typical
of a whole *unbelieving generation*, stands in sharp contrast to the vision
of glory so recently described in the Gospels.

In their accounts of the unfortunate boy's affliction the Gospels seem
to be describing the symptoms of epilepsy, which was popularly equated
with insanity and the possession of an evil spirit. Jesus' lament over the
general lack of faith is the more understandable as it becomes evident
that the disciples, too, were unbelieving. This, at least, is Matthew's explanation of their inability to exercise the power Jesus had given them
(see above on Mk 3:13–19 and parallels): he cites in this connection
a well-known saying of the Lord (cf. Mt 21:21; Mk 11:23; Lk 17:6),
here to imply that their faith is not even as great as *a mustard seed*
(see above on Mt 13:31 f. and parallels). Even the distraught father
mingles incredulity with his humble cry for help—*if you can.* Jesus' retort is an exasperated echo, the reaction of a weary Master who has done
so much with such little effect. *"If you can"! For one who believes,
everything is "can"!* The man's response in the consciousness of an
awakening faith remains an inspiration to the Christian surrounded by a
world of doubt: *I do believe; help my weak faith!*

Mark ascribes the failure of the disciples to heal the boy not so much
to their lack of faith as to their complacent exercise of a committed
power without due recognition of its source: *This kind cannot be cast
out except by prayer.* Most of our Greek manuscripts add here "and by

fasting," but the critical evidence leaves us in no doubt that this is an early expansion of the text. The text thus expanded served as a model for another early scribe who inserted what appears as verse 21 in the standard version of Matthew's Gospel.

Mk 9:30–32   At this point the evangelists have placed the second of
Mt 17:22–23   Jesus' predictions of his coming passion and death (see
Lk 9:43b–45   above on Mk 8:31–33 and parallels). The terms are
              somewhat less precise than those used on the former
occasion, which has led some to suppose that in this passage we may have a more primitive form of the same tradition. The Gospels feature here the disciples' uneasiness over what Jesus has said and their fear at enquiring more deeply into his meaning; this is undoubtedly an accurate portrayal of the state of mind of men who are only beginning to realize the implications of the commitments which they have made.

Mt 17:24–27   The story of the paying of the temple tax is told only by
              Matthew. Matthew's interest in Peter partly explains his
use of the story, but probably even more important to him was its subject matter, which involved a problem that was of deep concern to all the evangelists and the early Church (see below on Mt 22:15–22 and parallels).

The *didrachma* or double drachma was a Greek coin worth upwards of a half dollar in our money, though of course in those times its purchasing power would have been far greater. It was considered to be the equivalent of the half shekel which according to the Law (cf. Ex 30:11–16) was to be paid by every Israelite each year for the support of the temple; under Roman domination the Jews were not allowed to coin their own money, except for small pieces of little value. Paying the temple tax was both a duty and an honor. Priests were exempted, but all other males subject to the Law, even the Levites, were expected to render it. On the contrary, it was not accepted from Samaritans and others whose title to Jewish orthodoxy was rejected.

The question whether Jesus would pay the tax was doubtless asked without ulterior motive. The tax was collected locally, in this case by citizens of Capernaum, and then sent to Jerusalem by means of the pilgrim caravans. Peter's affirmative answer was probably based on his experience of Jesus as well as presumption. The payment of the tax is never at issue; the point of the story, however, is that it was paid freely and to avoid disedification, not as of obligation. The little parable suggests that Jesus —and with him, Peter—are *the sons* of whom *the kings of the earth* do not expect tribute. Jesus, in view of his unique relationship to his Father, did not recognize the temple tax as required of him. Presumably Matthew implies to his Christian readers that they are somewhat in the same position as regards the taxes imposed upon them by the law of Rome. As

children of the Father of all law and authority *they are free,* but other
serious considerations should persuade them to pay. Their Master had
given them no precedent for rebellion or anarchy.

The miracle story which concludes the episode—actually, not so much
the story of a miracle as the promise of one—is not open to the objection
that miracles are not to be expected where natural means will do. It is
consistent with Jesus' insistence that he, and Peter because of him, are
free of the tax, and that if he submits himself to it he does so entirely on
his own terms. The Roman silver *stater* had the value of four drachmas.

Mk 9:33–37   The three Synoptic Gospels now continue with a story
Mt 18:1–5   that admirably suits their intention of characterizing this
Lk 9:46–48   present stage of Jesus' career as one of the education of
               his disciples. Essentially, the story is the same in all three
Gospels. It must be observed, however, that in this instance it is Matthew
who has made the most of it, he has depended here on another source
besides Mark.

In the context of Jesus' reiterated pronouncements concerning the
true nature of his kingdom and his messiahship, there is something
ironical in the spectacle of the disciples' dispute over their relative dignity
in the messianic realm-to-be. Mark has the Lord first (vs. 35) make a
pronouncement which we find later in a somewhat ampler form (see below on Mk 10:43 f. and parallel). Then he preaches to them a parable in
action. It is easy to imagine the scene, bearing in mind once more the
informality of Palestinian life. Into the group of men sitting on the rush-
strewn floor in earnest conversation had wandered one of the village children. Jesus places the child in their midst, holds it in his arms, and tells
them that such they must become if they are to have any part in his kingdom. The saying that makes the point of the parable is Matthew's contribution: *unless you change and become like little children, you shall
not enter the kingdom of heaven.*

The sense of this saying has often been misunderstood. The Oriental
loves children, sometimes to excess, but he has no sentimental illusions
about them. The Lord is not extolling here any supposed childlike virtues
of humility or simplicity, virtues which many parents would be surprised
to learn are proper to children. *Whoever considers himself of little account like this little child* means exactly what it says. The child was
without rights to consideration in society, totally dependent upon the
good will of his elders, an "it" rather than a "he." By deliberate choice,
Jesus says, his disciples must become what the child is by necessity. This
is the only greatness allowable in the kingdom of him who came to be
the servant of all.

The other saying which concludes this passage is independent of the
foregoing (cf. Jn 13:20), but related to it conceptually. To *receive a*

child such as this—to succor the needy, the helpless, the abandoned—*in my name*, is truly to take in Christ and his revelation of the God of love and mercy (cf. Mt 25:31 ff.). This is likewise the teaching of 1 Jn 4:19–21.

Mk 9:38–41   The "in my name" of the immediately preceding verse
Lk 9:49–50   has led Mark and Luke to insert here the case of "the
Mt 10:40–42   strange exorcist." Acts 19:13–16 tells of certain Jewish
              exorcists who invoked Jesus' name as a kind of magical
formula, and a well-known exorcism papyrus now in the National Library of Paris, written about A.D. 300, includes among the efficacious names to be used that of "Jesu, the god of the Hebrews." The situation called to Jesus' attention by *John*, the son of Zebedee, does not seem to have been of such a character. Though unauthorized and unknown to the rest of the disciples, the man appears to have been successfully appealing to God with some kind of true faith in the person of Jesus. Jesus' argument is based on his exercise of a power for good, and it is rightly cited as a principle of tolerance. If the man was healing in Jesus' name he could hardly be counted as an enemy, *for he who is not against us is for us*. Obviously, this is not Jesus' only word on the often complicated issue of others' relationship to him and his teaching.

Matthew has omitted these verses, possibly because he was afraid that they might be misunderstood (cf. Mt 7:22 f.). In the context of his "missionary discourse" of Jesus, however, he has applied to the disciples a lengthier expression of the sentiment which Mark ascribes to the Lord in verse 41. Acceptance of Christ's followers and representatives is the measure of accepting Christ himself. Good works done in their behalf will be rewarded as having been done to the Lord. Such ideas were precious to the Church of the Gospels.

Mk 9:42–48   Building again on a verbal connection with the preced-
Mt 18:6–9   ing context, this time with the "child" of verse 37, Mark,
Lk 17:1–2   followed by Matthew, attaches a saying of Jesus on the
              scandal of the weak: *Whoever causes one of these little ones who believe to commit sin*. There is also a connection of ideas: if we are to be rewarded for doing good to God's children, we shall certainly be punished for doing them evil, and there is no greater evil we can do them than to cause them to sin against the faith by which they are saved. *Better for him if a millstone were hung from his neck and he were thrown in the sea*. The millstone of which Jesus speaks is the *mylos onikos*, "donkey mill," a huge stone three or four feet in diameter and weighing several hundred pounds, turned on a pivot by oxen or asses.

Scandals must come, Matthew adds. In this world, constituted as it is, they are inevitable. Yet no one is thereby excused from guilt in being the occasion whereby evil finds an outlet in the world. Thus far there is a

Lucan parallel to what Mark and Matthew have in this place, but put in another context which we shall understand better later on.

Mark and Matthew continue with a transition from the objective to the subjective aspect of scandal, that is, from the consideration of man as an occasion of sin to others to the consideration of how he can be a danger to himself. Basically, Matthew repeats here what he has already included in the Sermon on the Mount (see above on Mt 5:27–30). Mark's version is substantively the same, but in speaking of *gehenna* and its *unquenchable fire* he cites the final graphic verse of the Book of Isaiah (66:24), which originally referred quite literally to the rotting corpses and smouldering refuse of the Valley of Hinnom.

Mk 9:49–50   It is this citation which leads Mark into his final verses
Lk 14:34–35   which deal with "salt"—the connection, however, is diffi-
                  cult to see at best. *Everyone will be salted with fire*: apparently the association is purely verbal, leading to the enunciation of a new thought. Fire—now the fire of eschatological judgment and purification rather than the fire of destruction of the preceding verse—will preserve the people of God as salt preserves food. Mark now brings in the little parable on salt as a quality of the Christian character which Matthew used earlier in the Sermon on the Mount (see above on Mt 5:13–16) and which Luke has also placed in a context of the demands of discipleship, where it appears, however, as a grim warning against apostasy. *Have salt in yourselves*, Mark concludes. Salt is also figurative of the astringent qualities of practical wisdom and prudence required for social living: *thus you will be at peace with one another.*

Mt 18:10–14   During the past several passages we have lost contact
Lk 15:3–7   with Luke's continuity, as now we do with Mark's as
                  well. Shortly we shall rejoin these two evangelists to see how they continue the Gospel story. For the moment it is Matthew who provides the best unity. He has made the immediately preceding passages the beginning of his fourth major discourse into which he has gathered the Lord's teaching on the nature of the community life of the Church, and it is this that he now continues with the present parable of the lost sheep, which Luke has put in another context for a somewhat different purpose.

As Matthew tells the parable, it builds on the theme of the concern due to *the little ones* of the Church and is an exhortation to apostolic zeal; *their angels in heaven continually look on my heavenly Father's face* underlines the divine solicitude for even the least deserving and most erring of God's children, a solicitude which should serve as a model for that of the Church. The parable itself is quite clear and requires little explanation. Luke makes a more dramatic story of it: in his context it is told in rebuke of the Pharisaical scandal taken at the Lord's association with sinners.

Mt 18:15–18   Consideration of the erring brother leads Matthew to follow the parable of the lost sheep with these words of Jesus on fraternal correction and the discipline of the forgiveness of sin. The Gospel is speaking of real sin, not just social offenses: *if your brother sins* is the reading of the best manuscripts, and "against you" is recognized to be an addition to the text. Previously we have seen Jesus vindicate to himself as Son of Man authority on earth to forgive sins, and we also noted the Church's recognition that this authority continued as its own (see above on Mk 2:1–12 and parallels). This is one of the several Gospel passages in which Jesus' transmission of this power to his apostles is explicitly affirmed (cf. also Mt 16:19; Lk 17:3; Jn 20:23).

The exercise of this power must be above all pastoral. Private fraternal correction may suffice to bring the sinner to the repentance that is required for his forgiveness. *But if he will not listen, take one or two others:* the invocation of the legal precedent of Deut 19:15 indicates that a serious and public matter is in question. If even this does not suffice, the case should be referred *to the church,* to the entire community. Only when contumacy is proof against all these measures of suasion should the person be excommunicated from Christian society, declared to be, in Jewish terms, *like the heathen and the publican* (cf. Mt 5:46 f.). In verse 18 the same judicial power is affirmed for the Church through the apostles which in Mt 16:19 was ascribed to Peter.

Mt 18:19–20   The following two verses appear to interrupt the continuity of thought, for verse 21 takes up again the idea of forgiveness, but actually the connection is quite close and logical. Jesus has not been talking about fraternal correction on a private and individual level, but of a power over sin and its forgiveness exercised by the Church, a power that it can exercise only because *I am in their midst.* It is the same presence of Christ which guarantees a special dignity and efficacy to the prayer of the assembled Church. Previously Jesus described the proper spirit of prayer as one in which a man retires into the privacy of his room and asks God in secret for what he wants (see above on Mt 6:5–8). This was not a condemnation of public prayer, but his way of rebuking ostentation and insincerity. The public prayer of the Church does not depend simply on the fervor of the individual Christian who prays, but it partakes of the efficacy of the prayer of Christ himself living in his Church gathered together *in my name.*

Mt 18:21–22   From the public sin with which the Church is to deal with pastoral charity the discourse passes to the question of fraternal charity in regard to personal offenses. *Peter* asks how

often he is obliged to pardon someone who has offended him: *up to
seven times?* Apparently the rabbis taught that no one could be expected
to forgive an offender beyond three or at the most four times, and Peter
doubtless thought he had seized the spirit of Jesus' generous interpretation of the Law when he had raised the number to seven. But the Lord's
answer is that there is no law to regulate charity. As often as offense has
been given, so often is there need to forgive (cf. Lk 17:4); the *seventy
times seven* of verse 22 is a conscious reversal of Lamech's song of vengeance in Gen 4:24. Unrestricted vengeance had been banished by the
Law of Moses, but for him who loves as a Christian should there is no
need of law (see above on Mt 5:21–26).

Mt 18:23–35   Appropriately Matthew ends Jesus' discourse with another well-known parable, which forms a kind of com-
mentary on the petition of the Lord's Prayer, "forgive us our debts as we
forgive our debtors" (see below on Mt 6:9–15 and parallel). Far more
importantly, however, it gives the motivation for the extraordinary spirit
of forgivingness which is expected of Christians and which has just been
commended to Peter: they must forgive their brothers their trifling offenses because of the far greater offense which God has freely forgiven
them.

The parable in this instance takes almost the shape of a fairy tale. Most
of the details are somewhat fabulous. The *king*—more properly, "a kingly
person"—is an Oriental potentate who disposes of a debt of *ten thousand talents*—twenty million dollars might suggest the sum—as casually
as the next man might cast an alms to a beggar. The exaggerations
are all calculated. In contrast, the second debt of *a hundred denarii* was
paltry indeed. Though such details help to make the point of the story, we
must as usual resist the temptation to allegorize it. The lesson of the
parable is in verse 33 (positively) and in verse 35 (negatively), not in
the intervening verse that rounds out the story. The parable, in other
words, does not teach that God will take back a pardon he has once given
or deliver anyone over to a debtors' prison. Its message is that of 1 Jn
4:11.

Mt 19:1–2   Matthew concludes Jesus' discourse with his usual formula
Mk 10:1   (see above on Mt 7:28 f.) and takes us immediately *to
Lk 9:51   the district of Judea beyond the Jordan.* Here he is following Mark, who now begins what is sometimes called the
story of the "Perean ministry." Each in his own way, the Synoptists are
doing much the same thing. They have at last brought the Galilean ministry to a definitive close and now set the Lord on his way toward Jerusalem
for the last act of the drama of our salvation in his passion, death, and
resurrection.

Luke, who has made the most of this section in his Gospel, deserves the greatest attention. He has long been waiting for this moment, and now he announces it in the tones of a triumphant exordium. Up to this point, though we may not have always noticed it, he has been quietly preparing for this climactic turn of events. In the other Gospels it has been made evident that Jesus has left Galilee more than once; in Luke's it has not. Even in describing something as important as Peter's confession of the Lord at Caesarea Philippi (see above on Mk 8:27–30 and parallels), Luke carefully refrained from identifying the place, thus not to anticipate this instant when he departed his Galilean homeland and *set his face to go up to Jerusalem*. For the same reason, from now on he will suppress any geographical reference that would detract from the theme of Jesus' journey toward his destiny.

Luke designates this moment as *when the days had been fulfilled for him to be taken up*. This "being taken up," an expression which Luke uses for the Lord's ascension in Acts 1:2, 11, 22, employs the language which the Greek Old Testament applied to such events as the assumption of Elijah (2 Kgs 2:9–11; Sir 48:9; 1 Macc 2:58) and of Enoch (Sir 49:14), the latter a figure which was of intense interest for the later Judaism of New Testament times. Luke means by this term the summation of Jesus' atoning life in his suffering, death, resurrection, and ascension to the Father, the complex of events which have made possible the coming of the Spirit into the Church. The term is, therefore, analogous to John's speaking of Christ as "raised up" or "glorified" (see above on Jn 3:14–21).

Lk 9:52–56   Only Luke has recorded this episode of the hostile Samaritans: the last time we saw Jesus in Samaria, he had a more hospitable reception (cf. Jn 4:4 ff.). As we know, the animosity between Jews and Samaritans was always intense and reciprocal. It was apt to flare up into bloodshed at the times of the pilgrimages to Jerusalem for the great feasts, when religious differences became underlined and accentuated. Sometimes it was worth the life of a Jew to venture through Samaritan territory, and this fact made it all the more inconvenient for those who had to come from Galilee. Jesus ran into this kind of situation. Having prudently *sent messengers before him* to feel out the sentiment, he learnt that he would not be welcome in this place *because his face was set toward Jerusalem*, and therefore he directed his way *to another village* where there would be no trouble.

James and John (as "sons of thunder"? cf. Mk 3:17) ask the Lord if he would have them *call down fire from heaven to consume them*. The evangelist is thinking of the event in the life of Elijah according to 2 Kgs 1:10–12. But while Jesus is the great prophetic figure of the New Testament, his prophetic word did not take such a form at all; hence *he turned and rebuked them*. "The Son of Man did not come to destroy

the lives of men but to save them," found in a great number of manuscripts, is doubtless a gloss on the text, but an accurate reading of its
meaning. On the other hand, what appears in some manuscripts as verse
55b, "He said to them, 'You do not know of what spirit you are,'" is
probably a Marcionite interpolation. Marcion, a strange second-century
heretic who accepted for his Scriptures only a corrupted form of Luke's
Gospel and some of the Pauline epistles, taught that the main work of
Jesus, the God of mercy of the New Testament, was to undo all that
had been done by the God of justice of the Old Testament.

Jn 7:2–13   We shall interrupt the Lucan "journey" narrative at this
               point, however, to consider the continuation of the Johan-
nine version of Jesus' public life. John, of course, has not built up his
Gospel to show one climactic appearance of Jesus in Jerusalem; he has,
as a matter of fact, centered the story of Jesus in Jerusalem rather than
Galilee. This present passage concerns a pilgrimage to Jerusalem on the
occasion of *the Jewish feast of Tabernacles*, the importance of which
we noted when commenting on the story of the transfiguration (see
above on Mk 9:2–10 and parallels). The section conforms to the
Johannine pattern: the feast serves as the occasion for a discourse in
which Jesus is revealed as the sign of God's glory replacing Jewish pre-
figurements (see above on Jn 2:1–11, 2:13–17, etc.), here the light of
life shining in the darkness of an unbelieving world (Jn 1:4 f.).

Jesus' *brothers* in the sense of his family relations (see above on Mk
3:31–35 and parallels) appear only here in the Fourth Gospel (in Jn
2:12 and 20:17 Jesus' brothers=his disciples). For John they represent unbelievers of the type encountered in Jn 2:23–25, 6:15—that is, those who
misinterpreted Jesus' *works*, seeing in them a fulfillment of their own
aspirations rather than a revelation of God for their acceptance, and
whose incipient faith led therefore ultimately to a rejection of his word.
Here they ask him to *go up to* Jerusalem, to make the solemn pilgrimage entry into the Holy City, taking advantage of the nationalistic
overtones of the feast of Tabernacles to *manifest* himself *to the world*
as they thought he should. Jesus' answer is that the time for his manifestation has not yet come; and when it does come, it will be of a vastly
different kind, which can be perceived only through the eyes of true
faith. Therefore he will not go up to Jerusalem in their sense, but only in
his own way. The world has, as a matter of fact, already seen and rejected
him (see above on Jn 3:14–21). His brothers themselves belong to this
world.

Jn 7:14–39   When Jesus does come up to Jerusalem *secretly* and
               when the feast was already half over, he finds the usual
situation of controversy about his person, varying degrees of interest both
idle and serious, dominated by the hostility of *the Jews*, here quite

obviously the Jewish leadership which is distinguished from the crowds who are more confused than inimical. He begins to teach *in the temple* courts thronged with pilgrims to the feast and all *marveled* at this (here we have the Johannine parallel to Mk 6:2; Mt 13:54; Lk 4:22a). To the implied criticism that he is self-taught, Jesus replies that he teaches a doctrine that is from God, which would be recognized as such by anyone who was truly trying to do God's will. His argument strikingly parallels that of Jn 5:31–47 (see above).

He now addresses himself to the previous controversy of Jn 5:16–30 (see above), employing new arguments. In the name of the Law they condemn his supposed violation of the Sabbath, *yet not one of you observes the Law:* the Law, of course, forbade the taking of an innocent man's life, and they were seeking to kill him (cf. Jn 5:18, 7:1). Doubtless the protestation of many in the crowd was sincere: *Who is seeking to kill you?;* however, verse 25 shows that the intentions of Jesus' enemies were not entirely secret. *One work I did* refers back to the miracle of Jn 5:2–15 (see above). Jesus' argument here on the "breaking" of the Sabbath parallels such Synoptic passages as Mk 2:27; Mt 12:11; Lk 13:15. The principle that circumcision was to be administered on the eighth day (Lev 12:3, etc.) even though it might coincide with the Sabbath was commonly accepted by the rabbis. But if the Sabbath can be set aside in favor of one member of the body, why *are you angry with me because I made a whole man well on the Sabbath?*

The next stage of the discourse plays on the theme of another popular misunderstanding. *Some of the Jerusalemites,* who knew full well what Jesus' enemies had in mind for him, were impressed by his boldness and the reasonableness of what he had to say. They noted that their leaders had fallen silent. Was it because they had become convinced and were ready to acknowledge him as Messiah? Doubtless they knew better than that; but still, silence gives consent, and perhaps the leaders had been convinced even against their wills. Yet *we know where this man comes from; but the Messiah, when he comes, no one will know where he comes from.* One popular notion of the Messiah was that his origins would be unknown before his sudden manifestation to Israel. Here, however, was Jesus, whose career the crowds had long watched, and whose relatives were even now standing about.

The passage is fraught with Johannine irony. They know him, yes, but only in the most superficial way possible. As regards everything that is essential they do not know him at all. They cannot know him because they do not know God, the one who has sent him. Had they known God, they would have recognized his messenger. It is probably in the same ironic vein that John refers in verse 31 to the *many in the crowd* who *believed in him:* their faith depended on miraculous *signs,* the real significance of which they had not perceived (see above on Jn 2:23–25).

Even this passing interest, however, provoked *the Pharisees and chief priests* to try to take further measures against him. Thus Jesus is inspired to his final utterances to this people. *Yet a little while I am with you:* nothing that his enemies can do will determine his coming and going, but only his free decision as the agent of the Father. *I go back to him who sent me:* even when it will seem that his enemies have prevailed, in reality Jesus will have fulfilled the mission of salvation for which he is in the world. *You will see me . . . you cannot come:* the finality of this sentence contrasts with the promise to the disciples in Jn 13:33–36. As usual, his words are taken in a superficial sense. *Does he intend to go into the Diaspora?* The question is intended sarcastically: since Jesus has gained no hearing with his own people, perhaps he will now try his luck with the Gentiles. But John sees its ironic implications: Christ in the Christian Church has indeed passed irrevocably from Palestinian Judaism into the Gentile world.

Jesus' closing statement is somewhat obscure, especially since for some reason the passing of several days is presupposed. The theme of Christ as living water is familiar (see above on Jn 4:4–19), and has probably been introduced here in view of the extensive libations proper to *the last day* of Tabernacles. *As the Scripture says:* we have to do with a paraphrase rather than a quotation, the identification of which is the more difficult since it is not clear whether it is to be referred to Christ or to the believer in Christ. Some passage like Ex 17:6 (cf. 1 Cor 10:4), Zech 14:8 (cf. Ezek 47:1–12), or Is 58:11 are probably in the evangelist's mind. At all events, it is clear that Jesus spoke of the outpouring of *the Spirit* which would be consequent on his glorification.

Jn 7:40–52   The variety of messianic expectations is again made evident in the discussion incident to Jesus' discourse. On *the prophet,* see above on Jn 1:19–24. Here the objection to recognizing in Jesus *the Messiah* is based on the standard doctrine of a Davidic Messiah of Judean origin: in John as in the Synoptic Gospels Jesus is commonly regarded as "the Galilean" (see above on Jn 4:43–45). The evangelist doubtless presupposes the Synoptic information on Jesus' Judean birth and therefore finds in the crowds' remarks a further indication of how little they know in comparison to what they pretend to know (vs. 27).

Jesus remains in control of his situation, as he had implied (vs. 33); no one as yet dared *lay hands on him.* Even the temple police sent to harass him (vs. 32) returned to their masters somewhat dazed from having heard Jesus (we are dealing here with the Johannine parallel to Mk 1:22; Lk 4:32; Mt 7:28 f.). The Pharisees' reaction to this accurately reflects some scribal opinion on the condition of the ordinary Jew who was no professional student of the Law: *this crowd which does not know the*

Law is accursed. This time, however, they had overstepped themselves and invited a rebuke from one of their own. *None of the Pharisees has believed in him,* they say. Out steps a Pharisee—and a Pharisee of Pharisees, for he is a member of the Sanhedrin—who does believe in him. They did not know that he was a follower of Christ, and with his characteristic timidity Nicodemus (see above on Jn 3:1–13) did not dare to make more than an indirect defense of Jesus, but it was enough to show that they had gone too far and enough, therefore, to enrage them further. *Are you also from Galilee?* they ask with a sneer. This was hardly to address themselves to the serious question of law—the very Law that they pretended to reverence—that Nicodemus had raised. Their final statement is likewise bluster. *From Galilee a prophet* (some important manuscripts have *the prophet*) *does not arise* interposes regional prejudice between themselves and the word of God.

Jn 7:53–8:11   There seems to be no doubt that the beautiful little story that now follows and which interrupts Jesus' Tabernacles discourse did not originally belong to the Gospel of John. It is lacking in practically all of the best Greek manuscripts of John, but there is some good reason to think that it has been dislodged from the Gospel of Luke, whose language and viewpoints it suits much better (in some manuscripts it appears at the conclusion of Lk 21). It is possible that in early times it was transferred to this location in the Gospels as a kind of commentary on Jn 8:15 below. At any rate, it is a part of the Gospel which deserves consideration in its own right, regardless of its context.

A situation is supposed like that of the Synoptic account of Passion week, when Jesus was spending the nights on *the Mount of Olives,* the hill that overlooks Jerusalem on the east, separated from the Holy City by the narrow Kidron Valley (cf. Lk 21:37 f.). *In the early morning* he has returned *to the temple* and, as before, the people gather to hear him while he sits on the ground before them in the manner of Oriental teachers. Through the courtyard passes a group of *scribes and Pharisees,* dragging with them a woman accused of adultery. They are taking her to trial. Then they see Jesus and quickly they form a plan to use the woman to hurt him in the eyes of the people.

Jesus' foes present him with a dilemma not unlike others in the Synoptic Gospels (see below on Mt 22:15–22). If he says that she should be condemned to stoning as the Law directed (Deut 22:23 f.)—or was he being challenged to specify stoning where the Law was silent as to the method of punishment? (cf. Lev 20:10; Deut 22:22)—then what would be thought now of his gentle teaching, of his principles of love and mercy that had already made him suspect in their eyes of defying the Law? If, on the other hand, he asks for her release, is not this another clearcut proof of his disregard for the Law of Moses and God?

The text says that *Jesus bent down and wrote with his finger on the ground.* Since only here in the Gospels is Jesus ever said to have written anything, commentators have enjoyed speculating over the centuries as to what he wrote. Probably he wrote nothing, but merely traced idle lines in the dirt to show his lack of interest in their simulated concern over his opinion. This seems to be indicated by what follows. *As they continued to ask him,* he finally stood and gave them his answer in a seemingly careless way, as though he had been distracted from something more important, for he immediately returned to his tracings in the earth.

His answer was adequate to the situation, but by no means should it be extended beyond the situation nor sentimentalized to produce the portrait of a Christ indifferent to sin. He asked the woman's accusers to examine their own consciences before inflicting punishment on others, and here they were, prepared to exploit a wretched person's shame and humiliation simply to face down one of their adversaries. Though he himself judges no one, his very presence is judgment against them and their unworthy motives (cf. Jn 8:15). He likewise stands as a merciful judge of the woman, who is told to go and *sin no more.* Forgiveness of sin does not condone sin, but looks toward its eradication in the sinner.

Jn 8:12–20   After the interpolated story of the woman taken in adultery, Jesus' Tabernacles discourse continues with another theme suggested by the rites of the feast, this time the illumination of the temple area to symbolize the light of truth. *I am the light of the world* (see above on Jn 1:3b–5) and *the light of life* identify with Jesus concepts which the Old Testament (cf. Is 51:4), rabbinical Judaism, and the Qumran literature would use to describe the revelation of God in the Mosaic law.

Immediately there is a controversy. Previously (see above on Jn 5:31–47) Jesus had conceded the legal principle that a man testifying in his own behalf needs corroborating witnesses. Now, however, his approach is somewhat different: *Even if I am my own witness, my testimony is true.* The reason for this is that I *know where I came from and where I am going* (cf. Jn 7:14–39 above) while they clearly do not: the only testimony that is valid in his case only he can give, and they are incapable of receiving it. In this situation, since his testimony is at the same time that of *the Father who sent me,* the requirement of the two witnesses (Deut 17:6, 19:5) is met by the only two witnesses competent to testify. Jesus says *it is written in your Law:* the "your" is eloquent of the evangelist's idea of the separation from Judaism of the Christ of the Church. The Pharisees demand that Jesus produce his second witness, *your Father,* a puerile request which is their self-condemnation, confirmed by Jesus' reply, that they know neither God nor his Word.

Judgment is the other theme of this interchange. Jesus says *I judge no one* (as we saw, it may be this statement that occasioned the insertion of the preceding story). This does not really conflict with Jn 5:16–30 (see above), where Jesus defines his character as judge in that his presence in the world works judgment in the face of unbelief. Here he is contrasting his oneness of spirit with the Father with the superficial judgments of the Pharisees, *according to the flesh* (cf. Jn 7:24).

These words he spoke in the treasury while teaching in the temple. Jesus was probably standing at the door of the strong room adjoining the court of the women, the most public of the temple courtyards. If, as is likely, a crowd was assembled during this dispute, it would sufficiently explain why *no one arrested him.* The evangelist probably sees a further irony in the fact that it was in the temple that he spoke, and went unrecognized, who was to replace the temple (see above on Jn 2:18–22).

Jn 8:21–29   *Again* (on another occasion?) Jesus speaks to *them* (vs. 22: *the Jews*) in language that is strongly reminiscent of what we have already read above (see on Jn 7:14–39). As in Jn 7:33 f., Jesus tells them that he is *going away* and that they will seek him in vain; this time he adds that *you will die in your sins.* Putting the idea of death together with his assertion that *where I go you cannot come*, they arrive at an even more foolish conclusion than in Jn 7:35. He is going to commit suicide, thus go to hell and be out of reach of all righteous men! John's irony is found, of course, in the half-truth they have unwittingly stumbled on: Jesus will, indeed, lay down his life, and as a result he will be beyond their grasp forever.

Jesus has introduced the theme of their sin. They belong to the order that is *below* and *of this world*, which can lead only to death. He has come *from above* to bring them life. But the condition of this life is faith, and thus their unbelief proves that they will die in their sin. *You do not believe that I am* (see above on Jn 6:17b–21).

The Jews recognize Jesus' "I am" to be a title. But what does it mean? *Who are you?* they ask. The Greek of his reply is not too clear, but probably it should be translated: *From the beginning the same that I am now telling you.* All his words and deeds up to this point, in other words, have been consistent with his present assertion. They have not understood the one because they have not understood the others. It is, therefore, pointless for him to continue to speak to them, his words judging them the while. His testimony he continues to offer only because it was for this that he was sent into the world. The final testimony is coming, irrefutable for all who believe; though it, too, will be wasted on them. *When you have raised up the Son of Man* (see above on Jn 3:14–21), *then you will know that I am he.*

Jn 8:30–36   It is surprising to find in the midst of these polemical passages the notation that *while he was saying these*

things many believed in him, and even more surprising to learn that
Jesus spoke the words that follow *to the Jews who had come to believe
him*—who speedily demonstrate that they do not believe him at all and
who end by trying to kill him! However, we have by now seen it suggested more than once that this lengthy Tabernacles discourse is an artificial literary unity made up of elements in part disparate, in part dupli-
cated elsewhere in the Johannine discourse material. Hence, we should
not attach too much historical importance to the present editorial transition. It may serve as a reminder, nevertheless, even though it is little
relevant to this context, that Jesus' sermons did not always fall on
deaf ears and that there was a variety of dispositions among his hearers.

Jesus' initial statement could very well, as a matter of fact, have been
directed to his disciples or to those who would be his disciples (vss.
31 f.). The reaction to it, however, is not that of believers but of the will-
fully obtuse. *The truth shall make you free,* he had said. This man is
offering them freedom? Freedom to *the seed of Abraham?* The Jews had
been subjected to foreign conquerors for centuries—to Assyrians, Baby-
lonians, Syrians, Egyptians, Persians, Greeks of divers degrees, and lately
to Romans. Yet in a sense they had never surrendered. Secure in the conviction that the God of Israel was their truth, they had stubbornly preserved their national and religious identity despite all the odds, while
other religions and other peoples, including many of their oppressors,
had now been lost in time. There was a great deal of truth in their
proud retort: *We have never been enslaved to anybody!*

A great deal of truth, but also more than a little of the wrongheaded-
ness that made them deaf to the word of life. They were assuming that
the freedom of which Jesus spoke was theirs by birthright as Jews. But as
another great Jew would write: "The true Jew is not he who is such outwardly . . . the true Jew is he who is such inwardly" (Rom 2:28 f.).
Jews, too, can commit sin, and *everyone who commits sin is a slave of
sin.* Thus, Jesus implies, they are really slaves after all, and as slaves they
have no abiding home in the household of God along with his sons who
have received their freedom at the hands of his one Son (cf. Jn
1:12 f.).

Jn 8:37–47   If they are in reality slaves, he goes on, in what sense
can they claim to be *the seed of Abraham?* He repeats the
charge, *you are seeking to kill me* (cf. Jn 7:19). Does this mark them as
children of Abraham, inspired by Abraham's example? Just as Jesus'
words and deeds manifest him as the Son of his Father, so do their actions
show them to be children of another father, who is certainly not
Abraham.

Twice Jesus has managed to suggest that his adversaries are children of
a father other than the one they claim. At first they indignantly ex-

claimed, *Abraham is our father.* Now they cry, *We were not born out of wedlock*—implying that Jesus had been?—*we have one Father, who is God.* But, replies Jesus, just as their works prove that Abraham is not their father, their lack of love for God's Son shows that neither can he be their Father. If God were their Father they would recognize his Son. Their ears would be attuned to a message that clearly speaks the words of God. They have heard him speak, but it has only been sounds to them. This proves that they have no part with God.

Must he tell them who their real father is? It is *the devil,* and what they are doing is this father's will. Do they want proof? Very well, he has already convicted them of two things, that they are seeking to murder him and that they prefer falsehood to truth. Are not these the works of the devil? The devil *was a murderer from the beginning:* it was he who introduced death into the world (cf. Gen 3:3 f.; Wis 2:24). It is the devil whose very nature it is to lie. This, then, is why they will not listen to Jesus' word: they hate the truth. Jesus has proved his devotion to the truth, for there is none of them who can convict him of any sin. He therefore concludes his argument as he began it: if they were God's children they would hear his word; that they refuse shows that they have no part with God.

Jn 8:48–59 The discourse ends in recriminations and the threat of violence. In calling Jesus *a Samaritan* the crowd doubtless intended nothing more than a term of deep contempt (cf. Sir 50:25 f.); that he possessed *a demon,* that is, was insane, demented, had been suggested before (cf. Jn 7:20). From their point of view, they were merely paying Jesus back in his own coin. Had he not said that their father was the devil?

Jesus leaves to God the judgment of the issue between them. This is also a warning to his traducers. That he has nothing in common with the devil is proved by the honor he gives to God and his promise to all who receive his word that they will *never see death,* the death which is the very province of Satan. This assertion affords the Jews the occasion to bring in Abraham a final time. *Not taste death?* Abraham, whose patronage Jesus has tried to deny them, great as he was, died like any man. Is he making himself something greater than Abraham? He has spoken of his word that gives life. But *the prophets,* the men of the word, they too are dead. Is he greater than the prophets?

Jesus' answer is twofold. They have asked, *Whom do you make yourself?* He has said nothing for his own self-glorification; he has merely revealed the word of the Father. Is he greater than Abraham? Yes, since Abraham *rejoiced that he would see my day:* Abraham recognized that he was not the terminus of God's promises, but the beginning of a blessing that was to come (cf. Gen 12:3, 18:18; Gal 3:8 f.). *When he saw it, he was glad:*

probably the reference is to Gen 17:17, understanding Abraham's laughter as a sign of his joy over the birth of Isaac, the earnest of the fulfillment of God's promises; this was the ordinary Jewish interpretation of the passage.

This last bald statement not unnaturally provokes the ire of this hostile audience. *You are not yet fifty years old,* still a young man, *and you have seen Abraham?*: the reversal of subject and object (Jesus had said that Abraham saw him, or rather, his day) is doubtless to heighten the supposed absurdity. Jesus' response combines the "I am" of verses 24 and 28 with the significant variation in tenses used in the Prologue to distinguish contingent being from the divine endurance (see above on Jn 1:1 f.): *Before Abraham came to be, I am* (cf. also Ps 90:2); on the historicity of what is implied in such an assertion, see below on Lk 10:21 f. and parallel. At this apparent blasphemy the Jews begin to look about for means to stone Jesus, who therefore quickly departs from the scene.

15. THAT THEY WHO DO NOT SEE MAY SEE

Jn 9:1–34   The story with which John continues his Gospel is certainly intentionally connected with the feast of Tabernacles of the preceding chapter, whatever may have been its original context. Above (see on Jn 8:12–20) Jesus proclaimed himself Light of the World. In this, the sixth of Jesus' "signs" of John's Gospel (see above on Jn 2:1–11), we see a dramatic demonstration of the triumph of light over darkness (cf. Jn 1:5). For this reason, it is doubtless of especial importance to John that this story tells of the giving of sight to a man *blind from birth*: the light which Jesus has come to give is the grace of divine life of which men are deprived from birth. The narrative is one of John's best, told with a respect for all of its simple dramatic qualities.

The disciples (who have not been mentioned by John in the preceding chapters) enquire, as people casually will, on seeing something that is of passing interest: *Who committed the sin, he or his parents?* It was commonly assumed that physical afflictions were personal retributions for sin. Either the sins of his parents had been visited upon him (cf. Ex 20:5; Deut 5:9), or God had made him blind at birth in view of the sins that he would commit in his lifetime. Jesus does not bother to affirm or deny the theory behind the disciples' question, but restricts himself to the case at hand. Neither the man nor his parents have made him blind; he has been blind in order to this time, *that the works of God might be made manifest in him*, that he might become a sign of *the light of the world*. In the best manuscripts, Jesus says, *We must do the works of him who sent me*: the Christian reader is invited to join in the continuing work of Christ performed in the Church, of which the healing of this blind man is a sign.

The sacramental gestures employed by Jesus are not without precedent in the Synoptic accounts of his cures (see above on Mk 7:31–37 and parallel and Mk 8:22–26). *Spittle* was commonly thought to have medicinal qualities. In this instance, however, it is used to mix a clay with which Jesus proceeds to *anoint* the blind man's eyes. "Anoint" is a strange word to use in this connection (it is certainly used in vs. 11, and the best manuscripts have it also in vs. 6), but John has probably deliberately chosen it in allusion to the rites of primitive Christian baptism. The earliest Christian exegesis of this passage correctly recognized that the evangelist intended his readers to find the realization of Jesus' "sign" in the baptism of the Church. For the same reason, the point is made that the man receives his sight only after he has fulfilled the command to *wash in the pool of Siloam*. Siloam was within the walls of the Jerusalem of Jesus' time, in the southeast corner of the city; its waters were used in the libations of the feast of Tabernacles. John assigns to it the popular etymology of "[someone] sent": it is the light-giving means employed by Jesus, the one who has been sent by the Father to be the Light of the World. In view of the controversy that follows, John may also be thinking of an earlier time when Jerusalemites rejected the divine grace symbolized by the waters of Siloam (cf. Is 8:6).

John undoubtedly sees irony in the bystanders' failure to recognize the man to whom Jesus gave sight and in their dispute over his identity (cf. Jn 7:40–43): the world which does not know Christ does not know those who are Christ's (cf. Jn 15:18–21); in verse 9 the man uses Christ's *I am* to identify himself. The man himself passes through the customary stages of affirmation of his faith as he is called upon, like every Christian graced by Christ, to give testimony before a hostile world. The person who in verse 11 is for him merely *the man called Jesus* is in verse 17 confessed to be *a prophet*, preparatory to his recognition as Son of Man in the dialogue with Jesus in verses 35–44. The issue for *the Pharisees* is, as before both in the Synoptics and in John, violation of the Sabbath. In this instance, however, the problem is further complicated for them since simultaneously they are trying to cast doubt on the reality of the event that has violated the Sabbath.

In verse 22 it is explained that *the Jews*, that is, obviously, the Jewish leadership, had adopted a policy of excommunication of all who would confess Christ. The kind of pressures which they would have been able to bring to bear in Jesus' lifetime doubtless did correspond to the formal excommunication inflicted on Jewish Christians in the time of the Gospel. This was a dire penalty in the tightly knit communities of that day, as it could affect a man's social and economic existence as well as his religious identity. In verse 27 the man who has now had his eyes opened in more than one sense through his dialogue with the Pharisees, is emboldened to ask, ironically, *Do you, too, wish to become his disciples?* The "too" manages to suggest the extent of Jesus' proselytizing in the face of all that they have been able to do. In their reply they unconsciously confess to the charge made by Jesus in Jn 8:14.

Jn 9:35–41   In the conclusion of the story which now follows Jesus the
               Light is shown confronting both faith and unbelief, and
we see exemplified in what sense Jesus has *come into the world for*

judgment (see above on Jn 3:14–21). The man born blind asks only to have Jesus offer himself as the object of his faith, and immediately responds with the Christian confession. The Pharisees, on the contrary, who have witnessed Jesus' sign unseeing, show themselves to be those who are really blind, with a willful blindness that is inexcusable because the means of sight have been present to them. Just as the loss of life for the Christian is the paradoxical means by which he gains life, and he who would try to preserve his life at all costs discovers that he has lost it forever (see above on Mk 8:34–9:1 and parallels), so has Jesus come *that they who do not see may see, and they who see may become blind.*

Jn 10:1–21 Despite the abrupt change of pace as Jesus now begins to speak of himself under quite different figures, it seems to be certain that John intends the present important passage to be set in close relation to the preceding story and its sequel (cf. vs. 21). We can assume, therefore, that at least for literary purposes the audience of this discourse is the same as that of the preceding dialogue.

First of all, Jesus identifies himself as *the good shepherd,* contrasting himself with the Pharisees who proved themselves to be false leaders and teachers to the man born blind (cf. Ezek 34:1–16). In Palestinian practice the sheep of a given community are kept at night in a common sheepfold, watched over by a *gatekeeper.* The sheep belonging to individual owners are painted with distinguishing marks, and also they are given distinctive names by their own shepherd to which they respond. The shepherd to whom various sheep belong enters the fold, therefore, by the ordinary gate where he is recognized by the gatekeeper, calls his own sheep by name, who recognize him and follow him out. Only a thief would have occasion to climb over the wall after the sheep. This is the first lesson, then, that Jesus intends by the use of this familiar figure, that they who are the true sheep of the Shepherd of Israel will hear and heed his voice (cf. Jn 8:43); it is predictable that his adversaries *did not understand what he was saying to them.*

Jesus now shifts the figure somewhat: *I am the sheepgate.* If the true shepherd is to be distinguished from the false by his lawful entry through the gate, then *all who came before me are thieves and robbers.* This is not to reject indiscriminately Israel's shepherds of Old Testament and Jewish times, but to define as interlopers all who do not belong to the true prophetic line of which he is the supreme exemplar. The figure of the gate, therefore, signifies both the guarantee of true shepherding and the way of the sheep into safekeeping: *whoever enters through me will be saved.*

Jesus contrasts himself, the good shepherd, with *the hireling*—in this context, the Pharisees of the preceding story—whose only interest in the sheep is selfish. The true shepherd to whom the sheep belong *lays down his life for the sheep:* the Palestinian shepherd was often called on to do

just that (cf. 1 Sam 17:34f.; Is 31:4). The application of the figure to
Jesus in a most literal sense is obvious, as is the fact that *I know mine and
mine know me*: Jesus has often rebuked his adversaries for knowing neither
himself nor his Father, whereas in the Last Supper discourse (see below,
page 346 ff.) he will dwell on the mutual knowledge of himself and his
disciples as the extension of the shared knowledge of Father and Son.

Other sheep I have that do not belong to this fold: in context this
doubtless refers to the Gentile mission of the Church of which John was a
member. While Jesus in his earthly career had necessarily limited his
ministry to Jews, the Church which had become mainly Gentile rightly
recognized the universality of his Gospel and sought precedents for its
catholicity in both his remembered words and actions (see above on
Mk 7:24–30 and parallel). *There shall be one flock (poimnē) and one
shepherd (poimēn)*: though the Gospel of John, Jewish in its ultimate
origins (see above in Chapter 1, page 27 ff.), continually recognizes the
separation that had taken place between Church and Synagogue to the
extent that it habitually speaks of "the Jews" in the third person, it nevertheless conceives of the Church as one, Jewish and Gentile, united under
its one Shepherd (cf. Eph 2:11–22). What has made this possible is Jesus'
atoning sacrifice: his free acceptance of the will of the Father means a
resurrection to new life of himself and his sheep.

Lk 9:57–62   As Jesus' testimony leaves his hearers faced with the
Mt 8:19–22   decision of faith of which John so often makes a point, we
                 now return to the Synoptic Gospels for various passages
which Luke has connected with Jesus *on the way* to Jerusalem (see above,
page 210 f.). Matthew, as we see here and in what follows, has situated the
same events during the Galilean ministry in other parts of his Gospel.
For various reasons that will probably be evident of themselves it is much
more convenient for us to follow Luke's orderly account for the time being
rather than Matthew's more complicated and artificial disposition of the
material. It is with these two evangelists that we shall be mainly concerned
for a while, with traditions which they either possessed in common independently of Mark or which were proper to themselves individually;
later, however, we shall rejoin the Marcan tradition as well. These
passages, as far as Luke's Gospel is involved, are known as his "great
insertion" into the Marcan outline.

We have before us three sayings of the Lord, only the first two of which
are reported by Matthew. It is Matthew, however, who identifies the first
spokesman as *a scribe*, an avowal which is particularly interesting coming
from the First Gospel, that Jesus found followers even from a group which
generally was bitterly opposed to him. We are not told what was his
eventual reaction to Jesus' reply, the sense of which is not to point to his
poverty precisely but rather to the extreme uncertainty and insecurity of

his life lived in fulfillment of his mission. Anyone who would be his disciple must be prepared for a similar renunciation of worldly security, compared to which even the vagrant animals enjoy an ordered and serene existence. This is one of those deceptively idealistic statements of the Gospel which the casual reader is prone to take in without reflection. It was surely not unimportant to Matthew that the disciple in question was a person of status, one of the privileged classes in Jewish society.

The second saying is another of the "hard" ones whose very harshness is the best proof of its authenticity. *Leave the dead to bury their own dead* is, taken in one way, an absurdity. It is not that Jesus is suggesting, as some have thought, that all who are not at present his disciples are spiritually dead: this would imply a sweeping and uncharacteristically negative judgment that has no place in this context. It may be that in the Aramaic which Jesus used the same word did for "mortal" and "dead," thus: let those who are not yet concerned with the things of this world tend to its affairs. But most likely the sense is simply—or, perhaps, not so simply—that for the disciple of Jesus everything and everyone that could interfere with his call must be considered dead, his own parents included (see below on Lk 14:25–27). Inexorable as these words may sound to us, they could not have failed to sound even more so in the Oriental ears for which they were first uttered, conditioned as the people were to an intense, at times even exaggerated, veneration of the obligations of filial piety. By comparison the third saying reported by Luke, while it makes use of an expressive proverb to convey substantially the same message, comes as something of an anticlimax.

Lk 10:1–12   Only Luke has recorded the mission of another
Mt 9:36–38, 10:5–16a   and larger group of disciples than the Twelve.
Though there is no reason to question the reality of this group and its mission, it also seems to be evident that Luke had no really independent tradition that dealt with its activities. The saying of Jesus concerning *the harvest* which awaits its missionary zeal Matthew has brought into connection with the mission of the Twelve. Likewise, virtually every detail of the Lord's charge to this new group in the text that lies before us has either been copied from the common Synoptic account of the mission of the Twelve which we have already seen (above on Mk 6:6b–13 and parallels) or is additional material shared with Matthew who took that occasion to incorporate it into his missionary discourse of chapter 10.

It is not clear whether Luke speaks of this group of disciples as *seventy* or *seventy-two*: the evidence of the manuscripts is about evenly divided between the two readings and it is impossible to make a decision. Either number is intrinsically likely. Seventy had as venerable traditional associations as did twelve—the seventy elders of Israel (Num 11:16) come im-

mediately to mind. Luke, however, may very well be thinking of the traditional number of the nations of the earth, which following Gen 10 was
sometimes counted as seventy, sometimes as seventy-two. There is also the
possibility that the tradition of the Septuagint lies behind the selection of
the number. The Septuagint, whose name preserves the legend of its origin
at the hands of seventy(-two) translators, had once opened up to the
Gentile world the Scriptures of the Old Testament, and now the disciples
are being sent to bring the Gospel to the world. It is true, Luke respects
his historical sources and does not suggest that Jesus actually missioned his
disciples on this occasion to preach to Gentiles. But he carefully avoids
repeating what Matthew has in his parallel, applied to the mission of the
Twelve: *Go nowhere among the Gentiles and enter no town of the Samaritans, but go rather to the lost sheep of the house of Israel.* Also,
of course, it is not without significance that this mission takes place after
the conclusion of the Galilean ministry, in intimate association with Jesus'
coming death for universal salvation.

If Luke wants us to think of the Church's universal mission in thus recalling this story, the discourse he has utilized is aptly suited to the purpose.
It indulges in no romanticism, but combines prosaic advice with a realistic
appraisal of the magnitude and dangers of the task ahead—*lambs among
wolves*—and concludes with the perennial eschatological message of the
Church: *the kingdom of God is at hand.* Nor is the gentle Luke reluctant
on this occasion to cite the Lord's grim warning in time-honored Jewish
language: *It shall be more tolerable for Sodom* (Matthew adds, *and
Gomorrah*) *on that day—the day of judgment,* Matthew paraphrases—
than for that town which rejects the apostolic preaching. It is interesting
to note in these parallels how often it is Luke rather than Matthew who
has preserved the Semitic structure of Jesus' words.

Lk 10:13–16   The theme of judgment causes Jesus to advert to the
Mt 11:20–24   cities of the Galilean ministry and to marvel over the
                          unbelief that he had encountered there. The fact that
Chorazin is named here for the first time and nowhere else in the New
Testament, yet according to Matthew was one of *the cities in which his
greatest miracles were worked*, indicates to us again how fragmentary is
our Gospel account of Jesus' career. Matthew has placed this passage
within the Galilean ministry itself.

If *Tyre and Sidon*, the proverbially pagan cities of the Phoenician coast,
had received the graces showered on Galilee, they would surely have repented, says Jesus. So much the better will it be for Tyre and Sidon than
for Chorazin *and Bethsaida*, the city of Philip, Peter, and Andrew, according to Jn 1:44. It is for *Capernaum*, however, that his harshest judgment is reserved, in language recalling the fate of other proud cities of
the past (cf. Is 14:13, 15; Ezek 26:20, 28:6, 8)—Capernaum which he

had chosen as his own city, where he had lived and was most familiarly
known to the people, so much so that it had been made a reproach
against him (cf. Lk 4:23). It is probably worth noting that Tyre and Sidon
still prosper to this day as cities in Lebanon, while Chorazin (probably
Khirbet Kerazeh, about two miles northeast of Capernaum), Bethsaida,
and Capernaum have for centuries been nothing but uninhabited rock
piles.

Luke, who has included these apostrophes as part of Jesus' instruction to
the seventy(-two), in verse 16 concludes with a saying of the Lord which
appears often in the Gospels and in various forms (cf. Mt 10:40; Jn
13:20).

Lk 10:17-20   Luke immediately describes the return of the seventy-
                    (-two) disciples who were elated over the success of their
mission which had exceeded their most optimistic hopes. Jesus' reply on
this occasion has often been misunderstood. *I saw Satan fall like lightning
from the sky* is not said as a rebuke to their supposed pride in their ac-
complishment, but is, rather, a confirmation of their conquest of evil by
the use of powers they had not known they possessed. At the same time,
he does take the occasion to remind them of "the more excellent way"
(cf. 1 Cor 13:1). Far more important than the charismatic graces they
have received for their mission and the success they have achieved in it
is that *your names are written in heaven,* that they, too, are to be counted
among the elect who have accepted Christ's salvation (see on Lk 11:27 f.
below).

Lk 10:21-22   Though the specific contexts differ—in Matthew we are
Mt 11:25-27   in the midst of a section in which the mystery of the
                    kingdom is the theme following the missionary discourse
to the Twelve—the following passage has essentially the same meaning in
the two Gospels which have recorded it. It is, first of all, Jesus' paean of
praise to the Father whose *good pleasure it has been* to *reveal these things,*
the Gospel's message of salvation, to *little ones* (cf. above on Mk 9:33-37
and parallels) rather than to *the wise and learned* of this world: the
scribes and Pharisees to whom Jesus was one of "the accursed people who
know not the Law," the Judeans who despised him because he was a
Galilean, the Galileans who would not credit him because he was lowborn
and one of themselves. Of all the liberating effects of the Gospel message,
which came almost unheralded into the religious world of New Testament
times and still has its battle to fight for survival, undoubtedly the greatest
and most revolutionary was its insistence on salvation as a matter of heart
and soul rather than as an introduction into a system of esoteric "thinking," of a "wisdom" open only to elect "initiates" who have prepared
themselves for it by study and mental discipline. The Christian principle

has nothing to do with anti-intellectualism, but insists against every kind of Gnosticism or snobbish scribalism on the utter gratuity of God's grace (cf. 1 Cor 1:18 ff.).

Correlative with this principle is that of the source of what is Christian wisdom: *Everything has been handed over to me by my Father, and no one knows [who is] the Son except the Father, or [who is] the Father except the Son—and anyone to whom the Son chooses to reveal him.* The mystery which Christianity reveals, the knowledge with which it deals, does not concern things but persons. It is an introduction into a shared life and existence—such, on Semitic lips, is the meaning of "to know"— which is unique to a Father and Son; it is doubtless not without relevance that Luke also prefixed to Jesus' pronouncement the observation that *at that very moment he rejoiced in the Holy Spirit.* The participation in the life of the triune Godhead, this is grace and salvation; it is this that liberates us from purposeless existence and constitutes us new persons, children of God.

The Johannine flavor of this verse will not be missed by the attentive reader. "A meteorite from the Johannine heaven fallen upon the Synoptic earth," one commentator once called it. Others have remarked that it contains in essence all the christology of the Fourth Gospel. That this is not too great an exaggeration can be verified by comparing such passages as Jn 3:35, 6:46, 8:19, 10:15, 30, 14:9, 16:15, 17:6, 10. Above (see especially on Jn 8:48–59) and quite often in John's Gospel we hear Jesus claim an intimacy with the Father and a unique access to his being and will which can only be interpreted as John says it was interpreted, as the assertion of a divine Sonship transcending all human capabilities. Though we do not often hear the Synoptic Jesus speaking this language, we do hear him in this verse—and no verse is better authenticated in the Gospels of Matthew and Luke. Quite apart from its functional value in the Gospel context, therefore, this passage is a precious witness of historical tradition to the Christ of faith.

Lk 10:23–24   Most appropriately Luke follows the "Johannine" passage with a saying of Jesus which we have already seen Matthew use in a different context, in connection with the teaching in parables (see above on Mk 4:10–12 and parallels). The revelation of God which is to be found in Jesus' words and deeds, in the Christ-event, is the fullness for which the just of the Old Testament unconsciously yearned, walking in the light that was given to them. It is the same light that now shines in all its splendor (cf. Jn 1:17; Heb 1:1 f.).

Mt 11:28–30   Even more appropriate, however, is Matthew's continuation, drawn from a tradition proper to himself. Here again we hear an echo of the Christ of John's Gospel. *Come to me, all you who labor and are burdened, and I will give you rest:* Jesus addresses the *anawim* of the Beatitudes (see above on Mt 5:3–12 and parallel). He does not say, as any teacher could say, that he will endeavor to put his followers in touch with the God who alone can give spiritual peace and rest, who alone can satisfy the longings of our souls created to know and love him and to be happy with nothing else. He himself is the immediate source of peace and rest, for he embodies in his person all that was the ideal of the *anawim:* he is *meek and humble of heart* (cf. Zech 9:9). The *rest for your souls* which he promises (cf. Jer 6:16) is not, obviously, a passivity. It is a new way of life, a road to walk, even a *yoke:* Jesus throughout has been speaking as the Wisdom of God (cf. Prov 8:32; Sir 6:24–30, 24:18). But because of where the road leads, the *yoke is sweet and* the *burden is light.*

Lk 10:25–28   The story that next follows in Luke's outline is similar in many ways to one told later on by Matthew and Mark (see below on Mk 12:28–34 and parallel), and either we have separate versions of what was originally a single event or details of basically similar stories have been exchanged in the process of oral transmission (as we saw in the case of Lk 7:36–50 above). In view of the separate use made of the stories in the Gospels, for our purposes it is better to opt for the latter explanation.

As Luke tells the story, *a certain lawyer* decided to *put him to the test* as a teacher, asking what he should *do to inherit eternal life.* Though the question may have been put in good faith, it was somewhat inept. In the first place, Luke's context has put the accent on salvation not by "doing" in any legal or activist sense but by opening oneself in all simplicity to the God of salvation revealed in his Son. Secondly, the tenor of the question is the somewhat naïve assumption that salvation may be obtained once for all by the doing of some single thing. It is, therefore, very important that we understand correctly Jesus' reply. *In the Law what is written? How do you read?* elicits from the scribe what the Gospels would certainly endorse as an epitome of the spirit of the Law (see above on Mt 5:17–20), expressed in the *Shema,* the ancient prayer recited by devout Jews to this day, combining the precepts of Deut 6:4f. and Lev 19:18. *Keep doing this,* then, says Jesus, *and you will live.* It is not by performing any work, great or small, that a man can make himself worthy of eternal life; but when he lives according to the law of love he has the assurance of having passed from death into life through God's power (cf. 1 Jn 3:14, 4:10–12).

Lk 10:29–37   Of what does the lawyer now seek *to justify himself?* Probably, of the intimation that his question could be answered so simply. He therefore, and doubtless still in a legalistic vein, counters with the classic problem of Jewish casuistry: *And who is my*

neighbor? (see above on Mt 5:43–45). It is this question that introduces
perhaps the most famous of all the Lord's parables.

The Jerusalem-Jericho road descends from Jerusalem, some 2600 feet
high in the hills of Judea, down to the area of the Dead Sea basin in which
Jericho is situated, about 700 feet below sea level, passing through gorges
and hills which in spring have a thin layer of grass but the rest of the year
are barren. Almost every foot of the road provides a likely hiding place for
robbers, and as a result it has been a favorite with them for centuries. Even
in modern times it has not been unknown for travelers to be waylaid on
the pavements that have replaced the old Roman road. The none-too-
gentle way in which the man in the parable was handled by the bandits
was very typical; he was fortunate to escape with his life.

It has been thought by some that the story of the parable was taken by
Jesus from an actual event. It is, indeed, possible. Though *the priest* and
the Levite add bite to the lesson, we could easily imagine a priest passing
by, having left the Holy City after his period of duty in the temple, making
his way to Jericho which was traditionally inhabited by priestly families.
The point is, of course, that while these two eminently qualified under
the Law, by anybody's interpretation of it, as "neighbors" to the man who
is obviously supposed to be a Jew, it remained for the despised heretic
Samaritan to show him the mercy and kindness that were their duty. It
was he who applied the soothing balm of *oil and wine*, recognized as a
disinfectant long before anyone knew about germs. It was he who took him
to the *inn:* the "inn of the Good Samaritan" pointed out to the traveler
in Palestine today, actually a police station inhabiting the ruin of a Turkish
building constructed for the same purpose, probably does occupy a site
that would have had a *khan* in ancient times, half way between Jerusalem
and Jericho.

As the parable concludes, the lawyer's question has been answered; or
rather, he has been taught that it was the wrong question to ask. "Love
your neighbor" has not been commanded in order to put a limitation on
love to indicate its direction. Rather than "Who is my neighbor?," it asks:
"To whom am I neighbor?": *Which of these three*, asks Jesus, *proved himself to be a neighbor to the one who fell among thieves?* Whoever truly
lives by the law of love will never ask who his neighbor is, for he will
recognize him in every man. He will ask only what he must do here and
now in order that he, too, may deserve the name of neighbor. Neighbor
is a relative word: God has made every man a neighbor to us, and it remains for us to make ourselves a neighbor to every man according to his
need.

Lk 10:38–42   Though the connection is not immediately evident, it is
                 most likely that Luke intends the story that follows to be

a further elucidation of "What must I do to inherit eternal life?" This charming little episode from the Lord's life introduces us to characters whose personality traits are strikingly confirmed by the independent testimony of Jn 11. Luke speaks of *Martha and Mary* here for the first time and never again, but from the familiar way in which Martha and Jesus exchange remarks, each not hesitating to chide the other, though in perfect good humor, we can deduce that he had been a visitor in the sisters' house before and that they all knew one another very well. Luke sets the scene in *a certain village* not, probably, because he did not know it was Bethany (Jn 11:1), but because in his perspective Jesus is still on his journey to Jerusalem (see above on Mt 19:1 f. and parallels), and it would be anticlimactic to indicate his presence in the Holy City before the appointed time: Bethany, where Jesus habitually lodged when in Jerusalem (cf. Mt 21:17; Mk 11:11 f.), was actually one of its suburbs. We may suppose that what is described here took place during one of Jesus' multiple visits to Jerusalem about which the Synoptic Gospels are silent but which are recognized in John's Gospel.

While Mary adopts the posture of a disciple, *seated at the Lord's feet listening to his word* (cf. Acts 22:3), *Martha was distracted with much serving.* The situation is a familiar one. Probably Martha had already sent some meaningful glances in Mary's direction that had gone unheeded before she took her complaint to Jesus. His reply that she is *anxious and troubled about many things,* his reiterated *Martha, Martha,* tell us that he was smiling at a friend whose little failings and excesses were well known to him. It is not that Mary had simply shirked her duty and left her sister to do all the work. It is plain that Martha had imagined that a great deal more was to be done than was really needful. She is the eternal elder sister who has a household to run, the hustler and bustler determined to kill her guests with kindness.

All this being understood, we will not misinterpret Jesus' meaning, as though he were making light of the practical necessities of life in favor of a kind of selfish and parasitical contemplative state. *There is need of but one thing,* he says to Martha. The "one thing" is not what Mary is doing in contrast to what Martha is doing, but the essential of what Martha is doing in contrast to the "many things" over which she is troubled. *There is need of but few things, or even only one* is the reading of some good manuscripts and by many this is believed to be the original reading. Whatever was required by hospitality for himself and his disciples had already been taken care of. Martha's many little duties in which she now wanted Mary to share were quite superfluous. Then, with a slight play on words: *Mary has chosen the good portion, which shall not be taken from her.* Without condemning Martha he praises Mary who has recognized that the most important of all things is to hear the word of life.

Lk 11:1–4   It is not inappropriate that while Luke is concerned with
Mt 6:9–15   the Lord's teaching on the way to eternal life he should
now bring in the story of the introduction of what we know
traditionally as the Our Father or Lord's Prayer. Matthew, as we know, has
the same prayer in his Sermon on the Mount, where it appears as a kind
of appendix to various teachings of Jesus on prayer, interrupting a well-
balanced series of examples in which Christian simplicity is being contrasted with contemporary religiosity. Luke's story, while no point is to be
made of its chronology—he says, again, that it occurred *in a certain place*,
holding to his journey-to-Jerusalem outline—is perfectly credible in itself.
It is only to be supposed that Jesus, like every religious teacher, and *as
John* the Baptist *taught his disciples*, should have instructed his followers in prayer. There is an ancient adage, *lex orandi lex credendi*, which
is to say that every belief manifests itself in its own proper way of praying.
In the ancient Church the Our Father was learnt by catechumens but
could be recited only by the baptized, so much was it identified with the
profession of the Christian creed. We retain something of this tradition
in our rite of Baptism and in our recitation of the Our Father at the conclusion of the Canon of the Mass before Holy Communion.

The liturgical use of the Our Father is indeed ancient. It appears in the
Didache substantially in its Matthaean form, with the instruction that it
is to be prayed thrice daily. In the Didache a liturgical doxology has been
appended, "for yours is the power and the glory forever," which in one
form or another has made its way into many of the manuscripts of
Matthew's Gospel and thus into many of the older vernacular versions
of the Bible. It is doubtless liturgical use in the various local churches
rather than an individual evangelist's tendency to shorten or lengthen the
Prayer that accounts for the "longer" and "shorter" forms in which we find
it in Matthew's and Luke's Gospels respectively. Neither form, we may
be sure, corresponds precisely to the Aramaic original uttered by Jesus.
While Luke's shorter version probably represents a form of the Prayer
which had undergone less material expansion, in various instances it is
evidently farther removed from a Semitic original than is Matthew's. It is
well to note that the liturgical adaptation of the Prayer is by no means
restricted to its development prior to the canonical Gospels. As used in
public prayer today by people of whatever language, the Our Father
hardly if ever corresponds exactly to the text of either Luke or Matthew.
The standard English version that is recited with incidental variations by
most Protestants and Catholics seems to have been standardized in the
time of King Henry VIII. A history of this kind is by no means isolated.
Prayers such as the Jewish *Shema* mentioned above and the *Shemoneh
Esreh* (the "Eighteen Benedictions") have the same record of development and adaptation as does our distinctive Christian prayer.

We think of it as a distinctively Christian prayer, though as a matter of fact it was first offered to devout Jews who in reciting it were not conscious of departing from any tradition of their past. It is not so much in content as in context that it is Christian, as becomes evident when we begin to study its very first line. Matthew has *Our Father who are in heaven.* In Aramaic "who are in heaven" would be a single word, the equivalent of our adjective "heavenly." This is a fairly standard Jewish designation of God, the purpose of which is not to suggest his remoteness from the world but rather his omnipotent transcendence of it: the "kingdom of heaven," after all, as Matthew understands it, is the coming of God's power down upon earth. Luke has, simply, *Father,* and it is most likely that it was in this form that Jesus first uttered the prayer. The New Testament, the Gospel of John especially but by no means exclusively, retains a vivid memory of the intimate way in which Jesus addressed God as "Father" or "my Father" (see above on Lk 10:21 f. and parallel), a distinctive address that was a departure from normal Jewish usage. So much did this impress itself on tradition that *Abba,* the Aramaic word which he used, has also been remembered and recognized as peculiarly Christian (cf. Mk 14:36; Rom 8:15; Gal 4:6). It is to acknowledge the extraordinary intimacy into which we enter with God through Christ that, "taught by our Savior's command, . . . we *dare* to say, Our Father . . ."

May your name be sanctified. This is a typically Jewish *Qaddish* prayer which is paraphrased by the second petition (in Matthew and Luke) and the third (in Matthew only). To ask that God's *kingdom may come* upon earth and that his *will be done on earth as it is in heaven* is to ask much the same thing, and this same thing is the sanctification of God's name, that is to say, the public and universal acknowledgment of his holy and saving power (cf. Zech 14:9). In Jewish ears, and in the ears of the earliest Christian Church, there was doubtless a once-for-allness connected with these petitions that we miss today. Without losing sight of this original perspective, however, the Church has continued to pray in these terms as each age has revealed more of her destiny to herself, recognizing that the eschatological kingdom is also realized in each existential moment. God's name is made holy to the extent that his holiness enters more and more into the lives of men; in this sense his kingdom continually "comes."

In the next petition, common to both Matthew and Luke, the Prayer turns from the kingdom itself to its members. The two Gospel verses are sometimes translated as though they said precisely the same thing, but actually there is considerable difference between them. While Matthew has *Give us* (once for all) *today our _____ bread,* in Luke we read *Give us* (continually) *day by day our _____ bread.* It is easier to take Luke's version first, because it is probably an adaptation. In both verses I have substituted a dash for the adjective which we customarily translate "daily," simply because we do not know the exact meaning of the Greek word (*epiousion*). "Daily" was the translation which St. Jerome found in the

Old Latin version of the Gospels of Matthew and Luke when he began the life's work of revision and translation that eventuated in the Vulgate Bible. (The Old Latin Gospels, which may have appeared as early as the end of the second century, are among our earliest interpretations of the New Testament.) Jerome left "daily" as it stood in Luke, and probably rightly. Luke, as we know, displays a more than usual concern for the poor and their needs, and it is therefore most likely that he understood the petition in terms of their day-by-day concern for subsistence (cf. Lk 6:21). Following a suggestion by Jerome himself, some modern scholars have theorized that the Aramaic word underlying *epiousion* would have been *delimḥar*. If so, the request would be, literally, for "tomorrow's bread": this is the prayer of the poor. Obviously, this direction of attention toward physical needs does not exclude but rather presupposes the dependence of the poor on God for every good thing, spiritual as well as material (see above on Mt 5:3-12 and parallel).

It is not so evident, however, that this is the way Matthew understood the petition. Here Jerome changed the Old Latin translation of *epiousion* to *supersubstantialem*, relying on the supposed etymology of the Greek word. Whatever he may have wanted "supersubstantial" to mean for his readers, it is clear enough that he did not believe "daily" was right. What would *delimḥar* signify in this context, a "tomorrow's bread" that is asked for today and once for all? Very likely, it is the bread of the kingdom (cf. Mt 15:26; Lk 14:15, and see above on Jn 6:26-51a). If this is the correct interpretation, this fourth petition of the Our Father agrees strikingly with the first three. It is likewise easier to see why Christian tradition, as reflected in our liturgical usage, has always put the Our Father into such close relationship with the Eucharistic bread.

Forgive us our debts, the Prayer continues in Matthew's Gospel. This petition embodies a Semitism that is doubtless original, which is paraphrased by Luke as *forgive us our sins*. Luke, however, shows his awareness of the underlying figure in his next clause: *for we also forgive everyone who is in debt to us*. This clause, too, is something of a paraphrase, smoothing out the ruggedness of Matthew's *as we have also forgiven our debtors* and, probably, stating as a continuing principle of forgiveness what was first envisaged in Matthew's version as a once-for-all remission of sin in view of the coming final judgment. No one would be so foolhardy as to ask God's forgiveness only in proportion as he has forgiven others, for by that very fact he would be asking for something less than complete forgiveness, and furthermore there can be no real proportion between what we forgive and what we hope to be forgiven us by God. The point is, however, that God's forgiveness is for those who are disposed for it, who know the need of forgiveness and its value. Only the man who has himself forgiven knows what it means to ask for forgiveness and is prepared to receive it. This is why it is so important to forgive.

That is the meaning of the little commentary that Matthew has attached
to the Prayer at the end (vss. 14 f.), and that was the sense of the parable of the unforgiving servant that we saw in Chapter 14 (see above on
Mt 18:23–35).

Do not lead us into temptation we find in both Matthew and Luke.
Though there is a sense in which God tempts man, that is, puts him to
the test (cf. Gen 22:1), it is equally obvious that he is not a tempter in
the conventional sense, an inciter to evil (cf. Jas 1:13). The expression is
a Semitism, the intention of which is "Let us not succumb to temptation." But what is the temptation in question? As the prayer has developed in Christian usage, doubtless any temptation of any kind is
meant. The first Christians, however, probably thought first and foremost
of the final great trial coming upon the earth, the last onslaught of Satan
and his minions which must be overcome by the elect before the end of
all (cf. Apo 3:10). In keeping with this is Matthew's parallel, *but deliver
us from [the] evil,* which may also be translated *from the evil one.*

Lk 11:5–8   Luke also adds his own commentary on the Prayer by way
            of the parable of the importunate friend, the meaning of
which is fairly pellucid. A knowledge of the Palestinian scene only draws
its picture more sharply. The house besieged by the friend would have
consisted of a single room: kitchen, larder, and parlor by day, bedroom
by night. When the mats had been spread over the floor and everyone
was in bed, it would indeed be an inconvenience to disrupt the entire
household literally to dig out what was needed. Still, if only to ransom
a part of his night's rest, the householder will eventually give in if his
friend plagues him long enough. So persevering must be prayer, says the
Gospel. Not, of course, that God will not hear us the first time; that is
not the point of the parable. The point is that we must not lose heart
when, for reasons of his own, God delays, or seems to delay, the answer
to our prayers. The point is driven home by further sayings of the Lord
which we have already seen in the context of the Sermon on the Mount
(see above on Mt 7:7–11 and parallel).

16. FIRE ON THE EARTH

Lk 11:14–23
Mt 12:22–30
Mt 9:32–34
Mk 3:22–27

We continue with Luke's order of events: "chronology" would obviously be the wrong term to use in this connection. Both Luke and Matthew give us the occasion of the charge of diabolism made against Jesus in the exorcism of a man who was *dumb* (in Mt 12, *blind and dumb*), while Mark simply notes the charge as made by *scribes from Jerusalem*. Mark and Matthew, however, situate the controversy within the period of the Galilean ministry, where it doubtless belongs; for Matthew this is only one of a whole series of controversies between Jesus and his adversaries. For good measure, Matthew has a doublet of the same story which he has placed earlier in his Gospel, in a context which shows the manifestation of Jesus' power in the face of the growing animosity of *the Pharisees*.

Jesus is accused—in Luke's timeless sequence Mark's scribes and Matthew's Pharisees become *certain people in the crowds*—of being diabolically possessed (the same charge in Jn 7:20, 8:48, 52, 10:20 imputes insanity to him), in the sense that his power derived from *Beelzebul the prince of demons*. Beelzebul, originally *baʻal zebul* (Baal the Prince), had once been the name of a Philistine god; the Jews tended to identify the gods of the Gentiles with demons (cf. 1 Cor 10:20f.). In the Hebrew Bible the name was deliberately corrupted out of contempt to *baʻal zebub* (Baal [lord] of the flies), which explains the "Beelzebub" of many of the Gospel manuscripts. Luke also adds that *others were demanding from him a sign from heaven* (cf. Mt 12:38, 16:1; Mk 8:11; Jn 6:30).

Jesus first mocks the absurdity of their claim, born of desperation. Satan overthrowing the power of Satan would be like civil war in a kingdom or commonwealth. Satan is not so foolish as to destroy himself. Moreover, he asks, according to Matthew and Luke, if exorcism can so readily be ascribed to diabolical influence, what does this make of the exorcisms performed by the Pharisees' own *children*, that is, their disciples? *They will be your judges:* Jesus' adversaries will stand condemned by the very doctrine they have taught. It is, in fact, this widespread conviction of the power of exorcism through *the spirit of God* (=the power of God=Luke's *the finger of God*, cf. Ex 8:15; Deut 9:10; Ps 8:4) that must prove to Jesus' hearers that *the kingdom of God has come upon you*. The little parable common to the three Gospels concludes the illustration. The only way to enter a strong man's house and rob it at will is first to have the strong man tied securely. If Jesus is, in fact, now plundering Satan's stronghold, then Satan's power must have been definitively broken. We have seen all along that this is the essential message of Jesus' healing miracles and exorcisms.

Matthew and Luke conclude with a saying that is verbally the reverse of another uttered on an entirely different occasion and to an entirely different purpose (see above on Mk 9:38–41 and parallels). Jesus speaks here as the gatherer of the eschatological community (cf. Ezek 34:13), and the times permit only the option that is possible between Christ and Satan: *He who is not with me is against me, and he who does not gather with me scatters.*

Mt 12:31–32   Matthew and Mark quite properly continue this scene
Mk 3:28–30   with the Lord's words on blasphemy against the Spirit
Lk 12:10   of God, the so-called "unforgivable sin." Jesus does not,
                  of course, say that any sin is really unpardonable, for
such a statement would put limits both on God's mercy and his power. He does assert that there is sin that will not be forgiven. If God's mercy is without limit, neither is it mindless: to represent God as an overindulgent father who automatically condones every offense is not to hear the teaching of Christ. Blasphemy against the Spirit—deliberately and in cold blood to ascribe the manifest workings of God to the power of evil —is a perversion of spirit, a reprobate sense which deprives itself of the divine mercy simply by denying its existence.

The meaning of Jesus' pronouncement becomes clearer in Matthew's Gospel, where the distinction is drawn between speaking *against the Son of Man* and speaking *against the Holy Spirit*. St. Jerome's commentary is apposite: "He who speaks a word against the Son of Man is scandalized by my flesh . . . that I am the son of a carpenter, and have brethren, James, and Joseph, and Jude, and that as a man I eat and am a drinker of wine; such an opinion and blasphemy, though it lacks not the guilt of its error, will however be forgiven because of the weakness of the flesh. But he however who plainly perceives the works of God, who is unable to deny the power but is impelled by envy of the same to calumniate and ascribe the works of the Holy Spirit to Beelzebub—for him there is no forgiveness."

Neither in this age nor the one to come is an emphatic paraphrase of Mark's *never*. "The age to come" as distinguished from "this age" or "this world" is Jewish language for the messianic era, which in the New Testament has been used to refer to the age of the Church (cf. Heb 2:5).

Luke has put his version of this saying in the quite different context of Jesus' warnings to his disciples against the temptation to deny him in times of persecution. Following verse 9 the sense is: Whoever disowns Christ simply as another man, that is, who denies being a follower of Jesus of Nazareth as Peter did, commits sin; but only he who repudiates Christ's divine mission as God's emissary and Son blasphemes against the Holy Spirit whom Christ has manifested.

Mt 12:33–37   Matthew concludes this episode with the use of a parable which both he and Luke have already employed in other contexts (see above on Mt 7:15–20 and Lk 6:43–45). Here the purpose is to drive home the point that the evil and malicious speech of Jesus' adversaries is a true index to their character as men.

Jn 10:22–39   We may find it convenient to turn now to the last of Jesus' discourses to the Jerusalemites recorded in John's Gospel. The evangelist connects it with the mid-December feast of *the Dedication* (Hanukkah), the Jewish celebration which commemorates the reconsecration of the Jerusalem temple in 165 B.C. by Judah the Maccabee after its profanation by Antiochus Epiphanes (cf. 1 Macc 4:36–59; 2 Macc 1:18). Judaism did and does observe Hanukkah as a festival of freedom, "the feast of Lights." Lamps were lighted to symbolize the light of liberty, and in various other ways it was regarded as a kind of continuation of the feast of Tabernacles and was sometimes even called by this name (cf. 2 Macc 1:9, 10:6). These resemblances partially explain the similarity of this discourse to the lengthy ones centered about the feast of Tabernacles which we saw in our preceding two chapters. As before, Jesus is *in the temple* area, *in Solomon's porch*, an area protected against the winter cold on the east side of the outer temple court.

The Jews ask Jesus to *tell us in plain speech whether you are the Messiah*. Although John habitually makes Jesus' messianic affirmations more explicit than those in the Synoptics, that such a question could be asked by the Jerusalem crowds this late in the ministry is doubtless an indication of the same historical "messianic secret" that underlies both traditions (see above on Mk 1:22–28 and parallel). As in the Synoptics, Jesus avoids here any direct affirmation or denial of the messianic title. As before, he points to the witness of his works to his identity, a witness, however, which can only be seen by the eyes of faith (cf. Jn 8:12–20, etc.). He returns to the theme of the good shepherd (see on Jn 10:1–21 above), this time to speak of the "pasturage" of *eternal life* into which he leads his sheep, a result which is guaranteed by the omnipotence of the Father and his oneness with him.

I and the Father are one is more than an assertion of the harmony of will and action between Jesus and the Father (see on Jn 5:16–30 above); it presupposes the radical unity asserted in Jn 1:1. The Jews correctly perceive this: *You, who are a man, make yourself God* (cf. Jn 5:18, 8:58 f.). For the evangelist, of course, this is a superbly ironic conclusion, since in reality Jesus is a God who has made himself man (cf. Jn 1:14).

Jesus' continuing argument has often been misunderstood. *It is written in your Law* (cf. Jn 8:17), he reminds them, "*I have said, 'You are gods.'*" The citation is of Ps 82:6; the Jews sometimes spoke of the entire Old Testament as "the Law": cf. Jn 12:34, 15:25. The Jews are not asked for an exegesis of the Psalm, but simply to reflect that in the Scripture, the word of God itself, they can hear God the Father declaring others than himself to be "gods." The title itself, therefore, is not *ipso facto* the *blasphemy* which they are making it out to be. Rather, they must ask with what right and in what sense the title may be used. If it was used in Ps 82:6 in one legitimate way, may it not be used now in another? How it is now being used—*that the Father is in me and I am in the Father*—is, as always, being demonstrated in *the works and words* of a Son of God *whom the Father consecrated and sent into the world.*

Jn 10:40–42   With the conclusion of this discourse John marks a provisional termination of the period of Jesus' public ministry by taking him to the same Perean district presupposed in the Synoptic outline at this stage (see above on Mt 19:1 f. and parallels). To where the witness to the Word had first begun (see above on Jn 1:19–24) Jesus now returns; and the Baptist's witness continues in the *many* who *believed in him there.*

Lk 11:24–26   Resuming the Synoptic passage with which we began
Mt 12:43–45   this chapter (above on Lk 11:14–23 and parallels), we find an eschatological warning of Jesus which has been topically associated with the discussion of the implications of his exorcisms. The point of the parable is clearly set forth in its concluding words: *the final condition (ta eschata) of that man becomes worse than the first;* Matthew only underlines what is implied in Luke when he adds, *thus will it be with this evil generation.* The very perversity of those who confront Jesus with the charge that his works are Satanic rather than divine is the proof that, in their case, his proclamation of the kingdom in deeds of power will be only a temporary relaxation of the grip of evil. They will be the worse for their rejection of grace and of the prophetic word. The power of evil over them will increase rather than diminish because they have shown themselves incapable of distinguishing the kingdom of God from the rule of Satan. The expelled demon with

his reinforcements will, therefore, find it quite easy to gain admittance
with them, and so it will be.

The parable presupposes the popular Jewish demonology of the times.
The demons are pictured as wandering through the *dry* and desert *places*,
thought of as their natural habitat (cf. Lev 16:10; Tob 8:3; Is 13:21;
Bar 4:35; Apo 18:2), seeking *rest*, that is, a human person in whom they
can take up abode. The proprietary *my house* of the demon (cf. 2 Cor
5:1) strikes an intentionally ominous note. It is doubtless not to the point
of the parable to enquire who has *swept* the house and put it *in order*
as the demon finds it on his return. The point is that the "house" is
always an attractive lodging to Satan, who will take possession when he
can.

Lk 11:27–28   The connection in context of the following two verses
                   proper to Luke does not appear immediately, but in real-
ity it is quite close; the association of ideas is quite like that of a previous
passage we have already seen, which, as a matter of fact, Matthew places
in this very context (see above on Mk 3:31–35 and parallels). Struck with
admiration for Jesus' teaching, thinking to please him and, at the same
time, expressing her own holy envy, *a woman in the crowd* cries out:
Blessed the womb that bore you and the breasts you sucked! How fortunate to be the mother of such a son! The praise of Mary is in reality the
praise of Jesus.

Jesus does not deny the validity of the woman's honest words. He can
turn them, however, to an even more important consideration, and he
does so. *Rather, blessed they who hear the word of God and keep it!*
The way out of the evil and perverse generation whose last lot will be
worse than its first lies not through blood relationship with Jesus—an
evident impossibility for many—but through a spiritual relationship
available to all. This relationship consists in becoming Christ's disciple,
which means to take in his word wholly, with one's whole being, thus
becoming a new person: this is to do so as well as to hear the word of
God (cf. Jas 1:22–25). This was as true for Mary as for anyone else.
"More blessed is Mary for believing the faith of Christ," said St. Augustine, "than for conceiving the flesh of Christ."

Lk 11:33–36   It is at this point (Lk 11:29–32) that Luke introduces
                   the passage on the sign of Jonah which we have al-
ready seen (above on Mk 8:11 f. and parallels). The following verses are
also paralleled elsewhere (see above on Mk 4:21–25 and parallel, and on
Mt 6:22 f.). In their present context, Luke uses them to contrast with the
evil generation on whom all signs are wasted those who have an eye of
sincere faith to perceive the brilliant light of his word which can illumine
their whole being.

Lk 11:37–54   For topical reasons also, but possibly in virtue of an
original historical context as well, Luke now brings in
this fairly lengthy rebuke of Pharisaical piety. Much of the material is
reproduced by Matthew in his chapter 23, a passage which is likewise
paralleled by Luke. It would appear that Matthew has made use of the
same source employed by Luke, but has assimilated the material to that
of the later context, where it will be more convenient for us to consider
his parallel and variant application of the verses that we now have before
us. The situation described by Luke, not without precedent in his Gospel
(see above on Lk 7:36–50), presupposes the Pharisaical doctrine of the
"tradition of the ancients" which we have already had explained to us by
Matthew and Mark (see above on Mk 7:1–13 and parallel). It does not
seem likely that *the Pharisee* who *asked him to dine with him* (literally,
"to breakfast"—but the Greek word was commonly used for any meal)
was only pretending the hospitality he offered, attempting to trap Jesus
in some way. That *he was astonished that* Jesus *did not first wash* sounds
like genuine and honest surprise at the unexpected. On the other hand,
this fact alone indicates that he could have known little about Jesus that
did not go beyond polite curiosity. Of course, we have no way of knowing
when and where this event occurred.

Now you Pharisees. The reaction of the Pharisee, probably expressed
externally in some fashion, becomes the signal for quite plain words on
Jesus' part. Coming from a guest to a host, they were not altogether
diplomatic. Apart from their service to the truth, however, it is possible
that they had a salutary effect on this particular Pharisee. Jesus' first
attack centers on the underlying error that has occasioned the present instance of Pharisaical scandal. You people, he says, carefully *clean the outside of the cup and the dish,* but you are little concerned when your own
souls are filled with corruption. This is the peril to which legalism exposes
the religion of even honest men: a preoccupation with trifling externals
can easily pre-empt all their attention and lead to forgetfulness of the
realities they were once supposed to externalize (see above on Mt 6:1–4).
Jesus' next words are obscure, but their sense seems to be: *Give as alms
what is within* the vessels you wash so carefully, *then everything will be
really clean for you.* What is needful is that they themselves be inwardly
clean; if this were the case, the rest would take care of itself. The
best way for them to "clean" their cups and dishes is by emptying them
for the sake of the poor, as a work of mercy.

However, the three "woes" that follow (cf. above on Lk 6:24–26) entertain little hope for any such performance on the part of the Pharisees.
They *tithe mint and rue and every herb*—insignificant garden produce
of which neither the Law nor firm custom demanded the tithe—so eager
are they to show their devotion to religion, but they have no time for
justice and the love of God. In such pronouncements we hear the ancient

voice of Israel's prophets (cf. Is 1:10–17; Hos 6:4–7; Amos 5:21–24, etc.). *These you ought to have done without neglecting the others:* Jesus' condemnation of a distorted interpretation of the Law is not a condemnation of the Law itself, whose claims he recognizes (see above on Mt 5:17–20).

The Pharisees *love the first seat in the synagogues and the salutations* which accompany men of conspicuous religion. But in reality they *are like hidden graves over which men walk unawares.* The Law, dating from an age that had no sterile gauze or hermetical sealing to prevent the spreading of disease and corruption, wisely designated legally "unclean" anyone who came in contact with a corpse or a grave, which is to say that it segregated him from his neighbors for a week (cf. Num 19:16). Graves were, as a consequence, usually well marked, lest anyone should come in contact with them without knowing it. Thus the point of the comparison. The Pharisees' semblance of piety and the good esteem which they enjoyed concealed their corrupting influence from those who were inclined to put confidence in their example and counsel.

At this juncture one of the scribes (called *lawyers* here by Luke; cf. vs. 53) rightly remonstrates with Jesus, pointing out that his strictures are in reality addressed to his professional class. Rightly, that is, since the Pharisees were mainly dependent for their religious attitudes on the scribal students and teachers who belonged to their party (see the remarks on the Pharisees in Chapter 1). The association of scribes and Pharisees is, as we have seen, habitual in the Gospels and certainly to be expected at the meal which serves as the setting for this passage.

The scribe's intervention earns three "woes" for his class paralleling those addressed to the Pharisees. First, says Jesus, they *load men with intolerable burdens* (cf. Acts 15:10); we have seen ample evidence of this in considering, for example, the scribal rigor concerning the Sabbath, which could make its observance dehumanizing (see above on Mk 2:23–28 and parallels), or the elaborate rules of ritual purity which they derived from the Law and which were an impossibility for the generality of men. Yet at the same time, by clever dodges and tortuous subterfuges, they could excuse themselves from the Law's fundamental prescriptions: here we can remember the "korban" oath by which duties even to parents could be avoided (see above on Mk 7:1–13 and parallel).

The second "woe" is not as easy to understand as the first. The scribes, Jesus goes on, *build the tombs of the prophets.* Is this meant ironically, of the entombment of the dynamic prophecy of Israel in the frozen system of scribal legalism, the reduction of the prophetic word to the role of a source book for casuistic commentary? It is possible. More likely, however, is it that Jesus has in mind the actual building and rebuilding of physical tombs which were intended to honor the traditional grave sites of the prophets of old. By this means men professed reparation for the sins of their *fathers who killed* the prophets (cf. Mt 23:30). All in vain, however; their conduct otherwise shows how much they were of the same mind as their fathers, and however much they protest other dispositions, they approve their deeds in fact (cf. Acts 7:51–53). Therefore in reality they form, together with their ancestors, a consistent tradition of conduct: they complete the work of their fathers, as it were, by providing tombs for those whom the former slew.

The Gospel finds the history of the past being repeated in the Christian present, when once again prophets are being killed and entombed. *The divine wisdom* knew from the beginning that the *prophets and apostles* whom it sent into the world would be killed and persecuted. It will demand account of this innocent blood, just as of this present generation account will be demanded of all the innocent blood shed *from the blood of Abel to the blood of Zechariah.* This last is a reference to the salvation history of the Old Testament; Abel (Gen 4:8) was the first and Zechariah (2 Chron 24:20 f.) the last man whose murder is described in this history, since in the Jewish canon of Scripture the Book of Genesis stands at the beginning and the Second Book of Chronicles at the end.

Finally, Jesus returns to his earlier charge. The scribes, he says, are like men who have stolen the key to a door; they do not use the key to enter themselves, nor will they allow those to enter who want to. Here it is question of *the key of knowledge,* the knowledge of God to be found in his Law. They themselves strive neither to know nor to do God's will, and they have made access to it impossible for those who have trusted in their teaching. It is not surprising, in view of the uncompromising tone of Jesus' strictures, that Luke closes this passage on a scene of violence or near-violence. The text suggests that *the scribes and Pharisees* were prepared to assail him physically as well as to trap him in his speech.

Lk 12:2–9   Neither is it surprising that Luke brings in at this point
Mt 10:26–33   the saying of Jesus on the "leaven" of the Pharisees
               which we have seen above (on Mk 8:13–21 and paral-
lels). As we noted, in verse 49 above the evangelist moved quite naturally from the purview of Jesus' Palestinian audience to the situation of the Church for which he was writing his Gospel. The same association of ideas now prompts him to include Jesus' words to his disciples on their conduct in the face of persecution, a passage to which Matthew has given a similar context as part of the Lord's missionary discourse to the Twelve.

In both Gospels the discourse embodies a saying which we have seen before, in a different context and with a different meaning (above on Mk 4:21–25 and parallel). Here *the hidden thing that is to be revealed* refers to the apostolic preaching. This is certainly the case in Matthew's version, and probably in Luke's as well: that is, *whatever you have said in the dark* among yourselves and with me . . . *shall be proclaimed upon the housetops*. The verb "proclaim" (*kēryssō*) corresponds to the term used for the apostolic preaching, the *kerygma*. Jesus does not minimize the dangers that will await his disciples in their mission: they will face discrimination, torture, and death. Yet however fearful such things may be, they must *fear them not* but rather reserve their fear for God. Their enemies have power, indeed, to *kill the body*, but only God can *destroy body and soul* together and forever. This may sound like a harsh and ignoble kind of motivation, but it is not intended so. To die, after all, under whatever circumstances, is the common lot of man. No earthly power can do more to him than unassisted nature will eventually do. But what no earthly power can do, man can do to himself. He can destroy his own identity forever, taking occasion from the trials of life to reject the Author of his being who thus becomes his inexorable judge. The fearsome God who destroys and buries in hell appears only to him who has refused him as a loving Father and at the same time denied his own sonship.

Jesus has not spoken of God to frighten his disciples, though the thought of his power must frighten the weak and fearful. God loves them, wants them, watches over them. He uses a homely example reminiscent of the Sermon on the Mount (see above on Mt 6:25–34 and parallel). One of the commonest, most valueless creatures he could name was the Palestinian *sparrow: two for a farthing* (the Roman *as*)—about one cent—says Matthew; *five for two farthings*, says Luke. Yet God watches over each one of these, and *not even one of them* dies without his knowledge and permission. Christ's friends must realize, then, how precious is each one of them individually in God's eyes and how much the object of his solicitude which extends to the numbering of the hairs of their heads. When their trials come, therefore, let them stand fast, confident and fearless. Those who acknowledge him in the face of all their common enemies will be sustained before men and, above all, in the final judgment of God; those who reject him will be rejected (see above on Mk 8:34–9:1 and parallels). Here Luke has brought in Jesus' saying on blasphemy against the Spirit which we saw earlier in this chapter (above on Mt 12:31 f. and parallels).

Mt 10:16b–25   Earlier in this discourse Matthew has cited other
Lk 12:11–12   teachings of the Lord on the same subject which are
                  here partly paralleled by Luke in his conclusion (cf.
also Jn 14:26). To *be prudent as serpents and simple as doves*, to combine sagacity with ingenuous honesty in dealing with a hostile world— the Gospels, quite evidently, look beyond the immediate Palestinian

scene with which Jesus dealt into the continuing history of the Church
—this is surely not easy. It means to know when to be bold, when
reserved; when to speak, when to remain silent, yet never to be silent
when it is necessary to speak; when to act and when to let events take
their natural course. Hard though it be, however, the disciples must remember that they are not alone. They will have the assistance of *the
Holy Spirit* to guide them, *the Spirit of your Father*, as Matthew puts
it. On this promise the Church has lived ever since.

Brother will deliver up brother to death . . . It is not an attractive
picture that Jesus paints. The saving message of Christ will divide families, or rather belief and unbelief will divide them, and the ties of
blood will be forgotten in the ensuing strife. The rule still holds, that
the disciple must expect to receive the treatment of his Master, if he is
disciple indeed (cf. Lk 6:40; Jn 13:16). If they have dared *call* even
the master of the house Beelzebul (see Lk 11:14–23 and parallels at the
beginning of this chapter), *how much more* will they do so with *those
of his household!*

Jesus instances an example of the prudence to be exercised by his
disciples. *When they persecute you in one village, flee to another.* The
call to Christian witness is not a summons to fanaticism: removing oneself from the attentions of a persecutor can be an act of charity toward
him and qualify as the simplicity of the dove. *You will not have gone
through all the villages of Israel,* Jesus adds, *before the Son of Man
comes.* This is another of those puzzling statements of Jesus like that of
Mt 16:28 which we saw on page 200 f. above (on Mk 8:34–9:1 and
parallels; cf. also Mk 13:28–32 and parallels below). The early Church
most certainly understood it and other words of Jesus of its kind as
pointing to an imminent termination of "these last days" (Heb 1:2)
in the glorious consummation of God's kingdom; indeed, the continued
"delay" of this eagerly awaited end became a source of scandal to many
as the Church continued on (cf. 2 Pt 3:3–10). What did Jesus himself
mean by such a saying? We shall be in a better position to answer this
question when we come to consider his *ex professo* teaching on the last
days in our Chapter 21 below. For the moment, let us understand what
Matthew has taken it to mean. The evangelist's context supposes no
speedy conclusion of the Church's mission limited to the towns of Palestine, but a continuing witness before the governors and kings of the
Gentile world (vs. 18), a mission which extends to all the nations of
the earth (cf. Mt 28:19 f.). For Matthew, then, "Israel" here means
nothing less than the new people of God which the Church is sent to
form (cf. Mt 2:6, 19:28). Until the Lord comes, he says, there will always be another place for the Church to go, retreating before violence,
and in going there to bear yet further its testimony to the Gospel of
Christ.

Mt 10:34–36   Violence has been the theme of Jesus' warnings to his
Lk 12:49–53   disciples, and it is on this theme that he continues to
                   dwell. It is one of the paradoxes of all time that this
Man of peace, whom the New Testament can call peace itself (Eph
2:14), should be the source of strife and dissension, that he should have
occasioned some of the vilest as well as the noblest of the conduct possible to man. For this reason he can say that he has come not *to bring
peace on earth . . . but a sword*, not *to give peace on earth . . . but
division*. Both Matthew and Luke cite Mi 7:6 in illustration of his meaning, words by which the prophet intended to signify all that was ab-
normal and enormous in human relations.

The sense of the Gospel, however, is not merely to reiterate warnings
of things to come. *I came to cast fire on the earth*, cries Jesus—the figure
has changed, but the meaning remains the same—*and how I wish that it
were already kindled!* He not only anticipates the violence, he also wel-
comes it! The word of Christ is not all milk and water, sweetness and
light. If the kingdom is to come only through violence—a violence which
is not of its making—then, violence or no, let the kingdom come! If
the violent of this world are to have their way forever, then nothing of
good will ever be accomplished. If good men are to be dissuaded from
good because doing good provokes violence, then evil has triumphed for
all time. We have it from the lips of Christ that, when the cause is
right, it is the man of peace in whose wake and at the tips of whose
nerveless hands injustice and inhumanity pursue their untrammeled paths,
while the man who is attended by violence does the works of God. We
have it from his lips and we have it from his life: *I have a baptism with
which to be baptized, and how I am hemmed in till it is done!* This is
an "imitation of Christ" to which all too few Christians have been
equal.

Mt 10:37–39, 11:1   Matthew proceeds toward the end of his mis-
Lk 14:25–27, 17:33   sionary discourse by joining together three say-
                         ings of Jesus appropriate to this context, two of
which he has already used elsewhere taken from the common Synoptic
tradition (see above on Mk 8:34–9:1 and parallels). One of these two,
as we also noted before, is likewise proper to the Johannine tradition
(cf. Jn 12:25). The three sayings have been repeated by Luke as well,
at two intervals in his "timeless" sequence of the Perean ministry.

The difference in meaning caused by the changed contexts is not appreciable; it is mainly a question of specific applications. It will pay us
to examine, however, the third of the sayings which we have not seen
up to this point. Here again it is interesting to note that it is Luke,
rather than Matthew, who has preserved the Semitic rigor of Jesus'
words. *If anyone would come after me and not hate his father . . . is*

softened to *Whoever loves his father or mother more than me*. We are
not invited by pronouncements of this kind to weigh our separate loves
in a balance and compare them in the abstract. The sense is, rather,
that no earthly love or bond must ever be allowed to interfere with our
prime allegiance to Christ. This is made quite evident when in Luke's
version the Lord says that we must even hate ourselves. The Christian
finds his true fulfillment in complete surrender to his Savior, renouncing
in the process when called upon to do so all that men would consider
to be the claims of self-interest. It is perhaps worthy of comment that
while Matthew has put these lines in a discourse of Jesus to the Twelve,
Luke has them in an address to the *great multitudes* which were following him, among whom, presumably, were those who were on the verge
of committing themselves to discipleship. Neither Gospel can be accused of proposing the calling of a Christian as an easy one.

Lk 12:13–21   Matthew closes his discourse with his customary formula
              (see above on Mt 7:28 f.). In Luke, Jesus' teaching at
first directed to his disciples (vs. 1) is now interrupted by the request of
someone in the crowd, an intervention which focuses his attention on
the whole assembly and leads to a discussion closely related to the foregoing.

We do not know the circumstances involved in regard to *the inheritance* about which the man hoped that Jesus would arbitrate between
him and his brother. He had seized this opportunity of calling out to
Jesus as a respected rabbi whose authority would be worth something
if used in his behalf. Jesus, however, as we know, habitually refused to
intervene in such matters, leaving them to be handled in the conventional way, as he does now. He did take the occasion to warn against
covetousness, which is not to say either that the man's desire for his
property was inordinate or that he was dishonest. Jesus' teaching on the
Christian attitude to wealth is more far-reaching than that.

Covetousness—the word *pleonexia*, which is used in the New Testament mainly by Paul, means "the desire for more"—is an evil for man
not because it necessarily makes him defraud others or otherwise do
them an injury, but because it can lead him to miss the meaning of
life and thus to destroy himself. It can make him forget that *a man's life
does not consist in the abundance of his possessions*. It is for this reason
that Col 3:5 calls covetousness "idolatry": it worships a false god by
setting up another goal of life than that for which man was created.

What Jesus understands by covetousness we learn from his parable.
We see a certain rich farmer—today he might be growing wheat in Kan-
sas or corn in Iowa—who brings in a bumper crop, so great that he is
forced to tear down his available barns and build greater ones. This he
does, and with all his possessions snugly laid in, it seems that he can

quite justly congratulate himself on a good job well done. He has security; he can now take things easy and live off his accumulated capital.
The picture Jesus drew would have appealed to his hearers, and was so
intended, as that of a respectable, solid citizen, one of the bedrocks
on which a stable society rested. Nor should we imagine that the average
Christian reaction today would be much different. We, too, are inclined
to see in this man the prudent organizer, the good planner whom we
would trust with our own goods, the man of substance who has done
well for himself and his family.

God, however, calls him *fool*, and in doing so indicates how far apart
our judgments can be from those of Christ. As far as Jesus is concerned,
the man was neither wise nor prudent nor sensible, but a fool. The
very night he found himself at last prepared to lead the good life without fear of want, that night God decreed his life forfeit. He was *not
rich toward God*. This does not mean necessarily that he was an ir-
religious man who had consciously cut God out of his life: the parable
does not suggest this. He was a fool, rather, because he felt that his
future was in his own hands, that whatever he was to become, he would
be "self-made"; he was a fool because he thought to reckon with every
eventuality of life, only to find out too late that no single one of them
had really been under his control. Not only a crude love of riches cor-
rupts, but also a preoccupation with them—and this holds, of course,
for the poor as well as the rich man. It can lead to a practical forgetfulness of God that is perfectly compatible with public protestations of
thanksgiving to a God of bounty who smiles on success and industry
and who frowns, as all responsible men frown, on the shiftlessness and
lack of forethought that alone account for poverty and want. It is not
difficult to see why Luke continues in this context with certain words
of the Lord which Matthew has put in his Sermon on the Mount (see
above on Mt 6:25-34 and parallel).

Lk 12:32-34   Luke goes on in the same vein, including material that
has been paralleled in part in Mt 6:19-21 above. Con-
cern for worldly goods is not the only hindrance to a wholehearted and
purposeful seeking of the kingdom, but it is a major one. Jesus speaks
as the Good Shepherd (see above on Jn 10:1-21), affectionately address-
ing his *little flock*, that is, his disciples (vs. 22) as distinct from the
multitude present (vs. 1). *Do not be afraid*, he tells them. He had begun by warning them of what they had to fear, but he had also told
them why they should discount their fears. They are a little flock, small
in the eyes of the world and defenseless, but they have what the world
cannot see. They have God and they possess his kingdom if they will
receive it from him. What need have they of anything else? *Sell what you
have*, he directs, *and give alms*.

This command of the Lord was taken precisely at the letter by the primitive Christian Church that emerged in Jerusalem following Jesus' resurrection and ascension (cf. Acts 2:44 f.). This same mother church, we must add, itself speedily became impoverished and economically dependent on the more vigorous Christian communities which soon began to proliferate throughout the vast Gentile world (cf. Rom 15:25–28; 1 Cor 16:1–4; 2 Cor 8:1–4). In the fifties and sixties of the Pauline churches the charitable communism of the Jerusalem church of the thirties must already have seemed a quixotic anachronism from a never-to-be-repeated age of Christian innocence. This is not to say simply that Christians discovered Christ's law to be impossible and therefore settled for something less. Rather, as we said above in this chapter (on Mt 10:16b–25 and parallel), the Church had to rethink, and to rethink continually, the enduring meaning of a revealed word which, as the Holy Spirit had now made quite clear, was to guide it not for five or ten or twenty years but for an indeterminate future that was beyond calculation. Some would always be able to take this word at the letter and thus fulfill in their lives a vocation to anticipate the eschatological fulfillment of the Church, just as others would be able to do through a life of celibacy or some other charismatic calling; but the Church could not then and cannot now ignore its duty to perpetuate itself in a world that is not yet eschatological and in which an eschatological vocation will always be the exception rather than the rule. Again, therefore, we must ask: How did Luke construe this pronouncement for the Church he knew and for which he wrote?

The answer to this question is fairly obvious. Not every Christian can literally sell all that he has and distribute what he gets in alms, for if everyone did so there would be none left to carry on the ordinary life of society; and it is this ordinary life of society that Luke presupposes as he shows the Church fulfilling its destiny in Paul's hands throughout the Acts of the Apostles. Everyone can, however, take as his own the spirit in which Jesus uttered these words, and in doing so he can accomplish the end toward which they indicated a means. He can acquire the detachment from wealth of which the Lord has been speaking in the preceding passages. He can recognize that his duty to his neighbor is not defined by the extent of his surplus goods but must be fulfilled at cost to himself. He can learn, then, the function of Christian almsgiving, which is not only to relieve the need of the poor but also to benefit the giver by destroying in him the spirit of covetousness.

Lk 12:35–40   An exhortation to vigilance now follows in Luke's compilation. That part of what Luke reproduces here turns up again in the major eschatological discourse of the Synoptic tradition (see below on Mk 13:33–37 and parallels) reflects the eschatological heritage of Jesus' preaching of the kingdom and of the primitive Christian Church. Luke obviously does not exclude this perspective but neither does he consider the Lord's words to be confined to it. The eschatological moment in which the Christian encounters his Judge likewise overtakes him pre-eminently in death, whose precise instant no man can ever possibly know, but also in every wakeful minute of his life, when he forms the judgments and does the deeds on which his eternal destiny depends. Every moment of decision is, in this sense, eschatological.

The parable told by Jesus pictures a master who is to return from *a wedding feast* and who has charged his servants to be waiting for him: a wedding feast has been deliberately chosen because it was an event whose duration was entirely unpredictable, thus making the rest of the story plausible. The point of comparison is, of course, that the Lord is coming at no known or determined time. The servants, then, are to have their *waists girt and* their *lamps burning* at all times so that they will be in instant readiness to receive their master. The flowing garments of the time were worn loose when one was at leisure, but had to be girt close about the body when any active work had to be done. Doubtless no earthly master would actually have treated his faithful slaves as does the man in the parable, reversing the roles of master and man (cf. Jn 13:3–20). The very exaggeration of the story, however, points up its message: a reward far beyond our deserts is in store for those of us whom Christ our Judge finds ready at his summons. In verse 38 the uncertainty of the time of visitation is stressed—for a Church that had reconciled itself to a "delay" of the Lord's coming—*even if he comes in the second or the third watch* of the night. The Romans divided the night into four watches of roughly three hours each, depending on the season of the year, and the Jews in Palestine followed this system. Probably, however, the reference here is to the more ancient Jewish practice which knew only three night-watches (cf. Jgs 7:19).

The other little parable used by Jesus likewise dwells on the idea of uncertainty. No thief in his right mind, of course, announces his coming, so that his victim will be alert and on his guard. Just so, the Lord does not announce his coming, but appears unawares as *the thief* who *breaks into the house*. This "breaking into" the house, incidentally, is not precisely what is meant nowadays by the "breaking and entry" of a police blotter, implying the picking or the forcing of a Yale lock. Palestinian houses were, and sometimes still are, walled of mud and wattles, and a thief might easily find it more convenient to remove a wall than to get through a stout door.

Lk 12:41–48   In Luke's context *Peter* now asks whether *this parable*
Mt 24:45–51   of Jesus applies *to us*, the Twelve, *or to everyone*. The
                question might seem natural enough in view of what

has gone before, since the Lord's attention has been often divided between the disciples and the accompanying multitude. Actually, however, it is pointless. Peter had no doubt at all that what Jesus had said, especially in verse 37 regarding the reward for faithful service, was meant for the Twelve. What he was asking was whether others were to be included as well. This is the kind of question that he asked according to Jn 21:21, and equivalently he receives the same answer here. His duty is to take in the word as he receives it without concerning himself about what others do or are intended to do. Actually, it is difficult to decide whether the evangelists understand the parable above and the one that now unfolds as designating pre-eminently the Twelve and therefore said with reference to apostolic functions in the Church (cf. the apparent echo in 1 Cor 4:1-3), or expressive of the common eschatological lot of all Christians. Some of the details of context favor the former, most of the content favors the latter interpretation. For practical purposes we need not attach too much importance to the distinction.

The parable presupposes the situation of a trusted slave appointed as overseer of his master's estate, a not uncommon occurrence. It is much to the point to observe that the reward for faithful service is even greater responsibility in the same order. Whether uttered in specific reference to service in the Church or extending to the Christian's total activity in the world, the lesson is much the same and is quite an important one. Authentic Christian eschatology is not "pie in the sky" unrelated to this present world; when the Christian enters into the reward of his Master he begins a life for which he has been preparing all along and which he has even been leading already in all of his actions and involvements. Christian service, which has as its model the life of the Servant of all, is ordered toward the world which God has created and which he has loved to the extent of sending his own Son for its salvation.

Conversely, what of the servant who takes advantage of his master's absence, abuses his trust, plays havoc with his goods and abuses his fellow servants, doubtless planning to put things to rights again at some final moment that never comes? The day of reckoning arrives with the unexpected return of the master. He will, the Gospels say, *cut apart* the faithless servant. This is a strange expression, but perhaps some light is thrown on this word (*dichotomeō*) which occurs only here in the New Testament by a Hebrew expression (*yabdîl*) which etymologically is the same, and which was used by the Qumran sectaries to mean *separation* from the elect community. This idea, which has Old Testament precedents (cf. Is 56:3, 59:2), seems to be what is intended here: such a person will have *his lot with the faithless,* as Luke puts it; *with the hypocrites,* says Matthew, who also adds the expressive words found often in the Gospels to describe the hopelessness and desolation of eternal perdition: *where they weep and gnash their teeth* (cf. Mt 8:12, 13:42, 50, 22:13, 25:30; Lk 13:28).

Luke at the end has included some allegorical details which contribute a further lesson related to the foregoing and clarified by his conclusion. What he is saying is that there are degrees of punishment meted out in accord with the various degrees of guilt that are incurred.

Lk 12:57–59   Luke now introduces the Lord's words on the effect of his coming which we have seen earlier in this chapter (on Mt 10:34–36 above), and also the saying on "the signs of the times" which is as appropriate in this context as in the one where we saw it previously (above on Mk 8:11 f. and parallels). The final lines with which he closes this chapter we have also had in a Matthaean parallel (on Mt 5:21–26 above). It may be very well that in Luke's context we have this saying in its original emphasis, whereas Matthew has somewhat adapted it in applying it to fraternal charity. The time of decision is now, says Jesus; now *right judgment* must be made; after now will be too late. Now come to terms, now seek salvation in repentance. The judgment of God is ever near, and it is inexorable.

17. WAITING IN PEREA

Lk 13:1–9   The Lucan passages with which we begin have a general connection with the context of the last chapter. Jesus takes occasion from two recent disasters to issue a further eschatological warning and summons. Concerning the circumstances of the incidents themselves we have no further source of information beyond Luke's Gospel. *The Galileans whose blood Pilate had mixed with their sacrifices* evidently were Galilean pilgrims to Jerusalem who had committed what either was in fact or what Pilate imagined to be an insurrection and were therefore slaughtered by the Roman governor. Either possibility is likely: the Galileans were always restless under Roman domination, and Pilate was extremely suspicious of rebellion and merciless in dealing with it. The Roman garrison was situated on the very edge of the temple area (cf. Acts 21:30–32); obviously what happened was that the troops simply poured down upon the Galileans who were thronged together in the courtyard while their sacrifices were being carried out by the priests within.

An unexpected death, especially a violent death, was popularly regarded as God's punishment for personal sins. Perhaps in the case at hand the question of the lawfulness of rebellion was in the air. Jesus does not concern himself with these issues. All men, he reminds his listeners, are under judgment and subject to death *unless you repent.* The Galileans have died, for whatever cause, not because they were more egregious sinners than others, but their deaths can at least serve as object lessons for others. So also *the eighteen on whom the tower in Siloam fell:* the reference is to another misfortune about which we are not otherwise informed. Without repentance *all will perish in the same way*, not necessarily by Roman swords or falling stones, but violently and unexpectedly.

It is in this context that the parable of the barren *fig tree* follows. As respects God's judgment all men are in a sense living on borrowed time. At any time they could be cut down, and if they have not yet been, it is only because in his mercy they are always being given one final chance to show themselves worthy of his concern.

Lk 13:10–17   Luke intends the story of the healing of the crippled
               woman to have a topical connection with the foregoing,
though it resembles even more some of the controversy stories involving
the Sabbath that we have seen before (see above on Mk 3:1–5 and
parallels). The connection here is the demonstration of the proximity of
the kingdom of God in the loosing of Satan's power which had *bound
this daughter of Abraham for eighteen years*. Though this healing miracle
was not precisely an exorcism it was produced much to the same effect,
since afflictions of the woman's kind were popularly ascribed, as we see,
to a personal *spirit of infirmity*. When the event actually occurred we
of course do not know, though it probably belongs to the early part of
Jesus' ministry when *he was teaching in one of the synagogues*. The
story is told with the attention to detail that speaks for its having been
taken from life. This is particularly evident, perhaps, in the words of
the ruler of the synagogue who, rather than attack Jesus directly, tries
to lecture the crowds who would not presume to answer him back,
placing the blame on them as though they had come to the synagogue
expressly to be healed, which was not the case. His pompous *come on
those* six other *days to be healed and not on the Sabbath* even manages
to suggest that miracles of healing were going on everywhere on a
twenty-four-hour schedule and could be regulated at will. It was probably these devious courses as well as his Pharisaical scandal that earned
the Master's retort, *Hypocrites!*

Lk 13:22–30   In this appropriate context of controversy over the com-
               ing of the kingdom Luke has included the parables of
the kingdom which we have already seen (above on Mt 13:31 f. and
parallels; Mt 13:33 and parallel). Then, after reminding us that Jesus
is *journeying toward Jerusalem* (see above on Mt 19:1 f. and parallels),
he has him *teaching through towns and villages* till he reaches the scene
of this present passage.

Will only a few be saved? was a natural question which inevitably
Jesus must have been asked countless times in his preaching of the kingdom. The rabbis generally thought that the number of the saved would
be rather small—as, for that matter, many earnest souls have thought
throughout history, not always without a certain complacency concerning
their own status among the saved. Small or great, however, the number
was usually related exclusively to the Jews; the Gentiles, by and large,
were left out of consideration as a matter of course. Descent from Abraham and Moses was what counted (cf. Jn 8:31 ff., 9:28 f.), that and the
faithful observance of the Law and the traditions of the ancients. Since
ignorance of the Law and the traditions, from the standpoint of the professional scribe, was more the rule than the exception, it was not felt
that the number of the elect would be large (cf. Jn 7:49). It was a

certain smugness, therefore, that lay behind the posing of the question, Will many be saved?

It is this kind of irrelevant question that Jesus never answers. Neither does he respond to it here. His saying about *the narrow door* (here the door of a house rather than the gate of a city) has the same meaning as its parallel in Matthew (see above on Mt 7:13 f.). *Keep trying to get in,* he teaches them, for the time is late and the kingdom of God is like a room into which everyone must crowd at once: in such a press of people it is normal that *many will strive yet not be able to get in.* His accent is on the urgency of the situation and the need for effort; he does not speculate on the relative numbers within and without the door. And the door is soon to be shut! In verses 25–27 Luke applies to the present figure words of the Lord very like those which Matthew reproduced in another context but to the same purpose (see above on Mt 7:21–23 and parallel). In turn, this leads to the sternest warning of all, which strikes at the complacency in which the original question had been asked. Luke's verses 28 f. parallel Mt 8:11 f. and have the same function (see above on Lk 7:1–10 and parallel). Blood descent from Israel's ancestry is no guarantee of membership in the kingdom, which can be given instead to the Gentiles. *The last shall be first and the first shall be last* is a saying of Jesus which appears in several Gospel passages. Here it probably refers less to the possible substitution of Gentiles for the Jews—though in Luke's perspective the substitution now had in fact taken place, in the Church—than to the general theme of the entire passage, which is now summed up: in the pell-mell struggle that is involved in the entry to the kingdom, see that you are not among the last, the too late!

Lk 13:31–33   The next episode, which is told us only by Luke, is entirely at home in this story of the Perean ministry. Perea, like Galilee, was the domain of *Herod* Antipas, and it was here in Perea that Herod had had John the Baptist put to death (see above on Mk 6:14–29 and parallels). It is not entirely clear what role the *certain Pharisees* played in the little drama that unfolds before us. Jesus' telling them to bear his message back to the tyrant may have been merely rhetorical, but at the same time it seems to indicate that he put them in the same class with Herod. On the other hand, had they really been privy to Herod's plans and in sympathy with them, they would hardly have brought a warning to Jesus of any kind. Probably we are dealing with a case of a coincidence of interests rather than a plot. Herod, we know, had heard of Jesus and was curious about him, and whatever he had heard was doubtless not to his liking. To say that Herod had decreed his death is certainly to say too much: *He wishes to kill you,* the Pharisees related. But it is most likely that he had said something

to the effect that the land would be well enough off without Jesus—
"Will not someone rid me of this troublesome priest?" It was probably
intelligence of this kind that the Pharisees brought. It was to their interest to be rid of Jesus' presence, and news like this could easily send
a person hurrying across the nearest frontier, since in those days it was
extremely unhealthy to come to the unwelcome attention of a king.

Jesus, however, will not be intimidated. *That fox*, he calls Herod: in
the Bible a fox is a predator rather than an animal of guile. *Today and
tomorrow and the third day* is the time that remains to him: the expression means a determined period, but a period determined by God,
not by Herod (cf. Hos 6:2). Furthermore, he adds ironically, it can
hardly be destined that his life should end in Perea, for it is Jerusalem
that has the monopoly in the slaying of prophets!

Lk 13:34–35   It is the mention of Jerusalem that causes Luke to in-
Mt 23:37–39   troduce at this point Jesus' lament over the Holy City,
                 a passage which Matthew has reserved for the perora-
tion of a lengthy discourse delivered in Jerusalem itself against the
Pharisaical leadership of Judaism. The city is symptomatic of all rebellious Israel in this apostrophe, of course, as it is so often in the Old
Testament, *rejecting the prophets and stoning those sent to it*. But
symptomatic or not, it is of the city that Jesus speaks when he touchingly
compares the mercy shown through him to the tender solicitude of a
mother hen who spreads her wings to protect her young from harm.
His *how often* confirms the Johannine tradition complementing the
Synoptic, that Jesus' acquaintance with and ministry in Jerusalem was
not confined to the one week of his passion, death, and resurrection
toward which Luke is looking in his Gospel.

Your house is left forsaken, pronounces Jesus, echoing the words that
an earlier prophet spoke of an earlier Jerusalem and its king (cf. Jer
22:5). Jerusalem, having rejected its destiny, is desolate, whatever be
its present proud pretensions. *I say to you, you shall not see me* (cf. Jn
7:34, 8:21) *until you say, "Blessed is he who comes in the name of the
Lord!"* (Ps 118:26). Do the evangelists think that this will eventually
happen (an "until" does not necessarily imply a change of state, cf.
Mt 1:25), or do they look on this as the Lord's irrevocable judgment
on Jerusalem? We cannot be sure. Luke, however, by placing this passage
where he has, has evidently seen a partial fulfillment of Jesus' condition
in his triumphal entry into Jerusalem on Palm Sunday (cf. Lk 19:38),
and therefore, in all likelihood, an earnest of the salvation of Israel in
God's own time (cf. Rom 11:26f.).

Lk 14:1–6   Luke now offers something of a change of pace in his
               "great addition" as he begins to tell a story that we have
the initial impression of having heard before because of its resemblance

to a common type (see above in this chapter on Lk 13:10–17); actually, however, this seems to be a story apart. The scene is set *in the house of one of the leaders of the Pharisees* where Jesus has been invited *to eat a meal on the Sabbath*. The setting is natural enough—of course we do not know when or where it is to be placed in the life of Jesus—and there is no reason to suspect that the invitation was anything less than a gesture of honest hospitality or that Jesus was seated among people who were antecedently hostile to him. *The lawyers and Pharisees* who were present *were watching him,* it is true, but seemingly more out of curiosity and of interest than of evil intent. The *man with dropsy* who suddenly appeared *before him* would have had no problem in intruding upon an Oriental banquet, and there is no indication at all that he had been introduced to provide a provocation. His swollen condition as he stood there spoke eloquently of his need; he had no cause to put it in words.

It is Jesus who forces the issue: *Is it lawful to heal on the Sabbath, or not?* (cf. Lk 6:9). The doctors of the Law recognize that this is no theoretical question, for here stands the man who, they realize, is to be healed. They evidently accept his argument that since a man can retrieve *an ass or an ox from a well* on the Sabbath, it should be permitted to heal a man (see above on Mt 12:9–13). (Some of the better manuscripts have "a son" in place of "an ass"; but this would appear to be an attempt to make things a little too easy for the legal mind.) *They could not reply to this:* they were not necessarily seeking an answer at all costs which they could not find; it is possible that they were genuinely puzzled. This older generation of jurists had been conditioned to certain automatic responses according to ingrained custom, and it did not come easy to them to devise new answers to new questions. The Gospel leaves them in a quandary rather than in a state of obduracy.

Lk 14:7–11 Jesus now seizes the opportunity from the present occasion to inculcate another of his teachings. The background for what Luke calls his *parable* may strike us as a somewhat stilted and stuffy social atmosphere, if not downright childish. However, protocol of a different kind probably plays as pervasive a role in our lives as the seating arrangements at table did in the lives of Jesus' contemporaries. What we tend to reserve for extraordinary affairs and state occasions was for these Orientals part of the daily routine. There were dozens of converging titles by which one man could claim precedence over another and which by comparison might make the arrangements of a Washington hostess seem like informality itself. Age, public position, learning, attainments, wealth, all had their claims, conferring on one the right, and a jealously guarded right, to be seated at one of the first places, that is, nearer the host. It was seeing this familiar ceremonial being enacted before his eyes that prompted Jesus to speak.

Jesus speaks of *a marriage feast* possibly out of a concern not to point his finger too directly at those present on this occasion, also because an event of that kind was more formally and solemnly observed than an ordinary meal. He neither condemns nor approves the social customs in question, but simply takes them for granted. Everyone present could appreciate, perhaps from sad or happy experience, the situation that he describes. It would indeed be a humiliation for one who had confidently taken one of the first places to find himself obliged publicly to relinquish it to a later arrival of greater dignity and thus have to make his way to one of the places below. On the contrary, what a joy to be able to walk, at the host's invitation, from a lower to a higher place reserved for him! The wisdom of seeking *the lowest place*, therefore, could hardly have been better brought out. And that, of course, is the point of the parable: *everyone who exalts himself will be humbled, and he who humbles himself will be exalted* (cf. Mt 23:12). Jesus has been teaching neither social etiquette nor the methods of face-saving. Humility, pursued for the glory of God and not of man, is the only way into God's kingdom, while pride bars the way completely.

Lk 14:12–14   Jesus also has a word for his host that reiterates teaching we have seen above in the Sermon on the Mount (on Mt 5:46–48 and parallel). The duties of hospitality were precise and taken very seriously in the East, as they still are. We can probably presume that at this banquet there was a sprinkling of the four classes of people noted by Jesus: *friends, brothers* (close relatives), *kinsmen* of less degree, and *rich neighbors*. Friend was hospitable to friend, brother to brother, kinsman to kinsman, and a rich neighbor of course could always count on a hearty reception. All this was reciprocal, a comfortable charity that worked hardship on no one. All well and good, Jesus tells the Pharisee, but he must also allow that this kind of cautious generosity simply follows the dictates of self-interest and carries with it its own present recompense. If he would have the reward of God and not of man, let him do good to those who cannot repay him. True charity is disinterested; it *will be repaid at the resurrection of the just*.

Lk 14:15–24   Mention of "the resurrection of the just" calls forth an exclamation from *one of those at table*, the kind of mutual congratulation and blessing to which Orientals are prone in moments of joy and satisfaction. Throughout this encounter Jesus' comments, though pointed, have been given in a pleasant way, and there is no indication that any of his teaching had been taken amiss. *Blessed he who shall eat bread in the kingdom of God!* was, of course, uttered with some of that complacency we have already remarked. The man who said it obviously had no doubts that the kingdom of God would be a prolongation of the good-fellowship of this present table, a perpetual banquet prepared by the Lord on Mount Zion (cf. Is 25:6) for such good fellows as these.

Hence the point of Jesus' parable which now follows. It is in all likelihood the same in origin as that told in Mt 22:1–14 below. The two evangelists or the sources on which they depended have so altered and adapted it, however, and applied it to different contexts, that it is necessary to consider the two passages as independent of each other. Here the purpose is to apply another correction to Jewish complacency about the kingdom and to insinuate once more the consequence of Jewish rejection that is dear to Luke's heart, the mission of the Church to the Gentiles. Both of these emphases are historically authentic in the teaching of Jesus, and for this reason Luke's version of the parable may be closer to the primitive form than Matthew's which is heavily allegorized.

The parable tells of *a man* who *gave a great banquet* to which *he invited many.* Following this preliminary invitation, which the parable supposes to have been accepted, he then *sent his servant,* as was the custom, when the lavish preparations had been completed and the presence of the guests was now expected. Had the servant not been sent, the invitation would have been deemed cancelled, which would have been an insult to the guests. By the same token, the refusal of the invited guests to honor the summons is a grave violation of the laws of politeness. Their excuses are paltry. *They all as one began to make excuses* is probably calculated language in view of the parable's application: it suggests a concerted conspiracy of refusal. No one, naturally, would have bought a foot of land without first having inspected it thoroughly, nor would he have acquired a single ox without knowing all about it in advance. Furthermore, no newly wedded wife would have had the slightest say about the goings and comings of her husband. The man in question may have been citing Deut 24:5 in his own favor; if so, he was guilty of what Jesus has previously stigmatized, using the letter of the Law to violate its spirit in respect to his humane duties.

His banquet spurned, the man now turns first to the byways of the town, bringing in *the poor and maimed and blind and lame* to replace his able and affluent, but absent, guests. Here we are to think of the ones called "sinners" by those seated comfortably about the Pharisee's table, who were entering the kingdom in place of the doctors and students of the Law (cf. Lk 15:1; Mt 21:31). *And still there is room!* Thereupon the master of the house gives the order for his servant to leave the town itself and to fill up the empty places with people who are outsiders (cf. Rom 11:17–25; Eph 1:11–13). The parable ends abruptly. Nothing is said of what the Gentiles will make of the kingdom, for that is not to the Lord's purpose. The warning to Israel, however, hangs heavy in the air as he concludes.

Lk 14:28–33   Luke now abandons the banquet scene and takes Jesus on his journey surrounded by a huge crowd. These are people evidently of good disposition, but equally with the Pharisees in need of instruction on the conditions of the kingdom. This instruction Jesus proceeds to give, beginning with words which we have already seen in the preceding chapter (above on Mt 10:37–39 and parallels). No one must assume that it is easy to follow Christ. It means the renunciation of all that could stand in his way, whether this be father or mother or even his own life itself. Let no one venture on this path without first counting the cost. This warning he illustrates with two little parables. He first pictures a person of substance *about to build a tower*, that is, probably, a large farm building, who if he is wise will begin by calculating his resources, lest the end result be nothing more than an unfinished local "folly" decorating the landscape and he become a laughingstock. Possibly the parable originally referred to some notorious instance of such improvidence. Or a *king going to encounter another king in war*: it is unpardonable to begin a war that one cannot win. For those who cannot win wars, negotiated peace is a necessity. The point of the parables, of course, is not that one has the option of entering or declining to enter the kingdom of God, but that one must be forewarned of the terms of his commitment and be prepared to meet them. Otherwise he may begin well and end miserably: here Luke introduces the figure of salt that has lost its taste (see above on Mk 9:49 f. and parallel).

Lk 15:1–2   The kingdom of God continues to be the subject of these Lucan passages as the evangelist joins together three parables which both respond to a well-known situation in Jesus' life and have served ever after as a precious source of reassurance to the repentant sinner of the Church for which Luke wrote and of which we are the heirs. The situation is, again, the Pharisaical scandal taken at the low company for which Jesus had become famous and for which he seemed to have an attraction rather than for the respectable elements of the population. The text says, with something of an exaggeration no doubt, that *all the publicans and sinners were drawing near to hear him*; at least they were coming in such numbers that as a class they could be listed as his followers, whereas the Pharisees and scribes as a class would doubtless have to be numbered among his enemies (see also above on Mk 2:13–17 and parallels). Not all those whom the pillars of Jewish society regarded as sinners were necessarily more reprobate morally than their fellows, it is true, but it is also true that Jesus was undoubtedly being pursued by a motley assembly that included sinners by anyone's accounting as well as by Pharisaical election. As the parables go on to show, this was not to Jesus' discredit, but rather testified to the bankruptcy of the religious establishment that had lost its sense of mission and now had no higher ambition than to devote itself to the serious purpose of saving the saved.

Lk 15:8–10   The first parable is that of the lost sheep, which we have seen above in a different context (on Mt 18:10–14 and parallel). Luke has it that *there will be more joy in heaven over one sinner that repents than over ninety-nine righteous who need no repentance.* The righteous often find this a hard saying, but it will be explained in better detail in the third parable.

The second parable is like the first, except that it figures something that was lost through carelessness rather than through its own willfulness. The *drachma* was a Greek coin of the same value as the Roman denarius, worth comparatively little in itself, but representing much to the *woman* of the story whose total wealth consisted in ten of them. Possibly they were her dowry money. At any rate she goes to extraordinary measures to find it, illuminating the dark house and sweeping the dirt floor, sifting until she has found it. As the shepherd with his lost sheep, therefore, she lets everything else go in her all-out effort to find what was lost. And again her joy in finding it is intense—greater than had she never lost the coin.

There is joy before the angels of God over one sinner who repents. The implications of this pronouncement should not be overlooked. He who says "sinners" thinks in categories rather than of persons. It is easy to hate, to despise, or merely to dismiss categories, because they are abstractions independent of experience. He who says "one sinner" thinks of a person who has sinned. The lesson of all these parables is the value that God attaches to each human person, in whatever category he has placed himself.

Lk 15:11–32   The third parable, certainly the best known of this triad, has only one or two other rivals among the many passages of the Gospels for first place in the affections of most readers. We think of it traditionally as the parable of the Prodigal Son, though Lost Son would be the more apt title; the son's prodigality is only a detail of the story, not its point. Because of its multiple values and message, we sometimes forget that it, too, was told originally to justify Jesus' association with sinners. That purpose quickly becomes obscured, however, as our interest is focused on the personalities of its protagonists. The parables of the lost sheep and the drachma were concerned with objects whose recovery was a precious joy to their owners, but in this story we have to do with a living, human person who is as much affected by the process of loss and gain as is the father who loses and regains him.

This parable, then, which is in part allegorical, we think of first and foremost as a word of love and reassurance to the repentant sinner himself.

According to the Law the younger of two sons was entitled to one third of his father's estate as his *share of property* (cf. Deut 21:17). The father was under no obligation to make a distribution of his goods during his lifetime; the father in this story does agree to do so, contrary to the advice of one of Israel's sages (cf. Sir 33:19–24). Apparently the elder son does not take possession of his share, but leaves it under his father's administration while he continues to live in the family home. The foolish younger son quickly *squandered his property*, and it was not long before he was reduced to the occupation of a swineherd—the lowest level of degradation for a Jew. In speaking of the youth's subjection to the *citizen* of *a far country* who is obviously a pagan, is Luke thinking of the publicans —pre-eminent "sinners" in Jewish eyes—who had sold themselves to the Roman state?

The *pods* eaten by the swine are the fruit of the carob tree. They are insipid and hardly fit for human consumption; however, on these the youth *would gladly have fed* (some manuscripts have *fill his belly*), simply to stop the pangs of hunger rather than to gain real food and nourishment. It is in these straits that he at length comes to his senses and recognizes the enormity of what he has done. His resolution to return to his father is not, by his own accounting, based on any motive other than his miserable condition contrasted with the lot of the poorest in his father's house. The speech that he rehearses to recite to his father is, however, an expression of true repentance, and it is by this means that the parable makes its point. Similarly, we could hardly uphold the father of the story as a model of sobriety in his treatment of the boy either before or after his wild oats had been sown. He runs out to meet him, does not even permit him to complete his carefully prepared confession, and proceeds to lavish on him every honor, not stopping at necessities but indulging every exaggerated mark of affection that the Oriental reserves for a favorite son who can do no wrong. The parable is not telling fathers how to deal with wayward sons, however, but trying to convey how great is God's happiness at the return of a sinner and how incredible is his mercy that extends far beyond anyone's just deserts.

And it is this, of course, that others of God's children often find it hard to understand. The elder son in the story speaks like one of the Pharisees (cf. also Lk 18:1–14 below), as one who has *served many years*, who *never disobeyed a command*. Indignant at his father's treatment of the ne'er-do-well, he himself becomes prodigal in his comparisons. His brother, whom he designates obliquely as *this your son*, had not merely been good-for-nothing, but *devoured your living with harlots*. He accuses his father of meanness in his regard. We begin to see a not unfamiliar phenomenon in the life of religion. It is a fact that we can easily set a greater price on virtue than does God himself, because we forget that we are all equally the objects of God's mercy, some in one way, others in another. If we have led a righteous life, or at least middling righteous, which is doubtless what most of us would lay claim to, it is all too easy to give ourselves full credit for what we have done. It is all too easy to compare ourselves favorably with the wastrel who has made his peace with God at the last moment, a comparison that is usually compounded with envy of a man who has somehow had the best of both worlds. But *you are always with me, and all that is mine is yours:* the righteous man has been the recipient of God's mercy all along. How many times has he not been shielded from temptations that he never knew, strengthened when others were weak? Because God rejoices more over the repentant sinner than over the righteous who need no repentance does not mean that he values lightly either the righteous or righteousness. He alone values it rightly, for it was of his doing. He has rejoiced over the righteous all along, and now is the time for another rejoicing.

Lk 16:1–13   Righteousness continues to be the theme of Luke's Gospel in the passages that follow, with the Pharisees always standing somewhere in the background. Perhaps, too, there is a connection of thought centering on the dangers and responsibilities of wealth, one of Luke's characteristic concerns, as the parable of the prodigal is succeeded by the others of this chapter. This next parable is also popularly misnamed. We think of it as about a Dishonest Steward, which of course it is; but again, it is not the steward's dishonesty but his sagacity that is the point of the parable, as is shown at the end of the story.

The parable tells of an overseer, apparently a freeman in this case, who held the position of trust ascribed to the slave of the story we saw above in Lk 12:41–48 and parallel. Having been found out in some embezzlement, probably, he faces the prospect of losing his position and of being forced to find another in order to live. He has no talent for common labor and he is ashamed, or afraid, to have to beg. So he hits on another plan. *Calling his master's debtors one by one*, he systematically reduced their debts by about half. Some commentators have suggested that this did not constitute another act of dishonesty, by which he continued to defraud his master, but rather that he forewent his own commission on these debts as overseer. Even today promissory notes are sometimes written not in the amount of the principal but with advance interest and other extras already totaled in. This may be true, since otherwise his master displayed an admirable detachment with regard to his own property when he proceeded to commend the steward's resourcefulness. But in any event, *the master commended the dishonest steward because he acted prudently.* There is the lesson of the parable. Finding his security threatened, the steward made quick and efficient use of the means that were at hand to buy friends for himself against the lean years ahead. His dishonesty, whether before or after his discovery by his master, is not commended, merely his shrewdness. By his principles, whether crooked or not, he acted wisely.

Whether verse 8b is also part of the parable depends on the main thrust one is disposed to find in the story as it appears in Luke's context. If the Lord's lesson includes teaching on the prudent use of wealth—and this interpretation would seem to suppose that what the steward did with his master's bills of debt was not dishonest—then the parable doubtless ends with verse 8a. What follows would then be an application of the parable. But if, on the other hand, the main intention all along has been to illustrate to Christians the need of expeditious and prudent action on their part, the parable certainly includes these words: *for the children of this world are wiser in dealing with their own generation than are the children of light.* The alacrity and skill with which the steward dealt with the crisis facing him serve as a model to Christians facing their crises of decision, which must be dealt with on principles of divine rather than worldly wisdom.

By any accounting, the following verses represent applications of the parable, all of them concerned with wealth and its uses. *Make friends for yourselves with the mammon of wickedness,* Jesus says, which means: make wise use of your wealth that will be to your true good. Mammon, money, is qualified as wicked perhaps because the mammon of the parable was such, but certainly because in Luke's mind its tendency is to make men wicked. Similar expressions were used by the rabbis and at Qumran, just as we speak jocosely—and sometimes affectionately—of "filthy lucre." Jesus' teaching regards the Christians' eschatological future: their use of worldly goods is to be such that *when it* [wealth] *fails, they may receive you* (=you will be received; the "they" is impersonal) *into everlasting dwellings.* Again, the proportion by which we are faithful in our trust with worldly goods (*a little thing*) will be the measure of our chance at heavenly things (*a great thing*). If we do not know how to handle *the wicked mammon,* how shall we know what to do with *the true wealth?* Wealth, after all, always really *belongs to another:* it is ours only fleetingly and does not go with us. All the more reason, if we have proved ourselves faithless in this extraneous thing, not to be entrusted with what is our very own forever. Luke now brings this series to a close with the saying on God and mammon which can be seen at Mt 6:24 above.

Lk 16:14–18   Jesus has been talking to his disciples (vs. 1), but now his attention is diverted by *the Pharisees who had heard all this.* Luke says that they *were lovers of money* in the sense that their notion of wealth as a token of divine favor tended to an attitude toward it which was diametrically opposed to that of Jesus ("the mammon of [=which leads to] wickedness"); in their theoretical teaching and belief, the Pharisees were not materialists, but rather opposed the materialism of the Sadducees. The verses that follow are intended as the introduction to the parable beginning with verse 19, the rich man in which Luke doubt- less thinks of as a Pharisee; but the sequence of thought is somewhat difficult to follow, possibly because these verses represent only the high- lights of a once extended discourse.

Jesus begins with an insistence on religion as a matter of the heart, in language reminiscent of other New Testament condemnations of ostenta- tion and externalism (see especially above on Mt 6:1–4, 5–8, 16–18). Then follows in verses 16 f. the Lucan version of two sayings Matthew has reproduced elsewhere (Mt 11:12 f., 5:18; see above on Lk 7:24–35 and parallel and Mt 5:17–20). The sense seems to be here: *the Law and the prophets,* the old dispensation for which the Pharisees professed to speak, is now passing away, and with it all that could serve as the occasion for their legalism. The mission of *John* the Baptist marked the transition: now *the good news of the kingdom of God is being preached, and every- one is forcing his way into it with enthusiasm.* Nevertheless, all that the Law really stood for remains and will remain without change: the word of God endures. Perhaps as illustrative of this principle verse 18 cites the law on marriage and divorce in its Christian formulation (see above on Mt 5:31 f.). At all events, Christ's pronouncement on divorce seems to have come from a controversy with the Pharisees, as we shall see below (on Mt 19:3–9 and parallel).

Lk 16:19–31   After this introduction we have the parable, in which
                it may be easier to see how these verses have, indeed, been an introduction. The *rich man* in the parable, with his belief in retribution after death and in a resurrection, is undoubtedly a Pharisaical Jew. (In early tradition he was given a name—"Nineveh" or something similar—probably because in this parable the poor man also has a name. The familiar title "Dives" often applied to him is not a proper name, but the Latin noun for "rich man.") It is important to note that the parable does not make him out to be what we would call a bad man. Rather, he is quite like the rich farmer of whom Luke's Gospel told in our preceding chapter (see above on Lk 12:13–21). He spent his money on *purple and fine linen and feasted sumptuously every day,* it is true, but we ordinarily find nothing wrong with a man spending his own money on himself as he pleases, so long as he harms no one else by doing so. He doubtless even dispensed some kind of charity to the *poor man named Lazarus who lay at his gate.* The text says that Lazarus *desired to be fed with what fell from the rich man's table,* and we do not have to conclude that he de-

sired in vain. The later development of the story shows that he both knew Lazarus and felt some kind of claim on him. Therefore he had probably given him the leavings from his table and had permitted him to lie in the courtyard outside his door along with the dogs: he was such a man, we might say, as "helps the poor." And for all this, after death he is found in Hades suffering torments. Why? Because, as Abraham his "father" is pictured as telling him, *you in your lifetime received your good things . . . and now . . . you are tormented.*

The lesson, therefore, is of the danger inherent in wealth itself, not simply of the evil use to which a man may put wealth. A man who has an abundance of the world's goods is in great danger not merely of becoming avaricious, grasping, and oppressive, but also of becoming insulated from life and the meaning of life. The free-spending, good-natured playboy who has never had to give a serious thought to money at any time, to whom every outstretched hand has appeared one and the same, to be filled in consideration of his comfort alone, if this consists only in his finding it more convenient than to strike it aside, such a person may have done no evil; but has he ever done any good? Has he ever asked by what law of God or man he has been privileged to live in thoughtless luxury while other men go hungry and wretched outside his gate and his mind? Has he ever known what it is to be human, which is to acknowledge the common family of man?

Lazarus is a model of the *anawim,* the poor of the Lord (see above on Mt 5:3-12 and parallel). Despite his abject poverty, his physical sufferings, his degradation when even dogs, unclean animals, lick his sores, he shows no resentment, no despair or hatred, asking only the bare pittance of food necessary to keep him alive. In this alone of Jesus' parables does one of the characters receive a name, which has doubtless been carefully chosen for the occasion (Hebrew *el'azar*="God helps"); however, some have suggested that even here the name may have been picked up in oral tradition from the story of Lazarus of Bethany who returned from the dead and was not believed (vs. 31; cf. Jn 11:1-44, 12:9 f.).

Abraham's bosom does not appear to have been a conventional term for a place of repose for the dead, but rather expresses the idea of the messianic age as a banquet in the company of Abraham and the patriarchs of old (cf. Mt 8:11; Jn 13:23). It is hard to tell to what extent some of the details of the parable represent contemporary popular ideas about the afterlife and to what extent they have been made to order for the sake of the story. At all events, the parable has not been told to suggest that Hades is divided by a chasm over which conversation takes place between the wicked and the just, or that a lost soul can feel compassion for those who are to share his fate. The point is made in Abraham's response to the rich man's petition and in the latter's reaction to the response (vss. 29 f.): the way of salvation has been indicated by

Moses and the prophets, but the Pharisees will not heed it (cf. vss. 15–17 above). For this selfsame reason, the parable concludes, the "signs" for which Jesus was continually being asked (cf. Lk 11:16, etc.) would equally have been of no avail.

18. THE LAST JOURNEY

Lk 17:3–6   In this chapter we shall see the end of Luke's "great addition" to the Marcan outline and at last rejoin the other Synoptic Gospels to resume their common tradition. Luke's verses with which we begin seem to have no close connection with his preceding context nor, for that matter, among themselves, except in the sense that they respond to various catechetical purposes in this highly catechetical Gospel. As before, Jesus is speaking *to his disciples*. We first read three isolated sayings of Jesus, all of which appear elsewhere in the other Gospels. The first we have already seen above almost verbatim (on Mk 9:42–48 and parallels). The second, on forgiving one's brother, seems to synthesize two Matthaean passages (see above on Mt 18:15–18 and 18:21 f.) where the context was much more obviously ecclesial than it is here. The third, uttered in response to the disciples' request to *increase our faith*, we saw Matthew incorporate into a previous story told by the Synoptic Gospels (see on Mk 9:14–29 and parallels above), and both Matthew and Mark will use it again in a later context. The other instances of this saying speak of the power of faith to move "this mountain" (the mount of the transfiguration and the Mount of Olives, respectively); here it is *this mulberry tree* (the saying had doubtless got associated with a tree from the context of Mk 11:22 f.; Mt 21:21). The disciples seem to have been asking for a special charism of faith in view of the demands of their apostolate: Luke refers to them here as *apostles*. But Jesus assures them that faith itself, when it is true faith, is more than sufficient for the greatest works they will be called on to do, of whatever order.

Lk 17:7–10   The fourth saying brought in by Luke is a little parable proper to his Gospel. Neither does it appear to be closely connected with its surrounding context. Taking the contemporary institution of slavery as its point of departure, it teaches the eminently Pauline doctrine of justification through God's mercy and not through works. The *servants* in the parable are simply slaves who belonged to their master body and soul according to the laws of the time. They did not look for consideration from their master, nor for his thanks, and no matter what service they faithfully performed, the master regarded it as due him by right, with no credit to his slaves. As it happens, this was an intolerable social order which evolving man quite properly abolished. Neither does the Gospel intend to suggest, of course, that God has made this imperfect human institution the model of his way of acting with us, his servants. The point of the parable is, rather, that he would most rightly do so if he chose. For we do belong to God body and soul, in a way that no human being can really belong to another.

We can give nothing to God, for we can add nothing to his existence by our own efforts, and no matter how much we do it is only what he has the right to expect of us. We owe him our being and everything that we are and have. If the Gospel also frequently speaks of a heavenly reward (literally *misthos*, wages) that God will bestow on us in return for our service (cf. Mt 5:12; Mk 9:41; Lk 6:23, etc.), it is only because of the divine promise that our good works thereby possess a value. Without it, they would have none. The good works of the Christian, along with Christian justification and salvation itself, are alike the manifestation of God's grace and mercy.

Lk 17:11–19   Reminding us yet once more (cf. Lk 9:51 f., 13:22) that Jesus is *journeying toward Jerusalem,* Luke tells us that *he was passing between Samaria and Galilee.* This sounds very much as though Jesus had recently left Galilee and was traveling down the western side of the Jordan Valley toward Jericho (cf. Lk 18:35). If geography and chronology were really an issue for Luke at this point, we should have to suppose that at some undetermined time Jesus left Perea for a final visit to his Galilean homeland. However, we may be sure that the evangelist is merely preparing us for a story in which we find Jews and Samaritans associating together. In the case at hand, this fact is not remarkable. The life of the leper was usually one of utter hopelessness, in which he was little disposed to bother about social distinctions. Though this story has various resemblances to others in the Synoptic tradition, it seems to have its own proper identity as a narrative proper to Luke. Again the evangelist is permitted to record something favorable to a Samaritan in contrast to his Jewish brethren (cf. Lk 10:29–37), a presage of the success of the Church's later mission to the Samaritans (cf. Acts 8:4–25).

The lepers were careful to observe the sad rules under which they had to live, standing *at a distance* to beseech Jesus' aid. Jesus likewise instructs them to *go to the priests* (cf. Mk 1:44 and parallels) who were empowered to judge when a man no longer had leprosy and could be readmitted to society. As we have already noted, many different kinds of skin disorders were called "leprosy" along with the actual dread disease itself, and to be on the safe side all were treated the same. Since the Samaritan and the others, who presumably were all Jews, would have gone to separate priests for scrutiny, it is not surprising that the former returned by himself. The point that is made is not that he alone possessed faith: all ten lepers were doubtless healed, and for the same reason. Only he, however, displayed that gratitude for grace that is so much the heart of genuine religion and the cause of its vitality.

Lk 17:20–21   Jesus' answer to the Pharisees in this next section begins a short treatment on *the coming of the kingdom of God* which at first glance seems to be somewhat contradictory. Actually it is not; it does, however, reflect the same tension that exists throughout the entire New Testament between what is sometimes called "realized" eschatology and "final" or standard eschatology. Jewish eschatology itself was comparatively straightforward. Those Jews who possessed eschatological views (not all did, by any means) were looking for an end-time, "the age to come," when the Messiah would inaugurate God's kingdom or reign, putting an end to evil once for all and establishing good for all time. The kingdom would come through judgment, fire, and tribulation, but come it would surely and definitively, and when it came "this age" would be gone forever and there would be a new heaven and new earth for God's elect. Within this framework there was, of course, room for an infinite variety of theories about details—the fate of the dead, the role of the Gentiles, the number of the elect, the character of the Messiah, and so forth, and so forth; still, the basic essentials were simple enough. This age and the age to come. The now and the kingdom of the future. When was it to be? Every rabbi was doubtless asked the same question.

By contrast, Christian eschatology became far more complex. The earliest Jewish Christians did not at first realize that this was so: they thought of the kingdom as did their fellow Jews, and looked for Jesus, as the Messiah, to inaugurate it. When instead he died on the cross, they were puzzled and disillusioned; had they believed in vain? (cf. Lk 24:21). The resurrection reassured them. Jesus their Messiah still lived. Now, then, he would surely establish the kingdom? (cf. Acts 1:6). But the risen Lord departed from their sight, though he remained present with them through his Spirit. Obviously, then, his glorious coming, his *parousia*, was reserved for the future: then at last would come the resurrection of the dead, the judgment, the end of all, the kingdom (cf. Acts 3:19–21). Would this be quite soon? The early Christians thought so—why should the Messiah have come but to bring in the kingdom? But later, as time went on, they began to have doubts, and from these doubts and the abiding presence of the Spirit of Christ came far deeper insights into the purposes of God. Had Jesus' teaching on the kingdom been quite as routine as they had imagined? If he had spoken of it in conventional apocalyptic language as any rabbi would, had he not also spoken of it at

times in quite prosaic terms, as a reality that one might easily overlook
if he did not see aright? What did all those parables of the kingdom
mean—parables about growing seeds, of wheat awaiting a harvest, of
leaven mixed in dough, and all the rest? Was it not possible that Jesus,
the Messiah, had indeed already brought in his kingdom, even though the
kingdom was yet to come? Was this really a contradiction? What of his
teaching on life and law, on oaths and promises, on love and filial respect,
on divorce, and marriage, and humility—was this intended merely to help
them mark time over a few weeks or months till a final cataclysm would
send it all to oblivion? Or was it the laying down of an ethic designed to
enable them to witness to a world which God loves (cf. Jn 3:16), a world
of whose vastness no one at that time could have had the faintest idea?
And what of this Christian community, this *qāhāl*, this *ekklēsia* (see above
on Mk 8:27–30 and parallels), of which they were members and whose
quickening Spirit they knew; did they not find in it, in its life and love
and liturgy and sacraments, at least a beginning of the blessings which
God had prepared for the people of his kingdom? (See below on Mk
10:23–31 and parallels.)

Hence we have in the New Testament "final" and "realized" eschatology. The Christian knew that a kingdom that was yet to come had, somehow, already begun. He knew that this realization diminished neither the
one nor the other. He could look for the resurrection of the dead while
believing himself already to be one of the resurrected: such is the conviction of John's Gospel. Like Paul, he could say in one epistle—even
in one chapter of the same epistle—that he was looking forward to becoming one of God's sons and that he was already one of God's sons (cf.
Rom 8:15, 23). The final times are now (cf. Heb 1:2), and they will
continue to be now as long as God has intended that the Church shall
endure.

What does all this make of Jesus' reply to the Pharisees? *The kingdom
of God does not come so that it can be observed,* he says. We can imagine
a saying like this in the lifetime of Christ even though we can imagine
it much more readily in the life of the early Christian Church. Apocalyptic language (cf. 1 Thes 4:16) was recognized as being, at least in some
part, figurative. Furthermore, not everyone shared the apocalyptic viewpoint. Therefore, it might well be that *the kingdom of God is within you,*
that is to say, *among you,* already begun, in your midst. Jesus was certainly
well aware that his preaching and teaching, his miracles and exorcisms,
had already inaugurated the kingdom of God. And obviously, not all
recognized this.

Lk 17:22–37   With hardly a change of voice, though now his words
are addressed *to the disciples,* Jesus begins to speak of
the coming of the kingdom in somewhat different terms. What he says
is for the most part expressed in fairly conventional apocalyptic lan-

guage, and this together with the fact that a great deal of the speech is paralleled in the later eschatological discourse common to all three Synoptic Gospels makes it easy for us to see that Luke has composed it from various statements of Jesus made on different occasions.

From what has gone immediately before, we should be surprised to hear Jesus speaking of the kingdom's coming either as a remote or proximate future event, and indeed he does not. His emphasis is entirely on the suddenness and unexpectedness of the *parousia* and the culmination of the last days: in this way, the kingdom is always imminent and the eschatological moment is always now. *One of the days of the Son of Man* probably is a Semitism for "the first of the days of the Son of Man," that is to say, the beginning of the last times. They will come with the suddenness of a *lightning flash,* he points out, and only in view of the Son of Man first having achieved his destiny of service, which is by far the present consideration of greatest importance: *first he must suffer many things and be rejected by this generation.*

The practical conclusion from all this is perpetual vigilance. As in the days of Noah (Gen 6:9–9:17), as in the days of Lot (Gen 18:16–19: 27), judgment comes when men are least prepared. And when it comes, no concern for worldly affairs will any longer be relevant; those who look back will do so only to share the fate of Lot's wife (Gen 19:26). Two people going about their ordinary affairs, to all appearances entirely alike, yet one is marked for judgment and the other is not; and when it comes, no one knows. It is quite evident that, despite the language of future eschatology, Jesus' emphasis is on here-and-now readiness for God's summons, however it comes.

It is this emphasis that renders somewhat fatuous the disciples' question. *Where, Lord?* they ask—where will all these people *be taken* to have judgment executed on them? Jesus replies with a characteristic no-answer, doubtless having in mind biblical figures like those of Is 18:6 and Ezek 39:4, 17. The "eagles" of the text are undoubtedly *vultures:* neither Hebrew nor, curiously, Greek distinguished between the two birds.

Lk 18:1–8   Two passages remain of Luke's special material, both of them fairly well-known parables. The connection with the preceding context is not hard to find. Persevering and persistent prayer, which is the lesson of the first parable, is the obvious corollary of the vigilance of which Jesus has been speaking. The comparison of God with the *judge who neither feared God nor regarded man* is, of course, rather to contrast the two. If even an unjust judge will finally do justice in spite of himself for one who is sufficiently persistent, then all the more will the God of justice who loves his children hear their persistent prayers. Perhaps Jesus' question at the end is not as gloomy as it sounds. He has just spoken of God's vindication of his elect, therefore he does ex-

pect to find faith. Nevertheless, the question is a warning and drives home
the point of the parable, for without prayer there certainly will be no
faith.

Lk 18:9–14   There is more to prayer than persistence, of course. The
                   main thing is that it should be genuine prayer. This sec-
ond parable takes its place among numerous Gospel passages which inculcate the spirit of true religion at the expense of contemporary forms
of externalism. For Luke it is the culmination of an extended treatise on
Christian righteousness which he has systematically contrasted with the
formalism associated by him—somewhat uncritically, as we know—with
the Pharisees.

The two participants in the parable provide a contrast almost like that
in the parable of the Good Samaritan. The Pharisee, by his own standards, was all that was respectable and proper. The publican, by the same
standards, was quintessentially a sinner. But in the eyes of God the roles
are completely reversed. The Pharisee's words are more a proclamation
than a prayer: Luke says, indeed, that he *prayed to himself,* and perhaps
he intended this to be taken ironically. The Pharisee says all that we
would expect him to say, and more. He is a model of sobriety and external decorum. Not only does he keep the Law faithfully, he performs
works of supererogation which he feels should place God firmly in his
debt; he *fasts twice a week,* on Mondays and Thursdays following Pharisaical tradition, and *gives tithes of everything* and not merely of those
things specified in the Law. He asks God for nothing, for he feels the
need of nothing. And, of course, he receives nothing. He is left with the
righteousness that he has designed for himself, which is as nothing in the
eyes of God.

It is the prayer of the despised publican that is received by God. *Be
merciful to me the sinner* are his words, which match his humble mien.
This is the prayer of a man who truly knows himself as he stands before
God. He cannot know other men as the Pharisee thought he could; as
far as he is concerned and can testify, he is the only sinner in the world
standing in the presence of him who hates sin. The publican has
brought all that any man can bring and the only thing that any man
should bring if he would be *justified* in the sight of God. Conscious that
man's righteousness is like worthless rags (Is 64:5), he is disposed for
the grace of God which alone can give him righteousness. On this Pauline
note Luke brings his treatment of Christian justice to a temporary close.

Mt 19:3–9   And once again it is necessary to pick up the threads of
Mk 10:2–12   the Synoptic continuity where Luke left it toward the
                  beginning of his lengthy journey-section. Matthew and
Mark also, as it happens, attach great significance to this final **division of**

their Gospels preparatory to the passion and resurrection narratives. For Matthew, in particular, the Church as it were journeys along with Jesus and passes from Judaism into the liberty of the Gospel. It is for this reason that there are in this section so many conflict stories representing Jesus' controversies with the rabbis. This first episode is a case in point. Luke, doubtless because of its Jewish coloration, has omitted it, though he has already given above (16:18) the Lord's *logion* embedded in the story; essentially the same *logion* is recorded by Paul as the Lord's command in 1 Cor 7:10 f.

Here by exception it appears that the Matthaean version of this parallel account is the more original and that Mark's is a story that has been considerably adapted. This becomes evident from the very beginning in the question that is put to Jesus. The *Pharisees* must have asked Jesus *whether it is lawful to divorce one's wife for any cause,* as Matthew has it: the tenor of this question is, "What are the lawful grounds for divorce?" The question was one much debated by the rabbis. The legitimacy of divorce itself, sanctioned by the Law of Moses, was not a point at issue. Thus there is something unreal about the question as phrased by Mark (in a few manuscripts of Mark "Pharisees" is omitted and the question is anonymous), *whether it is lawful for a man to divorce a wife.* Mark is interested merely in giving the Lord's teaching on marriage and divorce and not in the circumstances of the Jewish legal discussion that originally prompted it.

The law of Deuteronomy (24:1) envisioned divorce as taking place when a husband found "something indecent" in his wife and thus decided to repudiate her. As we have already explained (above on Mt 5:31 f.), this law was mainly concerned with protecting woman's rights in some small way and was not a pronouncement on the grounds for divorce. Nowhere in the Law, as a matter of fact, is any such thing spelt out. Not unnaturally, however, the subject came up frequently in moral discussions, and the rabbis generally fixed on the "something indecent" of Deut 24:1 as offering some index of the divine will in the matter. But what was "something indecent"? In the time of Jesus there were two radically opposed interpretations current in the rabbinical schools. Those who followed the tradition of the liberal Rabbi Hillel—one of the formulators of the Golden Rule (see above on Mt 7:12)—did not restrict the "indecent" to the immoral. This school, which in practice was followed by most Jews (cf. Mt 1:19), held that a man was free to divorce a woman for anything that he found displeasing about her, even, say, if this should be only that she had spoilt his dinner or railed at him in public. Common sense and the Semitic love of family undoubtedly kept the application of the principle well within reasonable bounds, while the law of Deut 24:4 effectively discouraged the temptation to hasty divorce.

Nevertheless, at least in theory it could fairly be said that the school of Hillel taught that it was lawful for a man to divorce his wife for any cause whatever. Opposed was the school of Rabbi Shammai (Shammai was a contemporary of Hillel), which taught that "something indecent" meant unchastity and that alone. It was into this dispute that Jesus was invited to enter.

Jesus does not, now or ever, permit himself to be entangled in fruitless casuistry. The casuistry in this case, the determination of legitimate causes, was fruitless because divorce itself is no law of God; at the very best, the legislation on divorce in Deuteronomy represented a divine concession to human weakness and *stubbornness*, making the best possible of a very bad bargain. *At the beginning* God had no divorce in mind. Marriage, Jesus reminds his hearers, was first intended for one man and one woman, not for a man and a succession of wives (cf. Gen 1:27, 2:24). Marriage so constitutes *one flesh*—one body, one person—that to destroy it is as unnatural as dividing a man's body into parts (cf. Eph 5:31). Furthermore, God himself is the author of the marriage bond and, therefore, the third party to every marriage contract. Not even mutual consent between husband and wife, as a result, is of any avail to dissolve a marriage. *What God has joined together, let not man separate.*

This teaching was not altogether new in Jewish ears. Other prophetic voices had troubled Israel's conscience in the matter in the past, and the Old Testament is a reflection of it. The texts which Jesus quoted are typical of a prevailing Old Testament view which regarded marriage as in principle monogamous and indissoluble. (It is doubtless relevant at this point to observe that the Jews, without having any laws to forbid divorce among themselves, nevertheless have established and maintain an enviable history of marital stability.) No Jewish teacher had, however, as far as we know, ever dared formulate as the divine will what Jesus now does in all confidence: *Whoever divorces his wife and marries another, commits adultery.* When Mark goes on to apply the same pronouncement to the situation of a woman divorcing her husband, he is without doubt adapting the Lord's teaching to a Gentile Church. The situation did not exist under Jewish law and would hardly have come up in a discussion with Pharisees. A Jewish wife could not divorce her husband, though under certain conditions she could sue to force him to divorce her. Undoubtedly some Jewish women took advantage of Roman law which permitted women to institute divorce proceedings; however, they would have been regarded as nothing less than apostates.

In Matthew's quotation of the Lord's words occurs the well-known exceptive clause, *except for immorality*; an equivalent expression is found also in Matthew's use of the saying in the Sermon on the Mount (Mt 5:32). When we compare the Lucan, the Pauline, and the Marcan forms of Jesus' *logion* on divorce and remarriage with the Matthaean, we are left in no doubt that Matthew's version, as regards these clauses, is an adaptation. But an adaptation to what? Certainly not, as some have thought, to a positive exception to the absolute principle expressed in verse 6, permitting divorce and remarriage on the grounds of marital infidelity (essentially, the doctrine of the school of Shammai). In addition to the fact that "immorality" (*porneia*) is hardly the word that Matthew would have used to express this idea—rather he would have said "adultery" (*moicheia*)—such an interpretation would make him contradict himself. What, then, does *porneia* mean? Most likely it has the same meaning that it has in Acts 15:20, 29, where it refers to sexual unions within certain close degrees of kinship or legal relationship as listed in Lev 18:6–18. Such unions the rabbis called by the Hebrew word *zenuth*, "fornication," which is translated by the Greek *porneia*. Marriages of people so related were abhorrent to the Jews, but were often common enough among the Gentiles. So common, in fact, that the rabbis would sometimes permit them in the case of proselytes who had entered Judaism from a Gentile background. What Matthew seems to be saying, then, is that Gentile converts to Christianity could and should break off these illegal sexual unions, which in his eyes were no-marriages, without fear of thereby offending against Jesus' prohibition of divorce. This was not to weaken but rather to strengthen the force of this prohibition. The "exceptive" clauses inserted into Jesus' teaching by Matthew or his source are the kind of adaptation of the word which would have been expected in the Jewish-Gentile church of Antioch for which the First Gospel was in all likelihood written, the same church for which the apostolic decree of Acts 15:28 f. was formulated.

Mt 19:10–12   In Matthew's Gospel *the disciples* who have heard Jesus' reply to the Pharisees and his stern interdiction of divorce come to the conclusion that perhaps *it is better not to marry*. The same thought has doubtless occurred to many a Christian on the threshold of the altar: it is not necessarily a counsel of despair, but rather a recognition of all that marriage means, not as a selfish and casual liaison but as a commitment for life. Who is to presume himself equal to such a commitment? Thus we have the full force of our Lord's reply: *Not everyone can accept this teaching, but only those to whom it is given*. This is not to say, obviously, that marriage is for only a limited few, or that one is free to take or leave alone his teaching on the indissolubility of marriage. He is saying simply that Christian marriage is a grace—a sacrament, it would later be called—and not merely a natural contract arranged through the inevitability of the sexes. Marriage is one thing, Christian marriage is something else. The fate of marriage taken as a human arrangement and

nothing more—its history has been written mildly in the divorce regula-
tions of the Law of Moses, and a far more dismal history can be read in
the laws of the Gentiles long before and long after Moses. Christian
marriage is a grace: it is God who calls people to this life and who gives
them the power to live it.

There is here a rather important Gospel teaching that Christians have
not always properly understood. Graces cannot be legislated. Understandable though it may be that Christian nations will desire their laws
to reflect the religious convictions of their peoples, it is a very question-
able wisdom that has prompted a country or a state to translate into
civil and actionable law a divine word that has been sent into the soul
and conscience of Christian man. For Christian man such a thing is
unnecessary in the first place and a usurpation of the liberty with which
God has made him free; for non-Christian man—who is at least as
frequent in a Christian country as in any other—it is an intolerable
burden, the imposition (in the name of God) of a duty which God has
not revealed to him and which, therefore, he has not given him the
means to fulfill. A sad, sad record of hypocrisy and collusion has dogged
the footsteps of good, earnest people who have made the mistake of
confusing the Gospel with a *corpus iuris*.

As Jesus goes on to say, not everyone, then or now, has been called to
the state of Christian marriage. *There are men incapable of marriage
from birth*: such persons, by the Jews considered the most unfortunate
of all men, were of course well known. Well known, too, were those
who had been made such by the violence of other men. Less well known
were those who *for the sake of the kingdom of heaven* rendered themselves incapable of marriage. Jesus is not thinking now of the castrated
priests of the mother goddess Cybele: as he saw it, they were hardly
tending toward "the kingdom of heaven." It is impossible to believe
that he was not thinking of himself, of John the Baptist, of the Qumran
people, of those who, like Paul (cf. 1 Cor 7), would later form a great
Christian host who could find their fulfillment in renouncing marriage
rather than in embracing it. If marriage is a grace, it is not necessarily
given to all, for God has other graces as well. *Let him who can, accept
the grace he is given.*

Celibacy in itself is merely a negation, but a celibacy in which God's
will is seen and pursued is one of the graces of the kingdom. This can
be a source of great consolation to many, to enrich lives that would
otherwise have been empty. There are other ways than by physical
mutilation by which men or women may be made incapable of marriage
by other men. Celibacy for such people is the result of no conscious
choice but is the conclusion of circumstance. Yet the grace of God can
also be offered through circumstance, and if accepted can transform
sterility and futility into meaningful existence.

Mk 10:13–16   It is somewhat fitting that a pronouncement on mar-
Mt 19:13–15   riage should be followed by this rather appealing story
Lk 18:15–17   of Jesus and the children. Probably no association is
                 intended with *the house* which Mark mentioned in
verse 10 simply to distinguish, as he usually does, between Jesus' public
preaching and his private instruction of his disciples. The scene is perfectly natural and could have been enacted anywhere at any time. Mothers
in the admiring crowds about Jesus bring their children to a respected
teacher that he may *touch them* in prayer and blessing. Natural, too, is
the reaction of the disciples, who thought they were serving Jesus' best
interests by discouraging such flattering but also time-consuming attentions.

The vehemence of Jesus' reprimand of the disciples, on the other hand,
shows that in his eyes they were missing something very important concerning his ministry. *To such as these belongs the kingdom of God*, he
reminds them. Mark and Luke also include here a saying which Matthew
used in an earlier, similar episode (see above on Mk 9:33–37 and
parallels). Consultation of the earlier passage should also put us on our
guard against attaching to this pronouncement an unintended senti-
mentalist judgment on the supposed virtues of children that make them
worthy of the kingdom of God. The kingdom belongs to such as these,
and every Christian must be such as these, precisely because these receive
it as a free gift, bringing to it nothing but themselves, their openness
and receptivity to the workings of God, incapable as they are of helping
themselves in any way. What these children are by nature, all must become by free choice who will enter the kingdom of God. This is what
it is to be childlike; it has nothing to do with childishness.

Some commentators think that this passage served a further catechetical
purpose in the Church that transmitted it to the evangelists. In all
three Gospels when Jesus says of the children, *Do not hinder them*, a
Greek verb is used (*kōlyō*) which elsewhere in the New Testament
(Acts 8:36, 10:47, 11:17) appears in contexts involving baptism; another
form of the verb is likewise used in Mt 3:14. There are in addition a
few hints in other early Christian literature, all of which support the
theory that this word was a technical term employed in the ritual of
Christian baptism to render the *nihil obstat*, the "nothing hinders"
verdict on a catechumen presenting himself for the administration of
the sacrament. If this is the correct understanding of the background of
this expression, it is possible that the Church which used it to translate
whatever Aramaic term Jesus may have employed did so with the intention of finding in Jesus' acceptance of the children a precedent for
the baptism of infants. The passage was often invoked in the early
Church as providing such a precedent, we know. The question of the
baptism of infants was much fretted during the first ages of the Church,

and it is conceivable that the form-critical analysis of this Gospel pericope reveals one of the earliest answers to the question.

Mk 10:17–22   The *rich young ruler* of the next passage is something
Mt 19:16–22   of a composite figure. All three Gospels agree that he
Lk 18:18–23   was rich, it is true, but only Matthew says that he was
                  young, and only Luke identifies him as a ruler of some
unspecified kind. The story explores the by now well-worn Gospel theme of the danger of riches to the Christian life, but also contains certain teachings proper to itself which make it unique in the Synoptic tradition.

First of all, there is the man's greeting, *good master*, and Jesus' reply, as found in Mark and repeated almost verbatim by Luke, *Why do you call me good? No one is good except the one God.* Matthew was apparently sufficiently impressed by the difficulties involved in this answer, by which Jesus seemingly repudiated any claim to the divine attribute of goodness, that he paraphrased both question and answer so as to put the discussion on an abstract level, leaving Jesus' person out of it. However, Jesus' words here doubtless represent the Synoptic equivalent of various pronouncements with which we are already familiar from John's Gospel (for example, see above on Jn 5:16–30). Always he refers to his Father the attributes which he has been sent to reveal in his life and teaching. "Good master" was an unusual title, fulsome even though well meant. The young man's "good" rolled from his tongue far too readily. Since he is being asked about *eternal life* (another Johannine phrase), Jesus feels obliged to focus attention immediately on its only source. God alone is truly good, and everything good that man is or does can only reflect this goodness. The Son of Man is no exception to this rule.

As we have already seen brought out in a previous story recorded by Luke (above on Lk 10:25–28), it is most typical that the young man should ask what he must *do* in order that, once for all, he may have eternal life. Though expressed differently, Jesus' reply is not much different from that of the former occasion. There is no esoteric way to salvation that is not already known to all. The man *knows the commandments*. Keeping God's commandments is a mark of one's love for him (cf. Jn 14:15). And since a man is what he loves, whoever has embarked on this route is on the way to eternal life with God.

The young man of the story felt that he was on this way, as perhaps he was: Mark says that *Jesus looked on him with love.* Mark's and Luke's record of his reply as *all these things I have kept since childhood* might just possibly be an indication that he was a very young man indeed. It is for nothing up to this point in his life, however, that the young man is censurable. He himself, nevertheless, recognizes that something is lacking in his life, something of which he is capable and of which he senses the need. The explicit *What more must I do?* of

Matthew's Gospel is implicit in all that he has said according to Mark and Luke. Here we have a bold spirit who will not abide what is not final and total. Unfortunately, like so many good men before and after him, he discovers that it is easier to have high ideals than to live by them. His is the tragedy that a man of low ideals will never experience, when he finds that his reach has exceeded his grasp.

If you would be perfect, Jesus replies, there is indeed a course available to him, the *one thing remaining* by which he can realize the potentialities that God has given him: *follow after me*. Jesus invites him to do no less than share his own life as an immediate disciple, an invitation that was not given to all. For this young man the acceptance of this invitation necessitated his dispossessing himself of all he owned and sharing the poverty of Christ, a necessity that was not imposed upon all. And so, a face which a moment before was radiant with enthusiasm now becomes clouded over. The challenge has been offered, and is reluctantly refused. The young man went away *sad at heart*, but he did go away, *for he had great possessions*.

This passage has justifiably been used to provide an evangelical basis for the tradition of the "religious" life which is venerable in Christianity and which is represented in various ways in Protestantism as well as in Catholicism. "Religion," in this restricted (and doubtless unfortunately chosen) sense of the term, means a vocation not to a higher form of Christianity, which does not exist, but to a distinct form of Christian life that seeks to realize in some fashion—anticipate is one way of saying it, but perpetuate is perhaps even more accurate—the eschatological figure of the Church. Just as celibacy is obviously for the few rather than for the many, but in those few can show forth an aspect of the kingdom of God that marriage does not (cf. Mk 12:25 and parallels), so it is with the life of evangelical poverty (see above on Lk 12:32–34). What the Church as a whole cannot and should not do can be the vocation of some to do for the Church. Such is the distribution of graces in the Church (cf. 1 Cor 12:4–31).

Mk 10:23–27   Jesus takes the occasion of the departure of the rich
Mt 19:23–26   young man to warn once more about the dangers of
Lk 18:24–27   wealth in respect to the kingdom of God. Mark, whose
                 account is summarized by Matthew and Luke, records
that *the disciples were astonished at his words*. Then as now, the rich man was regarded as the one who had the easiest time of it, in salvation as in everything else. If the poor were in some special way under God's care, this was, after all, simply because there was no one else to watch out for them; the rich man could take care of himself. He had the leisure and the opportunity to know the Law and the means to fulfill

it by almsgiving and other good works. If he nevertheless is in danger, *then who can be saved?*

Predictably the Lord tells them that in their sense of the question no one can be saved, rich or poor. *But what is impossible with men is possible with God.* No man saves himself, but he is saved wholly by the grace of God. What is needful is that he remove the obstacles to grace, and a rich man has tremendous obstacles to remove. For this reason *it is easier for a camel to pass through the eye of a needle than for a rich man to enter the kingdom of God.* There is no point in attempting to mitigate the extreme hyperbole of this expressive figure by imagining that there was a well-known passageway called "the needle's eye" or by supposing *kamēlos,* "camel," to have been misread for *kamilos,* "hawser." The figure says what it has to say with complete Semitic extravagance.

Mk 10:28–31   In context, Peter's intervention is now quite under-
Mt 19:27–30   standable. Unlike the rich young man, he and the
Lk 18:28–30   other disciples *have given up all things and followed
Jesus.* The warning against the dangers of riches there-
fore holds no terrors for them. What, then, will be their reward? In his comments on this passage St. Jerome rather dryly reminds Peter that he was not a rich man but a fisherman: what he had left was a boat and a few nets. All the same, he had made the sacrifice that the rich man had refused, for he had left all that he had, and no man can do more than this. What is more important, as Jerome went on to say, he and the rest had really followed Jesus. We know with what generosity they had done so, without haggling over conditions or terms. They had gone where they knew not, simply out of faith and good will, and they had served him well, if imperfectly.

Matthew inserts at this juncture a saying of Jesus of which there is a variant parallel in Lk 22:28–30, a saying so "primitive" in the Jewish-ness of its formulations that it must be very nearly precisely as Jesus uttered it. *In the new creation* (cf. 2 Pt 3:10; Apo 21:1–5), promises Jesus, *when the Son of Man sits upon the throne of his glory,* these faithful Twelve *will themselves sit upon twelve thrones judging,* that is to say, ruling, *the twelve tribes of Israel.* Nowhere else in the New Testament is the kingdom of God described in more material and earthly terms. However the saying may have been initially understood (see above on Lk 17:20 f.), it is certain that Matthew interprets it of the apostolic government of the Church.

All three Gospels go on to record the Lord's promise not only to the Twelve but to *everyone* who has imitated their example in renouncing family, friends, and possessions for his sake. Each version has modifica-tions of its own: it is interesting to find that according to Mark, for example, Jesus included *persecutions* among the favors reserved for his friends (cf. 1 Thes 3:3; 2 Thes 1:5). Even more interesting, however, is what is made quite explicit in Mark and Luke, that besides *eternal life in the age to come* Jesus promises a here-and-now reward, and a reward that is of the same order of the things that have been renounced. Mark is most emphatic about it: *a hundredfold now, at this very time.* This does not mean, obviously, a hundred houses or a hundred wives for one. It does mean a more than compensating sense of possession, of social existence, of family relationship to be found within the kingdom (cf. Mk 3:35; Rom 16:13; Phlm 10, etc.). When we reflect that this exchange is often the material and social wealth of one who by this world's standards is both poor and alone—a man who has embraced monastic poverty for the sake of the kingdom has very literally "left house and wife and children"—we can again see the relevance of this entire sequence to those charismatic callings which prefigure the eschatological Church.

Matthew and Mark conclude with Jesus' saying about the first being last and the last first (cf. Mk 9:35; Lk 13:30, etc.). Here the purpose is probably to underline the divergence between the value judgments of God and of man. Many who in this life are held to be of little or no consequence, "last" by man's accounting, shall prove to be "first" in the eternal kingdom; and they who are the mighty of this earth, on whom the world's destiny has turned, may have no part at all in the world to come.

Mt 20:1–16   It is this saying and this theme that Matthew takes up in the parable of the Laborers in the Vineyard. If this parable continues to perplex a great number of readers who feel that the mode of conduct it depicts as God's is, from any human standpoint, eccentric and not altogether fair and square, it must be concluded that it deserves to rank among the most successful of Jesus' parables, for that is exactly the effect that it set out to produce. It shows how the last become first through a divine mercy that men find incomprehensible, yet with the preservation of justice for all. Jesus very likely intended it to be a cautionary story for the Pharisees, but its message is perennial, applicable equally well to any earnest soul who knows that he has deserved well of the Lord, who nevertheless finds his faithful service made of no more account than the momentary performance of him who answered the roll call at the last possible minute. It reminds us again that salvation is in any case God's free gift, and also warns against the assumption that membership in the eschatological kingdom and the pilgrim Church is one and the same thing. The Church, it is true, is ordained for the kingdom: it is a sign, a sacrament, of eternal election (cf. Rom 8, etc.); but the converse is not necessarily true, that where there is no perceptible sign there is also no election.

The parable, as parables so often do, combines a basically plausible story with some details that are too good to be true, which have been deliberately constructed to bring out the intended lesson. Thus, on the one hand, hiring workmen *in the early morning* for a day's work is natural enough. It is still common in the Near East for day laborers to assemble early in the public places of the town or village to bargain for their services with an employer or his agent. Settling for *a denarius*, the ordinary daily wage, was also to be expected. But it would have been unlikely that any vineyard would require the services of so many men, nor would they have been hired at different times during the day, much less at the very end. Here, to add climax to the story, laborers are engaged *at the third, the sixth,* and *the ninth hour,* that is, around nine o'clock in the morning, at noon, and three o'clock in the afternoon, and finally *at the eleventh hour,* only an hour before sunset, when work ceased for the day. We may be sure, too, that no real-life workers would have undertaken their job just on faith that the owner of the estate would pay them *whatever is fair.* Finally, the men would hardly have been paid in reverse order; Jesus tells the story this way to explain how the original group of workers can see what the others have received, since otherwise as soon as they had received their wages they would have gathered their tools together and gone home.

We see *the foreman,* then, passing out the coins of payment in the sight of all. Those who have worked only an hour, and that in the cool of the evening, receive a denarius, a truly generous wage far beyond their deserts. We are not told what the intervening groups received— they are not really important to the story except to contribute to the suspense—but presumably they also received a denarius from their rather single-minded employer. Those who have toiled since dawn now expect to receive more, since it seems to them that generosity should be extended to them in like proportion. But when it comes their turn to be paid, they too get each a denarius. Then begin the objections!

And, of course, those who object have not a leg to stand on. The man had agreed with them on a definite wage, and they had made a contract together. The contract had now been fulfilled on both sides, to the letter. There is no question of anyone having a claim in justice to anything further, not even if the owner of the vineyard had given the rest of his workers ten denarii each. The alternating liberality and strict application of justice that he has displayed may appear quite baffling to all, but there is precisely the point of the story. So does God's way of acting often seem baffling to us.

When the parable is applied, we begin to see the enormity that is involved in the workers' complaint: *Could it be that you are showing envy because of my generosity?* No objection whatever can be made against God's justice. What it amounts to, then, is that we can only feel chagrin that he has seen fit to deal more kindly with men than our mean natures deem proper. The reaction of the workers is a natural one, so natural that we must be constantly on guard against it, lest we find that with many high-sounding words and much righteous indignation we are really doing nothing more noble than to rail against the incomprehensible goodness of God.

19. BETHANY AND JERICHO

Jn 11:1–16   Somewhere paralleling the vague chronological sequence of the Synoptic events that have preceded and that will immediately follow, John intends us to read the story of the raising of Lazarus. This miracle is the last and greatest of the "signs" of Jesus which John has distributed over the first half of his Gospel (see above on Jn 2:1–11), quite literally fulfilling the words which Jesus uttered in Jn 5:28. All the "signs" reveal in some fashion the life-giving, saving power and presence of the Word of God, his "glory," but none other quite as definitely and directly as this one. Furthermore, in John's eyes it is this work of Jesus above all that sets in motion the chain of events that culminate in Jesus' ultimate work of salvation, his sacrificial death (cf. Jn 11:45–53, 12:9 f.), which for John is his "glorification" (see above on Jn 3:14–21). In view of its extreme importance for John, it is perhaps surprising that there is no parallel to the story in the Synoptic tradition. However, all the Synoptic Gospels make mention of similar miracles (cf. Mk 5:35–43; Mt 11:5; Lk 7:11–17), and we know by now how variously the Synoptic and the Johannine traditions have gathered and utilized their material (cf. also the remarks on Lk 16:19–31 above, on the name "Lazarus").

Bethany, today called by the Arabs *El-azariyeh* (an obvious corruption of the name "Lazarus"), is a village on the southeast of Jerusalem, separated from the Holy City by the Mount of Olives. John identified it as *the village of Mary and her sister Martha* who are known to us from the Gospel of Luke (see above on Lk 10:38–42). It was with this family, in all likelihood, that Jesus resided when he came to Jerusalem (cf. Mt 21:17; Mk 11:11 f.). John's reference to Mary as she *who anointed the Lord with ointment and wiped his feet with her hair* presupposes that the reader is already familiar with a story he himself has not yet related (Jn 12:1–8); the evangelist has no thought of connecting Mary with the incident described in Lk 7:37 f. Though Lazarus is not mentioned elsewhere in the Gospels, the text before us bears out what Luke tells us of Jesus' intimacy with his family in Bethany. The names of Lazarus, Martha, and Mary were quite common in

Palestine: a single Jewish tomb in the vicinity of Bethany discovered last century yielded all three names, together with those of Judas, Simon, and Jesus!

There are certain intentional resemblances between this story and that of Jesus' first sign in Jn 2:1–11. The message of the sisters to Jesus, *he whom you love is ill*, is a discreet and implied request, like Mary's statement at Cana (Jn 2:3). In the same way, Jesus at first appears to be on the point of disregarding their petition, though all the time he has in mind an action that will show forth his glory (cf. Jn 1:14, 2:11). There are also, as in so many of the Johannine dialogues, deeper levels of meaning—the Johannine irony—in various of Jesus' and the disciples' statements. When Jesus says that *Lazarus has fallen asleep*, for example, using the Christian euphemism for "has died" (cf. 1 Cor 15:6, 20, 51; 1 Thes 4:13, 15, etc.), the disciples take his meaning literally for the healthful sleep of convalescence, but also utter a truth that expresses the Christian belief in the resurrection: *Lord, if he has fallen asleep, he will be saved.* Lazarus appears in this story not merely as the brother of Martha and Mary and as the friend of Jesus, but as typical of every Christian to whom the Lord also gives life; hence the reiteration that he is one whom Jesus loved.

A subsidiary theme of the story is Jesus' impending death and the danger that he faces in returning to Judea (cf. Jn 10:31, 39). *Are there not twelve hours in the day?*: the daytime is the period of Jesus' ministry, before the coming of night and darkness (cf. Jn 1:5, 9:4); the time for this is determined by God, not by man (cf. also Lk 13:32). When Jesus shows himself resolute in going up to Judea, *Thomas*, a disciple merely named as one of the Twelve by the Synoptic Gospels, expresses a loyal willingness to share his Master's fate, which again echoes the formulas of Christian faith in Jesus' salvific death and resurrection (cf. Rom 6:3 f.).

Jn 11:17–32   John correctly observes that *Bethany was about fifteen stadia from Jerusalem*, that is, something under two miles. That Lazarus had been in the tomb *four days already* is stressed doubtless in order to emphasize the reality of his death: some of the rabbis taught that for three days after death the soul continued to hover over the body and only on the fourth day did it depart. As was true of Jesus' first manifestation of his glory at the end of the first week of the new creation (Jn 1:19–2:11), again it is on the seventh day that Jesus achieves this ultimate manifestation (cf. vss. 4 and 6).

This time it is Mary who *remained quietly at home* while Martha went out to greet Jesus as he entered the village. The Lucan portrayal of the sisters, however, is basically the same as that of this story. The large number of *the Jews* who were present is explained by the mourning rites of the time, which usually lasted seven days after death. Burial always took place as soon as possible, since there was no way of preventing the rapid decomposition of the body. On the other hand, travel was slow, and thus it would require a number of days for all the friends and relatives of the deceased to put in an appearance and console the bereaved family. It is noteworthy that in this passage "the Jews" simply means these concerned people and has no pejorative connotations as it so often does in John's Gospel.

Martha's conversation with Jesus is a singular combination of faith and lack of understanding. She greets him with the *Lord* of Christian faith, and her initial statement expresses her confidence in his power and a half-request that he will make use of it in respect to her brother. But when Jesus assures her that Lazarus will rise again she thinks only of the Jewish belief in the final resurrection of the dead. It is this belief, accepted by Christ and Christianity, which Jesus proceeds to reformulate in Christian terms: *I am the resurrection and the life; whoever believes in me, though he has died, shall live; and whoever lives and believes in me shall never die at all.* The source of the resurrection stands before Martha. It is he who will raise the dead on the last day because he is the very life of God come into the world (cf. Jn 5:26); and for the believer this selfsame eternal life is already a present reality (cf. Jn 6:40). Martha makes this formulation her own, and in doing so says more than she understands, since Jesus is about to signify what he has uttered by the raising of Lazarus from the dead. She now summons Mary with the call that will greet every Christian at the resurrection: *The Master is present* (the verb is *parestin,* from which comes *parousia*) *and calls for you.*

Jn 11:33–44   The magisterial Christ of John's Gospel is fully human for all that he is a divine person come into the world. He weeps in the presence of the grief of Mary and the other mourners. *He trembled,* says the text, and twice over an expression is used which denotes intense emotional involvement, of indignation or of anger. This seems to represent the Johannine equivalent of something we have already found in the Synoptic tradition (see above on Mk 1:40–45 and parallels) concerning Jesus' reaction to the reign of sin and its consequences and his recognition of the life-and-death struggle to which he is committed.

The more practical of the two sisters remonstrates with Jesus in what she takes to be his ill-advised desire to look for a last time on the features of his friend. Far from being a comfort, such a sight can be a repulsive shock. Thereupon Jesus tells her that the faith to which she had previously given utterance will now find an immediate realization: *you will see the glory of God.* His prayer to the Father is an accompanying sign *for the crowd:* his will is always one with the Father's and needs no leave

to be exercised, but it is necessary that this work be seen as the carrying
out of a life-giving mission (cf. Jn 5:19–24). Thus the men nearest the
vault roll back the stone that covers its entrance, and at the summons
of Jesus (cf. Jn 5:28 f.) Lazarus comes forth with the burial cloths still
loosely wrapped about his face and body. Jesus' further command to
loose him and let him go was probably not only a practical direction but
also intended to demonstrate the reality of the miracle. However, this
Gospel story is no exception to the rule that such events are briefly described with an economy of detail that wastes no time on incidentals.
Once the fact has been stated, the story is at an end.

Jn 11:45–57   As usual in John where the words and deeds of Jesus
are shown in their living character of revelation inviting
response, there is a mixed reaction to the raising of Lazarus. *Some of the
Jews . . . began to believe in him, but some of them also went off to the
Pharisees and told them what Jesus had done.* The latter did not necessarily have a hostile intent, but neither is it indicated that they were much
affected by what they had seen. Their report leads to a summoning of
the Sanhedrin by *the chief priests and the Pharisees* ("scribes" would
be more accurate here, as designating the second major component of the
supreme Jewish tribunal). It is not necessary to suppose that this was a
formal session of the Sanhedrin; it suffices that a cabal of Jesus' enemies
drawn from its members should have gathered together to discuss his case
and the threat which he offered.

The chief element of concern expressed on this occasion was the popular belief in Jesus as Messiah. For all of those present, Messiah could
only mean the leader of a Jewish liberation movement. To the Sadducean priesthood the idea of such a thing was abhorrent in principle;
to the scribes Jesus was unacceptable on other grounds. *Everyone will
believe in him, and the Romans will come and destroy our holy place
and our nation.* This is Johannine irony: this precise thing did happen,
though through a somewhat different causal connection than was then
imagined. The same irony reaches its height in the words of *Caiaphas,
who was high priest that year* of Jesus' death, whose part in the story of
Jesus' passion and death we shall see later on. Caiaphas' "prophecy" is
a study in cynical expediency, doubtless called forth to synthesize an opposition and policy on the part of men whose motives were disparate and
partly conflicting. He is willing to dismiss as irrelevant the question of
whether Jesus is guilty of any crime. Guilty or not, sincere or not, good
teacher or bad, miracle-worker or fraud, sent from God or from the devil
—the practical fact is that he is a danger to the established order. *It is
better for you that one man die for the people rather than that the whole
people should perish*; on such unlikely lips, and unconsciously, we find
the Christian doctrine of the atonement!

Caiaphas was evidently able to evoke a responsive chord in the minds and wills of those who were plotting against Jesus. John may very well have anticipated this conspiracy in order to connect it more closely with the story of the raising of Lazarus (cf. Mk 14:1). At all events, we now see Jesus withdraw once more from the danger zone *to a town called Ephraim,* doubtless to the great relief of the Twelve who had followed him to Bethany with such quaking hearts. Ephraim is usually identified with a little village on the borders of the Judean desert, about fifteen miles northeast of Jerusalem.

It is on this note of a temporary stay in impending violence that John makes his first mention of the last and decisive *Passover* of Jesus' public ministry. In his chronology, as we shall see (cf. Jn 12:1), the Passover is only a week away, and already throngs of people are gathering *in Jerusalem to purify themselves* of various ritual irregularities that would prevent their celebrating the feast. Again it is a matter of speculation whether Jesus will present himself in Jerusalem for a great feast (cf. Jn 7:11). Actually, of course, he was to celebrate this Passover in a way that none of them had imagined, but at the time it seemed scarcely likely that he would dare to make an appearance.

Mk 10:32–34   The Synoptic Gospels, too, are bringing us closer to
Mt 20:17–19   this last Passover, in their own more leisurely fashion.
Lk 18:31–34   Here we find them all together again "on the way to
Jerusalem," on a journey that is fast drawing to a close. This "third" prediction of the passion, it scarcely needs to be said, like the first two (see above on Mk 8:31–33 and parallels; Mk 9:30–32 and parallels) has put Jesus' intimations about his future into the explicit descriptions of the known Gospel fulfillments and has made no effort to preserve the precise language in which he spoke at that time. This is acknowledged plainly in Luke's account (vs. 34), though he also intends to say that the disciples were dull of understanding because of their preconceived ideas about the Messiah and the kingdom of God, as we see illustrated in the next episode told by Mark and Matthew. At all events, that Jesus' disciples were expecting his triumphal resurrection following his death is contrary to all of the later Gospel evidence.

Mark's account, considerably shortened by Matthew and Luke, pictures Jesus striding ahead of the somewhat reluctant disciples, who are puzzled and fearful. On the steep and narrow paths of Palestine most of the walking had to be done single file, and it was customary for disciples to let their master precede them. In this case, however, the evangelist seems to be suggesting the same kind of dispositions on the part of Jesus and the disciples that were recorded in Jn 11:8–16 above.

Mk 10:35–45   How little ready the Twelve were to accept Jesus' con-
Mt 20:20–28   ception of his mission as that of a Servant of the Lord
and of the kingdom of God as one of service in his

image and likeness, can be seen from this story about the two disciples who, after Peter, have the greatest prominence in the Synoptic tradition. That the story was something of an embarrassment to the same tradition that recorded it, seems to be evident from the various ways in which it has been treated in the Gospels. While Mark, as usual, records what he had to record without undue sensitivity to its implications, Matthew has taken advantage of a variant form of the tradition which ascribed ambition less directly to *James and John* and rather to *the mother of the sons of Zebedee*. The proverbial and often overpowering aspirations which mothers entertain for their favorite sons lend sufficient credibility to Matthew's version of the story; further, we know that among Jesus' intimate disciples, a category which extends beyond the Twelve, there were also many women (cf. Lk 8:1-3). Luke, for his part, finds it convenient to omit this story entirely, though in a later context (see below on Lk 22:24-30), doubtless under Johannine influence, he incorporates its lesson for the disciples into his story of the Last Supper.

To *sit at the right hand and the left hand* of the Lord *in* his *kingdom* or his *glory* obviously means to possess the best and second-best preferential places after Christ himself. It is not necessary to suppose that their ideas about the kingdom were completely and crassly materialistic: the Gospel has represented Jesus speaking in similar terms not long before this (see above on Mk 10:28-31 and parallels). Nevertheless they were, to say the least, extremely naïve, as the question itself shows best of all. Hence there is genuine and compassionate irony in Jesus' exclamation: *You don't know what you are asking!*

To *drink the cup* was a recognized figure for embracing one's destiny or undergoing it, as was, seemingly, *to be baptized* (cf. Lk 12:50), though this latter Marcan expression may be a Christian paraphrase (Old Testament precedents might be Pss 42:8, 69:2; Is 43:2; Cant 8:7). At any rate, Jesus demands of James and John whether they are prepared to share his fate, in terms that make it clear that it will be no easy one, and they reply confidently that they are ready. Thus the irony of their initial request is completed. Though Jesus says that only the Father, whose Servant he is, may assign places in his kingdom (see above on Jn 5:16-30), that they will indeed drink his cup and share in his baptism means that they will also have assured positions in his glory. The triumph and victory of the Christian is to be configured to Christ, and suffering and persecution thereby become a sign of divine predilection (cf. 1 Thes 3:3; Col 1:24). James, as a matter of fact, the elder of the two brothers, was beheaded by Herod Agrippa about A.D. 44 (Acts 12:2), the first of the Twelve to suffer martyrdom. John does not appear to have been martyred, but he was tortured, exiled to the island of Patmos, and died long after, among the last of the "first generation" Christians upon the earth.

The *indignation* felt against James and John by the rest of the Twelve may very well have been motivated by something less than a contrasting humility in the spirit of Christ's teaching (see above on Mk 9:33–37 and parallels). What Jesus says, therefore, he says to all. Previously he had spoken of the dispositions which must characterize every member of his kingdom. What he had taught then applies eminently to the present question of the leadership of the kingdom. Christ's Church must be governed, like any other organization of men. But in its government it cannot imitate the power structures of the kingdoms of the earth, for it is the kingdom of God whose head became the Servant of all. If the lot of every Christian is to be the servant of God, the lot of Church leadership is to be the servants of servants. In this passage the key words *servant* (*diakonos*, from which comes "deacon") and *slave* (*doulos*, used of Christ in Phil 2:7) were significant in the early Christian vocabulary.

The example, always, is Christ himself. *The Son of Man did not come to be served but to serve:* this epitome of Jesus' mission as he himself saw it is, in turn, the explanation of the second part of the statement that follows. *To give his life as a ransom for many* describes the extent and the end of Jesus' ministry of service: it is to perform the role of the suffering Servant of the Lord (Is 53:10 f., paraphrased here; cf. also Phil 2:6–11), whose sacrificial obedience is redemptive for the multitude of the people of God. (The "many" of the Gospel and Is 53 is descriptive, not exclusive: the life of the *one* Servant is offered for *many*, without implying that there are others for whom it is not offered.) Jesus' sacrificial life and death are called "ransom" (*lytron*: this word only here in the New Testament, though equivalent expressions are frequent) as a bold figure of speech that is not to be pressed: a parable rather than an allegory. While *lytron* was the money paid for the redemption of property that had been pawned or forfeited, its metaphorical meaning as applied to Christ's death is merely that by its means God once more came into complete possession of his people. Therefore we do not ask what third party was "paid" this "ransom" for the many, who it was that "owned" them before they were "bought back." Ultimately the figure is based on Old Testament types, according to which, for example, the God of Israel "ransomed" his people from the slavery of Egypt (Deut 7:8, etc.), not, obviously, by the payment of any price to anyone but by the revelation of his power and grace.

Mk 10:46–52   The "journey to Jerusalem" of the Synoptic
Mt 20:29–34, 9:27–31   Gospels now brings Jesus to Jericho, the city
Lk 18:35–43   mentioned before in the Gospels only as a detail in the parable of the Good Samaritan (Lk 10:30). This was not the famous Jericho of the Old Testament, which lay in ruins, but a more recent city built nearby and embellished by Herod the Great and his son Archelaus, some twenty miles away from Jerusalem in the tropical Jordan Valley. New Testament Jericho itself

has long since disappeared, but its site is contiguous with the modern town which still bears the same name.

Mark and Matthew, as it happens, mention Jericho only to dismiss it, since the event they describe along with Luke took place, in their view, *as he was leaving Jericho with his disciples and a considerable crowd.* Luke, who has a story to tell that took place in Jericho (Lk 19:1–10 below), prefers to set the scene *as he was drawing near to Jericho.* From a statistical point of view, there is scarcely any doubt that Mark and Matthew are correct. It would have been at the most frequented places, such as the Jericho-Jerusalem gate, that blind men would sit to beg, begging being the only means that such afflicted people had to gain their food. This is all the more likely if chronology is a real issue in this context, since the crowd which Mark mentions would probably have been the pilgrim throng making its way to Jerusalem and the Passover.

The other major discrepancy in the Gospel accounts involves the number of blind men who figure in the story. For Mark, followed by Luke, there is only one, whom Mark further calls by name, *Bartimaeus,* adding (he or a helpful scribe) the translation, *the son of Timaeus.* Matthew has two blind men. This is not, as we know (see above on Mk 5:1–20 and parallels), an isolated instance with the first evangelist. He omitted the previous story of a healing of a blind man in Mk 8:22–26. It is also possible that as, following Mark, he has made this episode the very last in Jesus' public life immediately preparatory to the triumphal entry into Jerusalem (see our next chapter), he has found it desirable to leave the testimony of *two* witnesses to Jesus as *Son of David* (vss. 30 f.) echoing in our ears as this part of the Gospel draws to a close. On the other hand, there seems to be no doubt that Mt 9:27–31, which also speaks of two blind men, is a doublet of this present passage, and therefore it may well be that Matthew depended on a tradition which differed from that of Mark. It may even be that it is more original than Mark's and that Mark's story has simply concentrated its attention on one of the central figures who was known by name to the early Church while the other had been forgotten. Matthew's earlier use of the story has been carefully integrated into the context of the Galilean ministry. There is a greater emphasis on the prerequisite of faith and an injunction to silence about the miracle (which is ignored), both of which are characteristics of the first days of the ministry.

Mark's account has all the vigor and freshness we have come to expect from the Second Gospel. We should probably conclude that Bartimaeus was a young man from the description given of him by Mark. Persistent in his crying out to Jesus after the crowd had tried to hush him up, at the Master's call he throws aside his outer garment, springs to his feet, and runs to his side. *Son of David* was a title which Jesus never used of himself because of its nationalistic overtones. Here, however, it is plain that Bartimaeus uses it without prejudice and that his faith, to which the healing wonder is ascribed, is faith in the merciful dispensation of God: restoration of sight to the blind is one of the works expected of the anointed Servant of the Lord according to the Greek text of Is 61:1.

Lk 19:1–10 Though Luke's is pre-eminently the Gospel of the poor, and though he has some stern things to say about the wealthy, it is interesting to see him interrupt Jesus' journey at this moment to tell the story of *a man named Zacchaeus, a chief publican who was rich*. Probably he intends a topical association with the preceding story: the *salvation* that comes to Zacchaeus' *house this day* is the spiritual counterpart of the physical sight restored to the blind man. The setting of such an event in Jericho is quite understandable. Jericho was an important commercial and trading junction on the main road between Judea and Perea, and King Herod had built a winter palace there. As a chief publican, Zacchaeus would have been in charge of the taxgathering and collection of duties over the entire district, having under his authority the various local publicans such as Levi had been, sitting in his little toll booth in Capernaum (Mk 2:13–17 and parallels).

There is something altogether charming about the story of Zacchaeus, the little man who wanted to see Jesus in his own way just as the blind man had wanted to see in another. Forgetting his dignity as a prominent official, he clambers up into the low-hanging branches of *a sycamore tree*, doubtless not without being observed by the semi-hostile crowd which drew Jesus' attention to him, but hardly expecting to be singled out as in fact he was when the Lord called him by name. There is a touch of humor in Jesus' calling out to Zacchaeus to *hurry down* from the perch that he had just gained with a bit of breathless effort. But Jesus knew Zacchaeus better than the man knew himself. He recognized in him *a son of Abraham*, a true Israelite without guile (Jn 1:47), whose single-minded and ingenuous conduct was evidence of something that went deeper than mere curiosity, whatever Zacchaeus himself may have thought of it at the time.

Zacchaeus' words are probably to be taken as an evidence of his conversion, another vindication of Jesus' habit of consorting with sinners (cf. Lk 15:1 f., etc.). The loose system of taxgathering made injustice almost an occupational hazard, and Zacchaeus is willing to concede the point without resort to casuistry: *if I have cheated anyone of anything—*as I doubtless have—*I restore it fourfold here and now* (fourfold restitution was traditional in cases of flagrant theft, cf. Ex 21:37; 2 Sam 12:6; but legally Zacchaeus could have been held to no such thing even if proof of a specific offense were possible). Furthermore, *I hereby give half of my possessions to the poor*. In a sense, Zacchaeus renounces his status as a rich man for the kingdom of heaven (cf. Lk 18:24–27); nevertheless,

Jesus accepts at face value this voluntary commitment and does not require of him that he sell all that he has and give to the poor (see above on Mk 10:17–22 and parallels). Even Luke's Gospel does not regard possessions of themselves or any occupation of itself inevitable hindrances to the salvation of the kingdom. Of Luke's various references to the publicans, as a matter of fact (here and in 3:12, 5:27, 7:29, 15:1, 18:10), all have been favorable.

Lk 19:11–28   The parable with which Luke continues may have been originally the same as another told later in a different context in Matthew's Gospel (see below on Mt 25:14–30). If so, however, the two traditions in which the parable was handed down have resulted in a considerable difference of details, even though the essential lesson still remains the same. In Luke's sequence there is only a tenuous connection between the theme of the uses of wealth as exemplified in Zacchaeus and the parable's subject matter which also involves the use of wealth. This, despite the fact that generations of homilists have understood the parable as an instruction on the right use of personal gifts— the "talents" of Matthew's version. While such an application of the story is not entirely foreign to its original intent, Luke nevertheless makes it quite clear that it was first uttered by Jesus *because he was near to Jerusalem, and because they supposed that the kingdom of God was to appear immediately.* It is a parable of eschatological decision, of the immediacy of the kingdom of God.

It is true, there are certain allegorical elements in the parable as reported by Luke, which were either in it from the beginning or, as is perhaps more likely, were introduced into it during the period of its oral transmission. The *certain man* who is the chief protagonist of the story is qualified as *a nobleman* who *went into a far country to receive kingly power and then return,* whose *citizens hated him and sent an embassy after him, saying, "We do not want this man to reign over us,"* and who nevertheless did receive the kingly power he had sought and ended by returning and putting to death those who had rebelled against his rule. None of this is really necessary to the parable, nor does it contribute anything to its lesson. It sounds very much like the story of Archelaus, who journeyed to Rome in 4 B.C. after the death of his father Herod to be confirmed as king of Judea and who was opposed there, rather unsuccessfully, by a delegation of Palestinian Jews. Archelaus returned and reigned as ethnarch of Judea for a few years, during which he added to the splendor of Jericho, in the environs of which Luke has placed this parable. It is easy enough to see why these details might have been added, therefore. They allegorize the parable by making its principal figure out as a king whose own natural subjects revolted against his rule and who were therefore punished: in Luke's eyes, the application to Christ and the Jews was obvious. This is an extension of the lesson that Jesus primarily intended, as we shall see in a moment.

What does the parable really say, first and foremost? The householder gives to *ten of his servants* each a like amount of money, *ten minas* for the ten, to each, therefore, a gold coin roughly the equivalent of twenty dollars. The amount is not important, nor is the number of the servants—that only three of them figure in the conclusion of the story shows how little interested it is in allegorical details. Neither, in all likelihood, is it significant to the story that one servant *by trading* has increased his master's money tenfold and another fivefold, and that they receive in recompense from this prince ten and five cities respectively (in vs. 25 the first servant's reward seems to be his master's money rather than authority over cities!). These servants appear in the parable only to underscore the slothfulness of the one who hid his gold piece *in a handkerchief,* who so much feared his master's wrath and the risk of loss that he did absolutely nothing with what had been entrusted to him. He thought to please his lord by preserving whole and entire exactly what he had received. But no, he has actually preserved nothing at all. Even what he thought he had is now taken from him. That it is given to another is a detail of the parable irrelevant to the main issue, except to the extent that it illustrates the parable of divine justice. In the parable it is given to the first servant, prompting the surprised exclamation (of the man's fellow servants? of those listening to Jesus?): *Lord, he already has ten minas!*

Thus the lesson of the parable: *To everyone who has, more will be given; but from him who has not, even what he has will be taken away.* Those who have prepared themselves for the kingdom will receive it, those who have not will not. And not to receive the kingdom means to lose everything. Jesus has in mind the kind of Pharisee for whom the Old Testament revelation was not a precious trust to be "traded" in for the salvation of Israel and the world, but a fossilized dogma to be hugged to sterile breasts in smugness and complacency and legalistic exclusivism (see above on Lk 13:22–30). It is such men, who fondly think that they have kept the faith pure and undefiled, who in reality are left with nothing, since what was once given to them they have stifled and smothered. The lesson of Jesus' parable, as should be evident, is equally applicable to the Christian awaiting Christ's coming for whom Luke wrote his Gospel. The Christian, too, can retreat into a barren contemplation of the truth which he possesses but which he will not allow to possess him, and with a mean conception of God's mercy and grace reduce his economy of salvation to a selfish kind of bookkeeping which he calls "saving his soul." Risking nothing in the mission field of the Church which is the world, he can end by losing all.

Concluding the parable, one final time Luke holds up for us his cherished view of the Christ of the Gospels *walking ahead, going up to Jerusalem.*

Jn 12:1-8   It is now necessary, however, to interrupt both the Lu-
Mk 14:3-9   can and the Synoptic sequence for an episode which
Mt 26:6-13 John places at this time, *six days before the Passover*.
Since, as we shall see later on, for John the Passover of
Jesus' death took place on a Sabbath day, he would be dating this
present event for us on the preceding Saturday evening, after the Sabbath
had officially closed with sunset. What is doubtless more important to him
is that the anointing at Bethany opens the "last week of the new cre-
ation" (see above on Jn 1:19-2:11). Jesus was crucified the day before
Passover (Jn 18:28, 19:31) and he rose on the following day following it
(Jn 20:1); therefore this event occurs seven days before the exaltation of
Christ (cf. Jn 20:19-22). There can be no doubt that this idea has influenced John in some of the descriptive details of his narrative.

John's chronology is thus symbolical. It is, nevertheless, intrinsically
more probable than that of the Synoptics, which has the event take place
two days before the Passover (Mk 14:1 and parallel). The Synoptic dating has been determined by the significance that Mark, followed by
Matthew, saw in the Lord's words concerning the woman at Bethany and
in the relation which he placed between her gesture and the hasty burial
of Jesus after the crucifixion. Mark, followed by Matthew, has consequently put this story into the most immediate possible proximity to the
narrative of Christ's passion and death. Luke, who avoids even apparent repetitions or doublets, has omitted the story entirely because of
his similar account involving the repentant action of a woman of Galilee
(see above on Lk 7:36-50).

The Lucan story, as we noted at the time, has evidently picked up in
oral transmission a few details that properly belong to the one that now
lies before us. We also noted that the exchange was not entirely one-
sided, and we can now find this contention verified especially in
John's version of the story. The most striking discrepancy, when John's
account is compared with the Synoptic telling of what happened at
Bethany, appears in the use to which each says that the ointment of
anointing was put. *She poured the perfume on his head*, say the Synoptics. Though the gesture was extravagant, as the story itself brings out,
this sort of thing was also quite straightforward and comprehensible: the
anointing of the head was and is in the Near East a customary and
conventional thing. But John writes that *she anointed Jesus' feet*.
This is as unlikely as the other is plausible; such an action would serve
no assignable purpose, and there is no known precedent for it. Even more
unlikely is what follows in John's Gospel, according to which *she dried
his feet with her hair*. In the first place, why? Beyond this, it would have
been unthinkable for a respectable Jewish woman to loose her hair in public for any reason. But these difficulties disappear if we assume that John

has made use of a tradition in which some details from the Lucan story have been intruded. In that story both the feet of Jesus and the hair of the woman figure both naturally and logically—there it is the anointing that seems to be out of place. Be this as it may be, John has taken the form of the narrative as it came to him and has found in it his own meaning which has enriched the message of the Gospel.

All the Gospels set the scene in *Bethany*. Somewhat unnecessarily John adds that it was here that *Lazarus was, whom Jesus had raised from the dead,* connecting this story with that of Jn 11:1-44 just as before he already looked forward to what he is now about to describe (cf. Jn 11:2). The presence of the resurrected Lazarus at the banquet undoubtedly contributes, in John's eyes, to the spiritual significance of what transpired there, helping to determine its character as a "sign." Who gave the banquet for Jesus is not made clear in John's Gospel; neither the fact that *Lazarus was one of those at table with him* nor that *Martha was serving* (cf. Lk 10:40) would necessarily mean that the banquet was in the house of Lazarus and his sisters, though this is often assumed. Matthew and Mark say that it was *in the house of Simon the leper*, who just possibly could have been a disciple of Jesus whom the Lord had cured of leprosy. The banquet may well have been a kind of civic affair.

Only John identifies the woman of the anointing as *Mary*, who thus acts in the character assigned her in Lk 10:38 ff. All the Gospels agree that she used an extraordinary quantity of very valuable perfume, valued at upwards of *three hundred denarii* (Mark and John): roughly ten months' wages! Presumably Mary would have stinted and saved for a long while to be able to make this great gesture, which would have recommended itself so highly to the Oriental's love of display. All the Gospels, too, record the disciples' initial displeasure at what has been done, their protest at the extravagance on the practical grounds that the money represented by it might better have been *given to the poor.* (So Martha objected to Mary's devotion on practical grounds according to Lk 10:40.) They also record Jesus' defense of Mary's *beautiful deed* (Matthew and Mark). The acts of love do not always respond to detached logic. Jesus yields to no one in his concern for the poor; however, there is more to religion—either as service of the Christ of the Gospels or the Christ continually living in his Church—than the alleviation of poverty. There is also room in religion for works which bespeak the heart rather than the mind, which are highly personal and uncalculated: *she did what she had to do* (Mark). John restricts the protest against Mary's action to *Judas the Iscariot*, meanwhile telling us for the first time that he kept the purse for Jesus' little band of disciples (cf. Jn 13:29). In ascribing it in his case to mean motives, however, we have the impression that, however justified the allegation may have been, John is attempting to lay the

foundation for an explanation of Judas' treason that will not prove adequate to account for all its complexities.

All the Gospels have Jesus offer an interpretation of the woman's deed
that has some relation to his burial. Mark and Matthew interpret his
words to mean that this anointing must take the place of the embalming
of his body that was later made impossible by the circumstances of the
crucifixion and resurrection (cf. Mk 16:1; Lk 24:1). John's interpretation is more difficult to make out. What he seems to give as Jesus'
words is: *Leave her alone, that she may keep it* [the ointment] *for the
day of my burial.* He does not, therefore, see this action as an anticipated
embalming of Jesus. In John's Gospel, as a matter of fact, the embalming
of Jesus' body for the tomb was not omitted but carried out with all
thoroughness (cf. Jn 19:39 f.). Rather, the "burial" of which John thinks
is that spiritual burial of Jesus which is the source of life for the Church
(see below on Jn 12:20–36). The anointing, in other words, has a continuing significance for the Christian who finds the living Christ in his
Church. This interpretation does not altogether differ from that of those
who believe that John looked on Mary's act as a symbolic anointing of
kingship preparatory to his triumphal entry when (according to John's
Gospel) he was hailed as "king of Israel" (see below on Mk 11:1–10
and parallels). In John's theology, Jesus' death and burial, triumph and
glorification, are one and the same.

If we may understand "the day of burial" for which Mary was to
"keep" the ointment as the period of the Church, then, just as John
so often connects water with Jesus, doubtless thinking of its sacramental
use in the Church which is the perpetuation of Christ in the world
(see above on Jn 2:1–11), he may also be thinking of the Church's
anointings in the same way (cf. Mk 6:13; Jas 5:14). Perhaps for the
same reason he alone has stressed the large amount of the ointment
which, poured on the Lord's feet rather than his head could then be
wiped off with Mary's hair so that, as she walked about, *the house was
filled with the odor of the perfume*: the ointment signifies the good
odor of the Lord's presence in his "house" (cf. Jn 2:21, 14:2).

Jn 12:9–11   John concludes the Bethany scene by speaking of the
               crowds of Jews who were coming there from Jerusalem
because of Lazarus, the witness in life to Jesus' life-giving power. He also
repeats what was said in Jn 11:53 about the plot against Jesus being
hatched by *the chief priests*—not "the Jews," who continue in this passage to represent the people in general—a plot which now extends, appropriately enough, to Lazarus as well. For the moment, however, they
are powerless to do anything. The brief period of Jesus' public triumph
is to begin on the morrow.

20. PALM SUNDAY

Mk 11:1–10   In the story of the anointing at Bethany which we saw
Mt 21:1–9   in our last chapter the Johannine and Synoptic tradi-
Lk 19:29–40   tions came together in what up to now has been the
Jn 12:12–19   rare exception to their rule of separate ways. From now
              on, though the ways will still remain quite distinct, they
will be less and less separate, and four-Gospel parallels will not be as
unusual as in the past. This situation reflects the unique character of
the narrative of Jesus' passion, death, and resurrection (which, strictly
speaking, John has not yet begun), a narrative which by all accounts
is the most primitive of all the Gospel "forms," for which, in varying
ways and with different emphases, all that has gone before in our literary
Gospels serves as introduction (the passion-resurrection narrative takes
up almost the entire second half of John's Gospel), a form which enjoyed greater rigidity and was less subject to variations than others in the
Gospel pattern. As we will see borne out in our remaining chapters,
while each of our Gospels retains its individuality and makes its own
contributions to what we discover to be a mainly consistent and coherent common narrative, it is basically from three related but independent historical traditions that the passion-resurrection story has been
drawn. The first of these is that of Mark-Matthew and, as before, it will
usually be obvious that priority in the use of the tradition must be assigned to Mark. Luke, who has made use of Mark's form of the tradition, nevertheless has one of his own proper to himself, which may have
been influenced in part by the Johannine tradition. John's story, finally,
continues to be uniquely his own, though in the opinion of most scholars John also not only knew and made use of the common Synoptic
tradition, but in addition was acquainted with the peculiarly Marcan
form of it.

If we follow John in thinking of this present event as taking place
on a Sunday, it is also because of his account that we call it Palm
Sunday. As John tells the story, Jesus, accompanied by a crowd of Jews
who had gone out to Bethany and were witnesses of the resurrection
of Lazarus, was met by another crowd from Jerusalem enthusiastic over

the report of the miracle who *took palm fronds and went out to meet him, crying, "Hosanna!"* The Synoptics really have nothing like this at all—neither do they ever explain the sudden welcome which Jesus receives in Jerusalem, a city with which they have shown him in no contact up to the present. Now palm trees are about as common in Jerusalem as they are in New York City or Chicago. Matthew says that some of the people *tore down branches from the trees,* olive trees, no doubt, which they strewed over the rutted and miry road in Jesus' path; Mark has it even more realistically that they *strewed reeds* (or rushes) *which they had cut in the fields,* that is, making a matting of grass or leaves; Luke includes nothing on this matter. It is difficult to avoid the conclusion that John has further adapted this story to the prophetic symbolism that already dominates it, seeing in it an anticipation of the eschatological feast of Tabernacles (cf. Zech 14:16–19). At Tabernacles, Hanukkah ("little Tabernacles," see above on Jn 10:22–39), and other joyous occasions palm fronds, brought in from Jericho usually, were waved in sign of joy and messianic triumph (cf. 1 Macc 13:51; Apo 7:9). The cries of the people, a mingling of Ps 118:25 f. and other Old Testament allusions, are taken by both John and the Synoptics as acclaim given to a messianic king. Both Matthew (vs. 10) and Luke (vs. 38) refer us back to their separate Gospels of the Infancy (cf. Mt 2:3; Lk 2:14).

The same eschatological significance has been found in the event by the Synoptics when they make the point that Jesus began his procession *at the Mount of Olives* (cf. Zech 14:4 f.), having passed from Jericho through Bethany to *Bethphage* on the slope of the mountain facing Jerusalem. John omits the story told by the Synoptics according to which Jesus consciously fulfilled the prophecy of Zech 9:9. As this is, seemingly, the only time in the Synoptic Gospels that Jesus unhesitatingly identifies himself with the King-Messiah of Jewish expectation (see above on Mk 1:22–28 and parallels), the incident deserves the closer attention that we shall give it below. The story itself is credible enough. Bethphage was a small village where everyone knew everybody else. The people of Bethphage immediately recognized Jesus' disciples and hence simply asked why the *colt* he had sent them for was being loosed; they knew it was not being stolen. Their answer, that Jesus wanted to make use of it, was enough. The owners were probably flattered to be of some help to the Master. The title *Lord* used by and of Jesus in this connection, however, is probably due to the later Christian transmission of the story.

Matthew's narrative is curious in that he speaks of two animals rather than one and even seems to have Jesus mount both of them, a rather evident impossibility. It seems that he, who alone of the Synoptists quotes Zech 9:9, wanted to stress an exact fulfillment of the prophecy even at the sacrifice of the logical probabilities. The text that he cited does, in fact, speak materially of two animals, but in Hebrew parallelism wherein *she-ass* and *colt* refer to one and the same beast. It is impossible to believe that Matthew did not know this; rather than as evidence of the misreading of a Semitic text by a Gentile evangelist (see page 26 above), what he has done corresponds to some of the exegetical techniques of the rabbis. His adjustment of the story to fit the text may also have something to do with his fondness for two's (see above on Mk 10:46–52 and parallels).

John, who also quotes the prophecy, states that its meaning was not understood at the time, but only later by the Church through the enlightenment of the Spirit (cf. Jn 2:22, 7:39, 13:7). At first such a remark seems strange. In the same breath John records the despair of *the Pharisees* at today's happenings, who utter another of the Johannine prophecies: *See! the whole world has begun to follow him!* This is in agreement with Luke, who shows the Pharisees indignant over the messianic acclamation being showered upon Jesus, but incapable of doing more in the face of it than remonstrate with Jesus himself, calling on him to put an end to the demonstration, which Jesus refuses to do. Since the Gospels without exception have represented the scene as a messianic proclamation, seemingly encouraged by Jesus himself, John is obviously suggesting that there is a messianic significance to the event that has not been grasped by the applauding multitude. This may, again, be not too far from what Luke means when he has the Lord tell the Pharisees: *If these were silent, the very stones would cry out!* The event, Jesus retorts, speaks for itself. The crowd is of good will and is not to be discouraged; but neither does Jesus necessarily accept its estimation of his present purpose in Jerusalem.

Mt 21:10–11, 14–17
Mk 11:11
Perhaps some additional light is thrown on the problem by Matthew's sequel to the Palm Sunday acclamation. When bystanders ask its meaning, they are told by those who have been crying out to Jesus, *This is the prophet Jesus from Nazareth of Galilee.* The thought of the evangelist may well extend to the eschatological prophet of Deut 18:18 (see above on Jn 1:19–24); but it is plain that the Jerusalemites are now testifying of Jesus in much less grandiloquent terms than they had used a few moments before in their enthusiasm. A few verses further on Matthew has a parallel to Luke's remonstration of the Pharisees when he pictures *the chief priests and the scribes* shocked over *the children* who were echoing the messianic cry they had heard from their elders, *Hosanna to the Son of David!* Jesus cites Ps 8:3 both to accept the children's praise and confound those who opposed it. The full quotation is: "Out of the mouths of babes and sucklings you have fashioned praise *because of your foes, to silence the hostile and the vengeful*." The main point is, however, that this is the praise of children, and for Jesus and

Matthew children represent those who are open to the designs of God, who are prepared to receive his Messiah on his terms rather than their own (see above on Mk 9:33–37 and parallels; Mk 10:13–16 and parallels).

The most suggestive contribution to our reconstruction, however, is that made by Mark, who possesses what is without doubt the oldest tradition about the events of this day. Here we see a suddenly solitary Jesus walking about the Holy City in the company of his disciples, *inspecting everything*, returning to his friends at Bethany as the evening draws on. The "many" and the "others" who had followed and preceded him into Jerusalem (vs. 8) have now melted away and disappeared; just how many they were in the first place, we have never really been told. The messianic fervor of only a moment ago appears to have been very ephemeral indeed.

A possible explanation of all this is that while Jesus accepted the messianic acclaim of his Galilean companions and of the Jerusalemites who participated in it up to a point, he adhered throughout to his own unique interpretation of his messianic character and demonstrated it in the gesture that he performed fulfilling Zech 9:9. It is perhaps significant that John has Jesus perform the gesture *after* he had been proclaimed "king of Israel" by the crowd, not to provoke such a proclamation. Zech 9:9, though accepted by the rabbis as in the authentic tradition of Davidic messianism, which in the time of Jesus was almost invariably a highly nationalistic messianism, does not really conform to the triumphalist tone that is the characteristic of the other Davidic oracles. Dependent on the exilic Isaiah of the Servant songs and on the other exilic and postexilic prophecies and experiences of Israel (especially, perhaps, on the prophecy of Zeph 3:14–17 which has also influenced the Lucan Gospel of the Infancy), Zech 9:9 pictures a messianic king who is less a conqueror than he is a sign of God's peace restored to his people. He is less a dispenser of judgment than he is the exemplar of God's saving mercy: he is savior not as a savior-king but as the leader of a saved people. He is called "humble," for he is first among the *anawim*, the poor of the Lord (see above on Mt 5:3–12 and parallel), and he enters the Holy City not on a war charger but on a lowly beast of burden. Such was Israel's kingly ideal as Jesus was prepared to fulfill it.

Once before Jesus had reacted to an attempt to proclaim him king by taking evasive action (see above on Jn 6:15 and Mk 6:45 f. and parallels). This time, the Gospels suggest, he did something much more positive and demonstrative. In both instances what he did was to repudiate a popular distortion of his mission, and in both instances he seems to have failed to channel the general enthusiasm in the direction toward which he had pointed.

Lk 19:41–44   It is in the vicinity of these events that the Synoptic Gospels, though variously, have located the story of Jesus'
invasion of the temple, an action which, we have already noted, might
better be placed in this context than in the one to which John has assigned it (see above on Jn 2:13–17 and parallels). Prior to this, however,
only Luke records Jesus' lament over Jerusalem which bears out, on his
part, the interpretation of the "triumphal" entry already ascribed to the
other Gospels. Luke never, in fact, shows Jesus actually enter the city in
procession, but has the Lord say to Jerusalem that *you did not know the
time of your visitation.* Apparently awaiting its Peacemaker with open
arms, Jerusalem in fact has not recognized what is God's peace. And
because of this, Jerusalem would be destroyed (see below on Mk
13:14–20 and parallels). All that lay before his eyes—the great temple
area with the beautiful temple of Herod, vast and priceless, the many
towers of the city, the wide walls, the teeming buildings of Jerusalem
the Golden—all would be leveled to the ground. *The days shall come
upon you*—it was to be just forty years later—when enemies shall surround Jerusalem *and build a rampart about you.* This the Romans did
with customary thoroughness. They laid total siege so that those within
perished under miserable and degrading conditions; and when they had
taken the city, they literally razed it to the ground so that nothing remained.

Mk 11:12–14   In a much more graphic fashion Mark and Matthew
Mt 21:18–19   convey the Lord's judgment on Jerusalem by means of
the story of the fig tree. The story causes all manner of
difficulties out of any proportion to its size, and it is easy to understand
why Luke chose to omit it. For one thing, this is the only instance in the
Gospels in which Jesus is shown exercising his miraculous powers in a de-
structive way. Such an objection is not, of course, peremptory. The divine
curse, anthropomorphism though it may be, is a corollary of the divine
blessing, and the caricature of Jesus as a kindly do-gooder whose lips
never moved except in benison grossly distorts the character of him who
came to cast fire on the earth. The action is presented as a kind of
parable, which certainly illustrates a genuine emphasis in Jesus' preaching
of the kingdom of God. On the other hand, taken as a factual account,
it comes uncomfortably close to picturing Jesus in the performance of
an arbitrary and petulant action, especially given Mark's characteristically honest but none too helpful observation that *it was not the season
for figs.* Figs in Palestine do not ripen till June, and the story is set
in the early spring of the Passover season. To what purpose would Jesus
have been looking for fruit from such an unlikely source? It is not
surprising that many students of the New Testament believe that for
this episode in his Gospel Mark depends ultimately on a parable of the

Lord (see above on Lk 13:1–9) which an early Christian tradition had transformed into a popular and uncritical narrative about Jesus.

While Mark narrates the story with careful attention to the detail in which it had come to him, Matthew tries to get at the point of it without delay. According to his Gospel the fig tree *withered up instantly*. There was ample prophetic precedent for the representation of Israel as figs or a fig tree (cf. Jer 24; Hos 9:10) and for the threat of divine judgment against it as the destruction of figs or of fig trees (cf. Is 34:4; Jer 29:18; Hos 2:14; Mi 7:10).

Jn 12:20–36   John, too, in his own way, is going to express the Lord's judgment on the unbelief that has greeted his manifestation of the kingdom of God (see below on Jn 12:37–50). Before doing so, however, he concludes the history of Jesus' ministry with an event and some sayings that both sum up its meaning and prepare for the adverse judgment that is about to be passed on the unbelieving generation among which the Word of God had appeared.

The *Greeks* who wanted to *see Jesus* were undoubtedly Jewish proselytes or Gentiles otherwise well-disposed to Judaism who were accustomed to assist at its great feast days. For John they undoubtedly represent the Gentile world which will later fulfill the unconscious prophecy of the Pharisees in verse 19, accepting the light which, for a final time, the crowds about Jesus are to prove themselves blind, the voice of God which they will not hear. Therefore the pertinence of Jesus' present teaching: it is by means of Christian faith that they will "see" Jesus. The Gentiles approach him through *Philip and Andrew*, the only two of the twelve disciples who bear Gentile names, and these consult together before speaking to Jesus in view of the fact that hithertofore his ministry had been, as it continued to be to the end, directed only to the Jewish world of Palestine.

The hour has come. John is now on the point of beginning the story of the passion, death, and resurrection of Christ, when *the Son of Man will be glorified* (see above on Jn 1:14, 2:1–11). At long last, the "hour" of which he had spoken (cf. Jn 2:4, 4:23, 5:25) is upon him, when he will show forth in his own person the paradox of Christian faith, that death is the source of life. This, he says, is the law of sacrifice, a law which can also be seen mirrored in nature. *The grain of wheat* sown in the ground must sacrifice its existence as seed if there is ever to be a new shaft of wheat and spurs of new grain. If it were to insist on its continued existence as a grain of wheat, it would remain alone and fruitless. So it is with the renunciation of Christ, whose death will mean the life of the world.

To express the same truth he uses a saying which we have already seen in various Synoptic contexts (Mk 8:34–9:1 and parallels; Mt 10:37–39;

Lk 17:22–37). What is nonsense when translated into this-worldly terms is Christian wisdom. One saves his life—the only life that truly matters —not by egoistically clinging to his separate identity as a good to be preserved at all costs, but by being willing to abandon and destroy it. This is the way of renunciation, of sacrifice, and of service which Jesus revealed as the genuine meaning of life, and this way of Christ must also be that of the Christian: *where I am, there shall my servant be.*

It is at this moment of his speaking of his sacrifice that Jesus undergoes in John's Gospel the experience which the Synoptic Gospels place in the garden of Gethsemane prior to his arrest and trial (see below on Mk 14:32–42 and parallels). *My soul is stirred:* the Greek verb is one used to express extreme mental and emotional anguish. The reference he has just made to his death and which seemed to be so lightly said, in reality cost him a great effort. *What shall I say?* We hear the voice of a Man seeking the consolation of the counsel of those who could never understand him. *Father, save me from this hour!* This is the alternative that was always open to Jesus, for the sacrifice asked of him had to be a free offering if it was to have any value, just as the commitment of Christian faith must also be free. Jesus' cry appears merely to consider the possibility, however, not to entertain it. It is immediately followed by the reaffirmation of his first resolve: *it was for this that I came to this hour.* Thus his final words are an epitome of his entire life of dedicated obedience: *Father, glorify your name!*

As in the Synoptic stories of Jesus' baptism (Lk 3:21 f. and parallels) and transfiguration (Mk 9:2–10 and parallels) *a voice from heaven* speaks the divine confirmation and interpretation of the event. The Father has already glorified his name by giving testimony to Jesus throughout his ministry of grace (cf. Jn 10:38, 11:40, etc.) by the many "signs" of the supreme glorification to be achieved in Jesus' triumph over death in his resurrection. It is typical of the crowd about Jesus that it cannot understand the divine voice (cf. Jn 8:43), even though Jesus says that it was directed to its ears rather than his own; he himself needs no reassurance, such is his oneness with the Father (cf. Jn 11:42).

Now is the judgment of this world. The glorification of Christ spells the end of the power of *the ruler of this world,* despite all the appearances there will soon be to the contrary. Through his death, when he is *lifted up* (cf. Jn 3:14), comes that triumph over evil whose enduring reality empowers the man of faith to escape divine condemnation while it condemns the unbeliever (cf. Jn 3:18). The people understand at least that he is talking of a going away. But he has said this of *the Son of Man.* This person can hardly be the Messiah, as they reason, since the messianic reign is to be everlasting according to *the Law* (that is, the Old Testament, cf. Jn 10:34: a typical reference would be Is 9:6 f.). This kind of fatuous half-truth has characterized the Johannine dialogues all along and has provided the basis for much of their irony. But Jesus has now brought his period of instruction to a close. He merely states the issue of light and darkness one final time (cf. Jn 8:12, 9:4 f.) and, as far as the Gospel of John is concerned, departs definitively from their presence.

Mk 11:18–19   The Synoptic Gospels have a rather more complicated
Lk 19:47–48   story to tell. John has previously connected the plot
               of *the chief priests and the scribes* of which Mark and
Luke now speak with the aftermath of Jesus' raising of Lazarus, the "sign" of Jesus which immediately precedes and occasions the hour of his glorification (see above on Jn 11:45–57). The Synoptics join it to the story of Jesus' cleansing of the temple. They also continue to stress the popularity which Jesus continued to enjoy with the people at large, which prevented any hostile action being taken against him immediately.

Mk 11:20–26   Mark and Matthew now conclude their story of the
Mt 21:20–22   withered fig tree, the denouement of which Mark
               alone has put *early in the morning* of a following day.
Actually, this passage addresses itself not to the why of the fig tree's destruction, a question which the Gospels allow the event itself to answer, but to the how. Jesus discourses first on the power of faith, in a saying which we have already seen in variant forms in both Matthew and Luke (see above on Lk 17:3–6). From faith the argument easily passes to the power of Christian prayer: such works as Jesus has done his disciples will also do provided their faith is unwavering. It is the magnitude of the works, of course, that interests the catechetical purpose of the Gospels, not their specific nature. Mark and Matthew here employ a saying of Jesus which appears several times in John's Last Supper discourse, where it contributes to one of the major themes developed by the Fourth Gospel (cf. Jn 14:13 f., 15:7, 16:23). Finally, Mark ends with a teaching of Jesus which Matthew placed in the context of the Sermon on the Mount (cf. Mt 6:14): not only confidence makes for effective prayer, but also a pure heart free of enmities and disposed to the grace of God which is the fruit of every prayer. (What appears as verse 26 in older translations of Mark is not in the better manuscripts, but has been borrowed from Mt 6:15.)

Mk 11:27–33   Just as John showed a demand made on Jesus by "the
Mt 21:23–27   Jews" to give evidence of the authority by which he had
Lk 20:1–8   presumed to interfere in the temple's business (see
               above on Jn 2:18–22), the Synoptic Gospels now tell
of a delegation which calls on him for the same purpose. The delegation was composed of *the chief priests and elders of the people* and, according to Mark and Luke, *the scribes.* Here we have representatives of the three groups that spoke for the three departments of Jewish life—though often

with some internecine rivalry—the religious and cultic, the national and civil, and the legal and doctrinal. They were also the three divisions of the Sanhedrin, and the present delegation may well have been official. The concern, after all, was legitimate, especially in the Synoptics' perspective of a first visit of Jesus to Jerusalem. He had intervened in the temple, his action had messianic overtones with possible political implications, and *he was teaching the people in the temple.*

All the same, their demand was a most tiresome one, given the total context of the Gospels. What Jesus had done in Galilee had not been hidden in a corner, and even though the Synoptic Gospels for reasons of their own have restricted his ministry in Jerusalem to this one Passover visit, at times they also reflect the viewpoint of John, namely that he was no longer attempting to convince people who had proved themselves to be incurably obdurate. Jesus, therefore, adopts the rabbinical expedient of countering a question with a question, shifting the initiative back to his questioners, and at the same time presenting them with a dilemma which they find insoluble. *Was John's baptism of divine or of human origin?* They want to say it was human, of course, for they were among those who had never accepted the Baptist and had been thoroughly repudiated by him (cf. Mt 3:7–10 and parallel). But they feared the consequences of such an answer. John the Baptist was almost universally regarded as *a prophet,* and doubtless all the more so now that he was safely dead. Yet they could not bring themselves to concur in the popular opinion. For one thing, their record was against them: *Why did you not believe him, then?* But more than this was involved. There was an uncomfortable parallel between Jesus and the Baptist, and the connection between the two was certainly known (see above on Lk 7:24–35 and parallel).

Jesus' hard question was not chosen at random simply to embarrass his adversaries. When these who claimed to be the spokesmen for Israel had to confess of the Baptist *we do not know,* they had placed themselves in the position of the Pharisees before the man born blind (see on Jn 9:1–34 above): "Why, here is a marvel!" Self-convicted of their inability to discern the presence of prophecy in Israel, they are as incompetent to judge the credentials of Jesus as they had been to judge those of the Baptist. It is the sign of Jonah all over again (see above on Mk 8:11 f. and parallels; Mt 12:38–42 and parallel).

Mt 21:28–32   In Matthew's Gospel Jesus quickly follows up his victory with a parable that underlines the lesson he has just made his enemies teach against themselves. The story is deceptively simple and utterly true to life, taking but a moment to tell. Suddenly another question is asked, and perhaps for a minute these leaders of the people were relieved because of the obvious answer that was expected, thinking that this time they could reply without incriminating themselves.

Which of the two sons *did what his father wanted,* the one who was all promises with no performance, or the one who did after all what was asked of him whatever his first reaction? The answer was, indeed, obvious, and in giving it the hostile embassy to its dismay again finds itself self-condemned. All through their history they have been shouting "yes" to God, yet they have not obeyed him, while those whom they despise as sinners are inheriting the kingdom in their place. It had first been so with John the Baptist, and now it was so with Jesus (cf. Lk 7:29 f.).

Jesus pointedly acknowledges the unsavory reputation borne by many of those who had turned with repentance to the preaching of the kingdom. Association with such people had more than once been held up to him in reproach, but he glories in their titles the better to demonstrate that the kingdom is the work of God's grace rather than of self-righteousness. The catechetical lesson was not lost on the Church, which in the time of the evangelists and subsequently had to justify itself to the fastidious on some other terms than as an exclusive club of the very best people. That with God there is no respect of persons is an honored Christian maxim that most respectable people find hard to believe deep down.

Mk 12:1–12   The next parable, included by all three of the Synoptic
Mt 21:33–46   Gospels, is as complicated as the preceding one of Mat-
Lk 20:9–19   thew's was simple. It contains numerous allegorical ele-
ments, including a pointed reference to the death of Jesus at the hands of the Jewish leadership, and largely for these reasons many scholars regard it as a story told by the Palestinian Church after the crucifixion rather than an actual part of Jesus' teaching. However, while allegorical, as is the parable of Is 5:1–7 on which it doubtless depends, it remains a parable rather than an allegory: there are more details that are not allegorical than those that are. If the story were a Christian invention the presence of some of these details and the lack of others would be hard to explain—nowhere, for example, is there any hint of the resurrection of Jesus. If we concede that Jesus foresaw his death as the end to which his course was inevitably leading, that he unhesitatingly placed himself within the prophetic succession of Israel yet at the same time thought of himself as in a special and unique way God's Son, there is nothing in the parable that is incompatible with his teaching as we otherwise know it. Its lesson is in large part that of Mt 21:28–32. Finally, while we have the parable only in its Marcan form as taken over by Matthew and Luke, it would seem that its substance was also known to the Q source utilized by these same two evangelists (see on the Gospel of Matthew in Chapter 1), as evidenced by a saying we have already found in Lk 11:49–51 and which we shall find later in Mt 23:34 f.

The story is true to the Palestinian life of Jesus' time. The *hedge,* the *vat,* and the *tower* mentioned by Matthew and Mark all had their essential roles to play in a Judean vineyard (the details are in Isaiah; Luke omitted them probably because they would have been meaningless to his readers). The hedge was not a neat row of shrubbery but a wall of stones tightly fitted together designed to keep out animals and to protect the vineyard from the flash floods which, in the rainy season, quickly form in the valleys and sweep away any cultivated area in the open. The vat was a winepress as well, or rather, the two were usually found in conjunction: in Palestinian vineyards the grapes were pressed and the fermenting juice was stored right on the scene. The tower was simply a rough shelter of stone, cylindrical in form, covered over at the top with branches, if at all. It was for the use of those who were to watch over the vineyard and protect it from trespassers as well as to give the vines what attention they needed.

The system of sharecroppers or tenant farmers presupposed in the story along with an absentee landlord actually existed, together with the often attendant evils of the system. It was by no means unheard of that tenants would at times forcibly take over the land they worked and whose produce they regarded as their own rather than as belonging to a distant owner. The more distant the owner the greater their temptation and chance of success. In such a situation even the seemingly stupid idea expressed by the tenants that by killing the owner's heir they would "inherit" his vineyard makes some kind of sense. In Isaiah's parable it was the vineyard itself that was unproductive: Israel had not been faithful to the care which God had expended on it. In Jesus' adaptation it is rather the keepers of the vineyard who are condemned, who undoubtedly represent the Jewish leadership.

The *servants* whom the owner of the vineyard sends at various times and whose fate is described with slight differences of detail by the three evangelists are beyond question the prophets sent to Israel by its God (cf. the Deuteronomic expression, "his servants the prophets," found in Apo 10:7, 11:18). At the end of the list the owner sends *his beloved son.* Here Jesus certainly means himself, but in the parable the son suffers precisely the same treatment as the others, neither more nor less. No attempt has been made to develop a christology from the figure, as later Christian theology would have tended to do.

A christology of sorts is developed, it is true, at the end of the parable, and this ending may very well be an adaptation made by the apostolic Church (cf. Acts 4:11; Rom 9:33; 1 Pt 2:6–8, etc.). The point of Jesus' parable is reached when he says (in Matthew, the listeners say it) that the owner of the vineyard *will come and destroy those vine-keepers and entrust his vineyard to others.* Were these "others" thought of by Jesus as another allegorical detail, or simply as a detail demanded by the logic of the story? Whatever may have been the original intent, the Gospels at least have taken it allegorically, Matthew most obviously of all, according to whom (vs. 43) *the kingdom of God will be taken from you and given to a people who will make it bear fruit* (cf. Mt 13:18–23): for Matthew more than for the other evangelists the kingdom has definitely passed to the Gentiles in the sense that the era of Israel is gone forever. All the Gospels insert at this point (in Luke it is a response to the *Not so!* of the crowd which has seen the application of Jesus' parable) a citation of Ps 118:22 f. which is obviously understood of Christ: he who was rejected by Israel has become the cornerstone of a new edifice of faith, the Church. Luke adds another thought topically related by the word "stone" and seemingly compounded from Is 8:14 and Dan 2:34 f., 44 (the parallel vs. 44 omitted in many manuscripts of Matthew is quite likely an intrusion from Luke): Christ is also a stone of stumbling for many, the occasion, all unwilling, of their destruction (cf. Lk 2:34).

The Gospels conclude with the note that those against whom Jesus had directed his parable understood it all too well. Matthew now joins the others in distinguishing *the crowds* with whom Jesus was popular from the leadership to whom he had become anathema.

Mt 22:1–14   Matthew, however, has yet another parable to contribute
                         to this theme, one which we have already seen in a considerably different form in Luke's Gospel (above on Lk 14:15–24). Both versions of the parable have been adapted and developed in oral tradition, Matthew's probably much more than Luke's. The most striking adaptation which we discover in Matthew's story is the introduction of an entirely new parable at the end.

As Matthew tells the story, it was *a king* who invited guests to a *wedding banquet for his son*. The messianic significance is thus brought out much more definitely from the very beginning (cf. Apo 19:9). Not once only but twice he sends out *his servants* to summon the guests, and now the guests not only decline the invitation but end by killing those who have been sent. The resemblances of this story to the one that precedes it are obvious, but it is not entirely certain that these details should be taken allegorically. In the present perspective of the parable we are not dealing with guests reluctant to attend the social affair of a friend but with subjects in rebellion against the proclamation of a crown prince. Thus when the king *sent his army to destroy those murderers and burn their city*, there may or there may not be a pointed reference to the destruction of Jerusalem by the Romans in A.D. 70. In any case, the teaching of the parable is as before.

But at the end, there is another teaching. As in Luke's version of the parable, substitutes are found for those who were first invited and who refused the invitation, but Matthew observes that those who were brought in were *both bad and good*. We are reminded here of some of Matthew's classic parables of the kingdom, such as that of the weeds and of the dragnet (see above on Mt 13:24–30, 13:47–50). The remark serves to introduce the additional parable that continues and concludes the story, and which we should read for its own proper lesson without expecting it to cohere closely with the parable that introduced it. We do not ask, for example, how someone who had been casually accosted and dragged off to a celebration he had not anticipated should be expected to appear in proper attire. The question now is: Is it conceivable that anyone invited to a royal wedding banquet should appear there and take his place in his working clothes—blue jeans and a sweat shirt at a White House reception, perhaps? The only thing to do with such a misfit is to chuck him out: the parable slips into its application as it specifies that he is to be cast into *the darkness outside where they wail and gnash their teeth* (cf. Mt 8:12).

Matthew (and Jesus) would not have us think that salvation consists solely in the acceptance of an invitation, as some "saved" people seem to believe. It is, on the one hand, God's free gift: no one can assure himself of it on his own merits. But neither may he appear before his Judge empty-handed. The guests *called* to the messianic banquet must have their *wedding garment* to be among the *chosen*. By "wedding garment" Matthew undoubtedly means not only faith—the response to the invitation—but also the evidence of that Christian righteousness which has been set forth especially in the teaching of the Sermon on the Mount. *Many* and *few*, of course, are not intended as terms of mathematical precision but as means of emphasis to warn the Christian against an abuse of God's grace.

Mk 12:13–17   The three Synoptic Gospels continue the interchange
Mt 22:15–22   between Jesus and the Jewish leadership of Jerusalem
Lk 20:20–26   with this story of the question of tribute to Caesar. Luke has it that the question was proposed as a trap by *spies* sent by the scribes and chief priests, while Matthew follows Mark in making the culprits *Pharisees and Herodians*. This same unlikely combination we have seen before (cf. Mk 3:6), and it is rendered plausible here by what Luke elsewhere tells us of the presence of Herod Antipas in Jerusalem for the Passover. However, as we have observed more than once, the Gospels are not always scrupulous in identifying and distinguishing the various elements that had made up the Jewish opposition to Jesus during his ministry.

It was not a particularly honorable means that had been chosen to get at Jesus, and the way it was gone about made it even less so. The spies pretended to be honestly troubled with doubts as to whether it was *lawful to pay taxes to Caesar*, whether such tribute went counter to their traditions and the Law of Moses. Scruples of conscience always have a claim of priority on any moral teacher, and his advice is consequently sought. The question was, without doubt, a genuine case of conscience for many God-fearing Jews, not simply a matter of reluctance to pay out money or of being forced to acknowledge the dominance of foreigners. In paying the tax to Rome and thereby acknowledging its government over the Jewish people, was one then denying the God who alone was ruler and Lord of Israel? Jesus was therefore being presented with a very live issue. The taxes would be paid in any case; Rome would see to that. But should they be paid? That Jesus saw through the feigned concern of his peti- tioners and brushed aside the fulsome compliments which they prefaced to their question did not make any less shabby their cynical exploitation of a truly moral problem. At the same time, because it was a truly moral problem the circumstances under which it was posed did not absolve him from giving his answer to it.

The dilemma was a real one. A simple reply that the tribute was lawful would have been odious to most of the people. A simple denial of its legality would have made him liable to denunciation to the Romans for sedition. But of course Jesus did not give a simple answer. *Render to Caesar the things that are Caesar's and to God the things that are God's* was his classic response.

It is to be noted that this answer was not only accepted as adequate by those about Jesus but that they even marveled at it. It was not, then, as some have later thought, merely a clever evasion which he was somehow allowed to get away with, to which no one thought to oppose the obvious sequel: what *is* Caesar's, and what *is* God's? His answer was, indeed, a good one, which evidently remained to guide the apostolic Church in its similar crises of conscience (cf. Rom 13:5-7; 1 Pt 2:13-17).

Jesus asked for one of the coins used in paying taxes, and of course he was handed a piece of Roman money, in this case *a denarius*. He asked *whose face and inscription* appeared on the coin, and of course he was given the obvious answer. By these dramatic gestures he had already forced his tempters to solve their own problem. Or rather, he had forced them to see what their real problem was, which they must now submit to their consciences. In submitting to the Roman state and in using its coinage as their own, they had both received the protection of Rome and had as- sumed obligations to it. It had been at the invitation of Jews that the Romans had first entered Palestine. Jews continued to derive considerable benefits from Roman rule, which for all its faults was infinitely preferable to the bloody anarchy it had replaced. Rather than question whether it was lawful to pay tribute, ought they not ask whether it was not required by conscience? Without abdicating his kingship over Israel God had used foreign princes before to further his designs on his people (cf. Is 44:28, 45:1; 2 Chron 36:22 f.; Ezra 1:1 ff., etc.); he was the Lord of all history, not merely Israel's, and by his authority kings ruled (cf. Dan 2:21, 37 f.;

Prov 8:15 f.; Wis 6:1–3). Political reservations there might be in plenty over the circumstances of the Roman domination of Palestine, but Jesus was not being asked political questions. On moral considerations, it should have been perfectly clear to a Palestinian Jew what it was that belonged to Caesar.

It would be an exaggeration to propose Jesus' teaching in this passage, admirable though it was in its circumstances, as the Gospel's final word on Church and State. The Gospel, as it happens, has no theology of Church and State, nor has a Christian theology of Church and State ever been elaborated in the spirit of the Gospel. Jesus' saying about God and Caesar was an adequate principle for a Palestinian Jew or a first-century Christian, to both of whom the state was completely extraneous, at the best a beneficent irrelevancy which God used to protect his saints, at the worst an occasion for patience and endurance and the discipline of chastisement. It could and should be submitted to in good conscience as part of the order of things willed by God, but its laws and polities were no more a subject for determination by the Jew or Christian than were the laws of nature: another part of the order of things willed by God. By the time the Apocalypse of John was written the principle was already in trouble, as more and more it became impossible to honor a Caesar who now was firmly convinced that he was God. It was most unfortunate for Christianity that when Caesar became Christian he found it hard to break the habits of his fathers, and that the Church's conquest of Antichrist could be thought of as its conversion to the kingdom of God. The Christian men who now formed the state's laws and polities made them seem even more God's order of things, and there the Christian theology of Church and State rested. How little prepared the Church was to cope with the modern state which emerged from the great revolutions that swept aside once and for all the Roman ideas of law and authority, is part of our sad history. It is only in modern times that Christian thinkers have begun to take up realistically once more the problem which Jesus faced realistically in the context of his times. But that is another story, not the Gospel's.

21. BEGINNING OF THE END

Mk 12:18–27   In our last chapter we left Jesus in the midst of con-
Mt 22:23–33   troversy with the Jews of Jerusalem, with hard questions
Lk 20:27–40   being asked on both sides. Here we find another hard
question asked in another controversy, this time in a
rare encounter of Jesus with *the Sadducees*. The connection of this passage
with the preceding is probably not incidental: of all the Jews of Palestine,
the Sadducees had the least difficulty in adjusting themselves to Roman
rule, not so much on principle, it is true, as on expediency, since as
largely representatives of the propertied class and the institutional side
of the Jewish religion they had a fierce instinct for maintaining the
status quo. Their question was aimed as much against their enemies the
Pharisees as it was against Jesus, who in their eyes was merely a Pharisaical
rabbi, but it obviously raised issues that remained actual for the Church of
the Gospels as well.

The Sadducees *hold that there is no resurrection*, says our text. Extremely conservative in religion, the Sadducees accepted only the Law of
Moses as divine revelation, rejecting alike the prophetic literature and
later writings of the Old Testament and the oral tradition on which the
Pharisees depended to integrate and explain the whole. Perforce they
rejected belief in a resurrection or in any kind of real survival after death,
both of which ideas developed in postexilic Judaism and are never taught
in the Torah. Cases such as the one they proposed to Jesus it was their
delight, as true believers rejecting the traditions of men, to use to bedevil
the orthodox rabbis. The case is on a level with one that a village atheist
might use today to ridicule the faith of the godly. Jesus eluded their trap
in the only way possible to him, by repudiating the fundamentalist naïveté
that is identified with orthodoxy by Sadducees, village atheists, and the
godly.

The Sadducees refer to Deut 25:5–10, the so-called levirate or brother-
in-law provision of the Torah (whether it was ever a strict law, may be
debated), designed both to preserve the name and memory of a man
who had been so unfortunate as to die without an heir and to prevent
family property from being alienated through his widow's marriage out-

side the clan. It seems to have been the intention of later laws like
Lev 18:16, 20:21 (dating from a time when women as well as men could
inherit property and pass it on) to do away with this ancient and somewhat primitive provision, but levirate marriages appear to have continued
among the Jews even into Christian times, and this Gospel passage probably indicates that they existed in the Palestine of Jesus. The Sadducees'
story stretches the long arm of coincidence in supposing seven so unlucky
brothers, but still it was always possible. How, then, does the rabbi answer?
If there be a resurrection, whose wife would the woman be?

Belief in the resurrection, in the time of the Gospels or in this twentieth
century, is belief in the creative *power of God*. This, Jesus replies, is
precisely what the Sadducees do not understand. The idea of a resurrection appears childish to them because they have never thought of it
except in childish terms, as though it meant the reanimation of corpses
which would continue the human processes of eating and drinking, loving
and hating, giving in marriage and taking wives. The resurrection, however, means first and foremost our translation into a new mode of
existence (cf. 1 Cor 15:51–53), when we shall be *like the angels* or, as
Paul would later write to the Corinthians, possessing spiritual rather than
fleshly bodies (cf. 1 Cor 15:42–50). The power of God which can call
men back from death is not limited by the materiality of man's ability to
conceive of it. The reference to the angels is, of course, another slap at
the Sadducees, who denied the existence of a spiritual order (cf. Acts 23:8).

The Sadducees also *do not know the Scriptures*. Jesus cites Ex 3:6, the
passage about Moses and the burning bush, because this was Scripture
also received by the Sadducees. That God identified himself to Moses as
the God of Abraham and the God of Isaac and the God of Jacob might
not occur to us as a proof of survival after death; however, it was evidently
an argument that was significant for the Jews. And, as a matter of fact,
there is more to it than meets the eye. *He is not the God of the dead but
of the living*. The experience of the living God was what had given
pious Jews their first groping thoughts about immortality, the conviction
that somehow the vital contact would be preserved, that this God would
never wholly abandon those whom he had made his own (cf. Pss 16:
8 ff., 49:15 f., 73:23 ff.).

Mk 12:28–34   Luke (vs. 39) concluded the story of the dialogue with
Mt 22:34–40   the Sadducees by noting the approval of *the scribes* who
                      were standing by, and as Mark tells the following story
of Jesus' conversation with *one of the scribes* we have a friendly dialogue
by honest enquiry. This fits somewhat strangely in the present context of
controversy, and it is likely that Mark has brought it in from some other
time and place simply to complete the sequence: Pharisees and Herodians,
Sadducees, and now scribes. Matthew has adjusted the story to its polemical

surroundings: in his Gospel the question of *the lawyer* is a test inspired by the Pharisees. Luke's earlier version of the story (see above on Lk 10:25–28) did not make it altogether clear in what spirit the question was asked.

Jesus is asked *what is the greatest commandment.* The question is posed in a legalist sense. As the rabbis analyzed the Law, it was made up of 613 distinct commandments, 248 of them positive (the "do's") and 365 negative (the "don't's"). They distinguished between great commandments and small, and even very great and very small. Jesus replies, however, by giving as the greatest commandment the spirit of what Matthew knows as *the Law and the prophets* (see above on Mt 5:17–20). Though he himself distinguishes two commandments, it is obviously only for the purpose of showing how they coalesce in one and are inseparable one from the other. He begins with the *Shema,* the words of Deut 6: 4 f., in which other high-minded rabbis had found a summation of the Law's spirit, and to this he adds Lev 19:18, the precept of the love of neighbor. It is disputed whether in the time of Jesus Lev 19:18 was already recited as part of the *Shema;* at all events, it is true that some of the rabbis regarded it as the greatest of the Law's commandments. The greatness of Jesus' teaching does not consist simply in his association of these two precepts and in the radical connection that he perceived between them, but also in the new dimension that he gave to both. If love of God above all is to be the motive and form of every act, and if experientially this love is to find itself in the love and service of the neighbor, it obviously matters very much who the neighbor is perceived to be (see above on Lk 10:29–37). Reciprocally, the dimension that is given to "neighbor" determines existentially who the God is that is loved and served in him.

In Mark's story Jesus discovers a kindred spirit in the scribe, who paraphrases his response with approval, recognizing in it the authentic voice of Israel's prophets (cf. 1 Sam 15:22; Hos 6:6, to which he alludes). In turn, Jesus tells him that he is *not far from the kingdom of God,* and we have every reason to hope that he followed him there.

Mk 12:35–37a   In all three Gospels Jesus terminates this series of inter-
Mt 22:41–46   changes by proposing a final enigma for solution. The
Lk 20:41–44   device appears to have proved eminently successful,
                since commentators on this passage have remained puzzled ever after. The question is, how would Jesus himself have answered what his adversaries are unable to answer? This is what the Gospels do not tell us, for what seems to be the quite sufficient reason that they did not know. The enigmatic quality of the passage makes it another of those about whose authentic connection with Jesus' teaching we have the least doubt in reading the Gospels. A saying of this kind, of

whose meaning no one is exactly sure, is hardly invented, though it is most easily remembered.

Whose son is the Messiah? The answer to that was easy, and it is given unhesitatingly. "The son of David" was doubtless the most commonly used title for the Messiah among Palestinian Jews. As we know, it is a title that Jesus never applies to himself, not even in John's Gospel where his teaching so often is phrased in the language and concepts of a developed Christian theology. His own view of his role in the economy of divine salvation was far too complex to be expressed by a simple identification with the Davidic Messiah. There was a sense in which he was the Messiah, and to this the Gospels and all of the New Testament testify. There was a sense in which he definitely was not, and it was this that necessitated the "messianic secret" (see above on Mk 1:22–28 and parallel). Certainly he was not the Messiah in the sense in which doubtless most of his contemporaries thought of the Messiah.

It seems that in this story Jesus tried to suggest some of the complexities of the messianic question as he knew it but which were bypassed in the conventional messianic thinking of Palestine. He quotes Ps 110:1, as it was commonly accepted among the Jews of his time, as a verse written by David under divine inspiration in referring to the Messiah: *The Lord said to my Lord* . . . If the Messiah is rightly called David's son, nevertheless how can David speak of him not as one whose greatest glory it will be to re-create the Davidic age as his worthy successor, but as his own Lord indeed? The paradox is brought out at its clearest in the Greek version of the Old Testament cited by the Gospels, where the same word *kyrios* is used to translate the first "Lord" (the God of Israel) and the second (the Messiah). However, much the same effect would have been produced by the use of the Hebrew text or an Aramaic translation, since it is the second "Lord" that poses the problem. Given the accepted meaning of the verse about which there was no dispute, in it David spoke of the Messiah as someone far more exalted than himself.

Jesus' question is left hanging in the air. It is answered neither by his audience nor by the Gospels. Since it is plain, however, that he asked it neither for curiosity's sake nor merely as a clever conundrum to discomfit his enemies, we may presume to find in it an attempt at self-revelation. In this passage we can discover, however obscurely, another of the Synoptic testimonials to Jesus' awareness of divine sonship that is the commonplace of John's Gospel.

Mt 23:1–14   The following discourse is somewhat embarrassing both
Mk 12:37b–40 in its length and in its harshness, but it must be faced
Lk 20:45–47   up to both as an historical record and as part of the
              Gospel message. It comes appositely enough at the
conclusion of a series of controversies with the Jewish leadership, and doubtless it does represent some kind of terminal judgment of Jesus on

his scribal opposition. The few verses of Mark and Luke have been
replaced in Matthew by a schematic arrangement that extends over
nearly an entire chapter, but the longer version is scarcely more bitter
than the shorter. For the First Gospel, as we have observed more than
once before, the question of Jewish opposition was still a much liver issue
than it was for the Christians for whom Mark and Luke wrote: this explains both the length of Matthew's treatment and the fact that he has
broadened the condemnation into a diatribe against both *the scribes and
the Pharisees*, against normative Jewry, in other words. Nevertheless, it is
not simply anti-Jewish. It can even be conceived as a kind of defense of
the Jews, among whom must be counted Jesus and his first disciples and
the earliest Christian tradition on which the discourse depends, against
those whom it regards as their betrayers and false guides: Jesus speaks *to*
the people *about* the scribes and Pharisees. Neither is it a condemnation
of all the scribes and far less of all the Pharisees. It is a repudiation of
certain of their tendencies that certainly existed, that were prevalent
enough to be taken as typical, and which were symptomatic of all that
was opposed to Christ and Christianity. The discourse should neither be
exaggerated beyond its intentions nor minimized because of them.

The scribes and Pharisees have taken their place on the chair of Moses,
Jesus begins. This is no blanket rejection of Pharisaism or of rabbinical
Judaism, the legitimacy of which Jesus did not question. By and large,
Jesus himself would have been regarded by his contemporary Jews as a
Pharisee and a scribe, though in neither instance a professional. The
Lord addresses himself to matters of practice, and immediately we are
reminded of various passages in the Sermon on the Mount. Luke has
also included some of the examples in his record of Jesus' denunciation
of Pharisaical piety (see above on Lk 11:37–54). New is the reference
to the widening of *phylacteries* and *tassels*. Phylacteries, still used at
times of prayer by conservative and orthodox Jews (by whom they are
called *tefillin*), were little boxes containing bits of parchment on which
were written various verses of the Law, which were bound with straps to
the left arm and on the forehead and worn in literalist obedience to
Deut 6:6–8. The "professional" Pharisee would wear them all day long
and be sure that they were large enough to be seen. So would they do
with the tassels which all good Jews wore (see above on Mk 5:21–43 and
parallels) in obedience to the Law (cf. Num 15:37–41; Deut 22:12).

Jesus mentions three titles in which these religionists took particular
pride: *rabbi, father,* and *teacher*. Properly, these were all titles borne by
the scribes, and essentially they amounted to the same thing. They were
honored names bestowed by a people who reverenced learning and who,
by using them, intended less to glorify the learned than the learning itself, which was the knowledge of the Law, the word of God. They were
applied, at various times, to Jesus himself, who never rejected them. And

of course, there was nothing wrong in them. What made them wrong was their being taken seriously, as titles of personal excellence, as though those whom we entitle "your honor" or "excellency" or "lordship" or "eminence" and the like should suddenly translate these honorifics of office to their own human selves as somehow setting them apart from other human selves. *You*, says Jesus, must *avoid* such things. The "you," there can be no doubt, is the Christian Church. The Church avoids what Jesus was talking about not by determining the nomenclature of office but by raising up doctors who know the difference between ministers of Christ and the lords of the Gentiles (see above on Mk 9:33–37 and parallels; Mk 10:35–45 and parallel).

In verse 13 Matthew begins a series of seven "woes" against the scribes and Pharisees, the first of which is a parallel of Lk 11:52. The second does not appear in verse 14, which on the manuscript evidence is an addition to his text from Mk 12:40 and Lk 20:47. It is no less a reproach to be brought against the scribes and Pharisees, however, who in any case *devour the savings of widows and recite long prayers to keep up appearances.* What seems to be involved in this change is that, contrary to the spirit of the laws of Num 27:5–11, 36:5–9 (which in principle guaranteed inheritance through female as well as male descendants), the Pharisees had decided that widows could not inherit from their husbands but rather must contract another marriage in order to guarantee their economic and social identity. They had even decreed that daughters could not inherit directly from their fathers but only through their sons. Contrary to such rules the early Christian Church regarded widows as a category of persons apart, possessed of rights on the whole community and to be honored in their own estate (cf. Acts 6:1, 9:39, 41; 1 Tim 5:3–16; Jas 1:27).

Mt 23:15–22   The second and third of Matthew's "woes" are proper to his Gospel. The *converts* of whom Jesus speaks were undoubtedly proselytes to Judaism out of paganism: in the first Christian century Judaism was an immensely successful proselytizing religion. It is not proselyting that is condemned here, but the "pharisaizing" of proselytes, evidently. What is meant by the proselytes becoming *sons of gehenna twice as bad* as the scribes and Pharisees is not specified, but it is well known that converts to a system are usually its staunchest supporters. The casuistry over oaths we have seen discussed in the Sermon on the Mount (above on Mt 5:33–37) and in respect to practices like the *korban* (see above on Mk 7:1–13 and parallel).

Mt 23:23–36   The remainder of the discourse is closely paralleled as to content in Lk 11:37–54. In Matthew's fourth "woe" Luke's "mint and rue and every herb" has become *mint and dill and cumin,* and Matthew has included the expressive saying about those who *filter out a gnat while swallowing a camel whole*—one of those inspired impossibilities like leading a camel through a needle's eye. A more serious difference with Luke appears in the fifth "woe" concerning those who *clean the outside of the cup and the dish* (Matthew used another word for the latter vessel, which is unimportant). Luke's version contrasted the Pharisees' zeal for the cleanliness of things with their lack of concern for their own interiors. Matthew's use of the saying turns it into a parable in which the cup and dish stand for the scribes and Pharisees themselves: outwardly they are clean, for they take great care to surround themselves with the signs of piety, but within they are guilty of all uncleanness. *Cleanse the inside of the cup so that the outside may also become clean* means, obviously, that if they would be sincere in their piety and practice genuine righteousness the externals would take care of themselves.

Luke spoke of the Pharisees as "hidden graves" by which men are contaminated unawares. Matthew's sixth "woe" varies the figure: they are like *whitewashed tombs*, nice to look at from the outside, but containing in themselves corruption. Tombs were customarily painted white so that they would be clearly visible even at night and thus the more easily avoided. The last of the "woes" is an expansion of one that Luke directs against the scribes, in which the Christ of the Matthaean Church speaks, condemning not only the murders of the past but also those that are to come, when he will send other *prophets and wise men and scribes* to be hunted down and crucified by these killers of the prophets. These titles should not be seized on as offering any indication of the constitution of the apostolic Church, however, since they are simply the applicable Old Testament terms extended into New Testament times. The most curious of the variants in Matthew's text is the identification of the *Zechariah* of 2 Chron 24:20–22 (whose father's name, according to the same passage, was Jehoiada) as *the son of Barachiah*. This is the result of a confusion with another, more famous prophet Zechariah (cf. Zech 1:1), and for this reason the phrase has been omitted in some of the manuscripts of Matthew's Gospel.

At the conclusion of this discourse Matthew has Jesus utter the words over Jerusalem which we have already seen placed in a somewhat better context by Luke (above on Lk 13:34f. and parallel).

Mk 12:41–44   Possibly because of the somber tone achieved in the dis-
Lk 21:1–4   course on the scribes and Pharisees which is to be sus-
              tained in the eschatological discourse that follows, Mat-
thew has omitted this little story about the widow and her gift which Mark and Luke have told. Though it has not always been given its proper place of honor in the Church, the evangelists surely intended that churchmen should reflect on it when considering to whom it is that the Church owes the most for the support of itself and its works. Most church-

men, whether or not they follow out its implications, know it to be a story that is profoundly true.

The treasury was in the temple courtyard, where there were thirteen chests for donations, each marked for a separate purpose. Particularly at the time of the great feasts there would be considerable activity about the treasury as the many pilgrims came to make their offerings. The Gospel does not necessarily imply that the wealthy were making a show of their large donations; generous giving was accepted as a matter of course. Jesus' saying simply regards the relative value of the gifts, depending on the sacrifice involved. The rich gave much because they could afford to do so, but the poor widow gave everything that she had. What she gave, in absolute figures, the Gospel calls *two lepta*, undoubtedly using the *lepton*, the smallest Greek coin in circulation, as the equivalent of the Palestinian *perutah*: two *perutoth* was the smallest offering accepted. Mark further translates the sum for his Roman readers as a *quadrans* which, as the name indicates, was the fourth part of a Roman *as*, a copper coin worth about one cent.

Jn 12:37–50   We are about to take up the Synoptic eschatological discourse, which in the three Synoptic Gospels represents Jesus' final words of teaching before the beginning of the passion story proper. Before we do this, it will be just as well that we see the corresponding section in John's Gospel, which appears immediately before he begins his story of the passion. There is little resemblance on the surface, yet a line of connection exists between the two endings in the two traditions. If it is with an eschatological message that the Synoptics leave us, John also concludes on a note of eschatology, the "realized" eschatology that is the emphasis of his Gospel.

But first, as John brings to a close the first half of his Gospel, his "book of signs," he offers his answer to a question that plagued the early Church more than did many others, namely, the scandal of Jewish incredulity. This Jesus Christ in whom a now largely Gentile Church believed as its risen Lord and so confidently proclaimed in Old Testament terms as Messiah, Son of God and Son of Man, the Word of prophecy incarnate, why had he ended by being rejected, generally speaking, by the people of the Old Testament? Why had it been that he came unto his own and his own received him not?

John insists, first of all, that the rejection of Jesus was foreseen by God and included in his plan of salvation. This was one of the earliest affirmations of the Church, that in his shameful death and repudiation Jesus had fulfilled the prophetic role of the suffering Servant of the Lord (cf. Acts 2:23, 3:13; 1 Cor 15:3; and Rom 10:16 which also cites Is 53:1 along with John). If this was the case, then in their unbelief the Jews were only bringing to pass God's prophetic word: *they could not believe*. In this connection, and to the same purpose, John quotes Is 6:10 which **the**

Synoptic Gospels use to explain Jesus' lack of success with his parabolic teaching (see above on Mk 4:10–12 and parallels). John adds that *Isaiah said this because he saw his glory and spoke of him.* It was the glory of Yahweh, the God and King of Israel, that Isaiah saw in vision (cf. Is 6:3). However, for John the glory of the Father and of the Son are one and the same (cf. vs. 28 above), and he doubtless thinks of the pre-existent Christ as active in the Old Testament. In announcing the failure of his own prophetic ministry Isaiah also spoke of Christ's, for they are two phases of the same word directed to the same recalcitrant people.

But why was this prophetic word uttered? Why did God have to include this obduracy in the construction of his economy of salvation? John can only say that *they loved the glory of men rather than the glory of God* (cf. Jn 5:44). We are left with the impression that John recognizes the inadequacy of this explanation, however true it may have been. In Rom 9–11 Paul explores the mystery of Israel more deeply than this, from the same standpoint of Jewish unbelief. But neither did Paul emerge with a definitive answer. The relation of Judaism to the Church in the final working out of God's kingdom is a matter on which the New Testament has uttered no ultimate word, and with it Christian theology continues to grapple.

In verse 36 John brought Jesus' public teaching to a close with the note that he now retired from the sight of men. It is doubtful, therefore, that the evangelist intends the concluding verses of this chapter of his Gospel to represent a new discourse, which in any case would be quite anticlimactic after his own peroration. Rather, they appear to be a summation drawn from the preceding discourses of the "book of signs" to allow John to portray dramatically and for one final time in the Lord's own words the light of revelation whose rejection he has just described. No new theme is introduced by these verses. Appropriately, the here-and-nowness of God's eternal judgment is brought to the fore, and we are left with the figure of the Christ of faith continuously present offering himself as eternal life for man's acceptance or refusal.

Mk 13:1–2   The Synoptic eschatological discourse begins in all three
Mt 24:1–2   Gospels with Jesus' prediction of the destruction of the
Lk 21:5–6   Jerusalem temple, a prophecy that was to be fulfilled some
             forty years later, on August 9, A.D. 70, to be exact. That
Jesus actually made such a prophecy, in view of his consistent eschatological teaching on the soonness of a divine visitation on Jerusalem and Judea, his conviction of the decisiveness of his own role in the workings of salvation history, and his reading of the temper of the times, there is absolutely no reason to question. His words are in the tradition of Israel's prophecy (cf. Jer 7:1–15; Ezek 24:15–23) and have not been simply made up by Christian writers in the light of later events. For one thing, the temple was not pulled down stone by stone, as a literalist interpretation of the proph-

ecy would suggest, but was destroyed by fire against the orders of the
Roman commander by the soldiers who were enraged at Jerusalem's having
held out so long against their siege. One of the charges made against Jesus
at his trial was that he had spoken of the destruction of the temple (cf.
Mk 14:58 and parallel).

The occasion of Jesus' prophecy is the exclamation of the disciples over
the grandeur of the temple and its annexed buildings. Even today when
one first looks over the temple area from the Mount of Olives he cannot
fail to be struck by the impressiveness of what he sees. However, the
singularly beautiful mosque called the Dome of the Rock which now
dominates the area could hardly be compared in any way with the sight
that greeted the eyes of him who looked down on Herod's temple. The
whiteness of its massive stones and the gold of its façade made it one of
the known wonders of the world, and no Jew could look upon it without
feeling a natural surge of pride in his race and his religion. Thus the
shock, such as we can hardly imagine, that must have been caused by
Jesus' words. Who could conceive a world without the temple? The end
of the temple would mean the end of sacrifice, and surely sacrifice would
end only with the world itself.

It is this association of related ideas that is reflected in Matthew's version
of the discourse as it continues, according to which the disciples ask the
time not of the destruction of the temple but *the sign of your parousia
and the end of the world*. This is much more precise than their question
as it appears in Mark and Luke. All the Gospels, of course, are far more
concerned with the eschatological question as it affected the Christian of
the first century than as it would have presented itself to a pre-Christian
Jew. Matthew, therefore, besides mentioning explicitly the two ideas that
were associated in the minds of the disciples, has also phrased their question
in Christian terms.

Mk 13:3–8   The two ideas, end of the temple and end of all, continue
Mt 24:3–8   to be associated in the discourse that now follows as the
Lk 21:7–11   Gospels tell of Jesus' answer to his disciples—only Mark
              notes that these were *Peter, James, and John,* his three
chosen intimates, together with *Andrew,* Peter's brother. Certainly in the
thought of the evangelists the destruction of Jerusalem and its temple—
an event which, for Matthew and Luke at least, had by now already taken
place—was the first act in the drama of the end-time in which the Church
was now living, the last act of which would be the Lord's glorious *parousia*
(see above on Lk 17:20 f.). In this view the New Testament is one.
Even in such a work as the Gospel of John with its strong emphasis on
"realized" eschatology that we know so well, the expectation of an
eventual end of this present order and beginning of a new age in a final
judgment and resurrection remains accepted doctrine. The only appreciable

difference among the New Testament writings in their views on the *parousia* and its aftermath is as regards when all this will take place, quite soon or in the indefinite future? This difference has no more complicated explanation than the process of continuing history, as the *parousia* was more and more "delayed" and as this or that "sign" that had been thought of as pointing to its coming proved to be no sign at all. Of course, the "delay" of the *parousia* had enormous influence on the development of New Testament theology, especially the theology of the Church. No one is disposed to bother much about organizing or theorizing on a Church that will at best be in existence for only a few months or years. It is a vastly different matter when the Church must think of itself, finally, in terms of becoming one of the semi-permanent institutions existing in this world.

But what of Jesus himself? Did he make the same association of ideas as did the early Church? Many today think that he did not, that the idea of a *parousia* and an end of this present world has been imposed on his teaching by an apocalyptically minded Church for reasons of its own contrary to, or at least not in accord with, his original intentions. (This is the exact reversal of a theory of a half-century or so ago, which wanted to explain everything in Jesus' teaching as derived from his obsession with the imminent end of the world.) According to these scholars, Jesus either believed that with him the kingdom of God had come into the world once and for all, with nothing more to follow, or that, at the most, the kingdom would be definitively brought in through some soon to come historical crisis, such as the end of Jerusalem. The Church apocalypticized Jesus' simple message either to explain away inconsistencies that had not yet become apparent in his lifetime, or merely because most of the early Christians thought in apocalyptic categories whereas Jesus had not.

Such a theory does violence to the New Testament evidence and to reason. Our first contact with Christian literature is from about A.D. 50, in Paul's first letter to the Thessalonian church. From this writing it is evident that the expectation of the *parousia* was already an "ancient" Christian doctrine, so much so that it had been made the occasion of a good deal of peripheral and bootless speculation about details and non-essentials. From then on, concern about it as a pressing event tends to decrease rather than increase. All this had occurred, independently of Jesus, within a period of some twenty years of his death? Suppose that it had: whence did it come? There was no precedent for it in Judaism—though both the word and the concept of *parousia* seem to be present in Dan 7:13—for the perfectly adequate reason that Judaism knew of no dying and resurrected Messiah, and therefore of no reason that he should return. It makes far better sense to credit the idea to Jesus than to anyone else. And why not to Jesus? That he believed that the kingdom of God had, in some fashion, begun with his preaching in Galilee, the Gospel seems to tell us on every page. That he also foresaw an imminent judgment of his own people, as we have just said, also seems to be inescapable. But that he should have made no pronouncement on his *parousia* is simply incredible. He knew that his death was necessary for the kingdom. But if death, resurrection; and if resurrection, *parousia*. Otherwise we find incomprehensible one of the affirmations on which all four Gospels are in the most solid agreement: that Jesus identified himself above all and by preference with the eschatological Son of Man, the judge and savior.

All this is said not to deny that here as elsewhere the evangelists have given us the Lord's words in the interpretation of the Church from which they had received them. In this passage which begins to speak of the time of the end of Jerusalem, Mark, followed by Matthew as usual, has responded with the doubtlet of a passage which he later uses in verses 21–25 where the reference is obviously to the last times; with his customary tidiness, Luke has avoided most of the repetition. What must be insisted upon is that the apocalyptic mentality reflected in these Synoptic passages and elsewhere in the New Testament was one in which Jesus shared. Apocalyptic, despite its to us at times bizarre imagery, was a way of thought with a high and serious purpose truly rooted in the Old Testament revelation. It was a way of thought that could get out of hand, obviously, as can any other. Jesus could not be called an apocalyptist in the sense that apocalyptic dominated all his thinking, just as he could not be called a legalist merely because he upheld the Law. But apocalyptic had a part in his teaching even as did historical and realized eschatology. It is part of the religion of Christianity. Remove it, and the vital New Testament concepts of prophetic witness and sacrifice are removed along with it. Apocalyptic affirms that this world is under judgment. Remove it, and the city of man becomes the city of God by its wishing so, while the transforming word of Christ is reduced to a "social gospel." The world is not evil, as some apocalyptists thought of it or think of it now, but it is the mission field of the Church in view of the kingdom of God, and there is a real sense in which it must come to an end and be changed.

Speaking of the "signs" that will precede "these things," Jesus refers to the *many* who *will come in my name*, pretending, in other words, to be the Messiah. There were, in fact, various persons who assumed this character before the fall of Jerusalem. The Acts of the Apostles names several: a certain Theudas and a Judas of Galilee (Acts 5:35–37) and an unnamed Egyptian Jew (Acts 21:38); and undoubtedly there were others. The times were filled with messianic hope, and it was inevitable that messiahs would come forward to satisfy it. However, this as well as the other warnings about *wars and rumors of wars, earthquakes*, and the like, borrow from standard apocalyptic imagery relating to the last times. *This is the beginning of the birthpangs*: this term and concept is borrowed from prophetic texts like Is 66:7–9; Hos 13:13. "The birthpangs of the

Messiah" referred to the travails that must be undergone by the world or by the messianic people as a condition for the birth of the messianic age.

Lk 21:12–19 From the general trials of the messianic times Jesus de-
Mk 13:9–13 scends to the specific sufferings to be undergone by his
Mt 24:9–14 disciples. Both Matthew and Luke have already partly paralleled this section in telling of earlier instructions and warnings given to the disciples (see above on Mt 10:16b–25 and parallel). It appears most likely that the original purview of Jesus' words had to do with what the disciples might expect in Jerusalem and Judea in the troubled times of the Jewish Church immediately following his crucifixion and resurrection, the period covered in the first chapters of the Acts of the Apostles. Luke and Mark tend to preserve this prospect, with its references to the *synagogues* and local Jewish *courts* into which the first Christians would be haled to give account of themselves (cf. 2 Cor 11:24). In verse 10, however, Mark has what is probably his own comment on the discourse which has adapted it to the later viewpoint of the Church to which the Gentile mission had been revealed: *but first the Gospel must be proclaimed to all the nations* (cf. Rom 11:11 f., 25 f.). In verse 14 Matthew repeats and expands on this idea, and in keeping with it describes the persecutions as emanating more from Gentiles than from Jews.

Mk 13:14–20 Jesus now speaks of the destruction of Jerusalem as a
Mt 24:15–22 pre-eminent sign of the last times. *When you see Jeru-*
Lk 21:20–24 *salem being surrounded by an army* in Luke is doubtless a free paraphrase in more prosaic terms of the Semitisms of Mark and Matthew, the paraphrase of a tradition that had been the fulfillment of the Lord's prediction (see also on Lk 19:41–44 above). Mark and Matthew quote Jesus as designating the sign by what has been traditionally translated *the abomination of desolation* (that is, an abominable thing which destroys) *standing where it ought not* (Matthew specifies, *in the holy place*). The reference is to Dan 9:27, 11:31, 12:11, and what was meant there was the desecration of the temple in 167 B.C. by the Syrian king Antiochus IV Epiphanes (cf. 1 Macc 1:54, 6:7), who had erected in it an altar and statue of the Olympian Zeus. Antiochus' terrible persecution of the Jews eventually led to the wars of the Maccabees and the establishment of an independent Jewish kingdom that was to exist until internal dissensions brought in the power of Rome. *Let him who reads take note!* means that what had occurred in Macaabean times will once more be a sign, and when the abomination of desolation again appears, *those who are in Judea should flee to the mountains*. Their flight must be precipitous and unhesitating, Jesus adds. Woe to him who has any kind of encumbrances! Simply pray that it be not necessary to flee *in winter*, when travel was virtually impossible, *or on the Sabbath*, when those bound by the Law were forbidden to travel.

Whatever may have been Jesus' precise intention in proposing "the abomination of desolation" as a sign, it appears that Luke's interpretation of it was commonly held by the Christians of Palestine. In A.D. 66 the first great Jewish revolt against the Romans broke out, and in the following year the Roman legions were already surrounding Jerusalem, occupying the rebellious towns of Galilee and Judea one by one. A reliable tradition has it that at that time the Christian population migrated across the Jordan to Pella in Perea (by some Pella was counted as part of the Decapolis), not to return to Jerusalem till after it had been seized and sacked by the Romans in A.D. 70.

Mk 13:21–27   Already in their references to the *shortening of the days*
Mt 24:23–31   of travail in favor of God's *elect*, lest all living creatures
Lk 21:25–28   should perish, the Gospels have shifted their view from
              the beginning of the last times to their continuation as
leading to the final appearance of *the Son of Man*. The highly apocalyptic description of the last times that now follows in Mark has been somewhat heightened by Matthew and toned down considerably by Luke. It is a mélange of prophetico-apocalyptic allusions from the Old Testament (cf. Is 13:10, 27:13, 34:4; Ezek 32:7 f.; Dan 7:13 f.; Joel 2:10; Hab 1:8, etc.): such an "anthological" style is one of the prime characteristics of apocalyptic as a literary form, as can easily be seen from its best exemplification in the New Testament Apocalypse of John, a book which is literally a tissue of such allusions.

It is conceivable that even in an apocalyptic passage of this intensity the Gospels, or perhaps Matthew and Luke, have historicized and realized the prophetic vision in events that had already taken place in the emergence of the Church, thus returning apocalyptic to its own origins, which were the prophecy of contemporary historical deeds and occurrences. Luke ends his description by the note that all these things are signs that *your redemption is near*. "Redemption," found only this once in the Gospels, is eminently a Pauline term which is usually, though not always, eschatological: the redemption of Christians is the object of their present hope, the consummation of God's kingdom in the resurrection of the just. Taken eschatologically here it makes admirable sense. It is just possible, however, that by it Luke means the liberation of Christianity from Judaism. The cataclysm of A.D. 70 was a sign of the eschatological age—it manifested, in some way, the kingdom of God—because out of it the Church came forth on its own, never more to be taken by anyone (as it had been taken in the beginning by outsider and insider alike) as merely another Jewish sect. It was now freed for the conquest of the Gentile world—*they will assemble his chosen ones from the four winds*, Matthew says. It might be considered, therefore, that in some real sense the Son of Man had in this event already been made manifest in his glory to the world, in the same kind of realized eschatology with which we are familiar from the Gospel of John.

Mk 13:28–32   Such an interpretation, if the Gospels were patient of it,
Mt 24:32–36   would remove all difficulties from the verses that follow.
Lk 21:29–33   Though it is not necessarily entirely wrong, however,
                neither is it adequate of itself alone to elucidate the full-
ness of Jesus' teaching as the Gospels seem to have understood it. Jesus evidently intends, now and finally, to respond to the disciples' initial question as to when "all these things" would come to pass. "All these things," as we saw, were not only the destruction of Jerusalem, but also the Lord's *parousia* and the end of the world, all of which together formed a single concept, in the mind of Jesus as well as in the mind of the disciples.

If *parousia* and the coming historical crisis formed a single concept, nevertheless it is not true to conclude that they were simply identified. All through his public preaching Jesus has been rebuking the Palestinians for their failure to read the signs of the times (for example, see above on Mk 8:11 f. and parallels), to recognize, in other words, that on historical grounds an intervention of God was inevitable and coming soon. This is also the lesson of *the parable of the fig tree,* which has been carefully chosen as a sign of things to come. In Palestine, where most of the trees are evergreen, the fig tree's sudden leaving into green indicates, as other trees do not, *that summer is near.* Luke accommodates the parable to a non-Palestinian audience when he simply equates the fig tree with *all the other trees.* So, Jesus applies the parable, *when you see these things happening, you will realize that he is near, standing at your door,* or, as Luke paraphrases, *the kingdom of God is near*—the "he" being the Son of Man, the eschatological judge and savior.

The difficulty is not only that Jesus seems to be speaking of the predictability of what in the next breath he says is unpredictable, but also that it is hard to know what is the antecedent of "these things." The apocalyptic "signs" in the moon and sun and stars, and so forth, of the preceding context are not thought of as indicative of the proximity of the *parousia* but rather of its presence as a *fait accompli;* by its very nature, an apocalyptic inbreaking of God into history and ending history is un-predictable, as indeed Jesus goes on to say. By now, however, it should have become plain that the eschatological discourse is a composite work in which not every verse now stands in its original historical context. As far as the Gospels are concerned, it is likely enough that their authors took the historical crisis to be a sign of the soon coming *parousia* and interpreted this verse accordingly, preserving the outlook of the primitive Christian community. It is equally likely that Jesus first uttered the verse in reference

to the coming historical crisis itself, in keeping with the sense of the parable and in the pattern of his other similar utterances. In the same way we
should probably understand his further word that *this generation will not
pass away before all these things come to be.* The following saying on
the passing away of heaven and earth has been obviously adapted to this
context for topical reasons (cf. Mt 5:18; Lk 16:17).

We are not saying that Jesus could not have looked on the coming
destruction of the temple as an immediate sign of the *parousia,* but that
he does not seem to have. If there is a series of words ascribed to him
in which the kingdom of God is presented as coming quite soon or, indeed, as already present in some fashion, there is an even more impressive
series in which its suddenness and unexpectedness is the theme: such
is the message of practically all of the "parables of the kingdom." We have
discussed this situation before (see above on Mk 8:34–9:1 and parallels;
Lk 17:20 f.). The final words of Jesus recorded by Mark and Matthew in
this section belong to this last series and even explain it: *Concerning that
day or its hour no one knows, not even the angels of heaven, nor even
the Son, but only the Father.*

Once more we are reading one of those absolutely convincing sayings
of Jesus that no one can imagine the early Christians having made up:
"nor even the Son" is missing from a significant number of important
manuscripts of Matthew's Gospel and that evangelist may in fact have
omitted the words; Luke certainly omitted the whole saying. It is, nevertheless, a most precious contribution to our understanding of the historical
process of God's revelation in Jesus Christ. At the very least, we are given
to know that the time of the *parousia* was not a part of what Christ had
come to reveal concerning God and his designs. But the text says more
than that. In his incarnational state Jesus did not play-act as man but
freely took upon himself the limitations of the human condition that he
embraced (cf. Heb 2:17, 4:15). Of what he did not reveal he himself had
no effective knowledge. Theoretically at least, he too could have shared the
Church's expectation of an early *parousia.*

Mk 13:33–37   Mark and Luke conclude the eschatological discourse
Lk 21:34–36   analogously but not in parallel. Mark's emphasis is on
              viligance in view of the uncertainty of the time of the
Lord's coming, and in the process he tells a parable which we have already
seen in more developed form in Luke's Gospel (above on Lk 19:11–28)
and will see again in Matthew's (below on Mt 25:14–30). Luke, too,
insists on vigilance, but in Pauline terms (cf. 1 Thes 5:1–11), moralizing
the eschatological message as he has done before (see above on Lk
3:10–14).

Mt 24:37–44   It is Matthew who has done the most with the same
              theme, for he has made the eschatological discourse the

fifth and last of his major discourses over which he has mainly divided the teachings of Jesus. He continues, therefore, with a series of sayings and parables, the first collection of which we have already seen at two places in Luke's Gospel with no appreciable difference in meaning (see above on Lk 17:22–37, 12:35–40). The parable with which he concludes his chapter 24 we have also already considered (see above on Lk 12:41–48 and parallel).

Mt 25:1–13   The following parable, however, is proper to Matthew's Gospel, aside from what may be a few echoes of it here and there in Mark and Luke. As in the preceding story, a point is made of the *delay* in an expected coming, a factor which serves to sharpen the stress on constant viligance and preparedness for an eschatologically minded Church.

The parable tells of *ten virgins who took their lamps and went outside to meet the bridegroom* (not "and his bride": this is an addition in some manuscripts made by someone who did not understand the background of the story). The wedding customs of Palestine have not changed greatly over the centuries. The festivities extended over several days, and their solemn conclusion took place when the bridegroom and his friends came in procession to the home of the bride, who was surrounded by her friends, the virgins of the parable; all then went into the wedding feast together. The circumstances of the story lend themselves readily to Jesus' message, and there is little if any allegorizing. The delay of the bridegroom's coming was the most natural thing in the world: among a people not notorious for their punctuality a bachelor is having a last fling with his male friends. The bride is not mentioned because she is irrelevant to the lesson: not the bride, but the virgins in the story represent the Church. They are not rebuked for sleeping—all of them sleep—but for being unprepared to meet the bridegroom on a moment's notice. In real life, of course, the improvident virgins could hardly have bought *oil for their lamps* in the middle of the night, nor, probably, would their more prudent sisters have shrugged off their plea so casually; these are devices to get the foolish virgins out of the way so that it can be made more evident how only the vigilant will enter into the kingdom: *watch, therefore, for you know neither the day nor the hour*. It is pointless to look for symbolism in the sellers of the oil, the oil itself, the number of the virgins, their relative division into wise and foolish, and so on.

Mt 25:14–30   The parable of *the talents* in Matthew has been allegorized, as has its companion piece in Luke (see above on Lk 19:11–28); it is not likely, however, that separate traditions had elaborated these lengthy stories out of any common source that we can now discern in the Gospels, certainly not the brief little comparison of Mk 13:34 which we saw above, though as regards the one basic point of vigilance against the coming of the kingdom it can be called the same parable.

In both Matthew's and Luke's telling of the story the lesson concerns the eschatological kingdom, stressing the need of both vigilance and preparedness. The original polemical direction of the parable against Pharisaism can perhaps be more readily perceived in Luke's version, however. Matthew has more obviously adapted it to the situation of the Christian awaiting the *parousia*: the master returns suddenly and *after a long time,* and he demands accounting from each servant for what has been committed to him *according to his abilities.* Furthermore, the reward awaiting the vigilant and deserving servant is not simply the kingdom itself, conceived as something that he has not previously possessed, but *greater things* of the same order as the *smaller* in which he has proved faithful: this it is to *share your lord's joy.* This teaching we have seen before (above on Lk 12:41–48 and parallel). The monetary terms used in Matthew's and Luke's separate parables are in striking contrast. The talent was a weight, not a coin. A talent of silver would have been roughly the equivalent of sixty *minas.* A talent of gold would have been simply a fabulous sum of money.

In keeping with the perspective which the parable has in Matthew's Gospel, significance is seen in the deprivation of the profitless servant of one talent and the further enrichment of the one of ten talents. The former has not simply lost his chance for what he never had; he is truly deprived of what he did possess. Thus there is a new point to the saying that *everyone who has will receive more and possess in abundance, while he who has nothing will be deprived of even what he has.* At the end the symbolism of the story is dropped, and the punishment of the useless servant is described in terms of the well-used figure of *the outer darkness where they weep and gnash their teeth* (cf. Mt 8:12, 13:42, 50, 22:13, 24:51; Lk 13:28).

Mt 25:31–46   These same ideas are continued in the magnificent passage with which Matthew concludes the eschatological discourse, a passage which fittingly takes the last judgment as its subject yet which is far more concerned with the here-and-now life of the Christian than with the ratifying judgment of the last day. The passage is not precisely a parable, though it contains a small and incidental parable of the sheep and the goats to which the elect and the condemned are compared. It is a parabolic story told by Jesus—its Aramaic origin shows through in more than one place—in which, however, the details of the story are not so much applied or allegorized as they are representational.

Several important lessons are included in this story. First of all, *the Son of Man,* the eschatological judge and savior, is recognized as *the King* and *Lord* because he has ascended *the throne* of *his glory:* the apoca-

lyptic vision of Dan 7:9–14 is simplified in that it now becomes evident
that the Son of Man is identical with Israel's God and Savior (cf.
Is 6:1–5). Early Christian theology used the royal and divine title Lord of
the resurrected Christ in testimony to this faith, for even though the
parousia was not yet, his glory had been proclaimed in the resurrection; the
Gospels have even, at times, applied the title to Jesus in their treatment
of his early life. This understandable development, another aspect of
realized eschatology, is here given a paradoxical twist. We are now called
on to recognize the exalted King and Lord present in the world as Son
of Man still. And he is present not only as Man and in man, but in the
most wretched and miserable of men.

Paul's doctrine of the Church as the Body of Christ has something to
do with this teaching: in part it was dependent on a revelation like this
one (cf. Acts 9:4 f.). However, the teaching is broader than the various
ecclesiological applications to which Paul put it. We are confronted by an
eschatological picture in which *all the nations will be assembled before
the God of all*. It is not only the reprobate, but also the elect, who have
failed to recognize who were *these least of my brethren* in whom
Christ was deserted or, all unknowingly, was served. Jesus is not merely
reiterating the venerable prophetic doctrine that religious people find it
so hard to learn, and so perplexing to them, that God is less impressed by
what they do for him than by what they do for one another (cf. Is
58:3–7). He not only singles out the poor and the wretched as objects of
his special solicitude, he identifies himself with them. Before he had
taught that the total dimension of "neighbor" is "man" (see above on
Lk 10:29–37). Now he teaches that he who serves man serves Christ.

Matthew is writing for the Church. It would not be foreign to his purpose to explore the implications of Jesus' teaching for those who lie outside the Church's pale, but it would be beyond it. The message for the
Church is quite enough to concern us. Christian apocalyptic does not
abandon this world that is passing away and that must be changed. Rather
it serves it, and in serving it serves Christ. The kingdom of God that comes
unexpectedly comes, however, through the prayers and the works of the
saints (cf. Col 1:24; Apo 8:2–6). The Church has, not as an avocation
but as its highest and most essential calling, the duty to serve man in all of
his needs spiritual and physical, and to fight all his ancient enemies—
ignorance, poverty, disease, injustice, bigotry, death of body or soul.
It is this whole man that Jesus became and remains forever. It is the wise
virgin, the profitable servant, who makes the Church's vocation his own.
He who does not deserves no name of Christian, and the Lord has said
that this name will be taken from him at the last.

22. A LAST SUPPER

Lk 21:37–38   Luke offers a summary statement on the Lord's practice while in Jerusalem for the days of the Passover (cf.
Jn 8:1 f.). Actually, the statement refers to the days preceding rather than
those that will follow. Jesus' practice was doubtless dictated by prudence,
to avoid the attentions of his enemies, but also by convenience: on *the
Mount of Olives* he could find solitude and privacy. As this was in the
direction of Bethany, it is not unlikely, too, that he enjoyed the
hospitality of the house of Martha and Mary.

Mk 14:1–2   The Synoptic Gospels now open the story of the passion
Mt 26:1–5   with a date; at least Matthew and Mark do, while Luke
Lk 22:1–2   contents himself with saying that *the feast of Unleavened
Bread called Passover was drawing near*. Matthew's and
Mark's *two days before*, for that matter, is not without its ambiguities, in
view of the Jewish practice of reckoning a new day's beginning from sunset and of counting any part of a day as a full day. Presumably they
mean that this was Wednesday of Holy Week, since for them the Passover meal was eaten by Jesus and his disciples on a Thursday evening after sunset. Matthew first makes his customary transitional ending to the
eschatological discourse (see above on Mt 7:28 f.). In all the preceding
instances this formula introduced a change of place in Jesus' mission. In
this case there can be no question of such a thing, and instead Jesus
speaks of his coming passion and death that are to terminate his mission
(see above on Mk 8:31–33 and parallels).

The Gospels go on to speak of a conspiracy of *the chief priests and
scribes* (for the latter, Matthew substitutes *the elders of the people*)
against the life of Jesus. There is nothing new in this (see above on
Mk 11:18 f. and parallel; Jn 11:45–57), though Matthew now has it for
the first time. It is also he who places the meeting at the house of the
high priest *Caiaphas*. We have no reason to think that for this reason the
conspiracy had any official status, however. It was simply a meeting of
some of Jesus' powerful enemies who were taking up an old item on their
agenda. Fear of the people persuaded them to be cautious. To act against

Jesus during the feast might provoke a riot, and a riot could easily bring in Roman martial law. They planned to defer any overt action till after the Passover, therefore, when the thousands of Galilean and other pilgrims would have left the city. What changed their plans to one of immediate action was the treason of Judas, the next act in the Synoptic drama (interrupted in Mark and Matthew by the story of the anointing at Bethany: see above on Jn 12:1–8 and parallels).

Mk 14:10–11   It was pointed out above (on Jn 12:1–8) that the Gos-
Mt 26:14–16   pels' scanty information on Judas Iscariot allows us no
Lk 22:3–6   adequate basis for an appraisal of his character and
                motivation, or rather, that what little they do say could
easily lead to a superficial and distorted assessment. Judas was, obviously, a source of extreme embarrassment to the early Church, which consequently thought about him and remembered about him only the little that was required by the statistical facts: that he had been a member of the Twelve and that, nevertheless, he had betrayed the Lord. That as one of the Twelve he should have made no particular imprint on Christian tradition is not, in itself, an isolated phenomenon (see above on Mk 3:13–19 and parallels); we know relatively little about most of the Twelve as regards their distinct personalities. In Judas' case there was positive cause to forget him as soon as possible, and when at last it became necessary to set down about him what had been remembered, it is not surprising that that was not very much nor entirely coherent.

Luke states that Judas did what he did because *Satan entered into* him, and with this judgment John agrees (Jn 13:2, 27; cf. Jn 6:70 f.). This is, however, a theological evaluation, not an historical explanation. John (cf. 12:6) has already called him a thief, an assertion which may depend on a creditable tradition yet which sheds little light on the matter at hand: it is doubtful that any of the Synoptic Gospels intend to suggest that the money which Judas received constituted the sole motive of his betrayal. Only Matthew mentions a specified amount, *thirty pieces of silver*, a paltry sum which has a symbolic value for him (cf. Zech 11:12) and to which he will return later. At all events, Judas could hardly have been paid a great deal. If we accept John's information that he was the treasurer for the apostolic band, we would have to conclude that even though their resources were not great he could without doubt have had at his disposal more than these few coins at almost any time during his period of service. Besides, he had already resolved on Jesus' betrayal when he approached the chief priests; the money was an afterthought and incidental, perhaps a matter of some haggling but definitely not a moving cause, for no one had sought Judas out to bribe him.

Perhaps we might reconstruct the succession of events as follows. Judas could easily have heard the *temple police* (Luke) discussing the troublesome reformer who had run afoul of their masters, whose popularity, however, had them baffled as to what action they could take. It was to these that Judas could first have offered his services, guaranteeing to find a way to turn Jesus over to them in secret before the people could know. The temple police would hasten to bring him before *the chief priests*, all too happy at this unexpected opportunity. Judas was given his token payment, and it remained for him to find his chance.

Because of this incident, the Wednesday of Holy Week has been traditionally known as "Spy Wednesday." There are all kinds of spies, it is true. Some serve for money, some for thrills, and some, probably the greater number, out of conviction. Judas' action, here and later, reads like that of a man who has changed sides. It is possible that Mark and Matthew have had some inkling of its meaning by placing his betrayal immediately after the story of the anointing at Bethany, when Jesus had spoken so forcefully about his coming death and burial. To think that Judas had first associated himself with Jesus from an erroneous persuasion of his messianic mission is to assert little more about him than has to be asserted about the Twelve in general (see above on Jn 6:5–15, 16–17a). That Jesus must suffer and die, that his messianic proclamation of the kingdom would, to all appearances, end in an ignominious anticlimax, had been an incomprehensible scandal to the Twelve (see on Mk 8:31–33 and parallels). They refused to accept it, and, as subsequent events will show, their refusal continued through the very events themselves, as Jesus had foretold them. It is conceivable that Judas took Jesus' words more seriously and at their face value than the rest of the Twelve did. As Peter thought on occasion, so did Judas: here was a Master who no longer talked like a Messiah, who was no longer pointing to a triumphant kingdom but to a miserable defeat of every messianic hope. The great difference, of course, is that Peter could believe without understanding or that his faith in Jesus' person could transcend the mystery of Jesus' words, while Judas' faith was not adequate to cover a prospect that boded only ignominy and shame in exchange for the life he had once committed to a great cause. The end of such a course could only be despair, disillusionment, and bitter resentment against one who had fed his hope in vain. Aside from hints and surmises like these, it has not been given to us to penetrate more deeply into the soul of Judas Iscariot.

Mk 14:12–17   Mark's and Matthew's *first day of the Unleavened*
Mt 26:17–20   *Bread*—Luke's *the day* is less precise, but means the
Lk 22:7–14   same thing—indicates the following day in the Synoptic
              chronology. It also seems to indicate that for them this
Thursday was the fourteenth day of the month Nisan, that is, the Preparation day for the Passover, which began with sunset; as the text goes on to show, the Synoptic Gospels quite definitely treat the Last Supper of Jesus

and his disciples as a Passover meal. Though originally the Passover and the Unleavened Bread were separate observances, throughout most of Israelite and Jewish history they were celebrated as one feast, with all the accumulated rites interpreted in relation to the circumstances of Israel's exodus from Egypt under Moses (cf. Ex 12:21–27, 37–42, 43–49, 13:4–10). On the Preparation day all leavened bread was removed from the house, for only unleavened bread was to be eaten during the entire week of the Passover. It was on this day, too, that the lambs were sacrificed which served as the *pièce de résistance* for the Passover meal. In the time of Jesus, with the scribal interpretation of the Torah as a unified and normative body of law, the lamb of the Passover meal was considered to be a sacrifice that could only be immolated in the Jerusalem temple, and for the same reason the Passover could be eaten only in Jerusalem (cf. Deut 16:1–8). In the evening, the slain lamb having been brought home from the temple and the other preparations made, the Passover was celebrated as of old, as a family feast of joy and freedom, on the beginning of the fifteenth of Nisan (the month also called Abib in the Old Testament).

Already we have entered upon one of the most fretted of New Testament questions and what is without doubt the most significant of the chronological discrepancies of the Gospels. Insistent as the Synoptic Gospels are on the Last Supper as a Passover meal, John is no less intent on showing that it was no such thing. All the Gospels agree that there was a Last Supper and that it was celebrated on a Thursday evening; all the Gospels agree that Jesus suffered and died on the following day, a Friday. For John alone, however, that Friday was the Preparation day, and it was not until that evening that the Passover was celebrated, therefore on the Sabbath. For John the Last Supper could not have been a Passover meal, and he does not present it as such.

Both chronologies are theological. While the Synoptics make much of the Last Supper as the origin of the Christian Passover, the Eucharist, John is understandably silent on this aspect of the meal. Instead, he finds it most significant and appropriate that Jesus should have died at the very time that the Passover lamb was being sacrificed. St. Paul in 1 Cor 5:7 seems to follow John in this.

If both are theological, obviously both cannot be equally historical. It is not true, incidentally, though often asserted in this connection, that the tradition of Western Christianity has favored the Synoptic chronology and the tradition of the East the Johannine, as though this followed from their separate disciplines of unleavened and leavened bread in the celebration of the Eucharist. In the oldest Western tradition leavened bread was used indifferently with unleavened, and though unleavened bread later became normative it may have begun as an innovation. Furthermore, though unleavened bread doubtless came to be used because of the supposed circumstances of the Last Supper as described by the Synoptics, there was never any serious attempt in the Church to make the institution of the Eucharist as annually celebrated coincide with the time of the Jewish Passover. Holy Thursday has always been observed as a Christian feast because of its relation to Easter, never as a continuation of the Jewish Passover. Always, that is, apart from some late patristic allegorizing.

All in all, the Johannine chronology has the most to recommend it historically. As we shall see, not only as told by John but also as told by the Synoptics the passion story makes good sense only on the assumption that the Passover feast had not yet begun. John's chronology, for that matter, has never caused any problems at all for the reader of the Gospels, except for the conflict that it creates when juxtaposed with the Synoptic story of a Passover meal. It is probably safe to say that the majority of scholars both past and present have always opted for the Johannine over the Synoptic chronology in this respect, and it is this option that we also shall take, without, obviously, being in any position at this time to do any kind of justice to the weighty arguments that have been and still are being proposed on both sides of the question, which remains a live one in New Testament studies. Accepting John's chronology as historical, we are probably able to assign with fair accuracy the date of Christ's crucifixion, in satisfying harmony with the few other meager indications we have of the time of the ministry of Jesus (see above on Lk 3:1 f.; Jn 2:18–22). The Passover, or fifteenth day of Nisan, coincided with a Sabbath, a Saturday, in the year 30 according to our reckoning, on April 8 to be precise. If this computation is correct, then Jesus who was born sometime after 8 B.C. (see above on Lk 2:1–7) died something in advance of his fortieth year.

What, then, are we to make of the Synoptic accounts which not only characterize the day of the Last Supper as the beginning of Passover, but add that Jesus *sent two of his diciples* (*Peter and John*, according to Luke) *into the city* of Jerusalem to prepare for their eating a Passover meal? There have been various attempts to harmonize their story with John's uncompromising chronology. Could not the Galileans have celebrated the Passover on a day differing from that of the Jerusalemites? Since the counting of the days of the lunar month depended on the observation of the new moon by the naked eye, might there not have been a difference of opinion on when the fifteenth day occurred? Might not a confluence of Sabbath and Passover call for special and variable rules and practices? All these are possibilities—there are few things that are not possible—but there is evidence for none of them, and much reason to deem them all improbable. Could there not have been a calendar dispute among the Jews of the first Christian century, as there is among so many other religions, the Christian included, which resulted in the observance of the same feast on different days? In recent years it has been discovered that there was indeed such a dispute. At least, it seems that the Qumran people followed a more ancient calendar than that in use by the official Jewry of the time, a solar calendar attested by both the Old Testament and by some later Jewish apocryphal literature, which may, as a matter of fact, have had some influence on early Christian practice. The Essenes of Qumran did keep the Passover on a different day from that of the Jerusalem hierarchy. Unfortunately for the hypothesis, however, it was on a day that has nothing to do with the Synoptic story of the Last Supper; as far as we can tell, this sectarian calendar was unknown to the Gospels.

It is extremely unlikely that in the Jerusalem of A.D. 30 any Passover meal could have been eaten except on the day officially recognized for it and without the lamb that had been immolated for it on the one day set aside for this purpose. It is equally unlikely that Jesus himself would have countenanced any such grave departure from the practice of normative Judaism. The Last Supper, therefore, could hardly have been a real Passover meal. It is worthy of note that though the Synoptic Gospels treat it as a Passover meal, they are strangely silent about what would have been its one main component, the Passover lamb, and that when they do speak of another of its important features, the bread, they use the common word *artos* rather than the technical term *azymos*, unleavened bread, which alone was permitted during the Passover season. Of most of the other rites proper to the celebration of the Passover there is also no trace in the Gospels.

What appears to have been true is that during this Passover time Jesus ate a farewell meal with his disciples which under the circumstances had the overtones of a Passover meal and partook of some of its elements. Because of these circumstances it was remembered as a Passover meal and is so treated in the Synoptic Gospels. We must treat it in the same way when studying them, for these elements which were no doubt intentionally present when Jesus instituted the Eucharist enter into their theological portrayal of this all-important event.

Matthew greatly summarizes the story told in more detail by Mark and Luke. The disciples were instructed to follow a man *carrying a water jar* and to ask for the master of the house which he entered. The servant would have been conspicuous: men ordinarily transported water in skins slung over their shoulders and left it to women to carry it in jars balanced on their heads—a graceful sight still quite familiar in the Near East, though gasoline tins have now generally replaced the earthenware jars. The disciples doubtless watched for the servant at the pool of Siloam and by this prearranged sign were led to the house with whose owner Jesus had spoken for the use of his *guest room*. The Passover retained its character as a family meal, even though in the vast concourse of pilgrims celebrating it together in Jerusalem the "families" would be rather temporary, and it was eaten in privacy. The *upper room* which the disciples found prepared might have been hired for the occasion, but it may also have been simply set aside by a pious Jewish householder for the use of some "family" of pilgrims during the Passover season. The upper room of a Palestinian house was not usually connected with the rest of the rooms of the building but was reached by an outside stairway only. The traditional site of the upper room of the Gospels, the Cenacle, can be seen on the map of Jerusalem, in what is now part of the Israeli sector of the city. The tradition is not particularly ancient and respects only the site occupied by the present building, which before the partition of Palestine between Jews and Arabs was a mosque.

Lk 22:15–18   The various accounts of the Last Supper are selective and not always mutually coherent. It is necessary, therefore, to perform a certain amount of suturing and reconstructing. On the assumption that the meal embodied some of the Passover ritual, however, Luke's introduction makes admirable sense. Wine was drunk at four different times during the Passover. At the beginning a blessing was invoked, the *kiddush,* and a cup of wine was then drunk in silence. This is no ordinary Passover meal, of course, and Jesus breaks the silence to determine the meaning of what is being done. *I have greatly desired to eat this Passover with you* and *I shall not eat it . . . till the kingdom of God comes* have been interpreted in many ways. Coupled with Jesus' injunction that the disciples *divide this among yourselves,* it appears that he is explaining his own abstinence from a meal to which he is attaching eschatological significance. As he is about to present the bread and wine of the meal as a memorial of his own body and blood, he himself does not partake of the meal. It is to be noticed that the Gospels speak of Jesus and his disciples as *reclining* at table. Though they sometimes did it at other times as well (see above on Lk 7:36–50), at Passover time the Jews made it a point of honor to dine in the reclining position introduced by the Romans. This was the position of free men, and the Passover was above all a celebration of freedom.

Lk 22:24–30   Though Luke topically connects the institution of the Eucharist with the inaugural cup that he has just described, his own choice of material makes it logical that we consider this following episode next. Jesus' mention of the kingdom could easily have provoked one of those childish disputes of which we have already seen one example above on Mk 9:33–37 and parallels. Or perhaps the question of precedence at table rose among them (see above on Lk 14:7–11). Once more Jesus must patiently remind them of what kind of Master they are disciples and of the scale of values that ought to govern his kingdom. For all practical purposes the words of Jesus that we read here have already been recorded in separate contexts by Matthew and Mark (see above on Mk 10:35-45 and parallel; Mt 19:27-30).

Jn 13:1–17   As is so often the case, John comes forward with a parallel to Luke in distinction to the other Synoptic Gospels. And what a parallel this is! What Luke has by precept, John records in action, an action which completely sums up the dedication of Jesus' life to be the servant of all. Laying aside his outer garments, he wraps a towel about him and proceeds, basin in hand and on his knees, about the outer circle of the reclining disciples, washing their feet one by one. It is well to recall that among the Jews not even a slave (if he was a Jew) could have been legally compelled to perform this act.

John keeps his distance from the Synoptic tradition: this took place *before the feast of the Passover.* Nevertheless, this supper was no less important to him than it was to the Synoptics. Hence his solemn exordium and his insistence that this great symbolic act took place *during a supper. Having loved his own who were in the world, he loved them to the end* doubtless is John's way of characterizing this entire evening: the sign of the foot-washing is merely the prelude to the great discourse that will follow.

We are left to imagine the stolid silence in which Judas, whose presence John has just emphasized, received the Lord's ministrations. Characteristically, it is Peter who finds something to say, recognizing the incongruity which Jesus himself points out in a moment. However, it is precisely this incongruity, this reversal of the roles of master and servant, that is folly to the world and wisdom to the Gospel. What Jesus now exemplifies is his own life, indeed, and also the life of every true Christian, but especially what must be the regimen of his Church: *What I do you do not now know, but later you will understand.* Peter, who definitely does not yet understand, responds naïvely in the pattern of the Johannine dialogues. First he will have nothing to do with his unseemly washing, then, when it is forcibly presented to him as the Lord's mysterious will, he would literally bathe in it!

Unless I wash you, you have no part with me obviously regards the Christian duty to share in the sacrificial life of Christ: the *command* of verse 15. It is from this command, *mandatum* in the Latin liturgy, that the name Maundy Thursday was derived. John with his habitual liking for multiple senses, may very well have intended Jesus' words to signify also the necessity of Christian baptism. Jesus' other response to Peter is more difficult to interpret, apart from its evident surface meaning. The text itself is not certain, but probably it should read: *he who has bathed needs only to wash his feet, then he is clean all over.* The disciples were not dirty; one of the virtues of rabbinical Judaism was the personal cleanliness on which it insisted. Before reclining at table they had thoroughly washed their face and hands from the dust of the street. But undoubtedly there is a spiritual and Christian depth to this state as there is to the former. Over and above baptism ("he who has bathed": various forms of this verb are used elsewhere in the New Testament to designate baptism, cf. 1 Cor 6:11; Eph 5:26; Tit 3:5; Heb 10:22), something else is required of the Christian if he is to be perfect. He must also have entered into the Lord's "washing" effectively, in work and performance, as well as having given assent to its high ideals. That "clean" does, indeed, have a spiritual meaning in this context, is shown by Jesus' contrast of Judas with the rest of the disciples.

Jn 13:18–30   That Jesus denounced the traitor on this occasion is the
Mk 14:18–21   testimony of all four Gospels. Mark and John have him
Mt 26:21–25   quote Ps 41:10, to the same effect of the statements
Lk 22:21–23   ascribed to him by Matthew and Luke: one of the
                Twelve, one of his familiar friends now sitting at table
with him in this family gathering, will betray him. The Gospels do not bother to explain the source of Jesus' knowledge; they simply take it for granted that he could and did know.

The action which involved *dipping into the dish* which now follows in Matthew and Mark on the one hand and in John on the other looks to be two variant recollections of the same event. In the Synoptics the action merely serves as a dramatic reinforcement of Jesus' assertion that one of his table-fellows will betray him. Doubtless even as he spoke several hands were in the common bowl together, and certainly all had been or soon would be there. On the assumption that this meal was following the Passover order, the dish may have been that of the *haroseth*, a sauce compounded of crushed fruits, spices, and vinegar whose color and consistency were supposed to make it a reminder of the clay from which the Israelites had moulded bricks during their slavery in Egypt (cf. Ex 1:13 f.). Into this bitter herbs were dipped and eaten as an hors d'oeuvre preliminary to the main Passover meal. Even in Matthew's Gospel where the traitor is at least identified to himself the result is ambiguous. To Judas' protestation, *Surely, rabbi, it is not I?*, Jesus' answer is, *As you say*. Did Matthew consider Judas' question to be one of sheer hypocrisy, or an indication that he was still wrestling with himself over his desertion?

In John's Gospel the situation is rather different. Judas is designated as the traitor, but only to *the disciple whom Jesus loved*, whom we generally assume to have been John the son of Zebedee, by the familiar gesture of a host's offering one of his guests a dipped morsel of food. The Gospel presupposes Jesus and the disciples reclining at the three sides of the low table or in a semicircle about it, with the beloved disciple on Jesus' right, almost literally *in his bosom* (in view of Jn 1:18, this expression is un-

doubtedly significant). In turn Peter would have been on John's right
and Judas, presumably, on Jesus' left. In the mind of the evangelist it was
at this moment that Judas made his irrevocable decision, spurning Jesus'
final gesture of love and grace.

John alone tells us that Judas left the Last Supper. *What you have to
do, do quickly* are important words for the evangelist, who wants to show
Jesus always in control of the situation during this hour of his glorification:
not even Judas can act against him till he has received "permission."
The interpretation put on Judas' departure by the rest of the disciples
indicates both their ignorance of the identity of the traitor and the assumption of the Gospel that the Passover feast had not yet begun, since
during such a time all the shops would have been tightly closed. *It was
night,* adds John: the time of darkness has come at last (cf. Jn 9:4).

Mk 14:22–25   We come now to what for the Synoptic Gospels is the
Mt 26:26–29   supreme moment of the Last Supper and has constituted
Lk 22:19–20   it forever the Christian Passover. The Passover ritual
                itself, to whatever extent it was really followed that
evening, has long been forgotten in view of larger realities; within the
format of a Passover meal, the institution of the Eucharist would in all
likelihood have coincided with the drinking of the third ritual cup, after
the meal proper had been concluded (cf. Luke's *after supper* introducing the consecration of the cup): this would not conflict with the
while they were eating of Matthew and Mark, since in the large sense the
meal continued until the final blessing and drinking of the fourth ritual
cup of wine.

Anyone who reads the Gospels attentively will see immediately that the
Synoptic tradition has preserved two distinct Eucharistic formulations
which agree substantively but also differ in some important details. For
all practical purposes, Matthew and Mark present one and the same text,
from which Luke diverges. He diverges even more if we accept the so-
called shorter Lucan formulation that appears in some manuscripts (the
omission of vss. 19b–20), which is held by many modern scholars to
represent the original text of Luke. But while it is true that the tendency
of scribes was to expand their text rather than to contract it, and that
therefore longer texts are rightly held suspect when there is a shorter
variant in the manuscripts, in this instance the shorter text is best explained
as the result of deliberate omission on the part of someone who misunderstood the function of the first, non-Eucharistic cup in Luke's story and
who took this means of harmonizing it with the other Gospels. Luke's
formulation is in substantial agreement with that of 1 Cor 11:12–25, the
fourth traditional account of the institution of the Eucharist given us
by the New Testament.

At the outset we should recognize that all the formulations, the Marcan-

Matthaean on one side and the Pauline-Lucan on the other, have without doubt been conditioned by liturgical usage, which varied somewhat
from local church to local church, just as in some respects it still does
today. Even Matthew, who has reproduced what Mark has almost
verbatim, seems to have done so not because he was copying Mark but
because he was in possession of his own Eucharistic narrative that was
very nearly the same as Mark's. Luke follows Paul closely, but not precisely.
Paul explicitly states that he was following ecclesiastical tradition, and the
same affirmation is implicit in everything that we know about the Gospels
and their formation.

Secondly, we must recognize that these formulations without exception
are those of Gentile churches. One import of this factor we have already
observed when treating of the Eucharistic doctrine of John (see above on
Jn 6:51b–59). John, who reproduces no Eucharistic formulation of his
own, nevertheless quotes the Lord as speaking of his *flesh* rather than
his *body*. It is altogether likely, in fact, that "flesh" is the word Jesus himself used to designate his Eucharistic presence under the sign of bread.
Neither Hebrew nor Aramaic—in one of which Jesus must have spoken—
possessed an acceptable word for what we understand by "body," for the
simple reason that the Semites did not distinguish the body from the
self. "Flesh" is about the only word that Jesus could have used. But
"flesh," as we know, also possessed some undesirable connotations, more
so for the Greek, but even for the Semite as well: it is this fact, we saw,
that made Jn 1:14 such an astounding utterance. It is not surprising,
therefore, that the Gentile churches soon took advantage of the greater
flexibility of the Greek language to substitute the more neutral term
"body" for the earlier "flesh" of the Eucharistic formulations.

These twin considerations regarding the transmission of our Eucharistic
narratives probably prove somewhat pointless a good deal of the discussion
that has gone on in the past concerning the "very words" used by Jesus
in the institution of the Eucharist as recoverable from the Gospels.
Here perhaps more than anywhere else in the Gospels the teaching of
Jesus comes to us refracted through the language of apostolic Christianity.
Whether such and such a specific expression can or cannot be "retrans-
lated" into Aramaic neither proves nor disproves that Jesus did or did not
say it or something substantively like it. It only indicates, as the variant
traditions themselves already indicate, how the Church of the Gospels
found meaningful ways of transmitting what it knew and testified to in
the Spirit that Jesus had taught. It is very doubtful that any scholar will
ever be able to reconstruct to the satisfaction of any other scholar the
ipsissima verba of Jesus at the Last Supper. The only test that we can
apply is what the words of the Gospels say. By that test we hear only
Jesus speaking in all of the Eucharistic formulations, in all of their
variations. This we must now try to show by examining them.

It is sometimes wondered why John, with his known sacramental interests, should have done nothing with the story of the institution of the Eucharist. We are by now familiar enough with his Gospel, however, to realize that it is not his way with the sacraments to have done what the Synoptics did. His sacramental doctrine, while pervasive, is communicated by indirection. Or rather, the direction it takes is to focus our attention on their here-and-now ecclesial significance and power instead of on their historical origins, on their realization of history instead of their evocation of it. There is also a special consideration in respect to the Eucharist. For John—and not, it seems, for the Synoptic tradition, for all its insistence on the Last Supper as a Passover meal—the sacrifice of the Passover lamb was a type of Jesus, who was put to death at the moment the lamb was being immolated. To describe the origin of the Christian Passover, the sacrament of Christ's death and resurrection, anterior to the Passover sacrifice might not have been impossible, but it would have been artistically awkward.

The first basic agreement of the Eucharistic narratives is that Jesus *took bread*—whether it was the unleavened bread of the Passover or leavened bread is immaterial—*and broke it* (so also in the Synoptic stories of the miracle of the loaves: cf. Mk 6:41 and parallels; Mk 8:6 and parallel; while John together with the Synoptics uses the Eucharistic word *klasmata*: see above on Mk 6:34–44 and parallels); this bread he then identified with himself: *this is my body*. With the cup of wine he did the same, identifying it with his blood. These elements, in other words, are the signs of his being and presence: "flesh and blood" are the sum and substance of the human person (cf. Mt 16:17; Gal 1:16, etc.).

But Jesus is not merely present in the bread and wine, he is present in a very special way. The body, says Luke, *is given for you* (Paul says simply, "is for you"). This may also be translated "will be given for you," but the difference is not too important. Jesus will die on the morrow, thus completing his atoning sacrifice for the sins of man, but his death will be only the termination of an entire life that has been and is now consecrated as this sacrifice (cf. Phil 2:7 f.). All the Gospels say of his blood that it *is* (or "will be") *poured out for you*: Matthew and Mark substitute here *for many* (Is 53:10 f.: see above on Mk 10:35–45 and parallel). Matthew adds, perhaps unnecessarily, *for the forgiveness of sins*: this was the traditional function of the spilling of blood (cf. Lev 17:11; Heb 9:22). Thus we find the first significance of this new Christian Passover. The Passover of the Jews commemorated the saving act by which God freed his people from the bondage of Egypt. The Christian Passover commemorates and signifies the sacrificial and saving act by which the Servant of the Lord has freed man from the bondage of sin. The broken bread and separated cup of wine, therefore, not improbably portray the broken body and shed blood of Christ's death (cf. 1 Cor 11:26). "Broken

body" and "shed blood" remain, of course, within the order of conventional terms for death: technically, crucifixion was a bloodless form of
execution, and according to John, Jesus' body was not broken (cf. Jn
20:36).

Jesus further specifies that his blood—his death—is the inaugural rite
of a new covenant between God and man. In Mark and Matthew we
read *this is my blood of the covenant*, which may be a Semitism for "this
is the blood of my covenant"; Paul and Luke have *this cup is the new
covenant in my blood.* The allusion here is to Ex 24:8 (cf. Zech 9:11),
the story of the ratification of the covenant of Sinai by Moses, who
sprinkled the people and the altar of God with the blood of bulls to
signify the blood-bond established by Yahweh's saving act and Israel's
acceptance of his law (cf. Heb 9:18–22). Just as the Jewish Passover
rejoiced in a covenant enacted in blood, so the Christian Passover is the
joyful covenant meal (cf. Ex 24:9–11) of a new covenant (cf. Jer 31:
31–34), again enacted in blood, this time the blood of the atoning
Servant of God (cf. Is 53:11 f.). Under this aspect of covenant meal
the Eucharist is sacrificial not in virtue of the Old Testament type—for
the blood of the bulls was not sacrificial—but in virtue of the sacrifice of
Christ which it represents.

The aspect of covenant meal, however, makes already implicit in all the
Gospel accounts the rubric stated explicitly only by Luke and Paul: the
command to repeat it *in my memory*. This "memory" (*anamnēsis*) is an
active word; the Eucharist does not merely call to mind, commemorate, the
saving act of Christ, it also re-presents it, makes it present in the sacrament
of his body and blood. It thus continues for the Christian the meaning
that the Passover has for the Jew when he recites at its beginning: "We
celebrate tonight because *we* were Pharaoh's bondmen in Egypt, and
the Lord our God delivered *us* with a mighty hand." By the same token
it is eschatological, a present sign of a future reality: what God has done
is the best guarantee of what he will do. Matthew and Mark bring in at
the end the same eschatological saying which Luke has attached to the
drinking of the first Passover cup. As St. Thomas said of all the sacraments,
the Eucharist "is a remembrance of what once took place, its manifestation
in the present, and a forecast of what is to come."

23. THE TRUE VINE AND ITS BRANCHES

Jn 13:31–35   With Judas now removed from the scene, John begins his own great contribution to the Last Supper story, the last discourse of Jesus which verbalizes so much of what the Synoptics have implied in their descriptions of the institution of the Eucharist. Here even more than elsewhere in the Fourth Gospel it is the *glorified* Christ who speaks to his chosen disciples, who are at one and the same time every Christian and the appointed leadership of the Church. These he now calls *little children*, a term found only here in the Gospel but which is characteristic of the First Epistle of John. The glorification of the Son of Man which is also the glory of God (cf. Jn 12:28, 14:13) comes *immediately*: for John the culmination of Christ's glory (see above on Jn 1:14) is his passion-death-resurrection, the basis of the realized eschatology which is the stress of his Gospel.

As I told the Jews. It is a technique of this discourse that in it statements from the earlier polemical discourses (here from Jn 7:33 f., 8:21) are taken up either to be reversed or employed in another sense. The disciples cannot follow Jesus as yet, for he refers now to himself as the principle and author of the Christian life, who must first return to the Father and prepare a place for them (Jn 14:2). How they will then "follow" him (cf. Jn 14:3), he immediately adds: *a new commandment I give you.* Love of neighbor is not unique to Christianity, nor does John suggest that it is. What is new is the dimension of both love and of the concept of neighbor as revealed in Jesus Christ (see above on Mk 12: 28–34 and parallel; Lk 10:29–37): *as I have loved you, you must love one another.* The love of Jesus, which is supreme (cf. Jn 15:13), is both the model and the principle of Christian love, and because of this it is a sign of the abiding presence of Christ, the witness of the pilgrim Church to what God has done. It is rightly called a new commandment in virtue of this character it confers on the Church.

Jn 13:36–38   Luke follows John in putting in this context of the Last
Lk 22:31–34   Supper Jesus' prediction that Peter will deny him be-

Mk 14:26–31   fore the night is out. The same episode occurs next
Mt 26:30–35   also in the Gospels of Mark and Matthew, but for these
                 evangelists only *after* Jesus and his disciples *had sung
a hymn* and *returned to the Mount of Olives.* The first two Gospels have
now done with the Last Supper; the "hymn" to which they refer, in
keeping with their perspective of the supper as a Passover meal, would
have been the second part of the *Hallel,* that is to say Psalms 115 through
118, which was sung after the fourth and last ritual cup of wine concluding the Passover. Luke and John still have more to tell about the
supper, and John a great deal more.

In John the occasion is one of those typical misunderstandings that
haunt the Johannine dialogues. Peter has heard Jesus say that he is going
away. Where can he possibly be going that his faithful disciples cannot
follow, as they ought? The misunderstanding is not complete: in some
vague way Peter realizes that the subject of death is in the air. *I will lay
down my life for you!* Jesus does not deny the possibility (Peter's
vehement assertion may be one of John's unconscious prophecies), but
sadly foretells his threefold denial before *a cock crows.* The third watch
of the night, the period from midnight till about three A.M., was
known as "cockcrow."

In Luke it is Jesus who takes the initiative, in one of those passages by
which all the Gospels consistently testify to Peter's priority among the
disciples. *Satan has petitioned* (and obtained permission) *to sift you,*
the plural: all the disciples, *like wheat,* Jesus tells Peter. It is God's will
that they will soon undergo a severe test of faith. But to counter Satan's
influence Jesus has *prayed* (successfully) that Peter's *faith may not fail;*
so that, once Peter has *turned back* from a deviation he is about to take,
he will again be a source of strength for his fellow disciples. The prediction recognizes Peter's pre-eminence, but it also speaks of his defection.
Thereupon Peter protests his loyalty and is told what is to happen, substantially as we read it in John.

In Matthew and Mark more is made of the coming general desertion
of Jesus by the disciples, seen as an illustration of Zech 13:7, and coupled
with this prediction is another of the post-resurrection reunion of Master
and disciples in Galilee, an important element in Matthew's Gospel (it
is possible that in Mark this part of Jesus' saying is an interpolation from
Matthew). All the disciples are offended at Jesus' lack of confidence in
them, Peter most of all. According to Mark Jesus looks for Peter's denial
before a cock crows twice. This would have designated the end of "cockcrow," or around three o'clock in the morning, and probably the other
Gospels have the same time in mind.

Lk 22:35–38   Luke continues with another saying of the Lord which he
                 doubtless sees in relation to the foregoing. The "sifting"

that the disciples are soon to undergo is one aspect of the greatly changed conditions to which they must reconcile themselves in the time that lies ahead if they will remain faithful to their calling. In former days, Jesus reminds them—though in words which Luke previously attached to the mission of the seventy(-two) disciples rather than of the Twelve (see above on Lk 10:1–12)—things had been relatively easy for them. When he had sent them forth they had taken nothing with them, relying on a hospitable reception in which they had not been disappointed. Jesus was in favor and they had shared in his popularity. Now they will again have to share the lot of their Master, and a vastly different one it will be. He is to be condemned as a common criminal, fulfilling once more the role of the Servant of the Lord (Is 53:12). They will be taken for nothing better. Henceforth they must shift for themselves as best they can, and fear for their lives in the bargain.

The disciple is advised to *sell his cloak and buy a sword*. Jesus employs a parable derived from the holy war, an institution that had once been deadly serious in Old Testament times and which remained something more than figurative for the Jewish zealots and the sectaries of Qumran, but which in the New Testament is a metaphor (cf. Mt 10:34 and parallel; Rom 13:12; 2 Cor 6:7; Eph 6:11–17). The Christian mission, he says, will be a battle in which not clothing or like possessions but survival itself will be at stake, and for this the disciple must prepare himself. The saying, therefore, has no relevance pro or con to the question of defensive warfare against persecution. Jesus' teaching on this matter has been expressed elsewhere (see above on Mt 5:38–42 and parallel). It is probably also implicit here in his reply to the disciples who triumphantly produce two real swords: *It is enough!* The disciples had reacted to his words without understanding as they so often do in the dialogues of John's Gospel, and Jesus' answer is appropriately ironical. The lesson will be completed when they see to what extent he permits the use of the sword in his own defense (cf. Lk 22:51 and parallels). The disciples' swords were doubtless not military weapons but long knives which served other utilitarian purposes than defense in the troubled Palestine of those days.

Jn 14:1–14   John now resumes the Lord's discourse, taking up from the point where Jesus had referred to an imminent departure. This must not sadden the disciples, he now adds, and immediately gives the reason. *As you believe in God, so you believe in me*: the Son and the Father are a common divine and personal principle of salvation (cf. Jn 10:30). It is this Christian faith in Jesus as divine Savior that explains what is entailed in his going away. He goes *to prepare a place* for them in the *Father's house*. There are *many rooms* in this house, therefore they must not fear that no place can be found for them—if such had been the case, he would have warned them of it. When he has prepared the place for them, he will *return* and take them along with him, so that *where I am you will also be*. Thus unlike that of the Jews (cf. Jn 13:33), their inability to follow him is only temporary.

All of this is said in the traditional language of Jewish and Christian eschatology. In John's realized eschatology, however, the language takes on new meaning. The inadequacy of human speech to convey divine realities is likewise clearly brought out. Jesus' "return" and their "joining" him are only two ways of saying the same thing; if they will be where he is, he could with equal ease tell them that he will be where they are, since the "places" in the Father's "house" are the Christians who together make up the resurrected body of Christ, the true house of God (cf. Jn 2:20f.). St. Augustine correctly perceived John's meaning when he commented that Jesus' going was not so much to prepare places as to prepare those who were to occupy the places. Hence the further significance of Christian faith. Faith in the glorified Christ not only identifies the objects of Christian hope as future realities, it is also the way whereby they become present here and now. In this sense, *the way to where I am going is known to you*.

The questions of *Thomas* and *Philip* afford the opportunity, as usual, for Jesus to explain his meaning more thoroughly. Whoever in faith knows and sees Jesus, whoever experiences the life of grace and is witness to Christ living and acting in his Church, has already achieved the heavenly goal, which is to know and to see God: *henceforth you know him and have seen him*. This is true because of the oneness of the Son with the Father, so that in Christ one finds *the way and the truth and the life*. The best commentary on these verses is John's own rhapsody on Christ as the Word of God which we treated in our Chapter 2.

Faith, then, is the key to all Jesus is now saying. And just as faith in the historical Jesus as God's Son rested upon his words and his works— which testified to him because they were really God's words and works (cf. Jn 7:16, 8:28)—in the same way faith in the Christ of the Church rests on the works of the Christian faithful which are really Christ's. Jesus speaks of them as *greater works*: his own historical ministry was sharply circumscribed by the circumstances of time and place, but in the Church his word will also gather in the sheep once lost to Israel (cf. Jn 4:35–38) and be heard throughout the entire Gentile world (cf. Jn 10:16f., 11:52, 12:20f.). They remain, of course, his works, since it is he who works in his Church: *whatever you ask in my name I will do*. This is not a blanket guarantee of infallible efficiency to every prayer of every Christian; "in my name" firmly grounds the promise in the condition of a communion of faith which leaves the initiative with Christ (cf. Jn 1:12). That the things of which he has spoken are possible, Jesus repeats, is due to his death and resurrection: *because I go to the Father*.

Jn 14:15–26   From the relation of the Son to the Father and the
faith by which the Christian also enters into the relationship, Jesus now passes to the Spirit and to the love which is the working
of the Spirit. Love itself, he has already said (Jn 13:34 f.), is the great
commandment by which the living presence of Christ is experienced by
the Christian and made known to the world. Let no one be deceived,
however, by what merely calls itself love and is not. True love shows itself
in its works: *if you love me, you will keep my commandments.* Where
this true love is present, there is the Spirit of God: *I will ask the Father,
and he will give you another Paraclete.* The meaning of "Paraclete" we
shall see better below; the Spirit is called "another" Paraclete because
the Son himself has been the first (cf. 1 Jn 2:1). It is through the Spirit,
Jesus goes on to say, that *I am coming back to you.* The presence of
Christ will be invisible to the world, visible to the eyes of faith which will
see him in the working of the Spirit. Just as the Son was sent into the
world by the Father to reveal God's saving presence, so the Spirit will be
sent to continue this revelation. In the possession of the Spirit will the
Christian recognize that a trinity of personality in the Godhead is not
simply an abstraction devised for the contemplation of the theologian,
but the effulgence of a divine love in which he has been caught up and
of which he is now a part: *in that day you will know that I am in my
Father, and you in me, and I in you.*

A further question, this time by *Judas* the son of James (see above on
Mk 3:13–19 and parallels) mentioned now for the first time by John, leads
to a restatement of the work of the Paraclete, *the Holy Spirit,* in
realized eschatology. In addition, mention is now made of his role in
completing the Christian revelation by enlightening the Church in its
understanding of Christ's teaching. The discourse which we are now reading in John's Gospel is, of course, one of the prime examples of the results
of the Spirit's activity which has moulded the tradition on which the
Gospel depends.

Jn 14:27–31   Jesus concludes the discourse with the classic Jewish
word both of farewell and of greeting (cf. Jn 20:19),
Peace. The basic concept of "peace" (*shalom*), in the Semitic sense, is
that of harmony, completeness, integration. Peace was the effect produced by covenant, thus the blessing bestowed by the God of election
(cf. Num 6:26), and thus, in an eschatological and messianic dimension,
virtually the equivalent of "salvation" (cf. Is 9:6). Eph 2:14 speaks of
the Christ in whom Jew and Gentile have been made one as "our
peace." Here it sums up the entire dispensation of saving divine love
which produces the new society of the Church, the final acts of which are
about to be played through in Jesus' passion, death, and resurrection, the
occasion of this leave-taking. *The Father is greater than I* is in the category
of similar soteriological statements we have encountered in John's Gospel

(see above on Jn 5:16–30): in the economy of salvation the Son is in the world to do the will of the Father.

The final words of this little section doubtless indicate that at one time it was the conclusion of the Last Supper discourse: bringing his remarks to a close, Jesus announces the imminent overthrow of *the ruler of the world* in the events of his glorification, and summons the disciples to depart with him from the banquet room. As John originally designed his Gospel, therefore, it is highly likely that what now appears as chapters 15–17 did not form a part of it. These chapters are, however, every bit as much the work of the evangelist as the rest of the Gospel; they are not additions to the Gospel but rather supplementary and parallel versions of Jesus' teaching brought in by the evangelist when composing the definitive edition of his work. Some of the parallels, though in part repetitious of much that has gone before, are precious in their own right, and the Gospel would be the poorer without them.

Jn 15:1–17   Precious indeed is the allegory of *the true vine and its branches* with which Jesus begins his discourse afresh. As has taken place in other instances—involving the shepherd and his sheep, for example, or the growth of a seed of life—here an Old Testament figure for the people of God (cf. Is 5:1–7; Jer 2:21; Ezek 15; Ps 80:9–16), which in the Synoptic Gospels Jesus takes up in one or another of his parables of the kingdom (cf. Mk 12:1–12 and parallels, for example), appears in a Johannine discourse simply identified with Jesus by one of his magisterial "I am's." Jesus *is* the eschatological Israel. On the sense in which he is the "true" vine, see above on Jn 1:9–13. The allegory, which is pellucid, strikingly illustrates the community of life shared by Christ and the Christian as well as the dynamic quality which is the character of this life: it must *produce much fruit.*

The comparison occasionally breaks down, of course. There is no exact correspondence between the pruning work of a *vine-dresser* and the fruit which the Father produces by tending the vine which is Christ and his Church. Neither would the injunction to *remain in me* apply to the prime analogue: unlike the branches of a vine which have no choice but to remain where they are, the followers of Christ must make their participation in his life the object of a deliberate commitment. As Jesus has been the instrument through whom God has reconciled the world of man to himself, his historical continuity in the Church remains the locale of the divine activity working in man. Remaining in Jesus the vine means adherence to his *words* by which his disciples are *clean,* well-tended branches capable of bearing fruit (cf. Jn 13:10): Jesus' words are all that has both taught and done as the prophetic Word of God, revealing the Father (cf. Jn 5:24).

Once again the theme of Christian life as an overflowing and com-

munication of God's love is introduced: the parallel with the discourses
in Jn 13–14 is close. Love has constituted the union of Christ and
Christian, and by love the union will be maintained. This love, as previously said, is proved by the keeping of Christ's commandments, even
as by fulfilling the will of his Father he proved his own love. By keeping
his commandments the disciples will not only show their love for Christ,
they will continue to be loved in turn by him, and thus their union will be
maintained.

This irrefutable conviction of God's love ought to be the source of a
great *joy* which should pervade all of Christian life. Even if this life be
one of privation and suffering, as Christ's was, there should be joy, for in
the revelation of the divine love in Christ suffering and sacrifice have
been given meaning. Jesus' command that the disciples *love one another
as I have loved you* takes on its fullness now that he refers to his death:
to lay down one's life for one's friends is the ultimate extension of love.
Once more the newness of his commandment of love is brought out (cf.
Jn 13:31–35). Only the Son of God could make such a demand which is
dictated by no natural law of life and which no other religious teacher
would dare assert on his own authority. It is such a concept of the duty
of the love of neighbor that is part of the folly of the Gospel (1 Cor
1:23)—a folly, we must add in all honesty, of which very few Christians
are prepared to be found guilty. Folly and paradox though it be (see
above on Jn 12:20–36), it is a law of life and death revealed in the Christ-
event and thereby constituted the law of Christianity (cf. 1 Jn 3:16).
Though by this-worldly standards it is a self-defeating principle, in fact
it has proved to be the source of all life. To accept it as such, to live by
its norm, requires great faith; but any faith that falls short of it is of
necessity something less than Christian.

Whoever can share in this love revealed in Christ is ennobled by it.
If God has loved us so much, if his love truly abides in us, then we
must be worthy of such attention, we must have been elevated by it
beyond our merely creaturely condition. He has *chosen* us. No longer is
the title *servant* applicable, honorable though it may be (cf. Jn 12:26,
13:16). We are now *friends*. Friendship with God is the result of God's
love, and the love of friendship is mutual, a love that is exchanged. We
enter into the intimate life of God and share it. We are introduced into
familiarity with him. No longer servants whose duty it is to obey simply
because it has been commanded, we return God's love in obedience to
his will because it is the desire of a friend. To *remain* in Christ's love
can thus be seen not only as the greatest but also, in a way, as the
only commandment. Jesus tells us what should be and what can be,
not necessarily what will be. To the extent that what can and should
be does become reality for any of us, to that extent we have remained in
his love, and to that extent only.

Jn 15:18–16:4a   As he does in the Synoptic Gospels (see above on Mt
10:16b–25 and parallel; Mk 13:9–13 and parallels),
Jesus now warns his disciples of the world's hatred and of coming persecutions. In John's context this warning appears as a further dimension of the way in which the Christian is assimilated to Christ in the life which God has been pleased to share with him. The Church's endurance of persecution and its rejection by the world, foreshadowed in Old Testament types (*they have hated me without cause*: Ps 69:5), are a continuation of the experience of Jesus; they are additional ways in which his prophetic *witness* to God's truth is lived out. This doctrine was also St. Paul's (cf. Rom 8:17, etc.). All the Gospels, and Paul too, for that matter, speak of hostility and persecution exclusively in Jewish terms. In the formative days of the Church that produced and shaped the Gospel materials the pressures brought against Christians—who, for all practical purposes remained identified as a Jewish sect even when, as speedily happened, Gentiles began to join them in great numbers—were measures taken by their fellow (but non-Christian) Jews. It is for this reason that we have such a prevalence of Jewish conflict stories in the Gospels (see page 19 f.), that in John's Gospel "the Jews" so often means nothing more or less than "the world," and even that the Gospels can at times exchange the terms "Pharisee," "Sadducee," "scribe," and the like, without too much bother about statistical accuracy. Historically, the first opposition to Christianity had come from the Jews. Later—but too late for most of the New Testament—it would come from the far greater world of the Roman empire, a world of much vaster resources of ruthlessness and the will to make use of them, as the second half of the Apocalypse of John bears witness.

Jn 16:4b–22   The discourse continues with what becomes ever more
obviously a reprise of the discourse of Jn 13:31–14:31.
While in Jn 13:36 and 14:5, however, the disciples did ask Jesus, *Where are you going*, here he reproaches them for not asking the question. Actually, these are two variant dialogistic devices to bring out the same teaching. The disciples have not yet asked the question rightly, namely by showing an awareness of the real meaning of Jesus' "going away" in terms of the history of salvation, the realization of the last times in the Church. This he now proceeds to explain once more, practically as we have seen it above. This time, however, much more is said in detail of the role of the Holy Spirit as *Paraclete*.

Both the Greek word *paraklētos* and its companion term *katēgoros* were available as loan words in the Palestinian Aramaic of Jesus' day. Borrowed from the language of the courts, they referred to what we would designate respectively as "defense counsel" and "prosecutor." In the jurisprudence of the Mosaic law, however, these functions were both assumed

by a single person, the "witness." The witness who testified against someone did so primarily as a witness *for* that which the accused was alleged
to have violated; there was no such thing as a disinterested witness. In
a capital case a witness for the prosecution quite literally testified to the
truth with his life, since if his testimony were proved false by the acquittal
of the accused it was he and not the defendant who would undergo
death. Thus it is that while the Holy Spirit is called *paraklētos* and never
katēgoros—the latter term was the equivalent of the native Hebrew and
Aramaic *sātān*, "accuser," and is so used in Apo 12:10—we should not be
surprised when we find that his function is seen to be as much prosecutor
of the world as it is defender of the Church.

The term is juridical, but the juridical background is not much stressed.
Rather, in the Fourth Gospel the concept of the Spirit as Paraclete continues and completes a pattern of *prophetic* witness which is one of its
stresses. This witness to truth, light, and life, against falsehood, darkness,
and death, the perennial witness of the prophetic word (cf. Jn 1:1–4),
has been the testimony of prophets like Abraham (Jn 8:56), Moses
(Jn 5:46 f.), Isaiah (Jn 12:38–41), and John the Baptist (Jn 1:19 ff.).
It reached its apex in the incarnation of the prophetic Word, in Jesus
Christ. But now Christ, about to withdraw his visible presence from the
world, leaves behind the prophetic Spirit of God to continue the testimony, the Spirit of prophecy itself now "incarnate" in his Church.

For it is in this "incarnational" state, as the "soul" of a Church of
living men, that the Holy Spirit *will convict the world of sin, and of
justice, and of judgment*—a conviction that is simultaneously a vindication of Christ, a witness to him. Of sin, first. Who was guilty of sin,
Christ who was put to death or the world which condemned him? The
lives of Christians, living by the power of the Spirit of God, must be
such as to demonstrate that nothing of Christ can have any part in sin;
their belief, then, must be the proof that it is with unbelief that sin lies:
because they do not believe in me. Next, of justice. Who was just, Christ
or the world? The just lives of Christians must show that it was and is
Christ who lives in them invisibly present in his Spirit: *because I go to the
Father and you see me no longer.* Finally, of judgment. Who has been
truly judged and condemned in the crisis in which Jesus was engaged
with the world? The lives of Christians, once more, must show that not
Christ but *the ruler of this world has been judged.* The work of the
Paraclete, therefore, is to inspire the Church as a body of prophetic witness which, in the words of the Fathers of the Second Vatican Council,
"shares in Christ's prophetic office by spreading abroad a living witness
to him by lives of faith and love, and by offering God the sacrifice of
praise, the fruit of lips that confess his name." The witness of the Spirit
and the witness of the Church is one and the same: "Those who bear

witness to Jesus have the spirit of the prophets" (Apo 19:10). From which it also becomes plain that realized eschatology as we find it in John's Gospel is not simply the Church's re-evaluation of the realities of its hope, but is at the same time its most profound recognition of its call to holiness, a call which has been heard by everyone who has believed.

Jesus also refers to the Paraclete as *the Spirit of truth* (cf. Jn 14:17, 15:26) *who will lead you into all truth*, bringing to completion, as a witness to Jesus, the witness which Jesus himself has given to the Father. The sense of this form of the Spirit's testimony we have already noted in Jn 14:15–26 above. It, and all other aspects of the life of the Church (cf. Jn 14:13), *glorifies* Jesus even as Jesus glorified and was glorified by the Father, as evidence of the saving divine presence still active in the world.

The disciples now do engage in a discussion like that of the questions of Jn 13:36 and 14:5, over the *little while* of which Jesus speaks, the parallel to which we have seen in Jn 14:18 f. above. Jesus' illustration of the woman in labor, apt in itself, may also be an allusion to the Jewish concept of "the birthpangs of the Messiah" (see above on Mk 13:3–8 and parallels). In this connection, the temporary sorrows of the disciples will herald the messianic age as realized in Christ's resurrection and glorification.

Jn 16:23–33   Jesus concludes with a final series of effects that are to be attributed to the work of the Paraclete. First of all, he tells the disciples, *in that day you will ask me about nothing*. The meaning of this is picked up by his comparison of their present understanding of his teachings—*in parables*—with the understanding that they will have "in that day" when he speaks to them—through the Holy Spirit —*plainly*. Further, he refers again (see on Jn 14:13 f.) to prayer *in my name*, that is to say, to prayer that will be addressed to Jesus as Lord of the Church, reigning over it by his Spirit as the triumphant Son of God who has *come forth from the Father* and *again* has *returned to the Father*.

All at once the disciples desert their somewhat studied obtuseness to take a spectacular leap into overconfidence. Though Jesus had just told them that the time for plain speech was coming and was not yet—the one thing out of his discourse that they might have been expected to hear plainly—they think they know their Master well enough to take from him in their own time what he has promised to give in his own. Their assured statement is a fine example of Johannine irony. Parroting Jesus' own formulations as though this were all of Christian faith, they merely reinforce what he has said about his words being parables to them. This forms the occasion of Jesus' prediction of the general defection of the disciples, an event which, as we saw at the beginning of this chapter, Matthew and Mark have also recorded. Yet withal, he ends on a note of consolation.

Jn 17:1–8   The final part of the Last Supper discourse of Jesus takes the form of a prayer, but in it his instruction certainly continues. We can imagine him and his disciples now standing, in the classic Jewish attitude of prayer, as *he raised his eyes to heaven* and began to address the Father. This passage has long been called Jesus' High Priestly Prayer, and rightly so, since in it he presents himself as consecrated for his great sacrifice of love and obedience; as both the victim and the priest of this sacrifice he prays for all the fruits that will derive from it. The prayer is for the consummation of all that he has been speaking of to the disciples, of the union between them and himself, the union which consists in faith and in the love of the disciples for him and the Father. So first of all he prays for himself, and for himself in union with the Father, the union which signifies and makes possible the unity of the Church with Christ. As *the hour has* now *come* for his passion, he prays that the Father may indeed *glorify* him, exalt him, that in his glorification he may bring with him into God's presence those who are united with him. The glorification of the Son, we know, likewise means the glorification of the Father. He has glorified the Father by the words and deeds of his earthly life, and now he will continue to glorify him in the extension of his person, in the Church, in the lives of those whom he will bring to sanctity.

This characterization of Jesus as a specifically priestly mediator is not one of the major stresses of the Gospels; in the New Testament it is almost a unique emphasis of the Epistle to the Hebrews. There may be a hint of it, however, in Jesus' own designation of himself, first in his "enigma of the Messiah" (see above on Mk 12:35–37a and parallels), later in his reply to the high priest (see below on Mk 14:62 and parallels). In both of these passages he applies to himself Ps 110 which, taken messianically, called the Lord of whom David had written "a priest forever, like Melchizedek." It is the same typology that the author of Hebrews exploits. There was a strand of Old Testament thinking which spoke of soteriological expectation in priestly terms, but in the normative Judaism of Jesus' time no way could be seen to combine in one person the royal figure of a Davidic Messiah and a priestly figure who, it was thought of necessity, must be Levitical. Some elements in Judaism solved this problem by looking for two Messiahs, one a king and the other a priest (the Qumran sectaries had an idea resembling this), or by featuring an eschatological high priest who would anoint the Messiah (it is possible that there is a trace of this idea in Luke's insistence on the priestly ancestry of John the Baptist). As the author of Hebrews perceived, however, he could apply to Jesus the Messiah a text that was an embarrassment to Judaism precisely because of the clean break which Christ's priesthood had effected with the Levitical priesthood of the Old Testament. Jesus' own use of Ps 110, his depreciation of the temple in respect to himself (Mt 12:6), his substitution of himself for the temple (Jn 2:19; the overall theme of Luke-Acts), and the priestly prayer that we are now reading, appear to point in the same direction. That direction is definitely away from any attempt to find precedents for the priesthood of Christ in the priestly legislation of the Mosaic law, despite the persistent efforts of some Christian writers to do just this. Christ's priesthood was and is a new thing, uniquely his in virtue of his unique consecration by the Father, and like Melchizedek's precisely because Melchizedek's priesthood was not that of Moses and Aaron. Significantly, the New Testament never applies the biblical (Old Testament) word "priest" (Greek *hiereus*= Hebrew *kōhēn*) to those who exercise the priesthood of Christ in his Church, though one of the words it does use, *presbyteros* (elder, translating the Hebrew *zāqēn*), became "priest" in English and other European languages under Christian influence.

Jn 17:9–19 Jesus' prayer now embraces the disciples, those whom the Father has given him. In praying *not for the world* he does not exclude the world from his prayer, since he will pray that his followers be consecrated for the service of the world; he does insist, however, that the disciples must be preserved from the world if they are to be preserved for it. Not only are they *in the world,* they are *sent into the world* even as the Son was sent into the world by the Father; but even as he, they must remain *not of the world:* the world is not its own salvation. They must be kept in God's *name,* with the *word* and life which Christ has bestowed on them; they must *be one even as we are one,* preserved in a love that has as its measure the love of the Father for the Son.

Not only is the relation of Father and Son the model of the disciple-and-Christ relationship, it is its principle. They must be *consecrated* with a priestly consecration, not, however, with anything less than the consecration of the Son himself, of *truth* and the *word. As you sent me into the world, so I sent them into the world:* the mission of Christ and the apostolic mission of the Church are one and the same, drawing their resources from the same source, with the same authority and powers.

Jn 17:20–26 Finally, Jesus prays for the Church of all time, for those who will believe through the preaching of his immediate disciples, *that they may be one, even as you, Father, in me and I in you.* In this unity of faith and love the world is to find a sign, and thus unity is by the divine will the great imperative for the Church's mission. The basis of this oneness is variously described as knowledge, recognition, faith, love, glory, but as the object of prayer it is *that where I am they may also be with me.* The prayer has subsumed the whole of the Last Supper discourses; in the world the Church communes with its heavenly Savior and finds realized in itself the divine presence even as Christ incarnated the divine Word through his communion with the Father.

24. AGONY

Mk 14:32a   Now that both John and Luke have completed their sto-
Mt 26:36a   ries of the Last Supper, they join Mark and Matthew in
Lk 22:39   taking Jesus and his disciples *across the valley of the*
Jn 18:1   *Kidron* (John) *to the Mount of Olives* (the Synoptics)
    to a place called Gethsemane (Mark and Matthew). Luke
and John (vs. 2) tell us that it was a place of ordinary resort for Jesus
(cf. Lk 21:37), and John speaks of it as *a garden*, evidently an enclosed
garden (vs. 1, *he entered*; vs. 4, *he went out*). Our sources converge
independently here in an obvious reference to a site that was well
known. It was doubtless the private garden of a friend containing an
olive grove and the oil press (*gath shemane* in Aramaic) for which it
was named. The Gethsemane of modern Jerusalem, a place of pilgrimage
from ancient times, can hardly be far removed from the garden that the
Gospels locate so precisely.

Mk 14:32b–42   The scene that follows, traditionally called "the agony
Mt 26:36b–46   in the garden" (from the word *agōnia* in Luke's ac-
Lk 22:40–46   count, vs. 43), is entirely omitted by John (who, how-
    ever, seems to refer to it in vs. 11); in the Fourth
Gospel the entire passion story from beginning to end is represented as
Jesus' triumph and exaltation, and episodes of this kind are bypassed. In
truth, John would have found it difficult to incorporate the story in any
way into his Gospel, though as we have seen (on Jn 12:20–36 above),
he does have something like it in another context. Here we are shown
a Jesus most nakedly human, bewildered, torn by conflicting emotions,
moved almost beyond endurance; and of course, this is as authentically a
Gospel portrait of Jesus as is that of the sublime and serene Teacher
that John likes to paint. The implications of the account in respect to the
psychological consciousness of the historical Jesus of Nazareth are for the
theologian to draw and to incorporate into his christology. We are concerned at the present merely with what the Gospels say and why they say
it. About the implications the New Testament writers, we may be sure,
were far more tranquil than later Christians have been. The author of

Hebrews, for example, for whom Jesus is without doubt the unique Son of God and celestial High Priest, completely sinless (4:15, 7:26, 9:14), was very likely thinking of this very story when he wrote: "In the days of his earthly life he offered up prayers and supplications, with loud cries and tears, to him who was able to save him from death . . . Son though he was, he learned obedience through suffering, and, once perfected, became the source of eternal salvation for all who obey him, being designated by God high priest in the order of Melchizedek" (5:7–10). For the Gospels this event is, before it is anything else, Jesus' priestly consecration (cf. Jn 17:19). From it he emerges with his sacrifice interiorly completed; the details of the passion that then begin to unfold he has already anticipated and accepted: they fulfill but do not constitute the offering that he has now made.

Luke's account differs considerably from that of Mark-Matthew. In the latter story only are the favored three disciples featured (see above on Mk 9:2–10 and parallels) as witnesses not of Jesus' agony itself—the Gospels agree that all were asleep during this—but of its most important prelude which Luke does not even mention explicitly. Matthew himself has somewhat toned down what Mark has written to describe this. *He went into a state of shock* would not be a translation too wide of the mark. What we are being told is that now Jesus experiences as a proximate reality the meaning of the destiny he had voluntarily assumed, to be the Servant of the Lord and to suffer an atoning death for the sins of man. It is one thing to embrace a vocation firmly and unequivocally with all its consequences clearly foreseen, and then to meet those consequences no longer as future abstractions but in the concrete present: in this instance to face an imminent death by torture. Yet even now more is involved than mere human repugnance to suffering and death. Jesus is fully aware of the vicarious nature of his suffering, which makes it not easier but all the more difficult to bear. All at once it is brought home to him how utterly alone he is in a world for which he is prepared to die and in which there is not another single person who can or will afford him the slightest consolation. For this reason he withdraws from the company of even the disciples of his choice and speaks with the Father who alone can understand him.

It is important to recognize that Jesus' agony is one of fear and horror, not of despair. *My heart is ready to break with sorrow,* his words to the disciples, evoke Pss 42:6, 12, 43:5, which is a psalm of confidence in God. Kneeling in the presence of his Father he prays not that he may be dispensed from his lot, nor does he rail against it; he only asks whether another way might yet be decreed by the one to whom all things are possible. And in his prayer he finds the strength he needs to go forward resolutely: *not as I will, but as you will.*

How long Jesus' prayer continued, the Gospels do not indicate. Luke does not prolong it over three stages as do Mark and Matthew. Luke makes his own contribution, however, both in personifying the divine consolation in the presence of *an angel from heaven* and in his graphic portrayal of the agony of Jesus in which *his sweat became like great drops of blood falling down upon the ground*. Whether this last he intends us to take quite literally or as an expressive figure of speech—the literal experience of bloody sweat seems to be an established pathological fact—in any case we cannot fail to grasp from it the reality of the agony itself. These two verses in Luke's account are missing in many of the early manuscripts. It is much easier to conceive of them as having been deliberately omitted, however, than as being a scribal invention; in all probability they formed an original part of Luke's text.

The sleeping disciples appear in ironic contrast to the Jesus who has just successfully survived his soul's crisis. Luke says that they were *sleeping for sorrow*. Although he had nothing about their witness of Jesus' shock and fear, he doubtless intends to suggest that they had had some surmise of it. Catching something of Jesus' mood they too experienced sorrow and, perhaps, depression. Unlike Jesus, however, they found prayer a task to which they were unequal, and thus they slept. Luke is quite as charitable as Jesus himself in interpreting their motives. The *temptation* against which they have been warned is, as in the Lord's Prayer (see above on Lk 11:1-4 and parallel), the hour of trial for the elect at the ushering in of the messianic age. In Matthew and Mark Jesus can tell the disciples, not without gentle sarcasm perhaps, that they may now sleep on and enjoy their rest, for the trial has been met and overcome by himself alone. And now the hour is at hand.

Mk 14:43–52   The story of Jesus' arrest is told dramatically by all the
Mt 26:47–56   evangelists, but with the kind of simple drama that ap-
Lk 22:47–53   pears to appeal to little more than an ultimate eyewit-
Jn 18:2–11   ness recollection. There have been a few embellishments
                acquired in oral tradition and through theological medi-
tation, but it is not difficult to reconstruct the event to the satisfaction of an historian, at least in its essential details. Of capital importance, however, is a detail on which our three passion-sources are not in agreement and which has considerable bearing on what is to follow. From Mark-Matthew we would judge that those who arrested Jesus were simply a hired mob—the kind of democracy in action never hard come by in any society at any time—sent *with swords* (or simply "knives") *and clubs* by the cabal of his inveterate enemies among the Sanhedrin which had plotted against him and bargained with Judas (see above on Mk 14:10 f. and parallels). Luke mentions, as he has before, the involvement of *the temple police*, one of whom may have been *the servant of the high priest* who figures in the accounts of all four Gospels. There is no reason to

question Luke's datum, which for that matter is confirmed by John. The temple police could have hardly been officially involved, it is true, for the Sanhedrin itself was not now acting officially. At the same time, they were the minions of those who had sent the mob, and it is not uncharitable to suppose that they included in their number men who were no better than their masters.

John's modification of this picture is most surprising. There was also present, he says, *the cohort*. He uses the Greek word normally employed for this Roman military unit of six hundred men (though this full muster was not necessarily normal), and by the article he evidently intends to say that they were soldiers of the Roman garrison at Jerusalem. Later (vs. 12) he adds that they were commanded by their *chiliarchos*: the term which designated a Roman *tribune*.

It is easy to say that John has, for theological reasons, magnified the array of worldly powers engaged in the arrest of Jesus: in an earlier age of Gospel criticism a judgment of this kind would have been routine. On the other hand, the introduction of Roman troops at this stage of the proceedings makes a good deal of sense in respect to the historical background of the passion story. John, be it noted, has no advantage to serve in inculpating the Romans of the events of this night. Neither was this a Roman arrest, according to John or any of the other Gospels. The Romans—most of whom, incidentally, were without doubt Syrians recruited from the neighboring province—could have been present only as "advisers." But that there were Romans privy to the plot against Jesus is not only not unlikely but almost inevitable. To mention only one thing at this time, it is hardly credible that any armed band of any size would have been permitted to pass through Jerusalem without prior Roman knowledge and approval. At the Passover season the Roman authorities were especially nervous about such things, but at no time did they look on unauthorized assemblies with a kindly eye. The Gospels have more than once included among the conspirators against Jesus certain Herodians (cf. Mk 3:6, 12:13; Mt 22:16), and the Herodians were Romanophiles. Suborning Roman officials in the provinces was neither unusual nor particularly expensive. All in all, there is ample cause to believe that the arms carried by the band that arrested Jesus were borne by Jewish and Roman soldiers, just as John tells us.

John's chronology of the Last Supper is likewise supported by this story and the ones that follow. It is hardly credible that any such thing could have taken place on the actual day of the Passover feast.

All the Gospels put Judas at the head of the arresting mob, even John's which has no account of the prior arrangement between Judas and Jesus' enemies. The Synoptics have the story of Judas' betrayal *with a kiss*; in Mark-Matthew the point is made that this was a prearranged signal. It is Luke who brings out the dreadful incongruity of the gesture, which, however, was a normal enough greeting between disciple and rabbi. In the dark of the garden—only John has thought to mention the *torches and lanterns* carried by the crowd—some identification of this kind was needful. Besides, most of those present did not know Jesus by sight; they were just simple mercenaries earning their pay with no especial interest in who was being arrested or why.

John omits the story of Judas' kiss and substitutes another which definitely does seem to be theologically motivated. In this account Jesus himself takes the entire initiative, while Judas stands helplessly by. The soldiers, awed by Jesus' commanding presence, arrest him only after he has identified himself and given them leave, and only after he has protected to the end those whom the Father has given him (cf. Jn 6:39, 17:12).

It is John who identifies the one who cut off the ear of the high priest's slave, and for good measure names the slave as well; neither identification causes any difficulty, and the first we might have suspected in any case. All the Gospels except Mark ascribe some saying to Jesus on this occasion, each of which is appropriate, and Luke tells us that he healed the wound; but the silence of the Lord is just as eloquent as his words. In the Synoptic Gospels he further rebukes the crowd for its armed hostility, seemingly presupposing his having been often in Jerusalem, as we know from John's Gospel.

The final lines in Mark's account are fascinating because of their obscurity and because Mark, who we know is not in the habit of wasting words, is the only evangelist to have kept the story. Theologically, it is pointless; it can only be the recollection of an eyewitness which Mark thought important enough to record. But why? Who was the *young man wrapped in a linen cloth*—apparently a sheet snatched from the bed by someone rudely awakened—who *fled away naked leaving the sheet* when an attempt was made to apprehend him? Perhaps the owner of the garden where the arrest took place, who suddenly found his villa invaded by a rabble of armed men. Perhaps Mark himself, who belonged to a Jerusalem family comfortable enough to support a town house (the upstairs room of the Last Supper?) and a garden on the Mount of Olives (cf. Acts 12:12). The possibilities are endless. At all events, whoever he was, he took the course of the rest of the disciples, surprised and dismayed as they were at the turn events had now taken. *They all deserted him and fled.*

Jn 18:12–14	We probably do well to be guided by John in the se-
Lk 22:54a	quence that follows. He alone tells us that after his ar-
Mk 14:53	rest Jesus was taken *first to Annas, for he was the father-*
Mt 26:57	*in-law of Caiaphas, who was high priest that year.* In
	saying that Caiaphas was high priest "that year" John

undoubtedly intends only to identify the high priest of the fateful year of Jesus' crucifixion, not to insinuate that the high priesthood changed hands every year—though as a matter of fact, between Annas and Caiaphas there had been a quick succession of three high priests, none of whom had lasted more than a year. John reminds us that it was Caiaphas who had uttered the cynical "prophecy" of Jn 11:50.

Annas himself had been high priest from A.D. 6 to 15, at which time he had been deposed by Valerius Gratus, Pontius Pilate's predecessor as governor of Judea during the years 15 to 26. He was patriarch of one of the half dozen families among which the high priesthood circulated, and himself appears to have had five sons, one grandson, and a son-in-law who at one time or another filled the office. There is no doubt, then, that he was the grey eminence behind the high priesthood throughout this entire period, and therefore it is not surprising that Lk 3:2 and Acts 4:6 speak of him as high priest. Probably in the minds of many Jews he was the legitimate high priest, since the Jews never quite reconciled themselves to the Roman governor's asserted right of deposing and appointing high priests at will, or, as it usually happened, for a bribe. Joseph Caiaphas was high priest from A.D. 18 to 36. He was deposed at just about the same time Pilate himself fell from favor and was removed from office, and the connection is probably more than casual. The Annas-Caiaphas family appear to have had an "arrangement" with the Roman governor, a fact which may help to explain the presence of Roman troops at the arrest of Jesus. It was certainly a fact that did not endear them to the great mass of Palestinian Jews. The Gospels are by no means alone in giving bad marks to these men. By the great majority of Jews of the time they were regarded as unworthy of their office and as more interested in perpetuating their political power than in preserving the faith of Moses.

At all events, that Jesus should have been taken to the house of Annas as John maintains is quite believable. Furthermore, it is most likely to Annas that Luke refers when he also narrates that Jesus was taken away *to the house of the high priest*. Luke agrees with John, therefore, when he is read apart from the other Synoptics. Luke further differs from Mark-Matthew in describing no trial of Jesus on this occasion; the trial, Luke insists (vss. 66–71), took place only on the following morning, and in the council chamber of the Sanhedrin, the proper place for a trial. All the historical probabilities are on Luke's side. The Sanhedrin could not pass judgment at night or in secret. Neither would the browbeating of a prisoner as the Gospels describe the treatment of Jesus have been tolerated in a regular and legal session of a Jewish court. What happened to Jesus this night after his arrest was not a trial by the Sanhedrin, but harassment at the hands of the Jewish conspirators and their lackeys who were detaining him against his trial in the morning. John, for his part, tells of

no trial either at night or in the morning. In his view it is not Jesus but
the world that is on trial during Jesus' passion-glorification.

But the Mark-Matthew narrative does describe the night detention of
Jesus as containing a trial; furthermore, Matthew speaks of it as taking
place in the house of Caiaphas rather than Annas. At the same time, both
Gospels do later on join Luke in recording an arraignment of Jesus before
a full session of the Sanhedrin on Friday morning. What seems to be our
best conclusion is that this narrative of the passion has telescoped the
events of Thursday night and Friday morning into one account, even
though it retained a memory of the separate Friday trial, since it was far
more interested in the drama of the story than in its correspondence
with Jewish legalities. Though two separate "high priests" were involved
in it, Annas in whose house Jesus was abused by his captors and where
Peter denied his Master, Caiaphas under whose presidency Jesus was
tried, Mark simply refers to *the high priest* throughout. By the time the
story had reached Matthew, who thought it necessary to call the high
priest by name, it had doubtless been forgotten that in the historical
sequence of events two high priests had figured in it in two different
capacities, and in the First Gospel, as a consequence, we find only the
name of Caiaphas, the official high priest. Having subsumed the sequence of events under the one heading, the Mark-Matthew narrative
does nothing with the actual trial except to refer to it summarily.

Jn 18:15–27   Following the reconstruction just proposed, we
Lk 22:54b–65   shall consider the four accounts as they lie be-
Mk 14:54–61a, 65–72   fore us, extracting from the Mark-Matthew
Mt 26:58–63a, 67–75   narrative only the solemn adjuration and ques-
                              tion put to Jesus by the high priest, which
served as the basis of his judicial condemnation and which we shall see
better where it belongs in parallel with Luke. What remains is the story
of the abuse of Jesus during the night of his detention and, coinciding
with this, the story of Peter's denial of his Lord. As we shall have already
surmised, John is interested in telling only the latter story, not at all the
former.

It is John who offers an explanation as to how Peter came to be in
the high priest's courtyard, an explanation, when we come to think of it,
that is really necessary. The arrest of Jesus, after all, was still secret and
unofficial, and it was not in the interests of his captors to admit just anyone to the scene of their machinations. By the same token, Luke's and
John's portrayal of the arrest as the work of hired soldiers makes very
good sense. Only John has it that besides Peter *another disciple had followed Jesus* after he had been taken. This cryptic anonymity from an
evangelist who is otherwise free with names makes us suspect that the disciple is deliberately unnamed and that he is that "disciple whom Jesus

loved" (cf. Jn 20:2), presumably John the son of Zebedee, the ultimate source of John's Gospel. At any rate, it was through this *other disciple known to the high priest* that Peter gained access to the high priest's house. "Known to the high priest" need not mean anything more than that he was known in the high priest's household, that is, among his servants, as, indeed, the story itself seems to suggest.

It is without doubt pointless to try to harmonize completely the Gospel accounts of Peter's multiple denial of Jesus. The Gospels agree that Peter denied Jesus three times, and on the circumstances of the first denial they are in fair agreement also. As for the subsequent denials, there are discrepancies both as to the circumstances and as to the precise individuals who put the question to Peter. These variations are such as would be expected to have occurred in separate oral transmissions of events that had been made known through hearsay—for certainly none of the evangelists was witness to them. Far more important than any attempt to reconcile stories that simply had in mind to relate the fulfillment of what Jesus had foretold (see above on Jn 13:36–38 and parallels) is it to make note of certain details in the stories that have something definite to tell us about the Gospel narrative, whether or not these were consciously thought of by the Gospel writers.

First of all, the character of Peter's denials should be properly understood. He was not, as Jesus was, being asked to declare himself before the world for its acceptance or rejection; he was probably being asked to do little more than satisfy the curiosity of uninvolved bystanders. While the curiosity was not precisely friendly, neither need we presume that it was especially hostile. These were the questions of servants milling about the high priest's courtyard, as much surprised as anyone else over the turn of events that had brought the man Jesus to their master's house. Peter's was a sin of cowardice and human respect (see above on Mt 12:31 f. and parallels). For the rest of it, matters like the open fire built against the cool of an early spring night, the persistence of the girl at the courtyard gate, Peter's Galilean accent which grated on Judean ears, seem to go back to eyewitness recollections all the more credible as such for having got somewhat mixed up, as eyewitness recollections generally do.

The only indignity which John allows to be shown to Jesus is in conjunction with the high priest's exploratory interrogation about his disciples. As an old political schemer himself, Annas could hardly think of anyone having messianic pretensions except in terms of political rebellion. Such thinking coincided with the interests of Rome, which Annas had long served for his own ends and which he would continue to exploit over the body of Jesus. Both in his disdainful reply to Annas, however, and in the mild but imperturbable reproof he administers to his sycophantic police officer, Jesus' dignity is shown enhanced all the more. It is he who controls the situation, not his captors exploring mare's nests for evidence and proving by their violence that they have run out of arguments.

What the Synoptic Gospels also describe is a searching for evidence against Jesus and the coaching of witnesses, not a formal presentation of a case that would hold in court. The abuse that was showered on him undoubtedly was intended as much to provoke some indictable response as to serve as an outlet for frustration and contempt. The one usable piece of evidence that was forthcoming, according to Mark-Matthew, was Jesus' prophecy of the destruction of the temple (see above on Mk 13:1 f. and parallels). That Jesus had not only made such a prophecy, but had connected himself intimately with the event and its consequences, is amply testified in the New Testament: once again by Mark-Matthew (Mk 15:29; Mt 27:40); by Luke not here but in Acts 6:14; for John's interpretation, see above on Jn 2:18–22. Therefore it is surprising that Mark insists that in bringing these words of Jesus against him *they testified falsely*. Evidently he means that they were quoting the prophecy in a garbled form and contrary to the spirit in which Jesus had uttered it, as though the temple were of no account except to serve as the occasion of a vulgar show of magical power. At any rate, whatever evidential value such a statement may have had seems to have vanished because of the faulty memories of those who had heard it: *even here their testimony was not the same.* To convict under the Mosaic law the agreed testimony of a minimum of two witnesses was required (cf. Deut 19:15). It may well be, however, as the Gospels suggest, that it was the implications of this saying of Jesus that led the high priest to put to him the question by which he became incriminated in the eyes of the Sanhedrin, and that it was the same that influenced the Sanhedrin to regard Jesus' answer as incriminating.

Lk 22:66–71   John has already said (vs. 24) that following
Mk 14:61b–64, 15:1a   the interrogation of Jesus at his house, *Annas*
Mt 26:63b–66, 27:1   *sent him bound to Caiaphas the high priest.*
                     Though John has no intention of describing
any trial of Jesus, his next passages will presuppose that such a thing has, indeed, taken place, and it is this that is now depicted for us by Luke, *when day came,* the only time that a trial could legally take place. Mark and Matthew, though they too preserved a tradition of a morning meeting of the Sanhedrin, now that they had already anticipated the judicial sentence of death passed on Jesus during the events of the night before, were somewhat at a loss what to do with the redundant session. At least Matthew was; Matthew is always more sensitive to such problems than Mark. Mark's source had it that *early the next morning . . . the whole Sanhedrin reached a verdict.* Though this might have given him pause in view of what he had already written about the verdict, he simply put

down what he had and went on to the next matter, the delivery of Jesus to the Roman governor. Matthew solved the difficulty by understanding the "verdict" as a new decision of the Sanhedrin to hand Jesus over to Pilate; this decision, however, would have been implied in the beginning in any sentence of death.

It is not much that the Gospels tell us about the trial of Jesus. We are left to imagine the title under which the Sanhedrin was convened, the nature of the charges that were proffered, how the seizure of Jesus and his harassment were legalized, and much else. Certainly Jesus was not friendless even among the Sanhedrin (cf. Jn 12:42 f.), to say nothing of his more general popularity with the people at large. His enemies were powerful and strategically placed; nevertheless, to accomplish what they did must have entailed much more maneuvering than we are able to follow in the Gospels. Of plots and plans we have been told, but without much detail. Of course, many of the details would have been unavailable to the Gospel sources.

One of the problems encountered by any commentator on the passion narrative is the time element. Events have moved very swiftly leading up to this Good Friday morning, and they will move even more swiftly hereafter. So swift is the tempo, in fact, many students of the Gospels refuse to believe that it can correspond to historical fact. They find it difficult to believe that Jesus could have eaten the Last Supper with his disciples, that he could then have gone to Gethsemane, have been arrested, carried off to detention and abused, have been tried and condemned, remanded to the Roman governor, sentenced, crucified, that he should then have breathed out his life, have been taken down from the cross and buried, all within the space of less than twenty-four hours; and from the list we have omitted several other episodes that the Gospels pack into this long day. An apparent way out of the supposed impasse has been found by some in the Qumran solar calendar which we mentioned above in connection with the date of the Passover (see on Mk 14:12-17 and parallels). If Jesus and his disciples did, indeed, keep the Passover according to the Qumran rule, the Last Supper would have taken place on a Tuesday evening, such being the peculiarity of its calendar. If the Last Supper occurred on a Tuesday and the crucifixion on a Friday—for the Gospels are at one on this—then we are afforded a more realistic time distribution for the events of Holy Week.

Though in the abstract this solution may have something to commend it, however, in fact it comes up against the Gospel chronology which knows nothing of such a possibility. This would not be a peremptory objection, it is true, but it is also true that there are many good reasons to believe that Jesus would never have followed the heterodox Qumran calendar. Furthermore, the very unlikeliness of the Gospel chronology may be the best proof of its authenticity and, perhaps, may help to explain the secret of the success of Jesus' enemies. If we take it at its face value, probably by the time that the news of Jesus' arrest had become known in any general way in Jerusalem he would have been already inexorably committed to death, beyond the hope of any remedial action by his friends and supporters. His powerful enemies had the advantage of surprise, they controlled much of the machinery of law in their own right, and they knew how to oil the machinery that they did not control but needed. What the Gospels describe is not impossible; it is simply obscure, and for the usual reason, that neither the Gospels nor their sources have bothered very much, if at all, with a great deal of what the modern historian considers to be of prime importance.

Another question that the Gospels do not solve concerns the legality of the sentence of death passed on Jesus by the Sanhedrin. Whether, indeed, the entire Sanhedrin was involved in the process is not certain —the Gospels' references to "all the chief priests," "all the elders of the people," "the whole Sanhedrin," and the like, have obviously not drawn on the official minutes of the supreme Jewish tribunal. We have argued above that Jesus' trial was held in the morning rather than at night for legality's sake not on any a priori basis, but because our sources for the passion-history, John, Luke, and even Mark-Matthew for that matter, indicate that such was the case. Psychologically considered, it makes very good sense that such should have been the case. A semblance of legality was needed by men who stood for the Law and the temple if they were to condemn Jesus in the name of the Law and the temple. But only a semblance was needed: no really successful criminal makes the mistake of violating obvious and easy laws which cost nothing. There remain many elements in what little of the trial we know about whose legality the scholars will long continue to debate. Was it lawful for the high priest to put a self-incriminating question to the accused? What precise legal ground was the basis for declaring Jesus' answer a "blasphemy"? In some part we are hampered by a lack of information concerning judicial procedure of the first Christian century, to what extent it corresponded with later Jewish jurisprudence that is better known. Was it lawful, for example, to pass sentence on the same day that judgment had been rendered? In later times, it certainly was not. But again, we ponder such questions without much help from the Gospels.

The Synoptic Gospels give us little more than the crucial question which the high priest asked of Jesus, together with Jesus' answer, on which the Sanhedrin passed its verdict. And even these they give us somewhat differently.

The high priest's question was: *Are you the Messiah?* This was to be, as we shall see, the title under which Jesus was handed over to the Romans as worthy of death and the title under which he was executed. In Roman eyes it was high treason to claim messiahship. But it was not a Jewish crime. Many in the Sadducean-dominated Sanhedrin might have been disposed to view it as a dangerous, even pernicious quixotism that could only bode disaster for the *status quo* of Roman Palestine (the sense of Caiaphas' "prophecy" in Jn 11:49f.); but it was not against the Law. The Pharisees present would certainly not have been much moved by the question as such. To claim falsely to be the Messiah might indeed be a cause for condemnation; but in that case the question was poorly phrased. They themselves had on more than one occasion required of Jesus testimonials to his messianic character, and he had always refused. They were doubtless not loath to see removed on any pretext one who had challenged their traditions and ridiculed their religiosity as hypocrisy. Still, on what pretext of Law? From the standpoint of Law Jesus was unassailably an orthodox Jew, and all the more so for his faith in messianism.

All the Gospels at one place or another make synonymous with Messiah in this passage the title *Son of God* (*Son of the Blessed One* in Mark's version has a more authentically Jewish ring to it). Students of the New Testament continue to dispute whether in pre-Christian Judaism this title was commonly used of the Messiah. Whatever may be the answer to this question, the Gospels evidently do consider it to be a messianic title (see above on Mk 8:27–30 and parallels), even though the evangelists quite obviously know of a deeper sense in which Jesus Christ was and is Son of God. Grounds for calling the Davidic Messiah Son of God could be found by any Jew in 2 Sam 7:14. At any rate, it is doubtful that the Gospels think of "Son of God" on the lips of the high priest as offering any greater challenge to Jesus than "Messiah."

And what is Jesus' answer to this solemn charge? In Luke, it is obviously non-committal. At first he dismisses their question as inutile, then when pressed he replies, *You say that I am.* This is likewise the meaning of his answer according to Matthew: *You have said so.* As we know very well, "Messiah" was not a name that Jesus could answer to without qualifications. He was the Messiah—as he understood the significance of this figure in the saving purposes of God—and he definitely was not the Messiah as most of those about him, whether approving or disapproving, thought of the Messiah (see above on Lk 4:3–13 and parallel). Hence the sense of his reply is the equivalent of "As you wish . . . You say it, not I."

Mark, however, has him say unequivocally, *I am.* Actually, there are Marcan manuscripts that read "You have said that I am," which some scholars believe to be the original wording of Mark's Gospel (thus better explaining Matthew's text which is otherwise usually an adaptation of Mark's). Still, we know that Mark has a special stake in the title "Messiah" as applied to Jesus: the "messianic secret" (see above on Mk 1:22–28) for him is a vital page of the Gospel. The secret has now been broken, and he would thereafter find it hard to deny this title to his Lord, even though he would understand it in a way quite different from that of the high priest. "I am," therefore, is probably what Mark originally wrote. In much the same manner, by an alternate arrangement of the dialogue between Jesus and his judges, Luke has given special prominence to the title "Son of God" (see above on Lk 1:34–38).

But having progressed thus far, we are still faced with the fact that, whether positively or negatively or neutrally, Jesus had committed himself to absolutely nothing that was actionable under Jewish law. If we are to look for an objective basis for the charge of "blasphemy" that was immediately hurled against him, we must seek it elsewhere in Jesus' reply.

In all three Gospels Jesus goes on to speak of himself in the language of Dan 7:13 and Ps 110:1. He is the Son of Man, he is the mysterious Lord of whose enthronement David had sung (see above on Mk 12:35–37a and parallels). In Mark-Matthew he speaks of his coming glorification, in Luke's version it is considered as already begun (cf. Jn 12:31). Technically, this was still not the language of blasphemy, but equivalent statements of Jesus had brought down this imputation before (cf. Jn 8:59, 10:31–33). It is important to observe that, not only in John's Gospel but in the Synoptic tradition as well, and in the most solemn of Jesus' declarations according to this tradition, he is represented as identifying himself by preference not as the Jewish Messiah but as the glorified Son of Man (see above on Jn 1:43–51). It was as such that he confronted the Sanhedrin, and as such that he was condemned.

By whatever evidence, probably on a confluence of motives and causes, Jesus was adjudged *deserving of death*. It was a judgment made by men who in separate ways saw him as a threat to their way of life, their profession, their religion, their nation, their God himself. It was undoubtedly the judgment of men sincere as well as men devious and guileful. It was a judgment made by Jews. It was not, however, the judgment made by a people.

Mt 27:3–10   Following the story of Jesus' trial, the Gospels proceed to the next inevitable step in the journey of Jesus to the cross, the ratification of his sentence by the Roman governor. Only Matthew, however, has inserted at this point a narrative which seems to have been drawn from a Jerusalem tradition about the subsequent fate of Judas Iscariot.

Probably a certain contrast is intended with the repentance of Simon Peter after his craven refusal to acknowledge his Master in the high priest's courtyard. When the enormity of what he had done was brought home to Peter, the Gospels tell us that *he went out and wept bitterly* over the collapse of the brave figure of loyal devotion in which he had once fancied himself. Judas, too, seeing what had happened to Jesus, *was* now *struck with remorse* over his betrayal. Just why, we are not sure, since we know little of the complexity of motives that had gone into Judas' action in the first place, and neither this Gospel passage nor any other informs us about them. At any rate, his bitter disillusionment is turned futilely against himself to a final act of self-destruction. Just as a murderer will sometimes try to destroy or to hide the weapon of death even from himself, as though doing so would cancel out the deed, Judas' first fixation is to rid himself of the incriminating *thirty pieces of silver*, the sum which Matthew alone mentioned before (Mt 26:15).

It seems to be Matthew's thought that Judas tried to return the money to the Sanhedrin itself, but it is *the chief priests* who make the final disposition of it as temple property. According to this tradition they used it to buy a tract of ground already known as *the potter's field*, doubtless because its clay had served the needs of one or several potters for some time, to turn it into *a burial place for strangers*. These "strangers" would be Jews from outside Jerusalem who would chance to die in the Holy City or who had come there expressly for their burial, and who were dependent on public charity. For this reason, says Matthew, the ground came to be known as *the field of blood*—Jesus' blood, that is, as bought with the blood money paid to Judas.

In Acts 1:16–20 Luke records an alternate tradition, both as to the origin of the name of the field and as to the circumstances of Judas' death. The field, according to Acts, got its name from *Judas'* blood, because he died some sort of violent death there on the land he had bought. It is not evident from Acts that Judas committed suicide. It is pointless to ask which tradition is "right." The only point is that early Christian tradition associated the field with the money of Judas' treachery and that it reflected on the end of the betrayer in terms of his Old Testament prototypes (cf. Wis 4:19; 2 Sam 17:23; cf. also Ps 69:26 in connection with the story in Acts). These reflections came from a Jewish, hardly from a Gentile Christian community.

Matthew's discovery of a prophetic precedent for this event is particularly interesting, the fruit of the same kind of reflection on the Old Testament we have just noted. Matthew refers to *Jeremiah the prophet*, but verbally his quotation begins with a reminiscence of Zech 11:12 f., a prophetic allegory which provided a certain typology for the matter at hand. Jeremiah is present in his mind, however, through a further association of ideas (cf. Jer 32:7–9, 18:2–10, 19:1 ff.): dominating the passage is the thought of the potter's field, the price of Jesus' blood, a standing witness forever against these false *sons of Israel* in Topheth, in the dismal valley of Ben-hinnom (gehenna: see above on Mt 5:27–30). This interweaving of disparate strands of scriptural word and idea resembles nothing so much as the midrashic interpretation of the rabbis.

25. "WHAT IS TRUTH?"

Mk 15:1b   After his trial before the Sanhedrin, Jesus was taken *to*
Mt 27:2   *Pilate the governor* and, as John specifies, *to the prae-*
Lk 23:1   *torium,* a term used later by Mark-Matthew also. The
Jn 18:28–32 Sanhedrin presumably had met in its customary meeting
hall on the western side of the temple area, in a sector
and near a market place which the Jews called Gazith (the corruption
of a Greek word, *xystos,* which meant a covered colonnade; similarly,
Sanhedrin itself was a corruption of the Greek word *synedrion,* council).
It is conceivable, however, that the trial of Jesus had been held in the
palace of Caiaphas the high priest, which was probably somewhere in
the southwestern part of New Testament Jerusalem, in the upper city
where the homes of the wealthy were. The geography of ancient Jerusalem is perforce often very conjectural, dependent on casual historical
references and a good deal of guesswork, since the continuous and dense
habitation of the city has made the investigation of much of its ground
difficult if not impossible. The location of the praetorium, for example,
which could be quite relevant to our understanding of the Gospel story,
is by no means certain.

The praetorium was the official residence of Roman authority, where
edicts were dispensed and judgments given. The seat of the Roman
governor of Judea was not Jerusalem but Caesarea; in Caesarea, then,
was the chief praetorium of Judea (cf. Acts 23:35). The governor also
maintained a residence in Jerusalem, however, which he visited especially
in times of potential danger to law and order, such as the great pilgrimage feasts of Judaism. This residence would be the praetorium of
the Gospels. As far as ancient records have anything to tell us about it,
the governor's residence would have been in the Palace of Herod (the
Great), on the western side of the city on an eminence now occupied
by a citadel known popularly as the Tower of David, near the Jaffa Gate.
Here was the second of the two garrisons maintained in Jerusalem, the
other being at the Fortress Antonia adjoining the temple area.

A persistent Christian tradition, however, has long associated Jesus'
passion with the Antonia region itself, and in the minds of many this

tradition has been confirmed by the findings of archaeology, to establish
that it was the Antonia that the Gospels call the praetorium. According
to Jn 19:13, the praetorium of the Gospels was given the name *Lithostrōton* (stone pavement), and in Hebrew (that is, Aramaic) it was
called *Gabbatha* (elevated place). Excavations many feet below the level
of modern Jerusalem have certainly revealed the courtyard of the Antonia, marvelously preserved, and the courtyard was certainly paved with
massive slabs of stone, on which it is still possible to see the marks left
by chariot wheels, the scars made by Roman lances, and even the designs
which the soldiers had sketched out for the games with which they whiled
away the time. The possible relevance of this last detail we shall see
later on. The Antonia was built on a rocky prominence, and therefore
seems to correspond with John's description. However, the question remains open. The Palace of Herod was on a higher elevation than the
Fortress Antonia, and while no excavations have brought to light its
stone pavement, it undoubtedly had one; furthermore the fact that John
speaks of it as *the* Stone Pavement might suggest that he had in mind
a place better known to the people at large than the barracks of the
Roman cohort.

Those who had brought Jesus to Pilate *did not enter the praetorium*,
John says, lest they contract a legal impurity from contact with Gentiles
and thus be unable to eat the Passover that evening (see above on Mk
14:12–17). Pilate does not hesitate to humor their scruples, as the Romans were usually careful to do. At the same time, the mutual contempt
in which he and the Jews held one another is quite evident from the
Gospel story. Neither does it appear, as we shall see, that Pilate is being
introduced to the problem of Jesus for the first time. It is wrong to read
the Gospels, as some have done, as though they conceived of Pilate
as a man fundamentally disposed to justice whose hand was forced against
Jesus. In a sense, his hand was forced, it is true, but if he had any thought
of saving Jesus' life it was not from any devotion to justice. Like most
of the provincial Roman governors, Pilate was selfish, rapacious, and
corrupt. If he held office as long as he did, it was because of Tiberius
Caesar's avowed and cynical principle that old governors governed best,
having now the leisure to govern once they had squeezed their personal
fortunes out of their subjects. In the drama of the passion Pilate plays
no role that does not serve his own sordid interests and his taste for
power. Jesus' enemies knew the temper of the man with whom they had
to negotiate. His high-handed despotism that had got him into trouble
before and would eventually bring about his downfall was this time kept
under control, but it was the calculated control of one who owed allegiance to no principle outside himself.

The initial exchange between Pilate and the Jews as reported by John
can be variously interpreted, depending on the sense of the avowal: *we*

are not permitted to put anyone to death. Ordinarily this is taken to mean that in Roman Palestine the sentence of death decreed by a Jewish court such as the Sanhedrin would be recognized as having no validity unless ratified by Roman authority. Such procedure obtained elsewhere in the provinces of the Roman empire. On the other hand, the Romans extended extraordinary privileges to the Jews, and we have no clear-cut evidence that they withheld the right of execution from the Sanhedrin; in fact, there are some events that might suggest that they did not (cf. Jn 8:7; Acts 7:58 f., 25:9–11). Even if they did, one might suppose that the limit of Roman interest would have been to certify the sentence and permit it to be carried out in the Jewish manner, by stoning, not to insist on a Roman trial and a Roman execution. Yet Jesus was executed in the Roman manner, by crucifixion, and for a crime against Roman law.

If this is, nevertheless, the meaning of the Jews' statement, as it may very well be, then we are treated to the rather unedifying spectacle of a sparring contest between two proud parties over the innocent person of Jesus, who matters to neither of them. Pilate asks, *What accusation do you bring against this man?*, insinuating, of course, that his trial begins here and now, that nothing that has been proved in any Jewish court can have the slightest bearing on his jeopardy to a death sentence. At this the Jews indignantly reply that he has, indeed, been shown to be an evildoer worthy of death. And thus Pilate is permitted to win the first round in a mutually hateful encounter. An evildoer? Well, then, *take him yourselves and judge him by your own law.* But this they cannot do, and they are forced to the humiliating admission that they cannot.

Others, however, understand John's story in another way. It was not merely that Jesus' enemies wanted him dead; they wanted him dead by Roman law and by a Roman execution. Not only did they not want to face their own people as responsible for his death, they hoped that he could also serve as a scapegoat to satisfy the Romans that they were being sufficiently vigilant over the rebellious people of Palestine, who now so obediently and loyally delivered over one of its own refractory members who had got out of hand (cf. Jn 11:49 f.). John himself seems to lean to this interpretation when he adds that *this was to fulfill the word which Jesus had spoken to show what kind of death he was to die* (cf. Jn 3:14, 8:28, 12:32 f.). In this construction, Pilate was simply demanding of the Jews a charge against Jesus that would stand up in a Roman court. Neither Pilate nor Roman law would take any cognizance of a merely Jewish crime (cf. Acts 18:14 f.). In either case, we might add, though in the latter especially, the possibility of prior collusion between Pilate and the Jewish leadership is always present.

Mk 15:2–5	The question which Pilate puts to Jesus according to
Mt 27:11–14	all four of the Gospels: *You are the king of the Jews?*

Lk 23:2–5   —probably with a tone of contempt on both "you"
Jn 18:33–38   and "the Jews"—presupposes some kind of denuncia-
                                    tion such as that which Luke alone records: *We caught
this fellow perverting our nation, forbidding them to pay taxes to Caesar,
and claiming to be Messiah, a king.* The charge is a mixture of truth,
half-truth, and the utter falsehood that is so often the progeny of both.
Jesus had made a pronouncement on tribute to Caesar (see above on
Mk 12:13–17 and parallels); this much was doubtless common knowledge,
whatever may have been the opinion about precisely what he had said.
He had been hailed as king on more than one occasion. The credentials
of most of those waiting on Pilate were probably quite acceptable for a
denunciation of this kind. Belonging mainly to the Sadducean priestly
families, their interests coincided with the Romans' in stamping out an
incipient messianism whenever it should arise. This Pilate knew, quite
in addition to whatever prior information he may have had about this
particular case.

Jesus' answer to Pilate's question, according to all four Gospels, is
again the non-committal *You say so;* John prefaces to it Jesus' explanation of the sense in which he may be considered a king. It is worthy of
remark that at this juncture both Luke and John have Pilate explicitly
affirm that he finds no cause for death in Jesus' teaching, and Mark-
Matthew imply much the same by showing the need that his accusers apparently felt to multiply the charges against him. Pilate was a Roman ad-
ministering justice, and the maintenance of the Roman system depended
on a strict adherence to the legal forms. He would later fall from favor, as
a matter of fact, through a miscalculation of this order, repressing as rebels
against Roman rule those who were able to convince his Roman superiors
they were no rebels at all. Jesus' reply was accepted as satisfactory: whatever his "kingship" meant, it was not deemed to constitute any threat to
the empire.

The more extended dialogue which John ascribes to Jesus and Pilate
is very important to this evangelist. Here, finally, the "world" to which
Jesus has come to bring life and light, and which of necessity has
hitherto been an exclusively Jewish world, now opens wide in the person
of the Roman governor who represents what to a first-century author
would have been the world par excellence, the *oikoumenē,* the inhabited
earth, the empire (cf. Lk 2:1). Pilate is an earnest of that vaster world
of men in which and before which the prophetic Word and Spirit
were now incarnated in the Johannine Church. But alas, Pilate is utterly
indifferent to the word. Jesus' invitation to him to consider the meaning
of this historical encounter and his part in it he dismisses with the contempt of a Roman skeptic: *Am I a Jew?* Though he can take in
Jesus' words on the surface, to know that this strange sort of king before
him has nothing to do with his world of intrigue and *Realpolitik,* his

What is truth? shows how completely he had missed the supreme opportunity of his life. *Everyone who is of the truth hears my voice,* was Jesus' final testimony. Pilate had heard nothing. He had not even paid the truth the compliment of a rejection, so little was his concern with it.

Lk 23:6–16   Luke alone tells the story of Jesus' being sent by Pilate to Herod Antipas, a story that is all the more credible because of our suspicion that more lies behind it than even Luke knew. We have already seen that the Herodians, Antipas' hangers-on and servants, were considered by the Gospels to have been involved in the plot against Jesus' life, for whatever reasons of their own. Herod certainly had cause to suspect Jesus' activity as adverse to his own interests (see above on Lk 13:31–33). It is not at all unlikely that if self-serving Jews and Romans could, to some degree at least, make common cause to rid themselves of one who disturbed them in various ways, Herod, who was a little of both Jew and Roman, might have found the same cause to his own advantage. Luke recalls that *Herod and Pilate became fast friends from that very day, whereas before they had been hostile to each other.* The friendship was, indeed, compounded over the body of Jesus, and it may well be that it was indicated rather than caused by Pilate's gesture, which really seems to have served little purpose beyond satisfying Herod's callous curiosity. The reason for their earlier enmity Luke does not explain, but it was quite likely some jurisdictional dispute or some action of Pilate's involving Galileans such as that described in Lk 13:1–9.

As Luke tells it, an apparently chance remark about Jesus' having begun his teaching in Galilee leads Pilate first to confirm that Jesus was a Galilean, *of Herod's jurisdiction,* and then to send him to the tetrarch who was in Jerusalem for the feast. Obviously this was nothing more than a courtesy on Pilate's part, as far as the legalities were concerned, since the governor retained full jurisdiction over any Jew in Judea. Evidently, too, however, he was looking for some help from Herod in determining what was to be the final disposition with regard to Jesus, against whom he now believed he had no capital case. Even though we pick up the Gospel hints that suggest a more complicated background to the death of Jesus than the dogged blood lust of a few Jewish plotters in high places, the same evidence prevents us from concluding that his fate had been irrevocably decided upon by others than these few. Roman soldiers might be easily hired for an illegal arrest, and Galilean officials might stand idly by when one of their subjects was bullied and harried, but there is no reason to think that the common interest extended on all sides to Jesus' literal destruction. That he should be discredited and repudiated, and his followers scattered, might be all that was needed. Murders, even judicial murders, have a way of remaining as evidence of untidy administration; Antipas seems to have had cause to regret the execution of John the Baptist (see above on Mk 6:14–29 and parallels). Thus, perhaps, Pilate's suggestion after Jesus was returned to him: *I will chastise him and then turn him loose.*

Whatever part Antipas was supposed to play in settling Pilate's mind, he seems to have contributed little or nothing. The tetrarch was almost certainly staying at the Palace of the Hasmonaeans, ancestral property of the Herod family, which Flavius Josephus locates for us as about equidistant from the Palace of Herod and the Antonia. Some, at least, of Jesus' accusers accompanied him to this place, but seemingly Herod paid little attention to them. His first interest in Jesus was as a captive magician who might enliven the boredom of the day by performing *some sign*. When, however, Jesus responded to his interrogation with the silence of the Lord's Servant that he had already shown before the Sanhedrin and before Pilate (cf. Is 53:7), Antipas quickly tired of the game and turned him over to the coarse amusement of *his soldiers* to be treated not as a dangerous criminal but as a lunatic and a fool. The *splendid apparel* in which Jesus was decked out to be sent back to Pilate was probably the clothing of royalty, by which his messianic pretensions were being mocked: these would have been as ludicrous to the Herodians as to the Romans. It is believed by some authors that it was at Herod's court that the sustained ridicule of Jesus as King of the Jews took place which Mark-Matthew and John, who have no story about Herod at all, later ascribe to the soldiers of Pilate. Luke himself prefers not to dwell on unpleasant scenes like this.

In verse 13 an anomaly is presented by Luke's text when Pilate is said to have *called together the chief priests and the rulers and the people* as those who had turned Jesus over to him for execution. Everywhere else in this Gospel, both prior to this verse (cf. 19:49, 20:6, 19, 26, 45, 21:38) and following it (cf. 23:27, 35, 48), the evangelist carefully distinguishes the people and its leaders as two opposed camps. It is the people who eagerly listen to Jesus, in fear of whom the leaders are hesitant to act against him, and who are shown never to have really consented to his death. Despite the lack of manuscript evidence, therefore, it has been plausibly suggested that Luke originally wrote here as he does elsewhere "the chief priests and the rulers *of* the people."

Mk 15:6–14   The four Gospels now tell of a development which
Mt 27:15–23   presupposes a custom at Jerusalem of which they are
Lk 23:17–23   our only historical informants, but which we have no
Jn 18:39–40   cause to doubt as having certain analogies elsewhere,
                        that *on the occasion of a festival* the governor *would release* to the people *one prisoner, the man they would ask for.* It has been conjectured that the custom began in Maccabean or Hasmonaean

times and that the Romans had found it convenient to retain it; presumably a prisoner that might hope to benefit from such an amnesty was not one already under actual sentence of death—ordinarily only the emperor himself could grant a pardon of this kind—but one awaiting trial or sentence. It occurs to Pilate that there is a way out of his present quandary if he can invoke the custom in Jesus' favor. What puts it into his head, according to Mark-Matthew, is the gathering of *the crowd* for this annual purpose. It is to be noted that this crowd now appears for the first time, having up to this point had nothing to do with the discussion over Jesus; in John and Luke (if we accept the emendation of Luke's vs. 13) there is no crowd: they have in view simply the chief priests and elders of the people who have since the early morning resolved on Jesus' death.

It is at this moment that the name of *Barabbas* briefly enters the Gospel. Actually, Barabbas is not a name but a patronymic, like Bar-Jona, the patronym of Simon Peter. Its meaning was "son of his father" —lest the distinction be thought pointless, the idea was that this man bore the same given name as his father, somewhat unusual at a time when there were no surnames and the name of the father was depended on to distinguish one Simon or John or Joseph from another. Barabbas' name was undoubtedly Jesus: "Jesus Barabbas" appears in a number of manuscripts of Mt 27:16 f., and it is impossible to account for it there except as a matter of historical record; on the other hand, it is easy enough to understand why Christian scribes got it out of most of the other manuscripts. *Jesus Barabbas or Jesus the so-called Messiah*, then, was the choice Pilate offered to the crowd.

But why Barabbas as a choice? Probably because it was for Barabbas that the crowd had come to petition in the first place, and Pilate merely attempted to divert its attention to Jesus instead. Mark says that Barabbas had been *imprisoned as one of the rebels who had committed murder in the uprising*—alluding in passing to some well-known event in which, as usual, the Gospels otherwise evince no interest. Luke's description agrees substantially with this, while Matthew simply states that Barabbas was *a prisoner of note*. John's characterization of Barabbas as *a bandit* is meant to underline the sordid type of person whom "the Jews" preferred to Jesus; however, "bandit" was the term commonly used for the zealots or partisans among the Jews who opposed Roman rule by recourse to violence. Barabbas was without doubt a popular patriot, a leader in one of the many nationalist movements against the Romans, and suspected by the latter of complicity in activities that had led to bloodshed. As shown by his designation of Jesus to the crowd as *Messiah* and *King of the Jews*, in Pilate's mind Barabbas and Jesus were two of a kind, though he was now convinced that Jesus was harmless and *knew that the chief priests had turned him in out of jealousy*. From his

standpoint it would make much better sense to release Jesus rather than
the popular hero who was far more dangerous. But of course, his di-
versionary tactic was doomed to failure. Jesus' enemies had no difficulty
in persuading the crowd to make a choice that was doubtless already to
its liking. Those who were in sympathy with Barabbas were not likely
to be enthusiastic over Jesus' kind of messianism.

Here and in subsequent passages the Gospels seem to go out of their
way to show Pilate more actively interested in sparing Jesus' life than
our knowledge of his character would have prepared us to expect. Often
this tendency is explained as anti-Jewish bias, an attempt to minimize the
part that Rome had played in the crucifixion, understandable in a Church
that was engaged in controversy with Judaism and which had to live in
the Roman empire and by Roman law. We have seen that there is, indeed, something of this tendency in the Gospels. However, it is also
true that we are hampered by a lack of background information that,
did we have it, might make Pilate's intervention quite comprehensible.
Of one thing we may be fairly sure, that it was not prompted by any
abstract devotion to justice. One tantalizing allusion—if it is that—to
the more complicated history behind the Gospel story may be seen in
the story told by Matthew, apparently making additional use of his series
of Jerusalem traditions, about the *message* sent to Pilate while *he was
presiding on the judgment seat* by *his wife*, a lady whom not too reliable
tradition identifies by the name of Claudia Procla. To many this story
is proof that the trial and passion of Jesus extended over a much longer
period of time than a single day and involved others than the few whom
the Gospels bring into it. It does at least suggest the possibility that the
name of Jesus had been mentioned in Pilate's household before this
fateful day.

Mk 15:15   Having made its choice of Barabbas, there was only one
Mt 27:24–26   reply for the crowd to give to the governor's further
Lk 23:24–25   question, which he doubtless put to it in frustration
                  and anger, not unmixed with contempt: What then
was to be done with the one some called the Messiah? *Crucify him!*
Preachers on the passion of Christ have often dwelt on the fickleness of
the people of Jerusalem who on Sunday hailed Jesus as their Messiah
and on the following Friday demanded his death. But in the first place,
it is impossible to know how many of the motley population of Jerusalem
at Passover time, nine tenths of which were pilgrims from every part of
Jewry, had participated in the enthusiasm of Palm Sunday; probably
most of it had been contributed by the Galileans who accompanied
Jesus, few of whom, if the Gospels' chronology is to be taken at face
value, were as yet even aware of his arrest. As for the present crowd
which, altogether contrary to Pilate's expectations, the chief priests were

able to turn into a mob demanding Jesus' blood, we have no reason to think that they either knew or cared much about Jesus. They had come to ransom a Jew held in a Roman prison, and they were not likely to be prejudiced in favor of someone whom the Romans evidently wanted to force on them and whom their own leaders were denouncing.

These remarks must be kept in mind when we evaluate the terrible cry which Matthew has recorded and which has been the cause of Jewish anguish ever since: *His blood on us and on our children!* Pilate's hand washing was a Jewish gesture, not Roman (cf. Deut 21:6 f.), and doubtless it needed no accompanying words to be understood. *All the people* present then assumed the responsibility which Pilate shirked. There is no doubt that Matthew heard in this cry a voice of prophecy echoed in the Synagogue of his day which was locked in struggle with the Church. It is for him a symbol of Jewish unbelief, a Jewish vale-dictory to Israel's hopes, the passing of the age of Israel which from now on becomes (as so often in John's Gospel) simply "the Jews" (cf. Mt 28:15), an alien religion. The solemnity of the passage as well as the structure of his Gospel as a whole forbid us to take Matthew's meaning in any other sense.

But to recognize the lesson that Matthew intended to draw from the passage for an embattled Church is not to dispense ourselves from the historical and theological task which his and the other Gospels set us in dealing with these events. "On us and on our children" was the legal formula by which liability was assumed that would also extend to one's heirs. In speaking thus the crowd intended, presumably, to acknowledge itself completely responsible for Jesus' death. But no one, of course, can make his children guilty of a crime he alone has committed. "All the people" who undertook this responsibility were Jews, it is true, but they were certainly not the whole Jewish people, nor even a very large part of the city of Jerusalem. They could speak only for themselves. Even the guilt which they must undeniably bear was unevenly divided among them. There is no basis in this or any other passage in the Gospels for a concept of the Jews, past or present, as a people laboring under an inherited curse: there is no such thing. Nor does the Jewish failure to accept Jesus as Messiah—which, in any case, he was in something of a non-Jewish sense—stem from these ill-considered words of a small mob or have any direct connection with the fortunes of the Jewish people throughout subsequent history. It must be candidly and humbly con-fessed that throughout most of their subsequent history the chief cause both of Jewish unbelief and of Jewish agony has been simply Christians.

In general, the Gospels do not say that Pilate sentenced Jesus to death, but rather that he *delivered him over* (Matthew and John both speak of the *bēma* or judgment seat, however, and Lk 23:24 used the word "sentenced"). The reason for this does not seem to be an intention on their part to minimize Pilate's part in the execution of Jesus but rather to stress the role of Jesus as the Servant of the Lord (cf. Is 53:12, "he was delivered over to death"); for the same reason, Judas is said to have "delivered Jesus over" (cf. Mk 14:18; Mt 26:46; Lk 22:21; Jn 12:4, etc.) and the Jews to have "delivered him over" to Pilate (cf. Mk 15:1; Mt 27:2; Jn 19:1; Acts 3:13, etc.). Jesus was certainly judicially sentenced by Pilate and suffered death at the hands of Roman soldiers and under Roman law.

Mk 15:16–20   At the end of the preceding section Mark-Matthew
Mt 27:27–31   tell us that, once Pilate had finally had his mind made
Jn 19:1–3   up for him, *he had Jesus scourged, then delivered him
                 over to be crucified.* The close sequence is undoubtedly
correct. Crucifixion, originally an Oriental mode of execution which the Romans had adopted as they did so much else and made peculiarly their own, was a disgusting and degrading torture reserved for non-Roman citizens convicted of exemplary crimes like treason. It was properly an occasion rather than a cause of death to the poor victim, who died—usually after several days—of exposure, exhaustion, hunger, and especially thirst. For this reason, some of the other brutalities that usually accompanied it, such as scourging and the breaking of bones that we will see later, were in their own way rough acts of mercy which would hasten death. Before crucifying a man the Romans would first give him a thorough lashing, then with whips drive him naked through the streets with the heavy wood of his cross across his shoulders until, half-dead already, he reached the place of execution.

The whipping which preceded crucifixion was a savage affair in which the victim frequently died. The whip, which could never be used on a Roman citizen, often had pieces of lead or bone attached to the multiple lashes, which tore the flesh horribly. There was no limit placed on the number of strokes: the soldier, or several soldiers consecutively who administered the punishment simply kept at it till their arms grew tired. The Roman practice was in contrast with the humane Jewish law which limited the number of lashes that a man could be given to forty (cf. Deut 25:1–3); scrupulous as ever on points of the Law, the Jews never went beyond thirty-nine (cf. 2 Cor 11:24).

All this taken into consideration, it is not probable that Pilate used the scourging as a means of placating those thirsty for Jesus' blood and, perhaps, of stirring up pity in their breasts, as John goes on to tell the story. The scourging, *flagellatio,* was not a cautionary but a terminative punishment. It would have taken place immediately before the crucifixion, as in Mark and Matthew. By the same token, however, neither in all likelihood would a man who had undergone a Roman scourging have been a fit subject for the cruel humor of Pilate's soldiers, as is now presupposed in the sequence of all three Gospels. The mockery itself is without doubt entirely historical, but there is much to commend the view that it had already taken place in the Palace of the Hasmonaeans, under the auspices of Herod Antipas (see above on Lk 23:6–16). Luke avoids saying anything directly about either of these indignities.

Whether administered by soldiers of Herod or those of the Roman garrison, the treatment accorded Jesus could hardly have differed very much. In both instances these were men recruited from the dregs of society, not Romans by birth but of every race and allegiance from the neighboring provinces, who by military duty could earn for themselves the coveted privileges of Roman citizenship. They shared a common hatred and contempt for the Jews: what was done to Jesus, we note, was as much an insult to the Jews as to himself personally. In this man who called himself—so they imagined—the King of the Jews, they saw a ludicrous object upon which they could vent their feelings for the whole race. The Gospels seem to describe a mock coronation. *They dressed him up in royal purple,* Mark says, which Matthew more realistically revises to *a scarlet cloak* of the type that soldiers wore: if sufficiently faded, it would resemble royal purple (John holds to *a purple robe*). The *crown of thorns* which they wove and crushed down on his head was probably in imitation of the laurel wreath affected by the Roman emperors. None of this grotesquerie, of course, was particularly subtle, nor is it therefore difficult for us to follow.

Those who locate the *Lithostrōton* at the Fortress Antonia, however, and who follow Mark-Matthew and John in identifying the soldiers who made mock of Jesus with the praetorian guard, may perhaps have some support for their views in the excavations that brought to light the paved courtyard of the Antonia. One of the games played by the Roman soldiers, the tracings for which may still be clearly discerned in the pavement (see above on Mk 15:1b and parallels), was the ancient Oriental jape of royalty called *Basilicus.* Having its origins in grim rites of myth and sympathetic magic, its sport consisted in the exaggerated ceremonial honors accorded a "king" chosen by lot who at the end was obliged to pay a forfeit—in ancient times his life itself, later a banquet or a round of drinks which he stood for his fellow players. Harmless vestiges of the ancient mythical ritual still exist under many forms in the folkways of various European peoples. The suggestion is that it was this customary game of the praetorian soldiers that dictated their treatment of the King of the Jews on this Good Friday.

Jn 19:4–16a   John has, by exception, repeated these repugnant details from the Synoptic tradition because they prepare for the scene that follows which is particularly suited to his portrayal of the Gospel story. We can easily imagine it as taking place after Jesus had been returned to Pilate by Herod Antipas, even though John in his Gospel has nothing about the confrontation of Jesus and Herod.

If it was Pilate's thought that the spectacle of the humiliated Jesus would satisfy the designs of the crowd, he could not have made a greater mistake; for John, "the Jews" who cry *Crucify him!* are *the chief priests and officials* who had arrested him (vs. 6), since this evangelist has nothing in his story about the crowd which had gathered to call for Barabbas. *Here is the man!* on Pilate's lips is a piece of Johannine irony. Pilate intends simply to point out a pitiable object, but John wants us to remember that the Son of Man is *the* Man.

Pilate's suggestion that the Jews *take him yourselves and crucify him* can only be sarcasm, for whatever power the Sanhedrin may have had to enforce capital punishment, crucifixion was a non-Jewish form of execution symbolic to them of their subjection to laws other than their own. The taunt does elicit from them a statement on the sentence passed on Jesus in the Jewish trial which John has not recorded: what had been done to Jesus thus far was all that Jewish law could do, and it now remained for Rome to do its part. *The Son of God* to Pilate would have had overtones far different from the biblical sense of this expression. Skeptic and cynic that he was, he doubtless shared in the superstitions of his class and age. Was this man somehow the offspring of a god, like the divine Caesar? *Where are you from?*, then, John sees as another piece of irony: Pilate is unconsciously demonstrating once more that he is part of that world which knows neither God nor his Son (cf. Jn 8:14, 9:29). Jesus maintains his customary silence during this as his other interrogations, for in the circumstances an answer would have been incomprehensible and have no point. He breaks his silence, however, when Pilate asserts his authority over life and death, to set the record straight, much to the satisfaction of John the evangelist: it is Jesus and not Pilate who is in real command of this situation. *The one who turned me over to you* is doubtless a reference to the Jewish leadership in general. It is the *more guilty* for having abused a God-given power, misleading rather than guiding the people entrusted to its care. As for Pilate, he has already proved himself to be only dimly aware of the magnitude of the drama taking place under his eyes, and in a moment it will become evident how hollow was his claim to have absolute discretion concerning what would happen to Jesus. It is now the judge who is under judgment.

If you turn this man loose you are no friend of Caesar. John's testimony to the ultimate persuasion used against Pilate has the ring of absolute authenticity. This was an argument which Pilate, who loved the glory of man rather than the glory of God (cf. Jn 12:43), found quite unanswerable. If he were to release Jesus against the will of those who had handed him over, what would be reported of him to Rome? That such reports were often made, and often heard, we know as a matter of record. Of a sudden, therefore, Pilate's vaunted power has melted away. He goes through the motions of the course laid out for him. He cannot resist one final fling at the Jews. Pointing to the outwardly dejected and degraded figure standing before him, he cries with all the hatred of his soul: *Look at your king!* From Pilate's point of vantage, this was merely a cry of frustrated rage. However, it goads the Jews into a counter-statement which John is able to report with his habitual irony. *We have no king but Caesar*, taken at face value, was the politic utterance of men prepared to deny their own heritage (cf. Jn 8:33) to gain their present objective through the power of Caesar. In John's day, a half dozen false messiahs later, with the temple in ruins and Jewish political power destroyed forever, the statement had its own more literal and more bitter truth.

Jn 19:16b–17a   The actual story of the way of the cross and the
Mk 15:21   crucifixion is told with relative brevity by all the
Mt 27:32   Gospels. The passion narrative, in the three versions
Lk 23:26–32   that we have in our Gospels, goes back to early
                 Christian meditation and *kerygma*, considerably in-
fluenced by the relevance of Old Testament figures and types such as that of Ps 22, the theme of the suffering just man. So much is this the case, it is not always possible to decide to what degree the type has determined the course of the narrative rather than been kept in its place as illustrative. The Gospels were no longer concerned with these events as statistical facts well known to their readers. From the beginning, the story had the liturgical and instructive character that it has ever after enjoyed in the Church.

John emphasizes that Jesus was *carrying his own cross* because he continues to insist on Jesus' complete control of his destiny at all times. Actually, this picture accords with the usual practice. Crucifixion was a degrading spectacle from beginning to end. The condemned person, stripped naked and beaten along with whips, was forced to bear the heavy crossbar on his shoulders, sometimes already fastened to his hands and arms; the upright of the cross, or of several crosses, for that matter, was already permanently fixed at the place of execution. However, there is no reason whatever to question the story of *Simon of Cyrene* found in the Synoptic Gospels. Obviously the cross was too much for Jesus to bear in his weakened condition, hence the soldiers forced a chance passerby to take up its burden instead. A highhanded action, but the Romans were used to this. The intimation of the Gospels is that Simon carried the cross by himself and that he carried it all the way to Golgotha. He was evidently a Jew of the Diaspora in Jerusalem for the feast day, *coming* into the city *from the country* (Mark and Luke). That Mark knows him as *the father of Alexander and Rufus* might mean that his sons, at least, later became Christians. The Gospels, at all events, say nothing further about him.

The story of Simon of Cyrene and that of *the women* of Jerusalem told only by Luke are two of the traditional "stations" of the cross. The stations, composed of incidents taken both from the Gospels and from apocryphal legends and introduced as a devotion into the West apparently in the thirteenth century, are faithful to the genre of the narrative we have before us. The women of whom Luke speaks were probably those who made it their pious custom to accompany condemned criminals and render them charitable services. The cup of wine that was ministered to Jesus before his crucifixion was probably handed him by one of these women. It is typical of Luke's concern for the feminine element in the Gospel that he alone has recorded this story. We note, too, that besides the women, *a great multitude of the people were following him;* with only the apparent exception of verse 13 above, in Luke's Gospel "the people" are Jesus' well-wishers.

Jesus does not rebuke the women for weeping over his plight, for their weeping was undoubtedly sincere; but somewhat in the language of the Synoptic eschatological discourse (see above on Mk 13:3–8 and parallels), he tells them of the coming things over which they will have to weep even more bitterly as affecting them the more directly. His citation of Hos 10:8 (describing the destruction of Samaria) specifies his reference to the devastation of Jerusalem by the Romans in A.D. 70. *If they do this with green wood, what will they do with dry?* has been variously interpreted. The general sense is clear: if green wood, which is tough and resilient and hard to burn, can nevertheless be so easily destroyed, by comparison what a blaze can be kindled with old dry wood! But who are the "they"? In context, Jesus is the green wood and Jerusalem the dry, and "they" are probably the Romans. If they so treat one who has offended them in no way, what will they not do with rebellious Judea?

Only Luke mentions at this point the presence of the others who were crucified with Jesus. Luke speaks, literally, of *two other criminals,* a choice of words that caused no end of embarrassment to early Christian scribes (and even to some modern translators as well); however, legally Jesus was a criminal, and he and his companions in suffering were on a common plane. Mark-Matthew later identify them as *bandits,* by the same word that John earlier used for Barabbas. It is conceivable that they, too, were part of the uprising of which Barabbas, presumably, had been leader (Mk 15:7). At all events, the association— together with the title which Pilate had affixed to Jesus' cross—without doubt gives us a strong factual indication of the meaning that the crucifixion had for Pilate and his Roman soldiers: the execution of a convicted rebel against the authority of the state.

Mk 15:22–26   According to Mark, who alone of the Synoptics makes
Mt 27:33–37   a point of it, *it was the third hour when they crucified*
Lk 23:33–34   *him.* This is one of the celebrated conflicts of the Gos-
Jn 19:17b–24   pels, since John has already said (vs. 14) that it was
               on the day of Preparation for the Passover about the
sixth hour that Jesus was condemned to death. John's chronology is theological: it was after noon (the sixth hour) that the Passover lamb was sacrificed on the day of Preparation (see above on Mk 14:12–17 and parallels). But Mark's chronology is probably equally theologically motivated: Jesus is crucified at the third hour, but then (vs. 33) there is darkness *from the sixth hour until the ninth hour* (the "darkness at noon" of Amos 8:9) when all is consummated; Mark's sequence divides itself into the three-hour periods of the Roman day (cf. the "terce," "sext," and "none" canonical hours of the Roman breviary). If we had to make a decision between the two timetables, which we do not, we should doubtless opt in favor of John's, since it is hard to imagine all that we have seen thus far having taken place by nine o'clock in the morning. On the other hand, the visitor to Palestine to this very day is perennially surprised to find that when he turns out of bed at eight o'clock or so in the morning the day is already half over for many natives of the place.

The place of execution is called by all the Gospels *the Skull*, for which all but Luke give the Aramaic name *Golgotha* (more accurately, *golgoltha*). The name "Calvary" in common English use comes from the translation in the Latin Vulgate *calvariae locus*, "the place of the Skull." The place was so called probably not from any fancied resemblance to the configurations of a human skull, but because it was a height, a headland. It is likely that there is no better authenticated site among all of those mentioned in the New Testament than that of Jesus' death and burial, which, according to John (vs. 41), was one and the same. Here Constantine built the first Basilica of the Holy Sepulcher in the fourth century, depending, as he usually did, on far more ancient and reliable tradition. There is not much that modern-day archaeology has been able to contribute to strengthen or weaken the tradition, but what little it has had to say has been in its favor. Some maps of "Jerusalem in the time of Christ" may still be found on which an encircling line has been drawn about the traditional site of the Sepulcher to indicate that in the first century it was within the city walls, thus impossibly the place of Jesus' execution and burial both from the known laws and customs of the time and on the testimony of the Gospel (cf. Jn 19:17, 20). But this line was drawn by unscholarly prejudice from the beginning, and subsequent scholarly prejudice has not availed to justify it; what little archaeological evidence there is, which is admittedly scanty, indicates that the traditional Golgotha and Sepulcher were safely outside the walls of New Testament Jerusalem. We must stress that it is the site only of which we are now speaking: nothing that is at present to be seen in the Church of the Holy Sepulcher in Jerusalem, several times demolished and rebuilt in the course of the centuries, goes back to New Testament times.

The *title* which Pilate affixed to Jesus' cross, which in John's Gospel is the occasion of a last bitter interchange between the governor and the Jews, was in accordance with Roman practice. That it was fastened to the cross rather than hung about his neck as was sometimes done may indicate that the form of Jesus' cross was "Latin," that is, that the upright beam projected beyond the crossbar. The cross was probably not very high; wood was and is a scarce commodity in Palestine. There was no footrest on the cross as later artists have imagined. The feet of the cruci-fied were either nailed separately to the wood or were tied there. In-stead, there was ordinarily a projecting peg which the condemned person straddled; this took the weight from his hands and arms and supported the body. The hands were sometimes nailed to the crossbeam, either at the wrists or through the palms, and sometimes they were tied. Or both methods might be used. John takes it for granted that Jesus was nailed to the cross (cf. Jn 20:25–27), and this seems to be Luke's meaning as well (cf. Lk 24:39). The *wine mixed with myrrh* which was offered to Jesus according to Mark was supposed to have a narcotic effect to deaden the pain of the torture. Matthew, by substituting *gall*, has seen in this gesture the fulfillment of another Old Testament type (cf. Ps 69:22).

All the Gospels mention the distribution of Jesus' garments by the soldiers (cf. Ps 22:19); custom gave the executed criminal's clothing to the executioners. Only John notes that the number of soldiers was *four*. This evangelist also makes a point of the *tunic without seam* worn by Christ for which the soldiers cast lots rather than destroy it. It is probable that he is again thinking of Jesus' priestly role on the cross, since it was the high priest's garment that could not be torn (cf. Lev 21:10).

Christians have long followed the devotional practice of collecting the last sayings of Jesus during his passion as recorded severally by the Gos-pels into "the seven last words." The first "word," Luke's verse 34a, is missing from some of both the oldest and the best manuscripts and may not be original to the Gospel; but it is one of those most in keeping with the spirit of the Jesus that is portrayed by the Gospels. *Father, forgive them, for they know not what they do* is not a condonation of evil but a plea for mercy. It does not deny the malice of those re-sponsible for the crucifixion, but it extends pity to those who are most in need of it, to those whose prejudices and hatreds have blinded them

to the enormity of the crimes they commit and which make them evil
men while they deem themselves righteous.

Mk 15:27–32   John has no room in his Gospel for the spectacle of
Mt 27:38–44   the crucified Christ prey to the insults and sneers of the
Lk 23:35–43   bystanders, *wagging their heads* in the Oriental way of
                 derision (cf. Pss 22:8, 109:25; Lam 2:15) and throwing
in his face his own words or deeds or words and deeds ascribed to him
(on Matthew's vs. 43 cf. also Ps 22:9). Luke has permitted us to see
some of it, but for his own purposes and in his own way. In the first
place, he distinguishes as usual between *the people* who *stood by watching* and *the rulers* who *scoffed at him.* Mark-Matthew supposes the cries
of raillery to have been initiated by chance passersby, which is natural
enough. Public executions, for a variety of psychological and other reasons, often enough bring out the very worst of which man is capable;
then, too, it is usually the very worst of men who find their recreation
in witnessing an execution. Natural, too, is Luke's information that the
soldiers joined in the mocking of Jesus. These were crude, rough men
who knew no way of dealing with criminals except cruelty. They merely
aped the cries that they heard about them, hoping to draw a reply from
the suffering man that would ease the boredom of their vigil. Luke brings
in here the incident of the *sour wine,* apparently taking it as another
instance of ridicule.

Luke makes another distinction. In Mark-Matthew's account, *those who
had been crucified with him also were taunting him.* Common misery
does not always ennoble men or make for brotherhood. According to
Luke, however, only one of the criminals joined in the abuse. Writhing
in pain on his cross, the poor devil was without doubt happy to find
that at least someone in the world was in a worse state than he. At
the same time, while his taunt was undoubtedly not to be taken seriously,
he made it practical. Yes, let Jesus indeed save himself—and save his
companions too. But the other one of the crucified, still according to
Luke, was prepared, despite the abject appearance now borne by Jesus,
to accept him at his own evaluation and recognize in him a Savior. His
profession of faith draws from Jesus the second "word" from the cross:
Today you will be with me in paradise. It would be beyond the evangelist's intention to read into this utterance a New Testament theology
of the afterlife. "Paradise" meant various things in Jewish apocalyptic
language, but always it had an association with a blessed immortality with
God. The "good thief" had put his faith in Jesus and asked to have a
share in his *kingdom*—we certainly need not presume that he had a better formed notion of what he was asking than Jesus' own intimate disciples had had (see above on Mk 10:35–45 and parallel). Jesus answers
his request in the spirit in which it was made: he will, indeed, be re-

membered by Jesus, and even more, he will share his glory as he has shared his suffering, and that beginning immediately. This immediacy of the kingdom is Luke's contribution to "realized eschatology." For him as for John the important thing is that Jesus reigns from the cross, the dispenser of salvation.

Jn 19:25–27   The third "word" from the cross is John's, and very
                much a part of his theology. All the Gospels speak of friends as well as enemies of Jesus who witnessed his execution. Luke (vs. 49) has it that *his acquaintances stood at a distance* (cf. Pss 38:12, 88:9 f.) along with *the women who had followed him from Galilee*. Mark (vs. 40) and Matthew (vs. 56) include among these women *Mary Magdalene, Mary the mother of James and Joses* (Matthew: *Joseph*), one of the "sisters" of Jesus as James and Joses were his "brothers" (see above on Mk 6:1–6a and parallels), and one or two others. *Salome* (Mk) may be *the mother of the sons of Zebedee* (Mt), and either John's *Mary the wife of Clopas* or *the sister of his mother* (if, indeed, John means to designate two women here) may be the mother of James and Joses; but we cannot be sure about these correspondences. At any rate, the Gospels presuppose various others present. John's most significant contribution to the list is Mary *the mother of Jesus*.

As in the only other passage of John's Gospel in which she plays a role, Mary is addressed by Jesus as *woman* (see above on Jn 2:1–11). Jesus' present action is not merely to provide a home for his mother as he is on the point of departing the world in death. His designation of *the disciple whom he loved* as her *son* is also a proclamation of Mary's spiritual motherhood of the faithful, as the new Eve, the mother of the living (Gen 3:20), a figure of the Church. The beloved disciple, whatever his historical identity, bears the character of every true Christian who is in the heart of Christ as Christ is in the heart of God (cf. Jn 1:18, 13:23). It is altogether fitting that this proclamation be made at the moment of Jesus' expiration (cf. John's vss. 30, 34 below), the beginning of the saving work of the Church through the power of the Spirit.

Mk 15:33–35   Quite different from this is Jesus' fourth "word" as
Mt 27:45–47   given by Mark-Matthew. This is another of those ut-
Lk 23:44–45a   terly authentic sayings ascribed to Jesus which, far from
                being the creation of early Christian theology, have posed problems for theology ever since. Luke no more than John can bring himself to transmit it, but restricts himself to the description of the *darkness over the whole earth from the sixth hour* until *the ninth hour* when Jesus spoke his word: the traditional *tre ore* of the passion, from noon till mid afternoon. As far as this and the subsequent phenomena described by the Gospels are concerned, while we need not conclude that they are purely symbolic, neither would it be faithful to

the Gospel accounts to interpret them as the record of statistical facts. They use the language of apocalyptic, which habitually described the great deeds of the Lord in terms of cosmic disturbances and perturbations, imitating in this the usage of the Old Testament prophets (cf. Is 2:2, 40:4 f.; Ezek 47:1-12; Mi 1:3 f., 4:1, etc.). On the "darkness at noon," cf. Amos 8:9; Jer 15:8 f.

Both Mark and Matthew quote Jesus' cry in two slightly varying forms of a Hebraized Aramaic; it is not possible to decide whether Jesus spoke in Hebrew that was Aramaized in the Gospel tradition, or vice versa. The words are the beginning of that Ps 22 which has so influenced the writing of the passion narrative. It has often been pointed out that this psalm is, in the ultimate analysis, a prayer of confidence in God and trust in his mercy, and that, whether or not Jesus recited the entire psalm, as is conceivable, his quotation of it was evocative of its final word of faith and trust. This is indeed true. But it is also true that these are words that express a sense of dereliction. It is the dereliction of a man of faith, but dereliction nonetheless. We must not attempt to explain the words away, but rather accept what they have to tell us about Jesus. They tell us that the Christ of Christian faith who suffered and died for us did so as a man in the fullest possible way, for all that this faith also assures us that he was something beyond man. It is the former rather than the latter affirmation of faith that this "word" impresses upon us. Just as at Gethsemane, Jesus' "loud cries and tears" (Heb 5:7) on the cross were wrung from a heart conscious of a terrible aloneness, an aloneness which even included that bewilderment before the inscrutable ways of God and his personal involvement in them that the man of faith knows as being abandoned by God.

Mk 15:36-37 The fifth, sixth, and seventh traditional "words" now
Mt 27:48-50 follow in quick succession. Mark and Matthew have their
Lk 23:46   casual bystanders catch Jesus' agonized prayer as a call
Jn 19:28-30 for help to *Elijah*, who was so often featured in messianic thought (see above on Jn 1:19-24). Perhaps the confusion may indicate that Jesus spoke the *Eli* of Matthew (Hebrew or Aramaic) rather than the *Elohi* of Mark (Hebrew, approaching the Aramaic *Elahi*). It has been often debated whether the mistake was in good faith or another form of ridicule, but the Gospels indicate that it was honest. These, after all, were uninvolved people, the "no opinion" percentage of the popular polls on good and evil, war and peace, God and Devil. Jesus' sufferings had provided them diversion against an idle afternoon and they had been the first to laugh at the pathetic spectacle on the cross, a demonstrated failure. But they had nothing against him, really. Perhaps, after all, he could bring off his summons of Elijah. It was certainly a possibility worth waiting for. Therefore they protested

vigorously when someone tried to put an end to Jesus' suffering by offering him drink—*Wait! let's see whether Elijah comes to save him.*

This relationship of events is somewhat obscured for us by Mark, who
may have misunderstood the purpose of the *sour wine;* in verse 36 Luke
also seems to have taken it as part of the persecution of Jesus (there is,
for that matter, an allusion to Ps 69:22 in the incident). But it is clear
from Matthew and, especially John, where the wine is offered in response
to Jesus' *I thirst,* that the gesture was kindly meant. It was popularly
believed, on whatever authority of experience, that drink hastened the
death of a crucified person. In John's Gospel Jesus takes the drink *knowing that all was now finished:* he himself decides when it is time for him
to die. Probably (explicitly so in Luke) it was one of the soldiers who
proffered the wine as an act of rough kindness. The wine in question
(*oxos*) was the cheap, vinegary thirst-quencher such as soldiers commonly
carried with them on duty. According to Mark-Matthew the wine was
raised to Jesus' lips by means of a soaked *sponge* thrust on *a reed.* For
"reed" John has substituted *hyssop.* This is initially incomprehensible,
since hyssop is a limp, leafy plant unsuited to be the conveyer of anything. However, John is still thinking of Jesus as the sacrificed Passover
lamb (see on Mk 14:12–17 and parallels and cf. Jn 19:14); it was with
hyssop that the blood of the Passover lamb was sprinkled on the door-
posts of the faithful (cf. Ex 12:22).

Immediately after drinking the wine, according to John, Jesus says,
It is finished. Again he himself pronounces that the moment of his death
has come; his sacrifice is ended with his carrying out of the divine
decree. The Synoptics mark the time of passing with Jesus' utterance
of *a loud cry* of sudden death, to which, nevertheless, Luke adds the
words of Ps 31:6. The *expired* (Mark and Luke) or *he gave up the
spirit* (Matthew) of the Synoptics probably means nothing more or less
than "he died"; but when John writes solemnly that *he handed over
the spirit,* we are probably meant to recall that through Jesus' glorious
death the Spirit has been delivered to the Church (cf. Jn 7:39, 20:23).

Mk 15:38–39   The Synoptics conclude their apocalyptic drama-
Mt 27:51–54   tization of the death of a Savior: if men do not
Lk 23:45b, 47–48   know how to mourn this thing that they have
                     done, then the elements do. *The veil of the temple
was split in two:* but which veil? One veil, at the entrance of the temple,
separated the interior of the temple from the profane gaze of Gentiles.
Are we to understand, then, that the death of Jesus has torn this veil
asunder as it also broke down the "wall of separation" (Eph 2:14),
uniting Jew and Gentile in one principle of salvation? There was also
the veil that separated the Holy Place of the temple, where the priests
offered incense, from the Holy of Holies, the most sacred spot in all

Israel, where God was thought especially to dwell, and which was entered by only the high priest once a year. Do we take the Gospels to mean that now the Old Testament priestly distinctions are at an end, their functions subsumed and fulfilled in the sacrifice of Jesus (cf. Heb 6:19, 10:20)? At all events, the death of Christ has changed the significance of the temple, and what now matters is no longer the temple, but Christ the Lord (cf. Jn 2:19).

Matthew's vision is the boldest of all. *The earth quaked, boulders split, tombs opened, and many bodies of saints who had fallen asleep were raised. Coming forth from their tombs after his resurrection, they entered the holy city and appeared to many.* This again is imagery (cf. Heb 12:26), utilizing Old Testament figures (cf. Is 26:19, 52:1; Ezek 37:12; Dan 12:2, etc.) in the perfect genre of New Testament apocalyptic (cf. Apo 11:11–13, 20:4–6, 21:2–4, etc.). In non-apocalyptic, non-descriptive language, Paul has put it otherwise: "Christ has been raised from the dead, the firstfruits of those who have fallen asleep" (1 Cor 15:20).

It is Mark, our oldest of the Gospel historians, who has told us what ultimately prompted the "confession" of *the centurion* in charge of the soldiers who saw to the execution of Jesus. It was, he says, *seeing how he died.* At the same time, Mark and Matthew after him have not resisted the temptation to put on the centurion's lips the affirmation of Christian faith—*Truly, he was Son of God*—in place of what comes much more naturally from Luke's account: *Surely, this man was innocent!* The centurion was undoubtedly a pagan, no better and no worse than the rest of his kind, whose level was not high. But he had seen what he had seen. Right is right, after all. Jesus had died no raving, screaming death of a maniac, but with the dignity fitting the claims he had made for himself. Equivalently, he had been proved right and his enemies wrong: the testimony of the Spirit had begun (cf. Jn 16:8–11).

26. GOD AND LORD OF ALL

Jn 19:31–37   This concluding chapter begins with the Gospel accounts of the immediate aftermath of the crucifixion. While the Romans had no scruples about letting an executed criminal gasp out his life for days, if necessary, the Jews did. The Law forbade a dead body to remain on the gibbet overnight (cf. Deut 21:22 f.: the Jewish law, of course, did not envision the impalement of a living person). Now the Sabbath would soon be upon Jerusalem, at sunset, after which the work of burying the dead could not take place. Besides, this coming Sabbath was *a solemn day*, the Passover, in fact. It was not to be tolerated that the solemnity of the feast should be marred by the sight of the three crosses with their sorrowful burdens on the hill of Golgotha just outside the walls of the festive city. Hence the Jews petitioned Pilate to hasten the death of the executed men that they might be safely laid away before the close of day. Pilate acceded to their request; he was no doubt as anxious as they were to avoid any potential trouble rising from the Passover celebration.

The customary manner of carrying out this apparently merciful measure was the brutal one of beating the helpless victim with iron rods. John calls it *breaking their legs*, because in fact that is what usually occurred; the legs were the part of the body the soldiers could most conveniently reach as the person hung on the cross. This beating was inflicted on the two others who had been crucified with Jesus, for they were still alive. But Jesus was already dead, and hence his bones were not broken. John sees in this fact another fulfillment of the typology of the Passover lamb, the bones of which were not to be broken (cf. Ex 12:46; Num 9:12).

Though the soldiers omitted the breaking of Jesus' bones, recognizing him to be dead, nevertheless one of them *pierced his side with a lance*, just to be sure. From the wound *immediately poured out blood and water*—the water, in medical opinion, would be actually either pericardial fluid or the clear serum of a pleural hemorrhage. For John this is another "sign" witnessing to the meaning of Christ's death. In 1 Jn 5:8 "water and blood" sums up the redemptive life and death of Jesus. It was

a common patristic interpretation that the flow of blood and water sym-
bolizes the life-giving ministry of the Church which derives its efficacy
from the death of Christ, and it is most likely that John had something
like this in mind. In fact, his previous use of the symbols of water (cf.
Jn 3:5, 4:10, 14, 7:38 f.) and blood (cf. Jn 6:53–57) encourages us in
the belief that he was thinking of the sacraments of Baptism and the
Eucharist, both of which he has featured in his Gospel. The piercing
of the side of Jesus itself he connects with Zech 12:10 (a word concerning one who, in John's thought, was probably identical with the Servant
of the Lord).

Thus even in death the Word of God rules and saves, as these mute
witnesses testify; and to their testimony the evangelist adds his own,
which is part of it.

Mk 15:40–47   The Synoptic Gospels have introduced the disciples and
Mt 27:55–61   Galilean followers of Jesus, and especially the women
Lk 23:49–56   (see above on Jn 19:25–27), as witnesses both of his
Jn 19:38–42   crucifixion and his burial. All our narrative sources
                are in agreement as to the identity of the man who
buried Jesus, though they describe him somewhat variously. *Joseph of
Arimathea,* a wealthy man who had come from an obscure little town
in Judea, was, it is agreed, a leading member of the Sanhedrin. Neither
Mark nor Luke ever says in so many words that he was a disciple of
Jesus, though Luke approaches such a statement in verse 51; both Matthew and John explicitly identify him as one of Jesus' followers. From
this variation some scholars have concluded that Mark had the right of
it at the beginning: that Joseph was simply a Jew faithful to the law of
Deut 21:22 f., who saw to the burial of Jesus as a disinterested work of
piety (so, too, the pious Jews—not Christians—of Acts 8:2 who buried
the protomartyr Stephen); the later Gospels which make Joseph a disciple contain the embellishments of an expanding tradition. While this
is conceivable, it would be difficult to explain even on Mark's account
why Joseph went to all the trouble he did for someone in whom he
did not take a personal interest; furthermore, Mark's observation that
he too was looking forward to the kingdom of God, we may be sure,
was not idly written.

As a disciple, however, he was not a particularly heroic one. Luke's
saying that *he was a good and just man* is not a blanket endorsement
of his life. We are left to imagine the figure he cut as a member of the
Sanhedrin that judged Jesus worthy of death—though, for that matter, his
involvement in that action may have taken no more positive form than
the flight of the Twelve who had left Jesus alone and defenseless. John
appropriately associates with him the timid *Nicodemus* (cf. Jn 3:1 ff.,
7:50 f.), also a member of the Sanhedrin and also a secret disciple of

Jesus. It was doubtless of these men among others that the evangelist was thinking in Jn 12:42. At least, they do now come forward and declare themselves by their actions.

As relatives or friends of the deceased had a right, Joseph petitioned the governor for the body of Jesus that he might save it from the common burial ground or charnel heap into which the bodies of executed criminals were commonly cast. The request may have been made at the same time that the Jews asked for the executions to be speeded up in view of the impending feast. Pilate, at first understandably surprised that Jesus was so soon dead, readily acceded to the proposal of an important man that cost him nothing.

The tomb, John says, was *in a garden near the place where he was crucified*, and, according to Matthew, it was Joseph's own tomb, probably one which he had had prepared for himself and his family: that it was *a new tomb in which no one had yet been laid* is perhaps John's and Luke's way of agreeing with Matthew. The proximity of the tomb to the place of execution is natural enough, since both had to be outside the city walls according to law. There are still visible in Palestine many tombs contemporary with and like the one the Gospels describe. It may have been at first a natural cave which was then further hollowed out till a sizable room was made, then fitted out with several individual resting places for the deceased. These were simply slabs of stone, sometimes with headrests, and sometimes with footrests as well. It was in such a tomb that the body of Lazarus had been laid according to the story of Jn 11:1-44, and the Gospels now describe Jesus as swathed in linen cloths as Lazarus' body had been. The opening of the tomb was, as usual, covered by a round flat stone—old millstones sometimes served the purpose—which could be rolled aside in a groove fixed for it.

The major discrepancy between the Johannine and the Synoptic accounts of the burial of Jesus concerns the circumstances of the embalming of his body. All the Gospels stress the haste of the burial, but while in the Synoptics this serves to explain the deferring of the customary preparation of the body for the tomb—a deferment which, in fact, was never actualized because of the intervention of the resurrection—John, nevertheless, insists that everything of *the burial custom of the Jews* was, indeed, done by means of the superabundant *mixture of myrrh and aloes, about a hundred pounds*, provided by Nicodemus. The reason for the difference, which is chiefly due to John's theology, we have already seen above (on Jn 12:1-8 and parallels). As John saw it, the burial for which Mary's precious ointment had been kept was not this "Jewish" interment of his dead body but his submersion in the life of the Church.

Mt 27:62-66   Matthew has another story (completed in Mt 28:11-15 below) from his collection of Jerusalem traditions which he uses to complete the narrative of Jesus' passion and death preparatory to the common Gospel testimony to the resurrection. The purpose of the story, as is obvious, is to counter an objection that the tomb of Jesus was found to be empty only because his disciples had come and spirited away his body. Even though the narrative is a free composition by the Christian community—the conversation between *the chief priests and Pharisees and Pilate*, for example, must have been reconstructed on imagination, since it is hardly to be thought that any one of the principals would have furnished a transcript for the Gospel tradition; furthermore, taken on the surface, the priests and Pharisees have a more vivid recollection of Jesus' promise of resurrection *after three days* and a greater expectation of its fulfillment than did his own intimate disciples!—still, in its own way it is a witness to the historicity of the empty tomb. That such a story had to be told shows that the point under debate between Christian and Jew was not the fact of the empty tomb, but rather how it came to be empty. The tradition of the empty tomb certainly belongs to the Jewish era of the Church: in Jewish thought, but not in the Greek thinking of the Gentile world, survival and reappearance after death necessitated a bodily resurrection.

Matthew's way of referring to Saturday as *the day after the Preparation* is curious—almost as though he was conscious that this was, indeed, the Passover as it appears in John's Gospel, but was inhibited from calling it this in view of his portrayal of the Last Supper as a Passover meal; otherwise we would expect him to have simply *the Sabbath*, as he later does in company with the other Gospels. Mk 15:42 also refers to the day of crucifixion as *the Preparation*, but there it is made to mean *the eve of the Sabbath*. The intervention of the Sabbath-Passover partly explains why a Roman *guard* (cf. Mt 28:14) was requested for the tomb when otherwise the temple police or other Jewish guards might have been employed: throughout for "guard" Matthew uses the Latin word *custodia*. Also, of course, the tomb was private property, and therefore some kind of official approval was needed. Pilate's *you have a guard* is to be taken to mean "here and now you are given a guard."

Mk 16:1–8	As is also the case with other Gospel events, both those
Mt 28:1–8	of great importance such as the institution of the Eucha-
Lk 24:1–12	rist and those of relatively secondary concern such as the
Jn 20:1–13	story of Peter's denials of the Lord, the resurrection nar-

ratives of the four Gospels are materially discordant and it is absolutely pointless to think of harmonizing their many variant details. Also, that kind of consistency was never within the purview of the Gospel writers, who wrote down the traditions as they had come to them without bothering their heads about such discrepancies or attempting to give us any help toward resolving them (some of their copyists, to be sure, did make the attempt). A fifth record of the tradition (1 Cor 15:3–8), the oldest of the lot as a written document, set down at a time when there were still living witnesses to the events recalled in it, merely compounds the confusion by contributing discordances of its own. We simply have to face the fact that such matters as to whom the risen Lord first appeared, and in the presence of whom, and under what precise circumstances, were not historical issues for the New Testament traditions of the resurrection.

Comparing the traditions one with the other, however, we find that there is a consensus not only on the underlying essentials, but even on certain points of detail. First of all, there is never any attempt—as there is in later apocryphal literature—to describe the resurrection itself. The resurrection is allowed to remain the mystery that it is, its "mechanics" unsubmitted to speculation. The empty tomb is a sign of the resurrection, but only after it has been determined by the revealed word: "He has been raised." The essence of the resurrection is not that a dead body left the tomb, but that a living person who had been dead, Jesus of Nazareth, lives once more, now transformed and glorified with God. He has passed from this earthly sphere and entered into the heavenly realm, for all that he continues to live in his Church through his Spirit. But both in the Semitic conception of things and, more than we often realize, according to our own "Western" conceptions as well, the body of man *is* his human personality. Thus the meaning of the empty tomb for the evangelists.

It does not seem to be true that the tradition of the empty tomb represents a later stage in resurrection theology, an attempt to provide objective evidence for the spiritual experience that the first Christians had of their living Lord after his death and burial. A resurrection without an empty tomb would have been as incomprehensible to St. Paul as to these other Christians: if the discussion in 1 Cor 15 is read attentively, this becomes very clear. Though the words "empty tomb" do not occur in the tradition which Paul recalls in verses 3–8, the idea is certainly there. That Jesus was known to have been raised up *on the third day* and not immediately indicates an awareness of the part played in the history of the resurrection by Jesus' burial and the tomb. The empty tomb does not figure in the Gospels as an argument to settle doubts and silence incredulity; rather, as Matthew has already shown, it was the occasion of controversy as well as a sign for belief.

Another point on which the Gospels are agreed is that the resurrection was wholly unexpected by Jesus' disciples. Though the Gospels have recorded Jesus' prophecies of his resurrection, they have also shown that the prophecies were not understood: these Gospel accounts are redactions of Jesus' words in the light of post-resurrection faith. Any idea of the resurrection of Jesus as a wish-fulfillment of the early Christian Church, therefore, must call for evidence that is contrary to that of the

Gospels, evidence which they had far less reason to invent than simply to remember with mixed emotions.

The time of the discovery of the empty tomb is roughly the same in all the Gospels: *very early in the morning on the first day of the week* (Mark *ad litteram*; the substance in Matthew, Luke, John). Only two of the Gospels offer an explanation of the coming to the tomb of *the women who had come with him from Galilee* (so Luke's "they," cf. Lk 23:55; Mark, Matthew, and John mention *Mary Magdalene* explicitly and certain other women—even John, cf. the "we" of vs. 2). According to Mark and Luke (cf. also Lk 23:55 f.), they came to anoint Jesus' body. John, we know, has reason to omit such a detail, and Matthew, for some reason of his own, omits it as well: perhaps he saw a difficulty in an anointing and embalming so long after burial. Even though Joseph of Arimathea has been, explicitly or implicitly, identified by the Gospels as one of Jesus' followers, he was evidently unknown to the women and there had been no communication between them (cf. Mk 15:47; Lk 23:55). The Gospels say nothing further about him or Nicodemus.

When the women reach the tomb they find *the stone* (mentioned now for the first time by John) already *rolled away* from the door. The purpose of this intervention was not to suggest the manner in which the Lord left the tomb, but to show that he had indeed left it; this is also the purpose of the much more graphic story by which Matthew describes the way in which the stone was rolled away and the Roman guards about the tomb were routed. This story as well as those which Mark and Luke go on to tell are variant forms of "angelic annunciation" (so also John's vss. 11–13), not dissimilar from others we have seen earlier in the Gospels, especially in the Gospel of the Infancy (see above on Lk 1:8–12). The descriptive details are fairly conventional for such stories (cf. Dan 10:5–9; 2 Macc 3:26, 33; Acts 1:10 f., 10:30–32; Apo 3:5, 7:9, 19:14, etc.), which have in view to communicate the word by which the empty tomb is constituted a sign to believers: *He is not here; he has been raised up!*

The most serious discrepancy in the Gospel accounts of this annunciation is as regards the indication they give of the locale of the post-resurrection appearances of Jesus. Mark and Matthew understood that the Lord would make himself known to his disciples once again *in Galilee*, where, as far as they were concerned, the Gospel had begun. Luke and John, however, take it for granted that he appeared to the disciples in Jerusalem (although John's ch. 21 without explanation shifts the scene to Galilee). Having once adopted these viewpoints, the Gospels stick to them fairly consistently. Since it does not seem possible that they can be harmonized, most commentators have felt that one or the other must be chosen as historical, and of these probably the majority has opted for the Galilean tradition. After the crucifixion, it is felt, the scattered disciples

fled to their Galilean homeland—a three days' journey from Jerusalem—
and it was here that the risen Lord gathered them again into his Church.
The post-resurrection focus of interest was later switched to Jerusalem,
according to this hypothesis, because the Church in Galilee did not long
flourish and the center of Palestinian Christianity speedily became Jerusalem in any case. It can be added that both Gospels which feature
Jerusalem do so for theological reasons: for Luke Jerusalem is both the
beginning and the end, and for John it is the center of Jesus' public life.
There is much to support this argument; however, it can neither be
proved nor disproved on the Gospel evidence, and contrary positions are
also tenable. We are reduced simply to taking the Gospel narratives singly
as we have them.

Mark disagrees with the rest of the Gospels at this point. According to
him, the women *fled from the tomb* and *said nothing to anyone because
they were very much afraid*. It is possible, however, that Mark is merely
emphasizing the awe that had gripped these first witnesses to the empty
tomb, and that he is not precluding their later report to *his disciples and
Peter* as they had been instructed. At any rate, the other Gospels say that
they did run to take the news to the disciples. Luke records that their
word was not believed (his vs. 12 is probably not original, but is an addition to his text modeled on Jn 20:3–10).

John's narrative becomes not only incoherent with the other Gospels
but also somewhat with his own sequence: it is not entirely clear how
verses 11–18 concerning Mary Magdalene are to be fitted into the chronology he has established for himself. According to his version of the
story, the news of the empty tomb was first brought by Mary Magdalene
(and other women?) *to Simon Peter and the other disciple whom Jesus
loved*, who hastened to verify the report with their own eyes. This story
itself, as it happens, there seems to be no reason to regard as anything
other than what was originally the recollection of an eyewitness; Lk 24:24
appears to refer to it. *He* (the beloved disciple) *saw* the linen cloths in
the empty tomb *and* (he also, along with Peter?) *believed* might suggest
that the mute evidence of the empty shrouds (preserving the outline of
the figure that had lain in them?) offered some kind of visual evidence
of a resurrection even though *they did not yet understand the Scripture*.
The "understanding" of the Old Testament as having relevance to the
resurrection of Christ (cf. Acts 2:24–36, etc.) is part of the rereading of
the Scripture in the light of Christian fulfillment (cf. Lk 24:27, 32, 45);
in precisely the same way, contemporary Judaism had reread the Old
Testament in its own favor.

Mt 28:9–10   With verse 8 above the original Gospel of Mark, to
Jn 20:14–18   the extent that we now possess it, has come to an
[Mk 16:9–11]   end. We say "to the extent that we now possess it,"
                    for hardly anyone is prepared to believe that the Gos-

pel originally ended so abruptly, even though it does end so abruptly in our oldest and best Greek manuscripts. For whatever reasons, it is agreed, the original ending of Mark's Gospel has disappeared, leaving behind no provable trace in the manuscripts. On the law of averages, it was not very lengthy, probably not even as lengthy as the verses 9–20 which are found in most of the manuscripts, which the Church has traditionally regarded as inspired and canonical, but which were assuredly not written by Mark. These verses the Church itself has contributed to serve as a conclusion to the Gospel: they are a composite of what is elsewhere found in Matthew, Luke, and John. By the critics they are sometimes called "the longer ending" in distinction to an ending of only a few lines substituted for or combined with it in some few manuscripts.

At least part of the lost ending of Mark's Gospel may have been preserved for us in the verses copied from it by Matthew, according to which Jesus himself appeared to the women hastening from the tomb to reinforce the angelic instruction that they carry the good news to his disciples. The passage fits better in Mark than it does in Matthew, as a matter of fact. In Mark it might have served to break the silence of fear that had descended upon them at the tomb, whereas in Matthew it somewhat interferes with the climax of the Galilean appearance of the Lord in the Gospel's final verses.

That the women who saw the risen Jesus are said to have *embraced his feet* is probably one indication that this passage is the Synoptic parallel to John's story of the appearance to Mary Magdalene. Mary at first does not recognize Jesus, taking him to be the one who owned the garden in which the tomb was situated (Jn 19:41). Partly this misunderstanding follows the pattern of the Johannine dialogues; however, Lk 24:16, 37 ff. also indicate that there was something about the appearance of the risen Lord that did not make him immediately recognizable. But perhaps we should not expect logical coherence in a story of this kind which is describing a human situation that need not be logical. Mary is distraught from grief and bewilderment. The thought that Jesus' body has been moved and that she must *take him away*—we do not ask how she expected to manage this—has become a fixation for her. In any case, it suffices for Jesus to call her by name for her to know him at last (cf. Jn 10:3 f.). She gives the glad cry of recognition, *Rabboni* (so Mk 10:51; an alternate form of the "rabbi" otherwise frequent in the Gospels), and falls to her knees at his feet. *Do not cling to me* is Jesus' way of telling her of the changed relationship in which they now stand, somewhat like his words to his mother in Jn 2:4, when the same kind of change was anticipated. No longer is he merely a rabbi with his disciples at his feet. His glorification is not yet complete. He must now *ascend to my Father and your Father, to my God and your God*: the disjunction is calculated, to remind us that God is our Father only because he is first the Father of Jesus

Christ, through whom we have eternal life. As in Mt 28:10, Jesus now calls the disciples *my brothers* (cf. also Jn 2:12 and Mt 12:49 f.).

The verses in the supplement to Mark, it seems to be evident, are a summary statement based on John's story, with the help of Lk 8:2 and 24:11.

Mt 28:11–15   Matthew now continues with another story that was not in Mark's Gospel, the conclusion of the Jerusalemite tradition about the empty tomb which he began in Mt 27:62–66 above. As we have already observed, a story of this kind can only be a free composition by which the Christian conviction as to what had taken place was translated into narrative form. The earliest Christian apologists of patristic times testify that the explanation of the empty tomb which Matthew ascribes to the suborning of the Roman guards was, indeed, current among the Jewish adversaries of Christianity.

Lk 24:13–35   Luke also has a proper story of his own concerning
[Mk 16:12–13]   the post-resurrection appearances of Jesus which has been hastily summarized—not, however, without some conflict—in the supplement to Mark. It is a rather strange story which he has not entirely integrated into his Gospel, but at the same time it contains a number of details which for that very reason are all the more interesting for their being quite uncalculated. Some have thought that it is the vestige of the tradition known also to Luke, though not used by him, that the word of the resurrected Savior was first brought to Jerusalem from outside. The reference in verse 34 to a prior appearance to Peter looks like an afterthought in line with 1 Cor 15:5, since there is nothing else in the Gospel about this. Whether or not this is so, Luke has repeated the story because of other values that it had for him. We shall try to see those values briefly.

That very day is presumably Sunday, the day following the Passover, when pilgrims to the Holy City could make their return to their homes far and near (so vss. 21b–24, if these were part of the original story). *Two of them* has no immediate antecedent; *Cleopas* (not the Clopas of Jn 19:25) and his companion were certainly disciples of Jesus, but their relation to the Twelve and the others of his intimate band of followers is not clear. Their conception of Jesus' mission was without doubt that of most of his disciples, including the Twelve, despite the hints that he may have given them of the larger dimensions of his character: *a prophet mighty in deed and word before God and all the people . . . we were hoping that he was the one who would redeem Israel*. Obviously they had no idea of a suffering Messiah, of Jesus as fulfilling the ideal of the Servant of the Lord. It is this same limited christology that Luke ascribes to the apostles at the very moment of the ascension (cf. Acts 1:6). The application to himself of the relevant themes of Old Testament prophecy Jesus now proceeds to reveal to them as he enters their company with the easy democracy of the East and engages them in conversation.

After *the breaking of the bread* the disciples recognize Jesus in the mysterious stranger and they also realize how *he opened to us the Scriptures.* It is unquestionably here that Luke sees the chief significance of this story, which he has used like one of the Johannine narratives to find in it a "sign." The meal that the disciples had with Jesus at Emmaus was, of course, not the Eucharist—"the breaking of bread" was a common idiom for taking a meal just as it later became a Christian term for the Eucharistic celebration. But even as Christ showed himself to his disciples in the breaking of the bread, Luke wants his readers to recognize how something of the same kind happens in their Eucharistic assemblies. Furthermore, it is on such occasions that the meaning of the Scripture is made clear.

From the historical point of view, certain details of the story cause problems. Most of them revolve about the location of *the village whose name was Emmaus, about sixty stadia from Jerusalem.* There is only one site in Palestine which can reasonably be identified as Emmaus, as it has been from the earliest Christian times; it is still known by that name, in the Arabic form *Amwas.* But Amwas is considerably farther away from Jerusalem than sixty stadia (say seven miles): the distance is more like twenty miles to the west. It is true, there are some manuscripts of Luke which read *one hundred and sixty stadia,* but this reading is generally thought to be an adjustment of the text to fit the geography of Amwas. On the other hand, it is possible that Luke did originally write "one hundred and sixty stadia" and that the figure was later altered to "sixty" for the same reason that would cause a modern commentator to question its accuracy, the improbability, namely, that having already traveled twenty miles and come to Emmaus toward evening (vs. 29), Cleopas and his companion could after supper return the twenty miles to Jerusalem and that same night find the apostolic band still gathered together. Improbabilities, it must be admitted, are not necessarily impossibilities. It is almost certain that Luke never adverted to the difficulty at all. Other proposed sites of "Emmaus" in Palestine have little to recommend them except that they are in closer proximity to Jerusalem and were close by the pilgrim routes of later times; the latter criterion has always been a powerful one in establishing alternate traditions for "the holy places."

Lk 24:36–43   It is as a sequel and continuation to the preceding story
Jn 20:19–23   that Luke now tells of the Lord's appearance in Jerusa-
[Mk 16:14]   lem to *the Eleven and those who were with them* (vs. 33). It is not certain whether the parallel story in John's

Gospel was intended to reflect precisely the same tradition; at any rate, there are several similarities between the two accounts other than the one of their general situation. As usual, copyists have tried to make the similarities even closer: Luke's verse 40 is suspect as an addition to the text modeled on Jn 20:20, and the greeting of Jesus in verse 36 has probably been borrowed from that of John's verse 19. The summary verse in Mark's supplement seems to refer to the Lucan story; however, the rebuke for disbelief in the resurrection has been considerably heightened in contrast to Luke's account, according to which *they still disbelieved for joy.*

Luke is intent on showing the reality of the resurrection, the idea of which was doubtless still somewhat grotesque to various of his Gentile readers, and consequently he lays emphasis on the signs which Jesus gave to the unbelieving. Lest they should think that they had experienced an hallucination, he had them note the wounds in his *hands* and his *feet* and *touch* the solidity of his body (this seems to be the meaning of vs. 39, even though only in Jn 20:25 is there explicit mention of nail wounds in his hands). Even then, as they could scarcely credit their senses, he ate in their presence, taking the food that they themselves had prepared that they might be sure there was no illusion. The story has as its obvious purpose to "objectivize" the resurrection in meaningful human terms (cf. 1 Jn 1:1); Luke offers no theories on the constitution of what Paul called the "spiritual body" of the raised (cf. 1 Cor 15:42–50).

John also brings in the physical evidence of the resurrection, though he makes a point of Jesus' appearance despite the fact that *the doors were shut* (so also in vs. 26 below). His main stress, however, is on the resurrection as fulfillment of Jesus' promises. *Peace be with you* is the conventional Jewish greeting, but it has added significance in view of Jn 14:27 and 16:33. Similarly, his consecration of which he spoke in Jn 17:18 now finds its culmination in the mission of his apostles: *As the Father has sent me, so I send you. He breathed on them* expresses sacramentally what is determined by the words: *Receive Holy Spirit* (cf. Gen 2:7; Jn 3:8). This action shows that, in John's view, the ascension to the Father of which Jesus spoke to Mary Magdalene in verse 17 above has now taken place, the glorification which is necessary for the giving of the Spirit (cf. Jn 7:39, 15:26, 16:7; 1 Cor 15:45). John has nothing in his Gospel of the symbolic chronology of Luke by which the resurrection is separated from the ascension by forty days, and the coming of the Spirit by another ten days (cf. Lk 24:49–53; Acts 1:3–11, 2:1 ff.). Christian liturgical celebration of these mysteries has followed the Lucan chronology for the same reason that the evangelist first employed it, to focus attention on one or the other separable aspect of a single spiritual reality. John, too, has separated the aspects, but without the chronology.

The specific activity to be exercised by the Church through the power of the Holy Spirit is here defined in terms of the forgiveness of sin (cf. Mt 9:8, 16:19, 18:18). This the Church does alike in its preaching of the Gospel of salvation and in its ministry of the sacraments of forgiveness, baptism, and repentance.

Jn 20:24–29   John has a complement to the story he has just told, with which he originally concluded his Gospel: the episode ends with the most explicit act of faith in Christ to be found in all of the New Testament. It takes place on the Sunday following, a device by which the evangelist is probably suggesting the rapidity with which the first day of the week became the time of Christian assembly in perpetuation of the Easter mystery. *Thomas called the Twin* has been introduced before (cf. Jn 11:16, 14:5) as a member of *the Twelve* (John still uses the traditional designation). In John's mind Thomas' objection was probably not one of skepticism with regard to the reality of the Lord's presence, but was concerned with its manner; as was Lk 24:37, John is disposed to make a point of the resurrectional appearance of Jesus as more than "spiritual."

Thomas' conditions for belief were rigorous, and Jesus' words are almost ironic as he invites the inspection which the disciple had demanded. But apparently the sight of the risen Savior was enough for Thomas. *My Lord and my God* is a culmination of the faith of apostolic Christianity expressed in a formula explicit both in the language of the Old Testament and in that of the Hellenistic world of the Gospels. This is the meaning of Jesus' acknowledgment: *Because you have seen me, you have believed. Blessed are they who have not seen, yet have believed.* The resurrection appearances, and the entire Gospel narrative itself, are the testimony of the first Christians to what they had seen. But though to believe was to see, to see was not necessarily to believe: John's "book of signs" is evidence of this. In the ultimate analysis, belief is the acceptance of a word, not on external proof but on the power of the word itself to convince. Those who followed Jesus in his earthly ministry did so because they believed in his word. Those who now follow him do so out of belief in the same word, which is the word of the Gospel.

Jn 20:30–31   And thus John gives us at the end the purpose of his Gospel: *that you may believe that Jesus is the Christ, the Son of God, and that believing you may have life in his name.* Once more we understand what he has meant by speaking of Jesus' *signs,* some of which he has written down, most of which he has not. What Jesus did and said—adequate motives for belief for all who are called by God and disposed to be his children (cf. Jn 8:47)—is available in the living witness that the Church gives in its ministry of the sacraments, its proclamation of the word of life, and its total life of the Spirit.

Jn 21:1–14   The final chapter of John's Gospel is a supplement,
though not in the same way as verses 9–20 are a supplement to the last chapter and the Gospel of Mark. These passages are
within the same tradition as that used by the evangelist of the Fourth
Gospel, and so much in its spirit and style that many have believed that
the original author himself has supplemented his own Gospel. It seems
more plausible, however, for reasons that will later become more apparent, to see in this chapter a parallel redaction of Johannine material that
was added to the Gospel after the death of the great John on whose
testimony it ultimately depends. Probably, for that matter, it was part of
the Gospel from the first in its published form. But there has been no
real attempt to integrate the chapter fully into the scheme of Jn 1–11.

We see this immediately when without any warning except that it was
after these things we suddenly find ourselves with the disciples *by the Sea
of Tiberias* (so called only here in the Gospels) in Galilee. Present,
among others, are Peter, Thomas the doubter, Nathanael, and *the sons
of Zebedee* (a Synoptic term not elsewhere used by John). No explanation is given for the transition from Jerusalem to Galilee. That the disciples did, indeed, go back to Galilee after the apparent disaster of
Golgotha, and that they would inevitably have reverted to their earlier
ways of living, these things are easily credited. It seems equally evident,
however, that the view of events reflected in this chapter is quite independent of that of the Jerusalem appearances of Luke and John's
chapter 20. What is being described here is a first appearance of Jesus
to his disciples, despite the "again" that has been inserted in verse 1 and
the "third time" in verse 14 which set up a perfunctory connection between chapters 20 and 21.

The encounter of Jesus and his disciples in this story bears certain
resemblances to that of Lk 5:1–11, there a narrative of the initial call of
the disciples to follow Jesus. As we saw (above on that text), there is
some difficulty in harmonizing Luke's account with that of the other
Synoptists (in any case, a Galilean call of the first disciples stands in
contrast to the Johannine chronicle of the ministry which is antecedently
more probable: see above on Jn 1:35–42), and some commentators even
believe that the Lucan story is a displaced narrative of a resurrection
appearance which the evangelist could no longer use because of its Galilean situation. Whatever the case may be, John's story is completely
natural in its details. After the disciples had fished all *night and had
caught nothing* they heard a stranger hailing them familiarly from the
shore. There is no more normal greeting in the world than that with
which the fisherman is habitually accosted: "Any luck?" And it was likewise normal for someone on shore to suggest likely places to cast the net,
for sometimes he could see fish in the water to which those in the boat

just above would be blind; besides, it is a rare fisherman who is unwilling to follow anyone's suggestion to try anywhere else, just once more.

But now *the disciple whom Jesus loved* recognizes in the stranger the risen Lord: the superabundant draught of fish is evidently seen as a "sign." He communicates his perception to Peter, and Peter the impulsive cannot wait for the boat to reach land: he throws himself into the water and rushes to meet Christ. The other disciples, no less eagerly but perhaps more practically, bring the boat in with the fish. They had been standing offshore *about two hundred cubits*—about a hundred yards—when they first saw the Lord. Their haul consisted of *a hundred and fifty-three large fish*. In view of the Johannine proclivity for symbolism, most commentators both ancient and modern have felt that this number means something of itself, but they have never been able to explain satisfactorily just what it does mean. In general, the scene is doubtless intended as a foreshadowing of the success of the apostles as "fishers of men." The Gospel also notes that *the net was not torn:* perhaps another symbolic detail (cf. Jn 19:23 f.), but also a practical consideration to fishermen who spent almost as much time repairing their delicate nets as they did casting them for fish.

The meal on the shore does not seem to have the same meaning as that of Lk 24:42 f. Here Jesus is not said to eat, but he *took the bread and gave it to them, and so with the fish*. This recalls the language of Jn 6:11, the miracle of the loaves which had taken place beside this same lake, and which was already established as a sign of the Eucharist. Thus the closer Lucan parallel is Lk 24:30–35.

Jn 21:15–19   Apart from telling of the appearance of the risen Lord to his disciples in Galilee—a version of the events which is probably more primitive than that adopted in the main part of the Gospel—the Johannine supplement also takes the occasion to conclude certain other unfinished business of the Gospel. First of all, it deals with Peter, whose name has once more been prominently introduced into the narrative.

The primacy of Peter in the apostolic Church is a common teaching of the Gospels (see above on Mk 8:27–30 and parallels), as it is, indeed, of the entire New Testament. If the testimony of Matthew's Gospel is the most detailed and explicit, it is nevertheless by no means unique or isolated. We have already proposed that the major Petrine passage of the Matthaean tradition is an artificial unity, combining the actual conferral of the primacy along with the change of Peter's name (which John has in Jn 1:42) and Peter's own great confession of the Lord (the Johannine equivalent of which is in Jn 6:68 f.). Specifically, that Christ should have explicitly designated Peter as head of the apostolic community that succeeded him accords better with this Johannine perspective of a post-resurrection experience of the risen Lord of the Church than with Matthew's context of Jesus' public ministry.

Three times—as Peter had denied him thrice—Jesus asks Peter if he loves him. The first time it is, *Do you love me more than these?*, perhaps a delicate reminder that Peter had never been slow to assert himself and to compare himself favorably with the other disciples (cf. Mt 14:29). With a sudden lack of impulsiveness, Peter is content to say only that he loves his Savior; for the others he dare not speak. Asked a second time for a declaration of his love, he replies humbly but confidently that the Lord knows he loves him. When he is asked the third time, possibly the full significance of these questions is brought home to him, and remembering his past weakness he cries out, troubled, that the Master who knows all things must know now that he does indeed love him, and that his betrayal has been bitterly repented. Each time Christ has repeated his commission to Peter: *Feed my lambs, tend my sheep.* To Peter Jesus transmits his own office as shepherd of the flock (cf. Jn 10:11 ff.; Acts 20:28; 1 Pt 5:2-4). As are all the offices in the Church, it is founded on love and service (see above on Mk 10:35-45 and parallel).

Jesus has an additional word for Peter. The true shepherd also lays down his life for his sheep (cf. Jn 10:11). There is no doubt, as verse 19 makes quite explicit, that the extent of Peter's following Jesus will be even to the end, to the death. Materially, Jesus says nothing more than that a man who is young and has all his faculties unimpaired girds himself and walks as he pleases, unaided, whereas an old man must stretch out his arms to be led, and needs others to care for him and help him. But this is Johannine irony. *You will stretch out your hands and another will tie you* would be recognized by John's readers as referring to Peter's crucifixion. There is good reason to accept the tradition—to which this Gospel passage is probably our oldest written attestation—that Peter was put to death in Rome under the emperor Nero either in A.D. 63 or 67.

Jn 21:20-23   The other bit of unfinished business concerned *the disciple whom Jesus loved*, who quite obviously in this passage emerges as the one on whom the Johannine tradition depends. What of him? This, indeed, is the question asked by Peter, who *turned and noticed him following them.*

It was an honest question, not born of envy but of friendly interest in a person who had often shared his confidences (cf. Jn 13:23 f., 18:15 f., 20:2 ff.). But it was not Jesus' practice to satisfy this kind of curiosity. *Suppose I would like him to remain until I come, what is that to you?* is as ambiguous as the prophecy of Peter's death. It neither affirms nor denies the possibility. What these verses are concerned with, however, is to lay to rest a popular belief that the Lord had, indeed, made a very firm commitment with regard to the beloved disciple.

The most logical interpretation of the background of this supplement is that this disciple—the John who is traditionally named the author of the Fourth Gospel—had recently died, the last, perhaps, of the known apostolic witnesses to the Jesus of Galilee and of the resurrection appearances, and that this event had upset a widely held conviction that such a thing could not occur before the *parousia* of the Lord. One of the stages in the Church's development of a theology of the "delay" of the *parousia* (see above on Mk 13:3–8 and parallels) without doubt involved the ever dwindling number of "first generation" Christians who had actually seen the Lord and lived with him. Surely, he would return before he had called all of them to himself? (That he had called any of them at all was problem enough to some, cf. 1 Thes 4:13–18.) Here we are being told, therefore, that Jesus had never really promised that the *parousia* would coincide with the end of the Johannine age.

Jn 21:24–25   Once again and finally, then, John's Gospel comes to a close. Those who are responsible for putting it in order testify to their dependence on an eyewitness authority—*he who wrote these things*—and to their acceptance of *his witness* as true. It is, as all the Gospels are, a fragmentary account: their intention is not so much to apologize for the brevity of the Gospel as to excuse their failure to plumb the full depths of all that Jesus had done and said.

Mt 28:16–20   Matthew also ends his Gospel in Galilee, at *that*
[Mk 16:15–18]   *mountain to which Jesus had summoned them* (see above on Mk 3:13–19 and parallels; Mt 5:1 f. and parallel). This evangelist shows no concern whatever for certifying the reality of the resurrection (except for the note that *some had doubted* before this event). He is intent, rather, on setting forth its consequences for the existing Church. These are: (1) That the apostles now go forth with the *authority* and in the person of Christ (cf. Mt 9:6, 11:27 [=Lk 10:22]; Lk 5:24; Jn 20:21–23). (2) That the Gospel may now be brought to *all the nations* of the earth (cf. Mt 24:14 [=Mk 13:10]; 26:13 [=Mk 14:9]; see above on Mk 7:24–30 and parallel, etc.), following its definitive rejection by Israel (cf. Mt 27:25). (3) That, on the one hand, this is a ministry of sacrament: *baptizing them in the name of the Father, and of the Son, and of the Holy Spirit.* This formula undoubtedly speaks for the Church of Matthew's time. While it had been sufficient to baptize "in the name of the Lord Jesus" in the earliest days of the Church (cf. Acts 10:48, 19:5, etc.), very soon it became necessary to employ a trinitarian formula to distinguish Christian baptism from the many alien rites of the Hellenistic world. (4) It is also a ministry of *teaching* as well as of proclaiming. As a semi-permanent institution awaiting *the end of the world*, the Church must present to man an ethical and moral doctrine

that is in conformity with the way of life. This Matthew has given, as one example, in the Sermon on the Mount.

The Marcan supplement adds to these essential characteristics certain signs that attended the apostolic Church (cf. Mk 6:13; Lk 10:19; Acts 2:3 f., 10:46, 19:6, 28:3 f.; 1 Cor 12:1–11, etc.) and which, on occasion, have attended the Church in every age, according to need. Miracles are not excluded from the life of the Church, but neither are they the life of the Church. This life Matthew has best described.

Lk 24:44–53   Luke's conclusion is a summary, and the ending of
[Mk 16:19–20] Mark's supplement is a summary of it. No indication
is given of a change of scene or of a passing of time since the immediately preceding episode of Jesus' appearance to the disciples in Jerusalem, still on that first day of his resurrection. The conversation which the Gospel ascribes to Jesus and the disciples on this occasion, however, corresponds to the forty days' instruction of which we read in Acts 1:3. Luke is preparing for the story of the apostolic Church, the Gospel of the Spirit, which begins where the Gospel leaves off, *in the temple* (cf. Acts 2:46) where the Gospel also began (cf. Lk 1:9). Through the Christ-event of the Gospel the temple, where we first saw Zechariah offering the sacrifices of the old dispensation, has now become a place of Christian worship; and through the Gospel of the Spirit the temple of Jewish Christianity will eventually be replaced by the world itself as the "place" of the Church's life and action.

Only Luke has felt it necessary to describe a departure of the risen Lord, a visible ascension (Acts 1:9; Lk 24:51b may be an addition to the Gospel text). Apparently it occurred neither to Matthew nor John, nor presumably to Mark, nor to their readers, to ask about the subsequent whereabouts of the resurrected Christ. But even Luke is only an apparent exception. The question, "Why do you stand looking into heaven?" (Acts 1:11), focuses our attention where it belongs, where Matthew and John would have it, where all the Gospels have placed it all along.

Despite their purpose of insisting on the reality of the resurrection as the bedrock of the Church's unshakable faith, by means that at this remove may seem at times somewhat naïve, the Gospels have never left us in doubt as to what is the real heart of this great mystery, to which no amount of description can be applied other than as an approximation. The risen Christ is to be seen in the members of his Church: this is not only the Church's glory, but also its most imperative call to holiness and to showing forth the God whom it incarnates. He is in the world, which often sees him not. He is in Galilee, preaching the word of life, the good news of the coming kingdom, healing, and bringing hope. He is in prison, in the hospitals, in hunger and in thirst, wherever there is human need, of whatever kind. He is the eternal Son of Man whom we see in every man, for whom Sabbaths were made, whom it is blasphemy to treat with contempt or injustice or lack of concern. When we would see the resurrected Christ the Gospels turn our eyes back to the ministry of Jesus of Nazareth. He is one and the same. That, after all, is what the resurrection stories intend to say. Christ lives, our Savior, our Teacher, our Judge.

INDEX OF GOSPEL PASSAGES

In each instance the first page number is given on which the relevant passage is under discussion.

MATTHEW

1:1–17	64	28–29	144	18–23	157
18–25	58	8:1–4	105	24–30	159
2:1–12	66	5–13	145	31–32	160
13–15	68	14–15	103	33	160
16–18	69	16–17	103	34–35	160
19–23	69	18	163	36–43	161
3:1–6	74	19–22	224	44–46	161
7–10	75	23–27	163	47–50	162
11–12	77	28–34	164	51–53	162
13–17	78	9:1–8	106	54–58	168
4:1–2	80	9–13	108	14:1–12	171
3–11	80	14–17	110	13	172
12	93	18–26	166	14–21	173
13–17	97	27–31	291	22–23a	175
18–22	100	32–34	236	23b–33	176
23–25	114	35	170	34–36	177
5:1–2	118	36–38	225	15:1–9	186
3–12	119	10:1–4	114	10–20	188
13–16	123	5–16a	225	21–28	190
17–20	124	7–11	170	29–31	191
21–26	126	14	170	32–39	192
27–30	127	16b–25	244	16:1–4	192
31–32	128	26–33	243	5–12	194
33–37	128	34–36	246	13–20	195
38–42	129	37–39	246	21–23	199
43–45	130	40–42	207	24–28	200
46–48	132	11:1	246	17:1–9	201
6:1–4	133	2–6	147	10–13	203
5–8	134	7–19	148	14–21	204
9–15	232	20–24	226	22–23	205
16–18	135	25–27	227	24–27	205
19–21	136	28–30	228	18:1–5	206
22–23	136	12:1–8	111	6–9	207
24	136	9–13	112	10–14	208
6:25–34	137	14	113	15–18	209
7:1–5	138	15–21	114	19–20	209
6	140	22–30	236	21–22	209
7–11	140	31–32	237	23–35	210
12	141	33–37	238	19:1–2	210
13–14	142	38–42	193	3–9	273
15–20	142	43–45	239	10–12	276
21–23	143	46–50	152	13–15	278
24–27	144	13:1–9	153	16–22	279
		10–17	156		

Passage	Page	Passage	Page	Passage	Page
23–26	280	38–44	389	8:1–10	192
27–30	281	45–47	390	11–12	192
20:1–16	282	48–50	391	13–21	194
17–19	289	51–54	392	22–26	195
20–28	289	55–61	395	27–30	195
29–34	291	62–66	396	31–33	199
21:1–9	299	28:1–8	397	34–9:1	200
10–11	301	9–10	400	9:2–10	201
12–13	88	11–15	402	11–13	203
14–17	301	16–20	409	14–29	204
18–19	303			30–32	205
20–22	306	**MARK**		33–37	206
23–27	306	1:1–6	74	38–41	207
28–32	307	7–8	77	42–48	207
33–46	308	9–11	78	49–50	208
22:1–14	310	12–13	80	10:1	210
15–22	311	14	93	2–12	273
22:23–33	314	15	97	13–16	278
34–40	315	16–21	100	17–22	279
41–46	316	22–28	101	10:23–27	280
23:1–14	317	29–31	103	28–31	281
15–22	319	32–34	103	32–34	289
23–36	319	35–39	104	35–45	289
37–39	256	40–45	105	46–52	291
24:1–2	322	2:1–12	106	11:1–10	299
3–8	323	13–17	108	11	301
9–14	326	18–22	110	12–14	303
15–22	326	23–28	111	15–17	88
23–31	327	3:1–5	112	18–19	306
32–36	328	6	113	20–26	306
37–44	329	7–12	114	27–33	306
45–51	250	13–19	114	12:1–12	308
25:1–13	330	20–21	151	13–17	311
14–30	330	22–27	236	18–27	314
31–46	331	28–30	237	28–34	315
26:1–5	333	31–35	152	35–37a	316
6–13	296	4:1–9	153	37b–40	317
14–16	334	4:10–12	156	41–44	320
17–20	335	13–20	157	13:1–2	322
21–25	341	21–25	158	3–8	323
26–29	342	26–29	159	9–13	326
30–35	347	30–32	160	14–20	326
36a	359	33–34	160	21–27	327
36b–46	359	35–41	163	28–32	328
47–56	361	5:1–20	164	33–37	329
57	363	21–43	166	14:1–2	333
58–63a	365	6:1–6a	168	3–9	296
63b–66	367	6b–13	170	10–11	334
67–75	365	14–29	171	12–17	335
27:1	367	30–33	172	18–21	341
2	373	34–44	173	22–25	342
3–10	371	45–46	175	26–31	347
11–14	375	47–52	176	32a	359
15–23	378	53–56	177	32b–42	359
24–26	380	7:1–13	186	43–52	361
27–31	382	14–23	188	53	363
27:32	385	24–30	190	54–61a	365
33–37	387	31–37	191		

61b–64	367	40–41	103	29–37	229
65–72	365	42–44	104	38–42	230
15:1a	367	5:1–11	104	11:1–4	232
1b	373	12–16	105	5–8	235
2–5	375	17–26	106	9–13	140
6–14	378	27–32	108	14–23	236
15	380	33–39	110	24–26	239
16–20	382	6:1–5	111	27–28	240
21	385	6–10	112	11:29–32	193
22–26	387	11	113	33–36	240
27–32	389	12–16	114	37–54	241
33–35	390	17–20a	118	12:1	194
36–37	391	20b–23	119	2–9	243
38–39	392	24–26	122	10	237
40–47	395	27–28	130	11–12	244
16:1–8	397	29–30	129	13–21	247
[9–11]	400	31	130	22–31	137
[12–13]	402	32–36	132	32–34	248
[14]	403	37–42	138	35–40	249
[15–18]	409	43–45	143	41–48	250
[19–20]	410	46	143	49–53	246
		47–49	144	54–56	192
LUKE		7:1–10	145	57–59	252
1:1–4	46	11–17	146	13:1–9	253
5–7	47	18–23	147	10–17	254
8–12	49	7:24–35	148	18–19	160
13–20	51	36–50	149	20–21	160
21–25	52	8:1–3	151	22–30	254
26–33	52	4–8	153	31–33	255
34–38	53	9–10	156	34–35	256
39–55	55	11–15	157	14:1–6	256
56–79	56	16–18	158	7–11	257
80	57	19–21	152	12–14	258
2:1–7	61	22–25	163	15–24	258
8–20	63	26–39	164	25–27	246
21–24	65	40–56	166	28–33	260
25–38	65	9:1–6	170	34–35	208
39–40	66	7–9	171	15:1–2	260
41–52	70	10–11	172	3–7	208
3:1–2	73	12–17	173	8–10	261
3–6	74	18–21	195	11–32	261
7–9	75	22	199	16:1–13	263
3:10–14	76	23–27	200	14–18	264
15	76	28–36	201	19–31	265
16–17	77	37–43a	204	17:1–2	207
18–20	78	43b–45	205	3–6	268
21–22	78	46–48	206	7–10	268
23–38	64	49–50	207	11–19	269
4:1–2	80	51	210	17:20–21	270
3–13	80	52–56	211	22–37	271
14a	93	57–62	224	33	246
14b–15	96	10:1–12	225	18:1–8	272
16–22a	98	13–16	226	9–14	273
22b–30	168	17–20	227	15–17	278
31	100	21–22	227	18–23	279
32–37	101	23–24	228	24–27	280
38–39	103	25–28	229	28–30	281

31–34	289	36–43	403	9:1–34	221
35–43	291	44–53	410	35–41	222
19:1–10	293			10:1–21	223
11–28	294	JOHN		22–39	238
29–40	299	1:1–2	37	10:40–42	239
41–44	303	3a	38	11:1–16	285
45–46	88	3b–5	39	17–32	286
47–48	306	6–8	41	33–44	287
20:1–8	306	9–13	41	45–57	288
9–19	308	14	43	12:1–8	296
20–26	311	15–18	45	9–11	298
27–40	314	19–24	76	12–19	299
41–44	316	25–27	77	20–36	304
45–47	317	28–34	82	37–50	321
21:1–4	320	35–42	83	13:1–17	340
5–6	322	43–51	84	18–30	341
7–11	323	2:1–11	85	31–35	346
12–19	326	12	88	36–38	346
20–24	326	2:13–17	88	14:1–14	348
25–28	327	18–22	89	15–26	350
29–33	328	23–25	90	27–31	350
34–36	329	3:1–13	90	15:1–17	351
37–38	333	14–21	91	18–16:4a	353
22:1–2	333	22–30	92	16:4b–22	353
3–6	334	31–36	93	23–33	355
7–14	335	4:1–3	93	17:1–8	356
15–18	339	4–19	94	9–19	357
19–20	342	20–38	95	20–26	357
21–23	341	39–42	96	18:1	359
24–30	339	43–45	96	2–11	361
31–34	346	46–54	97	12–14	363
22:35–38	347	5:1	182	15–27	365
39	359	2–15	182	28–32	373
40–46	359	16–30	184	33–38	376
47–53	361	31–47	185	39–40	378
54a	363	6:1–4	172	19:1–3	382
54b–65	365	5–15	173	4–16a	383
66–71	367	16–17a	175	16b–17a	385
23:1	373	17b–21	176	17b–24	387
2–5	376	22–25	177	25–27	390
6–16	377	26–51a	178	28–30	391
17–23	378	51b–59	179	31–37	394
24–25	380	60–66	181	38–42	395
26–32	385	67–71	181	20:1–13	397
33–34	387	7:1	186	20:14–18	400
35–43	389	2–13	212	19–23	403
44–45a	390	14–39	212	24–29	405
45b	392	40–52	214	30–31	405
46	391	53–8:11	215	21:1–14	406
47–48	392	8:12–20	216	15–19	407
49–56	395	21–29	217	20–23	408
24:1–12	397	30–36	217	24–25	409
13–35	402	37–47	218		
		48–59	219		

GENERAL INDEX

Aaron, 49, 53, 357
Abba, 233
Abel, 243
Abiathar, 111
Abijah, 49
Abilene, 73–74
Abraham, 58, 64, 266, 354; salvation and descent from, 218–20, 254, 293, 315
Acts of the Apostles, 18, 22, 24–26, 35, 46, 51, 61, 153; apostles named in, 115–16; Judas' death in, 372; messiahs named in, 325; Paul in, 24, 249; Peter in, 198; *porneia* in, 276; sermons of, 56
Adultery, 59, 127, 215–16, 275, 276
Agony, Jesus', 359–61, 391
Ahimelech, 111
Ain Karim, 52
Alexander (son of Simon of Cyrene), 386
Allegories, 111, 161, 252, 262, 294, 330, 351; distinguished from parables, 154–55
Allusion, use of, 80, 91, 328
Almsgiving, 133–34, 248–49, 281
Alphaeus, 115, 116, 169
Amwas, 403
Anawim, the, 120–22, 229, 266
Andrew, 83, 100, 103, 115, 116, 226, 323; and miracle of the loaves, 174
Angels, 80, 82, 315, 361; annunciation and, 50–55, 60, 63, 399, 401; belief in, 35, 183
Anna the prophetess, 66
Annas, 363–65, 366, 367
Annunciation, 48, 50–60 *passim*, 62, 399–400
Anointing, 150, 171, 221, 285, 296–98, 399
Antioch, 30, 276
Antiochus IV Epiphanes, 51, 238, 326
Antonia, the, 373–74, 387, 383
Anxiety, 137–38
Apocalypse of John, 20, 28, 327
Apocalyptic language and thinking, 108, 324–32, 391, 393

Apocryphal gospels, 47, 62, 71, 398
Apostles, 114–17, 170, 172, 281 (*see also* Disciples; Twelve, the; specific events, individuals); list of, 114–17; missioning and instruction of, 163, 168, 170–75, 207, 208, 225–26, 243–52, 404, 408–10; and resurrection, 402–10; significance of word, 116–17
Arabs, 285, 338
Aramaic language usage, 22, 25–26, 27, 28, 33, 48, 83, 91, 108, 112, 164, 168, 183, 198, 225, 331, 353, 354; in Eucharist, 180, 343, 345; in Lord's Prayer, 232, 233, 234; in passion narrative, 359, 374, 387, 391; in Sermon on the Mount, 134
Aretas, 172
Ark of the Covenant, 54, 55, 71
Arrest of Jesus, the, 361–64, 365, 377, 380
Ascension, 211, 401, 402, 404, 410
Askar, 94
Atonement, 288, 360
Augustine, St., 240, 349
Augustus, Emperor, 53, 73
Authorship, 123; of John, 28; of Luke, 23–24; of Mark, 22; of Matthew, 25–27

Baal, 236
Back-references, in John, 41
Balaam, 67
Baptism, 40, 75, 91, 191, 232, 395, 405, 409; infants, 278–79; Jesus and, 91, 92–93, 95, 222, 232, 246, 278–79, 290, 340–41; John the Baptist and, 75, 77–81, 82, 92–93
Barabbas, 379, 384, 386
Barachiah, 320
Bar Kokeba, 67
Bar mitzvah, 71
Barnabas, 22, 116
Bartholomew, 84, 115, 116
Bartimaeus, 292–93
Beatitudes, 119–24
Beelzebul (Beelzebub), 236, 237

Belief, unbelief. *See* Faith
Benedictus, 56, 57
Ben-hinnom, 372
Benjamin, 69
Bethany, 82, 231, 285–91, 296–98, 333
Bethesda, 183
Bethlehem, 58, 59, 62–70
Bethsaida, 84, 172–73, 175, 183, 195, 226–27
Binding and loosing, 198–99, 254
Birds, parables of, 137–38, 158, 244, 272
Birth (rebirth of man), in John, 42, 90, 91, 94
Birth, Virgin. *See* Virgin Birth
Birth and infancy narrative, 37ff., 47–60, 61–72; in John, 37ff.; in Luke, 25, 47–62 *passim*, 73, 85, 86; in Matthew, 47–49, 52, 53, 58–70 *passim*, 74; in Paul, 18
Blasphemy, 107, 220, 237–38, 239, 369, 371, 411
Blind, the, 139, 165, 188, 195, 221–22, 223, 236, 292–93
Blood of Jesus, 344–45, 372, 381, 394–95
Blood vengeance, 126. *See also* Murder
Boanerges, 117
Body of Christ: Church as, 332; Eucharist and, 180–81, 343–45
Bread: breaking of (in resurrection), 403; Last Supper and, 333, 335–45 *passim*; of life, 178, 179–81; Lord's Prayer and, 233–34; miracles and, 173–79 *passim*, 192, 195, 344
Bridegroom, 86, 110, 330
"Brother," use of word, 153, 402
Brothers and sisters of Jesus, 152–53, 169, 212, 237, 245, 258, 390, 402
Buddha, 53
Burial(s), 147, 164, 225, 242, 286–87, 320, 372; of Jesus, 387–88, 394–400

Caesarea, 24, 31, 33, 195, 373
Caesarea Philippi, 195, 198, 202
Caiaphas, Joseph, 288–89, 333, 363–65, 367, 369–70, 373
Calvary, 387
Camel and eye of needle, parable of, 281, 320
Cana of Galilee, 85, 97
Canticles, 56, 63, 66, 80
Capernaum, 84, 88, 97, 100, 103, 106, 107, 108, 152, 169; Jesus condemns, 226–27; miracle in, 166–68, 178–81; and temple tax, 205
Catechesis, 106, 107, 110, 278; in Luke, 46, 268; in Mark, 110, 189; Sermon on the Mount, 135, 137
Celibacy, 54, 277, 280

Cenacle, the, 339, 363
Centurion: confession of, 393; healing and, 145, 146
Cephas, 197–98
Charity, 76, 126–27, 133–34, 139, 143, 209–10, 249, 252, 258. *See also* Justice; Righteousness
Children, 264, 278–79; becoming like, 206–7, 278; disciples as, 346; feeding of, 191; lost sheep parable, 208–9
Chorazin, 226–27
Christ (*see also* Jesus): as title, 197
Christology, 40ff., 54ff., 79, 228, 359, 402. *See also* Theology; specific teachings
Chronology, 17, 21–30 *passim*, 38, 84, 89–90, 93, 170, 182, 192, 201, 289, 337 (*see also* specific events, Gospels); birth narrative, 61–62, 64, 67, 71, 73; passion, death, and resurrection narrative, 289, 292, 296, 333, 335–38, 362, 368–69, 387, 392, 397, 399, 400, 402, 404
Church: origins of, 17–36 *passim*, 58, 86, 89, 198; use of word in Gospels, 27, 198
Chuza, 151
Circumcision, 56, 57, 65, 213
Claudia Procla, 380
Cleanliness, 188–89, 241, 320, 340–41, 351
Cleopas, 402, 403
Clopas, 390, 402
Commandments, 316, 346, 350, 352. *See also* Law, the; Ten Commandments; specific teachings
Conflict (controversy) stories, 19–20, 27, 34–35, 89ff., 106–13ff., 183–89, 212ff., 236, 254, 274ff.; and passion, death, and resurrection narrative, 314ff., 353
Constantine, 387
Conversions, 75, 174, 293, 319
Corinthians, 81, 315
Covetousness, 247, 249
Creation, 37, 38–39, 42, 43, 82, 87; new, 281, 296
Criminals, crucifixion of, 386, 389, 396
Cross, Jesus', 388. *See also* Crucifixion
Crowd(s), 78, 81, 104, 107, 118, 122, 147, 148, 152, 166, 181, 193, 194, 196, 219, 247, 254, 287; feeding of, 173–75, 178, 179; in Jericho, 292; and passion narrative, 362, 363, 379–92 *passim*
Crown of thorns, 383
Crucifixion, the, 18, 200, 296, 298, 345, 375, 380–94 *passim*, 395, 408; chronology, 387
Cup of wine: Crucifixion, 386, 388, 389, 392; Last Supper (Eucharistic), 339, 342, 344–45; Passover, 339, 342

Dalmanutha, 192, 194

Daniel, 50, 54, 65, 108

Darkness: in John, 40, 42, 90, 92, 212, 221, 342; in Matthew, 331; in passion narrative, 390–91; in Sermon on the Mount, 136

David, 33, 111, 317, 356, 371; Jesus in line of, 53, 55, 57, 58, 60, 62, 64, 68, 292, 317

"Day of parables," 152, 153, 159, 160, 162, 168

Dead, the (death), 43, 225; of Jesus (see Passion, death, and resurrection); Jesus on, 244, 250, 253, 315, 325 (see also Eternal life; Resurrection); miracles, 146–47, 166–68, 185, 270–71, 285–88

Dead Sea, 57, 230

Dead Sea Scrolls, 28, 35–36

Debts, debtors, 127, 210, 234, 263

Decapolis, 32, 164, 165, 327

Demoniacs, 165–66

Demons (devils), 101–2, 104, 114, 151, 164, 165–66, 219, 236, 240. See also Satan

Denarii, 283, 297, 312

Desert (wilderness), 57–58, 73, 83, 240; temptation of Jesus in, 80–81

Deuteronomy, 81, 144, 274, 275, 314

Diaspora, the, 33, 34, 114, 214

Diatessaron, 15

Didache, the, 174, 232

Disciples (discipleship), 83–87, 88–99, 100ff., 112, 114–17, 147, 163–75, 176–203 passim, 204ff., 221, 222, 238 (see also specific disciples, events, teachings); call of, 100–1, 104–5, 108–10, 280; Last Supper and, 333–45 passim, 346ff.; missioning and instruction of, 163, 168, 170–75, 200ff., 206, 207, 208, 218, 225–26ff., 243–52ff., 268ff., 271ff., 276ff., 323, 346ff., 404, 408–9, 410; named, 114–17; parables and, 151, 156, 157, 160, 176, 264, 280, 355; passion, death, and resurrection narrative and, 289–98 passim, 333ff., 346ff., 360ff., 390, 395–410 passim; persecution, martyrdom of, 290, 326, 348, 353; preaching of, 151, 163; Sermon on the Mount and, 119ff., 139

Discourses, 19, 26, 27, 145ff., 153–62, 168, 170, 190, 317–20, 346 (see also specific occasions, teachings); eschatological, 321–32, 349; in John, 90, 91, 94, 177, 178ff., 212–21, 346, 348ff.; missionary, 163, 168, 207, 208, 225–26ff., 243–52ff., 268ff., 348ff.; Sermon on the Mount, 118–44, 145

"Dives," 265

Divorce, 59, 128, 265, 274–77

Dome of the Rock, 323

Doublets, 192, 292, 296, 325

Doves, 244, 245

Dreams, 60, 68. See also Visions

Easter, 55, 405

Edomites, 33

Egypt and the Egyptians, 49, 58, 62, 69, 291, 325, 344, 345

El-azariyeh, 285

Eli, 391

Elijah the prophet, 52, 57, 74, 77, 80, 83, 147, 148, 169, 171, 211; passion and, 391–92; transfiguration and, 202–3

Elisha the prophet, 147, 169

Elizabeth, 49, 51, 52, 54, 55, 56–57

Elliott-Binns, L. E., 33

Elohi, 391

Embalming of Jesus, 396, 399

Emmaus, 403

End of the world, discourse on, 323–32, 353, 409

Enoch, 211

Ephesus, 24, 28, 30

Ephraim, 69, 289

Ephrathites, 68

Eschatology, 36, 75, 108, 185, 200, 201, 202–3, 270–72, 321–22, 348, 349; miracles and, 165, 174, 264; parables and, 156, 157, 159, 249–50, 251; Sermon on the Mount, 119, 120, 121, 127, 143, 144

Essenes, 35–36, 54, 58, 75, 82, 338. See also Qumran

External life, teachings and beliefs on, 35, 92, 229, 231, 238, 279, 282, 287, 315, 402. See also Resurrection

Eucharist, the, 18, 87, 174, 234, 336–45, 346, 403; in John, 178–81, 336–37, 340–42, 343, 344, 346, 395, 407

Evil, 40, 42, 43, 81, 92, 198, 227, 235 (see also Sin); miracles and (see Exorcisms; Miracles); parables on, 159–60, 161, 264; in Sermon on the Mount, 122, 129–30

Excommunication, 209, 222

Exile, the, 50, 58, 69, 74

Exorcisms, 29, 101–2, 103–4, 164–66, 170, 207–8, 236–37, 254

Eye, in parables and teachings, 129, 136, 139, 281, 320

Faith (belief-unbelief), 114, 148, 167, 168, 169, 193, 197ff., 204, 240, 281, 286, 381, 405, 410 (see also Piety; Religion; specific events); in John, 40, 42–43, 54, 84, 89–92ff., 178, 185–86, 212, 217, 226; kerygma and, 17, 18; in Luke, 55, 66, 169, 240, 268, 270, 295, 347;

in Mark, 114, 169, 204; in Matthew, 58, 114, 143, 169; miracles and, 105, 107, 146, 148, 167, 169, 177, 204, 207, 222–23, 270, 273, 293 (*see also* Miracles); parables and, 145, 149, 157ff., 240, 268, 281 (*see also* Parables)

False prophets, 123, 142–43

Fasting, 80–81, 110, 135, 205, 273

Feasts, 182, 202, 250, 258, 259, 289, 297, 320, 333ff., 337. *See also* Passover; Tabernacles; Weddings

Feet: anointing of, 296–98; washing of, 150–51, 340–41

Fig tree, parable of, 253, 328

Fire, 78, 208, 246

First and last, 255, 282

"Firstborn," use of word, 62, 65

Fish, miracle of, 173–75

Fishermen, 100–1, 104–5, 162, 281, 406–7

Flesh (body); Eucharist and, 180–81, 343–45; Word of God as, 43–45

Flesh and spirit, Jesus on, 90–91

Food, 74–75, 81, 96, 137–38, 150, 173–74, 178–79, 191 (*see also* Fasting; Feasts; specific kinds, miracles); clean and unclean, 188–89; Last Supper, 338 (*see also* Last Supper)

Forgiving (forgiveness), 75, 79, 107, 139, 151, 209–10, 234–35, 237–38, 268. *See also under* Sin

Form criticism, critics, 19–21, 35, 279

Formgeschichte, 20

Friends, friendship, 352, 390. *See also* Neighbors

Fruit trees, parables of, 142–43, 268

Gabriel, 50, 51

Gadara, Gadarenes, 164–66, 168

Galilee, 24, 25, 32–34, 52, 59, 61ff., 71, 94–117 *passim*, 377, 380, 399ff.; ministry of Jesus in (*see* Ministry narrative)

Galilee, Sea of, 100, 105, 163–64, 175, 176, 191

Gamaliel, 35

Gaulanitis, 84

Gazith, 373

Gehenna, 126, 127, 198, 208, 319, 372. *See also* Hell

Genealogy, 58, 64–65

Gennesaret, 100, 178. *See also* Galilee, Sea of

Gentiles, 23–27, 33, 41, 43, 58, 65, 109, 116, 138, 140, 165, 166, 190–94, 214, 245, 254–55, 353 (*see also* specific events, Gospels, places, teachings); parables and, 145–46, 224, 226, 254; resurrection and, 404; salvation and, 254, 255, 259

Gerasa, Gerasenes, 164–66, 168, 175

Gerazim, 95

Gethsemane, 359, 391

Gideon, 51

Gifts: of the Magi, 68; widow's, 320–21

Girgashites, 164

Glory, glorification, 44, 82, 86, 87, 92, 123, 298, 342, 346, 349, 359; in passion narrative, 211, 298, 342, 346, 349, 356, 371, 404; signs and, 107, 214, 285, 286; transfiguration and, 202, 212

Gnosticism, 19, 142, 228

Goats, 331

Golden Rule, 125, 132, 141, 274

Golgotha, 385, 387–88, 394, 406

Gomorrah, 226

Good Samaritan parable, 33, 154, 230

Good will, 63

"Gospel," use of word, 17, 63, 74

Grace, 44, 45, 228, 239, 281; baptism and, 75; in John, 39, 40, 41, 42, 44–45, 94, 349; in Luke, 51, 53, 228, 239, 269, 270, 273; marriage and, 276–77; transfiguration and, 202

Greek language usage, 17, 30, 33, 100, 134, 234, 251, 278, 317, 320, 343, 373; John and, 38, 39, 44, 84, 91, 174, 353, 362; Luke and, 46, 48, 62, 63, 107, 359; Mark and, 107, 117, 152; Synoptic question and, 22, 23, 25, 26, 27

Greeks, 43. *See also* Greek language usage; Hellenism

Hades, 266. *See also* Gehenna; Hell

Hannah, 55

Hanukkah, 51, 238

Harvest: Jesus' words on, 96, 225; parables on, 155–56, 157–58, 159–60

Harvesting on the Sabbath, 111

Hasmonaeans, 32, 378, 383

Hatred, 126–27, 130–32

Healing miracles, 29, 101–8 *passim*, 112–13, 144–47, 164, 166–68, 169, 178, 182ff., 191, 204–5, 221–23, 254, 257, 270, 293; disciples and, 170, 171, 195, 207, 221

Heaven (paradise), 233, 389

Hebrew language usage, 25–26, 44, 48, 60, 62, 63, 64, 70, 75, 117, 124, 183, 197, 226, 251, 276, 350, 354 (*see also* Aramaic language usage; Semitisms); in Eucharist, 343, 345; in passion narrative, 374, 391; in Sermon on the Mount, 124, 137

Hebrews. *See* Hebrew language usage; Hebrews, Epistle to the; Jews

Hebrews, Epistle to the, 356, 360

Heli, 64

Hell, 127, 155, 198, 266. See also Gehenna

Hellenism, 24, 38, 42, 43. See also Greek language usage; Greeks

Heresy, heresies, 19, 40, 43, 44, 47, 142–43

Hermon, Mount, 195, 202

Herod Agrippa, 290

Herod Antipas, 32, 70, 73, 74, 78, 93, 97, 108, 113–14, 146, 151, 255–56; and John the Baptist, 171–72, 378; and passion narrative, 377–78, 383, 384

Herod Archelaus, 70, 73, 291, 294

Herod the Great, 32, 33, 48–49, 50, 62, 66, 68, 69, 70; Archelaus succeeds, 294; Jericho and, 291, 293; Palace of, 373, 374, 378

Herodians, 113–14, 362, 377

Herodias, 172

Herod Philip, 32, 73, 74, 172, 195

Hillel, Rabbi, 35, 274–75

Hinnom, Valley of, 208

History, historians, historical method, 16–17, 19, 29–30, 78, 171–72, 176, 201–2 (see also specific events, individuals, places); in John, 83, 84, 85, 100, 182, 337, 359, 362; in Luke, 47, 49, 50, 73, 74, 226, 241, 259, 327, 328, 329; in Mark, 100, 165, 190ff.; in Matthew, 68, 100, 190ff., 327, 328, 329; passion, death, and resurrection narrative and, 368, 369, 378, 381, 397, 403

"Holiness, Law of," 188

Holy of Holies (Holy Place), 392–93

Holy Sepulcher, Church of the, 388

Holy Spirit, 19, 24, 141, 228, 245, 249, 405, 409; blasphemy against, 237, 238; Mary and, 54, 59, 60; Paraclete as, 350, 353–55

Holy (Maundy) Thursday, 337, 340

Holy Week, 333, 335

Hosea, 69, 196

Householder, parables of, 162, 235, 295

Houses, parable of, 144

Humility, 258, 291

Hunger, 121, 173–74. See also Fasting; Food

Hymns, 347

Hyperbole, use of, 125, 139, 210, 281

Hypocrites, 134, 135, 139, 251, 254

"I am," use by Jesus, 96, 177, 179, 217, 220, 351, 370–71

Iatros, 24

Ignatius, St., 27

Immanuel, 60

Immorality, divorce and, 275–76

Immortality, 35, 315. See also Eternal life

"In the beginning," use in John, 37

Incarnation: in John, 38, 40, 41, 42, 43–45, 354, 358, 376; in Luke, 55, 329, 376, 410

Inclusion, use of device in Matthew, 26, 122

Infancy. See Birth and infancy

Infidelity, 276. See also Adultery

Inheritance, 247, 262, 315, 319

Innocents, slaughter of, 69

Irenaeus, St., 22, 25

Irony, 290, 348; in John, 95, 213, 217, 222, 239, 286, 288, 355, 384, 405, 408

Isaac, 49, 51, 220, 315

Isaiah the prophet, 18, 60, 74, 77, 82, 98, 99, 157, 208, 322; testimony of, 354

Israel (Jacob), 84

Israel, Israelites. See Jews; specific beliefs, events, individuals, places

Jacob, 64

Jacob (Israel), 67, 84, 94, 315

Jairus, 166–68

James (brother of Jesus), 169, 237, 390

James of Alphaeus, 115, 116, 169

James of Zebedee, 101, 103, 105, 115, 116, 117, 211, 290, 323; miracles and, 168, 201; passion narrative and, 360; resurrection and, 406; seating of, 290–91

Jehoiada, 320

Jeremiah, 50, 51–52, 69, 196, 372

Jericho, 230, 269, 291–92, 293

Jerome, St., 70, 233, 234, 237, 281

Jerusalem, 22, 24, 33, 76ff., 95, 256 (see also Temple of Jerusalem); burial of Jesus and, 387–88; end of, 325–29; Jesus and, 29, 52, 53, 55, 65, 67, 68, 71, 76, 88, 92, 96, 182ff., 231, 238, 322–29, 338ff.; "journey to," 291ff.; map of, in time of Christ, 13; passion, death, and resurrection narrative and, 211–20, 221, 256, 291ff., 363ff., 373–93 passim, 394, 399ff.

"Jesu, the god of the Hebrews," 207

Jesus, passim (see also Messiah; Savior; Servant of God; Son of God; Son of Man; specific events, individuals, places, practices, teachings in life of); age at death, 337; ascension (see Ascension); baptism of, 78–80, 82, 83, 93; birth, date of, 61, 62 (see also Birth and infancy narrative); called Lord, 146; as Christ, 197; chronology (see Chronology); disciples of (see Disciples); genealogy of (see Genealogy); Gospels as life of, 15–16ff., 47ff. (see also History; specific events, Gospels; Hebrew terms for, 70, 178, 318, 401; Incarnation (see

Incarnation); Jewish religion of, 34; as king of the Jews (see King of the Jews); language (speech), 29 (see also Language); Last Supper and (see Last Supper); ministry of (see Ministry); miracles (see Miracles); as a name, 51, 60; Palestine in time of, 12, 13, 31–36 (see also specific places); parables (see Parables); passion, death, and resurrection (see Passion, death, and resurrection narrative); prophecy and (see under Prophets, prophecy); as Son of David, 102, 292, 317; temptations of, 80–81, 235; transfiguration of, 201–3

Jesus Justus, 24

Jewish Antiquities, 31

Jews (Hebrews, Israelites), *passim* (see also Judaism; Judea; Palestine; specific concepts, events, Gospels, individuals, places, practices); birth narrative and, 51, 54, 59, 62, 63, 64, 65; conflict stories and (see Conflict [controversy] stories); ministry of Jesus and, 89–117 *passim*, 149, 176–89 *passim* (see also Ministry); parables and, 145ff. (see also Parables); passion, death, and resurrection narrative and, 212ff., 298, 362–72, 373–410 *passim*; priests (see Priests, priesthood); prophets, 38 (see also Prophets, prophecy); sects, denominations, 33–36

Joanna, 151

John, 28–30, 83 (see also Apocalypse of John; John, Epistles of; John, Gospel of); death of, 406, 409; John of Zebedee and, 366 (see also John of Zebedee)

John, Epistles of, 20, 28, 29, 346

John, Gospel of, *passim*; apostles in, 116 (see also specific apostles); authorship of, 28; birth narrative, 37ff.; characteristics of, 21–30 *passim*, 37ff., 90ff., 406, 407 (see also specific characteristics); compared to Synoptics, 17, 27, 28, 29, 39; Eucharist discourse, 178–81; Last Supper in, 336, 340–58 *passim*; ministry narrative (see under Ministry); miracles in (see under Miracles); passion, death, and resurrection in (see Passion, death, and resurrection narrative); prologue, 37–45; Sermon on the Mount in, 139; sources of, 30, 41, 94; theology in, 37–45, 54, 66, 88, 271, 298, 390 (see also specific doctrines, events)

"John," as a name, 51–52, 57

John the Baptist, 25, 38, 41, 44, 57–58, 74, 92–93, 354; birth narrative and, 47–51, 56–58, 65, 70–72; disciples and, 83, 84, 100, 110; execution of, 171–72, 378; imprisonment of, 78, 93, 113, 147–48;

messianism and, 147–49, 203, 356; preaching of, 73–81, 82, 83, 92–93, 97, 110, 265

John of Zebedee, 101, 103, 115, 116, 117, 211, 290, 323; Last Supper and, 290, 337, 341–42; miracles and, 168, 201, 207; passion narrative and, 360, 366; resurrection and, 406

Jonah, 193–94, 240

Jordan, river, 79, 82, 83, 195, 327

Jordan Valley, 269, 291

Joseph (or Joses; brother of Jesus), 169, 237, 390

Joseph (husband of Mary), 52, 53, 54–55, 58–60, 62–63, 69–71, 225; Davidic ancestry of, 62, 64; death of, 169

Joseph (son of Jacob), 69, 94

Joseph of Arimathea, 395–96, 399

Josephus, Flavius, 31, 35, 49, 61, 171, 172, 378

Joses. See Joseph (or Joses; brother of Jesus)

Joshua (Jeshua), 60

Judah (town), 55

Judah the Maccabee, 50–51, 238

Judaism, 33–36, 107, 183–89; John and, 38, 77, 90, 94–95, 183; Matthew and, 26, 67–68

Judas (or Jude; brother of Jesus), 169, 237

Judas of Galilee, 325

Judas Iscariot, 90, 115, 116, 117, 181; death of, 372; Last Supper and, 334–35, 341–42, 346; treason of, 298, 334–35, 341–42, 361, 362–63, 372

Judas (or Jude) of James, 115, 116, 169, 350

Judea, 31–33ff., 48, 52, 57, 62, 63, 70, 73, 92–93, 96, 182, 286, 322, 364; ministry in, 83ff., 92–93, 96, 104, 110, 114, 176–89, 210ff., 322ff.; passion narrative and, 367, 373ff.

Judging, judgment, 92, 185, 226, 252 (see also Justice); controversy over, 216–17, 219; final, 234, 250, 270, 324–25; Holy Spirit and, 354; parables, 127, 139–40, 143, 223, 272

Justice, 76, 79, 83, 114, 122, 129–32, 133, 241, 272, 282–84, 295 (see also Charity; Judging; Righteousness); Holy Spirit and, 354

Justification, 268, 273

Kefr Kenna, 85

Kerioth, 117

Kerygma, 17–23 *passim*, 29, 30, 46, 47, 53, 73, 85, 244

Khirbet Kerazeh, 227

Kidron Valley, 215, 359

Kingdom of God (of heaven), 73ff., 97–104ff., 118ff., 133–45, 159, 170, 190, 198, 200–1, 233, 237–52 passim, 278, 280, 291, 316; coming of, 270ff., 323–32 (see also Eschatology); in John, 41, 63, 90, 92; Last Supper and, 340; in Luke, 73ff., 118ff., 170, 226, 245, 250, 270ff., 280; in Mark, 74ff., 97ff., 174, 190, 280; in Matthew, 26, 58, 75ff., 97ff., 118ff., 128–45, 170, 174, 245, 280; parables of, 145–62 passim, 239–52 passim, 329

Knowledge, 40, 42, 95, 228, 243

Korban, 187, 242, 319

Kursi (Kersa; Gersa), 164

Kyrie, 95

Lamb(s) (see also Sheep): among wolves, 226; of God, 82–83; Passover, 336, 338, 344, 392

Lamech, 210

Language, 17, 28–45 passim, 48, 52, 53, 56, 62–64, 83–84, 91, 112, 124, 125, 180, 278, 317 (see also specific events, individuals, languages, phrases, words); apostles and, 116–17; Eucharist, 180, 343; parables (see Parables); passion, death, and resurrection, 211, 217, 270, 271, 289, 291, 353–54, 405; Sermon on the Mount, 119–32, 134–37ff.; Synoptic question and, 21–29 passim

Last Supper, 172, 224, 290, 333–45, 346, 351, 356–58, 362, 368. See also Eucharist

Latinisms, 23, 387

Law, the, 59, 94–113 passim, 124–32, 141, 146, 162, 239, 241ff., 316ff., 369–70, 382, 394 (see also Mosaic law; Torah; specific aspects); conflict stories and, 183–89, 274ff.; observance and salvation, 254, 279

Lazarus, in parable of the rich man, 265–66

Lazarus of Bethany, 106, 266, 285–88, 297, 396

Leaven, 160, 194, 243

Lebanon, 227

Lebbaeus, 116

Legion, 165–66

Lepers, leprosy, 105–6, 269–70, 297

Levirate marriage, 314–15

Levites, 77, 205, 356, 357

Levi (or Matthew) of the Twelve, 25, 108–9, 115, 116, 167, 293–94

Light (see also Darkness): enlightenment (in John), 39–42, 90, 92, 212, 216, 221; Jesus as the, 98, 123, 212, 216, 221, 222

Lights, feast of, 238

Lilies of the field, 138

Literary devices and forms, 25, 26, 28, 41, 49–50, 53, 80, 119, 122, 123, 153–57, 192 (see also specific devices, Gospels, stories); form criticism, 19–21; Synoptics and, 17, 21–27

Lithostrōton (Stone Pavement), 374, 383

Loaves, miracle of, 173–75, 177, 178, 179, 192, 195, 344

Logia (logion), 26, 274, 275. See also Discourses

Logos. See Word (logos) of God

"Lord," as title, 317, 332, 405

Lord's Prayer (Our Father), 135, 140, 210, 232–35, 361

Lost sheep, parable of, 208–9, 261

Lot, 272

Lot's wife, 272

Love, 44, 45, 92, 121, 185, 229, 230, 247, 316, 346, 350, 352–58, 408; in parables, 151, 229, 230, 279; in Sermon on the Mount, 121, 130–32, 139

Luke, 23–25, 46. See also Acts of the Apostles; Luke, Gospel of

Luke, Gospel of, 23–25, 30, 46–60, 73–82; authorship, 23–24; birth narrative (see under Birth and infancy narrative); catholicity, 24; characteristics, 21–27 passim, 46ff., 73; chronology, 23, 24, 47, 61, 64, 71, 73; "great addition," 224, 256, 268; "great omission," 177–78, 186, 190, 192, 203; Last Supper in, 333–45, 346–48; ministry narrative (see under Ministry narrative); miracles in (see under Miracles); parables of the kingdom, 149–51, 152–60, 248–52, 253ff.; passion narrative (see under Passion, death, and resurrection narrative); Sermon on the Mount, 114, 118–32, 133–45; sources, 22–27 passim, 46–48, 74, 113, 118–19, 170, 177, 200, 241

Lysanias, 73–74

Lytron, 291

Maccabeans, 50–51, 238, 326, 378

Magadan, 192, 194

Magi, the, 66–69

Magnificat, 55–56, 57

Mammon, 137, 264–65

Manger, 62

Manna, 179

Marcion, 212

Mark, 22, 23, 24, 363. See also Mark, Gospel of

Mark, Gospel of, 21–23, 47, 73, 74–82; apostles named in, 115–17, 152; authorship, 22; characteristics of, 21–27 passim, 74, 102 (see also specific characteristics, events); ending of, 400–2;

kingdom of God in, 74–82; Last Supper, 333–45, 347; ministry narrative in (*see under* Ministry narrative); miracles in (*see under* Miracles); parables, 152–61 (*see also* specific parables); passion, death, and resurrection in (*see under* Passion, death, and resurrection narrative); Sermon on the Mount, 118; source for other Gospels, 22, 23, 25, 26, 27, 30, 46, 114

Mark, John, 22

Mark Antony, 73

Marriage, 52, 59–60, 62, 128, 265, 274–77, 319; levirate system, 314–15

Martha, 231, 285–87, 297, 333

Mary (Mother of Jesus), 51, 52–60, 62–63, 65–70, 71, 153, 390; ministry of Jesus and, 85–86, 88, 169, 225, 240

Mary (wife of Clopas), 390

Mary of Bethany, 231, 285–87, 297–98, 333, 396

Mary Magdalene, 151, 390, 399, 400, 404

Matthew, 25–27. *See also* Matthew, Gospel of

Matthew, Gospel of, *passim*; apostles named in, 115–17; authorship, 25–27; birth narrative (*see under* Birth and infancy narrative); characteristics of, 21–27 *passim*, 58, 101, 197 (*see also* specific characteristics, events); Last Supper, 333–45, 347; ministry narrative (*see under* Ministry narrative); miracle accounts (*see under* Miracles); parables of the kingdom, 145–49, 152–62, 259, 330–31; passion, death, and resurrection narrative (*see under* Passion, death, and resurrection narrative); Peter and, 205–6, 407; Sermon on the Mount, 101, 103, 105, 118–32, 133–45

Matthew (or Levi) of the Twelve, 25, 108–9, 115, 116, 168, 293

Maundy (Holy) Thursday, 337, 340

Medicine, medical practice, 103, 167, 183, 221

Meek, the, 120–21, 229

Melchizedek, 356, 357, 360

Mercy (compassion), 56, 121, 129–32, 173, 263, 268, 269. *See also* Forgiving; Love

Messiah, messianism, 75ff., 196ff., 288; Jesus' interpretation of, 103, 108, 147–49, 174–75, 186, 196, 199, 206, 214, 317, 325–26; Jewish thought on, 49, 56, 65ff., 75–80 *passim*, 104ff., 147, 174–75, 196ff., 202, 213, 214, 238, 270, 288, 317, 324; John on, 83–96, 213, 214, 238–39; Luke on, 53–56, 64–66, 70–72, 75, 195ff.; Mark on, 102ff., 195ff.; Matthew on, 58, 64, 66–70, 85,

104, 114, 195ff.; "messianic secret," 23, 102ff., 106, 108, 114, 160, 168, 191, 195, 196, 238–39, 317, 370–71; passion, death, and resurrection narrative 335, 355, 356, 361, 366, 369–70, 375–81, 385

Metanoia, 75

Micah, 68

Midrash, 49, 68, 372

Ministry narrative, 18, 29–30, 82–87, 88–117, 118–44, 145, 151–75, 178–89, 190–252, 253–67, 268–98, 299–313, 314–32, 349; John, 29–30, 82–97 *passim*, 100, 145, 173–75, 178ff., 212–24, 228, 238–39, 285–89, 296–98, 299–306, 321–22; Luke, 25, 88, 97–132 *passim*, 145ff., 163–75, 177ff., 227, 229–35, 236–67 *passim*, 268–82, 291–95, 296, 299–313, 314–29; Mark, 84, 88, 97–117, 151ff., 163–75, 176, 178–89, 190ff., 236–37, 273–82, 289–98, 299–313, 314–29; Matthew, 84, 88, 97–117, 118ff., 163–75, 178–79, 190–210, 226, 232–52 *passim*, 256–82, 289–98, 299–313, 314–32; Palestine in time of, 12, 13, 31–36, 191 *see also* specific places); rejection of, 149, 163–75, 181, 186, 321–22

Miracles, 101–8, 112–13, 163–68, 171, 176, 191, 192ff., 205–6, 207–8, 221–23, 237, 285ff., 292–94, 409 (*see also* Signs; specific miracles); disciples and, 170, 171, 195, 207, 221, 222(*see also* specific disciples); faith and (*see under* Faith); in John, 29, 85–87, 90, 97, 173–75, 177ff., 221–23, 285ff.; in Luke, 103–4, 112–13, 145–47, 151, 163–68, 173–75, 254, 270; in Mark, 101–4, 113, 163–68, 173–75, 176, 191ff., 195, 204, 409; in Matthew, 145, 146, 163–68, 176, 191ff., 226

Missionary discourse, 163, 168, 207, 208, 225–26, 243–52ff., 268ff., 348ff., 410

Money, 88, 89, 205, 206, 261, 264, 291, 295, 297, 320, 331 (*see also* Riches [wealth]); Judas and, 334

Money-changers, 88, 89

Mosaic law, 45, 56, 65, 77, 84, 105–6, 165, 188–89, 215, 274, 357 (*see also* Law, the; Torah); divorce and, 277; Sadducees and, 314; Sermon on the Mount and 124–32, 133, 140

Moses, 27, 35, 38, 45, 51, 58, 65, 67, 69, 70, 84, 115, 179, 345 (*see also* Mosaic law); burning bush, 315; discourses of, 144; priesthood of, 357; prophecy of Jesus in, 186; salvation and, 254, 267; testimony of, 354; transfiguration and, 202–3

Mulberry tree, parable of, 268
Murder, 126, 219, 320, 377–78
Mustard seed, 160, 204

Naaman the Syrian, 169
Nabataeans, 172
Nain, 146–47
"Name, the," God as, 43
Naphtali, 97
Nathanael, 84, 85, 87, 97, 116, 181, 406
Nativity. See Birth and infancy narrative
"Nature" miracles, 164
Nazarene, 69–70, 98
Nazareth, 52, 58, 59, 69–70, 84, 98, 100; Jesus' "hidden life" at, 71–72; Jesus rejected in, 168–70
Nazirites, 52
Neighbor(s), 126–27, 130–32, 139, 155, 230; love of, 316, 332, 346, 352
New Testament, 18, 32, 42, 49, 73, 83, 148, 179, 194, 198, 278 (see also specific Books, Gospels, individuals, people, places); apostles and, 115; light-darkness in, 40; parables and, 153, 157; parousia and, 324, 325; resurrection and, 398, 405; salvation in, 40, 42, 73; Sermon on the Mount and, 122, 124, 125, 142
Nicodemus, 90–91, 92, 97, 178, 181, 215; and burial of Jesus, 395–96, 399
Nineveh, 193, 194, 265
Nisan, 335, 336, 337
Noah, 272

Obedience, 81, 92, 125
Oil, anointing, 171, 230, 330
Old Testament, 22, 34, 37, 78, 115, 179, 194, 202, 211, 228, 256, 275 (see also Jews; Prophets; specific Books, events, individuals, places); birth narrative and, 48, 49–60 passim, 64, 67; parables and, 153, 157, 160; resurrection and, 400; Sermon on the Mount and, 121, 122, 125, 128, 129, 141; testimonial collections, 74
Olives, Mount of, 215, 268, 333, 347, 359, 363

Palestine, passim (see also specific events, individuals, places); "holy places" of, 48; maps, 12, 13
Palm Sunday, 256, 299ff.
Papias, 22, 25, 26
Parables, 29, 33, 110–11, 123–24ff., 136–44, 174, 176, 189, 190, 194, 205ff., 239–52, 253–84 passim, 355 (see also specific parables, teachings); "day of," 152, 153, 159, 160, 162, 168; kinds of, 154–55; of the kingdom, 145–62, 179,

237, 253ff., 268ff., 294–95, 322, 330–32, 348 (see also specific parables); as teaching form, 153–57
Paraclete, 350, 353–55
Paradise (heaven), 233, 389
Parousia, 270–73, 287, 295, 323–32, 350, 409
Passion, death, and resurrection narrative, 18, 35, 110, 166, 195–204, 210–20, 221, 255–56, 270, 285, 286, 289, 291, 296–313 passim, 314–32 passim, 333–45, 346–72, 373–93, 394–411; agony (Gethsemane), 359–61, 391; arrest, 361–64, 365, 377, 381; ascension, 211, 401, 402, 404; burial, 387–88, 394–400; chief priests and, 298, 333, 334–35, 397; chronology, 289, 292, 296, 333, 335–36, 337–38, 362, 368–69, 387, 392, 397, 399, 400, 402, 404; crucifixion, 18, 200, 296, 298, 345, 375, 380–94 passim, 395; death, time of, 392–93; in John, 86, 91, 212–20, 221, 288, 289, 296–98, 336, 340–42, 343 344, 346–58, 359–67, 373–92, 393–411; in Luke, 25, 71, 195, 204, 210, 333–45, 346–48, 359–72, 373–92; in Mark, 25, 195, 204, 210, 333–45, 347, 359–72, 373–92, 396–410; in Matthew, 25, 195, 204, 210, 333–45, 347, 359–72, 373–93, 394–410; prophecy of, 193, 199, 201, 205, 289, 325–32 passim, 333, 335, 341–42, 397; resurrection, 393, 394–411; sites of, 387–88 (see also specific sites)
Passover, 71, 88, 173, 182, 333–45, 362, 394, 397; Christian, 342–45; last, 289, 292, 296, 333–45, 346ff., 368, 374, 380, 387
Patmos, 290
Paul, 37, 42, 43, 56, 62, 82, 116, 122, 129, 186, 189, 196, 198, 248, 268, 274, 322, 332, 353; Epistles, 18, 20, 47, 153, 271; Eucharist and, 174, 343, 344; Luke and, 23–24, 63; Mark known to, 22; Pharisees and, 34, 35; redemption and, 327; resurrection and, 393, 398, 404
Peace, peacemakers, 63, 122, 229, 350, 404
Pella, 327
Pentateuch, 188
Pentecost, 55, 78
Perea, 32, 73, 172, 255, 327. See also Perean ministry
Perean ministry, 210, 239, 246, 253–67
Perfume anointing, 296–98
Persia, 67, 68
Peter (Simon), 56, 83–84, 100–1, 103, 104, 107, 115, 116, 163, 196–99, 250–51, 281, 290; confession of, 181, 195,

196–99, 201, 202, 407; crucifixion of, 408; denies Jesus, 238, 346–47, 365–66, 371–72, 408; forgiveness and, 209–10; Last Supper and, 335, 337, 340, 342; Mark and, 22, 23; Matthew and, 205–6, 407; miracles and, 163, 168, 177, 201, 202, 205–6, 226; passion, death, and resurrection narrative and, 238, 323, 346–47, 360, 365–66, 371–72, 400, 406–8; primacy of (the Rock), 196–98, 347, 407–8; sermon to the Gentiles, 18

Pharisees, Pharisaism, 34–35, 36, 76, 90, 107–14 *passim*, 125–26, 186–89, 314, 318ff., 353 (*see also* Priests; Scribes); parables and, 150–51, 241–43, 255–56ff., 264–67ff.; passion and death of Jesus and, 214, 255–56ff., 260, 370, 397; signs and, 192–93, 267, 288

Philip, 84, 96, 115, 116, 226; faith of, 174, 349

Philistines, 33

Philo of Alexandria, 35

Phoenicia, 190, 226

Piety, 133–45, 242, 318, 320. *See also* Religion

Pigs (swine), 140, 165–66

Pilate, Pontius, 31, 73, 253, 364, 368, 373–88 *passim*; and burial of Jesus, 394, 396, 397

Pilgrims, pilgrimages, 67, 71, 88, 213, 373, 380, 402, 403; Last Supper and, 334, 338–39

Platonic aphorisms, 43

Pool, miracle at, 182–84, 222

Poor, the (poverty), 99, 118–21, 134, 136, 137, 174, 225, 234, 241, 265–66, 282, 297, 332 (*see also* Anawim; Riches); evangelical, 280; Mark as gospel of, 293–94

Possession, 101–2, 104, 165–66, 236–37. *See also* Demons

Praetorian soldiers, 383

Praetorium, 373, 374

Prayer(s), 204, 209, 229, 231, 232–35, 273, 332, 347 349; Jesus' agony in the garden, 360–61; Jesus' crucifixion, 391; Jesus' High Priestly, 356–58; Lord's (*see* Lord's Prayer); Sermon on the Mount on, 134–35, 140–41; transfiguration and, 201–2

Pride, 258, 318–19. *See also* Humility; Piety

Priests, priesthood, 19, 20, 31–35, 49, 50, 52, 89, 112, 214, 256, 269–70, 288 (*see also* Law, the; Pharisees; Sadducees; Sanhedrin; Scribes); Jesus as priestly mediator, 356–58, 360, 388, 393; passion and death narrative and, 298, 333, 334–35, 361ff., 376, 378–84ff., 393, 397

Prodigal Son, 154, 261–63

Prophets, prophecy, 38, 73ff., 95, 97–99, 168, 169, 171, 174, 179, 193, 239, 242–43, 246, 316, 354–55 (*see also* specific prophecies, prophets); birth narrative and, 46–60, 66; Jesus', 77, 80, 84, 89ff., 95, 98, 147, 211, 215, 256, 322–29, 333, 335, 337, 348, 366, 367, 397, 398, 408; in John, 41, 42, 45, 89ff., 93, 95, 215, 288, 321–22; kingdom of God and, 75ff., 97–99, 323–32; in Luke, 46–60, 66, 70–72, 73, 98–99, 241, 242, 243, 265; in Mark, 101ff.; in Matthew, 58–60, 66–70, 114; parables and, 147, 159, 160, 241, 242; Sermon on the Mount, 122, 124, 125, 126, 141, 142–43

Prostitutes, 150, 162, 262

Psalms, 89, 131, 239, 347, 360, 391

Publicans, 32, 76, 108, 113, 260, 262, 273

Purification, 65, 78, 86, 161, 187, 242, 289

Q (Quelle), 26–27. *See also* Logia

Qaddish prayer, 233

Quirinius, Publius Sulpicius, 61

Qumran, 35–36, 48, 49, 56, 57, 63, 92, 183, 198, 216, 252, 264 (*see also* Essenes); baptism and, 75, 83; calendar of, 338, 368; messianism and, 356; Sermon on the Mount and, 131

"Rabbi," Jesus addressed as, 178, 318, 401

Rabbis, 34, 71, 83, 90, 94, 107–13 *passim*, 124, 126, 144, 189, 274 (*see also* Priests; Sanhedrin; Scribes; specific individuals); parables and, 154, 210; salvation and, 254

Rachel, 52, 69

Ramah, 69

Redemption, 53, 82, 91, 291, 327, 394; birth narrative and, 65, 66, 67, 69

Relatives of Jesus, 152–53, 169, 258. *See also* Brothers and sisters of Jesus; specific members of family

Religion, true, 241, 242, 263, 265, 270, 280, 295, 332 (*see also* Faith; Piety); discourses on, 318–32 (*see also* specific discourses, occasions); John the Baptist's conception of, 76; Sermon on the Mount on, 133–45

Repentance, 75, 79, 97, 149, 151, 157; in Prodigal Son parable, 261–63; punishment by death and, 252, 253

Resurrection (*see also* Eternal life): belief in, 35, 315; of Jesus, 393, 394–411 (*see also* Passion, death, and resurrection narrative); of the just, 258–59; miracles, 146–47, 166–68, 185, 270–71, 285–88, 298

Revelation, 18, 78, 85, 197; in John, 38, 40, 45, 93, 322, 350; in Luke, 52, 53, 78; in Matthew, 60, 78; miracles and, 102

Riches (wealth), 122–23, 136–37, 247–49, 264–67, 279–81, 293–94, 331. *See also* Money

Righteousness, 125–27, 130, 133, 263, 273, 320. *See also* Charity; Justice

Romans (Rome and the Roman Empire), 20, 22, 24, 30–36, 42, 73, 76, 207, 275 (*see also* specific events, individuals); birth narrative and, 49, 61ff., 67, 70; crucifixion, passion, and death narrative, 200, 288, 334, 353, 362, 364, 366, 368, 369ff., 373ff., 387ff., 394; destruction of temple by, 24, 35, 90, 323, 326, 327; ministry narrative and, 90, 145, 146, 186

Rufus (son of Simon of Cyrene), 386

Sabbath controversies, 103–4, 111–13, 183ff., 213, 222, 242, 254, 257

Sacraments, 344, 345, 395, 405, 409. *See also* specific sacraments

Sacrifice(s), 50, 51, 65, 88–89, 95, 253, 323; Last Supper, 335, 344, 345

Sadducees, 35, 76, 187, 192, 194, 265, 288, 353, 370, 376; questioning of Jesus by, 314–15

Salome (daughter of Herodias), 172

Salome (wife of Zebedee), 390

Salt, 123, 208, 260

Salvation, 17, 73ff., 84–117 *passim*, 146, 196ff., 252ff., 266, 279, 280, 282–84, 317, 392–93, 405; Eucharist, 180; in John, 39–40, 42, 44–45, 86, 92, 93, 95, 183, 185, 214, 321–22, 348ff., 350–58; in Luke, 24, 47, 48, 52, 53, 54, 57, 73ff., 98ff., 227–28, 229, 254ff., 266, 269, 279, 293–94, 295, 389–90; in Mark, 74ff., 279; in Matthew, 58, 60, 69, 74ff., 190, 227–28, 279; Sermon on the Mount, 119

Samaria, Samaritans, 24, 31, 32, 33, 35, 73, 205, 211, 219, 269, 386; Jesus' ministry in 93–96; parables of, 33, 94–96, 154, 230

Samson, 49, 51, 52

Samuel, 49, 52

Sanhedrin, 33, 90, 126, 199, 215, 288 (*see also* Rabbis; Scribes); origin of word, 373; passion and death narrative and, 361–62, 364–75 *passim*, 377, 384, 395

Satan, 102, 158, 166, 181, 199, 219, 227, 235, 236, 239–40; Judas and, 334; Peter

and, 347; temptation in the wilderness and, 80–82

Saul, 111

Savior, 40, 44, 45, 55, 60, 69, 79ff., 108, 146, 348 (*see also* Messiah; Salvation); death of, 392–93 (*see also* Passion, death, and resurrection narrative); resurrection of, 405, 411

Schweitzer, Albert, 16

Scourging, 382–83

Scribes, 19, 33, 34, 35, 101, 107, 109, 112, 125–26, 152, 162, 186–89, 193, 198, 242, 243, 315–18ff.; passion, death, and resurrection narrative and, 199, 204, 215, 224, 260, 288, 333, 342, 353; salvation and, 254, 261

Second Vatican Council, 21, 354

Seeds, parables of, 155–56, 157–58, 159–60, 161

Semitisms, 23, 25, 26, 42, 48, 63, 234, 326, 345. *See also* Aramaic language usage; Hebrew language usage

Septuagint, the, 22, 48, 198, 226

Sepulcher, Holy, 387–88

Sermon on the Mount, 27, 101, 103, 105, 118–32, 133–45, 318

Servant canticles, 80

Servant of God, 72, 79, 82–83, 345, 378, 382

Servant of Man, Jesus as, 148, 340

Servants, 259, 263, 268–69, 291, 295, 331, 332, 340, 352

Service, Christian, 251, 291, 332, 408

"Seven last words," 388–92

Seventy(-two) disciples, 225–26, 227, 348

Shammai, Rabbi, 275, 276

Sheba, Queen of, 194

Shechem, 33, 94

Sheep Gate, 182

Sheep and shepherds, 113, 173, 208–9, 223–24, 226, 238–39, 248, 331; lost, parable of, 208–9, 261; Peter and, 408

Shema, 229, 232, 316

Shemoneh Esreh, 232

Shepherds. *See* Sheep and shepherds

Sick, the: healing miracles of (*see* Healing miracles); Jesus' call to, 109

Sidon, 190, 226–27

Signs, 83, 87–92, 97, 101, 102, 170, 174, 177–81 *passim*, 186, 192ff., 221ff., 240, 252, 267, 285ff., 297 (*see also* Miracles; Prophecy); birth narrative and, 52, 55, 63, 65; coming of the kingdom, 323–32; John's "book of signs," 321–22, 394–95, 405; messianism and, 147–48, 174; resurrection and, 394–95, 403, 405, 410

Siloam, 222, 253, 338

Simeon, 65–66, 71, 86

Simon (brother of Jesus), 169
Simon (later Peter). See Peter (Simon)
Simon the Cananaean (or Simon the
    Zealot), 115, 116
Simon of Cyrene, 385–86
Simon the leper, 150, 297
Sin, sinners, sinning, 109, 113, 127, 207–
    8, 218, 237, 238, 253, 259, 260, 261,
    287, 354 (see also Evil); forgiveness of,
    75, 79, 107, 139, 151, 184ff., 198–99,
    209, 216–17, 221, 234, 237–38, 405
    (see also Mercy); repentance and, 262;
    Sermon on the Mount on, 127–28, 132
Sisters. See Brothers and sisters of Jesus
Slaves, slavery, 218, 220, 250, 251, 263,
    268–69, 291, 341
Sodom, 226
Soldiers, Roman, 76, 362–63, 364, 365,
    374, 377, 381–93 passim, 394, 397, 399,
    402
Solomon, 33, 54
Son of David, 102, 292, 317
Son of God, 42–45, 53–55, 69, 79, 81, 84,
    92, 114, 184, 196, 197, 202–3, 205,
    219, 317, 349, 352, 356, 370–71, 384;
    in Hebrews, 360; miracles and, 177,
    184–85; in Paul, 271; resurrection and,
    405
Son of Man, 84, 91, 108, 112, 122, 161,
    184–85, 193, 197, 199, 200, 203, 211,
    217, 245, 272, 279, 291, 371, 384, 410–
    11; blasphemy against, 237, 411; new
    creation and, 281, 346; parousia and,
    327, 328, 331–32; passion and, 391,
    410–11
Soteriology, 40, 108, 350
Sources, 22–30 passim, 41, 74, 94, 118–
    19, 145, 170, 200, 241. See also specific
    events, Gospels, teachings
Sower, parable of, 153, 155–56, 157–58,
    159–60
Sparrows, 244
Spirit (life-giving), 82, 90–91, 92, 214,
    353–54, 392–93 (see also Holy Spirit);
    baptism and, 78, 79, 80, 83, 92, 93, 95;
    love and, 350; resurrection and, 405
Star of Bethlehem, 67, 68
Stations of the Cross, 386
Stephen, St., 56, 395
Steward, parable of, 263–64
Stoning, 215, 256, 375
Storm, quieting of, 163–64
Suetonius, 31
Susanna, 151
Swine (pigs), 140, 165–66, 262
Sychar, 94
Synagogues, 33, 34, 134, 166; Jesus' teach-
    ings and, 98–99, 100, 101, 104, 144,
    168, 170, 180, 188, 224, 254

Synoptic Gospels, 17–30, 37, 45 (see also
    specific Gospels); characteristics of, 17,
    21–30, 35 (see also specific character-
    istics, Gospels); chronology (see Chro-
    nology); defined, 17; form criticism, 19–
    21; history and, 16–17, 19, 29ff. (see
    also History); language and, 21–29 pas-
    sim (see also Language); literary con-
    nection ("Synoptic question"), 21ff.
    (see also Literary devices; specific events,
    Gospels, teaching); sources of (see
    Sources); why written, 18
Syria, Syrians, 31, 61, 62, 190, 326, 362;
    Legate of, 31, 32; Matthew and, 27

Tabernacles, Feast of, 202, 212–20, 221,
    238
Tabor, Mount, 202
Tacitus, Cornelius, 31
Talents, parable of, 210, 294, 330–31
Talion, law of, 129
Talmud, 34
Tatian, 15
Tax, taxgathering, 32, 76, 108–9, 132,
    162, 205–6, 293
Temple, Jerusalem, 32, 33, 36, 50, 323,
    410; birth narrative and, 49–51, 54, 66,
    71; destruction of, 24, 35, 90, 322–29,
    367; ministry narrative and, 88–90, 95,
    112, 212ff., 238, 321, 357; passion,
    death, and resurrection narrative and,
    334–35, 361–62, 367, 369, 373ff., 392–
    93, 410; prophecy of destruction of,
    322–29, 367
Temple police, 334–35, 361–62
Temple tax, 205–6
Temptation: denial of Jesus and, 238, 361;
    of Jesus in the wilderness, 80–82; prayer
    for delivery from, 235
Ten Commandments (Decalogue), 126,
    127. See also Mosaic law
Tent of Meeting, 44, 54
Thaddaeus, 115, 116
Theology, 23, 37–45, 49, 51, 53, 54, 58,
    66, 88, 271, 298, 317, 322, 390, 398
    (see also specific doctrines, Gospels,
    teachings); parousia and, 342–43
Theophany, 79, 177, 203
Theophilus, 46
Theudas, 325
Thieves, parables of, 230, 250
Thomas, St., 115, 116, 286, 345, 349;
    resurrection and, 405, 406
Tiberias, Sea of, 100, 406. See also Gal-
    ilee, Sea of
Tiberius Caesar, 73, 374, 376, 384, 385
"Till," use in Matthew, 60
Timaeus, 292
Tithes, 241, 273